Education and Culture

IN THE BARBARIAN WEST, SIXTH THROUGH EIGHTH CENTURIES

Published in Columbia, South Carolina,
during the
one hundred and seventy-fifth anniversary
of the establishment of
the University of South Carolina
and the two hundredth anniversary
of the establishment of the
United States of America.

The frontispiece reproduces folio 5 recto of the *Codex Amiatinus*, which Abbot Ceolfrid (690–716) of Wearmouth-Jarrow commissioned as a gift for the pope. Ceolfrid died at Langres on his journey to Rome, but his followers brought his manuscript to its destination. It came eventually to the abbey of Monte Amiata from where in 1782 it entered the Biblioteca Medicea Laurenziana in Florence. Ceolfrid's Bible was modelled on the Bibles of Cassiodorus that Benedict Biscop brought to England. The illustration on folio 5 recto is generally accepted to be a representation of Cassiodorus working on and surrounded by the three Vivarian Bibles he described in his *Institutiones*. The history of Ceolfrid's gift fittingly exemplifies one of the major themes of this book—the transmission of learning and culture from the Mediterranean world to the Anglo-Saxon world and from there to the Continent. The frontispiece appears here with the kind permission of the Biblioteca Medicea Laurenziana.

Education and Culture

IN THE BARBARIAN WEST SIXTH THROUGH EIGHTH CENTURIES

By Pierre Riché

Translated From the Third French Edition
By John J. Contreni

With a Foreword
By Richard E. Sullivan

UNIVERSITY OF SOUTH CAROLINA PRESS
COLUMBIA, SOUTH CAROLINA

Library of Congress Cataloging in Publication Data
Riché, Pierre.
    Education and culture in the barbarian West, sixth
through eighth centuries.

    Translation of Éducation et culture dans l'Occident
barbare, VIᵉ–VIIIᵉ siècles.
    Bibliography: p.
    Includes index.
    1. Education—Europe—History. 2. Educational
anthropology—History. 3. Education, Medieval.
4. Middle Ages. I. Title.
LA96.R5213   370'.94   76-25249
ISBN 0-87249-330-X

For My Wife

Contents

List of Maps

Foreword
to the English Edition

Writing on Saint Augustine in his *Condition of Man*, Lewis Mumford provided a metaphor that is extremely helpful in introducing Pierre Riché's study of early medieval education and culture to an English-reading audience. Summarizing the main thrust of historical development during the fifth and sixth centuries, Mumford wrote: "One by one, the old classic lamps went out; one by one, the new tapers of the Church were lighted." This adept generalization provides a clue to two dimensions of scholarly research into the history of the early Middle Ages over the past two generations, both brilliantly exemplified by Riché's book. One has to do with the substantive results of these investigations; the other relates to the methodology employed in producing them.

Mumford's statement reminds us, first, that it was indeed "one by one" that the essential elements of the old classical order passed and those of the new medieval world emerged. Those who have followed in any detail the investigations of historians studying the period bounded by the collapse of the Roman Empire in the fifth century and the emergence of the Carolingians in the eighth century know that there was no clear break marking the end of one civilizational pattern and the beginning of another. Rather, this epoch was characterized by the persistence of fragments of the classical order—institutions, techniques, ideas from another world, now standing "one by one" without much relationship to other surviving elements of the same old order and serving society in unaccustomed ways. Many, indeed most, of these vestiges of the classical world "went out" between the fifth and the eighth centuries, each in its own turn and in circumstances that bore little relationship to the older order. Often the fragmented, isolated survivals of the classical world vanished because some new institution, technique, or idea had been generated in an unstable world to take its place. This lighting of the "new tapers" likewise occurred piece by piece, willy-nilly, without any easily discernible order or pattern. In short, Mumford's statement points to a profound truth about the history of the early Middle Ages: the passing of the old order and the emergence of the new involved a process that was unpatterned, that was comprised of disparate parts seldom connected to one another, and that for the modern historian takes on meaning only when isolated pieces of the disordered process are given visibility in and of themselves.

Moreover, Mumford's generalization provides us with the clue to the scholarly approach which has yielded the clearest knowledge of and the deepest insight into the confused history of the early Middle Ages. That approach has involved isolating particular aspects of the classical world in order to trace each to its end and, likewise, singling out individual features of the emerging new society in order to depict each in its singularity. Rather than fashioning sweeping syntheses which try to fit the tangle of individual events into some hypothetical model explicating the death and birth of civilization, historians of the early Middle Ages have, over the last two generations, set themselves to the more modest tasks of tracing the details marking the end of particular remnants of the classical order that survived into the early Middle Ages and of ferreting out the precise circumstances marking the emergence of specific new institutions and ideas. They have worked on both the "old lamps" and the "new tapers," but have treated them "one by one." The result has been a remarkable deepening of our understanding of a critical age whose essence lies in a fragmented transformation of the conditions of human existence from one basis to another.

Pierre Riché's *Education and Culture in the Barbarian West, Sixth through Eighth Centuries*, is a landmark study in the quest for a better comprehension of what is often called the real "dark age." Since its original publication in French in 1962, it has served admirably to answer to those two ends suggested by Lewis Mumford's statement. The book has provided a definitive description of one crucial aspect of the changing order in Western European society between 500 and 750, namely, the way education was organized and executed. And it has illustrated in a superlative fashion the methodological approach required of the historian who wishes to make sense out of the chaotic, almost intractable records of human endeavor surviving from those confusing centuries. So basic is Riché's book to both the history and the historiography of the early Middle Ages that many—especially teachers of medieval history—have lamented its unavailability to English readers to the point of feeling that those who could not read the work in French (or, since 1966, in Italian) were being deprived of adequate knowledge of a significant aspect of early medieval history. It is therefore cause for genuine celebration that Riché's work now appears in English; Professor John Contreni has provided the English-reading world with an invaluable instrument to assist in deepening our understanding of one of the most enigmatic epochs in all of human history.

To mention the special qualities of Professor Riché's book would involve a long list, as will be obvious to all who read the book. From that extensive list, however, a few particular achievements make the book uniquely outstanding as a contribution to the ongoing quest for an understanding of the early medieval period. Their identification here might well serve not only as a special inducement to the reading of the book but also as a guide to those aspects of the study that will yield the richest profits to the careful reader.

First, there is the subject of the book. Riché asks his readers to inquire about a great subject, one that is universally and critically vital to the human condition: education. Without seeking or needing any explanation, readers will realize that they are being involved with a topic that is fundamental to any age and any society, including those that are remote in time and often judged to be dismal in terms of the quality of life. Likewise, they will instinctively sense that if anything happened in any historical period to change the character of education, it follows that the period has significance in the total stream of human history. This must be so because education is so fundamental to any civilizational order that its character and quality affect every other aspect of that order. Quite in keeping with the spirit of the modern approach to the early Middle Ages, Riché has isolated a significant aspect of the old classical order and has pursued that theme across a particular time span in order to illuminate any changes that occurred. He focuses attention on the extinguishing of old lamps and the lighting of new tapers, but he fixes on particular lamps and tapers in order to assure that an intelligible portion of an entire societal order can be seen clearly and precisely.

The effectiveness of Riché's treatment of his subject is enhanced by his disciplined conceptualization of education. He resists the modern temptation to define education as a process that embraces every experience which men and women, either individually or collectively, undergo —a definition that might make an historical exploration of the subject so diffuse and so demanding that the results would be incomprehensible. He avoids the pitfall of equating education with the productions, especially literary productions, of those who were educated—a confusion that often results in an inverted reconstruction of the educational process itself on the basis of what had to be in order to explain what was later written or spoken. For Riché, education is a very specific process, consciously structured and executed to produce a particular result. It is a social art by which elders seek to modify the behavior of the young by subjecting them formally to specific experiences that will permit them to do things previously beyond their capability. Within this framework, Riché can address himself to the specific issues constituting the essence of education as he sees it. He is able to concentrate on identifying those in early medieval society who were subjected to a specific process, to answer the question, Who was educated? He is able to identify those who executed the specific process, to respond to another basic question, Who did the educating? He is in a position to delineate a precise process, to answer the question, How was education carried out? He can search for those elements providing the substance of the process, and thus answer the question, What was taught? He is able to explore the motivating forces undergirding the process, to answer the question, Why was education undertaken? Such precise questions, emerging from a realistic conceptualization of education and pursued with admirable concentration, produce a study characterized both by that kind of clarity which results from dealing with simple but fundamental questions and by a substantive profundity which emerges from treating the real acts of human beings consciously engaged in a specific undertaking.

A third noteworthy feature of Riché's study is the meticulous attention given to the chronology of educational evolution. Too often, those who deal with the somewhat distant past are tempted to lump two or three centuries together into a conceptual entity and to treat events occurring within that period as if they occurred almost simultaneously.

Since this is not the way the human experience unfolds, such a condensation of time can breed serious distortions of the past. Riché avoids the aberrations that result from the indiscriminate placement of individual events within a preconceived scheme of periodization. With meticulous care, he locates events in the actual sequence in which they occurred. The result is a firm sense of the order of events within a three-century span and a meaningful presentation of change and development within that temporal framework.

Reinforcing Riché's attention to the temporal beat of the historical process is a fourth significant characteristic of this book: a rigorous concern with geography. Although his broad concern is with the West, Riché refuses to succumb to a temptation that has beguiled too many historians of the early Middle Ages—at great disadvantage to their studies. He avoids treating "the West" as a homogeneous geographic entity about which universally valid statements can be made. He constantly fastens his attention on where things actually happened, resisting the temptation to assume that an event occurring in a particular place in the West permits one to conclude that a comparable development occurred everywhere else in the West. The consequence is a much more nuanced and complex picture of the cultural history of the early Middle Ages than has been heretofore available. Especially dramatic to those who have some general sense of the history of educational institutions and practices during the sixth, seventh, and eighth centuries will be Riché's success in pinpointing the geographic centers of creative activity and in tracing the outreach of influences from those centers leading eventually to the pan-Western cultural phenomenon known as the Carolingian "renaissance." Equally illuminating will be the differences between regions of the West in this seminal age in the history of education, differences that ultimately served as stimulants to cultural growth once circumstances permitted interactions between the diverse educational institutions and practices of various localities.

As critical as they are to understanding the past, time and place do not make history. Only men do. Pierre Riché is always mindful of this fact, and his concern for the human dimensions of educational development provides a fifth remarkable feature of his book. Too often the history of the early Middle Ages has been told in terms of impersonal, faceless collectivities to which things happen or which cause things to happen, with the result that one gets no feel for the life forces that individuals bring to the historical process. This approach is easy to take with respect to the early Middle Ages because the surviving record is not only sparse and spotty, but also maddeningly impersonal. Riché refuses to take the easy path; he relentlessly pursues the individual. And he succeeds in filling his book with a range of individual human beings whose particular involvement in the processes of education make them real to the reader. The traditional heroes of early medieval cultural life—those that E. K. Rand would identify as "founders of the Middle Ages"—are all portrayed in full detail: Augustine, Cassiodorus, Boethius, Isidore of Seville, Gregory the Great, Bede, Gregory of Tours. So also are a host of lesser figures involved in the changing educational scene: aristocrats who tried to keep the classical educational system alive, bishops who struggled to find means of transmitting the skills needed to sustain the Christian heritage, abbots who labored to teach their monks to be saints, masters who worked with students of all sorts, the students themselves. Riché even draws our attention to the illiterates —a constantly growing legion representing all levels of society—and to the kind of education they received. His passion for discovering the individuals involved in educating or being educated and for making concrete and particular exactly what happened to each individual enriches and humanizes the book. His accomplishment in filling the era with living people may well make this the most remarkable book about the early Middle Ages the reader has ever encountered.

None of the admirable features mentioned thus far would have been possible without Riché's impressive ability to wrest from the surviving records of the early Middle Ages a rich harvest of information and to present this information with an amazing depth of understanding. Only those who have struggled to recreate the history of the sixth, seventh, and eighth centuries from those sources will appreciate the magnitude of this feat. For early medieval records are truly a miserable base from which to work. They are few; their provenance is usually uncertain; their language is imprecise and confused; most frustrating of all, they seldom discuss directly those topics with which the modern historian is concerned—education, for instance. Riché refuses to be frustrated by this seemingly intractable record. He has devoted immense energy to an exploration of the whole record, in whatever form it exists, in search of data relating to educational development. He has patiently scrutinized each shred of evidence in infinite detail to discover whatever minute fact it might reveal about educational history. He demonstrates an uncanny ability to extract vital information from records that seem little related to or concerned with educational matters. Frequently, he has translated an oblique remark deposited in the record by someone little mindful of the future historian into a rich comment on the educational system, an ability grounded in a profound understanding of human nature, human motivation, and human modes of thought and expression. All of this is achieved without straining the record. Riché is always objective, critical, and judicious as he goes about extracting new and revealing information from the witnesses who left records about how men and women were educated in the early Middle Ages. His performance as an information gatherer and interpreter is truly the fundamental key to every other outstanding feature of the book.

These special traits of Pierre Riché's book suggest a classic historical study—even though it usually takes a reading public longer than a decade or so to recognize and to accept a classic. This book's subject commands the reader's attention. The clarity with which that subject is conceived and the discipline with which it is pursued provides the book with an orderliness that compels admiration. The effort to discover and delineate time and place and human beings immerses the reader in those unique dimensions of the past that make history a mind-expanding enterprise. The consummate skill in exploiting nearly intractable records reflects an artistry that will bedazzle the casual reader and be the envy of scholars. One wonders what more can be said of the work of any historian.

To what Pierre Riché has wrought, Professor Contreni has detracted nothing in his translation. Like all translators, he has undertaken a thankless job, but he has performed his task in a manner that asks for approbation. He has rendered another language into impeccable English that conveys accurately and gracefully what Pierre Riché has said. His willingness to spend uncounted hours in the cause of giving a new audience access to a major historical study puts us in his debt.

RICHARD E. SULLIVAN
Michigan State University

Prefaces

PREFACE TO THE FIRST FRENCH EDITION

To write a book about education during the most obscure centuries in Western history would have been interpreted only a few years ago as a risky venture. The period which opens the Middle Ages has long been considered an uncultured and barbaric time, to which the historian, hurrying on to the Carolingian renaissance, would devote but a few scornful lines. Nevertheless, despite the paucity of sources, historians have begun to appreciate the significance, if not the richness, of those centuries which lie between the end of the ancient world and the beginnings of the Middle Ages.[1] An ever-increasing number of studies and even scholarly congresses[2] have tried to illuminate these "Dark Ages."[3] Already, the elements of a synthesis of the civilization of the Barbarian West are being brought together. The transmission of Roman culture to the Middle Ages has been the subject of several remarkable works which, however, have generally focused

---

[1] Numerous studies have dealt with this transitional period since the appearance of the classic work of Ferdinand Lot, *La fin du monde antique et le début du Moyen Age* (Paris, 1937; 2nd ed., 1951). See Hermann Aubin, *Vom Altertum zum Mittelalter: Absterben, Fortleben, und Erneuerung* (Munich, 1949); Karl F. Stroheker, "Um die Grenze zwischen Antike und abendländischem Mittelalter, ein Forschungsbericht," *Saeculum* 1 (1950): 433–65; P. Hübinger, "Spätantike und frühes Mittelalter," *Deutsche Vierteljahrsschrift für Literaturwissenschaft und Geistesgeschichte* 26 (1952): 1–48; Eugen Ewig, "Das Fortleben römischer Institutionen in Gallien und Germanien," in *X Congresso internazionale di scienze storiche, Relazioni VI* (Florence, 1955), pp. 561–98.

[2] Scholarly meetings devoted to the early Middle Ages have been held at Spoleto since 1954. Some of the meetings have focused on the Barbarian period; see the volumes of *Settimane* listed in the Bibliography.

[3] For this expression see the opening pages of W. P. Ker, *The Dark Ages* (New York, 1904).

on one country or on one man.[4] No study of the entirety of Western culture during the Barbarian period could have been attempted without these works.

As I, in turn, now approach this barren period, I have chosen not to study culture in the larger sense of the term,[5] or even one of its manifestations, the teaching of classical literature, which was the subject of a book now a half century old and, on many points, still authoritative.[6] Rather, I have chosen a too often neglected aspect of the history of civilization for the theme of my research: education. Antiquity created an educational system that is now well known.[7] The Carolingian epoch, a golden age of masters and schools, has long attracted the attention of researchers. It is indispensable to know how ancient education gave way to medieval education, how the Roman man of letters was replaced by the medieval cleric. What influence did the Barbarian invasions have on the fate of the school and of education in general? How did lay literary culture disappear? How did laymen receive their religious instruction? Did the schools of the clerics and monks inherit the program of the Roman school, as is so often claimed? Did ecclesiastical pedagogy adopt antique methods, or was it innovative? These questions, among many others, merit an answer.

Of course, it is easier to study education during a time when a system of values is well established. An adult who has charge of a child transmits to him that which seems most apt to form his body, his mind, and his religious faith in light of a well-defined ideal of life. But between the sixth and eighth centuries, traditional values were placed in question. The West knew not one type of civilization but, rather, several civilizations which coexisted and often rivaled each other in offering quite different paths to young people. What contrasts there were among the

[4] See the important study of Jacques Fontaine, *Isidore de Séville et la culture classique dans l'Espagne wisigothique* (Paris, 1959), a work to which I will often refer. Pierre Courcelle's thesis, *Les lettres grecques en Occident de Macrobe à Cassiodore* (Paris, 1948), studies one aspect of Western culture and ends with the sixth century.

[5] For the different meanings of the word *culture*, see Henri Marrou, *Saint Augustin et la fin de la culture antique* (Paris, 1938), pp. 549–60.

[6] In *L'enseignement des lettres classiques d'Ausone à Alcuin* (Paris, 1905), Maurice Roger limited his study to the intellectual culture of Gaul and the British Isles. Reacting against the optimism of romantic authors, he produced a very critical work. He wrote, on p. 146: "An accumulation of uncertain sources leading to negative results—such is the ungrateful task we are undertaking."

[7] See Henri Marrou, *Histoire de l'éducation dans l'Antiquité* (Paris, 1948). The epilogue of this significant work—the point of departure for the present study—is devoted to a brief but remarkable synthesis of education between the fifth and eighth centuries.

pupil leaving the charge of the Roman grammarian, the lector attached
to a cathedral church, the Barbarian raised in the entourage of his chief,
and the monk offered to his monastery as an infant!

The differences among these opposing types of education make this
study particularly interesting as well as difficult to present. I did not
want to write a history of literature or to concentrate on the culture of
the great men who dominated their period independently of the culture
of their contemporaries. Instead, I have studied the education of laymen,
clerics, and monks by placing them in the social and geographical
milieux to which they belonged. By adopting a plan which is more
historical than logical, I wanted to show how the education of Western
man gradually changed as a result of political and social changes.

In order to grasp more clearly the many facets of this history, I have
researched every region in the Barbarian West, including Byzantine
Italy, since the culture of this country is closely linked to that of the
West. The point of departure for my study coincides with the disappearance of the Empire in the West—not because I wished to bow to
the official and conventional chronology which makes the Middle Ages
begin in 476 but, rather, because it is necessary to await the triumph of
the Barbarians in order for the pedagogical problems which had long
been posed to be resolved. I conclude my study when the medieval
educational system is firmly in place, that is, at the beginning of the
Carolingian renaissance.

For this work, it has been necessary to gather and to compare evidence from the most diverse sources: narrative, diplomatic, juridical,
epigraphical, and archaeological. Even so, many aspects of this synthesis
remain obscure, and many of its hypotheses cannot be verified in the
absence of documentation. Nevertheless, I have taken a stand after
sifting all the evidence we possess. I have done so without hesitation in
the hope that my work might further the understanding of one aspect
of the civilization of Barbarian times and at the same time be useful
to those who undertake to write the history of medieval education.

I would like to thank all who have shown interest in this work: my
teachers at the Faculté des Lettres in Paris, Charles-Edmond Perrin and
Yves Renouard, professors of medieval history, who after the death of
Louis Halphen—whose memory I salute here—agreed to direct this
thesis; Gabriel Le Bras, dean of the Faculté de Droit in Paris, Pierre
Courcelle, professor at the Collège de France, and Jean Hubert, professor at the Ecole des Chartes, who have guided and encouraged me with

their advice; and also all those who in various capacities facilitated my research.

Finally, I must express my gratitude to Henri I. Marrou, professor of the history of Christianity at the Sorbonne, whose confidence and friendship have always meant much to me and who has accepted this work for the series which he directs. Although not devoted to the Church Fathers, this study shows how much the culture of the end of the ancient world and of the beginning of the Middle Ages was inspired by their teaching. In taking up the work of the Fathers, in adapting it to the conditions of their time, the "founders" of Western culture—Cassiodorus, Gregory the Great, Isidore, Bede the Venerable—transmitted to the Middle Ages a patristic tradition that was continued in monastic schools until the end of the twelfth century.

Carthage
22 June 1960

PREFACE TO THE SECOND FRENCH EDITION

Almost five years have passed since the publication of this book. The friendly welcome which the critics gave to the first edition and to the Italian edition (Rome, 1966) has persuaded me to present simply a corrected second edition. The reviews have generally been too kind for me to draw material from them for a true revision. On the other hand, publications on this subject during the last five years have not been numerous enough to lead me to modify my conclusions. I have, however, added several titles and an index and have particularly taken the opportunity to correct a few oversights and imperfections in details here and there. I do not know how to thank all those who have graciously helped me in many ways with this task.

Some critics have reproached me for not having given an important enough place to Celtic education. I am the first to be aware of this fault because I know how much the Celtic world contributed to the history of Western culture. As I have already said, however, one cannot undertake the study of Celtic culture without understanding Gaelic texts. Furthermore, it is difficult to use Celtic hagiography since the Irish, Welsh, and Amorican saints' *Lives* were written well after the period which concerns us. Other critics have thought my conclusions on monastic culture too optimistic and have reproached me for minimizing the importance of the Carolingian renaissance under Charlemagne. On this point, I remain faithful to my conclusions until someone demonstrates the profound originality of this renaissance.

It remains for me to hope that other historians will take note of the omissions and insufficiencies of this book and will complete it or redo it in one or another of its chapters. Thus, my work will have been useful if it opens up a field of research that has too often been neglected. Work on the education and culture of Late Antiquity and the Middle Ages ought not to be undertaken by one man but by an entire team of scholars, historians, philologists, archaeologists, and others. But this poses the problem of methods of historical research in France—a problem which has not yet found a satisfactory solution.

Rennes
January 1967

PREFACE TO THE THIRD FRENCH EDITION

I have taken the opportunity of a new edition, coming five years after the second edition, to enrich the general bibliography and to add to the footnotes wherever possible. Articles and even books that have appeared in the intervening five years have enabled me to add new material here and there. These additions, found at the end of the book, are signaled in the text by asterisks.

Paris
25 July 1972

TRANSLATOR'S NOTE

The material that Pierre Riché added at the end of the third French edition of his book has been incorporated into the text and notes of this translation. Also, for this translation, frequently cited works of modern scholarship have been designated by abbreviations; these abbreviated titles appear in the list of abbreviations that follows. The Bibliography includes references to English translations of works in modern foreign languages for the convenience of the reader. Citations in the footnotes, however, continue to refer to the editions used by Pierre Riché. I have translated quotations from these editions. The opportunity to revise the format of the notes has enabled me in many cases to furnish complete bibliographical references, to correct erroneous citations, and to catch typographical errors overlooked in the third French edition. A new index has been prepared for this translation, and the maps have been redrawn.

JOHN J. CONTRENI
August 1976

Abbreviations

I. JOURNALS

AB	*Analecta Bollandiana*, Brussels
AcIB	*Comptes rendus des séances de l'Académie des Inscriptions et Belles-Lettres*, Paris
AEA	*Archivo español de arqueologia*, Madrid
Aevum	*Aevum: Rassegna di scienze filologiche, linguistiche e storiche*, Milan
AFU	*Archiv für Urkundenforschung*, Leipzig
AHDE	*Anuario de historia del derecho español*, Madrid
AHMA	*Archives d'histoire doctrinale et littéraire du Moyen Age*, Paris
ALMA	*Archivum latinitatis Medii Aevi (Bulletin du Cange)*, Brussels
AM	*Annales du Midi*, Toulouse
AST	*Analecta sacra tarraconensia*, Barcelona
BAB	*Bulletin de la classe des Lettres de l'Académie royale de Belgique*, Brussels
BECh	*Bibliothèque de l'Ecole des Chartes*, Paris and Geneva
Bibl. HR	*Bibliothèque d'Humanisme et Renaissance*, Geneva
BSAF	*Bulletin de la Société nationale des antiquaires de France*, Paris
BTAM	*Bulletin de théologie ancienne et médiévale*, Louvain

Byzantion	*Byzantion: Revue internationale des études byzantines*, Brussels
BZ	*Byzantinische Zeitschrift*, Munich
CArch	*Cahiers archéologiques (fin de l'Antiquité et Moyen Age)*, Paris
CM	*Classica et mediaevalia: Revue danoise d'histoire et de philologie*, Copenhagen
CPh	*Classical Philology*, Chicago
CQ	*Classical Quarterly*, Oxford
CW	*Classical Weekly*, New York
DA	*Dissertation Abstracts: A Guide to Dissertations and Monographs Available in Microform*, Ann Arbor, University of Michigan Microfilms
EL	*Ephemerides liturgicae*, Rome
Emerita	*Emerita: Boletin de lingüística y filologia clásica*, Madrid
FS	*Frühmittelalterliche Studien: Jahrbuch des Instituts für Frühmittelalterforschung der Universität Münster*, Berlin
Germania	*Germania: Anzeiger der römisch-germanische Kommission des deutschen archäologischen Instituts*, Berlin
HJ	*Historisches Jahrbuch*, Cologne
HS	*Hispania sacra*, Madrid
MA	*Le Moyen Age: Revue trimestrielle d'histoire et de philologie*, Brussels
MEFR	*Mélanges d'archéologie et d'histoire de l'Ecole française de Rome*, Paris
MIOEG	*Mitteilungen des Instituts für Oesterreichische Geschichtsforschung*, Innsbruck
MS	*Mediaeval Studies*, Toronto
NA	*Neues Archiv der Gesellschaft für ältere deutsche Geschichtskunde*, Hannover, Berlin
NRTh	*Nouvelle revue théologique*, Louvain and Tournai
PhQ	*Philological Quarterly*, Iowa University Press
RA	*Revue archéologique*, Paris
RAE	*Revue archéologique de l'Est et du Centre-Est*, Dijon
RAM	*Revue d'ascétique et de mystique*, Toulouse

RB	*Revue bénédictine,* Abbey of Maredsous, Belgium
RBPh	*Revue belge de philologie et d'histoire,* Brussels
REA	*Revue des études anciennes,* Bordeaux
REL	*Revue des études latines,* Paris
Revue Mabillon	Abbey of Ligugé, Ligugé, France
RH	*Revue historique,* Paris
RHD	*Revue d'histoire du droit: Tidjschrift voor rechtsgeschiedenis,* Groningen, Brussels, and The Hague
RHDE	*Revue historique de Droit français et étranger,* Paris
RHE	*Revue d'histoire ecclésiastique,* Louvain
RHEF	*Revue d'histoire de l'Eglise de France,* Paris
RhM	*Rheinisches Museum für Philologie,* Frankfurt
RMAL	*Revue du Moyen Age latin,* Strasbourg
RPh	*Revue de philologie,* Paris
RQH	*Revue des questions historiques,* Paris
RSH	*Revue suisse d'histoire: Schweizerische Zeitschrift für Geschichte,* Zurich
RTAM	*Recherches de théologie ancienne et médiévale,* Gembloux
Scriptorium	*Scriptorium: Revue internationale des études relatives aux manuscrits,* Antwerp and Gand
SE	*Sacris Erudiri: Jaarboek voor Godsdienstwetenschappen,* St. Pietersabdij, Steenbrugge
SM	*Studi medievali,* Spoleto
Speculum	*Speculum: A Journal of Medieval Studies,* Cambridge, Mass.
Traditio	*Traditio: Studies in Ancient and Medieval History, Thought, and Religion,* New York
Vallesia	*Vallesia: Bulletin annuel de la Bibliothèque et des Archives cantonales du Valais et du Musée de Valère,* Sion
VChr	*Vigiliae christianae: A Review of Early Christian Life and Language,* Amsterdam
WS	*Wiener Studien: Zeitschrift für klassische Philologie,* Vienna
ZKG	*Zeitschrift für Kirchengeschichte,* Stuttgart

ZRGG	*Zeitschrift der Savigny-Stiftung für Rechtsgeschichte (Germanistiche Abteilung)*, Weimar
ZRGR	*Zeitschrift der Savigny-Stiftung für Rechtsgeschichte (Romanistiche Abteilung)*, Weimar
ZRPh	*Zeitschrift für romanische Philologie*, Tübingen

II. COLLECTIONS, DICTIONARIES, AND ENCYCLOPEDIAS

Anth. lat.	*Anthologia latina.* Ed. Franz Buecheler and Alexander Riese. Vol. 1, Leipzig, 1894.
AS	*Acta sanctorum bollandistarum.* Antwerp and Brussels, 1643–.
ASOB	*Acta sanctorum ordinis sancti Benedicti.* Ed. Jean Mabillon and Thierry Ruinart. 9 vols. Paris, 1668–1701.
Blaise	*Dictionnaire latin-français des auteurs chrétiens.* Ed. A. Blaise, rev. H. Chirat. Strasbourg, 1954.
CBEL	*The Cambridge Bibliography of English Literature.* Ed. F. W. Bateson. Cambridge, 1940.
CCL	*Corpus christianorum, series latina.* Turnhout, 1953–.
CDL	*Codice diplomatico longobardo.* Ed. Luigi Schiaparelli. Rome, 1929–33.
ChLA	*Chartae latinae antiquiores.* Ed. Albert T. Bruckner and Robert Marichal. Olten and Lausanne, 1954–.
CIG	*Corpus inscriptionum graecarum.* Berlin, 1873–.
CIL	*Corpus inscriptionum latinarum.* Berlin, 1869–.
CLA	*Codices latini antiquiores.* Ed. Elias Avery Lowe. 11 vols. with a *Supplement.* Oxford, 1934–71.
Clavis	Eligius Dekkers and Aemilius Gaar. *Clavis patrum latinorum. SE* 3 (1951); 2nd ed., 1961.
Cottineau	L. H. Cottineau. *Repértoire topo-bibliographique des abbayes et prieurés.* 2 vols. Mâcon, 1935–39.
CSEL	*Corpus scriptorum ecclesiasticorum latinorum.* Vienna, 1866–.

DACL	*Dictionnaire d'archéologie chrétienne et de liturgie.* Ed. Fernand Cabrol, Henri Leclercq, and, since 1947, Henri I. Marrou. Paris, 1907–58.
DDC	*Dictionnaire de droit canonique.* Ed. R. Naz. Paris, 1935–.
DHGE	*Dictionnaire d'histoire et de géographie ecclésiastiques.* Ed. Alfred Baudrillart, R. Aubert, E. Van Cauwenbergh, and A. De Meyer. Paris, 1912–.
DSp	*Dictionnaire de spiritualité, ascétique et mystique, doctrine et histoire.* Ed. Marcel Viller, F. Cavallera, J. de Guibert, Charles Baumgartner, and Michel Olphe-Galliard. Paris, 1937–.
DTC	*Dictionnaire de théologie catholique.* Ed. A. Vacant, E. Mangenot, and E. Amann. 15 vols. Paris, 1909–50.
Haddan-Stubbs	*Councils and Ecclesiastical Documents Relating to Great Britain and Ireland.* Ed. Arthur West Haddan and William Stubbs, 4 vols. Oxford, 1869–78.
Hoops	*Reallexikon der germanischen Altertumskunde.* Ed. Johannes Hoops. 4 vols. Strasbourg, 1911–19.
ICR	*Inscriptiones christianae urbis Romae septimo saeculo antiquiores.* Ed. J. B. de Rossi. Vols. 1–2. Rome, 1857/61–88.
Keil	*Grammatici latini.* Ed. Heinrich Keil. 7 vols. Leipzig, 1855–80.
Le Blant, *IC*	*Inscriptions chrétiennes de la Gaule antérieures au VIIIᵉ siècle.* Ed. Edmund Le Blant. 2 vols. Paris, 1856–65.
Le Blant, *NR*	*Nouveau recueil des inscriptions chrétiennes de la Gaule antérieures au VIIIᵉ siècle.* Ed. Edmund Le Blant. Paris, 1892.
Mansi	*Sacrorum conciliorum nova et amplissima collectio.* Ed. J. D. Mansi. Florence and Venice, 1759–98.
MGH	*Monumenta Germaniae historica.* Hannover and Leipzig, 1826–.
——, *AA*	*Auctores antiquissimi.*
——, *Capit.*	*Capitularia regum Francorum.*

——, *Dipl. karol.*	*Diplomata karolinarum.*
——, *Ep.*	*Epistolae.*
——, *Leges*	*Leges* (series in folio).
——, *Leg. sect.*	*Legum sectiones I–V*
——, *PAC*	*Poetae latini aevi carolini.*
——, *SRL*	*Scriptores rerum langobardicarum et italicarum saeculorum VI–IX.*
——, *SRM*	*Scriptores rerum merovingicarum.*
——, *SS*	*Scriptores.*
Pardessus	*Diplomata, chartae, epistolae, leges, aliaque instrumenta ad res Gallo-Francicas spectantia.* Ed. J. M. Pardessus. 2 vols. Paris, 1843–49.
PG	*Patrologia graeca.* Ed. J. P. Migne. Paris, 1856–66.
PL	*Patrologia latina.* Ed. J. P. Migne. Paris, 1844–64.
RE	*Real-Encyclopädie der classischen Altertumswissenschaft.* New ed. Begun by G. Wissowa; continued by W. Kroll, K. Mittelhaus, and K. Ziegler. Stuttgart, 1894–.
SC	*Sources chrétiennes.* Paris, 1942–.
ST	*Studi e testi.* Vatican City, 1900–.
ThLL	*Thesaurus linguae latinae.* Leipzig, 1900–.

III. SECONDARY WORKS

See the Bibliography for complete bibliographical information on the following works.

Bezzola	Reto R. Bezzola. *Les origines et la formation de la littérature courtoise en Occident, 500–1200.*
Courcelle, *LG*	Pierre Courcelle. *Les lettres grecques en Occident de Macrobe à Cassiodore.*
Courtois	Christian Courtois. *Les Vandales et l'Afrique.*
Coville	Alfred Coville. *Recherches sur l'histoire de Lyon du Ve au IXe siècle (450–800).*
Curtius	Ernst Robert Curtius. *La littérature européenne et le Moyen Age latin.*
Diaz y Diaz, *AW*	Manuel C. Diaz y Diaz, *Anecdota Wisigothica.*

Fliche-Martin	Augustin Fliche and Victor Martin, eds. *Histoire de l'Eglise depuis les origines jusqu'à nos jours.*
J. Fontaine, *IS*	Jacques Fontaine. *Isidore de Séville et la culture classique dans l'Espagne wisigothique.*
Levison, *England*	Wilhelm Levison. *England and the Continent in the Eighth Century.*
Manitius	Max Manitius, *Geschichte der lateinischen Literatur des Mittelalters.*
Menéndez Pidal, *HE*	Ramón Menéndez Pidal. *Historia de España.*
Roger	Maurice Roger. *L'enseignement des lettres classiques d'Ausone à Alcuin: Introduction à l'histoire des écoles carolingiennes.*
Salin	Edouard Salin. *La civilisation mérovingienne d'après les sépultres, les textes et le laboratoire.*
Schanz	Martin Schanz. *Geschichte der römischen Literatur.*
Settimane	*Settimane di studio del centro italiano di studi sull'alto medioevo.*
Stein	Ernst Stein. *Histoire du Bas-Empire.*
Stroheker	Karl Friedrich Stroheker. *Der senatorische Adel im spätantiken Gallien.*
Wattenbach-Levison	*Wattenbach-Levison: Deutschlands Geschichtsquellen im Mittelalter, Vorzeit und Karolinger.* Ed. Wilhelm Levison and Heinz Löwe.

Education and Culture

IN THE BARBARIAN WEST, SIXTH THROUGH EIGHTH CENTURIES

Introduction

THE PRESTIGE OF ROMAN EDUCATION IN THE FIFTH CENTURY

During the catastrophic fifth century, the century of the great invasions, Romans, whether pagan or Christian, continued to have confidence in an educational system that had been one of the greatest artisans of their success. Rome, through its educational institutions, had imposed its law and its culture on its far-flung empire. The written word, which did not extend beyond the Mediterranean regions before the Roman conquest, reached countries which had previously known only oral traditions. From Wales to the borders of the Sahara, Latin inscriptions on tombs, monuments, and the most ordinary objects bear witness to Rome's success. To learn to read and to write had become an obligation for all who wished to participate in the activities of *Romania*.

We cannot know exactly how far Roman culture penetrated society. Rome ruled with its elite class and could not envision the intellectual advancement of the masses it had conquered. Even in Italy, the "democratization of culture" had probably never extended very far.[1] Rome preferred to place its emphasis on the establishment of "secondary" schools, the schools of the grammarian and the rhetor, which alone would permit the formation of the type of man Rome desired.

Once a child could read and write correctly,[2] he was confided to a

---

[1] On this question see the very misleading report of Santo Mazzarino, "La democratizzazione della cultura nel 'Basso Impero,'" in *XIe Congrès international des sciences historiques (Stockholm . . . 1960): Rapports*, vol. 2, *Antiquité* (Uppsala, 1960), pp. 35–54.

[2] For the instruction provided by the *primus magister*, or the *litterator*, see Henri Mar-

4.

INTRODUCTION

grammarian who taught him to speak and write with style and introduced him to the classical authors. The last centuries of the Western Empire have been well designated as "the golden age of Latin *grammatica*."[3] At a time when the Latin language was undergoing a transformation, it is remarkable to note the appearance of a great number of grammatical works. Their authors seemingly wanted to arrest the evolution of the language and to impose on the educated class the rules which had once been Latin's strength. Although they differed in presentation, these manuals all dealt with the same questions. First, letters and syllables, then the "eight parts of speech" (noun, verb, participle, article, pronoun, preposition, adverb, conjunction) were minutely studied and categorized. Grammar, which originally was meant to teach the mechanics of the language, became a highly cultivated, almost speculative science. Instruction in spelling received particular attention. The grammarian warned his students against orthographic innovations carried over from the spoken language.[4] Grammarians also taught the rules of prosody and meter according to traditional literary norms, likewise without regard to changes in the pronunciation of words. Finally, they explicated the classical authors to the child (*enarratio auctorum*).[5] They devoted many hours to the verse-by-verse, line-by-line literal explication of a text. They did not limit themselves to a mere grammatical analysis of a text but went on to explore all the information it contained. Working with the historical, legal, and scientific allusions contained in the text, the grammarian introduced his pupil to the different branches of ancient learning and, in the process, gave him a vast general cultural background. At the same time, the pupil was invited to demonstrate his proficiency with preparatory exercises. He proved his knowledge of accentuation and of the rules of pronunciation by reading and reciting short passages.[6] He then had to transpose a poem into prose or to paraphrase a few moral maxims.[7]

---

rou, *Histoire de l'éducation dans l'Antiquité* (Paris, 1948), pp. 359–68 (hereafter cited as *Education*).

[3] Henri Marrou, *Saint Augustin et la fin de la culture antique* (Paris, 1938), p. 11, and *Education*, pp. 370–79. See also Charles Lambert, *La grammaire latine selon les grammairiens latins du IVe et du Ve siècle*, Revue bourguignonne publiée par l'Université de Dijon, vol. 18, nos. 1–2 (Dijon, 1908); and J. Fontaine, *IS*, pp. 27ff.

[4] See the preface to Agroecius' mid-fifth-century treatise, which revised Caper's work (Keil, 7: 112). The study of spelling and of the etymologies of nouns and verbs were combined; see Lambert, *La grammaire latine*, pp. 225–26.

[5] For the *enarratio*, see Marrou, *Education*, pp. 375ff.

[6] Lambert, *La grammaire latine*, pp. 42–44; Marrou, *Education*, p. 553, n. 30.

[7] See Quintillian, *Inst. orat.*, I, 9 (ed. Henri Bornecque, 4 vols. [Paris, 1933–34], 1:

Once he had acquired a basic knowledge of the Latin language and a good cultural background, the young man could end his studies. But if he had developed a taste for Latin speech and wished a more detailed understanding of its rules, he presented himself to the rhetor. Here, as he began a new stage in his studies, the student ran the risk of being deceived. Quite often the work of the rhetor overlapped that of the grammarian, since the borders between their disciplines were not clearly defined. The pupil also soon learned that rhetoric was a difficult skill that demanded a greater intellectual effort than grammar and a long period of training. He had first to learn oratorical rules and devices such as those which the manuals of the *Rhetores latini minores* of the fourth century preserve for us: how to "invent" commonplaces (*topoi*), how to construct a speech (*dispositio*) from the exordium to the peroration, and how to present it orally (*elocutio*) with gestures (*actio*).[8] In addition, he had to ornament his speech with rhythmic clausulae, thereby rounding out his knowledge of the laws of poetry to which the grammarian had already exposed him.[9]

The study of orators and historians gave him a rich storehouse of *exempla* which he drew upon for the practice exercises his master gave him. First, he practiced eulogizing a great person, describing a monument, or discussing a question on the moral order. Then, he tried more complex exercises, the *declamationes*. These fictitious speeches, presented either as arguments (*controversiae*) or as deliberations on a subject drawn from history or mythology (*suasoriae*), formed the most original part of rhetorical instruction.[10] The student not only had to utilize all the training acquired since his first grammatical studies but also had to draw on the science of discussion, that is, dialectic, which was considered the third liberal art.[11]

When he left the rhetor's school after four to six years of training, he could become a brilliant lecturer or, better, after some legal training,

---

126–28). Commentaries on the sayings of the philosophers provided the foundation for a young man's moral education; see Roger, pp. 16–17.

[8] For instruction in rhetorical theory, see Marrou, *Saint Augustin*, pp. 47ff., and *Education*, pp. 380ff.; also see J. Fontaine, *IS*, pp. 211ff., and Curtius, pp. 76ff.

[9] For the relationship between poetry and rhetoric, see Eduard Norden, *Die antike Kunstprosa vom VI. Jahrhundert v. Chr. bis in die Zeit der Renaissance* (Leipzig, 1918), 2: 894; and Curtius, p. 179. Karl Polheim, *Die lateinische Reimprosa* (Berlin, 1925), has studied metrical clausulae.

[10] For these exercises, see Marrou, *Education*, p. 383, and the classic work by Henri Bornecque, *Les Déclamations et les Déclamateurs d'après Sénèque le Père* (Lille, 1902).

[11] See Marrou, *Saint Augustin*, pp. 240–48.

a formidable lawyer.[12] Master of the art of oratory, the Roman felt himself as much a master of the world as he was of the word. Rhetoric provided him with "power, honors, friendships, and glory in the present life and in that to come."[13]

This eulogy, which ends Quintillian's *Oratorical Institutes*, is surprising to us who approach rhetoric from the outside through scholarly manuals. The study of the technique of oratorical devices seems to us dry and irrelevant.[14] It is true that rhetorical training during the last centuries of the western Empire no longer corresponded to the program traced by Cicero and Quintillian. They had hoped that the study of oratorical rules would be accompanied by a broader development which would complete the training the student had received from the grammarian and introduce him to philosophical inquiry. As a consequence of the abandonment of instruction in Greek, however, Romans no longer had access to philosophic training.[15] Only a few of the educated tried to save Hellenism in the West. Their efforts, as remarkable as they were, did not extend beyond the boundaries of small, privileged circles.[16]

The abandonment of philosophical training was inevitably accompanied by the abandonment of scientific studies. According to the program inherited from the Greek tradition, the four branches of mathematics (arithmetic, geometry, music, astronomy) were to be added to the three literary arts (grammar, rhetoric, dialectic) to form the ἐγχύχλιος παιδεία, or *artes liberales*.[17] Although some intellectuals from the fifth century on were still conscious of this unified program, they were unable to reintroduce it into the schools.[18] It sufficed to study the commentaries the grammarians gave when they explicated texts. While this kind of learning satisfied curiosity, it did not shape the mind. After years of study, the man of letters could add to his *eruditio* by consulting manuals, actually "digests," whose number steadily increased from the fourth century. Here he found not only lists of geographical names and historical anecdotes, but also a storehouse of

---

[12] For legal training, see Marrou, *Education*, pp. 380ff.

[13] Quintillian, *Inst. orat.*, XII, 11, 29 (Bornecque ed., 4: 390).

[14] Latin rhetoric has often been placed on trial. It has been defended, however, by Roger, p. 18, and especially by Marrou, *Education*, p. 384.

[15] For the retreat of Greek in the West, see Marrou, *Education*, pp. 351–55.

[16] The essentials on philosophical studies in the fifth-century West can be found in Courcelle, *LG*.

[17] Marrou, *Education*, pp. 243ff.

[18] Sidonius Apollinaris, *Carm.* XIV and XXII, prefaces (*MGH, AA*, VIII, 232, 244).

information on astronomy and its complement, astrology; the medical sciences; natural history; and other branches of knowledge.[19]

Thus, classical education in the West was uniquely literary. It sought to give the young Roman the means to take his place in a society that judged a man essentially on his qualities as an orator. It likewise permitted him to become a citizen capable of serving the State by directing the numerous offices upon which the organization of the Empire depended.

The State understandably supervised the organization of study and encouraged cities to open municipal schools.[20] Public officials nominated teachers. These masters enjoyed a variety of privileges and were protected from the competition of private teachers.[21] Some were admitted into the imperial entourage,[22] and one even briefly held the title of emperor.[23] Rome preserved its strength and prestige more by its teaching than by its armies. As much as they were able, its leaders watched over the orderly development of educational institutions.

The importance of the school in an Empire officially Christian since the fourth century is, at first glance, surprising. State control of the school should have disturbed the Church, whose mission was to teach Christian truth. Moreover, the moral principles of the Gospels were far removed from the humanist ideal fashioned by centuries of paganism. A Christian was apt to be scandalized by the immorality of the texts chosen by the grammarian and to consider studies whose essential goal was the art of speech as vain. The "cult of the Muses" threatened to turn the faithful from the cult of the true God.[24] Had not the Christian

---

[19] For the physical and natural sciences, we can cite the *Phenomena* of Aratus and Solinus' *Collection of Curiosities*; for history, Valerius Maximus' *Memorable Deeds and Sayings*; for geography, Vibius Sequester's *Dictionary*; for mythology, the *Mythographi vaticani* and Fulgentius' *Mitiologiarum libri*; and for the liberal arts, Martianus Capella's *De nuptiis Philologiae et Mercurii*. For the *eruditio* of the fourth century, see Marrou, *Saint Augustin*, pp. 105–57; for the fifth century, see André Loyen, *Sidoine Apollinaire et l'esprit précieux en Gaule aux derniers jours de l'Empire* (Paris, 1943), pp. 17ff.

[20] See Marrou, *Education*, pp. 398, 415, for the State and education.

[21] A law of 425—*Theodosian Code*, XIV, 8–3, in *Theodosiani libri XVI*, ed. Mommsen and Meyer, 1: 787—forbids those who teach "intra parietes domesticos" from teaching in public schools.

[22] The master of offices of Emperor Majorian (died 461) was a poet and rhetor; see Sidonius, *Ep.* IX, 13; *Carm.* IX, v. 308 (*MGH, AA*, VIII, 162, 225).

[23] Eugenius, a former rhetor, became emperor in 393. See Stein, 1: 211.

[24] There are countless studies of the opposition between classical culture and Christianity. To the references provided by Marrou, *Education*, pp. 423–24, add Jean Gaudemet, *L'Eglise dans l'Empire romain, IVe–Ve siècles* (Paris, 1958), pp. 582ff. A bibliography on the question is given in Gerard Leo Ellspermann's mediocre work *The Attitude of the*

everything in the sacred texts with which to satisfy his intellectual curiosity? Why should he go to the pagan rhetors, poets, scholars, and historians when he had the epistles of Saint Paul, the books of Genesis and Kings? The Bible was a work rich and varied enough to replace the liberal arts. This program, proposed in the *Didascalia apostolorum*[25] in the third century, was, in fact, adopted by monks in later centuries.[26]

The monks, however, still formed but a small minority living on the fringes of society. Although clerics and lay Christians admitted the superiority of the Bible over the liberal arts, they were so solidly attached to Roman civilization that they could not deny classical culture. Even those most intent upon denouncing the dangers of pagan literature saw the necessity of sending their children to school.[27] Christians themselves became grammarians and rhetors. They did not hesitate to transpose the Old and New Testaments into classical verse in order to prove that the biblical message could be successfully adapted to a literary form originally foreign to it. During the mid-fifth century, with Sedulius and the rhetor Claudius Marius Victorius, classical Christian poetry continued its brilliant course.[28]

No center for religious studies existed alongside the antique school. Young laymen received religious training within the family circle.[29] Those who felt a calling to clerical life were generally admitted into the ranks of the clergy after having gone only to the grammarian's school. It was in the service of the Church that they learned their trade: reading

---

Early Christian Latin Writers toward Pagan Literature and Learning (Washington, D.C., 1949). The *Journal of Classical Studies* 2 (1954): 103–11, even cites a work in Japanese by G. Mayeda with the English title *Classical Scholarship and Christianity: A Survey of Recent Studies.* Lastly, see Harald Hagendahl, *Latin Fathers and the Classics: A Study of the Apologists, Jerome, and Other Christian Writers,* Studia graeca et latina Gothoburgensia, vol. 6 (Göteborg, 1958).

[25] *Didascalia apostolorum: The Syriac Version . . . Accompanied by the Verona Latin Fragments,* trans. and ed. R. Hugh Connolly (Oxford, 1929), I, 6, 1–6 (p. 13).

[26] When he traced an educational program for a future nun, Jerome provided only for the study of the Bible; see C. Favez, "Saint Jérome, pédagogue," in *Mélanges de philologie, de littérature et d'histoire anciennes offerts à J. Marouzeau* (Paris, 1948), pp. 173–81.

[27] Marrou, *Education,* pp. 425–26.

[28] Pierre de Labriolle has studied Christian Latin poetry (*Histoire de la littérature latine chrétienne,* 2 vols. [Paris, 1947], 2: 466–94, 695–742). For Christian rhetoric, see below, chap. 3, sect. I.

[29] A passage in Ambrosiaster (*In epistolam Beati Pauli ad Ephesios, PL,* XVII, 387) suggests that originally the Church, like the synagogue, gave the child his first instruction. The author wrote: "Magistri . . . [sunt] ii qui litteris et lectionibus imbuendis infantes solebant imbuere sicut mos Iudeorum est, quorum traditio ad nos transitum fecit, quae per negligentiam obsolevit."

sacred texts, chanting Psalms and hymns, participating in the liturgy.[30] Neither exegesis nor theology was taught by specialized masters. The cleric interested in the sacred science had to educate himself outside his ecclesiastical service. He did not have the opportunity to take courses at an advanced school of religious sciences since none existed in the West.[31] The theological formation of the Latin Fathers of the Church occurred outside a school. It is this which accounts for the freedom of thought and richness of expression responsible for their success.

When, at the beginning of the fifth century, Augustine defined the principles of sacred learning in his *De doctrina christiana*, he did not intend to establish guidelines for a school but rather to offer the Christian intellectual rules for scriptural interpretation in an abbreviated format. He indicated how the Christian might utilize the skills he had acquired in school to deepen his religious culture.[32] Contrary to what has long been thought, Augustine did not have only the cleric in mind. He also invited laymen to become Christian scholars. In fact, laymen, following the examples of the emperors, became theologians, intervened in doctrinal quarrels, and commented on the Scriptures in both prose and verse. There were not two distinct cultures in the fifth century—one religious and reserved for the clergy, the other profane and the domain of the laity.[33] This concept of the unity of culture undoubtedly explains the absence of strictly clerical schools.

The only Christian school that could provide for a child's education and training was the monastic school. Coming from the East, monasticism implanted itself in the West during the fourth century. It attracted men who wished to flee the world and offered them a way of life completely opposed to that of the world. Obviously, then, secular knowledge had no place in the monasteries. Since one had only to be able to read in order to have access to the Bible, the monks limited their teaching to the rudiments for the children confided to them by their parents and for the adolescents who came to the monastery of their own volition.[34]

---

[30] Marrou, *Education*, p. 430. We will return to this question below, chap. 4, sect. II.A.

[31] Ibid., pp. 431ff.

[32] Marrou, *Saint Augustin*, pp. 331ff.

[33] Ibid., pp. 380–85.

[34] For the monastic school, see Marrou, *Education*, pp. 435ff. Gustave Bardy, "Les origines des écoles monastiques en Occident," *SE*, 5 (1953): 86–104, after having collected texts concerning the education of young monks, wrote, "We do not see monastic schools in the strict sense in the West"—a conclusion which seems to me to have been contradicted by the author's own research.

These schools can in no way be considered centers of sacred study. As we shall see, the monastery of Lérins, founded at the beginning of the fifth century and regarded by some as a school of theology, was really a school for asceticism.[35]

If Christianity did not influence the program of the Roman school, it might have modified the school's pedagogical methods and the Roman concept of the child. Romans, like Greeks, were not interested in the child or even in the adolescent. The goal of education (*humanitas*) was to form the adult "man" and not to preoccupy itself with the development of youth.[36] Only precocious children—that is, prodigies who already "thought like old men"—were worthy of interest.[37] Christianity could have recognized the distinctive attributes of childhood and transformed the spirit of education while remaining true to the teaching of its founder. In fact, however, Christians rarely praised the "spirit of childhood." Pope Leo the Great in the fifth century stood almost alone when he magnificently recalled that "Christ loved childhood, mistress of humility, rule of innocence, model of sweetness."[38] The Church

[35] See below, chap. 4, sect. I.A. The case of the monastery of Thagaste, which was created by Augustine, is different. If this was, in fact, a learned monastery, it was so because of the personality of its founder. The same can be said for the monastery founded by Jerome in Bethlehem.

[36] The subheading "L'homme contre l'enfant" is used by Marrou (*Education*, p. 299). There are few works on Roman pedagogical methods: see Violette De Cuyper's thesis, "L'attitude du Romain envers l'enfant en bas âge" (Louvain, 1947), cited in *RBPh* 27 (1949): 422; and Jean Gaudemet's article, "Parents et enfants dans la doctrine patristique et la législation conciliaire du Bas-Empire," in *Etudes d'histoire du droit privé offertes à Pierre Petot* (Paris, 1958), pp. 223–29.

[37] There are many epitaphs of child prodigies. See Henri Marrou, Μουσικὸς Ἀνήρ: *Etude sur les scènes de la vie intellectuelle figurant sur les monuments funéraires romains* (Grenoble, 1938), p. 304; Le Blant, *IC* I: 469–70 (no. 353); *Anth. Lat.*, no. 345. See also the topos *puer-senex* in Curtius, p. 124, to whose examples the following can be added: *Disticha Catonis*, IV, 18, ed. Marcus Boas and Johan Hendrik Botschuyver (Amsterdam, 1952); Ambrose, *Expositio evangelii secundam Lucam*, PL, XV, 1782; Eucherius, *De laude*, 3 (PL, L, 702: "Licet annis juvenem moribus senem").

[38] Leo the Great, *Serm.*, VII, 3–4 (SC, 22: 248): "Amat Christus infantiam, quam primum et animo suscepti et corpore. Amat Christus infantiam humilitatis magistram, innocentiae regulam, mansuetudinis formam. Amat Christus infantiam, ad quam majorum dirigit mores, ad quam senum reducit aetates et eos ad suum inclinat exemplum, quos ad regnum sublimat aeternum."
See also Hilary, *In Math.*, XVIII (PL, IX, 1018): Maximus of Turin, *Homilia* XVII (PL, LVII, 250); and Epiphanius of Beneventum, *Interpretatio Evangeliorum*, in *Sancti Epiphanii episcopi Interpretatio Evangeliorum*, ed. Alvar Erikson (Lund, 1939), p. 43: "Parvulus enim ira teneri vel irascere non novit, malum pro malo reddere nescit, non cogitat turpia non committit adulteria . . . quae audit, credit." In the East, Clement of Alexandria praised the spirit of childhood in his *The Pedagogue* (see Marrou, preface to the edition published in SC, 70: 23ff.). For the Fathers' attitude toward childhood, see Marie-François Berrouard, "Enfance spirituelle," *DSp*, 4, pt. 1: 696–705.

Fathers (in particular, Augustine), who followed the teaching of the Old Testament more than that of the New Testament, saw the mark of original sin in all the child's acts.[39] The best way to banish foolishness from the child's heart was to use the rod, according to a biblical text often cited.[40] Christian pedagogical principles thus complemented those of the Romans. The master was to be even more severe toward the adolescent in the "bubblings of puberty"[41] and was supposed to direct parents' attention to the dangers which too much freedom posed for young people.[42]

Christianity, then, wanted neither to modify the ancient school nor to transform the Roman who was still imbued with the ancient spirit. In fact, Christians were never more strongly attached to the ideal of life which Roman civilization proposed than when the Barbarian armies devastated the Empire. For the Roman Christian, the Barbarians were not only pagans or heretics but people totally alien to his concept of man. Barbarian education, what we know of it, had nothing in common with Roman education. It was an education for peasants and warriors like that characteristic of Homeric society or even of Rome in its early days.[43] The Barbarian child was kept under strict paternal supervision

---

[39] Augustine often alluded to the wickedness of children; see *En. in Ps.*, PL, XXXVI, 493, and, especially, *Confess.*, I, 7 (ed. Pierre de Labriolle, 2 vols. [Paris, 1925–26], pp. 19, 25). The Gospel of Pseudo-Matthew, which circulated at the end of the fifth century, described the wickedness of children, even of the child Jesus: see the *Evangiles apocryphes*, vol. 1, chaps. xxvi, xxviii–xxix, xxxiii, in *Protoévangile de Jacques, Pseudo-Matthieu, Evangile de Thomas*, ed. and trans. Charles Michel (Paris, 1911), p. 125. This pessimistic conception of infancy must be seen in light of the question of infant baptism championed by Augustine against the Pelagians (*De peccatorum meritis et remissione et de baptismo parvulorum*, in *CSEL*, vol. 40).

[40] Proverbs 22:15: "Stultitia colligata est in corde pueri et virga disciplinae fugabit eam." See also Proverbs 23:12–14, 29:15, and the advice of the *Constitutiones apostolorum*, IV, 11, in *Didascalia et Constitutiones apostolorum*, ed. Franz Xaver von Funk (Paderborn, 1905), pp. 230–32.

[41] Augustine, *Confess.*, II, 1 (de Labriolle ed., p. 30). In the same vein, see Ambrose, *De interpellatione Iob et David*, PL, XIV, 806; Paulinus of Périgueux, *Vita Martini*, IV, 500 (*CSEL*, 16, pt. 1: 100: "Lasciva juventus"); Avitus of Vienne, *Ep.* XVIII (16) (*MGH, AA*, VI-2, 49); Valerianus of Cimiez, *De bono disciplinae*, PL, XL, 1219.

[42] Advice to parents is contained in the *Constitutiones apostolorum*, ed. Funk, p. 230, and Fulgentius of Ruspe, *Ep.* I (*PL*, LXV, 310). Sidonius wrote, apropos of his daughter: "Et cum severitate nutritur, qua tamen tenerum non infirmatur aevum sed informatur ingenium" (*Ep.* V, 16 [*MGH, AA*, VIII, 89, l. 17]). It seems that he was making an exception. There are a few lines in his letters on education; see ibid., IV, 1; VII, 2 (pp. 53, 105).

[43] Marrou, *Education*, pp. 29, 315ff. For Germanic civilization, see the bibliography assembled by Courtois, p. 21, n. 2; see also Albert Fuchs, *Les débuts de la littérature allemande du VIIIᵉ au XIIIᵉ siècles* (Paris, 1952), p. 12; and Robert Latouche, *Les grandes invasions et la crise de l'Occident au Vᵉ siècle* (Paris, 1946), p. 297, who, however, unaccountably denies the Germans the privilege of a "civilization."

until he was worthy to participate in combat with adults. The ceremony of armament admitted him into the fellowship of warriors without, however, making him forget his ties with the family clan.[44] The military exploits of ancestors transmitted orally from generation to generation[45] and the belief in the complete power of the forces of nature were the bases of his moral and religious formation. Intellectual training was foreign to him. While Germanic writing—runic script—did exist, its knowledge was reserved to the priest, and its use was magical.[46]

The triumph of the Barbarians would spell the end of Roman culture because, as a Christian poet noted, "the difference between a Roman and a Barbarian is the same as that between a biped and a quadruped, between a being gifted with speech and a mute brute."[47] If some German chieftains in the service of the emperors were interested in letters, they became so only after they had adopted the lifestyle of the Romans.[48] No compromise was possible between Roman and Germanic civilization.[49] One can thus appreciate the ferocity with which the Romans resisted the Barbarian advance for a century and the reason that, despite the invasion and its destructions, Romans clung even more tenaciously to an educational system which had become a symbol for them. The provinces of the Empire were occupied by the Barbarians, and Rome was twice pillaged; but outside the regions completely abandoned to the Barbarians—Britain, northern Gaul, and Germany[50]—schools re-

---

[44] Tacitus, in *Germania*, 7, 3; 13, 1; 20, 1–2, described Germanic education. Most of our knowledge, however, comes from sources later than the invasions; see below, chap. 8, sect. I.D. For the military education of the Germans before the invasions, see Hans Delbrück, *Geschichte der Kriegkunst im Rahmen der politischen Geschichte*, 7 vols. (Berlin, 1907–36), 2: 317ff.

[45] Tacitus, *Germania*, 2, 3 (Perret ed., p. 71): "Celebrant carminibus antiquis quod unum apud illos memoriae et annalium genus est."

[46] Salvian, *De gubern. Dei*, V, 2–8 (*MGH, AA*, I-1, 56): "Barbari . . . qui totius litteraturae ac scientiae ignari." See Helmut Arntz, *Handbuch der Runenkunde* (Halle, 1935), for runes.

[47] Prudentius, *Contra Symmachum*, II, 816–17 (*CSEL*, 61: 276): "Sed tantum distant Romana et barbara quantum quadrupedes abiuncta est bipedi vel muta loquenti." For the feelings of Romans in the face of the Barbarian peril, see Pierre Courcelle, *Histoire littéraire des grandes invasions germaniques* (Paris, 1964), and J. Zeller, "Les sentiments du monde romain en face des invasions germaniques," *Journal des savants* (1949), p. 30.

[48] Marrou, *Education*, p. 411, has examples from the fourth century of Romanized and lettered Barbarians.

[49] German influence was felt in the Empire from the moment the Barbarians entered the West, if only in the agricultural and military spheres. We should note, too, that more than one comparison can be made between Germanic law and Roman "vulgar law"; see below, chap. 2, n. 135.

[50] Pockets of classical culture, like little islands of resistance, can be found even in these regions; see below, chap. 6, sect. III.A.

mained open. Retreating to their estates, the lettered gave themselves up to intellectual pastimes and forgot the misfortunes of the times.[51] They enjoyed peaceful people and shunned the Barbarians. They read a great deal and delighted in the companionship of learned men.[52] While their studies have the air of decadence,[53] they bear witness to an astonishing fidelity to what had been the glory of Rome.

Such was the situation when the Germans organized their states in the former Empire and when a Barbarian deposed the last emperor, Romulus Augustulus. The event of 476, which was not startling at the time, has a symbolic significance for us. It was at that moment that the educated generation represented by Sidonius Apollinaris, who died around 483, disappeared. The children born around 480 were called Caesarius, Benedict, Cassiodorus, and Boethius. Placed in new historical circumstances, they had to resolve the cultural and educational problems which their predecessors, convinced of the eternity of the Empire, had ignored.

[51] For educated society and schools in the fifth century, see Roger, pp. 65ff., and Loyen, *Sidoine Apollinaire*, pp. 56ff.

[52] Sidonius, *Ep.* VII, 14 (*MGH, AA*, VIII, 121–22).

[53] Claudian Mamertus, *Ep. ad Sapaudum, CSEL*, 11: 254. See Roger, pp. 49ff., for the decline of studies.

THE SURVIVAL OF THE ANTIQUE SCHOOL AND THE ESTABLISHMENT OF CHRISTIAN SCHOOLS IN THE MEDITERRANEAN BARBARIAN KINGDOMS (480–533)

Part One

1. Centers of Ecclesiastical and Lay Culture circa 533

CHAPTER ONE

The Survival
of the Antique School

I. HISTORICAL CONDITIONS

The deposition of the last Roman emperor and the establishment of the Barbarian kingdoms brought few important changes to the West. In the long-abandoned northern reaches of the former empire—Britain, Germany, and northern Gaul—the Barbarians continued to settle. As the traces of Romanization slowly disappeared, these regions returned to paganism and to clan life. In the lands bordering the Mediterranean, however, Roman civilization survived. The Burgundian, Visigothic, Ostrogothic, and even the Vandal princes did not settle in the former Empire as newcomers, for all through the fifth century they had been stamped by the civilizing influence of Rome.[1]

The Visigoths, converted to Christianity in the fourth century,[2] proudly recalled that their chieftain, Alaric, had not destroyed Rome in 410, as would have other Barbarians.[3] Ataulf, Alaric's successor, who married Galla Placidia, the daughter of Emperor Theodosius, even gave thought to the restoration of the Empire based on Gothic might.[4] In the middle of the fifth century, one of Ataulf's successors was killed defending the West against the armies of Attila. The Ostrogoths, who remained in the East longer than the other Barbarians, placed them-

---

[1] For the settlement of the Goths and the Burgundians in the Empire, see Ludwig Schmidt, *Die Ostgermanen* (Munich, 1934).

[2] Ibid., p. 233; Hans von Schubert, *Geschichte der christlichen Kirche im Frühmittelalter* (Tübingen, 1921), pp. 132ff., 225ff.

[3] Jordanes, *Getica*, XXX, 156 (*MGH*, *AA*, V-1, 98, ll. 17–18): "Spoliant tantum, non autem, ut solent gentes, igne supponunt." See Orosius, *Adv. pag.*, VII, 39, 15 (*CSEL*, 5: 548), and Augustine, *De civitate Dei*, I, 1 (*CSEL*, 40: 4–5).

[4] Orosius, *Adv. pag.*, VII, 43 (p. 559). See also Courcelle, *Histoire littéraire*, p. 91.

selves in the service of the emperor. In 490, at Zeno's request, Theodoric the Amalian conquered Italy, where Odoacer had ruled since 476.[5] The Burgundians, relatively recent settlers in the Empire, were not less favorably disposed to Roman civilization. Allied to the Romans from the fourth century, they liked to say that they were also linked to the Romans by ties of kinship.[6] The evidence of the fifth and sixth centuries does, in fact, attest to their moderation and to their desire to establish good relations with the Gallo-Romans.[7] They were Arians, like the Goths, but only after having first known Catholicism.[8] Also like the Gothic princes, their chieftains intervened in the political life of the Empire, and one of them, Gundobad, lived for a long while in Italy.[9] The Vandals, lastly, do not entirely deserve the reputation for savagery that has been given them.[10] Despite their religious fanaticism, they too appreciated Roman civilization. When they crossed over into Africa in 429 after a long stay in Spain, they preserved the institutions of the Empire.[11]

    The territorial unity of the Mediterranean region was not broken by the establishment of four Barbarian kingdoms. Close family ties existed among the Barbarian princes. Political borders were easily crossed. The son of Sidonius Apollinaris, a Visigothic subject, was in contact with Avitus of Vienne, in Burgundian territory. Avitus corresponded with friends in Milan and Ravenna, in Ostrogothic territory, while Ennodius in Pavia corresponded with scholars in Lyon. One could still believe that one was living in the time of imperial unity—especially after 507, when Theodoric partially restored that unity by annexing Provence and protecting the Visigothic kingdom against the attacks of the Franks.

    Within this political framework, Romans could maintain the illusion

---

[5] Schmidt, *Die Ostgermanen*, pp. 287ff.

[6] Ammianus Marcellinus, *Rerum gestarum libri qui supersunt*, XXVIII, 5 (ed. Charles U. Clark [Berlin, 1915], p. 153): "Jam inde a temporibus priscis subolem se esse romanam Burgondii sciunt." For the Burgundians, see Coville, pp. 79–101.

[7] Socrates, *Hist. eccles.*, VII, 30 (in *Socratis Scholastici Ecclesiastica historia*, ed. Robert Hussey, 3 vols. [Oxford, 1853], 2: 801); Orosius, *Adv. pag.*, VII, 32 (p. 278); Gregory of Tours, *Historia Francorum*, II, 33 (*MGH, SRM*, I, 81). (Hereafter *HF*; parenthetical page references are to the edition in *MGH, SRM*, I, 1–537.) Sidonius complained of their presence, not of their barbarism. It is incorrect, however, to believe that he defined them as the "most merciful of the Barbarians." See Courcelle, *Histoire littéraire*, p. 179, n. 5, who corrects Coville, p. 202.

[8] Orosius, *Adv. pag.*, VII, 32; see Coville, pp. 139, 147.

[9] Gundobad, a relative of Ricimer, participated in Anthemius' deposition and received the title of patricius; see Schmidt, *Die Ostgermanen*, p. 147. For Sigismund, see Avitus, *Ep.* LXXXIV (84) (*MGH, AA*, VI-2, 101).

[10] Courtois, pp. 168ff.

[11] See Heinrich Brunner, *Deutsche Rechtsgeschichte* (Leipzig, 1906), I: 1, on the survival of Roman institutions.

that nothing had really changed. In the first place, their contacts with Barbarian troops were practically nonexistent, since the relatively small number of Barbarians were quartered in well-defined regions—undoubtedly the least Romanized. The Ostrogoths occupied northern Italy,[12] the Burgundians settled on the plains of the Jura,[13] and the Visigoths on the plains of Old Castile.[14] The Vandals in Africa were the only Barbarians who found themselves in a heavily Romanized area, but even they were not very numerous.[15]

Roman life went on much as it always had. The ruins of the fifth century had been repaired, sometimes even with the help of Barbarian kings. Theodoric's building programs at Rome, Verona, and Ravenna are well known.[16] It should be remembered that Gundobad at Geneva,[17] Ruric at Merida,[18] and the Vandal princes at Carthage[19] were also

[12] See Ludo Moritz Hartmann, *Geschichte Italiens im Mittelalter*, 2 vols. (Leipzig, 1879–1900), 1: 128. For the settlement of the Barbarians in the West, see Ernst Gamillscheg, *Romania germanica: Sprach- und Siedlungsgeschichte der Germanen auf dem Boden des alten Römerreichs*, 3 vols. (Berlin and Leipzig, 1934–36), a work historians have criticized. See also F. Lot, "Que nous apprennent sur le peuplement germanique les récents travaux de toponymie?" *AcIB* (1945), pp. 289–98.

[13] Excavations and toponymy have traced the Burgundians to the peripheral regions: the upper valley of the Doubs, the regions on the Saône and of the Yonne. See the maps in Maurice Chaume, *Les origines du duché de Bourgogne*, 2 vols. (Dijon, 1925–31), 2: 161, 171; and Pierre Bouffard, *Nécropoles burgondes de la Suisse: Les garnitures de ceintures* (Geneva and Nyon, 1945). See also Salin, 1: 344ff.

[14] Wilhelm Reinhart, "Sobre el asentamiento de los Visigodos en la Peninsula," *Archivo español de arqueologia* 18 (1945): 124–39; Ramon de Abadal y Vinyals, "A propos du legs visigothique en Espagne," *Settimane*, 5: 545. For the settlement of the Visigoths in Gaul, see Salin, 1: 387ff., and Maurice Broëns, "Le peuplement germanique de la Gaule entre la Méditerranée et l'Océan," *AM* 68 (1956): 17–38. Broëns has shown that tombs formerly attributed to Visigoths are in actuality tombs of Franks who had rapidly become Romanized.

[15] Courtois, pp. 215–16.

[16] Cassiodorus, *Variarum libri xii*, I, 28; II, 39; III, 30–53; IV, 51 (*MGH, AA*, XII, 29, 67, 94, 108). See in particular ibid., I, 28 (pp. 29–30), on the restoration of towns: "Laus est temporum reparatio urbium vetustarum: in quibus et ornatus pacis adquiritur et bellorum necessitas praecavetur." This text was inspired by a novel of Majorian, *De aedificis publicis*, of 458. See Fedor Schneider, *Rom und Romgedanke im Mittelalter* (Munich, 1926), p. 60.

[17] For Gundobad's restorations at Geneva, see Louis Blondel, "Praetorium, palais burgonde et château comtal," *Genava* 18 (1940): 60–87. The two texts that we have on this subject are a mutilated inscription (*CIL*, XII, 2643) and the following mention in four manuscripts of the *Notitia Galliarum*: "Civitas Genavensium quae nunc Geneva a Gundebado rege Burgundionum restaurata" (*MGH, AA*, IX, 600). The Burgundian kings had their *pretorium* in the towns: for Lyon, see Sidonius, *Ep.* IV, 20 (*MGH, AA*, VIII, 70–71; "Sigismerem . . . praetorium soceri expetere vidisses"); for Vienne, see *Vita beati Aviti episc. Viennensis*, V (*MGH, AA*, VI-2, 180–81).

[18] José Vives, *Revista del centro de Estudios extremeños* 13 (1939): 1–7, has correctly shown that the manuscript referring to the restoration of the bridge at Merida dates from 483. Thus, it refers to Euric and not, as the copyist wrote, to Erwig. See also José Vives,

builders. In the towns, a rich citizen could still divide his time among the forum, the business and legal center,[20] the baths, whose benefits even the Barbarians appreciated,[21] the dinners accompanied by gossip and games, the theater, and the races.[22] The Roman home kept its traditional plan and decoration.[23] Life in the great rural domains in Italy,[24] Spain,[25] and Africa[26] is reminiscent of Sidonius' fifth-century descriptions.

The picture was not entirely optimistic, however. Certainly, Barbarian rule was difficult for some to take. Furthermore, the Barbarians were Arians and persecuted Catholics in Spain and Africa. Nevertheless, compared to the tragic years of the invasions, the last two decades of the fifth century and the beginning of the sixth century can stand as a period of relative peace.[27] Italy was not disrupted by Theodoric's overthrow of Odoacer and remained peaceful until Theodoric's death in 526 and even afterwards. Euric, who guided the Visigothic kingdom to its apogee, passed it to his son Alaric II without difficulty in 484. In the Rhône basin, the two Burgundian kingdoms of Geneva and Lyon were united by Gundobad and his brother Godegisil in 485.[28] Finally, in

---

Inscripciones cristianas de la España romana y visigoda (Barcelona, 1942), no. 363. Urban life went on: Hydatius mentioned a *conventus* at Lugo (102, 194, 202) and at Braga (179, 214a); see *Continuatio Chronicorum Hieronymianorum, MGH, AA*, XI, 22, 31–32.

[19] See Courtois, pp. 313–14.

[20] See Cassiodorus' praise of urban life in *Var.*, VIII, 31 (*MGH, AA*, XII, 259).

[21] Theodahat had baths constructed near Viterbo (Otto Fiebiger and Ludwig Schmidt, *Inschriftensammlung zur Geschichte der Ostgermanen* [Vienna, 1917], II, no. 41), as did Thrasamund at Carthage (*Anth. lat.*, p. 181).

[22] For Rome, see Cassiodorus, *Var.*, I, 27, 33; IV, 51; V, 42 (pp. 29, 33, 138, 168). In 536, Theophanes noted the presence of an Italian player in Byzantium (*Theophanis Chronographia*, ed. Johan Classen, 2 vols. [Bonn, 1839–41], 1: 347). See also the allusion of Gregory the Great in *Reg. past.*, III, 20 (*PL*, LXXVII, 85). Caesarius reproached the faithful of Arles for attending "spectacula cruenta" (*Sermo* CL [Morin ed., p. 581]; see *Sermo* XII [pp. 59] and LXXXIX [p. 353]). See also the epitaph of the Milanese goldsmith Lucifer: "Fabolarum socius, laetitiae semper amicus . . . ilaris, jocundus" (Ugo Monneret de Villard, *Catalogo delle iscrizioni cristiane anteriori al secolo XI* [Milan, 1915], p. 207, no. 10).

[23] See Ennodius' epigrams on the various rooms of a house in *Carm.* 2, 37–43 (*MGH, AA*, VII, 147–49), and 2, 17 (ibid., p. 127).

[24] Ennodius, *Ep.* VII, 22 (*MGH, AA*, VII, 248, 24–26), an allusion to falconry; Council of Agde, 506, c. 55 (Mansi, VIII, 534).

[25] See, for the villa of Daragoleja in the province of Granada, Menéndez Pidal, *HE*, 3: 460–61, and for the villa of Cuevas de Soria near Numantia, which was restored in the fifth century, ibid., 2: 239.

[26] Courtois, p. 228.

[27] See Ferdinand Lot, *Les destinées de l'Empire en Occident de 395 à 888*, 2nd ed. (Paris, 1940), pp. 131ff.

[28] Coville, p. 165.

Africa, the accession of Gunthamund in 484 marked the beginning of a détente between Vandals and Afro-Romans.

This period of stability came to an end around 533. In that year, the Franks annexed the Burgundian kingdom and, two years later, occupied Provence. Also in 533, Justinian undertook his reconquest of the West, first seizing Vandal Africa, then attacking Italy, which for almost twenty years fought the invader. The Visigothic kingdom also suffered political crises beginning in 531 and was threatened by Frankish incursions before it fell victim to the Byzantine reconquest.[29]

Thus, we find the best conditions for studying the survival of the antique school between 480 and 533.

II. LITERARY CIRCLES AND SCHOOLS

Could the Romans—who, after the triumph of the Barbarians, preserved their monuments, their baths, and their theaters—also maintain their schools? In order to answer this question, we would like to have all the varied sources which the modern historian of Antiquity has at his disposal: inscriptions, biographies of masters, students' notebooks, and other source materials. Unfortunately, we no longer have anything like this. The educational institution escapes our analysis. We can only study the different levels of educational activity indirectly by studying the men who went through the schools and the works produced in them in the form of literary works or simply as notes.

A. Elementary Instruction

No direct source describes the fate of the elementary school. No text, no inscription introduces us to a schoolmaster, the *magister ludi*, a person well known in Antiquity. Does this mean that elementary instruction was available only to aristocratic families?[30] This is hardly probable. To be able to read and to write was always a necessity, especially in the cities. The Barbarian invasions did not obliterate what had characterized all Antiquity—the civilization of the written word. As in the past, the city-dweller's attention was continually solicited by inscriptions on civil

---

[29] Menéndez Pidal, *HE*, 3: 92.

[30] Placidia of Verona (*CIL*, V, 3897) was no doubt taught in this atmosphere: "Placidia inlustris puella instructa litteris." This little girl died in 532, when she was eight years old.

and religious monuments[31] and especially on tombstones. It is unthinkable that engravers slavishly adhered to a tradition, fully aware that their work was no longer understood. Later, we will have the occasion to underscore the close relationship that existed everywhere between inscriptions and intellectual culture.

Other indices prove that the written word still played an important role in the life of the Barbarian kingdoms. At Rome and Ravenna, for example, the custom of publicly posting documents had not disappeared in the middle or at the end of the sixth century.[32] In the commercial realm, trade continued to demand a minimum of writing. If some merchants were illiterate, they had scribes who helped them with their accounts and correspondence.[33] Sales, donations, and wills were inconceivable without the preparation of a document, whose value was no longer simply probative but tended to become contractual.[34]

Elementary instruction must have survived outside the big cities. Only one piece of evidence has come down to us, but it is an important one: deeds of sale written on wooden tablets in the region of Tebessa during the reign of the Vandal king Gunthamund. Some owners signed the contracts while others indicated that they were unable to sign, proving that this ignorance was considered exceptional.[35] The same

---

[31] Ennodius, *Carm.* 2, 17, and 2, 38–43 (*MGH, AA*, VII, 127, 147–48).

[32] In 440 at Rome, a novel of Valentinian III called on Romans to resist Genseric (*Theodosiani libri XVI: Novellae*, ed. Meyer, pp. 90–94). When Totila besieged Rome in 546, he had a proclamation posted in several quarters of the city; see Procopius, *Bell. goth.*, III, 9 (Haury ed., p. 335). See also Athalaric's letter to the Roman people in *Var.*, VIII, 3 (*MGH, AA*, XII, 233) and the royal decree against simony in ibid., IX, 15 (pp. 279–81). In 595, a *libellus* hostile to Gregory the Great was posted in Ravenna (Gregory, *Ep.* VII, 42 [*MGH, Ep.*, I, 490]). The plates in Jean Mallon, *L'écriture de la chancellerie impériale romaine*, Acta Salmanticensia, Filosofia y letras, vol. 4, no. 2 (Salamanca, 1948), give specimens of fifth- and sixth-century poster script.

[33] A Roman epitaph of 535 speaks of a John, "vir honestus," who was secretary to Isidore, a tavern owner ("olografus pronine isidori"); see *ICR*, 1: 478, no. 1055. In Provence, Caesarius of Arles alluded to "negotiatores qui cum litteras non noverint requirunt sibi mercenarios litteratos" (*Sermo* VI, 8; VIII [Morin ed., pp. 38, 42]).

[34] André Piganiol, *L'Empire chrétien, 325–395* (Paris, 1947), p. 409. See Charles Lécrivain, "Remarques sur l'*Interpretatio* de la Lex Romana Visigothorum," *AM* 1 (1889): 181; and Alain de Boüard, *L'acte privé* (Paris, 1948), p. 41. Julius Paulus the lawyer had already begun to react against the tendency toward literal formalism in his *Libri quinque sententiarum*, II, 17, 14 (in *Corpus iuris civilis academicum parisiense*, ed. Charles M. Galisset, 7th ed. [Paris, 1862]).

[35] C. Courtois et al., *Tablettes Albertini* (Paris, 1952), preface, p. 206. See also Louis Stouff, *Etude sur la formation des contrats par l'écriture dans le droit des formules du Ve au XIIe siècle* (Paris, 1887); and, more recently, Veikko I. Väänänen, *Etude sur le texte et la langue des "tablettes Albertini"* (Helsinki, 1965). Additional tablets have since come to light; see Y. Duval and P. A. Février, "Procès-verbal de déposition de reliques de la région de Telergma (VIIe s.)," *MEFR* 81 (1969): 257–320.

observation applies for documents prepared in Italy during the reigns of Odoacer and Theodoric.[36] They were drawn up in the *stationes* of the *tabelliones* of Ravenna and Rome and then inscribed on the curial registers by a clerk.[37] These documents carried the autograph subscriptions of the interested parties and their witnesses. If some did not know how to write (*litteras nescientes*),[38] they said so and traced a monogram by hand or with the aid of a signet ring.[39] We should note that the use of this ring, which spread in the Late Empire and enjoyed great success in the Barbarian world, does not necessarily imply, as some would have it,[40] that those who used it were ignorant. The signet ring was a jewel that could be worn and which, at the same time, permitted one to authenticate a document quickly or to lock a jewelry box.[41]

We can conclude, then, that elementary education did not disappear. The situation had undoubtedly changed little from the imperial period: among the middle classes, a certain number attended school in order to acquire the rudiments of an education. The privilege of a more extensive education acquired from the grammarian and the rhetor was reserved for the aristocratic classes.

B. The Grammarian and Rhetor as Teachers

The young aristocrat's education followed the earlier pattern. The child, having left the care of his nurse[42] and been schooled in the basics, was sent to the grammarian and then to the rhetor. Although we know only a few masters, we can learn what their teaching was like by ex-

---

[36] Gaetano Marini, *I papiri diplomatici* (Rome, 1805), no. 84; Jan Olof Tjäder, ed., *Die nichtliterarischen lateinischen Papyri Italiens* (Lund, 1954–55), nos. 12, 113, 115, etc.

[37] For the practice of insinuation, see Felix Martel, *Etude sur l'enregistrement des actes de droit privé dans les "Gesta municipalia," en droit roman* (Paris, 1877); Bruno Hirschfield, *Die "gesta municipalia" in römischer und frühgermanischer Zeit* (Marburg, 1904); and, most recently, L. Santifaller, "Die Urkunde des Königs Odovakar vom Jahre 489," *MIOEG* 60 (1952): 1–30.

[38] Theodoric's edict provided for just such an occurrence by including an article from the novels of Valentinian III; see *Edictum*, 29 (*MGH, Leges*, V, 155). There are not many diplomas without autograph signatures, however; see Marini, *I papiri*, nos. 115 and 26; and Tjäder, *Papyri*, p. 271.

[39] Marini, *I papiri*, no. 74, "signaculum anuli mei"; no. 86, "jugalis meus" (in Tjäder, *Papyri*, pp. 204, 306).

[40] Maximin Deloche, *Etude historique et archéologique sur les anneaux sigillaires et autres des premiers siècles du Moyen Age* (Paris, 1900), p. 5.

[41] Avitus of Vienne described one signet ring in *Ep.* LXXXVII (78) (*MGH, AA*, VI-2, 97); see also Cassian, *De institutis coenobiorum*, IV, 12 (*CSEL*, 17: 55).

[42] We have two epitaphs of nurses from the sixth century, one for 509 (*ICR*, vol. 1, no. 943), the other for 558 (ibid., no. 1093); for Saint Benedict's nurse, see Gregory the Great, *Dial.*, II, 1 (Morrica ed., p. 73).

amining the schools and lettered circles their former pupils generated in the various Barbarian kingdoms.

1. IN NORTHERN ITALY

Even though we know nothing of the entire educational system of northern Italy in the fifth century, a happy accident, the preservation of Ennodius of Pavia's work, allows us to verify the existence of schools at the beginning of the sixth century.

Ennodius, a member of an aristocratic family from Provence, settled in Pavia as a youth around 490. When he was twenty years old, he entered the clergy of Pavia and then that of Milan before ending his career as bishop of Pavia in 511.[43] The literary culture which he had acquired before and perhaps even after his entrance into orders[44] made him a renowned figure in the literary circles of Liguria. The location of his correspondents shows that his reputation also reached as far as Rome and to the province of his birth.[45] Even before Theodoric's annexation of Provence, some of Ennodius' cousins sent their sons to him for guidance during their study of the liberal arts,[46] as did Italian families both in the north and in the south.[47] Altogether, then, we know about a dozen youths who were recommended to the good care of the deacon. Does this mean that we can speak of "Ennodius' school" at

[43] For Ennodius of Pavia, see Schanz, IV-2, 131.

[44] This is according to Vogel. See the preface to his edition (*MGH, AA*, VII, xi). Ennodius made very vague allusions to his studies as a young man: "Adulescentiae meae memini me legisse temporibus de quodam dictum" (he was referring to *Medea* and Seneca; *Libellus pro synodo*, ibid., p. 54, ll. 14–15); in the beginning of his *Eucharisticon de vita sua*, ibid., p. 301, l. 15, he recalled his fondness for poetry. A certain Servilio seems to have been his master (*Ep.* V, 14 [ibid., p. 183]). M. L. W. Laistner, *Thought and Letters in Western Europe, A.D. 500 to 900* (London, 1957), p. 111, incorrectly thought that he was a pupil of Deuterius.

[45] Of his approximately fifty correspondents, about twenty lived in Rome, fifteen in northern Italy, ten in Provence, and only one in Africa. Those remaining came from undetermined regions in Italy.

[46] These were his nephews Lupicinus (*Ep.* III, 15 [*MGH, AA*, VII, 111]; *Dictio* VIII [ibid., p. 78]) and Parthenius (*Dictio* X [p. 118]), and the sons of his cousin Camilla (*Ep.* IX, 9 [p. 297]).

[47] The most famous of Ennodius' charges was Arator; see Johannes Sundwall's note, *Abhandlungen zur Geschichte des ausgehenden Römertums* (Helsingfors, 1919), p. 92, and Schanz, IV-2, 291–394. Avienus, son of the quaestor Faustus, should also be cited: "Hic [Liguria] eruditione patefactus" (Ennodius, *Ep.* IX, 32 [p. 320]). The son of Eusebius, a noble (*Dictio* XI [p. 132]), and the brothers Paterius and Severus (ibid. XIII [p. 309]) should also be listed, along with Ambrose, the son of Faustinus, and Beatus, to whom Ennodius dedicated a pedagogical treatise (*Paraenesis didascalica, MGH, AA*, VII, 310).

Milan?[48] I do not think so. Ennodius has been cast as the master of an episcopal school at Milan[49] without any evidence in the sources. Ennodius, who from at least 499 was a deacon in the church of Milan, was not interested in opening an educational center, since the town school had not disappeared.

In fact, we even know the teacher's name: Deuterius. Although he held the title of *grammaticus*, he also taught rhetoric, an increasingly common tendency.[50] Deuterius established his school in the forum of Milan. Admission to his *auditorium* was a great event marked with a ceremony.[51] When Lupicinus, the nephew of Ennodius; Arator, the protégé of the bishop of Milan; and Eusebius, Paterius, and Severus were admitted to it, Ennodius composed *dictiones* for them which he later included among his works.[52] He continued to follow the young men in their studies and helped them with their rhetorical exercises,[53] the traditional suasoriae or controversiae. Ennodius himself may have participated in the classes and improvised speeches on themes suggested by Deuterius.[54] Thus, we see Ennodius more as a counselor and tutor than as a teacher. These functions allowed him to remain in contact with his "pupils" when they left Deuterius' school to finish their studies elsewhere.

Let us first accompany the young Arator to Ravenna. The political capital of Italy must also have had schools, even though no text expressly mentions them. The presence of the court, of the offices, and of

---

[48] See Francesco Magani, *Ennodio*, 3 vols. (Pavia, 1886), 1: 285; St. Léglise, "S. Ennodius et la haute éducation littéraire dans le monde romain au commencement du VIe siècle," *Université catholique de Bordeaux* 5 (1890): 214.

[49] Stein, 2: 276; Schmidt, *Die Ostgermanen*, p. 396.

[50] "Dictio data Deuterio v. s. grammatico" (Ennodius, *Carm.* 1, 2 [*MGH, AA*, VII, 170]); "Deuterius qui ubertate linguarum germina tibi multiplicatus seminibus" (*Dictio* IX [ibid., p. 114]). For his teaching of rhetoric, see *Carm.* 2, 104 (pp. 182–83), and *Dictio* VII (p. 7, l. 30), where he is described as "eloquentiae doctor."

[51] Ennodius, "Dictio in dedicatione auditorii quando ad forum translatio facta est," *Dictio* VII (p. 6). F. Ermini's hypothesis that this forum was located in Rome cannot be accepted (see "La scuola in Roma nel VI. secolo," *Archivium Romanicum* 18 [1934]: 150), since Deuterius does not seem to have taught in Rome. The passage from *Carm.* 1, 2 (p. 170) cannot be brought into evidence since it is addressed, not to Deuterius, but rather to Eugenetes through the intermediary of Deuterius ("Dictio data Deuterio v. s. grammatico nomine ipsius Eugeneti v. i. mittenda").

[52] Ennodius, "Praefatio dicta Lipicino quando in auditorio traditus est Deuterio v.s.," *Dictio* VIII (p. 78). See ibid. IX (p. 112) for Arator; XI (p. 132) for Eusebius; and XIII (p. 309) for Paterius and Severus.

[53] *Dictiones* for Arator appear at ibid., XII, XVII–XVIII, XXII (pp. 138, 184, 191, 271). For Ambrose, see XIX (p. 201).

[54] "Dictio ex tempore quam ipse Deuterius injunxit," ibid. XXIV (p. 167).

the high functionaries employed in royal administration necessitated the existence of schools. Law must have been taught there, since this is what attracted Arator, destined for a career as a lawyer, to Ravenna.[55] There, an older fellow student introduced him to the works of Caesar, the classical poets, the hymns of Ambrose, and the poems of Sidonius.[56] This student, Parthenius—who should not be confused with his homonym, Ennodius' nephew[57]—came from Gaul and was the grandson of Bishop Ruricius of Limoges and of Avitus, a former emperor.[58] He, too, no doubt came to Ravenna to finish the studies which would prepare him for a high administrative post. We find him later in the service of a Merovingian king.

We should add that cultivated men outside the school devoted themselves to the classics, whose texts they carefully revised. A Macrobius manuscript bears the subscription of Senator Symmachus and of the grandson of the author of the *Saturnalia*. Two manuscripts of Pomponius Mela and Valerius Maximus bear the subscription of Helpidius, count of the consistory.[59] This kind of activity proves that Ravenna was still a vibrant literary center.

2. IN ROME

Many young people preferred Rome, the historical capital of the kingdom, to the political capital. In the sixth century, Ennodius and Cassiodorus, like Sidonius in the previous century, celebrated the merits of Rome's schools, which alone could offer a real education in rhetoric.[60]

[55] Cassiodorus, *Var.*, VIII, 12 (*MGH, AA*, XII, 242, l. 33).

[56] Arator, *Ep. ad Parthenium*, CSEL, 72: 150, ll. 35–48: "His quoniam laribus tenebamur in urbe Ravennae / Hospes hians aderam nocte dieque tibi / Quos mihi tu libros quae nomina docte sonabas."

[57] As has generally been done after Hartmann, *Geschichte*, 1: 190, despite the correction of Rudolf Buchner, *Die Provence in merowingischer Zeit* (Stuttgart, 1933), p. 91, n. 25, which was repeated by Stroheker, pp. 199–200, no. 284.

[58] Ruricius, *Ep.* II, 37 (*MGH, AA*, VIII, 339, l. 26). See the table devoted to the Ruricii in Stroheker, p. 236.

[59] Otto Jahn, "Ueber die Subscriptionen in der Handschriften römischer Classiker," *Berichte d. k.-sächsischen Gesells. d. Wiss. zu Leipzig, philol. hist. Classe* 3 (1851): 347. For Helpidius, see Giuseppe Billanovich, "Dall'antica Ravenna alle biblioteche umanistiche," *Annuario dell'Università cattolica del S. Cuore* (Milan, 1955–56), pp. 74ff.

[60] Ennodius' remarks on Rome include "Natalis scientia sedis" (*Ep.*, VI, 15 [*MGH, AA*, VII, 222, l. 26]); "urbs amica liberalibus studiis" (ibid., VI, 23 [p. 225, l. 17]); and "urbs in qua natalis eruditio" (ibid., V, 9 [p. 179, l. 28]). Cassiodorus wrote (*Var.*, X, 7 [*MGH, AA*, XII, 302, ll. 29–30]): "Cujus affluentem facundiam studia romana genuerunt. . . . Ibi defaecatus sermo latinus est, ibi discuntur verba toto nitore lucentia." See also ibid., V, 22, VI, 4 (pp. 156, 177); and Sidonius, *Carm.* VIII, v. 10 (ibid., VIII, 218).

Arator was exceptional among young lawyers in not having pursued his studies at Rome.[61] When Deuterius' pupils left Milan, Ennodius gave them letters of recommendation in order to open Roman circles to them.[62] To the young Ligurians Ambrose and Beatus he even addressed a short pedagogical treatise, the *Paraenesis didascalica*,[63] to which he appended a list of the most highly recommended scholars. It would help us also to become acquainted with these scholars.

There were two groups of scholars or, better, two families of opposing political positions: the circle of Senator Faustus, on the one hand, and that of Senator Symmachus on the other. Faustus, one of the first to rally to the cause of Theodoric, was named to high administrative posts by the grateful king.[64] His position, however, did not stop him from being a poet on his own time[65] and from spending long stretches in his library, which Ennodius has described for us in a few unfortunately sketchy verses.[66] Faustus was also concerned with the education of his sons,[67] particularly that of Avienus, who at one point studied at the side of Ennodius.[68] Even Faustus' sister, the widow Stephania, tried her hand at scholarly exercises.[69] She had previously been married to Asterius, a poet and man of letters who revised a manuscript of Virgil during his consulate and, a little later, a work of Sedulius.[70]

As for the Symmachi, who were less well disposed to the government of Theodoric and maintained their contacts with the Eastern Empire,[71] we find two remarkable scholars: Symmachus and Boethius. In this family, already made illustrious by the great Symmachus, the cult of

[61] Cassiodorus, *Var.*, VIII, 12 (p. 243): "Paterno igitur exemplo ingenium extendisse credendus es qui in Romano foro eloquentiam non nutristi . . . ubi sunt qui latinas litteras Romae non etiam alibi asserunt esse discendas."

[62] Ennodius, *Ep. IX*, 2 and 4 (pp. 294–95), to Probinus and Faustus recommending Ambrose; V, 9 and 11 (pp. 179–80), to Faustus and Luminosus for Parthenius; VI, 15 (p. 222), to Faustus for Simplicianus; VIII, 38 (p. 290), to Symmachus for Beatus; IX, 8 (p. 296), recommending Paul's son to Victor.

[63] Ennodius, *Paraenesis didascalica*, MGH, AA, VII, 310.

[64] See Stein, 2: 125.

[65] Ennodius, *Ep.* I, 6 (p. 15, l. 34), and *Carm.* 1, 7, v. 13 (p. 28): "In veterum morem pangit nova carmina Faustus."

[66] Ennodius, *Carm.* 2, 3 (p. 80): "De epigrammatis per armaria domni Fausti factis."

[67] Ennodius, *Ep.* IX, 32 (p. 320, l. 28).

[68] Ibid. I, 5 (p. 14).

[69] Ibid. IX, 18 (p. 305).

[70] The terms used by Ennodius in a letter to Marcianus, the son of Asterius (*Ep.* V, 2 [p. 154, l. 20]), and in another letter to Stephania (*Ep.* VIII, 17 [p. 382, l. 10]), support Sundwall's hypothesis in *Abhandlungen*, p. 95. For Asterius' subscription, see Jahn, "Ueber die Subscriptionen," p. 350. See also *Anth. lat.*, p. 48, for several verses by Asterius.

[71] Stein, 2: 130.

letters was a tradition. Symmachus' great-grandson could not fail but to
maintain the family tradition. A philologist, historian, and philosopher,
the younger Symmachus' cultural training was vast.[72] He corresponded
with Priscian, the grammarian from Constantinople and, together with
him, had considered applying Greek methods of work at Rome.[73] Young
Boethius, orphaned at an early age, found a counselor in Symmachus,
who, recognizing the character and intellectual precocity of the young
man, gave his daughter to him in marriage.[74] When Ennodius wrote
to his two pupils, Ambrose and Beatus, Boethius had already published
his great works.[75] Senator Festus, who is also mentioned by Ennodius,
belonged to the circle of the Symmachi. He helped Symmachus supervise
some young Syracusans, sons of important functionaries from Ravenna,
who came to Rome to study.[76]

Thus, Rome drew young provincials from the north and the south,
who found tutors in the city to help them with their work. Did they also
find teachers in Rome? It is quite surprising that Ennodius never mentions a teacher in his correspondence.[77] We know, however, that teachers of grammar, rhetoric, and law were listed in the public budget under
Theodoric[78] and his successor Athalaric.[79] During the latter's reign,
Felix, a rhetor, and his pupil, Deuterius, revised a Martianus Capella
manuscript.[80] Felix is not the only teacher whose name has been preserved. Maximianus the poet tells us that in his youth he too had been
an illustrious *orator*, a term which at that time was synonymous with
rhetor.[81] Boethius gives us the name of another rhetor, his friend Patricius.[82] Three known teachers, admittedly, are not many. Even if we

---

[72] See Schanz, IV-2, 84.

[73] Courcelle, *LG*, pp. 304ff.

[74] For Boethius' youth, see P. Courcelle, "Boèce et l'école d'Alexandrie," *MEFR* 52
(1935): 185, and the article on Boethius by Claudio Leonardi et al. in *Dizionario biogra-
fico degli Italiani* (Rome, 1970).

[75] Courcelle, *LG*, pp. 258ff.

[76] Cassiodorus, *Var.*, I, 39, and IV, 6 (*MGH, AA*, XII, 36, 117). Theodoric refused to
allow these youths to leave Rome for Sicily "studiorum causa."

[77] The only allusion to a teacher, who was called a *praeceptor*, is found in a letter to
Meribaudus (*Ep.* IX, 3 [*MGH, AA*, VII, 295, l. 4]).

[78] Justinian referred to them in the *Pragmatic Sanction*; see below, chap. 5, n. 4.

[79] Cassiodorus, *Var.*, IX, 21 (p. 286).

[80] Jahn, "Ueber die Subscriptionen," p. 351; H. I. Marrou, "Autour de la bibliothéque
du pape Agapit," *MEFR* 48 (1931): 160.

[81] Maximianus, *Eleg.* I, 19, in *Poetae latini minores*, ed. Emil Baehrens, 6 vols. (Leipzig, 1879–86), 5: 317: "Dum juvenile decus dum mens senusque maneret / Orator toto
clarus in orbe fuit." For this poet, see Schanz, IV-2, 76–78, and E. Merone, "Per la bio-
grafia di Massimiano," *Giornale italiana di filologia* I (1948): 337–52.

[82] Boethius, *Commentaria in Ciceronis Topica, PL*, LXIV, 1039. Boethius called him
"peritissimus rhetorum."

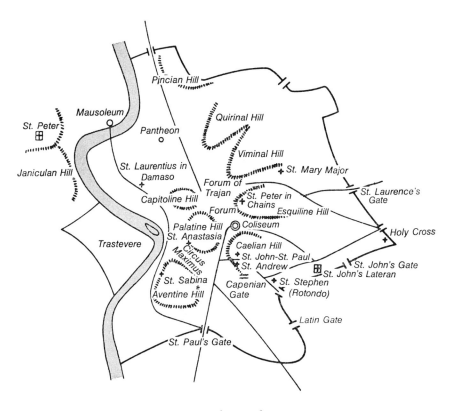

St. Peter

Mausoleum

Janiculan Hill

Pincian Hill

Quirinal Hill

Pantheon

St. Laurentius in
Damaso

Viminal Hill

St. Mary Major

Capitoline Hill

Forum of
Trajan

St. Peter in
Chains

St. Laurence's
Gate

Forum

Esquiline Hill

Trastevere

Palatine Hill
St. Anastasia

Coliseum

Holy Cross

Circus
Maximus

Caelian Hill

St. John-St. Paul

St. Andrew

St. John's Gate
St. John's Lateran

St. Sabina
Aventine Hill

Capenian
Gate

St. Stephen
(Rotondo)

Latin Gate

St. Paul's Gate

2. *Rome in the Sixth Century*

take into consideration the fact that other names might not have been preserved, still the list of masters must not have been very long, since there were no longer a great number of students. Even though we by no means know all the students, they nevertheless do not seem to have formed a large segment of the Roman population. When Cassiodorus enumerated the different responsibilities of the Roman magistrates, he did not mention the supervision of students, as had Emperor Valentinian I at the end of the fourth century.[83] Then, too, scholars must have hesitated to become teachers at a time when the pay continually decreased. The Senate took such great advantage from the turnover in personnel to lower salaries that King Athalaric was forced to remind them to pay the new masters the same amount they had given the masters' predecessors.[84] In order to replace the diminishing number of teachers, more than one semi-educated person without the proper competency tried to open a school.[85]

A final question ought to be asked: where was the center of school life located in Rome? The usual answer is that it was still in Trajan's forum. This is probable but not certain. Fortunatus, the poet, is the only one to mention it, and his allusions must be treated with caution.[86] Ulpian's famous library was still in this forum at the end of the fifth century.[87] Perhaps the son of Priscian the grammarian came to research among its "stacks" at the beginning of the following century.[88] Nevertheless, the small number of teachers and students leads one to suspect that schools were no longer concentrated in one place but, rather, that the pupils worked at the homes of their masters. Felix the rhetor and his disciples were settled at the foot of Mount Caelius "near the Capenian

---

[83] See Marrou, *Education*, p. 412, and André Chastagnol, *La préfecture urbaine à Rome sous le Bas-Empire* (Paris, 1960), pp. 283–89.

[84] Cassiodorus, *Var.*, IX, 21 (p. 286): "Qua de re, Patres conscripti, hanc vobis curam . . . ut successor scholae liberalium . . . litterarum commoda sui decessoris percepiat."

[85] Ennodius, *Carm.* 2, 96 (*MGH, AA*, VII, 172): "De quodam Romano qui magister voluit esse."

[86] Fortunatus, *Carm.* III, 18, v. 7; VII, 8, v. 25 (*MGH, AA*, IV-1, 70, 162). But are not these allusions simply literary devices? H. Marrou uses Fortunatus' evidence in "La vie intellectuelle au Forum de Trajan et au Forum d'Auguste," *MEFR* 49 (1932): 99. For a contrary opinion, see Stein, 2: 694, n. 1.

[87] Sidonius mentioned this library (*Ep.* IX, 16 [*MGH, AA*, VIII, 171]). It was still in existence at the end of the sixth century. See below, chap. 5, n. 254.

[88] Priscian, *Institutio*, in Keil, 3: 407, l. 14: "Filio meo Romae in praesenti degente optans dicam: utinam Romae filius meus legisset actores, propter quos nunc ibi moratur." Pierre Courcelle has concluded from this that the young man's research was in vain (*LG*, p. 311). I do not think that conclusion is warranted.

gate," quite far from the forum.[89] Perhaps Ennodius' young friends also worked in the homes of their correspondents, which might explain why the deacon never tells us anything about teachers.

Rome, then, still had some schools at the beginning of the sixth century, although university life tended to break down. It would have necessitated a real effort on the part of public officials for the city to have become once again the great cultural center of the West.

3. IN SOUTHERN GAUL

In passing from Italy to Provence, we remain in the same kingdom, since this region was under Ostrogothic domination from 508, after having been part of the Visigothic kingdom for thirty-two years.[90] Scholars suffered little from these political changes. The culture of those known to us through Ennodius in the sixth century compares well to that of Sidonius' friends.[91] Ennodius' sister, Euprepia,[92] and his cousin, the *senatrix* Archotamia,[93] were correspondents worthy of him. We have already noted that Ennodius' relatives sent their sons to Milan so that they might receive a classical education there.[94] The father of the consul Felix, who devoted his life to Greek and Latin letters and to "scientific" studies, also probably belonged to Ennodius' family. Cassiodorus calls him the "Cato of our times," but we know nothing more of him.[95]

Firminus, an Arlesian, is better known to us. As early as 481, Sidonius Apollinaris dedicated the last book of his correspondence to him.[96] His eloquence and the purity of his language later made him a friend of

[89] See above, n. 80.

[90] Stein, 2: 152. Theodoric proclaimed that he restored liberty to the Provençals; see Cassiodorus, *Var.*, III, 17 (*MGH*, *AA*, XII, 88): "In antiquam libertatem . . . exuite barbariem."

[91] We know of them through Sidonius' letters; see Loyen, *Sidoine Apollinaire*. See also the *Vita Hilarii*, *PL*, L, 1232, which mentions Silvius, Eusebius, and Domnulus: "Praeclari auctores . . . qui suis scriptis merito claruerunt."

[92] Ennodius, *Ep.* II, 15; III, 15; III, 28; V, 7; VI, 3; VII, 8 (*MGH*, *AA*, VII, 68, 111, 125, 173, 216, 234).

[93] Ibid. VI, 24; VII, 14 (pp. 226, 237).

[94] See above, n. 46.

[95] Cassiodorus, *Var.*, II, 3 (p. 48): "Litterarum quippe studiis dedicatus, perpetuam doctissimis disciplinis mancipavit aetatem. . . . Vehemens disputator in libris, amoenus declamator in fabulis . . . fuit quidam nostrorum temporum Cato. . . . Rerum quoque naturalium causas subtilissime perscrutator Cecropii dogmatis Attico se melle saginavit." This passage concerns Felix's father rather than Felix himself, as Courcelle contends (*LG*, p. 259, n. 2).

[96] Sidonius, *Ep.* IX, 1 (*MGH*, *AA*, VIII, 149).

Ennodius.[97] It was Firminus who, in 498, welcomed Caesarius, the young monk from Lérins and future bishop of Arles. Firminus wanted to familiarize him with classical culture in order, according to the *Vita Caesarii*, "to make his monastic simplicity less ignorant by the study of profane disciplines."[98] Firminus thus entrusted Caesarius to his friend, Julianus Pomerius, but the experiment was unsuccessful. We shall see why.

Certainly, Pomerius' talent was not to blame. Coming from Africa—doubtless fleeing Vandal persecution—he was renowned as a teacher of rhetoric and grammar.[99] He was a friend of Ennodius.[100] Ruricius, the famous patrician from southern Gaul, corresponded with him.[101] Like his predecessors in the fifth century, Pomerius probably ran a private school in Arles.[102] Around 503, he left Arles to take orders[103] and put his rhetor's pen to the service of the Church.[104] While we do not find another master after him, this does not mean that men of letters had also disappeared.[105]

If we go up the Rhône through Avignon, we enter the Burgundian kingdom. There we find the same situation: small groups of scholars and few teachers. That at least is how it appears in our sole source, the correspondence of Avitus of Vienne.

Avitus straddled two epochs. In age, he was close to the generation of his relative and model, Sidonius Apollinaris. Yet, in many ways, he resembles Ennodius, who was thirty years younger than he.[106] Born

---

97 Ennodius, *Ep.* I, 8 (*MGH, AA*, VII, 17, l. 1): "Jucunda sunt commercia litterarum . . . in quibus ad unguem politi sermonis splendor effulgorat." *Ep.* II, 7 (p. 39): "Vos . . . quibus ubertas linguae castigatus sermo latiaris ductus quadrata constat elocutio." For the identity of this Firminus, see Stroheker, p. 174, no. 157.

98 *Vita Caesarii*, I, 9 (Morin ed., p. 300): "Ut saecularis scientiae disciplinis monasterialis in eo simplicitas poliretur."

99 Ibid.: "Quidam Pomerius nomine scientia rhetor Afer genere quem singularem et clarum grammaticae artis doctrina reddebat."

100 Ennodius, *Ep.* II, 6 (*MGH, AA*, VII, 37).

101 Ruricius, *Ep.* I, 17; II, 10 (*MGH, AA*, VIII, 309, 318).

102 Little is known about the schools of Arles in the fifth century. The *Vita Hilarii* mentions a poet, Edesius, who lived before 450 and was described as "rhetoricae facundiae et metricae artis peritissimus vir" (*PL*, L, 1233). But we do not know whether he was an official rhetor.

103 At least this is what the letters of Ruricius (II, 9 [*MGH, AA*, VIII, 385]) and of Ennodius (II, 6 [*MGH, AA*, VII, 44]) imply.

104 Pseudo-Gennadius, *De viris inlustris*, III, 99 (Richardson ed., p. 96). For Pomerius and his work, see Schanz, IV-2, 554–56; and the preface to Mary Josephine Suelzer's edition, *The Vita Contemplativa of Julianus Pomerius* (Westminster, 1947).

105 See below, chap. 6, sect. II.A.

106 For Avitus of Vienne, see Schanz, IV-2, 269; Stroheker, pp. 154–55, no. 60; and Max Burckhardt, *Die Briefsammlung des Bischofs Avitus von Vienne* (Berlin, 1938).

in 460 at Vienne, Avitus came from a family in which classical education was a tradition. His affected style and archaic taste bear witness
to an education comparable to that of Ennodius.[107] Like Ennodius, he
wrote some *epigrammata* and perhaps even some school dictiones, in
addition to a collection of letters.[108] When he became bishop in 494, he
took his religious duties seriously yet at the same time kept his taste for
good style[109] and for grammatical discussions.[110]

Only the personality of the poet Heraclius[111] emerges clearly from
among Avitus' correspondents, who, on the whole, seem little different
from the aristocrats, landowners, and functionaries in contact with
Ennodius.[112]

Classical education was still available in Burgundy outside family
circles. It has been assumed that one of Avitus' masters was Sapaudus,
the friend of Sidonius and Claudian Mamertus.[113] It would first have
to be proved, however, that this rhetor was still alive in 475. Sapaudus
did, nevertheless, have some successors in Vienne, among whom was
Pantagathus, who became bishop of Vienne and died around 538.[114] At
the beginning of the sixth century, the rhetor Viventiolus was at Lyon,
according to one of Avitus' letters. He reproached the bishop of Vienne
for having "treated the middle syllable of *potitur* as a long and for not

---

[107] For Avitus' style, see Henri Goelzer's *Le latin de saint Avit, évêque de Vienne* (Paris,
1909).

[108] The *epigrammata* were lost during the siege of Vienne in 500, as Avitus himself
said in the preface to his poems (*Prologus, MGH, AA*, VI-2, 201). The catalogue of the
Codex Dietzianus (Berlin, Staatsbibliothek, Diez B. Sant. 66) from the ninth century
contains the following citation: "Libri Alchimi. sic incipit In adulescentiam qui In publico
patre cadente risisset et languenti puellae amatorium dedit. De controversia fullonis vel
calvi." Is this a reference to our Alcimus Avitus? See preface, *Oper., MGH, AA*, VI-2, lii.

[109] See the note to the prefect Liberius (*Ep.* XXXV [32], *MGH, AA*, VI-2, 65), and
the letter to Sidonius Apollinaris' son (*Ep.* XXXVI [33], ibid., p. 66).

[110] *Ep., Viventiolo rhetori, Ep.* LVII (51), p. 85. See below, n. 115.

[111] *Ep.* LIII (47), XCV (85), pp. 81, 102. Heraclius' replies are still extant; see *Ep.*
LIV (48), XCVI (86), pp. 83, 102.

[112] See the letters to Duke Ansemundus, Helladius, and the deacon-physician Helpidius
(Avitus, *Ep.* LXXX [71], LXXXIII [75], XXXVIII [35], pp. 93, 95, 67).

[113] This opinion is shared by Goelzer, *Le latin de saint Avit*, p. 4; Schanz, IV-2, 381;
and Roger, p. 69, n. 14. The death of the rhetor, recorded in two sources—a letter of
Sidonius (V, 10 [*MGH, AA*, VIII, 85]) and the letter-preface of Claudian Mamertus
Ep. ad Sapaudum (*CSEL*, 11: 203)—is difficult to date. See Schanz, IV-2, 269–70. The
Sapaudus to whom an archdeacon wrote in the name of Avitus (*Ep.* LXXXVI [77], pp.
95–96) should not be confused with the rhetor; see Goelzer, p. 15.

[114] See Stroheker, p. 198, no. 279. The epitaph of Pantagathus reads as follows: "Orator
magnus vates et ipse fuit / his igitur studiis primaevo flore virente / inter summatos esse
prior studuit" (Le Blant, *IC*, 2: 101–2. [no. 429]). This passage can be compared with
what Maximianus the orator told us of himself; see above, n. 81. Lampridius, a rhetor at
Bordeaux, was also an orator and poet; see Sidonius, *Ep.* VIII, 11 (p. 139).

having followed the example of Virgil" in a sermon. Avitus, sharply stung, replied by defending himself against having committed a barbarism and urged Viventiolus to go back to his own school: "I hope that in the ancient authors, which you rightly teach to your pupils, you will easily find what you are looking for."[115]

Our search becomes more difficult as we pass into the Visigothic kingdom. We would like to know what became of the lettered circles of Aquitaine and of the Narbonnaise, known to us through Sidonius.[116] Did they abruptly disintegrate at the end of the fifth century after having earlier survived a more critical period? What became, for example, of young Burgundio, whose precocious talent Sidonius praised around 480? We do not know, since Sidonius' correspondence ends in 483, with his death about the same time.[117] Yet, from other sources, we can divine that the sons of Sidonius and of his friends remained faithful to family traditions. Young Apollinaris—for whom his father, then bishop of Clermont, reread Terence[118]—was competent to judge the poems which his relative Avitus of Vienne sent to him.[119] In one letter, Ruricius, who became bishop of Limoges in 485, recalled the good education which this young man had received.[120] Ruricius' sons, who were equally well educated, do not seem to have inherited the literary talents of their father.[121] Ruricius' grandson, Parthenius, rescued the family honor by studying at Ravenna.[122] The same continuity can be observed among

[115] Avitus, Ep. LVII (51) (MGH, AA, VI-2, 85–86): "Avitus episcopo Viventiolo rhetori. . . . Spero, ut de priscis magis oratoribus, quo discipulis merito traditis, perquisitum diligentius . . . pandatis." This Viventiolus ought not to be confused with the bishop of Lyon of the same name. See my article, "La survivance des écoles publiques en Gaule au Ve siècle," MA 63 (1957): 426.

[116] See Courtenay Edward Stevens, Sidonius Apollinaris and His Age (Oxford, 1933), and Loyen, Sidoine Apollinaire.

[117] Sidonius, Ep. IX, 14 (MGH, AA, VIII, 168). Coville, p. 204, thought that this Burgundio was none other than Syagrius, the legal counselor of the Burgundians. Loyen agreed (Sidoine Apollinaire, p. 53, n. 27). In fact, however, Syagrius was a mature adult when Burgundio was an adolescent: "Adulescentem vel, quod est pulchrius, paene adhuc puerum" (Sidonius, Ep. IX, 14 MGH, AA, VIII, 168, ll. 9–10). The name Burgundio is again found in the sixth century; see Gregory of Tours, HF, VI, 15 (p. 285), and Vitae patrum, VIII, 9 (MGH, SRM, I-2, 699). It also appears in the seventh century in Vienne (CIL, XII, 2097). For the date of Sidonius' death, see Stevens, Sidonius Apollinaris, p. 166.

[118] Sidonius, Ep. IV, 12 (p. 64). Apollinaris was born around 460; see Stevens, Sidonius Apollinaris, p. 87, n. 7.

[119] Avitus, Ep. LI (45) (MGH, AA, VI-2, 80).

[120] Ruricius, Ep. II, 26, 27, 41 (MGH, AA, VIII, 332, 333, 341).

[121] Ruricius rebuked one of his sons for his dissipation: "Quamlibet Baccho, symphoniis et diversis musicis nec non etiam puellarum choris te deditum esse cognoverim" (Ep. II, 24 [p. 332]). The young man had been taught by Hesperius, the rhetor of Clermont; see ibid. I, 3 and 5 (pp. 301–2). Ruricius' other two sons were clerics at Clermont's cathedral (ibid. II, 40 and 49 [pp. 341, 345]).

[122] See above, sect. II.B.1.

the Ferreoli: Sidonius praised the culture of Tonantius Ferreolus in 481, and later, in the sixth century, we meet with lettered descendents of this humanist.[123]

Were there any professors in Aquitaine after 480? Lampridius, the rhetor who taught at Bordeaux, died between 475 and 479.[124] We know of no master[125] at Narbonne, a town which had maintained its grandeur and intellectual life during Sidonius' time.[126] The only grammarian known at the end of the fifth century was a certain John who ran a school somewhere in southern Gaul.[127] So, for this part of the Visigothic kingdom, we have hardly any information after 480. This silence ought not to lead us to the conclusion that every teacher had disappeared. What has disappeared is our source, Sidonius' correspondence.

Coming to the end of our investigation of southern Gaul, we can conclude that teachers continued to ply their trade, at least in the big cities. But did they teach in public? This question has been asked before, and since Roger's work, it has been thought that public instruction ceased in Gaul around 430.[128] Roger, however, based his conclusion on very weak evidence and perhaps overgeneralized the case of Sidonius' master, who taught at home.[129] Lampridius at Bordeaux, Domitius at Clermont, Sapaudus at Vienne, and Viventiolus at Lyon were all masters who gathered many students around themselves. Furthermore, Sidonius, in two letters dating from 472 to 474, still spoke of educational institutions. For him, the school was still part of the municipality, like the tribunal or the offices of the tax collectors. He even mentions the "municipal rhetors, titulars of a chair" ("municipales et cathedrarios oratores") in a letter to Claudian Mamertus. Unfortunately, he did not specify the city, but his testimony nevertheless proves that public schools still existed in certain centers. Thus, we can now date the end of public schools in Gaul from 474 at the earliest.[130]

On what authority did the masters depend? On royal power? We

---

[123] Sidonius, *Ep.* I, 13 (p. 163). For his family library, see *Ep.* II, 9 (p. 31), and *Carm.* XXIV, v. 90 (p. 264). For his descendents, see below, chap. 6, sect. II.A.

[124] Sidonius, *Ep.* IX, 13 (p. 163, vv. 22–23). Roger cites this text (p. 86) but discredits it without sufficient reason.

[125] Leo, the minister of the Visigothic king, was not a teacher as Loyen thought (*Sidoine Apollinaire*, p. 86), but a legal counselor. For this Leo, see below, chap. 2, n. 136.

[126] Sidonius, *Carm.* XXIII, vv. 37 ff. (p. 251). See Loyen, *Sidoine Apollinaire*, pp. 77–78.

[127] Sidonius, *Ep.* VIII, 2 (p. 127).

[128] Roger, p. 87, who was followed by Marrou, *Education*, p. 453.

[129] Sidonius, *Ep.* IV, 1 (p. 52).

[130] See my article, "La survivance des écoles publiques," pp. 421–36.

will see later that the Barbarian kings had very little interest in classical studies. From the municipality, then, as in Italy? Certainly, because the cities tried to hold on as long as possible to that which made them little Romes. Municipal institutions did not disappear simultaneously, and as long as they existed, the school remained open.[131] When the cities were unable to provide the salary of the teacher, parents replaced the city and paid the master, who then worked as a private individual.

4. IN SPAIN AND AFRICA

Let us finish our quest with Spain and Africa. From 476, the Iberian peninsula was divided between Suevian and Visigothic kings without, however, being completely occupied.[132] As archaeological and epigraphical maps prove, certain regions, in fact, never saw the Barbarians.[133] Spain preserved many of the traces of its Roman past. Roman roads, whose outline can still be seen in the Spanish highway system, were used by the Barbarians. The major cities kept their Roman architectural décor, and would keep it for a long time to come.[134] In Betica, in particular, less ravaged than other provinces by the wars of the fifth century, Roman traditions were maintained.[135] Could Spain—which had received so much in the intellectual realm from Rome[136] and had in return given Rome Seneca, Lucan, Quintillian, Martial, and others—forget Roman culture? According to Sidonius, Cordova was still well endowed with pupils (*praepotens alumnis*).[137] Unfortunately, aside from this tiny shred of evidence, we know nothing about the culture of laymen during this period.

What undoubtedly allowed Spain to preserve its traditions was the Ostrogothic influence in the Visigothic kingdom. Beaten by Clovis

[131] The texts pertaining to the survival of municipal institutions in Gaul are collected in ibid.

[132] Lot, *Les destinées*, p. 166; Menéndez Pidal, *HE*, 3: 37ff.

[133] See sect. I of this chapter. Vives, *Inscripciones*, cites only about ten Gothic names for the peninsula, most of which come from the seventh century. He found only one Gothic name at Tarragona (ibid., no. 214).

[134] See the sketches of Alexandre Louis Joseph, comte de Laborde, in *Voyage pittoresque et historique en Espagne*, 2 vols. in 4 (Paris, 1806–20).

[135] For the Romanization of Betica, see Raymond Thouvenot, *Essai sur la province romaine de Bétique* (Paris, 1940). Betica seems to have suffered but one incurison by Theodoric II, in 459. See Hydatius, *Continuatio Chronicorum Hieronymianorum, MGH, AA*, XI, 31.

[136] J. L. Cassani, "Aportes al estudio des proceso de la romanización de España: Las Institutiones educativas," *Cuadernos de Hispaña* 18 (1952): 50–70; Marrou, *Education*, p. 392.

[137] Sidonius, *Carm.* IX, v. 230 (*MGH, AA*, VIII, 224): "Corduba praepotens alumnis."

in 507, the Visigothic kings were rescued by the powerful Theodoric. In 531, the Ostrogoth Theudis, who acted as regent, was named king and resided at Barcelona until his death in 548.[138] The Ostrogoths extended the reorganization they had undertaken in Italy to Spain and thus kept Roman life alive in that country.[139] The written word, in particular, was to survive until the end of the Visigothic period, as we shall see below.[140]

We are much better informed about the intellectual centers of Vandal Africa. Despite property confiscations and religious persecutions, Afro-Romans remained loyal to their customs and to antique culture. Moreover, at the end of the fifth century during the reigns of Gunthamund and Thrasamund, persecutions were rare, the Barbarians were becoming Romanized, and the Romans began to hope for peace and, perhaps, for the conversion of their princes.[141] During this period teachers and scholars were once again in evidence; consequently, some have called it the "Vandal renaissance."[142]

Carthage's schools, which played such an important role in the history of Latin culture during the Empire, were still renowned when Genseric took the city in 439.[143] Martianus Capella had just drawn up his encyclopedia without ever imagining that his guidebook, written for the instruction of his son, was going to become the textbook for students throughout the Middle Ages.[144] The physician Cassius Felix translated Galen's works into Latin around 447, likewise for his son.[145]

---

[138] Menéndez Pidal, *HE*, 3: 91ff.

[139] See Cassiodorus, *Var.*, V, 35 and 39 (*MGH, AA*, XII, 162 and 164), for Theodoric's letters to the counts in charge of Spain.

[140] See chap. 6, sect. IV.B.

[141] Courtois, p. 300.

[142] For example, Courtois, pp. 228–29, and M. Simonetti, "Studi sulla letteratura cristiana d'Africa in età vandalica," *Rendiconti dell'Instituto lombardo di scienze e lettere* . . . (Milan) 83 (1950): 407.

[143] Salvian, *De gubern. Dei*, VII, 16, 68 (*MGH, AA*, I-1, 96): "Illic artium liberalium scolae, illic philosophorum officinae."

[144] Philologists have generally agreed that the *De nuptiis* was written between 410 and 430. See Schanz, IV-2, 169, and Maieul Cappuyns, "Capella" in the *DHGE*, 11: 842–43. The *terminus post quem* for the work was established by an allusion to the proconsul of Carthage. This post did not disappear during the Vandal domination, however; see Courtois, p. 528. Thus, Martianus could have composed his work after 430. For Martianus Capella's influence in the Middle Ages, see C. Leonardi, "Nota introduttiva per un'indagine sulla fortuna di Marziano Capella nel Medioevo," *Bullettino dell'Istituto Storico Italiano per il Medio Evo* 67 (1955): 265–88; Claudio Leonardi, *I codici di Marziano Capella* (Milan, 1960); and W. H. Stahl and R. Johnson, *Martianus Capella and the Seven Liberal Arts*, vol. 1, *The Quadrivium* (New York, 1971).

[145] Schanz, IV-2, 284. Caelius Aurelianus and Mustio, the translator of Soranus, must have lived at the same time; see ibid., pp. 286, 289.

The Vandal conquest thus surprised Carthaginians, who, despite the invasions, had not changed their way of life. Schools probably entered a period of decline at this time. The exile or imprisonment of the senators deprived them of a large part of their clientele.

One can thus understand the joy of the educated classes when the schools reopened at the end of the fifth century during the reign of Gunthamund. Felicianus, the grammarian, was praised for having "brought back to Africa the literature which had fled."[146] He was not alone. While almost the entire professorial corps at Rome is unknown to us, we can cite the names of several Carthaginian masters: Faustus, who held school in the forum and had the poet Luxorius for a pupil;[147] Coronatus; Cato; Chalcidius; and, perhaps, Pompey.[148] Poets gravitated to these schools. Dracontius wrote some school exercises for Felicianus' *auditorium*, just as Ennodius had for Deuterius at Milan.[149] The *Latin Anthology*, a *florilegium* collecting the poems of the African pleiad, was probably composed during Hilderic's reign for use in school.[150] The manuscript which preserves the *Latin Anthology* also contains a hundred enigmas composed by the *scolasticus* Symphosius. He seems to have been an African professor who, during this period, worked either for his own pupils or for those eternal pupils, the scholars of his day.[151] Thus, Carthage well merits the poet Florentinus' description of it as a city of masters and studies ("Carthago studiis, Carthago ornata magistris").[152]

[146] Dracontius, *Romulea*, I, v. 13 (*MGH, AA*, XIV, 132): "Qui fugatas Africanae reddis urbi litteras."

[147] Luxorius, *Anth. lat.*, p. 247, no. 287: "Tantus grammaticae magister artis." In reference to a poem of his youth, Luxorius wrote: "Quos olim puer in foro paravi versus" (ibid., v. 5). For Faustus, see Schanz, IV-2, 73; for Luxorius, Morris Rosenblum, *Luxorius: A Latin Poet among the Vandals* (New York, 1961).

[148] Coronatus wrote a work entitled *De ultimis syllabis partium orationis* (Keil, 4: 50). See *Anth. lat.*, p. 295, for Cato; the preface to Fulgentius' *Expositio sermonum antiquorum* (Helm ed., p. 105), for Chalcidius; and Schanz, IV-2, 209, for Pompey. For Pompey see also the recent work by L. Holtz, "Tradition et diffusion de l'oeuvre grammaticale de Pompée, commentateur de Donat," *RPh* 3rd ser. 45 (1971): 48–83.

[149] Dracontius, *Romulea*, III (*MGH, AA*, XIV, 137): "Incipit praefatio ad Felicianum grammaticum, cuius supra in auditorio, cum adlocutione." See also poems IV, V, and IX ("deliberativa Achillis, an corpus Hectoris vendat"). For Dracontius, see most recently, F. Chatillon, "Dracontiana," *RMAL*, 8 (1952): 177–212.

[150] For the *Anth. lat.*, see Schanz, IV-2, 69–74, and R. T. Ohl, "Some Remarks on the Latin Anthology," *CW* 42 (1948–49): 147. The preface to the *Anth. lat.*, no. 90, clearly states the purpose for which the anthology was intended: "Parvola quod lusit, sensit quod junior aetas . . . hoc opus inclusit."

[151] See Schanz, IV-2, 74–76, and R. T. Ohl, "Symphosius and the Latin Riddle," *CW* 25 (1932): 209–12.

[152] *Anth. lat.*, p. 289, no. 376.

The capital of Vandal Africa, however, did not monopolize all scholarly life. There were still important schools in the provinces which produced famous scholars. During Genseric's reign, Victor of Vita acquired his literary training outside the capital.[153] Around 480, Fulgentius, the future bishop of Ruspe, was sent to school, perhaps at Theleptus, after having begun his studies at home.[154] Later, the poet and grammarian Corippus taught in the provinces before coming to Carthage.[155] After the Byzantine reconquest, provincial schools trained educated men, who then entered the service of the Church: the future quaestor Junilius, whose style has an antique flavor; Primasius of Hadrumetum; Verecundus of Junca.[156]

In Africa, then, scholarly life was maintained more substantially than elsewhere. The literary achievements of the poets of the *Latin Anthology*, of course, were without issue. That, however, is not the essential point. Historians who have spoken of a "renewal" have perhaps concentrated too much on this literary episode. The important point is that the antique school survived the Vandal occupation. When Carthage again became "Roman," Justinian provided for the support of two grammarians and two rhetors.[157] His action represents more a nationalization than a restoration of learning. Until the Arabs took Carthage in 698, young Africans could pursue classical studies. Consequently, as we shall see, Africa would be able to contribute to the creation of Western culture.

III. CHARACTERISTICS OF CLASSICAL CULTURE AT THE BEGINNING OF THE SIXTH CENTURY

In our inquiry into the various Barbarian kingdoms, we have observed that educated men everywhere still had the means to instruct

---

[153] For the literary culture of Victor of Vita, see Christian Courtois, *Victor de Vita et son oeuvre* (Algiers, 1954), pp. 66ff.

[154] Ferrandus, *Vita Fulgentii*, I, 5 (Lapeyre ed., p. 13): "Latinis litteris ... in domo edoctus artis etiam grammaticae traditus auditorio."

[155] Schanz, IV-2, 78; Laistner, *Thought and Letters*, pp. 113–14.

[156] According to Isidore of Seville, *De viris illustribus*, 7 (*PL*, LXXXIII, 1088), Verecundus received a liberal education: "Studiis liberalium litterarum disertus." See Schanz, IV-2, 394ff. Junilius reports a remark in the preface of the *Institutiones, PL*, LXVIII, 15, of Primasius of Hadrumetum on the schools of Africa: "Apud nos in mundanis studiis grammatica et rhetorica . . . traditur."

[157] *Corpus iuris civilis*, I, 27 (1, 42) (Krüger ed., p. 79).

themselves. When we look inside the schools of the grammarian and the rhetor, we can observe that the program and methods of instruction also had not changed.

A. MAINTENANCE OF TRADITIONS

As in previous centuries, cultural life was essentially literary and oratorical. For Cassiodorus and Ennodius, grammar remained "the foundation of literature, the glorious mother of eloquence," the "nurse-maid of the other arts."[158] As in the past, the student began his studies with grammatical treatises, especially that of Donatus.[159] Because grammar led to "the art of speaking well according to the example of the illustrious poets and authors,"[160] the student had also to enrich his mind by reading the classics. Judging from the citations or reminiscences found in Cassiodorus, Ennodius, Arator, and Avitus, among others, the classical authors they knew were the same ones Augustine and Sidonius Apollinaris cited.[161]

The teaching methods the student faced in the rhetor's class were likewise traditional. Like his fathers, he learned which topics provided the arguments demanded by the *inventio*; he studied the six parts of a speech and then how to speak affectedly and elegantly.[162] He also discovered the secrets of meter, since rhythmic prose was considered a stylistic ornament.[163] He studied dialectic, the tool of eloquence.[164]

---

[158] Ennodius, *Opusc.* VI (*MGH, AA*, VII, 313, ll. 8–9): "Istae . . . prae foribus quasi nutricem ceterarum [artium] anteponunt grammaticam." Cassiodorus, *Var.*, IX, 21 (*MGH, AA*, XII, 286): "Fundatum pulcherrimum litterarum mater gloriosa facundiae quae cogitare novit ad laudem, loqui sine vitio."

[159] Cassiodorus, *Institutiones*, II (Mynors ed., p. 94): "Donatus qui et pueris specialiter aptus." Donatus' commentary was also used for children by the African Pompey; see the preface in Keil, 5: 90. For the relationship between grammar and culture, see J. Fontaine, *IS*, pp. 29ff.

[160] Cassiodorus, *Inst.*, II (p. 94): "Grammatica vero est peritia pulchre loquendi ex poetis illustribus auctoribusque collecta."

[161] Especially, among the poets, Virgil (cited sixty times by Ennodius, more than two hundred times by Arator, and more than sixty by Avitus) and his imitator, Silius Italicus, who was cited by Ennodius and Arator. Next came Terence, Horace, Ovid, Tibullus, Lucan, and Statius. Among prose authors we can list Cicero (cited by Cassiodorus and Ennodius), Sallust, Caesar, and Valerius Maximus. See Schanz, IV-2, 311–12.

[162] For instruction in rhetoric, see Cassiodorus, *Inst.*, II, 2 (p. 100).

[163] In the fifth century, Edesius was "rhetoricae facundiae et metricae artis peritissimus vir" at Arles (*Vita Hilarii*, PL, L, 1233). Ennodius, in the sixth century, had *poetica* depend upon rhetoric (*Ep.* VI [*MGH, AA*, VII, 314, l. 10]). See, however, Cassiodorus, *Var.*, IX, 21 (p. 286): "Dispositis congruenter accentibus metrum novit decantare grammaticus." For poetic prose, see Norden, *Antike Kunstprosa*, 2: 894, and M. Nicolau, "Les deux sources de la versification latine accentuelle," *ALMA* 9 (1934): 77. For a more recent treatment, see Curtius, p. 179. For Ennodius' rhythmic clausulae, see

When it came to practice, our student performed classic exercises: the suasoria and the controversia. Ennodius and Dracontius have left us examples of these exercises which in every particular recall those of Seneca the Elder and are just as artificial.[165] For example, they tried to imagine the speeches of Dido abandoned by Aeneas or the complaints of Menelaus before the burning of Troy and to make a case against a man who placed a statue of Minerva in a brothel or against another who wanted to buy the innocence of a vestal with gold.[166] The student of the sixth century was satisfied with a rhetoric that seems quite vacuous to us, and yet this rhetorical instruction marked the entire literature of the period. It has been pointed out that Martianus Capella and Fronto were used as models much more than Cicero and Quintillian.[167] Writers sought to use rare words and obscure and obsolete expressions.[168] The sixth-century school tremendously influenced the future of Western culture: it preserved the tradition of mannerism, whose traces we find throughout the Middle Ages.[169]

The educated man of the sixth century, like his predecessors of previous centuries, sought not only to be *eloquentissimus* but also to be *doctissimus*. His curiosity knew no bounds. He collected everything from his extensive reading that could enrich him. A man like Cassiodorus is the type of the erudite scholar. Paradoxically, the most technical of his works, the *Variae*, provides examples of this kind of erudition.[170] The paradox, however, is only apparent, because the letters drawn up

---

Armand Fougnies, *Een studien over de clausulen bij Ennodius* (Brussels, 1951), and idem, "Resultats d'une étude sur les clausules chez Ennodius," *RBPh* 26 (1948): 1048. For the clausulae of Ruricius, see Harald Hagendahl, *La correspondance de Ruricius* (Göteborg, 1952), p. 49.

[164] When Fulgentius enumerated the arts (*Mitol.*, III, 8 [Helm ed., pp. 77–78]), he made dialectic a rhetorical skill: "In omnibus igitur artibus sunt primae artes, sunt secundae . . . in rhetoricis prima rethorica, secunda dialectica." According to Martianus Capella and, no doubt, to his compatriot Tullius Marcellus of Carthage, dialectical syllogisms were part of rhetorical training, as they had been in Augustine's time. See J. Fontaine, *IS*, pp. 622ff., for the influence of African treatises in the West.

[165] See Marrou, *Education*, pp. 277, 282, for these exercises. For sixth-century rhetoric, see Edgar de Bruyne, *Etudes d'esthétique médiévale* (Bruges, 1946), 1: 43–62.

[166] Ennodius, *Dictiones* XIV–XV, XVII–XXIII (*MGH, AA*, VII, 175–76, 184, 191, 201, 220, 260, 271, 325). Ennodius' letter IV, 4 (ibid., p. 130), can also be added to this list, since it contains arguments put forth by a sister for naming her brother as her heir.

[167] Curtius, p. 359; René Marache, *La critique littéraire de langue latine et le développement du goût archaïsant au IIe siècle de notre ère* (Rennes, 1952), pp. 335–39. We have a manuscript of Fronto from the sixth century; see *CLA*, I, 27.

[168] See Fulgentius' treatise, *Expositio sermonum antiquorum*, ed. Helm, pp. 111–26, which is a glossary of sixty-two words.

[169] Curtius, pp. 331ff.

[170] For the erudition of the fourth century, see Marrou, *Saint Augustin*, pp. 110–11.

by the royal chancery largely obeyed the laws of rhetoric.[171] It is interesting to note that Cassiodorus did not incorporate learned digressions only in his letters to his most cultured correspondents.[172] Boethius, Faustus, and Symmachus were not the only ones to benefit from his letters: the minister also provided functionaries recently appointed to a new post or to a particular province with curious details on the origins of their new duties or on the country which they were to administer.[173]

If we classify these various *excursi* according to types, we see that Cassiodorus' curiosity took him into very divergent fields: praise of the liberal arts,[174] descriptions of certain regions in Italy[175] and of the natural phenomena found there (volcanoes, geysers),[176] information on animal life (the chameleon, the elephant, the quail)[177] or on the manufacture of certain products (papyrus, chalk, wine).[178] In general, Cassiodorus was particularly interested in the origin of war, of the *annona*, of money, of letters, of geometry and theater,[179] and in the invention of products such as bread, purple dye, and lead.[180] In reading these learned digressions we meet once again with the literary atmosphere of Macrobius' *Saturnalia*, and also with the erudition of a Saint Augustine.[181]

Cassiodorus was one erudite scholar among many. The father of the consul Felix, a Provençal, was praised for having closely studied the origin of natural events ("rerum quoque naturalium causas subtilissime perscrutatus").[182] Ennodius has a poetic evocation of the famous

[171] See Åke J. Fridh, *Terminologie et formules dans les "Variae" de Cassiodore: Etudes sur le développement du style administratif aux derniers siècles de l'Antiquité*, Studia graeca et latina Gothoburgensia, vol. 2 (Stockholm, 1956).

[172] H. Nickstadt studied only the sources of the digressions in *De digressionibus quibus in Variis usus est Cassiodorus* (Marburg, 1921).

[173] Cassiodorus, *Var.*, VII, 8; VI, 19; VII, 15 (*MGH, AA*, XII, 207, 191, 211).

[174] Arithmetic (ibid., I, 10), geometry (III, 52), and astronomy (XI, 36). See ibid., pp. 19, 107, 350.

[175] Mount Lactarius (XI, 10), Lake Como (XI, 14), Bruttium (XII, 14), and the lagoons of Venetia (XII, 24). See ibid., pp. 340, 342, 371, 380.

[176] Volcanoes (III, 47; IV, 50), the fountains of Aponus (II, 39) and of Arethusa (VIII, 32). See ibid., pp. 102, 137, 68, 261.

[177] Ibid., V, 34 (p. 162); X, 30 (p. 317).

[178] Ibid., XI, 38 (p. 351); VII, 17 (p. 213); XII, 4 (p. 362).

[179] Ibid., I, 30 (p. 31); VI, 18 (p. 191); VII, 32 (p. 219); VIII, 12 (p. 243); IV, 51 (p. 138).

[180] Ibid., VI, 18 (p. 191); I, 2 (p. 11); III, 31 (p. 95).

[181] See Marrou, *Saint Augustin*, pp. 125–57. Alexander T. Heerklotz, *Die Variae des Cassiodorus Senator als kulturgeschichtliche Quelle* (Heidelberg, 1926), p. 41, thought, without any real proof, that this scientific curiosity derived especially from Christian influence.

[182] Cassiodorus, *Var.*, II, 3 (p. 48, l. 20).

Aponus fountain, which Cassiodorus also liked to describe.[183] Avitus digressed on the Nile's floods,[184] a classical theme of "natural treatises." In his *Commentary on the Ecclesiastical Canticles*, the African Verecundus of Junca referred the reader to the "histories of the learned physicians Pliny the Elder, Solinus, and many others" and to the contemporary work of John of Constantinople on the "nature of animals."[185] Pliny and Solinus were still sources for the man of erudition and would long remain so.

The scholar plundered not only scientific works. Geography remained what it had been in the fourth and fifth centuries, either a collection of names for the use of a grammarian or a collection of travel descriptions *(itineraria)*.[186] History continued to provide exempla for the rhetor and the moralist.[187] Certainly the erudition of these authors is not as rich as that of their predecessors, but they do bear witness nonetheless to the same taste for compiling, a taste which these scholars transmitted to the Middle Ages.

B. Impoverishment and Dislocation of the Program

The Roman subjects of the Barbarian kings deluded themselves about the culture which they received and transmitted: they apparently thought that it was the same as that which their fathers had possessed and passed on to them. They seem not to have taken into account its increasing impoverishment. The time spent with the grammarian and the rhetor seems to us to have often been wasted. We should not blame the grammarian, however, for not teaching Ciceronian Latin at a time when the vocabulary and syntax of Latin was changing.[188] In fact, our

---

183 Ennodius, *Ep.* V, 8 (*MGH, AA*, VIII, 178, l. 33); Cassiodorus, *Var.*, II, 39 (p. 68).

184 Avitus, *De mundi initio*, 262–89 (*MGH, AA*, VI-2, 210–11).

185 Verecundus, *Commentarii super Cantica ecclesiastica*, in *Spicilegium solesmense*, ed. Jean-Baptiste Pitra, vol. 4, pt. 1 (Paris, 1858), p. 104. See Schanz, IV-2, 395, and Manitius, 1: 117.

186 For geography in the fourth century, see Marrou, *Saint Augustin*, p. 136, and, for the fifth century, Loyen, *Sidoine Apollinaire*, pp. 20–25. Ennodius has left us some poetical *itineraria* in *Carm.* 1, 1 and 5 (*MGH, AA*, VII, 193 and 292). Pomponius Mela's work was revised at Ravenna. For the maps Jordanes used, see Mommsen's preface to his edition of Jordanes' *Romana* and *Getica* (*MGH, AA*, V-1, xxxi–xxxii).

187 Ennodius, *Paraenesis didascalica*, *MGH, AA*, VII, 314, l. 8: "De virorum fortium factis quod volumus creditur." Cassiodorus, *Var.*, III, 6 (p. 82, l. 28): "In libris veterum Decios cognovit antiquos nobilemque progeniem gloriosae mortis beneficio viventem."

188 For the transformation of Latin during this period, see Einar Löfstedt, *Late Latin* (Oslo, 1959), as well as the following studies of Christian texts: Pieter Willem Hoogterp, *Etude sur le latin du Codex bobiensis (k) des Evangiles* (Wageningen, 1930); Christine

authors still tried to respect the authority of the classics.[189] Nevertheless, classical authors would have criticized sixth-century authors for the poverty of their inspiration, which they tried to mask by an excessive complication of form.

Even more serious for the future was the growing ignorance of Greek and, thus, the abandonment of an entire segment of ancient culture. Pierre Courcelle has correctly shown how Greek culture disappeared in Gaul at the end of the fifth century after the death of its last representative, Claudian Mamertus (474).[190] Yet, he insists on what he calls the "renaissance of Hellenism under the Ostrogoths."[191] But, in fact, all that this "renaissance" amounts to in terms of profane learning is the abortive efforts of Boethius and his group to restore Greek philosophical and literary culture. This remarkable effort, which had such important consequences beginning in the ninth century, could not be grasped by Boethius' contemporaries. There were simply not enough people who could read Greek or who were even interested in the translations produced during this period.[192] The rupture between the Latin and the Greek worlds was almost complete. At the beginning of his reign, Theodoric and, later, his daughter Amalasuntha attempted to reestablish contact with Byzantium. But Gothic nationalism and the passivity of the Latins provoked a political and cultural split that Justinian's reconquest could not remedy.[193]

The only land where we still find an interest in Greek is Africa, but

Mohrmann, "Les formes du latin dit 'vulgaire,'" in *Actes du premier Congrès de la Fédération internationale des associations des études classiques, 1950* (Paris, 1951), pp. 207–29; idem, "La latinité de saint Benoît: Etude linguistique sur la tradition manuscrite de la Règle," *RB* 62 (1952): 114; Philip B. Corbett, Introduction to *Regula Magistri*, ed. Hubert Vanderhoven and François Masai (Brussels, 1953), p. 69; idem, *The Latin of the Regula Magistri* (Louvain, 1958).

[189] See Augustin Dubois, *La latinité d'Ennodius: Contribution à l'étude du latin littéraire à la fin de l'Empire romain d'Occident* (Paris, 1903); Goelzer, *Le latin de saint Avit*; Bernard Henry Skahill, *The Syntax of the "Variae" of Cassiodorus* (Washington, D.C., 1934); and Åke J. Fridh, *Etudes critiques et syntaxiques sur les "Variae" de Cassiodore* (Göteborg, 1950).

[190] Courcelle, *LG*, pp. 246–52. For Claudian Mamertus, see E. L. Fortin's *Christianisme et culture philosophique au Ve siècle: La querelle de l'âme humaine en Occident* (Paris, 1959).

[191] Courcelle, *LG*, pp. 257ff.

[192] For sixth-century translations, see F. Blatt, "Remarques sur l'histoire des traductions latines," *CM* 1 (1936): 217–42, and Albert Siegmund, *Die Ueberlieferung der griechischen christlichen Literatur in der lateinischen Kirche bis zum zwölften Jahrhundert* (Munich, 1949). Arnaldo Momigliano has studied aristocrats' knowledge of Greek in *Secundo contributo alla storia degli studi classici*, Storia e letteratura, vol. 77 (Rome, 1960).

[193] See Stein, 2: 254, 328, for the political break of the sixth century.

we cannot really speak of the study of this language. Greek novels[194] and medical treatises[195] were translated for the Latin public. Faithful to an old tradition,[196] the young Fulgentius learned Greek about 490 even before studying Latin. Homer and Menander were familiar to him.[197] Once beyond his childhood years, however, he no longer read or spoke this foreign tongue.[198] The only reason Greek was not totally forgotten in Africa was because certain Catholics, persecuted by the Vandals, maintained contacts with the Empire. They were awaiting their liberation, which came in 535 with Justinian's reconquest of Africa. The survival of Greek culture in this part of the West is thus tied to particular political conditions.

Having forgotten Greek, the lettered of the sixth century had no contact with the culture which previously had come to them from the East, that is, philosophical culture. At the end of the fifth century, Sidonius Apollinaris could still appreciate the work of Claudian Mamertus even though, like many, he was not philosophically inclined. Matters were completely different a few years later. Boethius' work interested no one but a few intimate friends.[199] Cassiodorus praised the translator but ignored the philosopher.[200] In his correspondence with Boethius, a relative, Ennodius busied himself with the acquisition of a house owned by the philosopher rather than with Boethius' work.[201] Philosophy was so unfamiliar to Boethius' contemporaries that they confused it with the occult sciences condemned by both the Church and the state.[202] Cassiodorus himself contributed to this confusion when

194 The *Aegritudo Perdicae* could be by Dracontius; see Chatillon, "Dracontiana," *RMAL* 8 (1952): 192. Fulgentius, *Mitol.* III, 2 (Helm ed., p. 61), treats the same subject, as well as the story of Eros and Leander and of Berecintha and Attis. For literary exchanges between Egypt and Vandal Africa, see H. Stern, "A propos des poésies des mois dans l'Anthologie latine," *Revue des études grecques* 65 (1952): 374–82.

195 See below, chapt. 2, n. 122.

196 Marrou, *Education*, p. 355.

197 Ferrandus, *Vita Fulgentii*, ed. Lapeyre, p. 10.

198 Courcelle, *LG*, pp. 206–9, has reduced Fulgentius' knowledge of Greek to proper proportions.

199 Symmachus, Novatus Renatus, and Fabius were among Boethius' intimates. Novatus read and corrected a copy of the *Topics* (see Schanz, IV-2, 151) and was perhaps the Renatus "vir spectabilis" mentioned in a letter from John to Senarius (*PL*, LIX, 399). Boethius is supposed to have engaged in a dialogue with Fabius in his commentary on Porphyry (*PL*, LXIV, 70). Boethius dedicated his *De syllogismo hypothetico* to an unidentified friend (ibid., 831).

200 Cassiodorus, *Var.*, I, 45 (*MGH, AA*, XII, 39).

201 Ennodius, *Ep.* VI, 6; VII, 13; VIII, 1; VIII, 36 (*MGH, AA*, VII, 217, 236, 268, 288). See also the ironic epigram "De Boetio spata cincto," which Ennodius undoubtedly wrote apropos of Boethius' consulate in 510 (*Carm.* 2, 132 [ibid., p. 249]).

202 For astrology in fifth-century Gaul, see the article by H. de la Ville de Mirmont,

he called philosophers those who "say that one should venerate the sun, the moon, and the other stars."[203] The cosmology dear to the Neoplatonists was likewise suspect.[204] In fact, Boethius, who did not conceal his taste for this discipline, was accused at his trial of being an astrologer and magician.[205]

When Ennodius and Cassiodorus used the word "philosophy," they had in mind "natural philosophy," physics, and medicine.[206] A little-known passage from Jordanes' *History of the Goths* gives the same interpretation.[207] Recalling that a certain Dicineus had given the Goths an introduction to philosophy, Jordanes, with the help of the classic definition of the Stoics, specified that philosophy consisted of ethics, physics, and logic. Then he spoke of *pratice* and *theorice*, a division similarly classic.[208] This is perfect so far. But when we read what Jordanes entered under each of the branches of philosophy, we are quickly disappointed. For him, philosophy is reduced to the knowledge of physical phenomena: the twelve signs of the zodiac, the revolutions of the moon and the sun, the study of vegetation. Such are the *doctrinae philosophiae* in which the ancient Goths were to have been schooled. Did not their descendent, Theodoric, want to pass for a philosopher-king by examining his minister on such questions? Philosophy had

---

"L'Astrologie chez les gallo-romains," *REA* II (1909): 301–27. Senators were prosecuted in Rome in 510 for having practiced magic (Cassiodorus, *Var.*, IV, 22, 23 [p. 124]).

[203] Cassiodorus, *Complexiones*, PL, LXX, 1351: "Commonens ut nemo eos seducat per inanem sapientiam philosophorum qui dicunt solem atque lunam vel astra cetera esse veneranda."

[204] Emile Bréhier, "La cosmologie stoicienne à la fin du paganisme," *Revue de l'histoire des religions* 64 (1911): 1–20.

[205] Boethius, *Philosophiae consolationis*, I, 4; I, 5 (ed. Rudolf Peiper [Leipzig, 1871], pp. 15–16). See L. Alfonsi, "Romanità e barbarie nell'Apologia di Boezio," *Studi Romani* I (1953): 605.

[206] Ennodius, *Eucharisticon de vita sua*, MGH, AA, VII, 301–2: "Tunc illa saecularis pompae philosophia Hippocrates et Galeni contrita." The equation of *philosophus* and *medicus* is also found in Cassiodorus, *Var.*, II, 39 (p. 68, l. 13). See Curtius, pp. 213ff., for the different meanings of *philosophi*.

[207] Jordanes, *Getica*, XI (MGH, AA, V-1, 74, ll. 2–9): "Qui . . . omnem pene phylosophiam eos instruxit . . . nam ethicam eos erudiens barbaricos mores conpescuit; fysicam tradens naturaliter propriis legibus vivere fecit, quas usque nunc conscriptas belagines nuncupant; logicam instruens rationis eos supra ceteras gentes fecit expertes; praticen ostendens in bonis actibus conversare suasit; theoreticen demonstrans signorum duodecim et per ea planetarum cursus omnemque astronomiam contemplari edocuit."

[208] The robe of philosophy bore π and θ; see Boethius, *Philosophiae consolationis*, I, 1 (Peiper ed., p. 4, l. 18). See also Fulgentius, *Mitol.*, II, 1 (Helm ed., p. 36, ll. 1–5): "Philosophi tripertitam humanitatis voluerunt vitam ex quibus primam theoreticam, secundam praticam, tertiam filargicam voluerunt, quos nos Latine contemplativam, activam, voluptariam nuncupamus."

become physical science, and a degraded form of physical science at that, since it became part of the eruditio already discussed.

We are far from the thought of the Hellenic masters, who saw in philosophy the coronation of the liberal arts. Boethius had attempted to revive this notion when, in the preface of his *De arithmetica*, he wrote that four disciplines—arithmetic, music, geometry, and astronomy—led to philosophy. These four avenues comprised what he called the *quadrivium*, a term which was to have a great history in the Middle Ages.[209] A program of scientific studies was thus laid out. Boethius then translated the essential texts that were studied in the East at that time,[210] so that his program might be applied; but no one was to read his work. Even Cassiodorus had only a very vague understanding of the different branches of the quadrivium. Ennodius of Pavia oddly linked arithmetic to rhetoric.[211] In Africa, Fulgentius presented a fantastic tableau of the liberal arts that included astrology, medicine, haruspicy, and other sciences which certainly meant nothing to him.[212] The exact sciences were no longer interesting. Only the applied sciences, as we shall see in the next chapter, still attracted attention.

Can one then speak of an "intellectual renaissance" in the Barbarian kingdoms? Historians have been so astonished that studies were not totally abandoned in the aftermath of the great invasions that they believe a renaissance did indeed take place. Yes, the antique school still existed. Where public instruction had disappeared, private instruction took up its methods. But the preservation of the routine traditions of the school and the increasing dislocation of the program of studies did

[209] Boethius, *De institutione arithmetica*, preface (Friedlein ed., pp. 9–10): "Quibus quattuor partibus si careat inquisitor verum invenire non possit. . . . Hoc igitur illud quadruvium est quo his viandum sit quibus excellentior animus a nobiscum procreatus sensibus ad intelligentiae certiora perducitur." Cassiodorus, *Var.*, I, 45 (p. 40): "Tu artem praedictam ex disciplinis nobilibus notam per quadrifarias mathesis januas introisti." See Pio Rajna, "Le denominazione trivium e quadrivium," *SM* 1 (1920): 5ff., and A. Viscardi, "Boezio e la conservazione e trasmissione dell'eridità del pensiero antico," *Settimane*, 3: 329.

[210] Courcelle, *LG*, pp. 262–63. Boethius' treatise *De institutione musica* has been studied by Leo Schrade ("Die Stellung der Musik in der Philosophie des Boethius als Grundlage der ontologischen Musikerziehung," *Archiv für Geschichte der Philosophie* 41 [1932]: 360–400), and by Henri Potiron (*Boèce: Théoricien de la musique grecque* [Paris, 1961]).

[211] Ennodius, *Paraenesis didascalica*, MGH, AA, VII, 314, l. 11.

[212] Fulgentius, *Mitol.*, III, 8 (Helm ed., pp. 77–78): "In geometricis prima geometrica, secunda arithmetica, in astrologicis prima mathesis, secunda astronomia, in medicinis prima gnostice, secunda dinamice, in aruspicinis prima aruspicina, secunda parallaxis, in musicis prima musica, secunda apostelesmatice."

not presage well for the future. The antique school was unable to reverse the decline it had undergone since the fourth century. The culture it dispensed was dull and lifeless and, thus, in grave danger.

IV. CLASSICAL CULTURE ENDANGERED

Classical culture, as we have seen, was the privilege of the aristocracy. All the students and scholars mentioned thus far belonged to the Roman and provincial senatorial classes. As in previous centuries, the goal of studies was not simply to furnish the mind and to form character,[213] but also to prove that one was worthy enough to belong to the good society.[214] Morally and intellectually trained, the young man could enter literary circles.[215] He put his literary training to use in his worldly affairs and used a trip,[216] a gift either sent or received,[217] a wedding, or a death[218] to display his poetical talents and his erudition. The friendships which united members of these circles were primarily literary. They exchanged "art letters," which, unfortunately for the historian, teach us nothing about the events to which the authors were witnesses but are simply compliments, mundane trifles, or literary advice.[219]

The lettered seem to have been eternal students or tireless pedagogues. Ennodius distributed some dictiones to his correspondents,[220] criticized their style,[221] or asked for a critique of his own but, like a petty schoolmaster, became angry when a mistake was uncovered in

[213] Cassiodorus, *Var.*, III, 33 (p. 96): "Gloriosa scientia litterarum . . . mores purgat." Ennodius, *Opusc.* 6 (*MGH, AA*, VII, 313): "De praefatis virtutibus [verecundia, castitas et fides] facessat studiorum liberalium deesse diligentiam."

[214] Ennodius, *Ep.* VIII, 32 (*MGH, AA*, VII, 287, l. 6): "Ortus nobiliter profutura ad testimonium ingenuitatis studia romana requirit." See also *Ep.* I, 18 (p. 25, l. 32).

[215] Ennodius, *Ep.* IX, 10 (p. 297, l. 17); ibid IV, 12 (p. 140, l. 13).

[216] Senator Faustus wrote a poem recounting his trip on Lake Como; see Ennodius, *Ep.* I, 6 (p. 15, l. 34). See also the *Itinerarium* of Ennodius, *Carm.* 1, 5 (ibid., p. 292), and the description of an island in Lake Bolsena by an unknown poet, H. W. Garrod, "Poeseos saeculi sexti fragmenta quattuor" *CQ* 4 (1910): 266.

[217] Ennodius, *Carm.* 2, 144 and 146 (p. 269); 2, 98 (p. 181).

[218] Ibid. 1, 4 (p. 276), is an epithalamium for Maximus. See Ennodius' epitaphs in *Ep.* VII, 29 (p. 260), his letters of consolation in *Ep.* III, 2 (p. 77), and those of Ruricius in *Ep.* II, 29 (*MGH, AA*, VIII, 340).

[219] For the friendship shown in these letters, see Ennodius, *Ep.* IV, 2, 17; V, 22; VI, 19 (pp. 129, 196, 224).

[220] Ibid. VIII, 11 (p. 276, l. 20). Ennodius suggested a theme for Arator to develop and thanked Olybrius for a *dictio* on Hercules and Antaeus (ibid. I, 9 [p. 18]).

[221] In a letter to Stephania, Faustus' sister: "Rogo . . . ut numquam scholasticorum indociles conpositiones sanctis dictationibus misceatis" (ibid. IX, 18 [p. 305, l. 23]).

one of his poems.[222] Cassiodorus, the minister, as we have seen, revealed the treasures of his erudition when he wrote to subordinates. Highly placed functionaries, like the grammarians, collected precious books[223] and occupied their leisure with revising poorly established manuscript texts.[224] The fate of this isolated, worldly culture depended on the existence of the aristocratic class. Should a political crisis test this social group, classical culture could very well disappear.

Classical culture had already suffered from the invasions of the fifth century. Educated men in the last years of the fifth century no longer possessed the culture of Sidonius' contemporaries. What would it be like, then, for their children? Teachers were fewer and were obliged to teach grammar as well as rhetoric, thus confusing secondary instruction with more advanced instruction. Students, also less numerous, were neither competitive nor greatly interested in their work. The eagerness of young Boethius for study struck Ennodius as something quite exceptional.[225] The Milanese deacon most often complained about the laziness of his young correspondents.[226] Once away from him, they no longer did anything. One of them, his nephew Parthenius, profited from the absence of Senator Faustus, to whom he was entrusted, to lead a rather gay life.[227] In Gaul, Ruricius scolded his son for "thinking too much of the girls' choir and of Bacchus."[228] From Constantinople,

[222] See ibid. VII, 28; VIII, 21 and 29 (pp. 259, 283, 285). Young Beatus discovered the mistake in a funeral poem by Ennodius. The poet vigorously defended himself but was forced to admit his error.

[223] A manuscript of Pliny the Younger, of which some fragments have come down to us, was copied during this period (see E. K. Rand and E. A. Lowe, *A VIth Century Fragment of the Letters of Plinius the Younger* [Washington, D.C., 1922]), as was perhaps the Vatican Virgil (see Vanderhoven and Masai, *Regula Magistri*, pp. 52–53). The daughter of the former emperor Olybrius, Juliana Anicia, had a manuscript of Dioscorides illustrated; see E. Riez, *Die Miniaturen des Wiener Dioscorides* (Vienna, 1907).

[224] Helpidius, *comes consistorianus* at Ravenna, revised a manuscript of Pomponius Mela and Valerius Maximus. Also at Ravenna, Senator Symmachus revised the commentary of Macrobius on the *Dream of Scipio*; see Jahn, "Ueber die Subscriptionen," p. 347. Lupicinus, a nephew and disciple of Ennodius, revised a manuscript of the *Gallic Wars*; see Jahn, p. 359, and Friedrich Vogel, the editor of Ennodius' works, *MGH, AA*, VII, 356. In 494 Asterius revised the *Bucolics* as well as the work of Sedulius; see Jahn, pp. 348–53. In 527, Mavortius revised the *Epodes* of Horace and the poems of Prudentius.

[225] Ennodius, *Ep.* VII, 13 (*MGH, AA*, VII, 236): "Cui inter vitae exordia ludus est lectionis assiduitas et deliciae sudor alienus."

[226] Ibid. IX, 6 (p. 296), to Beatus; VIII, 3 (p. 270), to Messala; VIII, 4 and 11 (pp. 271, 276), to Arator. See especially V, 19 (p. 195, l. 7): "Taciturnitatis imperitiam prodit et infabricata confabulatio manifestat infantiam"; and VI, 23 (p. 225, l. 28): "Labora ergo . . . eos qui consortio [te] suo polluunt . . . fuge."

[227] Ibid. VII, 30 (p. 267, l. 1), to Faustus: "Nunc per absentiam vestram venerandae solutus lege formidinis molitur obscena."

[228] See above, n. 121.

Priscian the grammarian wrote to Symmachus in the hope that the latter might excite the zeal of young Romans.[229]

These are not simply clichés. The absence of great literary works is silent proof of disinterest in studies; indeed, some students became rapidly disgusted with the artificiality and triviality of culture. Young Benedict of Nursia, hardly settled in Rome, fled the city and its schools around 500, appalled by what was being taught to him.[230] Benedict's lofty reasons were, of course, not those of all students.[231] Most students, after spending time in school, were often content to return to the family property and forget all that they had learned. Cassiodorus complained of this in a letter that has been dated 527: "What use is it that so many men brought up on literature remain hidden? Their children want to go to secondary schools and could soon be worthy of the activities of the forum; as soon as they return to their homes in the country, they begin no longer to know anything. They make progress in school, only to unlearn everything. They educate themselves so that they never have to bother with it again, and while they love their fields, they no longer know how to love themselves." In conclusion, "it is scandalous that a noble bring his children up in the middle of a desert."[232] Cassiodorus was perceptive. The abandonment of the cities by the aristocrats was prejudicial to literary culture. On their rural properties, young people unfortunately were interested only in what pertained to their farms. Even if they had a library at their disposal, were they not likely to lock the richly bound codices in their armoires, as did those book-loving bishops and scholars Caesarius of Arles described?[233]

The promise of a career would have compensated the student for his efforts, kept him in the city, and given him the necessary enthusiasm

---

[229] Priscian, in Keil, 3: 405: "Et Romanorum diligentiam vestrorum ad artes suorum alacriorem reddatis auctorum."

[230] Gregory the Great, *Dial.*, II, prologue (Moricca ed., p. 71): "Sed cum in eis [studiis] multos ire per abrupta vitiorum cerneret eum quem quasi in ingressum mundi posuerat retraxit pedem ne si quid de scientia ejus adtingeret ipse quoque postmodum in inmane praecipitium totus iret."

[231] See below, chap. 3, sect. III.

[232] Cassiodorus, *Var.*, VIII, 31 (*MGH, AA*, XII, 260): "Quid prodest tantos viros latere litteris defaecatos? Pueri liberalium scholarum conventum quaerunt et mox foro potuerint esse digni, statim incipiunt agresti habitatione nesciri: proficiunt, ut dediscant: erudiuntur, ut neglegant et cum agros diligunt, se amare non norunt. . . . Foedum ergo nimis est nobili filios in desolationibus educare."

[233] Caesarius, *Sermo* II (Morin ed., p. 201, ll. 5–10): "Multi sunt . . . qui plures libros et satis nitidos et pulchre ligatos habere volunt et eos ita armariis clausos tenent ut illis nec ipsi legant nec aliis ad legendum tribuant."

for his studies. In the Late Empire, the immediate goal of classical studies was service in public administration.[234] Cassiodorus liked to say that it was still so.[235] But could students still hope to have access to important posts? Everything depended on the policies of the government at the time, the Barbarian princes, and their attitude vis-à-vis classical education.

[234] Marrou, *Education*, p. 412; Massimiliano Pavan, *La crisi della scuola nel IV secolo* (Bari, 1952), p. 88.

[235] See Cassiodorus, *Var.*, X, 7 (p. 302, l. 31), in reference to the lawyer Patricius, who became quaestor in 534: "Sic bonis artibus eruditus mox est forensibus aptatus excubiis"; and ibid., IX, 21 (p. 287, l. 1): "Per quos [magistros] et honesti mores proveniunt et palatio nostro facunda nutriuntur ingenia." In several nominating letters Cassiodorus took care to recall the training of new functionaries: see *Var.*, VI, 5 (p. 178, l. 33); VI, 17 (p. 190, l. 1); VIII, 31 (p. 259, l. 9). Deuterius' school was situated in the forum at Milan in order, undoubtedly, to be close to the center of public business; see Ennodius, *Dictio* VII (*MGH, AA*, VII, 6). Faustus' school at Carthage was also located in the forum.

CHAPTER TWO

The Barbarians and Antique Culture
at the Beginning of the Sixth Century

W e have already observed that the establishment of the Barbarians in the Mediterranean world did not really transform the Roman way of life. In particular, the political domination of the invaders did not result in the disappearance of classical culture and education. Now, however, we must try to determine whether the Barbarians, as self-styled heirs of the emperors, showed any interest in classical intellectual training or, on the other hand, whether they chose to ignore it out of contempt or because of their inability to comprehend it.

The question deserves to be asked. Of course, the adoption of the culture of the conquered by the conquerors is a well-known historical phenomenon. "Barbarous Latium," victorious over Greece, was not alone in recognizing the cultural superiority of its subjects. The Mongols, triumphant over the Chinese, and the Aztecs, victors over the Toltecs, did likewise. One might argue, however, that the Germans were accustomed to the harsh life of warriors and peasants and thus did not share the same faculty for adaptation. Yet, during the fourth and at the beginning of the fifth century, Barbarian chiefs who settled in the Empire rapidly forgot their origins in order to profit from the prestige of Latin culture.[1] Would the Barbarian chieftains remain faithful to this tradition? German historians think so, but they have often tended to see in the sixth century a situation that prevailed only in earlier centuries. Also, we must insist on the distinction between the protection which the princes were able to provide scholars and the princes' personal

[1] Marrou, *Education*, p. 411.

intellectual formation. Were they simply, in short, adopting the role of a Maecenas, or were they themselves men of letters? Had the Barbarian aristocracy been won over to classical culture?

I. BARBARIAN KINGS AND CLASSICAL EDUCATION

A. Visigothic Kings

If the court at Toulouse had been favorable to scholars during the first half of the fifth century,[2] it was no longer so beginning with the reign of Euric (466-84). This king was above all a soldier, and the Visigothic kingdom attained its furthest boundaries as a result of Euric's conquests.[3] Euric's religious fanaticism especially hindered any possible exchanges with Roman men of letters. Except for his minister, Leo, we know of no scholars at Euric's court. Rather than supporting scholars, he assigned them to military duties.[4] Namatius commanded part of his fleet;[5] Victorius received the submission of Clermont and governed the city.[6] Sidonius Apollinaris, the prince of Gallo-Roman scholars, vainly defended the city against the Visigoths and was imprisoned in a fortress after its fall. He tried to gain the king's grace by addressing a flattering poem to him and by composing a few verses for a *missorium* given to Queen Ragnahilda, but his efforts were of doubtful success.[7] In fact, he refused shortly afterwards to write a history of the Goths for his friend Leo of Narbonne.[8] Could King Euric even have understood Sidonius? He must not have known Latin well, since he needed an interpreter in order to respond to the envoy of Emperor Julius Nepos.[9] Alaric II,

---

[2] Sidonius, *Carm.* VII, v. 497 (*MGH, AA,* VIII, 215).

[3] For Euric's reign see Karl F. Stroheker, *Eurich, König der Westgoten* (Tübingen, 1937).

[4] I cannot agree with the statement of Theodore Haarhoff, *Schools of Gaul* (Oxford, 1920), p. 24, that "Euric encourages the teaching of classical literature," or with his view of the court of Toulouse as "the last refuge of Roman letters." Schmidt's opinion (*Die Ostgermanen*, p. 528) is more moderate but still too optimistic.

[5] Sidonius forwarded Varro's *libri logistorici* and Eusebius' *Chronicle* to Namatius so that he could occupy his leisure time when he was with the fleet (*Ep.* VIII, 6 [*MGH, AA,* VIII, 133, ll. 14-15]).

[6] Sidonius, *Ep.* V, 21 (p. 93); Gregory of Tours, *HF*, II, 20 (*MGH, SRM*, I, 65).

[7] Sidonius wrote this letter (*Ep.* VIII, 9 [p. 135]) to the rhetor Lampridius, who had himself composed a poem of this type for the glory of the king. The poem on the *missorium* is found in *Ep.* IV, 8 (pp. 59–60).

[8] Sidonius, *Ep.* IV, 22 (p. 72).

[9] Ennodius, *Vita Epifani*, 90 (*MGH, AA,* VII, 95), wrote that the king needed an inter-

Euric's successor—who spent his youth in laziness and at parties, according to Isidore of Seville[10]—was no more interested in Latin culture than his father had been. When his lawyers went through the *Theodosian Code* to make an abbreviated version of it (*Breviary of Alaric*), they left aside articles pertaining to teaching and masters.[11]

B. BURGUNDIAN KINGS

If we move to the court of the Burgundian kings, who were more tolerant toward Catholics, we find a few Gallo-Romans around the princes, among them several scholars: the poet Heraclius; the quaestor Pantagathus, who no doubt was a rhetor at Vienne;[12] and especially Avitus of Vienne, whom we have already mentioned. At no time, however, did Gundobad and Sigismund play the role of a Maecenas. Their education, whatever one might say about it, appears, in fact, to have been quite elementary.

Gundobad was articulate, according to Ennodius,[13] but that does not mean that he had learned rhetoric and dialectic.[14] It cannot be argued that he had a philosophical culture simply because Avitus counseled him to have "a serenity worthy of a philosopher"[15] after his daughter's death. He did not know Greek.[16] For that matter, nothing permits us to think that he might have read profane authors. The passage by Avitus

---

preter in order to answer Bishop Epiphanius of Pavia: "Taliter tamen fertur ad interpretem rex locutus."

[10] Isidore of Seville, *Historia Gothorum, Wandalorum, Sueborum*, 36 (*MGH, AA*, XI, 281–82): "Cum a pueritia vitam in otio et convivio peregisset." Alaric exiled Ruricius of Limoges and Caesarius of Arles to Bordeaux; see Schmidt, *Die Ostgermanen*, p. 499.

[11] That is, those articles in chapter XII, 3–11, of the *Theodosian Code* (see *Theodosiani libri XVI*, ed. Mommsen and Meyer, vol. 1). The preparation of the *Breviary* is discussed in sect. III. B, below.

[12] Heraclius is mentioned in Avitus' correspondence (*Ep.* LIII [47], and XCV [85] [*MGH, AA*, VI-2, 81 and 102]). See also Stroheker's notice, pp. 180–81, no. 186. Pantagathus' epitaph reads "Arbitrio regum quaesturae cingula sumpsit." See above, chap. 1, sect. II.B.3, for more on him.

[13] Ennodius, *Vita Epifani*, 164 (*MGH, AA*, VII, 105): "Fando locuples et ex eloquentiae dives, opibus et facundus adsertor." Ennodius furnished many details on Epiphanius' trip from Pavia to Lyon, but nothing permits us to think that he might have accompanied the bishop, as Coville (p. 206) seemed to believe.

[14] Binding, *Das Burgundisch-romanische Königreich* (Leipzig, 1868), p. 222, thought so.

[15] Avitus, *Ep.* V (*MGH, AA*, VI-2, 32): "Neque porro cadit in regiam quidem sed philosophicam mentem maeroris abjectio."

[16] Despite what M. Burckhardt said in his *Die Briefsammlung des Bischofs Avitus von Vienne* (Berlin, 1938), p. 75, n. 5, after citing the following sentence by Avitus: "Quod, ut nostis, convenientius exprimit uno vocabulo Graecus dicens cenos" (*Contra Arrianos*, 30 [*MGH, AA*, VI-2, 13, l. 12]). This remark is much too vague to be used as a proof of Gundobad's knowledge of Greek.

used to support this thesis is deceptive: wishing to explain the sense of *missum facitis* to the king, Avitus told him that he could have read this expression in the profane authors and added immediately, "unless, having abandoned their reading because of your duties, it might have escaped your memory"—the language of a courtier, full of polite irony.[17] If Gundobad had had a good education, the bishop of Vienne would have been the first to congratulate him on it, as was the custom of the age. As we shall see later, only religion attracted Gundobad's intellectual curiosity. Sigismund, his son, shared the same interest. If Avitus was indeed his preceptor, it was in religious matters alone.[18] There is no reason to speak of "the protection and encouragement of Latin culture" apropos of the Burgundian kings.[19] They passively accepted what still existed; they could not do otherwise.

C. Vandal Kings

Paradoxically, the Vandal sovereigns, convinced Arians and persecutors, paraded as lettered princes at least from the time of Thrasamund (496–523). Until that time, the Vandals did not have a reputation for being sympathetic to Latin culture. As Fulgentius said to Thrasamund, they "claimed ignorance as their birthright."[20] Genseric perhaps knew Latin, but the circumstances of his takeover in Africa did not endear him to the educated.[21] Vandal princes after him were Romanized. We know at least two lettered men among Genseric's descendents: a nephew of Hunneric[22] and Thrasamund. We know nothing about Gunthamund except that he threw the poet Dracontius into prison for having celebrated the glory of a foreign prince rather than that of the Asdings.[23]

---

[17] The entire passage is as follows: "A cujus proprietate sermonis in ecclesiis (palatiisque sive praetoriis) missa fieri pronuntiatur, cum populus ab observatione dimittitur. Nam genus hoc nominis etiam in saecularis linguae auctoribus, nisi memoriam vestram per occupationes lectio desueta subterfugit, invenitis" (*MGH, AA*, VI-2, 13, ll. 2–5).

[18] See Avitus' letter to Sigismund, *Ep.* XCII (82) (*MGH, AA*, VI-2, 99).

[19] As Schmidt does (*Die Ostgermanen*, p. 192).

[20] Fulgentius, *Ep. ad Thrasamund*, 1, 2 (*PL*, LXV, 226) spoke thus of the Barbarian nation: "Quae sibi velut vernacula proprietate solet inscitiam vindicare." This passage can be compared to a passage from Fulgentius the Mythographer (*Mitol.*, I, 17 [Helm ed., p. 9]) in which the muse Calliope speaks to the author: "Cum barbarorum morem auscultaverim ita litterarios mercatos penitus abdicare ut hos qui primis elementorum figuris vel proprium discripserint nomen cassata inquisitione mutum in carnificiana reptarent."

[21] For Genseric's culture, see Courtois, p. 222, nn. 3–4.

[22] Victor of Vita, *Historia persecutionis Africanae provinciae*, II, 13 (*CSEL*, 7: 28): "Magnis litteris institutus."

[23] Dracontius, *Satisf.*, 21–22, 93–96 (*MGH, AA*, XIV, 114–18). For Dracontius, see Schanz, IV-2, 58ff.

King Thrasamund, on the other hand, was praised by poets. He had married Amalafrida, Theodoric's sister. Raised at the Byzantine court in the entourage of the Empress Ariadne, the princess must have helped to open the court at Carthage to scholars.[24] As for Thrasamund, he played the role of a patron of culture like Theodoric, his brother-in-law. Unfortunately, all this tells us little about the culture of the prince himself.[25] The poet Florentinus, who created an idealized portrait of the delightful life at Carthage, is not helpful.[26] We know that the king, like Gundobad, was interested in religious questions. He asked Bishop Fulgentius of Ruspe theological questions even while he continued to persecute Catholics.[27] This interest thrilled the bishop, who had already portrayed the king as "promoting studies among the Barbarian people."[28] Unfortunately, the episode was illusory. Even under Thrasamund's successor, Hilderic, who through his mother was the grandson of Emperor Valentinian III and was completely devoted to Byzantium, the only scholars were Romans.[29] The one new fact is that poets were welcomed not only by the king but also by certain aristocratic Vandals. We can hardly conclude from this that even the most Romanized Vandal princes patronized a literary "renaissance" of any sort. They permitted poet-courtiers to sing their praises and the clergy to hope, in vain as it turned out, for their conversion to Catholicism.[30]

D. OSTROGOTHIC KINGS

Theodoric, the last Barbarian prince to settle in the West, was a genuine Maecenas. Of course, he was in control of Italy, the source and center of Latin culture. At the same time that he rescued Roman monuments from destruction, this "new Trajan"[31] protected writers and

[24] For Amalafrida, see L. M. Hartmann's article in *RE*, 1: 1714–15.

[25] For Thrasamund's culture, see the evidence of Procopius, Cassiodorus, and Fulgentius that Gabriel G. Lapeyre collected in *Saint Fulgence de Ruspe* (Paris, 1929), pp. 160–61.

[26] *Anth. lat.*, p. 88, no. 376: "In quo concordant . . . decus animus senusque virilis / Invigilans animo sollers super omnia sensus."

[27] See sect. II.C. below.

[28] Fulgentius, *Ep. ad Thrasamund*, I, 2 (*PL*, LXV, 226): "Per te . . . disciplinae studia moliuntur jura barbaricae gentis invadere."

[29] See above, chap. I, sect. II.B.4, for these men of letters. We should especially note the presence of the royal referendary among them; see *Anth. lat.*, p. 292, no. 30.

[30] Procopius relates that the last Vandal king, Gelimer, sang of his misfortunes while accompanying himself on the cithara; see *Bell. vand.*, II, 6, 33 (Haury ed., I, 443). He does not tell us whether the king sang in Latin or in the Germanic tongue. Perhaps Gelimer, who represented the "nationalist party," wanted to restore Germanic traditions.

[31] So he was called by Romans, according to *Anonymus Valesianus*, 12. 60 (*MGH, AA*, IX, 322).

guaranteed a salary for teachers in Rome's schools. Nevertheless, having argued for a general decline in studies, we find it difficult to speak of an "Ostrogothic renaissance." We can grant, though, that the Barbarian prince realized the importance of classical culture. Of course, Theodoric had the good fortune to find Romans who would help him, among them Cassiodorus Senator. Still, the Barbarian would have to have been disposed to follow Cassiodorus' advice in the first place. We must first, then, examine Theodoric's educational background—a question which still continues to excite the keen interest of historians.

Was the king illiterate, as some argue?[32] This opinion rests on only one text, which has been interpreted much too literally. An anonymous chronicler twice described the king as illiterate and further reported that, since he did not know how to write, Theodoric had to use a golden pattern in which was engraved the word *legi*, which he would mechanically trace when he had to sign an act.[33] Many historians have believed the chronicler. Others, particularly the German historian Ludo Schmidt, have rightly regarded the chronicler's account as a mere calumny. The chronicler is, in fact, patently hostile to Theodoric on many points. Furthermore, he seems to have misunderstood the use of the royal seal, which must have resembled the one used in the Byzantine chancellery.[34] This famous anecdote then, I think, is too suspect to be probable, since we have other sources which describe the king's education for us. These sources tell us that in his youth, from age eight to eighteen, Theodoric was a hostage at the court at Constantinople. There, the intelligent young man (*puerulus elegans*)[35] gained the friendship of emperors, who undoubtedly provided him with the kind of education a young aristocrat received in order to hold his own among the educated.[36] A passage in one of Cassiodorus' letters proves that Theodoric

[32] For the literature, both pro and con, on this subject, see R. Lessi, "Theodoricus inlitteratus," in *Miscellanea di studi critici in onore di Vincenzo Crescini* (Cividale, 1927), p. 221; L. Schmidt, "Cassiodor an Theodorich," *HJ* 47 (1927): 727; idem, *Die Ostgermanen*, p. 273; W. Stach, "Die geschichtliche Bedeutung der westgotischen Reichsgründung," *Hist. Vierteljahrschrift* 30 (1935): 439; W. Ensslin, "Rex Theodoricus inlitteratus," *HJ* 60 (1940): 391–96; idem, *Theodorich der Grosse* (Munich, 1947), pp. 25–26; Stein, 2: 791.

[33] *Anon. Vales.* 12. 61 and 13. 79 (*MGH, AA,* IX, 322, 326): "Dum inlitteratus esset tantae sapientiae fuit ut . . . ; Igitur rex Theodoricus inlitteratus erat et sic obruto sensu ut in decem annos regni sui quattuor litteras subscriptionis edicti sui discere nullatenus potuisset."

[34] See Procopius, *Anecdota,* VI (Haury ed., p. 40), concerning Justin.

[35] See Jordanes, *Getica,* LVII, 289 (*MGH, AA,* V-1, 132), and Stein, 2: 12. *Elegans* often connoted intellectual qualities; see *ThLL,* V-2, 334.

[36] Ennodius, *Panegyricus dictus Theoderico,* III (*MGH, AA,* VII, 204, l. 29): "Educavit

was marked by his early studies. Cassiodorus recounted that the king, wanting to put aside his public duties, asked Cassiodorus to read him the maxims of the ancient sages, to discuss the courses of the stars, the movements of the seas, and the wonders of fountains with him so that he might be called a "philosopher king."[37] Just as it did for many other educated men of his time, philosophy for Theodoric meant only physical science, or more precisely, curiosity about strange natural phenomena.

Not only did Theodoric pretend to imitate Roman scholars; he also wanted to maintain the tradition of his Gothic ancestors, who, in Dicineus' school, were given to philosophizing,[38] and thus became "the most educated of all the Barbarians and almost like Greeks."[39] At least, this is what the official historian recorded at the king's request.[40] The Goths were worthy enough to occupy Italian soil, and their prince had to care for intellectual activities, as did all civilized princes. The first responsibility of a cultured king was to give his family a solid education. Education had made Theodoric, and he was no doubt more demanding than others had been with him. Amalasuntha, his daughter, who was to succeed him on the throne in 523, knew not only Latin but also Greek. The praise which Cassiodorus lavished on her suggests that her education was above average.[41] She understood the value of classical culture, since at the outset of her regency she entrusted the education of her son to a Roman preceptor.[42]

The children of Amalafrida, the king's sister and wife of the Vandal Thrasamund, likewise received an extensive education. Amalabirga,

---

te in gremio civilitatis Graecia." Cassiodorus, *Var.*, I, 1 (*MGH, AA*, XII, 10): "Nos maxime, qui divino auxilio in re publica vestra didicimus."

[37] Cassiodorus, *Var.*, IX, 24 (p. 290): "Nam cum esset publica cura vacuatus sententias prudentium a tuis fabulis exigebat ut factis propriis se aequaret antiquis. Stellarum cursus maris sinus fontium miracula rimator acutissimus inquirebat, ut rerum naturis diligentius perscrutatis quidam purpuratus videtur esse philosophus."

[38] Jordanes, *Getica*, XI, 69 (*MGH, AA*, V-1, 74). This Dicineus appears in the story as a magician in the service of the Dacian king Byrebistas, who attempted to form an empire around 60 B.C. (Strabo, *Geog.*, XVI, ii, 39). Through the "Geographer of Ravenna" we know of other Gothic "philosophers," such as Athanarit, Hildebald, and Marcomir, who, if they ever really did exist, were only geographers. See *Wattenbach-Levison*, 1: 69.

[39] Jordanes, *Getica*, V, 39 (p. 64): "Unde et pene omnibus barbaris Gothi sapientiores semper extiterunt Grecisque pene consimiles, ut refert Dio." The reference is to Dio Chrysostom, author of a history of the Goths. For Jordanes' sources, see Mommsen's preface to his edition, *MGH, AA*, V-1, xxxff.

[40] *Anecd. Holderi, MGH, AA*, XII, vi: "Scripsit praecipiente Theodorico rege historiam Gothicam originem eorum et loca mores in libris enuntians." See Schanz, IV-2, 97.

[41] Cassiodorus, *Var.*, XI, 1 (p. 328, l. 18): "Qua enim lingua non probatur esse doctissima? Atticae facundiae claritate diserta est, Romani eloquii pompa resplendet. . . . Jungitur his rebus . . . notitia litterarum." See also ibid., X, 4 (p. 299).

[42] Procopius, *Bell. goth.*, I, 2 (Haury ed., p. 11).

whom Theodoric married to the king of the Thuringians, was called
"litteris docta, moribus erudita."[43] Her brother, Theodahat, a great
Tuscan landowner and later associated with the throne through his
marriage to Amalasuntha,[44] had acquired great wisdom and self-mastery
through reading. Rome could say that it "had never had a king as
learned."[45] Procopius, the Byzantine historian, tells us that this prince
was more learned in Plato's philosophy than he was in military science.[46] Theodahat, more a scholar than a strategist, did not in fact know
how to defend his kingdom against Justinian. Theodahat's deposition
and death (536) mark an important date for the history of this period
because that date represents the end of an experiment: the adoption by
Barbarian princes of classical culture.

The Ostrogothic kings who succeeded the Amals were not only alien
to classical culture, like the Visigothic and Burgundian kings, but they
were even hostile to it. Cassiodorus could carry out the illusion for a
while and continue to play the role of learned counselor to Vitigis. But
when he praised the king, it was solely for his military qualities.[47] In
537, when he realized that he was serving only a brutal soldier, Cassiodorus left him.[48] Totila, who after the defeat of Vitigis continued
the battle against Byzantium (542), was likewise a stranger to Roman
civilization and culture. Did Totila plan, as an unknown Greek historian tells us, to initiate instruction in the Gothic tongue in Italy?[49]
We do not know, but it is not impossible. The project would not have
contradicted the clearly anti-Roman policy of this king, who, after he
first captured Rome, thought of destroying it (546) and at the very least
had the city completely evacuated.[50] It has been said that Totila, after

[43] Cassiodorus, *Var.*, IV, 1 (p. 114).
[44] Jordanes, *Getica*, LIX, 306 (*MGH, AA*, V-1, 136). See Stein, 2: 335.
[45] Cassiodorus, *Var.*, X, 3 (p. 299): "Patiens in adversis, moderatus in prosperis . . .
olim rector sui. Accessit his bonis desiderabilis eruditio litterarum. . . . Princeps vester
etiam ecclesiasticis est litteris eruditus." Ibid., XI, 13 (p. 342): "Habui multos reges sed
neminem hujusmodi litteratum." A court poet spoke to the same theme: "Solers Theodatus
. . . Theodate potens, cujus sapientia mundo prospiciens." See H. W. Garrod, "Poeseos
saeculi sexti fragmenta quattuor," *CQ* 4 (1910): 263–66.
[46] Procopius, *Bell. goth.*, I, 3 (Haury ed., p. 19).
[47] Cassiodorus, *Var.*, X, 31 (p. 318): "Non enim in cubilis angustiis sed in campis late
patentibus electum me esse noveritis, nec inter blandientium delicata colloquia sed tubis
concrepantibus sum quaesitus." See also the *Orationum reliquiae, MGH, AA*, XII, 476.
Procopius' eulogy (*Bell. goth.*, I, 11 [Haury ed., p. 59]) was of the same tenor.
[48] Cassiodorus undoubtedly left the service of Vitigis after the massacre of the Roman
senators who were taken from Rome as hostages; see Stein, 2: 353.
[49] See S. Reinach, in *Rev. Germanique* 2 (1906): 472–78, *contra* L. Schmidt, *Hist.
Vierteljahrschrift* 30 (1935): 433, and *Wattenbach-Levison*, 1: 78, n. 151.
[50] Stein, 2: 585.

once again becoming master of Rome in 550, revived Roman traditions by organizing chariot races in the *Circus Maximus*. In fact, however, as Procopius, to whom we owe this information, noted, Totila had uppermost in his mind the training of his men for the projected Sicilian campaign when he organized this sporting competition.[51]

Thus, the attitude of the last Ostrogothic kings toward Roman culture does not at all resemble that of the Amalian princes. Although political circumstances no doubt explain this difference, there is yet another determining factor. Vitigis and Totila issued from the Gothic aristocracy and represented, as we shall now show, the deliberate tendency of this class to remain separate from Roman culture, at least in its intellectual manifestations.

II. THE BARBARIAN ARISTOCRACY AND CLASSICAL EDUCATION

A. Romanized Barbarians

We have very little information on the lifestyle of the companions of the Barbarian kings, that aristocracy of warriors and functionaries.[52] We know that some, after settling on Roman soil, adopted the habits of wealthy Romans. They knew how to take good advantage of the material comforts they found.[53] Life on the Roman domains they confiscated domesticated the Germans.[54] Theodoric's observation that the "poor Roman imitates the Goth and the rich Goth imitates the Roman"[55] rings true. If the Barbarian princes deliberately settled most of their people in superficially Romanized regions, some noble Germans more attuned to Roman civilization were able nonetheless to mix with their conquered subjects without actually merging with them.

The fairly numerous epitaphs that have been collected prove that some Barbarians wished to be taken for Romans even in death.[56] These

---

[51] Procopius, *Bell. goth.*, III, 37 (Haury ed., p. 463).

[52] Burgundian texts refer to them as *optimates* and *proceres*; see the preface to *Liber const.*, *MGH, Leg. sect. I*, II, 29–30.

[53] See the poetical description of Theodahat's villa at Bolsena in one of the poems published by Garrod, "Poeseos saeculi sexti fragmenta," p. 263.

[54] The epitaph of Manneleubus from Briord records that this Burgundian freed six slaves upon his death in 487 (*CIL*, XIII, 2472). For the division of land and labor, see F. Lot, "Du régime de l'hospitalité," *RBPh* 7 (1928): 975–1011.

[55] "Romanus miser imitatur Gothum et utilis Gothus imitatur Romanum" (*Anon. Vales.*, 12. 61 [*MGH, AA*, IX, 322]).

[56] They have been collected by Fiebiger and Schmidt, *Inschriftensammlung*. Vandal

inscriptions were, first of all, written in Latin. Archaeologists have not yet succeeded in finding any in the Gothic tongue.[57] Secondly, the Barbarians applied traditional Roman titles to themselves, such as *vir honestus, vir venerabilis, vir illustris, spectabilis femina*. If we did not have the German name, it would be difficult to distinguish these tombstones from those of the autochthonous population. In addition, we should also mention the Burgundian strap buckles which carry mottoes, not in a Barbarian tongue, but in Latin.[58] Only a few German words have been preserved; they are in an epigram in the *Latin Anthology*[59] and in two subscriptions to acts from Ravenna.[60] Did the Germans, following the lead of their kings, go so far as to learn Latin? Probably. The counts, the *saiones*, sent on missions to Roman functionaries must have known a few Latin sentences which they could have picked up just as any officer or soldier would have done in an occupied country over a period of time. It is significant that none of our sources mention an interpreter.[61]

The Romanization of certain Barbarians is further confirmed by the

---

epitaphs in Latin have been restudied by Courtois, pp. 376ff. See, more recently, S. Lancel, "Une épitaphe de Tebessa," *Libica* 4 (1956): 328–31, and, for Hippo, H. I. Marrou, "La basilique chrétienne d'Hippone d'après le résultat des dernières fouilles," *Revue des études augustiniennes* 6 (1960): 136–43.

[57] The inscription in the "Gothic tongue" that could still be seen in the sixteenth century in the church of Sant' Agatha de' Goti could only have been imaginary according to F. X. Zimmermann, "Der Grabstein der ostgotischen Königstochter Amalafrida Theodenanda," in *Festschrift für Rudolf Egger: Beiträge zur älteren europäischen Kulturgeschichte*, ed. G. Moro, 3 vols. (Klagenfurt, 1952–54). 2: 348. For the Ostrogothic tongue in Italy, see Ferdinand Wrede, *Ueber die Sprache der Ostgoten in Italien*, Quellen und Forschungen zur Sprach- und Culturgeschichte der germanischen Volken, vol. 68 (Strasbourg, 1891), and C. Battisti, "L'elemento gotico nella toponomastica e nel lessico italiano," *Settimane*, 3: 621–49, who notes the very weak influence of Gothic on spoken Italian.

[58] For the mottoes on these buckles, see, most recently, W. Deonna, "Inscriptions de plaques de ceinturons 'burgondes,'" *RSH*, 25 (1945): 305–19. For the date of the inscriptions, see Hans Zeiss, *Studien zu den Grabfunden aus dem Burgundenreiche an der Rhone* (Munich, 1938), and A. de Molin, "Etude sur les agrafes de ceinturon burgondes à inscriptions," *RA*, 3rd ser. 40 (1902): 371. The only non-Latin inscription was found on a fibula decorated with runic characters from Charnay; see Le Blant, *IC*, 1: 216 (no. 146).

[59] *Anth. lat.*, p. 221, no. 285, 1 and 2: "Inter eils goticum scapia matzia ia drincan / Non audet quisquam dignos edicere versus." This poet's disgust is reminiscent of Sidonius' attitude toward Burgundians; see *Carm.* XII (*MGH, AA*, VIII, 230–31). See Courtois, pp. 222–23, for spoken Vandal in Africa.

[60] See the Gothic inscriptions in Marini, *I papiri*, pp. 118–19.

[61] There is a rare allusion to an interpreter in a letter of Sidonius from about the year 474 (*Ep.* V, 5 [*MGH, AA*, VIII, 81, ll. 5–6]): "Adstupet tibi [Syagrio] epistulas interpretanti curva Germanorum senectus et negotiis mutuis arbitrum te disceptatoremque desumit." See also a text already cited above, in n. 9.

law codes which Euric, Gundobad, and Theodoric drew up for their people. These laws were written in Latin. Specific chapters in them provide for instances when Barbarians would need legal documents for donations, wills, acts of sale, and the like, as in Roman practice.[62] These law codes, then, presuppose some familiarity on the part of German aristocrats with Roman culture, especially since we know that the codes were used: Italian papyri from this period mention Goths' having acts drawn up that they subscribed either with their signatures[63] or with a seal.[64] The Goths kept these documents in their personal archives and, like Romans, locked them in *scrinia*.[65]

The very rapid Romanization of some aristocratic Barbarians, then, is a fact. Yet it is equally certain that this process can only have affected a minority. The majority of the Barbarians conserved their own customs and practices.

B. The Refusal of the Aristocracy to Adopt Classical Culture

Did the Barbarian minority we have just described attempt to imitate the most essential characteristic of the Roman aristocracy, its classical culture? We have already noted that some Barbarian chiefs did imitate the Roman aristocracy in this respect in the fourth and at the beginning of the fifth century when they were in the service of the Empire. There is nothing like this, however, at the end of the fifth century or at the beginning of the following century. We find no trace of any interest in Latin letters among the Visigoths, the Burgundians, or even the Ostrogoths themselves. Not one Goth or Burgundian is among the correspondents of Ennodius, Avitus, or Ruricius.[66] These scholars did not attempt to introduce the Barbarians to Latin letters. When Sidonius related that the traitor Seronatus taught literature to Goths, it was his

---

[62] *Codex Euricianus: de venditionibus* (286–304), *de donationibus* (305–319); *Liber const.*, 43, 45, 99 (*MGH, Leg., sect. I*, I, 11, 16ff.; II, 74, 75, 113).

[63] "Hildevara inl. femina" (Marini, *I papiri*, no. 85 [Tjäder, *Papyri*, no. 20 (p. 348)]); "Signum Sisiverae" (ibid., no. 93); "Runilo sublimis femina, Felithanc subl. vir." (ibid., no. 86 [Tjäder, no. 13]); "Gundihild Leudarit" (ibid., no. 79 [Tjäder, no. 7]).

[64] For Burgundian signet rings, see Marius Besson, *L'art barbare dans l'ancien diocèse de Lausanne* (Lausanne, 1909), p. 164, and Maximin Deloche, *Etude historique et archéologique sur les anneaux sigillaires* (Paris, 1900). Thrasamund's seal has come down to us; see Courtois, p. 401. For the signet rings of Alaric II and Theodoric, see Percy E. Schramm, *Herrschaftszeichen und Staatssymbolik* (Stuttgart, 1954), 1: 213–37.

[65] *Liber const.*, 29, 3 (*MGH, Leg. sect. I*, II, 66, l. 11).

[66] Vittamer, one of Ruricius' correspondents, seems to have been a Roman with a German name; see *Ep.* II, 60 and 62 (*MGH, AA*, VIII, 349).

way of saying that the usual order of things had been overturned.[67] The Arvernian was too well aware of the gulf which separated Barbarian from Roman to believe that Barbarians could really adopt classical culture. What was not possible in Sidonius' time was even less so during Ennodius'. The high functionaries at the court of Ravenna—the *majores domus*, Gudila and Bedeulf;[68] Count Arigern;[69] Pitzia;[70] and even the counselor Tuluin, who had been raised at the king's court[71]— showed no taste for classical culture.

The only Goth, as far as we know, who might have been an author is Jordanes, to whom we owe a resumé of the *Roman History* and a compilation of Cassiodorus' *History of the Goths*. Yet Jordanes most probably did not live in Italy, but in the Eastern Empire, and must have made Cassiodorus' acquaintance at Constantinople.[72] He himself admits that he never attended a Roman school, and his style proves it. If he had acquired Latin culture, it was because he had been secretary (*notarius*) to an Ostrogothic prince who had been named *magister militum* by the Imperial government.[73]

How could the Gothic aristocracy have had a Latin education when their prince forbade them to attend Roman schools? According to Procopius, representatives of the aristocracy, disturbed when Queen Amalasuntha confided her son to a Roman pedagogue, reminded her that her father, Theodoric, had never permitted Goths to place their

---

[67] Sidonius, *Ep.* II, 1 (*MGH*, *AA*, VIII, 21, l. 10). In *Ep.* I, 8 (p. 13, l. 17), he painted a catastrophic picture of Ravenna and noted that "eunuchs practiced with weapons while the federates practiced with literature." (This is an example of the rhetorical process of *adynaton*.)

[68] Both played a role in the business of the Laurentian schism. See Cassiodorus, *Var.*, *MGH*, *AA*, XII, 422–23. An inscription records that Gudila had an ancient statue reset at Faventina on Theodoric's orders; see *CIL*, XI, 268.

[69] Arigern was in charge of municipal administration in Rome; see Cassiodorus, *Var.*, III, 36, 45; IV, 23 (pp. 97, 101, 124).

[70] Ennodius described him as a courageous soldier (*Panegyricus dictus Theoderico*, XII [*MGH*, *AA*, VII, 210]).

[71] Cassiodorus, *Var.*, VIII, 9–10 (pp. 237–39) praised him without referring to his culture—something unusual for Cassiodorus.

[72] Mommsen's study in the introduction to his edition of the *Romana* and *Getica* (*MGH*, *AA*, V-1, 1) is still valuable. He was wrong, however, to think that Jordanes was an Alan; see *Wattenbach-Levison*, 1: 76. Francesco Giunta, *Jordanes e la cultura dell'alto medioevo* (Palermo, 1952), p. 163, tried to prove that Jordanes was very cultured. For a more recent view of Jordanes, see A. Momigliano, "Cassiodorus and the Italian Culture of His Time," *Proceedings of the British Academy* 41 (1955): 207–45.

[73] Jordanes, *Getica*, L (p. 126): "Ego item quamvis agramatus." For Jordanes' origins, see Mommsen's preface, *MGH*, *AA*, V-1, iv-vii, and, more recently, Norbert Wagner, *Getica: Untersuchungen zum Leben des Jordanes und zur frühen Geschichte der Goten* (Berlin, 1967).

children in Roman schools.[74] Theodoric indeed did have such a policy. His interdict is in accord with the general policy of a Barbarian king who, as king of Italy, accepted Roman culture for himself and for his family but refused it to his people in order to preserve their identity. Barbarians in contact with Roman aristocrats might have been won over to antique ways, but barred from the schools, they remained alien to true classical culture, a culture which it was difficult to acquire outside the school.

We have a proof to the contrary when we consider the Vandal kingdom. Only there do we find Barbarian aristocrats sensitive to the poems Roman scholars addressed to them.[75] The Vandal aristocracy had long been won over to Roman civilization—at least at the beginning of the sixth century. Procopius tells us that they had a passion for the theater, the hippodrome, the dances, and the mimes.[76] Living in Carthage, they also might have frequented the schools. Dracontius, in fact, tells us that the grammarian Felicianus welcomed young Vandals among the young Romans in his *auditorium.*[77] This exceptional fact is explained by its time and locale. We are at the end of the fifth century, a time when the schools were reviving, and what is more, we are at Carthage, a privileged cultural center.

Now that we have come to the end of our inquiry, it appears that except for the Amalian royal family and certain Vandal nobles, the Barbarian aristocracy did not wish to acquire that which had been the glory of the Romans, classical literature. Did they realize the uselessness of literary studies? Perhaps. There was, however, a more positive reason for their rejection of classical culture. The Barbarian aristocracy possessed its own culture, a culture to which it remained faithful. The Barbarian people formed a minority in the West which, in order to preserve its strength, refused to integrate with the Roman population. The aristocracy worked to preserve its originality and to give its children an education that conformed to Germanic tradition.

[74] Procopius, *Bell. goth.*, I, 2 (Haury ed., p. 12): Ἔλεγον δὲ ὡς οὐδὲ Θευδέριχός ποτὲ Γότθων τινὰς τοὺς παῖδας ἐς γραμματιστοῦ πέμπειν ἐῴη.

[75] *Anth. lat.*, no. 18 (poem dedicated to Fridus); nos. 304–5 (dedicated to Fridamal); no. 326 (for Blumarit); nos. 332, 345, and 369 (to Hoageis) (pp. 79, 256, 57, 266, 268, 274, 285).

[76] Procopius, *Bell. vand.*, II, 6, 7 (Haury ed., I, 444). See Courtois, pp. 227–28.

[77] Dracontius, *Romulea*, I, 12–14 (*MGH, AA*, XIV, 132): "O magister . . . barbaris qui Romulidas iungis auditorio." Schanz, IV-2, 58, thought that this passage referred to natives but never provided reasons for this interpretation. The evidence of Felicianus' school ought not to be generalized as Audollent, *Carthage romaine* (Paris, 1901), p. 757, who spoke of an "auditoire compact," and even Courtois, p. 222, n. 5, have done.

C. The Education of Barbarian Youth

Since Germanic society was a warrior society, the education young men received was primarily military. Physical training was the principal element of this education during peacetime. Theodoric reminded the Goths that they ought to look to the physical education of their sons[78] and that a child could attain his majority more by his skills as a warrior than by the law.[79] The general Tuluin, who spent his own youth at court, according to Cassiodorus, perhaps later became the master of the young Gothic men at Ravenna.[80] As in all warrior societies, the king's court did in fact attract adolescents who wanted to enter the prince's service and who knew that the post of squire (*spatarius*) was a stepping stone to a brilliant career.[81] Athalaric was brought up in the midst of these young men after he left his Roman teacher.[82] Groups of young warriors raised in the entourage of the prince can also be found at other Barbarian courts.[83] Only the Vandals neglected military training for their youth—and paid dearly for it.[84]

Military education was complemented by moral training. The Barbarians provided their sons with the examples they were to follow by reminding them of the virtues of national heroes. The old tales and legends had long been passed from generation to generation as songs.[85]

[78] Cassiodorus, *Var.*, I, 24 (*MGH, AA*, XII, 27, l. 29): "Producite juvenes vestros in Martiam disciplinam"; and V, 23 (ibid., p. 157, l. 23): "Ostentent juvenes nostri bellis quod in gymnasio didicere virtutis. Schola Martia mittat examina, pugnaturus ludo qui se exercere consuevit in otio."

[79] Ibid., I, 38 (p. 36, l. 7): "Juvenes nostri qui ad exercitum probantur idonei, indignum est ut ad vitam suam disponendam dicantur infirmi et putentur domum suam non regere qui creduntur bella posse tractare. Gothis aetatem legitimam virtus facit."

[80] Ibid., VIII, 10 (p. 239): "Qui mox inter parentes infantiam reliquit statim rudes annos ad sacri cubili secreta portavit. . . . Cujus ut coepit aetas adulescere tenerique anni in robustam gentis audaciam condurari ad expeditionem directus est Sirmensem."

[81] As was true of the future King Vitigis. See Jordanes, *Getica*, LX, 309 (*MGH, AA*, V-I, 137, l. 14).

[82] Procopius, *Bell. goth.*, I, 3 (Haury ed., p. 13). Actually, the Greek historian tells us that Athalaric devoted himself primarily to debauchery.

[83] See Procopius, *Bell. vand.*, I, 2 (Haury ed., p. 313), for the role played by young Visigoths during the siege of Rome in 410. We can assume that young Ebrovaceus, whose ransom was paid by King Gundomar of Burgundy (*CIL*, XXI, 2504), was among them. He would have been thirteen years old at the time.

[84] Courtois, p. 232.

[85] For these national songs, see Andreas Heusler, *Die altgermanische Dichtung* (Wildpark-Potsdam, 1926), and the older work of Wilhelm Streitberg, *Gotische Literatur*, in *Grundriss der germanischen Philologie*, ed. Hermann Paul, 3 vols. in 4 (Strassburg, 1900–1909), 2, pt. 1: 1–3. There is a little information on the subject in Hermann Schneider, *Geschichte der deutschen Dichtung*, vol. 1, *Die altgermanische Dichtung* (Bonn, 1949). See more recently, Ramón Menéndez Pidal, "Los godos y el origen de la epopeya española," *Settimane*, 3: 285–322.

Young Ostrogoths had many models to imitate, from King Berig, who led the Goths out of Scandinavia, to contemporary princes, especially Theodoric.[86] It would be interesting to know how Germanic heroes were portrayed to the young men. Unfortunately, however, while we know of the existence of national songs during this period, we are ignorant of their content.[87] The young "Dietrich of Berne," none other than Theodoric himself, quickly became a national hero, but we cannot tell whether or not the elaboration of his legend immediately followed the Ostrogothic king's death.[88]

Religious training comprised the third element of Barbarian education. Even though we know little about it, we cannot let it pass in silence, since it was primarily the Barbarian's religious training which prohibited the fusion of the German and Roman aristocracies. The Germans, we should never forget, were Arians. As far as we can tell, their churches seem to have been well organized.[89] Kings like Euric and Gundobad, who had only a slight interest in cultural affairs, were quite excited by religious problems.[90] The Burgundian king Gundobad, in particular, discussed questions dealing with the Trinity with Avitus of Vienne and with the poet Heraclius and asked for explications of biblical passages.[91] He vacillated until his death between the doctrines of the Catholic clergy and those of the Arian clergy.[92] The Vandal Thrasamund was more intolerant than Gundobad, but he too liked to discuss theology

[86] Cassiodorus' list of kings probably comes from these legends; see *Var.*, I, 1 (*MGH, AA*, XII, 330).

[87] See the references given by Sidonius (*Carm.* XII, v. 6 [*MGH, AA*, VIII, 231]: "Quod Burgundio cantat esculentus"), Cassiodorus (*Var.*, VIII, 9), and especially by Jordanes, (*Getica*, IV, 25; IV, 28; XII, 72; XIV, 79 [*MGH, AA*, V-1, 60, 61, 72, 79]).

[88] For this legend, see Hermann Schneider, *Germanische Heldensage*, 2 vols. (Berlin and Leipzig, 1928–34), 1: 315–22; and A. Heusler's article, "Dietrich von Berne," in Hoops, 1: 464–68.

[89] Except for the information in von Schubert's classic work, *Geschichte*, 1: 17–31, there is nothing on the Arianism of the Burgundians and Goths. Courtois, pp. 225–27, sketched the history of Vandal Arianism. See also Heinz Eberhart Giesecke, *Die Ostgermanen und der Arianismus* (Leipzig, 1939).

[90] Sidonius portrayed Euric as a fanatic (*Ep.* VII, 6 [*MGH, AA*, VIII, 109, l. 23]).

[91] For these discussions, see Burckhardt, *Die Briefsammlung des Bischofs Avitus von Vienne*, pp. 55ff., and especially Avitus' letter to Heraclius, *Ep.* LIII (47) (*MGH, AA*, VI-2, 82): "Habuistis igitur, ut audio, cum rege tractatum. . . . Discussum est nuto divino."

[92] See Avitus, *Contra Arrianos*, 30 (*MGH, AA*, VI-2, 13), for the priests who advised Gundobad. The fact that the episcopal library of Lyon contained manuscripts of Hilary's works (E. A. Lowe, *Codices lugdunenses antiquissimi* [Lyon, 1924], pp. 26ff.) can perhaps be explained by the controversies between Arians and Catholics. Hilary was one of the most widely read authors in southern Gaul during this period. See Ruricius, *Ep.* I, 6 (*MGH, AA*, VIII, 303).

with the Catholics. He brought Fulgentius of Ruspe back out of exile so that he could have a worthy adversary.[93] In Italy, religious tolerance was official policy. Except for the last years of his reign, Theodoric respected his mother's religion.[94] Still, that did not prevent controversies between Arians and Catholics. Gregory of Tours recorded a discussion between an Arian priest and two Catholic deacons from Ravenna.[95] Caesarius of Arles described the efforts of the Arians in Provence to convert Catholics. He wrote his *De Trinitate* to help the latter.[96] Hilary's and Augustine's treatises of the same title were restudied and their manuscripts revised.[97] The Arians were also busy. Ulfila's Bible was recopied: the famous *Codex argenteus* copy probably dates from Theodoric's reign.[98] Finally, bilingual texts of the Gospels and Epistles prove that real exchanges were carried on between Arians and Catholics.[99] The religious strength of Arianism has too often been underestimated. The Germans sought not only to preserve their faith but also to attract adherents to it. Thus, religious instruction certainly occupied a high place in the education of youth.

III. WHAT THE BARBARIANS RETAINED OF ANTIQUE CULTURE

The Barbarians' contempt for classical culture is reminiscent in a relative sense of the reaction of the "Old Romans" of the second century B.C. when Hellenic education was introduced to Rome.[100] Like the Romans, who were also warriors and peasants, the Barbarians tolerated

[93] Ferrandus, *Vita Fulgentii*, XX–XXI (Lapeyre ed., pp. 99–107). See *Vie de saint Fulgence de Ruspe*, ed. and trans. G.-G. Lapeyre (Paris, 1929), pp. 160ff. Victor of Tunnuna (*MGH, AA*, XI, 193) reported that theology was even discussed in the baths. Fulgentius had a manuscript of Hilary's *De Trinitate* copied at Cagliari (*CLA*, I, 2).

[94] *Anon. Vales.*, 12 (*MGH, AA*, IX, 322). See also Cassiodorus' famous statement on tolerance in *Var.*, II, 27 (*MGH, AA*, XII, 62): "Religionem imperare non possumus, quia nemo cogitur ut credat invitus."

[95] Gregory of Tours, *Glor. martyr.*, I, 80 (*MGH, SRM*, I-2, 542).

[96] Caesarius of Arles, *S. Caesarii opera omnia*, ed. Morin, 2: 165.

[97] See below, chap. 5, sect. IV.A.

[98] G. W. S. Friedrichsen, *The Gothic Version of the Gospels: A Study of Its Style and Textual History* (London, 1926), p. 161; Ensslin, *Theodorich*, pp. 287–88. The *Codex argenteus* can be compared with the *purpureus* Latin Evangeliary of Brescia; see *CLA*, III, 281.

[99] For these fragments, see Theodor Wilhelm Braune, *Gotische Grammatik*, 12th rev. ed. by Karl Helm (Halle, 1947), pp. 119ff., and J. W. Marchand, "Notes on Gothic Manuscripts," *Journal of English and Germanic Philology* 56 (1957): 213.

[100] Marrou, *Education*, p. 333.

only a culture that dealt with practical and concrete realities.[101] These great realists preferred whatever could help them in their administrative duties, applied sciences, medical practice, and law, to rhetoric and poetry.

A. APPLIED SCIENCES

The Ostrogothic government was particularly interested in the applied sciences. On several occasions, Cassiodorus, speaking in Theodoric's name, insisted on the practical applications of geometry (mechanics,[102] surveying,[103] architecture[104]) and arithmetic (fixing of coinage, weights and measures[105]). Surveying occupied a special place in his heart. In a letter to an *agrimensor*, Cassiodorus even contrasted the theoretical sciences of the quadrivium, which were the domain of the *studiosi* and not under the protection of the state (*publica auctoritas*), to the surveyor's art, which enjoyed the complete support of the government.[106] The establishment and revision of the cadaster upon which property taxes were based depended, of course, on the surveyors.[107] In addition, surveyors were called in to effect the division of land between the conquered and the conquerors after the Barbarian settlement.[108] Surveying, a highly technical skill, was always reserved for specialists who were trained in theory and practice at an early age.[109]

[101] For the Greeks' distaste for technology, see ibid., pp. 303–5. Roman science was not as speculative as Greek science; see A. Raymond, *Histoire des sciences exactes et naturelles dans l'Antiquité* (Paris, 1955), pp. 103ff.

[102] Cassiodorus, *Var.*, I, 45 (*MGH, AA*, XII, 41, l. 25): "Mechanicus, si fas est dicere, paene socius est naturae, occulta reserans, manifesta convertens, miraculis ludens."

[103] Ibid., III, 52 (p. 107).

[104] Ibid., VII, 5 (p. 204, l. 21).

[105] Ibid., I, 10 (p. 18).

[106] Ibid., III, 52 (p. 107): "Videant artis hujus periti [he means surveying] quid de ipsis publica sentit auctoritas. Nam disciplinae illae toto orbe celebratae non habent hunc honorem. Arithmeticam indicas, auditoriis vacat, geometria cum tantum de caelestibus disputat, tantum studiosis exponitur, astronomia et musica discuntur ad scientiam solam." The passage is followed by a eulogy of surveying.

[107] André Deléage, *Les cadastres antiques jusqu'à Dioclétian: Etudes de Papyrologie* (Cairo, 1934), 2: 73–225; idem, *La capitation du Bas-Empire* (Mâcon, 1945).

[108] Ennodius referred to surveying in a letter to Liberius, the patricius who was in charge of this project (*Ep.* IX, 23 [*MGH, AA*, VII, 307]). See Hartmann, *Geschichte*, I: 91–94, on this subject.

[109] Aggenus Urbicus' commentary on the *De agrorum qualitate* of Frontinus was written for children: "Volumus ut ea quae a veteribus obscuro sermone conscripta sunt, apertius et intelligibilius exponere ad erudiendam posteritatis infantiam" (in *Corpus agrimensorum romanorum*, ed. Carl A. Thulin [Leipzig, 1913], p. 517). For this literature, see Schanz, IV-2, 303–5, and especially C. Thulin, "Der Frontinus Kommentar: Ein Lehrbuch der Gromatik aus dem 5–6 Jahr.," *RhM* 68 (1913): 110.

The manuscript which contains the school manuals that were used, the *Codex Arcerianus*, dates from the first half of the sixth century.[110] It was not the only one composed during this period.[111] Surveyors continued to function during the Byzantine occupation. In 597, Gregory the Great wrote to the bishop of Syracuse that he was sending him an agrimensor from Rome to settle a boundary dispute between two neighboring monasteries.[112]

Architecture was another branch of the applied sciences which interested the Barbarians. They employed architects to continue or to restore the monumental works of the emperors.[113] Architecture could have been studied from the manuals of Greek geometers, in particular that of Euclid, which had just been translated in Italy by Boethius.[114] But, in fact, architects made greater use of formularies like the extant one on the measurement of columns.[115] Instruction in architecture was primarily practical and was to remain so throughout the entire Middle Ages.[116]

At the beginning of the sixth century, medicine continued to be practiced in many urban centers in Italy and southern Gaul. Centers famous for their physicians drew patients from afar, like Bishop Maximian, undoubtedly from Trier, who went to Arles to take care of his

---

[110] This manuscript, which contains the *Corpus gromaticorum*, was discovered at Bobbio, where it had been from at least the fifteenth century. For its date, see Åke Josephson, *Casae litterarum: Studien zum Corpus agrimensorum romanorum* (Uppsala, 1950), and Carl Thulin, *Die Handschriften des Corpus agrimensorum romanorum*, Abhandlungen der könglich preussischen Akad. der Wissensch., Philos.-hist. Klasse, 2 (Berlin, 1911), both of whom agree that it dates from the first half of the sixth century. For a different opinion, though hardly a probable one, see Charles H. Beeson, "The Archetype of the Roman Agrimensores," *CPh* 23 (1928): 1–14, who thinks the manuscript had an Irish archetype.

[111] Vatican, Biblioteca apostolica vaticana, Palatinus 1564, was copied in the tenth century from a sixth- or seventh-century Italian manuscript. See Theodor Mommsen, "Die interpolationen des gromatischen Corpus," *Bonner Jahrbucher* 96 (1895): 275.

[112] Gregory the Great, *Ep.* VII, 36 (*MGH, Ep.*, I, 484, ll. 23–25).

[113] See Cassiodorus, *Var.*, II, 39 (*MGH, AA*, XII, 67), for a letter to Aloiosus, an architect; VII, 5 (p. 204), for a letter of nomination to the *curator palatii*; VII, 15 (p. 211), for a letter "de architecto faciendo in urbe Roma." The building projects princes undertook are mentioned above, chap. 1, sect. I.

[114] In ibid., VII, 5 (p. 204) Cassiodorus recommended Euclid to the *curator palatii*: "Ad quae sic poterit idoneus inveniri, si frequenter geometriam legas Euclidem."

[115] V. Mortet, "La mesure des colonnes à la fin de l'époque romaine d'après un très ancien formulaire," *BECh* 57 (1896): 289.

[116] For the science of architecture and geometry in the early Middle Ages, see the remarks of Jean Hubert in Raymond Lantier and Jean Hubert, *Les origines de l'art français* (Paris, 1947), p. 149, and in "Les peintures murales de Vic et la tradition géométrique," *CArch* 1 (1945): 85–88. The *Vita Eligii*, I, 17 (*MGH, SRM*, IV, 683), mentions surveyors in Paris during the seventh century.

sight.[117] From the time they came into the Empire, the Barbarians showed great interest in medicine and protected those who devoted themselves to it. A Roman inscription reminds us that after the Visigoths took Rome in 410, they carried the deacon-physician Dionysius away with them and that they "were subject to him by his art."[118] The sixth century was no different. Physicians were particularly honored at the court at Ravenna. We know that Deacon Helpidius, the friend of Ennodius and Avitus,[119] enjoyed Theodoric's favors and that Anthimus, who came from the East (perhaps with Theodoric[120]), was later sent as an ambassador to the court of the Merovingian Theodoric.[121] It was also at this time that Greek medical works, especially those of Oribasius, were translated at Ravenna.[122]

Although medical classics were still being translated, they became less influential as medicine became increasingly empirical. Many illnesses were cared for with an air cure[123] or by the waters.[124] In 535, at

[117] Avitus, *Ep*. XI (9) (*MGH, AA*, VI-2, 45), referred Maximian to Caesarius of Arles: "Causa veniendi est ut peritiorem medicum quocumque perquirat qui imbecillitati corporeorum luminum cujuscumque remedio artis succurrat." Dom Morin places this bishop in the see of Trier; see "Maximien, évêque de Trèves, dans une lettre d'Avit de Vienne," *RB* 47 (1935): 207–10. Caesarius himself went to Arles for reasons of health (*Vita Caesarii*, I, 7 [Morin ed., p. 299]).

[118] *ICR*, 1: 106, no. 49; Fiebiger and Schmidt, *Inschriftensammlung*, p. 224. See also Courcelle, *Histoire littéraire*, p. 56.

[119] This important individual was mentioned in a letter of Cassiodorus (*Var.*, IV, 24 [*MGH, AA*, XII, 124]), in four letters of Ennodius (VII, 7; VIII, 8; IX, 14; and IX, 21 [*MGH, AA*, VII, 234, 275, 300, 306]), in a letter of Avitus (XXXVIII [35] [*MGH, AA*, VI-2, 67]), and in a passage of the *Vita Caesarii* (I, 41 [p. 313]). He is nowhere described as a native of Lyon, as Coville, p. 227, would interpret a passage in the *Vita Aviti*. Helpidius seems rather, to have been an Easterner; see Ennodius, *Ep.* IX, 21 (p. 306, l. 19).

[120] Stein, 2: 11, does not accept this hypothesis. But certain terms in Anthimus' *De observatione ciborum* show that the author lived among Goths; see Schanz, IV-2, 293. Like many others, Anthimus entered the Amalian's service after he had first been the physician of Theodoric Strabo, who died in 481. See Ensslin, *Theodorich*, p. 292.

[121] See the dedication to his work: "Epistula Anthimi viri inlustris comitis et legatarii ad gloriosissimum Theudoricum regem Francorum de observatione ciborum." See Schanz, IV-2, 291–93.

[122] See Paul Thomas, "Notes lexicographiques sur la plus ancienne traduction latine des oeuvres d'Oribase," in *Philologie et linguistique: Mélanges offerts à Louis Havet par ses anciens élèves et ses amis, à l'occasion du 60e anniversaire de sa naissance, le 6 janvier 1909* (Paris, 1909), p. 504; Courcelle, *LG*, p. 259, n. 2. Hennig Mørland (*Die lateinischen Oribasiusübersetzungen* [Oslo, 1932]) is the most recent editor of the *Oribasius latinus*. Like his predecessors, he dates the translation to the beginning of the sixth century and attributes it to northern Italy. Milan, Bibl. ambros., G 108, inf., part of which was copied from a Ravennate archetype, mentions an Agnellus *yatrosophesta* and a Simplicius *medicus*. See Augusto Beccaria, *I codici di medicina del periodo presalernitano, secoli IX–X–XI* (Rome, 1956), p. 290.

[123] Cassiodorus, *Var.*, XI, 10 (p. 340).

[124] Ibid., II, 39 (p. 67); VIII, 33 (p. 261); X, 29 (p. 315); XI, 10 (p. 340). In *Dial.*,

the beginning of the war of reconquest, Wisibald, the count of Ticinum (Pavia), received King Vitigis' permission to take care of his gout in the waters of Aquae Bormiae (today Bourbon-l'Archambault).[125] Pharmacy, on the other hand, fared better than medicine. The work of Dioscorides, a first-century physician and botanist, enjoyed a vogue at Byzantium and was translated into Latin, most probably in Vandal Africa.[126] The Germans also liked to cure themselves with herbs. One Vandal prince grew medicinal plants in his garden.[127]

The adoption of this kind of therapy, however, endangered the medical science taught in the schools. Cassiodorus was aware of this, and in a letter to the *comes archiatrorum*, he recommended that doctors not abandon their books after years of study and that they continue to follow the teaching of the ancients.[128]

B. Law

Once settled in a land where political, social, and economic life had long depended on written law, German sovereigns understood the need to have the customs of their own people drawn up[129]—customs which traditionally (except perhaps for the mysterious *belagines* of the Goths) had been transmitted orally.[130] Euric the Visigoth (466–84) was no doubt following the lead of his brother, Theodoric II, when he had a legal code composed for his people.[131] Gundobad the Burgundian in his *Liber constitutionum*, better known as the *Gombetta Law*, also brought

---

IV, 42 (Moricca ed., p. 299) Gregory the Great mentioned that Bishop Germanus of Capua, who died in 541, was sent by his physician to the sulfur baths at Angulum (Samnium). Thrasamund had medical baths constructed in Carthage; see *Anth. lat.*, p. 181, no. 212, v. 10.

[125] Cassiodorus, *Var.*, X, 29 (p. 315).

[126] Schanz, IV-2, 296–97. This translation also came into Gaul; see *CLA*, VIII, 1191.

[127] *Anth. lat.*, p. 285, no. 369: "De horto domni Oageis ubi omnes herbae medicinales plantatae sunt."

[128] Cassiodorus, *Var.*, VI, 19 (p. 191, l. 34): "Habeant itaque medici pro incolumitate omnium et post scholas magistrum, vacent libris, delectentur antiquis: nullus justius assidue legit quam qui de humana salute tractaverit."

[129] The evolution of written law in the Barbarian kingdoms has been ably described by Bruno Paradisi, *Storia del diritto* (Naples, 1951), pp. 245ff.

[130] The *belagines* were written laws which, according to Jordanes, were given to the Goths by Dicineus. See *Getica*, XI (*MGH, AA*, V-1, 74, ll. 5–6): "[Dicineus eos] naturaliter propriis legibus vivere fecit, quas usque nunc [the mid-sixth century] conscriptas belagines nuncupant." Rudolf Buchner, *Die Rechtsquellen* (Weimar, 1953), p. 2, thinks that *belagines* is a Germanic word and translates it as *Satzungen* (statutes).

[131] See Buchner, *Die Rechtsquellen*, pp. 7–8, for Euric's code. Sidonius, *Ep.* II, 1 (*MGH, AA*, VIII, 21–22) referred to the legislation of Theodoric II; see Alvaro D'Ors, "La territorialidad del derecho de los Visigodos," *Settimane*, 3: 389.

together constitutions promulgated before his reign by his predecessor Hilperic.[132] On the other hand, Gundobad, Alaric II the Visigoth, and Theodoric the Ostrogoth continued the legislative work of the last emperors by adapting Roman law to the new circumstances in the "breviaries" prepared for the use of their Roman subjects.[133] The kings used Roman jurists for both Roman and German legal work. Consequently, legislative texts destined solely for Germans were influenced by Roman law[134] or, at least, by provincial law, which was not so different from Germanic law.[135] The names of some of the jurists the kings enlisted in their service have survived: Leo of Narbonne, *consiliarus* of Euric and Alaric, was at Toulouse,[136] with the referendary Anianus;[137] while Syagrius, whom Sidonius ironically dubbed the "new Solon of the Burgundians,"[138] worked at Lyon during the reign of Hilperic.

[132] Brunner, *Deutsche Rechtsgeschichte*, 1: 497; Buchner, *Die Rechtsquellen*, pp. 11–12. Hilperic, who died in 475, played a legislative role, as a passage in the *Vita Lupicini* (*MGH, SRM*, III, 149) attests: "Sub quo principe ditionis regiae jus publicum tempore illo redactum est." See also an allusion by Gundobad to the "priores leges et constitutiones" of his ancestors (*MGH, Leg. sect. I*, II-1, 5) and Sidonius, *Ep*. V, 5 (p. 81).

[133] See Buchner, *Die Rechtsquellen*, pp. 12–13, for the *Lex Romana Burgundionum*, which is perhaps contemporary with the *Lex Romana Visigothorum*, also known as the *Breviary of Alaric* (ibid., pp. 9–10). For the *Edictum Theodorici*, see ibid., pp. 13–14, and Schanz, IV-2, 187–89.

[134] Alfred von Halban, *Das römische Recht in den Germanischen Volksstaaten*, 3 vols. (Breslau, 1899–1907), discusses the influence of Roman law in the Barbarian kingdoms. For the Gombetta Law, see H. Ruegger, *Einfluss des römischen Rechts in der Lex Burgundionum* (Bern, 1949), and Wilfried Roels, *Onderzoek naar het gebruik van de aangehaalde bronnen van Romeins recht in de Lex Romana Burgundionum* (Antwerp, 1958).

[135] According to Ernst Lévy, the laws of the Barbarian kingdoms were inspired more by "vulgar provincial law" than by classical law. For this "vulgar law," see the various works by Lévy, especially "Vulgarisation of Roman Law in the Early Middle Ages," *Medievalia et Humanistica* 1 (1943): 14–40, and *West Roman Vulgar Law: The Law of Property*, Memoirs of the American Philosophical Society, vol. 29 (Philadelphia, 1951). See also Alvaro D'Ors, "La territorialidad," *Settimane*, 3: 363–408; Franz Wieacker, *Vulgarismus und Klassizmus im Recht der Spätantike* (Heidelberg, 1955); and B. Paradisi, "Quelques observations sur un thème célèbre," *RHD* 27 (1959): 75–98.

[136] This individual is known to us through the letters and poems of Sidonius (*Ep*. IV, 22; VIII, 3; *Carm*. XXIII, v. 446) and through Ennodius (*Vita Epifani, MGH, AA*, VII, 85–89). See Schanz, IV-2, 57–58, and Stroheker, p. 187, no. 212.

[137] According to a subscription, Anianus was Alaric's referendary: "Anianus vir spectabilis ex praeceptione domni nostri gloriosissimi regis Alarici . . . hunc codicem legum juris secundum authenticum subscriptum vel in thesauris editum." See the *Theodosian Code*, in *Theodosiani libri XVI*, ed. Mommsen and Meyer, 1: xxxv. F. Beyerle, "Zur Frühgeschichte des Westgotischen Gesetzebung," *ZRGG* 63 (1950): 1–33, thinks that Magnus of Narbonne also contributed, but we have no real proof. There is also no reason to see the influence of Caesarius of Arles in these law codes, as does E. F. Bruck, "Caesarius von Arles und die *Lex Romana Visigothorum*," in *Studi in onore di Vincenzo Arangio-Ruiz nel 45 anno del suo insegnamento*, 4 vols. (Naples, 1953), 1: 201–17.

[138] Sidonius, *Ep*. V, 5 (p. 81): "Novus Burgundionum Solon in legibus disserendis." According to Stroheker, p. 221, no. 369, this letter dates from 470. Coville, p. 197,

But most of the *prudentes*[139] who worked at compiling the laws are anonymous. The tone of some of their legal definitions suggests that most of them came from some sort of academic milieu.[140] Could it be that the law schools, which had been severely tested by the crisis of the fifth century,[141] once again opened their doors?

It is difficult to say for Gaul. Several texts of a scholarly cast still survive with their resumés, glosses, and interpretations of the great monuments of Roman jurisprudence, particularly the *Theodosian Code*, of which there are some sixth-century Gallo-Roman manuscripts.[142] The *interpretatio* which accompanies and predates the *Lex Romana Visigothorum*, or the *Breviary of Alaric*, is one of these texts.[143] So too are another interpretatio—the commentary of Gaius from an Autun manuscript generally dated to the fifth century—and the *Epitome Gaii*, which contains the *Lex Romana Visigothorum* and could have been used in teaching "first-year" law.[144] Yet another famous text, the *Consultatio veteris cujusdam jurisconsulti*, which dates from the beginning of the sixth century and is perhaps from Arles,[145] also seems to me to

---

argues for a date of 475. In either case, the letter was written when Gundobad was not yet king (he became king in 485); see Schmidt, *Die Ostgermanen*, p. 146. Syagrius, therefore, was in the service of Hilperic.

[139] This is what the preface of Alaric's *Breviary* calls them: "Quibus omnibus enucleatis atque in librum unum prudentium electione collectis." See the *Theodosian Code*, *Theodosiani libri XVI*, ed. Mommsen and Meyer, I: xxxiii–xxxiv.

[140] See, for example, the *Lex Romana Burgundionum*, which appealed to such authorities as Gaius, Paul, and Hermogenus, as would a school synopsis. Note also the use of the following phrases: "secundum Gaii regulam" (X, 1 [*MGH, Leges*, III, 602]); "Pauli regulam" (XV, 1 [p. 606]); "sciendum est" (XI, 2; XXII, 5 [pp. 603, 610]); and others.

[141] Valentinian III complained in 451 that he could not find competent jurists: "Notum est post fatalem hostium ruinam, qua Italia laboravit, in quibusdam regionibus et causidicas et judices defuisse hodieque gnaras juris et legum aut raro aut minime repperiri" (*Theodosiani libri XVI: Novella* 32 [Meyer ed., p. 77]). See *Novella* 10; Fritz Schulz, *History of Roman Legal Science* (Oxford, 1946), p. 270; and Max Conrat, "Zur Kultur des römischen Rechts im Westen der römischen Rechts im vierten und fünften Jahr. n. C.," in *Mélanges Fitting: LXXVe anniversaire de M. le professeur Hermann Fitting*, ed. E. Meynial, 2 vols. (Montpellier, 1907–8), 1: 289–320.

[142] See the *Theodosian Code*, in *Theodosiani libri XVI*, ed. Mommsen and Meyer 1: lxxxiv. The presence of these manuscripts in Lyon has led to the too hasty conclusion that there was a law school in this city.

[143] Charles Lécrivain, "Remarques sur l'*Interpretatio* de la Lex Romana Visigothorum," *AM* I (1889): 150. Haarhoff, *Schools of Gaul*, p. 24, has incorrectly attributed the *interpretatio* to Euric.

[144] Paul Frédéric Girard, *Textes de droit romain*, 6th ed., rev. Félix Senn (Paris, 1937), p. 224; Schulz, *Roman Legal Science*, pp. 301–2. See also G. Archi, *L'Epitome Gai* (Milan, 1937). Gaius' *Institutiones* were considered the student's first manual. See Paul Collinet, *Histoire de l'école de droit de Beyrouth* (Paris, 1925).

[145] Schanz, IV-2, 175; Vincenzo Arangio-Ruiz, *Storia del diritto romano*, 2nd ed. (Naples, 1950), p. 372. Petronius, to whom Sidonius dedicated the eighth book of his

have a didactic character. This text is a *responsa* and undoubtedly originated in one of those consultation offices (such as the one Sidonius
frequented in his youth at Arles) that were open to young people who
wished to acquire a legal background.[146] By the end of the fifth century,
it must have become the rule in Gaul to prepare for law by practice.

During Sidonius' time and even earlier, those wishing to take courses
at an actual school went to Rome.[147] What happened to Rome's legal
school in the sixth century? Apparently, it was still in existence. The
juris expositores were among the professors for whom Athalaric sought
a decent salary in 533.[148] The following year, Justinian's *Constitutio
omnem* suppressed all law schools except those at Beirut and in the
urbes regiae[149]—that is, in Constantinople and in Rome. Finally, in 555,
Justinian reestablished the law professors' salaries with the *Pragmatic
Sanction*.[150] Despite this evidence, we have no idea how the school at
Rome operated. There is no reason to believe that its program was based
on that of the school at Beirut.[151] We cannot even point to a text that
might have been used in the school unless the commentary on the
Theodosian Code known as the *Vatican Summary* is dated to the sixth
century, a date which can be defended only with some difficulty.[152]

Ravenna, first as a center of Ostrogothic administrative offices and
later after the Byzantine reconquest, must have been a center for legal
training. Theodoric's *Edictum* undoubtedly came from these offices

---

correspondence around 480, is the last known jurisconsult from Arles; see *Ep.* VIII, 1
(*MGH, AA*, VIII, 126).

[146] Sidonius, *Ep.* VIII, 6 (p. 131). See Marrou, *Education*, pp. 264, 387, for these
offices.

[147] Marrou, *Education*, p. 387. Germanus of Auxerre may have studied law in Rome
at the beginning of the fifth century; see Jean Gaudemet, "La carrière civile de saint
Germain," in *Saint Germain d'Auxerre et son temps*, ed. Gabriel Le Bras (Auxerre, 1950),
pp. 117-18.

[148] Cassiodorus, *Var.*, IX, 21 (*MGH, AA*, XII, 286, l. 21).

[149] *Corpus iuris civilis*, I, *Digest*, c. 89-12. Collinet, *Histoire de l'école*, p. 193, thinks
that there was only one professor of law in Rome. If we were to follow the same reasoning,
since Cassiodorus employs the singular ("ut successor scholae liberalium litterarum tam
grammaticus quam orator nec non juris expositor"), Rome would have had only one
grammarian and one rhetor. Moreover, the *Pragmatic Sanction* mentioned teachers of
law. It is difficult otherwise to explain the additional chairs between 533 and 555.

[150] See below, chap. 5, n. 4.

[151] This is what Enrico Besta thought (*Storia del diritto italiano* [Milan, 1949],
1: 105).

[152] Besta dates it to the sixth century and argues that it comes from Ravenna (*Fonti
del diritto italiano dalla caduta dell'Impero romano sino ai tempi nostri*, 2nd ed. rev.
[Milan, 1950], 1: 95-96). Fitting believes, however, that it is contemporary with the
Consultatio—that is, from the end of the fifth or the beginning of the sixth century. See
A. Rivier, "La science du droit dans la première partie du Moyen Age," *RHD* (1877), p. 2.

under the direction of a quaestor.[153] Pavia's school, however, seems only to have existed in the imaginations of certain historians.[154]

In Italy as well as in Gaul, instruction in the law tended to drift farther and farther away from general cultural training, especially from rhetorical training, to become a very exact speciality which one learned through practice. The Barbarian princes asked for no more and perhaps even applauded this tendency. Emperors who wished to honor the world of letters gave high administrative posts to former rhetors or at least to their pupils.[155] The Barbarian kings, however, disdained the learned and rather preferred men with technical competence. They had been taught their lesson by Boethius, the minister-philosopher, whose political experience at Ravenna ended in a tragic drama. If some alumni of the schools of Milan and Rome still could obtain positions in the Ostrogothic administration, it was because they were lawyers.[156] Their legal knowledge, however, added more to the stock of their *eruditio* than to their profession. Lawyers by this time were more rhetoricians than jurisconsults.[157]

The number of bureaucrats thus increased—bureaucrats who, trained in the offices since their childhood, had no classical background. The official texts even congratulate them for their limited education. Cyprian, the referendary and Boethius' opponent, was congratulated for "having learned more by action than by reading" ("agendo potius instructus est quam legendo").[158] Senarius, count of the patrimony, likewise was in the service of the king from his youth.[159] So too was Argolicus, prefect

---

[153] The *interpretatio* was consulted more than the text of the *Theodosian Code* in the elaboration of this *edictum*; see A. Ponchielli, *Commento all'editto di Theodorico* (Milan, 1923). For its date, perhaps 524, see Guido Astuti, *Lezioni di storia del diritto italiano* (Padua, 1953), pp. 39–42. Some historians think that it could not have been promulgated by Theodoric. Giulio Vismara, "Romani e Goti di fronte al diritto nel regno ostrogoto," *Settimane*, 3: 409–63, supposes that Theodoric II, the Visigoth, was responsible for the *edictum*, but his thesis does not seem to have prevailed.

[154] Antonio Viscardi, *Le origini* (Milan, 1939), p. 215, makes Epiphanius of Pavia a lawyer. He was really only an ecclesiastical notary; see below, chap. 4, n. 152.

[155] Marrou, *Education*, p. 409.

[156] Many of the bureaucrats of Ostrogothic kings were chosen from among lawyers, e.g., the quaestors Fidelis (Cassiodorus, *Var.*, VIII, 19 [MGH, AA, XII, 250, l. 11]), Patricius (*ibid.*, X, 7 [p. 302]), Decoratus (ibid., V, 4 [p. 145]), Eugenius (ibid., I, 12; VIII, 19 [p. 20, l. 250]), and Count Ambrose (ibid., VIII, 13, 4 [p. 243]). Thrasamund's referendary in Carthage was a poet; see *Anth. lat.*, p. 282, no. 300.

[157] See Schulz, *Roman Legal Science*, p. 270.

[158] Cassiodorus, *Var.*, V, 40 (p. 167, l. 7). Cyprian knew Greek as well as the Gothic language, which he must have picked up in the royal offices: "Instructus enim trifariis linguis."

[159] Ibid., IV, 4 (p. 116). The long epitaph for Senarius (ibid., p. 499) makes no mention of his education.

of the city in 510.[160] Even Cassiodorus joined the administration as a youth during the prefecture of his father and acquired legal knowledge only when he became quaestor at age twenty-one.[161] One can thus understand why he praised administrative practice and experience when he wrote to the *cancellarius* of Campania that he who learned by working was more educated than the scholar who knew only a few definitions.[162]

The functionaries, obviously, were not totally uneducated; the documents that issued from the royal offices prove that.[163] Trained in their métier from an early age, however, they were all the more under the control of the kings, who molded them to provide for royal interests. Bureaucrats had become essentially technicians. Like the *tabellion* who worked in his *statio* drawing up documents or the court clerk who registered them, the bureaucrat did not see beyond the walls of his office. Like them, he trained his successor by transmitting essentially routine methods to him, teaching him to use the formularies which facilitated the task, but while conserving the letter of a legal or administrative document, killing its spirit.[164] And yet, it was due to the survival of these offices that the Roman administrative tradition survived during the early Middle Ages.

In remaining loyal to their traditional oratorical and literary culture, the Roman aristocracy could not hope to play an important role in public affairs. Some Romans understandably neglected to pass their culture on to their descendents and instead adopted the lifestyle of the Germans. Some dressed *à la barbare*,[165] while others went farther and gave their children an education that emphasized sports more than letters. Even before the invasions, Romans, after the example of the

---

[160] Ibid., III, 11 (p. 85, ll. 22–24): "Apud nos [Theodoric] faciunt studia litterarum ubi cognovisti omne quod deceat et ad usum vitae gloriosae animum . . . formasti."

[161] Ibid., IX, 24 (p. 289, ll. 27–28): "Quem primaevum recipiens ad quaestoris officium, mox repperit conscientia praeditum et legum eruditione maturum." For Cassiodorus' beginnings, see Sundwall, *Abhandlungen*, p. 154, and Stein, 2: 109, 128.

[162] *Var.*, XI, 37 (p. 351, ll. 13–16): "Splendescunt usu ipso laboribus attributi qui reddunt homines semper instructos: labores inquam, violenti magistri, solliciti paedagogi, per quos cautior qui efficitur, dum incurri pericula formidantur, erudiatur quis forensibus litteris; alter qualibet disciplina doceatur, ille tamen instructior redditur qui actu continuae devotionis eruditur."

[163] See Tjäder, *Papyri*, p. 149.

[164] See C. Saumagne's remarks on juridical formularies in the preface to Christian Courtois et al., eds., *Tablettes Albertini* (Paris, 1952), p. 148.

[165] See Ennodius' epigram against Jovinianus, *Carm.* 2, 57 (*MGH, AA*, VII, 157): "Qui cum haberet barbam gothicam lacerna vestitus processit ex tempore." Certain Romans dressed in the Barbarian style from the fourth century on. See Ambrose, *Ep.* 10, 9 (*PL*, XVI, 983).

Barbarians, assigned greater importance than had previous generations to the military education of their sons. Young Honorius, the son of Theodosius, appears in Claudian's poem as a young "knight" eager to bear arms.[166] Aetius' education was completely military and quasi-barbarian.[167] Avitus and Majorian were trained under military orders at an early age.[168] Even when Sidonius spoke of his friends' talents, he did not neglect to weigh their athletic accomplishments.[169] Physical education gained in importance after the settlement of the Burgundians and Goths in Roman territory. Parents began to encourage their children in athletic exercises during the reign of Theodoric, when Romans were no longer allowed to bear arms. At Ravenna, a meeting place for Gothic and Roman youth, Cyprian the referendary raised his sons among young Barbarians.[170] Without going quite as far, Basilius Venantius completed the literary education of his children by developing their bodies with stadium exercises.[171]

The war which broke out in 535 only reinforced these tendencies. Although it is not known whether the Italians helped the Byzantines with their reconquest, military events nevertheless affected them profoundly. Children and adolescents especially were unable to remain indifferent during the conflict. Procopius tells us that during the siege of

---

[166] Claudian *Panegyricus de quarto cons. Honorii Augusti*, 364ff. (*MGH, AA*, X, 164). On Honorius, he wrote:

> Per strages equitare libet. Da protinus arma.
> Cur annos obicis? Pugnae cur arguor impar?
> Aequalis mihi Pyrrhus erat, cum Pergama solus. . . .

And on Theodosius,

> Laudanda petisti
> Sed festinus amor. Vaniet robustior aetas.

[167] Gregory of Tours, *HF*, II, 8 (p. 51), who here cites Renatus Frigeridus ("A puero praetorianus. . . .")

[168] For Majorian's youth, see Sidonius, *Panegyric* for Majorian, in *Carm.* V, v. 204 (*MGH, AA*, VII, 192). For Avitus' early years, see *Carm.* VII, 172 (ibid., p. 207).

[169] Sidonius, *Ep.* III, 3 (ibid., p. 41, l. 12): "Hic primum tibi pila pyrgus accipiter canis equus arcus ludo fuere." See also "Ad Consentium," *Carm.* XXIII, vv. 214ff. (p. 255).

[170] Cassiodorus, *Var.*, VIII, 21 (*MGH, AA*, XII, 253): "Sic fetus tui . . . regales oculos ab ipsis . . . cunabulis pertulerunt. Relucent etiam gratia gentili nec cessant armorum imbui fortibus institutis. Pueri stirpis Romanae nostra lingua loquuntur."

[171] Ibid., IX, 23 (p. 288): "Quorum infantia bonis artibus enutria juventutem quoque armis exercuit, formans animum litteris membra gymnasiis." We know nothing about the athletic activities of young Romans, nor do we know what became of the *collegia juvenum* of the Late Empire (see Marrou, *Education*, pp. 399–400). I have been able to find only one sentence in Cassiodorus which alludes to a stadium, and even here it is only a metaphor: "Quis enim palaestricae artis ignarus in stadium luctaturus introeat?" See *Var.*, IV, 25 (p. 125, l. 14). Also see Sidonius, *Carm.* XXIII, vv. 214ff. (p. 255).

Rome, some young shepherds from Samnium played at "Belisarius and Vitigis."[172] For many other youngsters, the game must have been much more true to life.[173] During the troubles which followed 535, a new aristocracy was born, an aristocracy more warlike and less cultivated— the ancestors of the medieval nobility.

Ancient education was also endangered from another quarter. Not all young Romans "turned to the Barbarians." Some of them, dis-oriented by political crises, fled the world and entered the ranks of the clergy or the monasteries. The Church offered them another kind of education, the principles of which it established at the end of the fifth and the beginning of the sixth century.

[172] Procopius, *Bell. goth.*, I, 20 (Haury ed., p. 102).

[173] Ibid., IV, 34 (p. 667) relates that Totila had the sons of notables brought to his court on the pretext that they would live with him. Actually, he used them as hostages. They were later massacred by Teias; see Stein, 2: 303.

CHAPTER THREE

Christians and the Antique School
at the Beginning of the Sixth Century

C hristians throughout the fifth century courageously fought to save the Empire and its civilization, even though there were those who would have allowed the Barbarians into *Romania* in the belief that their conversion to Catholicism would thus have been facilitated.[1] The settlement of the Barbarians in the Empire should have led the Church to reorganize Christian education on new foundations, if only to combat heretical Arian propaganda. In fact, however, the "conversion" to a uniquely religious culture did not come immediately. As long as the antique school survived intact, Christian aristocrats were unable to imagine any culture but Christian classical culture. In the new political and social context, however, opposition to this culture, which had previously been confined to monasteries, became stronger. The resulting crisis of conscience that we are going to study led to the establishment of the first Christian schools.

I. MAINTENANCE OF CHRISTIAN CLASSICAL CULTURE

As in the fourth and fifth centuries, the religious culture available to lay and clerical Christians at the beginning of the sixth century closely resembled classical culture. Aristocratic laymen made it a duty

---

[1] Orosius, *Adv. pag.*, VII, 41 (*CSEL,* 5: 554). For this attitude, see Fliche-Martin, 4: 362ff.

to deepen their faith through reading and studying. At the end of the fifth century some friends of Sidonius Apollinaris asked the bishop of Clermont for explications of certain religious texts.[2] At the beginning of the sixth century, Proba, an illustrious noblewoman, received a *florilegium* of Augustine's works from Abbot Eugippius.[3] During the same period, the patricius Senarius questioned John the Deacon on the baptismal liturgy.[4] In Africa, Bishop Fulgentius of Ruspe addressed theological works to various laymen.[5] When he settled at Cagliari during his exile in Sardinia, the aristocrats there came to hear the lessons he gave to monks.[6] Clergymen, for their part, could sometimes find copies of works they needed in the libraries of laymen. Bishop Ruricius of Limoges asked a certain Taurentius for a papyrus copy of the *City of God* which the latter had long promised to send the bishop.[7]

Not only did laymen interest themselves in studying religious texts, but they also put their pens to the service of the Church. About 525, Rusticius Helpidius, a former quaestor at Ravenna, composed two poems dealing with Christ and various biblical passages.[8] A few years later a Campanian aristocrat specialized in hagiography.[9] At Rome,

[2] Namatius asked Sidonius for Eusebius' chronicle (*Ep.* IV, 3 [*MGH, AA*, VIII, 54]). While Ruricius was still a layman he requested a copy of the Heptateuch from Sidonius (ibid. V, 15 [p. 88, l. 10]). Count Arbogast of Trier questioned Sidonius (ibid. VIII, 17, 3; see Schanz, IV-2, 378). Felix the Provençal asked Faustus of Riez for a treatise on the "fear of God"; see Gennadius, *De viris inlustris*, 86 (85) (Richardson ed., p. 91).

[3] Eugippius, preface to *Excerpta ex operibus s. Augustini, CSEL*, 9, pt. 2: 1. For Proba, see Sundwall, *Abhandlungen*, p. 161. She was also in contact with Fulgentius of Ruspe (*PL*, LXV, 320).

[4] John the Deacon, *Ep. ad Senarium, PL*, LIX, 399. See Sundwall, *Abhandlungen*, p. 153, for Senarius. Avitus wrote to him apropos of Eastern theological quarrels; see Avitus, *Ep.* XXXIX (36) (*MGH, AA*, VI-2, 68).

[5] Fulgentius, *Ad Monimum, PL*, LXV, 151; *Ad Felicem notarium*, ibid., 497; *Ad Theodorum senatorem*, ibid., 348. See Schanz, IV-2, 576.

[6] Ferrandus, *Vita Fugentii*, XIX (Lapeyre ed., p. 95): "Delectabat nobiles viros si fieri posset, cotidie beatum Fulgentium cernere disputantem."

[7] Ruricius, *Ep.* II, 27 (*MGH, AA*, VIII, 327): "Rogo, sicut promittere dignati estis, librum nobis sancti Augustini de civitate dei per portitorem harum sine dilatione mittatis." We have Taurentius' reply (ibid., p. 272). He recommended this precious book to Ruricius because it was on papyprus ("chartaceus liber").

[8] Dirk Hendrik Groen, *Rusticii Helpidii Carmina notis criticis, versione batava, commentarioque exegetico instructa* (Groningen, 1942). This editor provides a résumé of the discussion on the person of the poet who—as Brandes, in *WS* 12 (1890): 306, already saw —seems to have been the person who was responsible for the Ravennate recensions (see above, chap. I, sect. II.B.1). A veiled allusion to Boethius' death suggests 524 as the date of Rusticius' work. See L. Alfonsi, "Note ad Elpidio Rustico," *Atti dell'Istituto Veneto* (1941), p. 339. More recently, see S. Cavallin, "Le poète Domnulus:·Étude prosopographique," *SE* 7 (1955): 49–65, who thinks that the Christian poet and Sidonius' friend, Domnulus (*Ep.* IX, 13 [*MGH, AA*, VIII, 164, l. 5]), were one and the same individual.

[9] Eugippius, *Ep. ad Paschasium diaconum, MGH, AA*, I-2, 1: "Epistola cujusdam laici nobilis . . . continens vitam Bassi monachi, qui quondam in monasterio montis, cui vocabu-

Boethius composed theological treatises refuting the Nestorian heresy.[10]
At Lyon, the poet Heraclius used his talents in dialectic to try to convert Gundobad.[11] Junilius, a mid-sixth century African who became
quaestor at Byzantium, wrote an introduction to the study of Holy
Scripture.[12]

These Christian scholars, former students of grammarians and rhetors, naturally wrote in a classic manner, since it seemed impossible to
them to express Christian truth in any way except through traditional
forms. For example, the adaptation of books of the Bible into hexameters, which for a century had been very successful in the West and
in the East, was continued into the sixth century.[13] Not only were
Sedulius and Prudentius still in vogue,[14] but new poets imitated them.
Dracontius in Africa and Avitus of Vienne in Gaul paraphrased the
first books of the Old Testament in verse.[15] Avitus even noted that
children could use his work.[16] One can imagine the pleasure with which
the young pupil of the *grammaticus* read verses which portrayed a God
who like Jupiter threw thunderbolts, or an angel who like Iris the
messenger came to deliver instructions to Noah, or Adam and Eve
amidst the joys of their wedding.[17] These pagan-Christian wonder
stories reconciled the two cultures. The Christian epic compared well

---

lum est Titas, super Ariminum commoratus, post in Lucaniae regione defunctus est."
For this *vita*, see below, sect. II.

[10] Boethius, *Opuscula sacra*, edited by Rudolf Peiper in the Teubner series (Leipzig,
1871). See Schanz, IV-2, 159.

[11] Avitus, *Ep.* LIII (47) (*MGH, AA*, VI-2, 82). See above, Chap. 2, sect. II.C.

[12] Schanz, IV-2, 583.

[13] For the East, see O. Bardenhewer, *Geschichte der altkirchlichen Literatur*, 5 vols.
(Freiburg-im-Breisgau, 1913–31), 4: 86, 395. For the West, see Max Manitius, *Geschichte
der christlich-lateinischen Poesie bis zur Mitte des 8. Jahrhunderts* (Stuttgart, 1891); de
Labriolle, *La littérature latine chrétienne*, 2: 465–94, 695–742; Christine Mohrmann, "Le
vocabulaire et le style de la poésie chrétienne," *REL* 25 (1947): 243; and idem, "Le latin,
langue de la chrétienté occidentale," *Aevum* 24 (1950): 133–61.

[14] Their manuscripts were revised in 494 and 527; see above, chap. 1, n. 224.

[15] For Dracontius' poem, see de Labriolle, *La littérature latine chrétienne*, 2: 731, and
F. Chatillon, "Dracontiana," *RMAL* 8 (1952): 179ff. For Avitus' poem, see Schanz, IV-2,
383, 385, and Stanislas Gamber, *Le livre de la Genèse dans la poésie latine au Vᵉ siècle*
(Paris, 1899).

[16] Avitus, *Ep.* XLIII (38) (*MGH, AA*, VI-2, 73, ll. 6–8): "Quocirca volumen per vos
temperatius ingerendum si supradictus frater [Sidonius' son, Apollinaris] vel infantibus
legi debere censuerit, possum . . . cognoscere." I do not think, given the context, that
infans means here "one who is unbaptized." Fulgentius used the word *infans* to designate
the children to whom he dedicated his *Expositio virgilianae continentiae*: "Ergo et infantibus quibus haec nostra materia traditur" (Helm ed., p. 96). We should also mention
that Claudius Marius Victorius put Genesis into verse in the fifth century for his son
(*CSEL*, 16, pt. 1: 359).

[17] Avitus, *Carm.* I, 144ff.; IV, 133, (*MGH, AA*, VI-2, 207, 239).

with Virgil, the schoolbook par excellence. Furthermore, in these paraphrases one could challenge the "lies of the poets"[18] with a "truth" expressed much more poetically than in the "rustic" Gospels.[19]

In the mid-sixth century, during the heat of the Byzantine-Gothic war, this poetic genre continued to enjoy the same success. In 544 Arator, who became a subdeacon in Rome after he abandoned his public duties, offered the pope his famous poetic paraphrase of the Acts of the Apostles. The pope, who liked poetry,[20] had the work deposited in the archives of Saint Peter's basilica. In addition, Arator gave readings of the entire poem for four days in the church of Saint Peter in Chains before an audience of laymen and clerics.[21] During a dark hour for Rome, a Christian Virgil reenacted the traditional *recitationes* for the last time in an episode which has often been recalled. Elsewhere, educated Christians' taste for religious poetry in classic vocabulary and form[22] was revealed in a whole series of metrical inscriptions, often embodying Virgilian reminiscences, on the walls of churches and on tombs.[23] Not even dogma escaped the laws of poetry. At the beginning of the sixth century, an African put the story of the Resurrection and the Last Judgment into dactylic verse,[24] while an anonymous poet in Rome meditated on the Incarnation.[25]

---

[18] This expression was a commonplace from Plato's time on. For its use, see Ruricius, *Ep.* I, 10 (*MGH, AA*, VIII, 306); Ennodius, *Ep.* I, 9 (ibid., VII, 18, l. 15); and Maximianus, *Eleg.*, ed. Baehrens, in *Poet. lat. min.*, 5: 316: "Saepe poetarum mendacia dulcia finxi."

[19] *Alethia* ("Truth") is the title of Claudius Marius Victorius' poem on Genesis (*CSEL*, 16, pt. 1: 359).

[20] See the metrical inscriptions he had composed on the occasion of the restoration of the catacombs of *Via Salaria* (*ICR*, 2: 100, 137).

[21] The circumstances of this poem's reading are reported in several manuscripts; see Arator, *Hist. Apos.*, *CSEL*, 72: xxviii ff.: "In ecclesia beati Petri quae vocatur ad vincula religiosorum simul ac laicorum nobilium sed et e populo diversorum turba convenit. Atque eodem Aratore recitante distinctis diebus ambo libri quattuor vicibus sunt auditi."

[22] E.g., Ennodius' poem for the Milan baptistery (*Carm.* 2, 56 [*MGH, AA*, VII, 157]) and his poems decorating the effigies of the bishops of Milan (*Carm.* 2, 77–78); the epitaphs of the bishops of Spoleto prepared by or on the order of Bishop Flavian in 542 (*CIL*, V, 6722ff.); Pope Hormidas' son's metrical inscription in honor of his father (*ICR*, vol. 1, no. 108).

[23] See especially Hilary of Arles' epitaph (Ernst Diehl, *Instcriptiones latinae Christianae veteres* [Berlin, 1924], pp. 204–5, no. 1062), the last verse of which repeats Virgil (*Ecl.*, V, 56). See also the contemporary African epitaph of young Constantina in Marrou, "Epitaphe chrétienne d'Hippone à réminiscences virgiliennes," *Libyca* I (1953): 215–320. For the East, see Pierre Waltz, "L'inspiration païenne et les sentiments chrétiens dans les épigrammes funéraires du VIᵉ siècle," in *L'Acropole: Revue du monde hellénique* 6 (1931): 3–21.

[24] See Schanz, IV-2, 394–95, and *Clavis*, no. 1453.

[25] *De Maria virgine ad Rusticianam carmen*, *ICR*, vol. 2, no. 109. According to a

With respect to preaching, the rhetor's art had an immediate appeal to educated bishops. The use of rhetoric in preaching had been a well-established tradition since the fourth century.[26] The sermons of Valerian of Cimiez were a model of the genre during the mid-fifth century.[27] His colleague, Hilary of Arles, reportedly elevated the tone of his preaching whenever scholars came into his church.[28] Charmed by the beauty of his speech, the faithful sometimes applauded the sacred orator as if they were in a rhetor's *auditorium*.[29] At the end of the fifth century, rhetorical rules were still observed by preachers. When Sidonius sent a sermon to Bishop Perpetuus of Tours, he begged indulgence for having worked too hastily and for having left out everything classic —"the figures of style, the authority of historical examples, poetical turns," and so on.[30] Despite this disclaimer, Sidonius' sermon is a rhetorical gem. The same could be said for the plea Ennodius made in favor of the synod that recognized the innocence of Pope Symmachus[31] or for the letters of condolence customarily sent to intimate friends.[32] Of course, the Bible was cited in all these eloquent pieces—but alongside profane authors.[33] The sacred text was one among many texts.

Our scholars did not seek, however, to deepen the message of Chris-

---

ninth-century manuscript, the author of this meditation on the Incarnation was an orator named Andreas. Rusticiana may have been Boethius' widow, but this identification is highly speculative.

[26] Marrou, *Saint Augustin*, pp. 512, 528. See Jean Leclercq, "Prédication et rhétorique au temps de saint Augustin," *RB* 57 (1947): 116–31.

[27] See Schanz, IV-2, 529; Gustav Bardy, "Valérien de Cimélium," *DTC*, 15, pt. 2: 2520–22; and Haarhoff, *Schools of Gaul*, p. 165.

[28] Honoratus, *Vita Hilarii*, PL, L, 1231: "At ubi instructos supervenisse vidisset, sermone ac vultu pariter in quadam gratia insolita excitatur."

[29] Sidonius, *Ep.* IX, 3 (*MGH, AA*, VIII, 152, l. 8). This tradition dates back much further; see Johannes Zellinger, "Der Beifall in der altchristl. Predigt," in *Festgabe Alois Knöpfler zur vollendung des 70. Lebensjahres gewidmet*, ed. H. M. Gietl and G. Pfeilschifter (Freiburg, 1917).

[30] Sidonius, *Ep.* VII, 9 (p. 112): "[Oratio] cui non rhetorica partitio, non oratoriae minae, non grammaticales figurae congruentem decorem disciplinamque suppeditaverunt, neque enim illic, ut exacte perorantibus mos est, aut pondera historica aut poetica schemata scintillasve controversalium clausularum libuit aptari."

[31] Ennodius, *Libellus pro synodo*, *MGH, AA*, VII, 48.

[32] Ruricius, *Ep.* II, 3 (*MGH, AA*, VIII, 312); Ennodius, *Ep.* III, 2 (ibid., VII, 76); Avitus (letter to Gundobad), *Ep.* V (5) (ibid., VI-2, 32). See also from the same period Remigius' letter to Clovis on the death of the king's sister, *Ep.* 1, (*MGH, Ep.*, III, 112).

[33] Ennodius cited Virgil, Seneca, and Terence in his *Libellus contra eos qui contra synodum scribere praesumpserunt, MGH, AA*, VII, 48–67. See also a reminiscence from the *Bucolics* in a sermon from this period published by Germain Morin ("Deux petits discours d'un évêque Pétronius du Vᵉ siècle," *RB* 14 [1897]: 3–8), who attributed it to Petronius of Verona or Bologna; Avitus, *Homilia in rogationibus, MGH, AA*, VI-2, 112, ll. 12–14, for a citation from Virgil (*Aeneid*, I, 204 and 122); and ibid., p. 117, l. 5, for a quote from Valerius Maximus.

tian revelation or to draw philosophical reflections from it. They were no more interested in theology than they were in philosophy. Theological studies had been vigorous in the fifth century.[34] Even at the end of the century, Sidonius hailed Faustus of Riez as a man who had subjected ancient philosophy to Christian law—a bit too flattering a compliment—and Claudian Mamertus as the "most remarkable Christian philosopher."[35] A few years later, the picture had changed. Avitus of Vienne so ineptly interpreted the doctrinal quarrels of his time that his theological training cannot be judged very highly.[36] Ennodius was no more a theologian than he was a philosopher. Only in Rome, in the persons of two men nourished on Greek thought, Dionysius Exiguus and Boethius, do we confront theologians.

Dionysius, a Scythian monk, had been called from Constantinople by Pope Gelasius, who had decided to organize the canonical collections.[37] After Gelasius' death in 496, Dionysius translated canonical texts as well as works dealing with the heresies the papacy was combatting.[38] Cassiodorus, who studied dialectic with Dionysius, probably in Rome, praised the monk's profound religious culture and his influence.[39] Abbot Eugippius and Julian, a learned priest, were also numbered among Dionysius' friends.[40] But even though Dionysius' canonical and

[34] Courcelle, *LG*, pp. 221ff., and, more recently, E. L. Fortin, *Christianisme et culture philosophique au V* siècle: La querelle de l'âme humaine en Occident* (Paris, 1959).

[35] Sidonius, *Ep.* V, 2; IX, 9, 18 (*MGH, AA*, VIII, 62, l. 158): "Peritissimus Christianorum philosophus."

[36] Courcelle, *LG*, p. 251.

[37] This pontificate merits a historian's attention. For the liturgical work of the period, see B. Capelle, "Retouches gélasiennes dans le sacramentaire léonien," *RB* 61 (1951): 3–14, and the preface to G. Pomarès' edition of *Adversus Andromachum senatorem et ceteros Romanos qui lupercalia secundum morem pristinum colenda constituunt*, in *SC*, vol. 65 (Paris, 1960). For the canonical collections, see Gabriel Le Bras, "La renaissance gélasienne," *RHD* (1930), pp. 506–18, and Paul Fournier and Gabriel Le Bras, *Histoire des Collections canoniques en Occident* (Paris, 1931), I: 23ff.

[38] Schanz, IV-2, 589.

[39] Cassiodorus, *Inst.*, I, 23 (Mynors ed., pp. 62–63). He must have known Dionysius between 512 and 522 in Rome and certainly not at Vivarium (which was founded after 555), as André van de Vyver thinks (see "Cassiodore et son oeuvre," *Speculum* 6 [1931]: 262).

[40] Dionysius, *Ep. ad Eugippium*, *PL*, LXVII, 345, and *Praefatio ad Julianum*, ibid., 231. According to Dionysius, Julian was Gelasius' disciple: "Per vos alumnos ejus [Gelasius] facilius aestimamus; cujus eruditione formati gradum presbyteri sancta conversatione decoratis." Wilhelm M. Peitz thinks that Dionysius lived with Julian in the buildings of the church of Saint Anastasia at the foot of the Palatine and that he collaborated in the preparation of the *Symmachan Errors*, the *Liber pontificalis*, and the *Liber diurnus*; see "Dionysius Exiguus als Kanonist," *Schweizer Rundschau* 45 (1945): 3. For Peitz's revolutionary theories, see P. Blet, "Collections canoniques et critiques textuelles: Note sur les recherches de W. M. Peitz," *MA* 60 (1954): 163–74; J. Rambaud-Buhot, "Denys le Petit," *DDC*, 4: 1131–52; and E. Munier, "L'oeuvre canonique de Denis le Petit," *SE* 14 (1963):

theological work was important, he left no disciples after his death in 525.

Boethius' attempts were just as ephemeral. This philosopher tried to apply Aristotelian methods to the investigation of the mystery of the Trinity.[41] He wanted to show that the study of theology necessitated rules just as precise as those used in the study of mathematics.[42] But he was not understood, and he lamented the ignorance of his contemporaries, particularly the clergy.[43] He deliberately adopted an esoteric style to protect his writings from the criticisms of fools.[44] The only cleric-theologian we find around Boethius was a Deacon John, whose advice he sought concerning his fifth opuscule.[45]

The Byzantine reconquest did not revive theological studies in Rome. The affair of the *Three Chapters* might have provided the occasion for a theological revival, but neither Pope Vigilius nor Pelagius, his successor, were theologians.[46] Only Vigilius' nephew, a theologian who also knew profane authors,[47] left us a treatise against the Acephalites.[48] In 545, the Roman clergy had to request clarifications from the two

---

236–50. Peitz's articles have been collected in his *Dionysius Exiguus-Studien* (Berlin, 1960).

[41] Courcelle, *LG*, p. 305; Emanuele Rapisarda, *La crisi spirituale di Boezio* (Florence, 1947).

[42] Boethius, *Opuscula sacra*, III (Peiper ed., p. 168: "Ut igitur in mathematica fieri solet ceterisque etiam disciplinis, praeposui terminos regulasque quibus cuncta quae secuntur efficiam.") See idem, *De Trinitate*, II, in *Opuscula sacra*, ed. Peiper, p. 152.

[43] Boethius, *Contra Eutychen et Nestorium*, in *Opuscula sacra*, ed. Peiper, p. 187, l. 29: "Tuli aegerrime fateor compressusque indoctorum grege conticui metuens ne jure viderer insanus, si sanus inter furiosos haberi contenderem." Boethius was undoubtedly alluding to the clerics who participated in the council of 512 and who brought knowledge of the letters of Eastern bishops to Pope Symmachus. See also ibid., p. 186, ll. 5–6: "Meministi cum in concilio legeretur epistola."

[44] Boethius, *De Trinitate*, in *Opuscula sacra*, ed. Peiper, p. 150, 16: "Idcirco stilum brevitate contraho et ex intimis sumpta philosophiae disciplinis novorum verborum significationibus velo, ut haec mihi tantum vobisque, si quando ad ea convertitis oculos, conloquantur."

[45] Boethius, *Opuscula sacra*, II (Peiper ed., p. 167): "Haec si se recte et ex fide habent, ut me instruas peto . . . fidem si poteris rationemque conjunge." This John, perhaps the author of the letter to Senarius, undoubtedly became pope under the name John I (523–26). See E. K. Rand, *Fleckeis Jahrbuch* 26 (1901): 442; *contra* Schanz, IV-2, 595. Courcelle, *LG*, p. 340, n. 4, prefers to identify this John with John III (560–73).

[46] See Louis M. Duchesne, *L'Eglise au VIe siècle* (Paris, 1925), pp. 173ff., for this affair. We should note, however, that we owe a canon on the origin of the soul to Vigilius (Mansi, IX, 533). The palinodes of Pelagius I do not prove deep theological learning on his part; see Duchesne, *L'Eglise*, p. 236. He knew Greek and translated the *Verba seniorum*; see Schanz, IV-2, 596, and Robert Devreesse, *Pelagii diaconi ecclesiae romanae: In defensione trium capitulorum, ST* vol., 57 (Vatican City, 1932).

[47] At least this is what his uncle criticized him for: "Tu Rustice dum aliqua nobis ignorantibus legeres, quae hominem loci tui omnino legere non decebat" (*PL*, LXIX, 43).

[48] Rusticus, *Contra Acephalos disputatio, PL*, LXVII, 1167. See Schanz, IV-2, 596.

Africans[49] Ferrandus of Carthage and Facundus of Hermianus. Some have called the latter the last theologian of Antiquity.[50] The African clergy had, in fact, never abandoned theological studies. During the Vandal domination, Fulgentius of Ruspe—who perhaps has too often been portrayed as a pale disciple of Saint Augustine[51]—and then, after the Byzantine reconquest, a whole series of theologians proved that, in Africa at least, Catholic thought was not represented merely by poets and orators.[52]

But Africa was an exception. Everywhere else, scholars' religious culture, like their profane culture, was uniquely literary and oratorical. The exile of philosophy necessarily entailed that of theology. As a result, religious culture could appeal only to a small number of Christian aristocrats with close ties to the antique school. Those who received only an elementary education or who chose to neglect their secondary studies were incapable of either appreciating classical culture, whether profane or religious, or criticizing its weaknesses. Thus, a fertile ground was prepared for the challenge of the Christian rigorists, who drew their recruits primarily from the monastic world.

II. OPPOSITION TO CHRISTIAN CLASSICAL CULTURE

Caesarius of Arles, who was a monk before he became bishop, indicted profane knowledge. Comparing the liberal arts to the plagues of Egypt, he argued that the songs of poets served only to fuel sensuality and that the teachings of philosophers misled untrained minds and thus were responsible for doctrinal deviations.[53] Philosophy was no longer what it had been for Claudian Mamertus—an intellectual stimulus invented by God—but, rather, a source of heresies. By philosophy,

---

[49] PL, LXVII, 921. See Duchesne, L'Eglise au VIe siècle, pp. 625ff., for the African Church.

[50] Schanz, IV-2, 581.

[51] For Fulgentius, see Lapeyre, Saint Fulgence de Ruspe, and F. di Sciascio, Fulgenzio di Ruspe e i massimi problemi della grazia (Rome, 1941).

[52] See Schanz, IV-2, 583ff., for Liberatus of Carthage and Primasius of Hadrumetum.

[53] Caesarius, Sermo, XCIX (Morin ed., p. 589): "Et in eis [scinifes] philosophae artis astutia et infelicium hereticorum venena vel commenta subtilissima designantur." Caesarius was repeating Origen, In Exod., 4, 6, in Überlieferung und textgeschichte der lateinisch erhaltenen Origeneshomilien zum Alten Testament, ed. Willem A. Baehrens, (Leipzig, 1916), p. 178. Cassian, De incarnatione Domini contra Nestorium, III, 15, 2 (CSEL, 17: 280), contrasted Thomas' ignorance and simplicity with the learning of the heretic Nestorius. Tertullian had earlier typed philosophers as "the patriarchs of heretics" (De anima, III, 1 [PL, II, 651]).

Caesarius meant the entire profane legacy. Of course, the arguments Caesarius borrowed from previous adversaries of antique culture were classic. Nevertheless, attacks against the immorality of poets and the errors of philosophers did not stop the Greek and Latin Fathers from using the poets and philosophers in the schools and from finding a *via media* which permitted the rational use of the riches of profane culture. This prudent solution, however, was possible only for men like the Fathers, men who had been profoundly nourished on antique culture. At the end of the fifth and during the sixth century, as a result of the decline of studies, only a warped version of classical culture remained; its essential humanism was obscured by an excessively complicated form as well as by the paganism of its thought. Classical training thus seemed both to menace the Christian faith and to bar the less instructed from access to the Gospel message.

The rigorists first presented their arguments on a moral plane and criticized Christian scholars for the equivocal nature of their cultural formation. One had to choose between paganism and Christianity. The Christian scholars of whom we have spoken, however, passed from the profane to the sacred without scruple.[54] Whenever Sidonius, Ennodius, Cassiodorus, or Dracontius offered an epithalamium to a friend,[55] they did not hesitate to use traditional mythological images in order to evoke the activities of Venus and Cupid, as the law of the genre required. How could one speak of a woman's beauty without comparing her to Helen or to Venus?[56] How could one aim an epigram at

[54] Umberto Morricca, in reference to these men of letters, spoke of the existence of a "double conscience"; see *Storia della letteratura latina cristiana* (Turin, 1932), 3: 194, and Chatillon, "Dracontiana," *RMAL* 8 (1952): 184–85, n. 8. This ambiguity has long cast doubt on Boethius' religious faith (see Courcelle's discussion in *LG*, p. 300) and on the identification of Bishop Fulgentius with Fulgentius the Mythographer (for this question, see Schanz, IV-2, 205; Franz Skutsch, "Fulgentius," *RE*, 7: 215; and P. Langlois, "Les oeuvres de Fulgence le mythographe et le problème des deux Fulgence," *Jahrbuch für Antike und Christentum* 7 [1964]: 127). Other periods have witnessed a similar dualism; see Lucien Febvre, *Autour de l'Heptaméron: Amour sacré, amour profane* (Paris, 1944).

[55] Sidonius, epithalamium for Ruricius, *Carm.* XI (*MGH, AA*, VIII, 227–30), analyzed by Loyen, *Sidoine Apollinaire*, pp. 115–17; Ennodius, "Epithalamium dictum Maximo v.s.," *Carm.* 1, 4 (ibid., p. 276); Cassiodorus, epithalamium for Vitigis, fragment in *MGH, AA*, XII, 480; Dracontius, *Romulea*, VI, VII (*MGH, AA*, XIV, 148–56).

[56] Anonymous poem, ed. H. W. Garrod, "Poeseos saeculi sexti fragmenta quattuor," *CQ* 4 (1910): 263 (I, 5–6):

> Esse Paris vellem. Helenae quid fama teneris
> In pretio? poterit cedere nuda Venus . . .
> Quisne parum tumidas delecto ventre papillas
> Non tractet manibus, poma fecunda, suis?

an enemy without emphasizing an immoral aspect of his personality?[57] Praise of the human body and of youth were also part of a literary tradition which our scholars could not forsake entirely.[58] Likewise they unabashedly admired artistic works of pagan inspiration. The platters and cups which Ennodius enjoyed describing were often decorated with salacious subjects.[59] The ivory pyxidia and coffers of newlyweds were adorned with designs inspired by mythological scenes.[60] Some Christians even had themselves buried in tombs which formerly housed the remains of pagans. The body of the noble Provençal Felix Ennodius was laid to rest at Gayole in a sarcophagus whose décor depicted the murder of Egisthus and Clytemnestra.[61]

For some, none of this was compromising. Aristocrats at the beginning of the sixth century were well aware that the ancient gods were dead. Myths had become artistic and literary themes whose symbolism alone was retained by aristocrats. Fulgentius the African devoted much of his work to the exegesis of ancient myths without disturbing his faith.[62] The rigorists, however, were not of the same mind. For them, paganism was still a religious force which the Christian must continue to combat. Recent events had proved them correct: had not Theodoric, on the pretext of saving the antique heritage, set up statues and restored

---

[57] The titles of Ennodius' epigrams are evocative: there is the "Epigramma de adultero et molle" (*Carm.* 2, 52–55 [*MGH, AA,* VII, 156–57]) and "Virsus de eo qui dicebatur meretricis filius et asellionis esse" (*Carm.* 2, 24 [p. 135]). See also *Carm.* 2, 97 (p. 172) and 69 (p. 160); as well as Luxorius' epigrams in *Anth. lat.,* p. 247. Peter, a referendary, was the author of an epigram *ad meretricem* (*Anth. lat.,* no. 382) and a poem on the "palace basilica" (ibid., no. 380).

[58] See the praise of youth in Maximianus' elegy (*Poet. lat. min.,* ed. Baehrens, vol. 5). For this poet, who probably lived during the first half of the sixth century, see Schanz, IV-2, 76, and, more recently, R. Anastasi, "La IIe elegia de Massimiano," in *Miscellanea di studi di letteratura cristiana antica,* ed. R. Anastasi, F. Corsaro, and C. Rapisarda (Catania, 1951), p. 81. Maximianus was probably a Christian (*Eleg.,* V, 91, ed. Baehrens, *Poet. lat. min.,* vol. 5), but his poetry is erotic more than once (ibid., V, 57); this, however, did not bar it from being used in medieval schools (see L. Traube, "Zur Ueberlieferung der Elegien des Maximianus," *RhM* 48 [1893]: 287).

[59] Ennodius, *Carm.* 2, 25 (p. 136): "Versus de cauco cujusdam habente Pasiphae et taurum"; ibid., 29 and 30 (pp. 137–38); ibid., 21 (p. 135): "Epigramma de scutellis septem habentibus feras vel Dianam"; ibid., 101, 102, 103 (p. 182). See also the *Anth. lat.,* p. 262, no. 317.

[60] There are many pyxidia from this period. Jewelry boxes of the period must have been like the one owned by Projecta, which dates from the end of the fourth century. Henri Stern, *Le calendrier de 354: Etude sur son texte et ses illustrations* (Paris, 1953), pp. 115–16, has studied pagan-Christian syncretism of the fourth century, a tendency which was to persist much longer.

[61] See H. Stern, "Un sarcophage de la Gayole découvert par Peiresc," *Gallia* 15 (1957): 73–85, and *Anth. lat.,* p. 263, no. 319: "De sarcophago ubi turpia sculpta fuerant."

[62] Schanz, IV-2, 196–98; see pp. 243ff. for the *Mythographi vaticani.*

the temples "at the request of several persons"?[63] In 495, several Roman aristocrats wanted to restore the celebration of the Lupercalia in Rome according to the ancient ceremonial.[64] During the siege of the city by Vitigis, some Romans wanted to reopen the temple of Janus.[65] Magic and astrology still had their adherents.[66] Finally, pagan beliefs were still solidly rooted among the rural and urban populace.[67] If Christians were to purify their faith, should not learned laymen and clergy point the way by purging their own works of any hint of paganism?

Furthermore, if the purification the rigorists sought was to be effected, scholars' works would have to be read and understood by great numbers of believers, not only by the educated. But the scholars could claim only a limited audience, and therefore the rigorists' complaint that classical religious culture was artificial was justified. Christians, of course, were aware of this problem before the sixth century. Many, following Augustine's example, said that they preferred *res* to *verba*[68] and preferred "to see themselves reprimanded by grammarians rather than misunderstood by the people."[69] But while they affirmed in the prefaces of their

[63] Cassiodorus, *Var.*, III, 31 (*MGH, AA*, XII, 95, l. 30); ibid., II, 35–36 (p. 66). For the statues erected in the sixth century, see *CIL*, XI, 268.

[64] Gelasius I, *Adversus Andromachum senatorem et ceteros Romanos qui lupercalia secundum morem pristinum colenda constituunt*, ed. G. Pomarès, in *SC*, vol. 65 (Paris, 1960): 163–69. Christians continued to participate in the celebrations despite the pope's warning. Pomarès skillfully compared the text of this letter with the masses from the *Leonine Sacramentary* which also allude to the survival of paganism. The masses were written by Gelasius in 495.

[65] Procopius, *Bell. goth.*, I, 25 (Haury ed., p. 126).

[66] Cassiodorus, *Var.*, IV, 22–23 (p. 124). See Schneider, *Rom und Romgedanke*, pp. 28ff.

[67] Caesarius of Arles' sermons contain the best information on pagan practices. See Arthur Malnory, *Saint Césaire, évêque d'Arles, 503–543* (Paris, 1894), pp. 221–28.

[68] Jerome, *Comm. in Ezech.*, XII, 50 (*PL*, XXV, 394): "In ecclesiasticis rebus non quaerantur verba sed sensus, id est panibus sit vita sustentanda, non siliquis." False eloquence was often compared to the pods the swine ate in the parable of the prodigal son; see Bernhard Blumenkranz, "*Siliquae porcorum*: l'exégèse médiévale et les sciences profanes," in *Mélanges d'histoire du Moyen Age dediés à la mémoire de Louis Halphen* (Paris, 1951), pp. 11–17. See also Ambrose, *Expositio evangelii secundum Lucam*, II, 42 (*CSEL*, 32, pt. 4: 65); Augustine, passim (see Marrou, *Saint Augustin*, p. 349); Victricius of Rouen, *De laude sanctorum*, X, 20 (*PL*, XX, 452); Salvian, preface to *De gubern. Dei, MGH, AA*, I-1, 1: "Nos autem qui rerum magisquam verborum amatores"; Sidonius, *Ep.* VII, 13 (*MGH, AA*, VIII, 119): "In quibus [litteris] eum magis occupat medulla sensuum quam spuma verborum."

[69] See, in the same spirit, Constantius, preface to *Vita Germani episc. Autissiodorensis*, *MGH, SRM*, VII-1, 220: "Cui verborum abjectio displicuerit, sensu placebit." See also the list of examples which K. Sittl gave in *Archiv für lateinische Lexicographie* 6 (1889): 560. This list is far from complete, however. For those "admissions of incapacity," see Hagendahl, *La correspondance de Ruricius*, p. 96; Leonid Arbusow, *Colores rhetorici: Eine Auswahl rhetorischen Figuren und Gemeinplätze als Hilfsmittel für akademische Übungen an mittelalterlichen Texten* (Göttingen, 1948), p. 105; and Curtius, p. 509.

works their intention to adopt *rusticitas* rather than *sermo scholasticus*,[70] in practice it proved more difficult for them to abandon the intellectual habits they had developed in the rhetor's school and to adapt their writings and speeches for the popular public. But this failure was precisely the core of the problem: Christians had to preach a truth which would be accessible to everyone. This need was more acutely felt at the end of the fifth and the beginning of the sixth centuries. More than ever, the old theme of "the Gospels preached to sinners and not to rhetors" was an extremely relevant one.[71]

Thus, the classical poetical form whose success we have described became suspect even in its Christian adaptation. Arator and Ennodius tried to legitimize their own poetry by recalling that poetry was not foreign to the Old Testament.[72] Avitus of Vienne went even further, however, when he announced to his brother in the second preface to his poetical works that he was abandoning the genre "because too few understand the measure of syllables."[73] A few years later the same ignorance led Bishop Leo of Nola to ask one of his clerics to render into prose Paulinus' poem on the virtues of Saint Felix.[74] The first re-

---

[70] See the famous formula of Augustine, *In Ps.*, 138, 20 (*CCL*, XL, 2004): "Melius est reprehendant nos grammatici quam non intelligant populi." See also the *De doctrina christiana*, XV, X, 24–25, with Marrou's comments (*Saint Augustin*, p. 525); Jerome, *Comm. in Ezech.*, XII, 40 (*PL*, XXV, 370); Ruricius, *Ep.* II, 38 (*MGH, AA*, VIII, 339): "Rusticitatem meam malo prodere quam perdere caritatem"; Claudius Marius Victorius, *Alethia*, preface, 119 (*CSEL*, 16, pt. 1: 363); Avitus of Vienne, *Prologus, MGH, AA*, VI-2, 201–2: "Si religionis propositae stilum non minus fidei quam metri lege servaverit, vix aptus esse poemati queat"; and G. Bartelink, "*Sermo piscatorius*," *Studia Catholica* 35 (1960): 267–73.

[71] This theme was frequently evoked. See Sulpicius Severus, *Vita Martini*, I, 4 (*CSEL*, vol. 1); Paulinus of Nola, *Ep.* V, 6 (*CSEL*, 29: 28). For the sixth century, see Justus of Urgel: "Ille [Christus] admonuit qui regnum Dei non in sermone sed in veritate" (ed. Zacarias Garcia Villada, in *Historia eclesiástica de España*, 2, pt. 2 [Madrid, 1933]: 265).

[72] Arator, *Ep. ad Vigilium*, 23–26 (*CSEL*, 72: 4):

> Metrica vis sacris non est incognita libris;
> Psalterium lyrici composuere pedes;
> Hexametris constare sonis in origine linguae
> Cantica, Hieremiae, Job quoque ducta ferunt.

Arator undoubtedly had in mind Sedulius, *Pasc. Carm.*, I, 23 (ibid., 10: 17) and even Jerome, *Interpretatio chronicae Eusebii Pamphili*, preface (*PL*, XXVII, 36). See also Ennodius, *Carm.* 1, 6 (*MGH, AA*, VII, 4): "Prophetarum insignissimi sub legem versuum verba redigentes carmine desideria sua et vota cecinerunt."

[73] Avitus, *Prologus, MGH, AA*, VI-2, 275: "Quod paucis intelligentibus mensuram syllabarum servando canat."

[74] *AS*, Jan., I, 946: "Prosae sensibus explicare vitam Felicis Paulino heroico versus digestans." Leo of Nola was a contemporary of Pope Agapitus. They were together in Constantinople.

quirement for a hagiographic work was that it be understood by a large public.

Hagiography as a literary form was destined from its origins for a popular audience, but classical writers who took over the genre divorced it from the public with the inevitable result. As early as the fifth century, two priests—Verus, who wrote the *Life of Saint Eutropius*, and Constantius, the author of the *Life of Saint Germanus*—tell us that they tried to write more simply.[75]

Eugippius was troubled by the same problems at the beginning of the sixth century, when he tried to write a *Life of Saint Severinus*. The history of the evolution of this text merits telling because it illustrates well the demand for clarity during this period. A noble layman who was a hagiographer in his leisure moments had asked Eugippius for documentation on Saint Severinus, the apostle of Noricum whose remains had been restored to Naples. Eugippius complied, but he revealed to one of his Roman friends, Deacon Paschasius, that he felt a bit uneasy about confiding the redaction of Severinus' *Life* to a layman whose literary style he already knew. Eugippius feared that the work would be incomprehensible to the masses and that the obscurity of the author's eloquence would not permit the admirable deeds of the saint's life to shine through.[76] Judging himself incompetent to write the *Life*, Eugippius asked Paschasius to take charge of it. But the Roman deacon replied that he could not do it any better than Eugippius, whose version already possessed the desired qualities of simplicity and clarity.[77] Eugippius, who as we shall see was a learned man, had lucidly anticipated the danger.

Simplicity of form was also required of preachers. Pomerius of Arles, a former rhetor, contrasted the *declamatores* with the *doctores* in a

75 Verus, *Vita s. Eutropii episc. Arausicani*, in *Gallia christiana novissima: Histoire des archévêchés, évêchés, et abbayes de France*, ed. Joseph H. Albanés, 6 (Montbéliard and Valence, 1916): 10; Constantius, *Vita Germani episc. Autissiodorensis*, preface and chap. 46 (*MGH, SRM*, VII-1, 250, 283). Gustave Bardy, "Constantius de Lyon, biographe de saint Germain," in *Saint Germain d'Auxerre et son temps*, ed. Gabriel Le Bras (Auxerre, 1950), p. 96, does not take these statements seriously and prefers to see in them the effects of rhetorical training. His opinion is too absolute. Constantius' *Vita* should be compared to Ennodius' *Vita* of Epiphanius.

76 Eugippius, *Ep. ad Paschasium diaconum, MGH, AA*, I-2, 1: "Ne forsitan saeculari tantum litteratura politus tali vitam sermone conscriberet in quo multorum plurimum laboraret inscitia et res mirabiles . . . obscura disertitudine non lucerent."

77 Ibid., p. 3: "Direxisti commemoratorium cui nihil possit adicere facundia peritorum et opus quod ecclesiae possit universitas recensere, brevi reserasti compendio . . . elocutus es simplicius, explicasti facilius, nihil adiciendum labori vestro studio nostro credidimus."

passage of his *De vita contemplativa*: "The former try with all the strength of their verbiage for a carefully worked declamation, while the latter seek the glory of Christ with a sober and fluent style."[78] Pomerius is thought to have had some influence on his former, though ephemeral, student Caesarius of Arles after the latter became an abbot.[79] Could it, rather, have been the other way about? Caesarius, the monk from Lérins without any classical culture, always adopted a popular tone in his sermons:

> I humbly ask that the ears of the learned tolerate some rustic expressions without complaining, so that the Lord's flock might receive celestial nourishment in a simple and down-to-earth language. Since the ignorant and simple cannot raise themselves to the heights of the learned, let the learned deign to lower themselves to the ignorance of the simple. Educated men can understand what has been said to the simple, while the simple are incapable of profiting from what would have been said to the learned.[80]

A reading of Caesarius' sermons furnishes convincing proof that this celebrated passage was not merely a matter of form.[81] His sermons, of course, are not entirely devoid of eloquence, but their eloquence is not studied: rather, it derives from the subject treated. Caesarius recommended simplicity of form to bishops: "It matters little that they know not the art of eloquence; they can explicate the obscurities of Scripture

---

[78] Pomerius, *De vita contemplativa*, I, 22 (*PL*, LIX, 439): "Denique alia est ratio declamatorum et alia debet esse doctorum. . . . Illi affectant suorum sensuum deformitatem tanquam velamine quodam phalerati sermonis abscondere, isti eloquiorum suorum rusticitatem student pretiosis sensibus venustare."

[79] Carl Franklin Arnold, *Caesarius von Arelate und die gallische Kirche seiner Zeit* (Leipzig, 1894), pp. 120–21.

[80] Caesarius, *Sermo* LXXXVI (Morin ed., p. 353): "Et ideo rogo humiliter ut contentae sint eruditae aures rustica aequanimiter sustinere, dummodo totus grex domini simplici et ut ita dixerim, pedestri sermone pabulum spiritale possit accipere. Et quia imperiti et simplices ad scholasticorum altitudinem non possunt ascendere, eruditi se dignentur ad illorum ignorantiam inclinare."

Louis Furman Sas sees this speech, perhaps with a bit of hyperbole, as "the manifest of the linguistic revolution of the sixth century" ("Changing Linguistic Attitudes in the Merovingian Period," *Word: Journal of the Linguistic Society of New York* 5 [1949]: 132).

[81] There have been various, even conflicting, assessments of the style of the sermons. Malnory speaks of a "complete lack of skill in the art of writing" (*Saint Césaire*, p. 18), while Maurice Pontet finds that "Caesarius presents and drapes his prose in the toga of antique eloquence" (*L'exégèse de saint Augustin, prédicateur* [Paris, 1946], p. 86). Buchner *Die Provence*, pp. 66–67, goes so far as to compare a page from Caesarius to Ennodius' style. See, however, Morin's preface to his edition of the sermons (*S. Caesarii opera omnia*, 1: viii), and I. Bonini, "Lo Stile nei sermoni di Cesario d'Arles," *Aevum* 36 (1962): 240–57.

with their own resources."[82] To take the expression of Saint Jerome, "the preacher should arouse wailing rather than applause."[83] These counsels belong to all periods and were voiced in other times when false eloquence and preciosity invaded the pulpit.[84] At the beginning of the sixth century, they accompanied a renewal of evangelism.

How can the desire for greater and greater simplicity be explained? By a diminution of the learned clientele? Undoubtedly. By a reaction against the excesses of an overly complicated style? Certainly.[85] But there is more to it than this. There remains a more positive explanation, which has not yet received the attention it deserves.

The Church was turning wholeheartedly to the urban and rural masses. In order to reach them it needed a language adapted to their usage. With the Constantinian peace, the Church bent itself to the conversion of the aristocracy, a task which it had almost completed with State support in the form of antipagan legislation.[86] But the rural masses were yet to be evangelized. The settlement of semi-Christianized Barbarians in the interior of the Empire threatened to encourage the rebirth of pagan customs.[87] Rural churches were organized in the fifth century, and many texts from the beginning of the sixth century show that that effort continued, particularly in Provence and Spain. Caesarius of Arles himself was preoccupied with the evangelization of the countryside and the instruction of the rural masses.[88] In order to make sermon

---

[82] *Vita Caesarii*, II (ed. Morin, p. 300, l. 13): "Sciens quia non deesset illis perfectae loquutionis ornatus quibus spiritalis eminet intellectus." Caesarius, *Sermo* I, 12 (Morin ed., p. 10, ll. 5–10): "Sed forte dicit aliquis: non sum eloquens, ideo non possum aliquid de scripturis sanctis exponere . . . ut etiam si sit in aliquo eloquentia saecularis, non oportet pontificali eloquio praedicare quod vix ad paucorum potest intelligentiam pervenire."

[83] Jerome, *Ep.* LII, 8 (*CSEL*, 54: 428). Caesarius, *Sermo* I, 20 (Morin ed., p. 19): "Sacerdote praedicante oportet ut magis gemitus suscitentur quam plausus."

[84] Origen, *Contre Celse*, VII, 59–60 (ed. Marcel Borret, *SC*, vol. 150 [Paris, 1969]). See, for the fourth century, Lucifer of Cagliari, *Moriendum esse pro Dei filio*, PL, XIII, 1028, and, for the fifth century, Peter Chrysologus, *Sermo* XLIII (*PL*, LII, 320): "Populis populariter est loquendum." For the seventeenth century, see Vincent de Paul, *Saint Vincent de Paul: Correspondance, Entretiens, Documents . . .* , ed. Pierre Coste, 13 vols. (Paris, 1920–24), 11: 342ff.

[85] See Marrou, *Education*, p. 445. Beginning in this period, classical Latin must not have been understood by the people. See Ferdinand Lot, "A quelle époque a-t-on cessé de parler latin?" *ALMA* 6 (1931): 99ff., and Einar Löfstedt's reservations in *Late Latin* (Oslo, 1959), pp. 11ff.

[86] Fliche-Martin, 4: 1–30.

[87] Ibid., pp. 586ff., with extensive bibliography.

[88] Ibid., p. 580. For the sixth century, see the Council of Agde, 53–54 (Mansi, VIII, 333–34); Third Council of Vaison, 1 (ibid., 726); Council of Tarragona, 511, c. 7 (ibid., 542). For Provence, see Malnory, *Saint Césaire*, p. 133, and H. G. J. Beck, *The Pastoral Care of Souls* (Rome, 1950). For Spain, see Garcia Villada, *Historia eclesiástica*, 2, pt. 1:

themes suitable for everyone available to preachers, Caesarius composed a homilary inspired by Augustine's sermons and assured its
diffusion.[89]

The urban population, if it was converted, often possessed only a
rudimentary Christianity. Caesarius was equally concerned with the
religious instruction of the faithful of Arles. His sermons reveal what
he demanded of them: in addition to attendance at numerous offices,
he asked them to study the sacred text at home, to "ruminate" on the
message they heard in church,[90] to read at dinner and during the long
winter nights,[91] and to meditate on religious texts. If they were unable
to read, they were to have the reading done by someone else, even if
they had to pay him.[92] They were also to sing psalms and hymns, for
two reasons.[93] Singing especially facilitated the religious instruction of
the faithful.[94] Heretics were the first to see that they could attract interest by singing hymns to the people,[95] and so Catholics imitated them.
In Africa at the beginning of the sixth century, Fulgentius wrote an
abecedarian psalm against the Arians, which was inspired by Augustine's famous *Psalmus contra partem Donati*.[96] At the same time at
Arles, Caesarius introduced the use of antiphonal chant, which Ambrose had first used at Milan in the fourth century.[97] Rhyming hymnic
poetry, those *quasi versus* despised by learned men, also circulated and
was much more popular than Christian classical poetry.

Sacred chant, secondly, represented the best means to combat traditional music, whether sacred or profane. The Eastern and Western
Church Fathers rose up against the flourishes of chromatic music and
the use of various instruments in liturgical music.[98] Monodic melody,

---

230, and Justo Fernandez Alonso, *La cura pastoral en la España romano-visigoda* (Rome,
1955), p. 396.

[89] Caesarius, *Sermo* CXCVIII, 5 (Morin ed., p. 579): "Lectiones divinas . . . in domibus
vestris relegite . . . verbum Dei . . . ruminantes."

[90] Ibid., VII, 1; VIII, 2 (pp. 39, 44).

[91] Ibid., VI, 2 (p. 33): "Quando noctes longiores sunt qui erit qui tantum possit dormire
ut lectionem divinam vel tribus horis non possit aut ipse legere aut alios legentes audire?"

[92] Ibid., VI, 8 (p. 36).

[93] Ibid., XV, 3; CI, 5 (pp. 73, 402).

[94] Cassiodorus, *Expositio psalmorum*, CCL, 97: 5: "Cantus qui aures oblectat et animas
instruit."

[95] Henri Leclercq, "Historiens du christianisme," *DACL*, VI-2, 2859.

[96] "Un psaume abécédaire inédit de S. Fulgence de Ruspe contra les Vandales ariens,"
ed. C. Lambot, *RB* 48 (1936): 221–34.

[97] *Vita Caesarii*, I, 19 (Morin ed., p. 303).

[98] For the East, see Ego Wellesz, *A History of Byzantine Music and Hymnography*
(Oxford, 1949). For the West, see *Les Pères de l'Eglise et la Musique* (Paris, 1931) by
Théodore Gerold, and Solange Corbin, *L'Eglise à la conquête de sa musique* (Paris, 1960).

which the Church borrowed from the synagogue, appeared to them to be a more authentic expression of prayer to God. On the other hand, the singing of hymns and Psalms could also rival profane and popular songs, whose couplets were often immoral. As Saint Jerome and many monastic leaders after him said, Psalms ought to be veritable "love songs."[99]

III. THE SOLUTION: A UNIQUELY RELIGIOUS CULTURE

For the rigorists, then, there was no possible compromise between antique and Christian culture. If one wanted to place his mind at the service of God, he began by rejecting classical literature, since one could not simultaneously sacrifice to the cult of the Muses and to God. Whoever, like the monk, turned his back on worldly wisdom and abandoned the world, renouncing his family, his wealth, his trade, and even the baths,[100] also had to bid farewell to profane learning.

Caesarius, a Gallo-Roman, and the Italian Benedict took these steps almost simultaneously. Caesarius settled in Arles around 500 and was encouraged by his friends to take lessons from Pomerius, the grammarian. One night, his biographers tell us, while Caesarius slept on a book, he dreamed that a dragon came out of the book to murder him.[101] The anecdote, of course, reminds one of the famous dream of Jerome. Still, it does indicate Caesarius' disgust for classical studies. Young Benedict of Nursia was sent by his parents to the schools of Rome also around 500. Gregory the Great, his biographer, relates that hardly had Benedict begun his studies when he stopped them, frightened by the dangers which menaced him.[102] We will see later that Caesarius and Benedict were never to return to these studies.

Monastic influence was so great at the end of the fifth century that the clergy, especially the bishops, gradually became aware of the incompatibility of profane and Christian culture. An old principle of the Church held that bishops were supposed to abstain from reading pagan works,[103] but, as we have seen, the concept was rarely honored.

[99] See below, chap. 4, n. 99, and chap. 10, sect. III.C, for these popular songs.
[100] Ferrandus, *Vita Fulgentii*, II, 6 (Lapeyre ed., p. 19).
[101] *Vita Caesarii*, I, 9 (Morin ed., p. 300).
[102] Gregory the Great, *Dial.*, II (Moricca ed., p. 71). See above, chap. 1, n. 230.
[103] *Didascalia Apostolorum*, I, 6 (ed. R. Rugh Conolly [Oxford, 1929], p. 13).

Even in the middle of the fifth century, Bishop Hilary of Arles unashamedly composed occasional verses inspired by pagan poets.[104] His colleague, Agroecius of Sens, wrote a treatise on orthography,[105] while Remigius of Reims composed school exercises which attracted Sidonius' admiration.[106]

In southern Gaul toward the end of the century, however, we begin to see a different trend. Former students of rhetors, who later became bishops there, were quite aware of the incompatibility of sacred and profane culture. Consider the case of Sidonius Apollinaris. When he became bishop of Clermont around 470, he worked for his church by composing masses and religious hymns.[107] Certain formulae he used suggest that he might have had some scruples in taking up his former intellectual habits. When he reworked Terence for his son's education, for example, he confessed that nature had triumphed over his *professio*.[108] He admitted that the reputation of a poet tainted the cleric's dignity and decided to write only religious poetry.[109] When we turn next to Ennodius, who thirty years later, in 511, became bishop of Pavia, we see the same reaction. He, too, was of the opinion that his vocation prohibited him from using an overly mannered style[110] and declared that he detested even the names of the liberal arts.[111] He wanted to devote himself to true wisdom,[112] contrasting Christian severity with profane softness.[113] His colleague, Bishop Avitus of Vienne,

[104] Hilary, *Versus fontis ardentis*, in *Anth. lat.*, no. 487. See Schanz, IV-2, 528.

[105] Schanz, IV-2, 206. The treatise published in Keil, 7: 112, was addressed to Bishop Eucherius of Lyon (died 450), who had sent the grammarian Caper's book to Agroecius.

[106] Sidonius, *Ep*. IX, 7 (*MGH, AA*, VIII, 154). These declamationes are no longer extant. See Roger, pp. 72, 78.

[107] See Schanz, IV-2, 46.

[108] Sidonius, *Ep*. IV, 12 (p. 64): "Naturae meminens et professionis oblitus." For the different meanings of *professio*, see Cyrille Vogel, *La discipline pénitentielle en Gaule* (Paris, 1952), pp. 128–29.

[109] Sidonius, *Ep*. IX, 16 (p. 171): "Clerici ne quid maculet rigorem fama poetae." See also *Ep*. IX, 12 (p. 162): "Primum ab exordio religiosae professionis huic principaliter exercitio renuntiavi, quia nimirum facilitati posset accommodari, si me occupasset levitas versuum . . . Post mortem non opuscula sed opera pensanda."

[110] Ennodius, *Ep*. II, 6 (*MGH, AA*, VII, 38): "Periculum facere de eloquentiae pompa non debeo nec praesumo qualiter quis valeat experiri, cum professionem meam simplici sufficiat studere doctrinae."

[111] Ibid., IX, 1 (p. 292, l. 22), to Arator: "Ego ipsa studiorum liberalium nomina jam detestor."

[112] Ennodius, *Eucharisticon de vita sua*, MGH, AA, VII, 301, l. 23: "Sic dum me concinnationis superfluae in rhetoricis et poeticis campis lepos agitaret, a vera sapientia mentitam secutus abcesseram." See especially paragraphs 5–8 of this "confession."

[113] Ennodius, *Paraenesis didascalica*, ibid. p. 311, ll. 21–23: "Christi militis insitum rigorem / Elumbem patimur cavere ductum."

was of the same mind gave up writing profane poetry because of his vocation.[114]

These three examples, occurring so close to one another, are significant. They would seem to indicate that, by this time, the injunction against the reading of pagan works by bishops was an actuality. In fact, one article in the *Statuta ecclesiae antiqua*, a collection which undoubtedly issued from the Provençal clergy during the second half of the fifth century, mentions this very matter.[115] Sidonius, Avitus, and Ennodius must have known this canon, whose existence would explain at least their formal reticence.

The injunction, furthermore, was part of a whole. Other articles forbade bishops anything that smacked of the laity, or of worldly affairs, sumptuous dinners, and relations with women.[116] Profane culture was one of those habits the bishop had to abandon when he left the lay state. We should not forget, however, that, as under the Empire, many bishops came rather late to the episcopacy and had been chosen from among rich lay aristocrats.[117] In order to assure their fidelity, the Church demanded that they be ordained after a year of *probatio*.[118] "Intellectual conversion" was one of the elements of the *conversio morum* that bishops had to undergo during this testing period.

Once ordained, bishops more or less kept their pledges, as Sidonius' case demonstrates.[119] Avitus' renunciation came several years after

[114] Avitus, *Prologus*, MGH, AA, VI-2, 275: "Decet enim dudum professionem, nunc etiam aetatem nostram, si quid scriptitandum est, graviori potius stilo operam."

[115] *Statuta ecclesiae antiqua*, 5, in *S. Caesarii opera omnia*, ed. Morin, 2: 91: "Ut episcopus gentilium libros non legat, haereticum autem pro necessitate temporis." For the evolution of this famous collection, see Fournier and Le Bras, *Histoire des collections canoniques*, 1: 20, n. 1, and, especially, Charles Munier, *Les Statuta ecclesiae antiqua . . .* (Strasbourg and Paris, 1960). Munier thinks that Gennadius of Marseille was the author. Historians are not in agreement on the meaning of canon 5. Dom Botte thinks that, like the *Didascalia*, it did not involve the authority of the Church; see his review of Marrou, *Education*, in *BTAM* 6 (1950): 89, no. 283.

[116] *Statuta ecclesiae antiqua*, chaps. 4, 6, 8, and the preface to the *Statuta*, p. 90, in *S. Caesarii opera omnia*, ed. Morin, vol. 2.

[117] See Beck, *The Pastoral Care of Souls*, pp. 6–9, for the aristocratic origins of sixth-century bishops from southern Gaul. There is no similar general work for Italy. We should note, though, that Bishop Julianus of Sabina (beginning of the sixth century) was a former *defensor*; see Gregory the Great, *Dial.*, I, 4 (pp. 33–34). Agnellus of Ravenna, in the middle of the sixth century, was a former military officer (*Liber pont. eccl. Ravenn.*, 84 [*MGH, SRL*, p. 333]).

[118] Council of Sardicca, c. 13: *De laicis non faciendis episcopis*, PL, LVI, 407. For the sixth century, Council of Agde, c. 16, in *S. Caesarii opera omnia*, ed. Morin, 2: 45: "Ut nullus ex laicis clericus ordinetur nisi ante aliquos annos vel unius spatio fuerit praemissa conversio." See Vogel, *La discipline pénitentielle*, pp. 130–31, and Gaudemet, *L'Eglise dans l'Empire romain*, pp. 149–52. For the *conversi*, see Paul Galtier, in *DSp*, 2: 1218–24.

[119] Mommsen, *MGH, AA*, VIII, xlviii, thinks that Sidonius abandoned poetry after

his ordination and then with some reservations.[120] If he seemed to exclude Virgil from his circle of acquaintances, he nevertheless used him as an authority in a discussion with Viventiolus, the rhetor.[121] As for Ennodius, it is not entirely certain, as has been assumed, that he forbade himself all contact with profane culture after 511.[122] It was just as difficult for the bishops to keep their pledges as it had been for other accomplished scholars. The monk's way of life could not be imposed on bishops. If they were to be asked to renounce classical letters, they would have to be recruited differently.

The demands placed on the bishops were also placed on clerics in major orders. Once in the clericature, they too had to renounce the world—at least in principle. Actually, those we can observe mixed dangerously close with the faithful, from whom they were not yet differentiated by distinctive clerical garb.[123] Commodian and Salvian, following Jerome and Sulpicius Severus, denounced the relaxation of clerical morality.[124] One of the chief reasons for this crisis stemmed from hasty recruitment of the clergy. As we have seen, the Church tried to win the greatest number of people over to Christ. In 524, the Council of Arles stated that the multiplication of churches necessitated the ordination of more clerics.[125] In order to obviate the more pressing situations, clerics were named without having been tested by a probationary year. Their religious and moral training was thus imperfect,

---

468, but there is no proof that he did so. As a bishop he studied the *Life of Apollonius of Tyana*; see *Ep.* VIII, 3 (p. 128): "cum Tyaneo nostro. . . ."

[120] Avitus, *Prologus, MGH, AA*, VI-2, 275, ll. 6–8: "Sane a faciendis versibus pedibusque jugendis pedem de cetero relaturus nisi forte evidentis causae ratio extorserit alicujus epigrammatis necessitatem."

[121] Avitus, *Ep.* LI (45) (*MGH, AA*, VI-2, 80, l. 6): "vester poeta." See above, chap. I, sect. II.B.3, for the letter to Viventiolus.

[122] Marrou, *Education*, p. 457, seems to follow Schanz, IV-2, 316, on this point. In order to be certain, we would have to establish the chronology of Ennodius' works. Vogel tried this in his preface (p. xxviii), but Sundwall came to a different conclusion (*Abhandlungen*, pp. 1–83). We have no works from Ennodius after 513, but this does not mean that he did not write any.

[123] See Pope Celestine's letter in 455 to the Viennoise and Narbonnaise bishops: "Discernendi a plebe vel caeteris sumus doctrina non veste" (*PL*, L, 431). The *Statuta ecclesiae antiqua*, from the same period, ordered clerics to wear a very simple costume (chap. 26, in *S. Caesarii opera omnia* ed. Morin, vol. 2).

[124] Sulpicius Severus, *Dial.*, I, 21–23 (*CSEL*, 1: 173); Commodian, *Instructiones*, II, passim (ibid., 15: 57ff.); Salvian, *De gubern. Dei*, III (ibid., 8: 57). These canons denounced clerics who were usurers, drunkards, magicians, soldiers, married men, and vagabonds. See the references in Vogel, *La discipline pénitentielle*, pp. 55–67.

[125] Council of Arles, 524, in *S. Caesarii opera omnia*, ed. Morin, 2: 61: "Tamen quia crescente ecclesiarum numero necesse est nobis plures clericos ordinare."

and quite often they were priests in name only. Just as often they were illiterate[126] or overeducated.

The overeducated, like the bishops, had to turn away from the liberal arts. As early as the mid-fifth century, the priest Rusticius confessed to Eucherius his fear of citing verses which he remembered from his youth.[127] At the beginning of the sixth century, Ennodius, a deacon at the time, said as much in a moment of intellectual humility. If he found it difficult to apply the principle to himself, however, he at least wanted it applied to others. When his relative Camilla sent her son to him for instruction in the liberal arts, Ennodius demurred on the grounds that the young child was already dedicated to the Church.[128] "Christ," he told her, "does not spurn those who come to him from liberal studies, but he does not tolerate those who leave his Splendor for them. I am ashamed to embellish with secular ornaments someone who has professed in the Church."[129] His use of the present indicative and the rest of his letter tell us that Ennodius, in fact, had nevertheless accepted the charge of the young cleric.[130]

This incident is a new proof of the malaise weighing on the clergy who were confronted with the problem of education. Educated clergy knew that it was necessary to break with classical culture but could not manage it despite conciliar decisions. Success would require the organization of special training for the clerics which would assure them a solid religious foundation. The monastic school would provide the model for the establishment of clerical schools.

---

126 See Siricius to Genesius (end of the fourth century), *PL*, XIII, 1130: *De presbytero qui ignorat orationem dominicam*; Council of Rome, 465, c. 3: "Inscii litterarum ad sacros ordines aspirans non audeant"; Gelasius I, *Ep. ad episc. Lucaniae, PL*, LIX, 53: "Ut nemo litteras nesciens vel aliqua parte corporis minutus provehatur ad clerum"; and ibid., 102. See also the imperial laws (*Corpus iuris civilis: Novellae*, VI, 4; CXXIII, 12; CXXXVII, 1). Some bishops at the Roman synod of 499 could not sign their names. Was this solely on account of illness? See *Var., MGH, AA*, XII, 408, n. 36.

127 Rusticius, *Ep. ad Eucherium*, 3 (*CSEL*, 31: 199): "Et vere dummodo orationibus tuis culpa caream, quod inter sacras apices commemorationesque sanctorum mundalium a me scripturarum promantur exempla."

128 Ennodius, *Ep.* IX, 9 (*MGH, AA*, VII, 297): "Nam parvulum tuum quem studiorum liberalium debuit cura suscepisse ante judicii convenientis tempora religionis titulis insignisti."

129 Ibid.: "Properantes ad se de disciplinis saecularibus salutis opifex non refutat, sed ire ad illas quemquam de suo nitore non patitur. . . . Erubesco ecclesiastica profitentem ornamentis saecularibus expolire."

130 Ibid.: "Suscepi tamen Deo auspice sanguinis mei vernulam." This letter would date from 511, according to Sundwall, *Abhandlungen*, p. 65.

The First Christian Schools at the Beginning
of the Sixth Century

I. MONASTIC EDUCATION

A. THE HERITAGE OF THE FIFTH CENTURY

From the beginning of the monastic movement, monks tried to fashion for themselves an original educational program. All the diverse activities of monastic life—prayer, the liturgy, reading, manual labor—had but one goal: the total transformation of the culture and habits of the men who left the world for the monastery. Monastic discipline was not so much an end in itself as it was a means to achieve perfection. Monasteries were actually schools—in the broad sense of that word—that taught the practical science of asceticism, which led to the theoretical science of contemplation. Monastic life presented hurdles to overcome and degrees to obtain. As Cassian said, the *coenobium* was a preparatory school (*juniorum schola*) which led to a superior degree, hermitical life.[1]

Monasteries had always accepted children and adolescents who came to them either in fulfillment of their parents' vows or because of their own inclinations to leave the world.[2] The education of these young people was the responsibility of abbots and, above all, of authors of monastic rules such as Pachomius or Basil. There were no other alternatives in the West. Martin at Ligugé and Tours, Honoratus at

---

[1] Cassian, *Conlationes*, XVII, 16 (*CSEL*, 13: 531): "De primis coenobii scolis, ad secundum anachoreseos gradum tendere." See also ibid., XIX, 2 (p. 536), where he spoke of the *coenobium* as a *juniorum schola*, a phrase which Owen W. Chadwick has translated rather more humorously than exactly as "kindergarten" (*John Cassian* [Cambridge, 1950], p. 49).

[2] Concern for young oblates grew in the mid-fifth century; see Leo the Great, *Ep.* LIV, 1208); Salvian, *Ad Ecclesiam*, II, 4, and III, 4 (*MGH*, *AA*, I-1, 133, l. 29, and 146, ll. 36–38); Gaudentius of Brescia, *Sermo VIII: De evangelii lectione primus*, PL, XX, 889.

Lérins, and the African abbots of the fifth century took upon themselves the moral, intellectual, and spiritual training of the youths who
came to them.[3] Elementary instruction, the study of biblical texts, and
sometimes the copying of manuscripts, an activity that was really more
manual than intellectual, formed the bases of this training.

Did anyone ever go beyond this basic training? Can we, in other
words, point to important centers of religious study in the West during
the fifth century? Lérins, founded around 410, has long been viewed
as just such a center. Thus, before proceeding further, we must first
consider the character of Lérinian culture, particularly since many monasteries of the first half of the sixth century were greatly influenced by
the spirit of this monastery.

Although many controversies have arisen over the so-called school of
Lérins, they have not resulted in a true understanding of the facts.
Lérins' first historians thought the monastery a center of both profane
and secular studies.[4] Roger and other scholars disputed this opinion
and depicted Lérins as a theological school partial to "semi-Pelagian"
theories.[5] I think that this is still going too far. In order to recapture
the true spirit of Lérinian culture, we must first describe the conditions
under which the monastery was founded.

Honoratus, the first abbot of Lérins, fled the world to live like the
desert ascetics. After a stay in the East, he chose the island of Lérins,
with the authorization of Bishop Leontius of Fréjus, as a place to retire
from the world like the solitaries on other western Mediterranean islands (Capraria, Gorgona, Palmaria, Galinaria, and the Hyères islands,
among others), who mortified their bodies by rigorous asceticism,
prayed day and night, recited the Psalms, and meditated on sacred
texts. A monastery was created for cenobites, while those who felt they
were strong enough for the life of an anchorite could settle in small,

---

[3] For monastic schools, see above, Introduction. *Vita Fulgentii*, XII (Lapeyre ed., p.
63), and Victor of Vita, *Historia persecutionis Africanae provinciae*, III, 65 (*CSEL*, 7:
105), should be added to the texts given by Bardy in "Origines des écoles monastiques
en Occident."

[4] L. Alliez, *Histoire du monastère de Lérins* (Paris, 1862), p. 26; Paul Lahargou, *De
schola lerinensi aetate merovingiaca* (Paris, 1892).

[5] Georg Kaufmann, *Rhetorenschulen und Klosterschulen oder heidnische und christliche
Cultur in Gallien während des 5. und 6. Jahrhunderts* (Leipzig, 1869), p. 69; Roger, p.
149. A. Loyen, "Sidoine Apollinaire et les derniers éclats de la culture classique dans la
Gaule occupée par les Goths," *Settimane*, 3: 278, speaks cautiously of a "center of intense
Christian meditation" without being more precise. P. Courcelle, in his "Nouveaux aspects
de la culture lérinienne," *REL* 46 (1969): 379–409, thinks that the Lérinians had a large
library.

isolated cells.[6] What we see at Lérins, then, is a monastic establishment organized along Eastern lines. Shortly after Lérins was founded, Cassian, who also came from the East, founded Saint Victor on the Continent at Marseilles,[7] while Castor, bishop of Apt and brother of Leontius of Fréjus, established a monastery at Ménerbes. Cassian's arrival was a major boon for Provençal monasticism. The great monk sent directives to Castor and dedicated two of his collections of "conferences" to Honoratus.[8] The rule of Lérins, whose text we no longer possess, must have been inspired by Eastern customs that had been adapted on Cassian's advice to conditions in the West.[9]

These influences affected the character of Lérinian culture. Lérins was first and foremost a center of asceticism. This is what the clergy and laymen sought when they came to Lérins for a short stay[10] or to retire there forever. Married men like Lupus, Eucherius, and Salvian came to Lérins, as did adolescents like Hilary, a relative of Honoratus, and Faustus, who perhaps came from Britain. These men had already received their intellectual training in the world and, thus, did not go to Lérins with that purpose in mind. Eucherius' taste for dialectic and grammar[11] and Salvian's and Hilary's talent for rhetoric[12] had already been acquired before they came to Lérins. It might seem surprising that they returned to these intellectual habits when they reentered the secular world. We should remember, however, that we are still in the first half of the fifth century, when the influence of the *Statuta ecclesiae antiqua* was not yet felt.

Did prospective monks, then, come to Lérins for biblical training? Probably, but not certainly. There is no explicit reference to the scientific study of Scripture in any text of Eucherius, of Hilary of Arles, or of Caesarius.[13] In their works they spoke only of silence, isolation, absti-

---

[6] Hilary, *Sermo de vita Honorati*, PL, L, 1249. See Jean Martial Leon Besse, *Les moines de l'ancienne France* (Paris, 1906), p. 37. Martin stayed for a time at Capraria; see Sulpicius Severus, *Vita Martini*, 6 (*CSEL*, 1: 116).

[7] For Cassian, see the excellent work by Chadwick, *John Cassian: A Study in Primitive Monasticism*. For Cassian's arrival in Marseille, see Henri Marrou, "Jean Cassien à Marseille," *RMAL* 1 (1945): 5–17.

[8] See Cassian, *De institutis coenobiorum*, CSEL, vol. 17, and *Conlationes*, XI, 17 (*CSEL*, vol. 13). *Conl.* 18 was dedicated to the monks of Hyères (ibid., p. 503).

[9] Carl Franklin Arnold argues this; see *Caesarius von Arelate und die gallische Kirche seiner Zeit* (Leipzig, 1894), p. 509 ("Die Lerinenser Regel").

[10] They undoubtedly came to Lérins as *conversi*. See Vogel, *La discipline pénitentielle*, pp. 134–35.

[11] Schanz, IV-2, 518.

[12] Ibid., p. 523. Hilary was a poet whose sermons were built on rhetoric.

[13] See especially a passage in Eucherius' *De laude heremi*, CSEL, 31: 193, where

nence, and prayer.[14] The only possible evidence for the scientific study of the Bible comes from Eucherius, who, when he sent his *Instructions* to his son, Salonius, recalled that Honoratus, then Hilary, and lastly Salvian and Vincent had introduced the young man to the "spiritualium rerum disciplinae."[15] The expression is vague and can refer to spiritual training as well as to intellectual research. Salonius, who became bishop of Geneva, later wrote an exegetical treatise in which his learning seems to owe more to his father's lessons than to those of his masters at Lérins.[16] The only works which issued from Lérins itself are those of the priest, Vincent.[17]

What really contributed to the celebrity of Lérins was its intervention in the mid-fifth century anti-Augustinian quarrel, although perhaps its true role in this dispute has been exaggerated.[18] Semi-Pelagianism, as it has been called, undoubtedly enjoyed some success at Lérins and other monastic environments, where asceticism demanded a great effort of the will. Only two Lérinians, however, threw themselves directly

---

Eucherius gave an overview of monastic life without mentioning studies. Instead, he contrasted those who devote themselves to "philosophy" to those who seek true wisdom in the desert: "Clari apud veteres saeculi hujus viri defatigati laboribus negotiorum suorum, in philosophiam se tamquam in domum suam recipiebant. Quanto pulchrius ad haec manifestissimae sapientiae studia divertunt, magnificentiusque ad solitudinum libertatem et desertorum secreta secedunt, ut philosophiae tantum vacantes, in illius heremi deambulacris tanquam in suis gymnasiis, exerceantur?" (ibid., 32 [p. 188]).

[14] Hilary, *Sermo de vita Honorati*, PL, L, 1259; *Vita Hilarii*, ibid., 1226–28. See also the *Vita Caesarii*, I, 6 (Morin ed., p. 299).

[15] Eucherius, *Instructionum ad Salonium, CSEL*, 31: 65: "Vixdum decem annos heremum ingressus inter illas sanctorum manus non solum imbutus verum etiam enutritus es sub Honorato patre illo inquam primo insularum postea etiam ecclesiarum magistro; cum illic beatissimi Hilari tunc insulari tironis sed jam nunc summi pontificis, doctrina formaret per omnes spiritualium rerum disciplinas, ad hoc etiam te postea consummantibus sanctis viris Salviano atque Vincentio eloquentia pariter scientia praeeminentibus." See Hilary's letter to Eucherius, *PL*, L, 1271: "Sed unum me de juvenibus tuis quorum haec eruditione ordinasti." Salvian likewise recalled this fact (*De gubern. Dei*, preface [*MGH, AA*, I-1, 1]), but it is hard to believe that he was ever a "Novice Master," as Nora K. Chadwick calls him (*Poetry and Letters in Early Christian Gaul* [London, 1955], p. 150).

[16] Salonius, *Expositiones mysticae in parabolas Salomonis et in Ecclesiasten, PL*, LIII, 967. See ibid., col. 998, for the definition of *Sapiens*: "Nonnunquam saecularis prudentia inimica Deo est et carnalis sapientia quamvis eloquentiae floribus exornetur, nullum tamen in se spiritualem . . . fructum continet."

[17] See José Madoz, *Excerpta Vincentii Lirinensis*, Estudios Onienses, vol. 1, pt. 1 (Madrid, 1940). Vincent perhaps owed his "humanist culture" to Augustine's works; see J. Madoz, "Cultura humanistica de San Vicente de Lerins," *Recherches de science religieuse* 39 (1951): 461–71 (also in *Mélanges Lebreton*, vol. 1). Vincent also wrote the *Commonitorium*, which contains several definitions that were to become famous; see Schanz, IV-2, 521, and the introduction to Michel Meslin's translation, *Saint Vincent de Lérins: Le Commonitorium* (Namur, 1959).

[18] For the "semi-Pelagian" affair, see Malnory, *Saint Césaire*, pp. 143ff., and Fliche-Martin, 4: 399.

into the quarrel—the famous Vincent, a priest at Lérins during the abbacy of Faustus, and Faustus himself. Faustus openly joined the fray only when he published his *De gratia Dei* after he had left Lérins to become bishop of Riez.[19] One can hardly speak of a "theological school"[20] and "Lérinian thought" apropos of the episodic intervention of two monks. Furthermore, one can scarcely speak of the continuity of "Lérinian thought." When the quarrel emerged again at the opening of the sixth century, Caesarius of Arles—a former Lérinian, to be sure—intervened, but in his capacity as bishop of Arles and, this time, in a totally different manner, since he rehabilitated the Augustinian doctrine.[21]

Lastly, we should add that at the end of the fifth and at the beginning of the sixth centuries, Lérins was still primarily a school for asceticism, as it had always been. When, about 490, the young Caesarius fled his family home for the refuge of Lérins, that was exactly what he sought.[22] We do have some information from Sidonius and Ennodius about the situation at Lérins during this period. Neither one ever spoke of the island as a scriptural or theological training center. In his poetic description of life at Lérins, Sidonius evoked, as had Eucherius, the fasting, vigils, and psalmody.[23] He congratulated Faustus for having kept to "the rigors of the old discipline" even after his election to the episcopate.[24] Elsewhere, he compared life at Lérins to military training. In another letter, he explicitly stated that Lérinians followed the traditions of Egyptian and Palestinian monks.[25] Ennodius of Pavia repeated the same information three times in different texts.[26] In his biography of Antony of Lérins, he portrayed his subject as an ascetic who had re-

---

[19] The *De gratia Dei* dates from 475. Faustus was definitely a bishop by 462; see Schanz, IV-2, 541.

[20] As did Roger, p. 149, and many others after him.

[21] Paul Lejay, *Le role théologique de Césaire d'Arles: Etude sur l'histoire du dogme chrétien en Occident au temps des royaumes barbares* (Paris, 1906).

[22] *Vita Caesarii*, I, 5 (Morin ed., p. 298).

[23] Sidonius, *Carm.* XVI, vv. 104–8 (*MGH, AA*, VIII, 241).

[24] Sidonius, *Ep.* IX, 3 (ibid., p. 152): "Rigorem veteris disciplinae non relaxaveris." This is the expression which Haarhoff, *Schools of Gaul*, p. 193, interpreted as an allusion to scholarly discipline.

[25] Sidonius, *Ep.* VI, 1 (pp. 94–95): "Post desudatas militiae Lirinensis excubias"; and ibid., VIII, 14 (pp. 145–46): "Affectans Memphiticos et Palaestinos archimandritas." See also Dynamius' *Vita sancti Maximi, PL*, LXXX, 31–40, which has recently been reedited by S. Gennaro (*Dinamii Vita sancti Maximi episcopi Reiensis: Fausti Reiensis Sermo de sancto Maximo episcopo et abbate* [Catania, 1966]). Maximus died around 460.

[26] Ennodius, *Ep.* VII, 14 (*MGH, AA*, VII, 237), in which he consoled Archotamia, whose son had left for Lérins. See also his *Vita Epifani*, ibid., pp. 93–95.

discovered at Lérins the lifestyle he previously knew with his master, Severinus.[27]

Was Lérins then a school for religious culture? Certainly, if by religious culture one means ascetical exercises and spiritual meditation on the Bible rather than learned exegesis and theology. If so many bishops were chosen from among former Lérinians, perhaps it was more for their spiritual and ascetical qualities than for their doctrinal learning.

B. Monastic Spirituality in the Sixth Century

The spirit of Lérins profoundly marked the monasteries established in Gaul and Italy during the first half of the sixth century. Caesarius was influenced by Lérinian customs when he organized his Arlesian monasteries.[28] Consequently, rules patterned after his—such as those of Aurelian of Arles, of Ferreolus, and even the *Regula Tarnantensis*[29] —also reflected this spirit. What was true for Provençal monasticism also applied to those monasteries in the kingdom of Burgundy about which we have some information. The monastery at Condat (later Saint Claude) was founded around 450 by Romanus, a former monk from Lyon who, like Honoratus, wanted to live the life of a desert monk.[30] When Romanus' disciple Eugendus became abbot of the monastery, he had his monks read the rule of Lérins and the works of Cassian.[31] In the sixth century, an anonymous monk wrote the *Lives*

---

[27] Ennodius, *Vita Antoni*, ibid., pp. 189–90 (written for Abbot Leontius): "Sanctorum expetamus exercitum et illam Lirinensis insulae cohortem irriguo inquiramus ardore." He called the island "nutrix sanctorum insula." For Severinus' ascetic monasticism, see Eugippius, *Vita Severini, MGH, AA*, I-2, 18, l. 24, and 19, l. 29.

[28] Caesarius, *Statuta sanctarum virginum*, 66 (Morin ed., 2: 120): "Secundum regulam monasterii Lyrinensis," and *Reg. monac.* (ibid., p. 153). See also Malnory, *Saint Césaire*, pp. 252ff.

[29] See Carlo De Clercq, *La législation religieuse franque de Clovis à Charlemagne* (Louvain and Paris, 1938), and Besse, *Les moines de l'ancienne France*, pp. 44ff., for these rules. The rule of Tarnant, whose provenance is unknown—Ternay near Vienne perhaps, but certainly not Agaune (see Jean-Marie Theurillat, "L'abbaye de Saint-Maurice d'Agaune des origines à la réforme canoniale (515–830 env.)," *Vallesia* 9 [1954]: 27) was influenced by Augustine's *Regula*. This rule is known as the *Regula Tarnatensis*, even though the Munich manuscript has *Tarnantensis*. For Ferreolus' rule, see Georg Holzherr, *Regula Ferioli: Ein Beitrag zur Entstehungsgeschichte und zur Sinndeutung des Benediktinerregels* (Einsiedeln, 1961).

[30] *Vita Romani*, 2 (*MGH, SRM*, III, 133). Bruno Krusch's arguments in favor of dating this text to the tenth century succumb to those of Louis Duchesne, René Poupardin, and P. W. Hoogterp, who unanimously date it to the sixth century. See P. W. Hoogterp, "Les Vies des Pères du Jura: Etude sur la langue," *ALMA* 9 (1934): 129–251.

[31] *Vita Eugendi*, 23 (*MGH, SRM*, III, 165).

of Romanus, Lupicinus, and Eugendus at the request of Abbot Marinus of Lérins.[32] The monasteries at Grigny, whose exact location still escapes us,[33] followed customs close to those of Lérins, according to Sidonius.[34] In 515, monks from Grigny founded the monastery of Agaune (Saint-Maurice-en-Valais) at the request of King Sigismund.[35] The *laus perennis*, a practice which began with this foundation, was unknown at Lérins, but its undeniably Eastern origins link it to the same ascetic spirituality found at Lérins.[36]

Numerous monastic centers, of which the most famous was Monte Cassino, were founded in the same spirit in Italy. After fleeing the schools of Rome around 500, Benedict, the founder of Monte Cassino, spent three years in solitude at Subiaco before he founded twelve monasteries of twelve monks each in imitation of Pachomius. He left Subiaco around 520 and finally established himself at Monte Cassino, according to Gregory the Great.[37] In reading Gregory's account, we do not see any major differences among Benedict, Honoratus, and Romanus, since all three took their models from the East. The rule which with all probability has been attributed to the abbot of Monte Cassino lends support to this statement. Its author was influenced by the *Vitae patrum*; by the rules of Basil, Cassian, and Caesarius; and perhaps by the customs of Lérins.[38] But Saint Benedict was not the only representative of this kind of monasticism in Italy. The acclaim which the great abbot was later to enjoy, thanks to Gregory the Great, has warped perspectives. Benedict must be assigned a more modest position among

---

[32] Ibid., p. 166: "Sancto Marino presbytero insulae Lirinensis abbate compellente."

[33] They were undoubtedly located on the right bank of the Rhône, in the diocese of Vienne. See M. Besson, *Monasterium Acaunensium* (Freiburg, 1913), pp. 152ff. Avitus liked to go there (*Ep.* LXXIV [65] [*MGH, AA*, VI-2, 91]).

[34] Sidonius, *Ep.* VII, 17 (*MGH, AA*, VIII, 124): "Secundum statuta Lirinensium patrum vel Grinincensium." Sidonius made this comparison apropos of the coming of a Lérinian to the Arvernian monastery of Saint-Cirgues—in itself further proof of the dissemination of Lérinian customs.

[35] *Vitae Abbatum Acaunensium*, MGH, SRM, III, 176. See Theurillat, "L'abbaye de Saint-Maurice d'Agaune," p. 32.

[36] Theurillat, "L'abbaye de Saint-Maurice d'Agaune," pp. 103–4. Agaune was in contact with Condat in the sixth century. See *Vita Abbatum Iurensium, prologus, MGH, SRM*, III, 131, l. 20.

[37] Gregory the Great, *Dial.*, II, prologue (Moricca ed., p. 71). See Philibert Schmitz, "Benoît de Nursie," *DHGE*, 7: 137–65, for the chronology of Benedict's life.

[38] Among the numerous articles discussing Cassian's influence on Benedict, see, in particular, B. Capelle, "Les oeuvres de Jean Cassien et la Règle bénédictine," *Revue liturgique et monastique* 7–8 (1929): 305, and idem, "Cassien, le Maître et Saint Benoît," *RTAM* 11 (1939): 110–18. See, more recently, Chadwick, *John Cassian*, pp. 174–78. For Lérinian influence, see Basilius Steidle, "Das Inselkloster Lerins und die Regel St. Benedikts," in *Benediktinische Monatschrift* 27 (1951): 376–87.

his predecessors and contemporaries in Italy, without, however, detracting any merit from the "Patriarch of Western Monks."

Except for the hermitages of the Tyrrhenian Sea, we know very little about Italian monasticism in the fifth century.[39] The translations of Jerome and Rufinus undoubtedly kindled some vocations. This body of literature was especially influential at the opening of the sixth century: the Gelasian Decree recommended Jerome's translations;[40] Dionysius Exiguus translated the *Life of Saint Pachomius*; the Roman deacon Paschasius translated the *Apophtegmata patrum*.[41] The political troubles which accompanied the demise of imperial power only served to encourage monastic vocations. When Benedict left the schools of Rome, he first joined some "honestiores viri" who were perfecting themselves in the Christian life at Enfide (Affile), perhaps under the direction of a priest.[42] In his *Dialogues*, Gregory the Great named a number of monasteries, nearly all of which were situated in the environs of Rome. The farthest one was that of Abbot Spes at Campello near Nursia;[43] others were located in the Sabine hills, in *provincia Valeria*, at the foot of the Lepini hills, and in the Alban hills.[44] In each monastery a uniform monastic routine embracing manual work, singing of hymns, and psalmody was observed. Unfortunately, Gregory limited his inquiries to the regions around Rome.

The rules which survive from this period fill in the gaps and provide information on ascetic life in monasteries that we cannot locate. Such is the case for the *Regula Tarnantensis* and especially for the equally mysterious *Regula Magistri*, which according to some historians was Benedict's model. The *Regula Magistri* can be dated to before the sev-

---

[39] See T. Leccisotti, "Aspetti e problemi del monachesimo in Italia," *Settimane*, 4: 312.

[40] *Decretum Gelasianum de libris recipiendis et non recipiendis, PL*, LIX, 157: "Vitas patrum Pauli Antonii Hilarionis et omnium heremitarum quas tamen vir beatissimus descripsit Hieronymus cum honore suscipimus." This so-called "Gelasian decretal" is perhaps from Provence and dates from the beginning of the sixth century; see *Clavis*, no. 1676.

[41] Courcelle, *LG*, p. 314.

[42] Gregory the Great, *Dial.*, II, 1 (p. 74). See Ildefons Herwegen, *Saint Benoît* (Paris, 1935), p. 31.

[43] Gregory the Great, *Dial.*, IV, 11 (p. 242, ll. 23–24).

[44] Monte Soracte (*Dial.*, I, 7 [p. 43]), presided over by Nonnosus; Subiaco (ibid., II, 1 [p. 76]), where Deodatus settled when Benedict came; Alatri (ibid., II, 35 [p. 128]), founded by the patricius Liberus; the monastery of Aequitius in "provincia Valeria" (ibid., I [p. 27]); Vicovaro (ibid., II, 3 [p. 80]), between Tivoli and Subiaco; Terracina (ibid., II, 22), founded by Benedict; Fondi (ibid., I, 1 [p. 17]), founded by the patricius Venantius at the beginning of the sixth century and directed by Honoratus, the son of one of his *coloni*; Tusculum (ibid., I, 3 [p. 27]), presided over by Abbot Fortunatus.

enth century on the basis of its surviving manuscripts, but its origin is still a matter for debate.[45] It has not yet been determined whether it came from Italy or from southern Gaul.[46] In any event, it is of the same tenor as the other rules. Influenced by the same texts, it organized an identical kind of spiritual life.

Some authors have traced the *Regula Magistri* to Spain.[47] What we know of Spanish monasticism does not contradict this hypothesis, and indeed, Spain could claim many monasteries before the invasions. Those in western Spain frequently served as refuges for the disciples of Priscillian.[48] Although they were severely tried during the fifth century, these monasteries did manage to survive. Furthermore, they could have been inspired by Eastern practices, since relations between Spain and the East had never been broken.[49] The Councils of Barcelona and Tarragona at the beginning of the following century spoke of monks without specifying their mode of life.[50] We know from Braulio of Saragossa, however, that the monastery of Asan was founded by Emilian. Emilian, a disciple of the hermit Felix, sought to imitate the great models of monasticism, Antony and Martin.[51] Shortly afterwards, Victorian, whose epitaph was written by Fortunatus,[52] came to Asan and founded numerous monasteries on both sides of the Pyrenees. According to some historians, Asan had the same impact as Lérins and became a nursery for bishops.[53]

[45] The abundant literature on the *Regula Magistri* is listed in *BTAM* 6 (1950–53), nos. 1027–66; in the preface to the edition prepared by Vanderhoven and Masai; in E. Franceschini, "La questione della regola di S. Benedetto," *Settimane*, 4: 221–25; in Holzherr, *Regula Ferioli*; and in B. Jaspert, "*Regula Magistri—Regula Benedicti*: Bibliographie ihrer Erforschung, 1938–1970," *Studia Monastica* 13 (1971): 129–71.

[46] The editors of the *Rule* are inclined toward southern Italy (*Regula Magistri*, ed. Vanderhoven and Masai, pp. 6off.). But several hints of "semi-Pelagianism" point to Provence. See D. Andriessen, "Si fratri impossibilia injungantur," in *Horae Monasticae: Sive studia et documenta vitam fulgurantem inradiantemque doctrinam divi patris Benedicti eiusque filiorumque conversationem illustrantia* (Tielt, 1947), pp. 81–93. The *Rule's* most recent editor, Adalbert de Vogüé, thinks that the Master's monastery was located to the south of Rome; see his introduction, *La Règle du Maître*, 1: 125ff.

[47] Anscari Mundó, "Il monachesimo nelle penisola iberica fino al sec. VII: Questioni ideologiche e letterarie," *Settimane*, 4: 92ff.

[48] Justo Perez de Urbel, *Los moñjes españoles en la edad media*, I (Madrid, 1933): 87–162.

[49] See Garcia Villada, *Historia eclesiástica*, 1, pt. 2: 255ff.

[50] Mansi, VIII, 543, and IX, 110; and Vives, *Inscripciones*, nos. 277, 278.

[51] Braulio, *Vita Aemiliani*, V, 12 (*PL*, LXXX, 706): "A caelicolis Antonio Martinoque vocatione, educatione atque miraculis omnia similis."

[52] Vives, *Inscripciones*, no. 283. We read "Pauli Antonique meritis quoequandus" in another epitaph (no. 284).

[53] D. Lambert, "Asan," *DHGE*, 4: 867–70; Mundó, "Il monachesimo," pp. 89–90.

Thus, in Gaul, Italy, and Spain the same spirit animated monastic life. If we turn to Africa, the same is true. There were many monasteries in the Vandal kingdom at the end of the fifth century. Unfortunately, of the fifty or so that we know, all that we do know about most of them are their names.[54] But one valuable text, the *Vita Fulgentii*, gives us entry to some of these foundations. When Fulgentius, future bishop of Ruspe, decided to abandon the world, he began by following the example of some monks he knew and fasted, prayed, and read on his estates.[55] Upon entering the monastery of Faustus, he lived like an Eastern ascetic.[56] When he became abbot, he shared the pleasure of reading Cassian's works with his brothers.[57] He later wanted to set out for Egypt, the home of monasticism, but the bishop of Syracuse dissuaded him, so he then joined a group of African solitaries at Junca. There he devoted himself to manual labor, studied in his little cell, made fans, and recopied manuscripts.[58] When he became bishop despite himself in 507, Fulgentius remained a monk, like Caesarius, and near his cathedral built a monastery, to which he often retreated.[59] Thus, the principles of spiritual life of Emilian, Benedict, Caesarius, and Fulgentius did not differ in essentials. One can truly speak of "Mediterranean monasticism." The monastic school, which we must now examine, likewise shared the same organization everywhere.

C. The Monastic School in the Sixth Century

Like the Eastern Fathers and Cassian, sixth-century monks thought of their monasteries as schools. In a sermon to the monks of Lérins, Caesarius of Arles cried out: "This holy island once welcomed my insignificant self into its affectionate arms. Like an illustrious and incomparable mother and a nurse who gives all good things, she made every effort to educate and to nourish me."[60] Upon opening Saint

---

[54] See Lapeyre, *Saint Fulgence de Ruspe*, p. 110, in the absence of a general study of African monasticism. For the site of Fulgentius' monastery, see J. Cintas and P. Cintas, "Un monastère de saint Fulgence," *Revue Tunisienne* (1940), pp. 243–50; ibid. (1942), pp. 252–55.

[55] Ferrandus, *Vita Fulgentii*, II (Lapeyre ed., pp. 15–16, 19).

[56] Ibid., II (p. 29).

[57] Ibid., V (p. 33): "Docendis fratribus peculiariter vacabat." Ibid., VIII (p. 47): "Aegyptiorum monachorum vitas admirabiles legens, Institutionum simul atque Collationum spiritali meditatione succensus."

[58] Ibid., XII (p. 65): "Nam et scriptoris arte laudabiliter utebatur."

[59] Ibid., XV (p. 79).

[60] Caesarius, *Sermo ad monachos*, CCXXXVI, 1 and 2 (Morin ed., p. 894): "Haec est quae et eximios nutrit monachos . . . et quos nutrit parvulos, reddit magnos. . . . Cum enim parvitatem meam haec sancta insula velut praeclara mater et unica ac singularis

Benedict's *Rule*, we see that the abbot of Monte Cassino was even more precise when he used the word *scola* to refer to his monastery. In the preface to the *Rule*, he said he wanted to found a "scola dominici servitii."[61] Some historians have equated the word *scola* with *militia* and consequently argue that Benedict was using an image which had been classic since Saint Paul's time in order to depict his monks training themselves like soldiers for spiritual combat.[62] Benedict certainly referred to military training more than once, but in this passage he described a monastery as a place where one acquires a science.[63] Perhaps, as others before him had done, he was even deliberately contrasting his monastic "school" to the one he had abandoned in his youth, the school of Christ to the antique school.[64] Furthermore, in several passages of his *Rule*, the legislator insisted on monastic pedagogy. The abbot is a master and father who speaks to his disciples: "Ausculta, o fili, pracepta magistri."[65] He is a master who must know and teach doctrine,[66] reprimand the undisciplined,[67] and adapt his methods to the different

bonorum omnium nutrix brachiis quondam pietatis exceperit et non parvo spatio educare vel nutrire contenderit."

[61] Benedict, *Regula*, prologue (Schmitz ed., p. 5): "Constituenda est ergo nobis scola dominici servitii." This sentence is found only in the Saint Gall manuscript and its family. But it is not very probable that the *Oxoniensis* represents the primitive version of the text. See Edward Cuthbert Butler, *Le monachisme bénédictin* (Paris, 1914), p. 180.

[62] Etienne Delaruelle, "Saint Benoît," in *Le Christianisme et l'Occident barbare*, ed. J. R. Palanque et al. (Paris, 1945), 2: 413, follows Rothenhausler's and Schuster's interpretation.

[63] Anselmo Lentini, *S. Benedetto: La Regola (testo, versione e commento)* (Montecassino, 1947), pp. 27–28, and Ildefons Herwegen, *Sinn und Geist der Benediktinerregel* (Einsiedeln, 1944), p. 39, use the word *scola* to refer to a school of Christian perfection and asceticism. See also Basilius Steidle, "Dominici schola servitii," *Benediktinische Monatsschrift* (1952), pp. 397–406, who studied the various sixth-century meanings of *schola* (or *scola*).

[64] Augustine, *Sermo* 177, 2 (*PL*, XXXVIII, 954), contrasted philosophers with the "scola Christi." See as well *Sermo* 17, 2, in Germain Morin, "Sancti Augustini sermones post Maurinas reperti . . . nunc primum disquisiti in unum collecti et codicum fide instaurati," in *Miscellanea agostiniana*, ed. Antonio Cassamassa, 2 vols. (Rome, 1930–31), 1: 82 ("Christus ille est enim omnium magister . . . sub illo in unam scholam convenimus."); and ibid., p. 112, l. 5; p. 566, l. 24. See further Peter Chrysologus, *Sermones* XI, XII, and XXX (*PL*, LII, 219, 224, 284); Facundus Hermianensis, *Pro defensione*, XII-1 (*PL*, LXVII, 825: "Nam si nunc ecclesia quaedam Christi scola est."); and de Vogüé, ed., *La Règle du Maître*, 1: 115.

[65] Benedict, *Regula*, prologue (p. 1). This text can be compared with Proverbs 1:8 ("Audi fili mi disciplinam patris tui") and with Proverbs 4:20 and 6:20. For the pedagogical tone of the rule, see A. Ceccarelli, "Note di pedagogia sulla Regola si S. Benedetto," *Benedictina* 4 (1950): 296–322.

[66] Benedict, *Regula*, II; ibid., VI, 15 (p. 21): "Nam loqui et docere magistrum concede tacere et audire disciplum convenit."

[67] Ibid., II, 64–65 (p. 11); IV, 72 (p. 17); V, 17–18 (p. 19); III, 16 (p. 14).

3. Monastic Cultural Centers circa 550

temperaments of his monks.[68] The pedagogical tone in the *Regula Magistri*, which bears many close resemblances to Benedict's rule, is even more pronounced. Here, a master answers the questions of his disciple, and several times the word *schola* is also used in the sense of a school.[69]

Our monasteries, then, were schools that fashioned a new life for those who were being "converted." Among these converts were some very young people whose presence, in turn, necessitated the formation of schools in the limited sense of the word. Eugendus became a monk at Condat when seven years old. Achivus, third abbot of Agaune, entered Grigny as an adolescent, over the objections of his parents.[70] Gregory of Tours referred to young monks at Agaune itself.[71] A school was organized under the direction of a *primiceria* or a *formaria* exclusively for young nuns at Saint John of Arles, where only girls at least six or seven years old were normally accepted—that is, girls who, according to the rule of Caesarius, were "at an age where they could learn to read and obey." Aurelian of Arles pushed the age of admission for young boys ahead to ten or twelve years,[72] while the *Regula Magistri*, which, as we shall see, reserved a large place in the life of the monastery for the *infantuli*, seems to have received children at an earlier age.[73] Saint Benedict also gave thought in his rule to young children offered to monasteries by their parents although he did not stipulate an age limit for admission.[74] After settling at Subiaco and, later, at Monte Cassino, Benedict received the sons of senators and curiales.[75] There can be no doubt then that our monasteries were generally open to children.

[68] Ibid., II, 85 (p. 12).

[69] *Regula Magistri*, ed. Vanderhoven and Masai, pp. 154, 192; 294, 25; 296, 64; 297, 110; 305, 35; 306, 41; 308, 104. See also the preface, p. 148: "Constituenda est ergo nobis dominici schola servitii ut ab ipsius numquam magisterio descendentes et in hujus doctrina usque ad mortem in monasterio perseverantes."

[70] *Vita Eugendi, MGH, SRM*, III, 100; *Vitae Abbatum Acaunensium*, ibid., p. 179.

[71] Gregory of Tours, *Glor. martyr.*, 75 (*MGH, SRM*, I-2, 538).

[72] Caesarius, *Statuta sanctarum virginum*, 7 (Morin ed., 2: 104): "Et si potest fieri aut difficile aut nulla umquam in monasterio infantula parvula nisi ab annis sex aut septem quae iam et litteras discere et obedientiae possit obtemperare suscipiatur." See Caesarius' letter to a young nun, *Epistulam horatoria ad virginem Deo dicatam*, ibid., p. 145, 17-19: "Ab ipsis paene cunabulis per annos infantiae atque adolescentiae ad juventutem usque studiis regularibus exercuisti vitam." See also Aurelian, *Regula*, 17 (*PL*, LXVIII, 38); In chap. 22 he describes the work of the "perparvuli infantes."

[73] *Regula Magistri*, LIX (Vanderhoven and Masai ed., p. 263): "Infantuli vero infra duodecim annos."

[74] Benedict, *Regula*, LIX (p. 83): "Si ipse puer minori aetate est." There are numerous allusions to young people in the *Rule*: e.g., LXIII (p. 88); LXX (p. 97); XXX (p. 50): "De pueris minori aetate qualiter corripiantur"; XXXVII (p. 57): "De senibus vel infantibus."

[75] Gregory the Great, *Dial.*, II, 3 (Moricca ed., p. 85), reports the arrival at Subiaco of

Let us now try to reconstruct from the sources the instructional program designed for young monks. First of all, they had to learn the rudiments—in essence, reading: "Let all nuns learn to read; let no monk ignore his letters," demanded the rules of Caesarius, Aurelian, and Ferreolus.[76] According to the *Regula Magistri*, small children grouped in a *decada* were to study their letters three hours a day under the supervision of a learned monk.[77] They undoubtedly had to learn to write at the same time. The Master was demanding on this score, since he also exhorted unlettered monks less than fifty years old to take up this study as well.[78] Benedict, although not as precise, provided that books, styli, and tablets were to be available for every monk's use.[79] Like the Master, however, he had in mind those who would not or could not read because of their laziness or inability.[80] Among the monks, there must have been some hard-core cases who could achieve salvation in the cloister while remaining completely unlettered. In this regard, Western monasticism resembled that of the East.[81]

Once he had acquired the elementary means to educate himself, would the young monk pursue his studies further? The culture for which he was destined, it must be repeated, was a uniquely religious culture. Having abandoned the world, the young monk cut his ties with one of the ornaments of the world, classical letters. Benedict, for example, apparently retained no remembrance of his past studies:[82] his rule is

---

Maurus, Euthicius' son, and Placidus, son of the patricius Tertullus. The son of a *curialis* was admitted to Monte Cassino (*Dial.*, II, 11 [p. 98, l. 4]).

[76] Caesarius, *Statuta sanctarum viriginum*, 7 and 8 (Morin ed., 2: 104–5); Aurelian, *Regula*, 32 (PL, LXVIII, 391); Ferreolus, *Regula*, PL, LXVI, 963–64.

[77] *Regula Magistri*, L (Vanderhoven and Masai ed., p. 247): "In his tribus horis infantuli in decada sua in tabulis suis ab uno litterato litteras meditentur."

[78] Ibid.: "Nam et inalfabetos majores usque vel quinquagenariam aetatem litteras meditentur."

[79] Benedict, *Regula*, LV (p. 78). Marrou, *Education*, p. 440, remarked that "the objects mentioned, among others, are part of monastic décor." See also Jean Leclercq, *L'amour des lettres et le désir de Dieu* (Paris, 1957), p. 20.

[80] Benedict, *Regula*, LVIII (p. 71): "Si quis vero ita negligens et desidiosus fuerit ut non velit aut non possit meditare aut legere." In chapter L (p. 251), the Master speaks of "duri cordes et simplices fratres vel qui litteras discere nolunt et non possunt."

[81] Marrou (*Education*, p. 493) seems to me to have forced the contrast between a learned Western monasticism and a relatively uncultured Eastern monasticism. Eastern cenobites cared as much as those in the West for instruction. See the rules of Pachomius and Basil and the frequent examples of lettered monks in Palladius, *Histoire lausiaque: Vies d'ascètes et de pères du désert*, LX, 2; XI, 4; XXXVII, 12; LV, 3; LXIV, 1–2; LVIII, 3; I, 1–3 (ed. and trans. Arthur Lucot [Paris, 1912]). Conversely, one could point to illiterate monks in the West.

[82] There are numerous articles on Benedict's "classical culture." See Schanz, IV-2, 593, and, more recently, Suso Brechter, "Benedike und die Antike," in *Benedictus, der Vater*

written in clear language—*luculentus* Gregory the Great called it—
stripped of all rhetoric.[83] No trace of profane reading has been found
in this text, except perhaps for some borrowings from legal works, which
was not at all uncommon in monastic legislation.[84] Those who have
wished to enhance Benedict's memory have searched in vain for classical reminiscences.[85] They attribute his "ne quid nimis" to a reading
of Terence, when in reality it is a proverbial expression borrowed from
Jerome and Augustine.[86]

Nor are there many references to profane readings in the works
of Caesarius, Benedict's Provençal contemporary. As we have already seen, the former Lérinian monk had quite early become disgusted with the study of the liberal arts. When he became a bishop,
he faithfully refrained from alluding to them. His style is simple, too
simple for some.[87] He made no allusion to classical works except
for a citation from Juvenal which had long been proverbial[88] and a

---

des Abendlandes (Munich, 1947), p. 147. Brechter's very prudent conclusion should be
retained. Anscari Mundó, on the other hand, is wrong in thinking that Benedict's library
contained profane works ("*Bibliotheca*, Bible et lecture du Carême d'après saint Benoît,"
RB 60 [1950]: 65–91).

83 There are also numerous studies of the Latin of the *Rule*: see Schanz, IV-2, 593, and,
most recently, Christine Mohrmann in the preface to P. Schmitz's edition (Maredsous,
1955), pp. 9–39. For the importance of the text of the Saint Gall manuscript, see Mohrmann, "La latinité de saint Benoît," *RB* 62 (1952): 108–39, responding to B. Paringer,
"Le manuscrit de Saint Gall 914 représente-t-il le latin original de la Règle de saint
Benoît?" *RB* 61 (1951): 81–140. See also A. Mundó, "Authenticité de la Règle de saint
Benoît," *Studia Anselmiana* 42 (1957): 105.

84 Ildefons Herwegen, "Vom Geiste des Römischen Rechtes in der Benediktinerregel,"
in *Christliche Verwirklichung Romano Guardini zum 50. Geburtstag dargebracht von
seinen Freuden und Schülern*, ed. Karlheinz Schmidthues (Rothenfels am Main, 1935),
pp. 184–88. There is a definite relationship between Dionysius' canonical works, Justinian's
Code, and the *Rule*. See John Chapman, *Saint Benedict and the Sixth Century* (London,
1929), p. 37 (chap. III).

85 See the *index scriptorum* in Edward Cuthbert Butler's edition, *Sancti Benedicti
Regula monachorum* (Freiburg-im-Breisgau and St. Louis, Mo., 1912).

86 *Regula*, LXIV, 30 (p. 90). Medieval commentators were the first to remark the
expression; see Leclercq, *L'amour des lettres*, p. 114. Moreover, the phrase "melius est
silere quam loqui" (*Regula*, I, 34 [p. 8]) is not from Sallust (*Jugurtha*, 19, 2). It is
absurd to make Monte Cassino the heir of imperial schools, as does M. di Martino Fusco,
"Le scuole benedictine continuatrici di quelle imperiali," *Mouseion* 2 (1925): 88.

87 Malnory, *Saint Césaire*, p. 18, wrongly deplores Caesarius' total lack of experience
in the art of writing. See above, chap. 3, n. 81.

88 Caesarius, *Sermo* CCXXII (Morin ed., p. 836): "Unde bene quidam dixit: crescit
amor nummi quantum ipsa pecunia crescit," a sentence perhaps borrowed from a sermon
by Faustus of Riez (*CSEL*, 21: 242, l. 27). See also this prudent citation from a profane
author (Symmachus) in *Sermo* CCXXXVI, (p. 897): 'Sed magis illam sententiam saecularem quidem sed valde utilem cogitemus: ut vera laus ornat ita falsa castigat." Likewise,
Sermo CCXVII (p. 818, l. 28): "Et quia vera illa sapientis viri sententia, sicut vera laus."
Caesarius must not have known who the author was when he borrowed from popular

Virgilian reminiscence borrowed no doubt from a Church Father.[89]

What was simple for a Benedict or a Caesarius, however, was un-doubtedly less so for former scholars, who had long been nourished on profane authors.[90] They must have reminded themselves of the advice which Abbot Nestor, according to Cassian, gave to a young monk who could not excise recollections of school from his memory: meditate continually on Scripture with as much zeal as had been for-merly given to profane books in order to banish unfruitful memories and replace them with spiritual preoccupations.[91]

Monastic legislators gave a prime place to psalmody as a means of imbuing the monk with the word of God. The novice had to learn his Psalter by heart in order to follow the offices. Monastic rules repeatedly linked the study of letters with the Psalms: "May he who wishes to claim the name of monk not forget his letters; may he also remember all the Psalms by heart."[92] The Master was very precise on this subject: after having demonstrated the advantage of knowing the Psalms by heart,[93] he recommended that monks help each other in this study. "For three hours of study in the morning, may they read and listen, may they learn letters and the Psalms."[94] When the three hours devoted to this "spiritual work" ("in spiritali opere") expired, the monks "re-placed the tablets and books so that they might get up to go to tierce."[95] A little further along, the Master, speaking of summer work, again referred to these studies and even provided for an examination before

---

sources. Even more surprising is a reminiscence from Sidonius apropos of Lérins in *Sermo* CCXXXVI (Morin ed., p. 940); see Sidonius, *Carm.* XVI, v. 110 (*MGH, AA*, VIII, 241), and Ennodius, *Vita Epifani*, 93 (*MGH, AA*, VII, 95).

[89] This is the famous "mille, mille nocendi artes" (*Aeneid*, VII, 337–38) which Caesarius used three times (*Sermo* L, 2 [p. 216, l. 19]; CLII, 2 [p. 590, l. 1]; CCVII [p. 785, 11]). See Jerome, *Ep.* XIV, 4 (*PL*, XXII, 349). This reminiscence is also found in a letter written by Abbess Caesaria of Arles to Radegunda at Poitiers (587) (*Ep.* 11 [*MGH, Ep.*, III, 451, l. 14]), amidst scriptural citations.

[90] For example, the monks Gregory the Great spoke of in *Dial.*, IV, 9 (p. 240): "Duo nobiles viri atque exterioribus studiis eruditi germani fratres." Benedict sent them to found Terracina.

[91] Cassian, *Conlationes*, XIV, 12, 13 (*CSEL*, 13: 414). See Roger, p. 145.

[92] Ferreolus, *Regula*, 11 (*PL*, LXVI, 959): "Omnis qui nomen vult monachi vindicare, litteras ei ignorare non liceat."

[93] *Regula Magistri*, XLIV (Vanderhoven and Masai ed., p. 241): "Ut quando in quovis loco codix deest textum lectionis vel pagine si opus fuerit memoria recitetur."

[94] Ibid., L (p. 250): "Ordinatione praepositorum suorum sequestrate a se per loca diversae decadae alii legant, alii audiant, alii litteras discant et doceant, alii psalmos quos habent superpositos meditentur." (Texts written on tablets are meant.)

[95] Ibid., L (p. 247): "In hoc spiritali opere has tres horas peregerint repositis tabulis et codicibus divinis ad tertiam laudibus surgant."

the abbot: when the monks knew their Psalms well, they were brought forward by their *prepositus* to recite a Psalm, a canticle, or a reading of their choice. The recitation over, a little ceremony ended the examination.[96]

Once they knew the Psalter perfectly, the monks, like the desert ascetics, could "ruminate" day and night on the sacred word.[97] During manual labor, especially in the fields,[98] the Psalms the monks recited were real "love songs" (*amatoriae cantiones*), according to Saint Jerome and the *Regula Tarnantensis*.[99] From the Psalms the monk drew strength against his adversary and the world: "If we have recourse to our Psalms, we will bar the way to worldly thought; the Psalms are truly weapons of the servants of God."[100] Whoever knew the Psalms— the true buckler of the Christian, rather than grammar and rhetoric, as Ennodius had said in his *Laus litterarum*—need not fear the enemy.[101]

This impregnation with the word of God continued during common readings at mealtimes or before complines. Abbot Eugendus introduced mealtime readings at Condat "in imitation of the ancient fathers."[102] Caesarius insisted on this point at Arles and required nuns to read during their work.[103] Aurelian and the author of the *Regula Tarnantensis* echoed these recommendations.[104] Saint Benedict and the Master even devoted a chapter to weekly readings and had readings for the guests of the monastery.[105] Common readings also accompanied the eve-

[96] Ibid., L (pp. 250–51).

[97] Caesarius, *Statuta sanctarum virginum*, 22 (Morin ed., 2: 106, l. 16): "Quodcumque operis feceritis quando lectio non legitur de divinis scripturis semper aliquid ruminate."

[98] Ferreolus, *Regula*, 11 (*PL*, LXVI, 959): "Similiter etiam his qui pastores pecorum . . . mittentur curae erit vacare psalmis."

[99] *Reg. mon. Tarnantensis*, 8 (*PL*, LXVI, 980): "Haec sint vestra carmina, haec ut vulgo aiunt amatoriae cantiones." See Jerome, *Ep.* XLVI, 12 (*CSEL*, 54: 342–43) apropos of the peasants of Bethlehem.

[100] Caesarius, *Sermo ad monachos*, CCXXXVIII, 2 (Morin ed., p. 904, ll. 2–5): "Fratres si frequentius psalmos nostros recurrimus cogitationibus mundanis aditum claudimus. . . . Psalmi vero arma sunt servorum dei, qui tenet psalmos adversarium non timet." See Evagrius Ponticus, Cassian's master, cited by Irénée Hausherr, "Le traité de l'oraison d'Evagre le Pontique," *RAM* 15 (1934): 127: "Psalmody conquers the passions and calms the intemperance of the body."

[101] Ennodius, *Dictio* XII, *Laus litterarum*, *MGH*, *AA*, VII, 239, ll. 24–26: "Vestris umbonibus directa ab adversariis tela repelluntur, nec spiculis peritiae vestrae ulla clipeorum crates obponitur."

[102] *Vita Eugendi*, 20 (*MGH, SRM*, III, 163).

[103] Caesarius, *Statuta sanctarum virginum*, 18 (Morin ed., 2: 105, l. 13): "Sedentes ad mensam taceant et animum lectioni intendant." See also idem, *Reg. monac.*, ed. Morin, 2: 150, l. 25, and *Statuta sanctarum virginum*, 20 (pp. 105, l. 25).

[104] Aurelian, *Regula*, 49 (on reading at table) and 29 (on reading at work), *PL* LXVIII, 393–99; *Reg. mon. Tarnantensis*, 8 (*PL*, LXVI, 980).

[105] Benedict, *Regula*, XXXVIII (p. 58): "De hebdomario lectore"; and LIII (p. 74,

ning meal, at least in Benedictine monasteries. The abbot would recommend Cassian's *Conferences*, the *Lives* of the Eastern Fathers, and, of course, the Bible, with the exception that the Book of Kings and the Heptateuch were not read during complines.[106] Benedict remembered Cassian's advice[107] and feared that less stable minds, those of the young in particular, would be troubled during the night by overly vivid stories.

Knowing his Psalter by heart and attentive to the common readings, the monk was indeed imbued with the divine word, but in a rather passive way.[108] Monastic legislators demanded still more of him: personal reading. What seems to us today an ordinary habit required a genuine effort then, perhaps even for cultivated men. Educated men during this period either had a text read to them, or they read it aloud.[109] Saint Augustine was quite astonished to see Saint Ambrose reading only with his eyes ("legere in silentio").[110] This practice, which was contrary to the ancient way of reading, first appeared in the monastery, where relative silence reigned.[111] Although monks continued to read aloud in the classroom,[112] Benedict asked them to do their personal reading without disturbing the repose of the others.[113]

Personal reading occupied an important place in monastic life: during winter more than three hours were spent reading in the morning; in the summertime two hours in the morning were devoted to reading, in addition to afternoon reading on a personal basis; a good part of Sunday was spent reading.[114] On the average, then, more than twenty hours a week were spent reading. During Easter, the time of penitence, the monks were to read *in extenso* from a book selected at the beginning of the period. Benedict insisted that personal reading be done under the

---

18): "Legatur coram hospite lex divina." *Regula Magistri*, XXIV (Vanderhoven and Masai ed., p. 217), recommends that spiritual reading be chosen with the guest's spiritual level in mind.

[106] Benedict, *Regula*, XLII (p. 63).

[107] Cassian, *Conlationes*, XIX, 2 (*CSEL*, 13: 55).

[108] See Cassian on the operation of the unconscious (*Conlationes*, XIV, 10).

[109] For this reading technique, see J. Balogh, "*Voces paginarum*: Beiträge zur Geschichte des lauten Lesens und Schreibens," *Philologus* 82 (1927): 83–202.

[110] Augustine, *Confess.*, VI, 3, 3 (de Labriolle ed., p. 120).

[111] Neither Benedict's rule nor any other imposes "perpetual silence." See Butler, *Le monachisme bénédictin*, pp. 300–303, and Pierre Salmon, "Le silence religieux: Pratique et théorie," in *Mélanges bénédictins* (Abbey of Saint Wandrille, 1947), p. 23.

[112] *Regula Magistri*, L (Vanderhoven and Masai ed., p. 247, 26): "Unus de decem . . . legat et residui de suo numero audiant."

[113] Benedict, *Regula*, XLVIII (p. 69): "Aut forte qui voluerit legere sibi sic legat ut alium non inquietet."

[114] Ibid., XLVIII (pp. 69–70).

constant supervision of one or two older monks and that slackers and babblers be punished.[115] This advice says a great deal about the difficulty of reading as an intellectual exercise. The *Regula Magistri* also insisted on reading and even provided for an illuminated *atrium lectorum* at night so that the abbot or monks could read. Monks were to carry a small book (*codiciclum modicum*) along with them on trips away from the monastery so they could read while resting.[116] Thus Abbot Aequitius, a rather picturesque figure in Gregory the Great's description, carried the Holy Books about with him in a leather pouch in order to have material at hand for his itinerant preaching.[117]

Personal reading was also the rule in other monasteries. Eugendus particularly insisted on reading at Condat and set a personal example for his monks.[118] A room (*scola*), which could not be left without permission, was reserved for study at Tarnant.[119] Nuns at Arles had to read for two hours in the morning, while monks were to devote three hours to reading.[120] In his sermon to monks, Caesarius encouraged the lazy to read and pointed out that the *lectio* had its place in monastic life alongside virginity, vigils, fasting, and prayer.[121] Like Benedict, he thought that Easter was an especially appropriate time for reading.[122]

Scattered references enable us to reconstruct what the monks read. The Bible heads the list, closely followed by the rule of the monastery.[123] Other rules, such as those of Basil and Pachomius, were read,[124] along with Cassian's works and the *Lives* of the Eastern Fathers.[125] The

---

[115] Ibid. (p. 70): "Ante omnia sane deputentur unus aut duo seniores qui circumeant monasterium horis quibus vacant fratres lectioni et videant ne forte inveniatur frater acediosus qui vacat otio aut fabulis et non intentus lectioni et non solum sibi inutilis est sed etiam alios distollit."

[116] *Regula Magistri*, XLIV (Vanderhoven and Masai ed., p. 241) and ibid., LVII (p. 261): "Codiciclum modicum cum aliquibus lectionibus de monastherium secum portet ut quavis hora in via repausaverit aliquantulum tamen legat."

[117] Gregory the Great, *Dial.*, I, 4 (p. 33, ll. 8–10).

[118] *Vita Eugendi*, 22 (*MGH, SRM*, III, 164).

[119] *Reg. mon. Tarnantensis*, 7 (PL, LXVI, 980): "Meditantibus etiam fratribus nulli liceat rebus se aliis implicare nec liberum judicet a scola vel ubi meditantur fratres discedere."

[120] Caesarius, *Statuta sanctarum virginum*, 19 (Morin ed., 2: 105, 19–20); idem, *Reg. monac.*, ibid., p. 151, l. 25. See also Aurelian, *Regula*, 28 (PL, LXVIII, 399), and Ferreolus, *Regula*, 19–26 (PL, LXVI, 966 and 968).

[121] Caesarius, *Sermo* CCXXXIV (Morin ed., p. 887, ll. 17–18). See also the *Reg. monac.*, 3 (ibid., 2: 136, ll. 21–23) and 7 (ibid., p. 140, l. 11).

[122] *Sermo* CCXXXVIII (p. 905, l. 26): "Maxime diebus istis sanctae quadragesimae nemo se excuset."

[123] This was especially true for novices. See Caesarius, *Statuta sanctarum virginum*, 58 (Morin ed., 2: 117, l. 7); Benedict, *Regula*, LVIII (p. 81).

[124] Benedict, *Regula*, LXXIII (p. 100); *Vita Eugendi*, 23 (*MGH, SRM*, III, 165, l. 4).

[125] Benedict, *Regula*, XLII (p. 63); LXXIII (p. 100).

Deeds of the Martyrs were even read in the monastery that followed Ferreolus' rule.[126] Benedict also mentioned the works of the Church Fathers,[127] whose presence in the monastic library is attested by a study of the sources of the *Regula*.[128] The anonymous monk who wrote the *Lives of the Fathers of the Jura* at the beginning of the sixth century owed his culture to a reading of the Fathers.[129] He must have borrowed from the library of his friend Eugendus, whose taste for Latin and Greek books he extolled.[130]

Although, unfortunately, we do not have any library catalogues, we do have some information on the organization of libraries. A librarian was in charge of distributing the books, at fixed hours in certain cases, by taking them out of the chests (*arcae*), the keys to which were in his keeping.[131] Nearly all monasteries established *scriptoria*.[132] Saint Benedict's rule alone neglects to mention them and speaks only of the library.[133] This silence is surprising, since there were *antiquarii* at work

[126] Ferreolus, *Regula*, 18 (*PL*, LXVI, 965). As Baudouin de Gaiffier has noted, the reference is to a public reading ("La lecture des Actes des Martyrs dans la prière liturgique en Occident," *AB* 72 [1954]; 146).

[127] Benedict, *Regula*, IX (p. 31): "Expositiones . . . quae a nominatis et orthodoxis catholicis Patribus factae sunt."

[128] See Dom Butler's edition of Benedict's *Rule* for a list of the *Rule*'s sources. They include Cyprian, Jerome, Augustine, and Leo the Great. See also Herwegen, *Sinn und Geist*, p. 289.

[129] P. W. Hoogterp, "Les Vies des Pères du Jura," *ALMA* 9 (1934): 130–31; introduction to François Martine, ed., *Vies des Pères du Jura*, in *SC*, vol. 142 (Paris, 1968).

[130] *Vita Eugendi*, 4 (*MGH, SRM*, III, 155, l. 28): "Lectione namque in tantum se die noctuque . . . dedit et inpendit ut praeter Latinis voluminibus etiam graeca facundia redderetur instructus." It is hardly probable that Eugendus, who entered the monastery at age seven, knew Greek in a period when it was forgotten. See Courcelle, *LG*, p. 221. He undoubtedly read translations of the Greek Fathers. The phrase *graecitatis facundia* ("Greek") is known from the *Theodosian Code*, XIV, 9–3, in *Theodosiani libri XVI*, ed. Mommsen and Meyer, 1: 187.

[131] Caesarius, *Statuta sanctarum virginum*, 32 (Morin ed., 2: 109, ll. 26–27); *Reg. mon. Tarnantensis*, 22 (*PL*, LXVI, 986): "Codices qui extra horam petierint non accipiant, et qui apud se habuerint amplius quam constitutum est retinere non audeant"; *Regula Magistri*, XVII (Vanderhoven and Masai ed., p. 206, l. 20): "Arca cum diversis codicibus membranis et chartis monastherii." The fixed hours mentioned in the *Regula Tarnantensis* is a borrowing from the Augustinian rule (Augustine, *Ep.* CCXI [*CSEL*, 57: 368]).

[132] There was one at Arles under Abbess Caesaria: "Libros divinos pulchre scriptitent virgines Christi" (*Vita Caesarii*, I, 58 [Morin ed., p. 320, l. 23]). Monks at Uzès who did not till the earth were scribes; see Ferreolus, *Regula*, 28 (*PL*, LXVI, 969). Also, "scribtores litteram non integrent" during the time for prayer, according to the *Regula Magistri*, LII (Vanderhoven and Masai ed., p. 257, l. 5).

[133] A. Mundó's thesis, according to which *bibliotheca* here refers to the books of the Bible, seems without foundation to me (see "*Bibliotheca*, Bible et lecture du Carême d'après saint Benoît," *RB* 60 [1950]: 65–91). The expression "accipere codices de bibliotheca" is sufficiently clear that one need not search for another meaning. See also Dom N. van Assche, "Divinae vacari lectioni: De *ratio studiorum* volgens sint Benedictus," *SE* 1 (1948): 13–34.

in monasteries in the vicinity of Monte Cassino.[134] It could be that Benedict counted the scribes of the scriptorium among the *artifices* he spoke of in Chapter LVII. This is an attractive hypothesis, although there is no way to verify it.[135]

Thus, we know the conditions in which religious culture developed in the monasteries. But we would like to know not only the level of this culture but also its goal. To what end did frequent reading of the Bible and the other texts we have cited lead? Historians have taken quite different and even opposing positions on this subject, especially insofar as the beginnings of Benedictine monasticism are concerned. According to some, monks read the Bible without ever truly appreciating its meaning.[136] Others claim that the monks abandoned themselves to learned study and portray Benedict as the "initiator of Biblical studies in the West."[137]

We have only the texts with which to settle this debate—in particular, the *regulae*, which speak of *lectio*, especially of *lectio divina* and *meditatio*. But what do these terms mean? The intellectual vocabulary of the period was quite rich but rather imprecise. For example, *meditatio*, which for the Church Fathers often meant "prayer,"[138] in the rules meant "study," especially "preparatory study." *Meditari litteras, meditari psalmos* meant to learn to read and to learn the Psalter by reading it aloud in order to become thoroughly familiar with it.[139] *Meditari* was also synonymous with *legere*, which ordinarily meant "to read"; but when Benedict spoke of the *lectio divina*, did he not mean something

---

[134] Gregory the Great, *Dial.*, I, 44 (p. 34, l. 6): "Julianus . . . ad ejus monasterium cucurrit ibique absente illo [abbate] antiquarius repperit qui dixerunt." The use of the plural indicates that the reading of most of the manuscripts ("antiquarios scribentes") should be adopted.

[135] When the monks fled Monte Cassino around 580, they must have taken other books in addition to the *Rule* with them; see Paul the Deacon, *Historia Langobardorum* (hereafter, *HL*), IV, 17 (*MGH, SRL*, p. 114). No sixth-century manuscript from Monte Cassino is extant, however.

[136] Roger, p. 175.

[137] L. Coletta, "S. Benedetto promotore degli studi biblici in occidente," *La scienza e la fede* 40 (1880).

[138] Jerome, *Ep.* L, 1; CXXVII, 7 (*CSEL*, 54: 389); Cassian, *Conlationes*, I, 17–18 (ibid., 13: 26–27). See Chadwick, *John Cassian*, p. 151. For the meaning of *meditari*, see E. von Severus, "Das Wort 'meditari' im Sprachgebrauch der heiligen Schrift," *Geist und Leben* (1953), p. 365; idem, "Das Wesen der Meditatio und der Mensch der Gegenwart," ibid. (1956), pp. 109–13; H. Bacht, "Meditatio in den ältesten Mönchsquellen," ibid. (1955), pp. 360–75.

[139] Benedict, *Regula*, LVIII, 11 (p. 80), in reference to novices; ibid., VIII, 8 ("qui psalterii vel lectionum aliquid indigent meditationi inserviatur"); *Regula Magistri*, L (Vanderhoven and Masai ed., p. 247). The same meaning is also found in Cassiodorus, *Inst.*, ed. Mynors, pp. 5, 7.

more than simply reading?[140] *Lectio,* for the grammarians, was the beginning of interpretation. "To read" the Bible, then, could mean to study it intensively under the direction of the abbot. Was the abbot to explicate the hidden meaning of the Scriptures to the monks and to be, as was said of Achivus of Agaune, an "interpretator insignis?"[141] All that is certain is that the abbot was primarily charged with directing the spiritual and moral life of the monks. He was more a "physician for the soul" than a teacher; a passage in the *Regula Magistri* portrays him curing an "illness" with words and appropriate readings.[142] I see no place for the establishment of "Christian learning" as Saint Augustine understood it in the ascetic climate described by the *regulae.*

According to Cassian, who borrowed the thought from Evagrius Ponticus, purity of heart was preferable to learning when it came to delving into the meaning of Scripture.[143] The cenobites of Gaul and Italy remained true to this advice. Caesarius said that humility, obedience, and charity were the primary conditions necessary for *lectio* and *oratio,* while Benedict, like Cassian, insisted on "puritas cordis."[144] Cenobites, beginners in the art of asceticism,[145] were apprentices under the direction of their abbot. Their final goal was real *meditatio,* the contemplation of God.[146] *Legere* and *meditari* meant more "to taste" than "to understand."

Thus the monk's religious culture was an exclusively ascetic culture. While there is no doubt that Benedict founded an original monastic organization, he was somewhat less original in the realm of religious

---

[140] For the meaning of this phrase, see Denys Gorce, *La "lectio divina" des origines du cénobitisme à St. Benoît et Cassidore,* I (Paris and Wépion-sur-Meuse, 1925): iii; Herwegen, *Saint Benoît,* p. 150; and A. Mundó, "La reglas monásticas latinas del siglo VI y la *lectio divina,*" *Studia Monastica* 9 (1967): 229–55.

[141] *Vitae Abbatum Acaunensium, MGH, SRM,* III, 179: "Libros ecclesiasticos corde receperit quarum scripturarum ex affectu divino interpretator insignis effectus est."

[142] *Regula Magistri,* XV (Vanderhoven and Masai ed., p. 200).

[143] Cassian, *De institutis coenobiorum,* V, 34 (*CSEL,* 17: 107). See Evagrius Ponticus, "Knowledge of Christ does not require a soul fortified by study but rather a soul that seeks . . . ," cited by Hausherr, "Le traité de l'oraison d'Evagre le Pontique," *RAM* 15 (1934): 90. For "purity of heart according to Cassian," see M. Olphe-Galliard, "La science spirituelle d'après Cassian," *RAM* 17 (1936): 36.

[144] Caesarius, *Sermo* CCXXXIV, 3 (Morin ed., p. 887): "Nemo sibi virginitatem lectionem orationem vigilias vel jejunia sine caritate vel oboedientia prodesse credat"; and ibid., pp. 879ff. See Benedict, *Regula,* XX, 7 (p. 43).

[145] Benedict, *Regula,* prologue (p. 7).

[146] Cassian, *Conlationes,* IX, 3, 1 (*CSEL,* 13: 277): "Non est . . . perfecta oratio in qua se monachus vel hoc ipsum quod orat intellegit." See Olphe-Galliard, "La science spirituelle d'après Cassien," p. 143, and idem, "Cassien: La doctrine spirituelle," *DSp,* 2: 225ff.

culture. He compares in this respect more with the Eastern cenobites than with Cassiodorus.[147] This monastic culture, which, as we have described it, was completely opposed to profane culture, was also proposed as a model for clerics.

II. THE FIRST EPISCOPAL AND
PARISH SCHOOLS

A. CLERICAL EDUCATION AT THE CLOSE
OF THE FIFTH CENTURY

Let us first try to reconstruct the way in which clerics were trained at the close of the fifth century, even though our information on this subject is very sketchy.[148]

A layman who wished to serve the Church joined the clergy of his town and passed step by step through the different minor and major orders enumerated in the *Statuta ecclesiae antiqua*: porter, lector, exorcist, acolyte, subdeacon, deacon, priest.[149] Clerics below the subdiaconate could marry and live as laymen when not performing their ecclesiastical duties. Young children were admitted to orders as lectors because of the purity of their voices, thus taking the first step in a career which for some culminated in the episcopate. As lectors, children were introduced to Christian letters[150] because their duties required thorough literary training, if only to master the punctuation of the texts they read. We have several mid-fifth-century examples of clerical careers which began with the lectorate in those of Bishop John of Chalon, Bishop Vivianus of Saintes, and Bishop Epiphanius of Pavia.[151] Epiphanius,

---

[147] This opinion is shared by Jean Martial Léon Besse, *Les moines d'Orient antérieurs au concile de Chalcédoine* (Paris, 1900), p. 391; Jacques Winandy, "La spiritualité bénédictine," in *La spiritualité catholique*, ed. J. Gautier (Paris, 1953); and J. Leclercq, *L'amour des lettres*, pp. 87–88.

[148] Some information can be found in Gustave Bardy, "Le sacerdoce chrétien du Ier au Ve siècle," in *Prêtres d'hier et d'aujourd'hui*, ed. Gustave Bardy et al. (Paris, 1954), pp. 23–63. Von Schubert, *Geschichte*, p. 70, devotes a few lines to the subject, as does Beck, *The Pastoral Care of Souls*, p. 30.

[149] In *S. Caesarii opera omnia*, ed. Morin, 2: 95–96.

[150] See Louis M. Duchesne, *Origines du culte chrétien*, 5th ed. (Paris, 1925), pp. 366ff.; Marrou, *Education*, p. 440; E. Josi, "Lectores, schola cantorum clerici," *EL* 44 (1930): 282–90; and Johannes Quasten, *Musik und Gesang in den Kulten der heidnischen Antike und christlichen Frühzeit*, Liturgiegeschichtliche Quellen und Forschungen, 25 (Münster, 1930), pp. 133–41.

[151] Sidonius, *Ep.* IV, 25 (*MGH, AA*, VIII, 76); *Vita Viviani, MGH, SRM*, III, 94; Ennodius, *Vita Epifani*, 8 (*MGH, AA*, VII, 85).

who became a lector when about eight years old, simultaneously served as a notary to Bishop Crispinus.[152] Was the notariate, then, an ecclesiastical grade?[153] Perhaps more in fact than in principle, since, toward the end of the fifth century, Gelasius equated the grade of lector with that of notary.[154] These confusions, however, probably never arose in the important churches, where, as in the civil bureaucracy, the notaries were grouped in a *schola*.[155] Notaries must have continued to live like laymen without being admitted to clerical orders.

It has been assumed on the basis of an example from the Church of Carthage, on the other hand, that the young lector served simultaneously as a cantor.[156] We should differentiate the two functions, however. At the close of the fifth century, young cantors were directed by a *primicerius cantorum* at Joviacum on the Danube, at Naples, and in Spain.[157] The *Statuta* clearly specify that the function of the cantor is different from that of the lector. The cantor had particular responsibility for psalmody and seems to have taken no part in minor orders.[158] Laymen, on occasion, could even direct the study of chant, as did Claudian Mamertus, who put aside his philosophical research to help his brother, the bishop of Vienne, with this task.[159]

[152] Ennodius, *Vita Epifani*, 8 (ibid., p. 85, ll. 29–31). This passage has led some historians to conclude that Pavia had a law school at the end of the fifth century—a conclusion that obviously forces the text.

[153] See Marco Magistretti, *La liturgia della chiesa milanese nel secolo IV: Note illustrative alla conferenza "Il rito ambrosiano"* (Milan, 1899), p. 36. According to an inscription, the father of Pope Damasus had been an "exceptor, lector, levita, sacerdos" (*Liber pont.*, ed. Duchesne and Vogel, 1: 213).

[154] Gelasius, *Ep. ad episc. Lucaniae*, 2 (*PL*, LIX, 49): "Continuo lector vel notarius aut certe defensor effectus post tres menses existat acolytus."

[155] Louis Halphen, *Études sur l'administration de Rome au Moyen Age*, Bibliothèque de l'Ecole des hautes études, vol. 166 (Paris, 1907), pp. 89–90.

[156] Duchesne, *Origines du culte chrétien*, p. 368, which depends on a passage from Victor of Vita (*Historia*, III, 39 [*CSEL*, 7: 91]) that mentions a lector directing twelve children gifted in chant ("aptos moduli cantilenae").

[157] Eugippius, *Vita Severini*, XXIV, 1, and XLVI, 5 (*MGA*, *AA*, I-2, 20 and 30). See, at Mertola in Spain about 525: "Andreas princeps cantorum sacrosanctae ecclesiae Mertillanae" (Vives, *Inscripciones*, p. 93).

[158] Council of Lerida (524), c. 2, Mansi, VIII, 612. A cleric guilty of infanticide could become a cantor only after seven years' penance. In the *Statuta ecclesiae antiqua* (*S. Caesarii opera omnia*, ed. Morin, 2: 96), "Psalmista id est cantor" comes before the porter and thus is outside minor orders. It was more a function than an order. The *Statuta*, chap. 10, specify that a cantor could receive his office without the intervention of a bishop. For the distinction between a lector and cantor, see, most recently, Corbin, *L'Eglise à la conquête de sa musique*, pp. 150ff.

[159] Sidonius, *Ep.* IV, 11 (*MGH*, *AA*, VIII, 63, vv. 13–15): "Psalmorum hic modulator et phonascus / ante altaria fratre gratulante / instructas docuit sonare classes." "Instructas classes" perhaps means "catechumens." See Gelasius, *Dicta Gelasii papae*, PL, LIX, 140: "Catechumeni, latine dicuntur instructi."

The entrance of young children into the ranks of the clergy bore with it certain advantages. Leo the Great saw in this practice a guarantee of the religious quality of priests.[160] But whether he was a lector, notary, or cantor, the young man was never a resident in a religious community during this period.[161] His professional training was assured by the Church, but his intellectual training no doubt was still left to the antique school, while his moral training took place within his family. Only those born into a family of ecclesiastics received a more complete religious education, as in the cases of certain clerics who were confided at an early age to an uncle-bishop.[162]

B. THE FIRST EPISCOPAL SCHOOLS

In order to deepen the religious training of all young clerics, a new institution was created under the influence of monasticism: the system of communal residencies for future clerics. There had been several attempts at these kinds of groups during the fourth and fifth centuries at Vercelli, perhaps at Tours, and certainly at Hippo, where a *monasterium clericorum* had been founded.[163] At the beginning of the sixth century, Fulgentius followed Augustine's lead at Ruspe, while Caesarius did the same at Arles in Provence.

We do not know whether all the clerics of the Church of Arles were constrained to live as a community, but we know from the *Vita Caesarii* that a small group lived with the bishop day and night.[164] Furthermore,

---

[160] Leo, *Ep.* XII (*PL*, LIV, 650): "Merito sanctorum patrum venerabiles sanctiones cum de sacerdotum elatione [electione?] loquerentur eosdem ut idoneos sacris administrationibus censuerunt, quorum omnis aetas a puerilibus exordiis usque ad provectiores annos per disciplinae ecclesiasticae stipendia cucurrisset ut unicuique testimonium prior vita praeberet."

[161] This is illustrated by the case of Caesarius, who, though attached to the church of Mâcon, lived with his family (*Vita*, I, 4 [Morin ed., p. 298]). See also the lector who sought a business in Marseille (Sidonius, *Ep.* VI, 8 [p. 99]).

[162] This was the situation of Epiphanius, a relative of Bishop Crispinus (Ennodius, *Vita Epifani*, p. 85), and of the nephew of the African bishop, Maximus ("Ab ipsis cunabulis militem Christi" [*Ep. ad Theophilum*, in *PL: Supplementum*, ed. Adalbert Hamman, I, pt. 3 (Paris, 1959): 1094]).

[163] Paul Monceaux, "Saint Augustin et saint Antoine," in Cassamassa, *Miscellanea agostiniana*, 2: 78ff. See Marrou, *Education*, p. 440, and Frederik van der Meer, *Saint Augustin, pasteur d'âmes*, French trans., 2 vols. (Paris, 1949), 1: 311–12. The same organization seems to have existed at Marseille under Bishop Proculus (Elie Griffe, *La Gaule chrétienne à l'époque romaine* [Paris, 1947], 1: 43), as well as in the church at Arles under Hilary (*Vita Hilarii*, *PL*, L, 1229, 1235, 1240). Gaudemet, *L'Eglise dans l'Empire Romain*, p. 164, views these groups as a means primarily to respect the law of poverty—a view which would thus limit the scope of the reform.

[164] *Vita Caesarii*, II, 5–6 (Morin ed., pp. 325–26). Fulgentius was doing as much at Ruspe; see Ferrandus, *Vita Fulgentii*, XXVII (Lapeyre ed., p. 129).

the clerics took their meals with Caesarius and participated in the offices of tierce, sext, and nones, which the bishop celebrated in the monastic fashion.[165] Although they did not benefit from a rule such as governed the community at Hippo, the Arlesian clerics lived as a group in the *domus ecclesiae* and were thus more separated from the world.[166] This kind of life imposed celibacy on the clerics in minor orders and made the observation of chastity easier for those in major orders.[167]

The culture of this clergy also benefited from more frequent contact with Scriptures. Caesarius wanted to be the master of his clerics and to instruct them through readings during mealtimes and through discussions that he directed.[168] He answered questions, explained obscurities in the Scriptures, and at night asked the clerics, "What have you eaten today?" by way of alluding to the spiritual nourishment he had given them.[169] Finally, he required those who were destined for the diaconate to read in order the books of the Old and New Testaments at least four times.[170]

Caesarius' community was definitely open to very young clerics. Two of Caesarius' biographers had been in his service since their adolescence, beginning as notaries, no doubt at the age of the lectorate.[171] Alongside them were the equally young scribes who recopied the sermons Caesarius addressed to his colleagues. They were undoubtedly chosen from among lectors, as was the practice at Verona during the same period.[172]

---

[165] *Vita Caesarii*, I, 62 (p. 322); ibid., I, 15 (p. 301). See Malnory, *Saint Césaire*, pp. 28ff.

[166] For the location of the *domus ecclesiae* at Arles, see J. Hubert, "La topographie religieuse d'Arles au VIe siècle," *CArch* 2 (1947): 17–27.

[167] See canon 9 of the Council of Agde, in *S. Caesarii opera omnia*, ed. Morin, 2: 40, and Malnory, *Saint Césaire*, pp. 75ff., on this question.

[168] *Vita Caesarii*, I, 62 (p. 322, l. 25): "Ad prandium vero et ad cenam mensae suae sine cessatione cotidie legebatur." Also, ibid., I, 52 (p. 317, l. 27): "In disserendis autem scripturis et in elucidandis obscuritatibus quanta gratia in illo emicuerit qui poterit enarrare?"

[169] Ibid., II, 31 (pp. 337–38).

[170] Ibid., I, 56 (p. 320, ll. 3–5): "Nisi quattuor vicibus in ordine libros Veteris Testamenti legerit et quattuor Novi."

[171] Ibid., preface (p. 297, l. 1): "Qui ei ab adolescentia servierunt"; I, 63 (p. 323, l. 20): "Pro eo quod ab adolescentia in obsequio ipsius fuistis"; I, 40 (p. 312, l. 20): "Notario suo illo tempore nunc venerabili viro presbytero Messiano"; II, 22 (p. 334): "Notariorum in quo ministerio inutilis ego serviebam." Malnory believed that these passages concern Deacon Stephen, the redactor of this part of the *vita* (*Saint Césaire*, p. iv). Notaries were also responsible for carrying the bishop's staff: "Clericus cui cura erat baculum illius portare, quod notariorum officium erat" (*Vita Caesarii*, II, 22 [p. 334]).

[172] Caesarius, *Sermones*, preface (ed. Morin, p. 20): "Et quia adhuc scriptores nostri incipientes sunt . . . literis melioribus transscribere jubete." For Verona, see the subscription of a manuscript from that town (*CLA*, IV, 494): "Scr. per me Ursicinum lectorem ecclesiae Veronensis" (an. 517).

Young children were also taught in the *domus ecclesiae*. We have the example of Florianus, whom Ennodius of Pavia baptized and Caesarius taught to read and to pray.[173] We can conclude, then, that Arles had an episcopal school where the clerics not only received professional training but also were taught and educated.

Were there similar experiments elsewhere? The future Bishop Epiphanius was raised at Pavia in the monastic fashion from his eighth year by Bishop Crispinus,[174] but his case is an isolated one. Some popes from the mid-sixth century had been clerics in Rome since their childhood, which assured them an advantage over other clerics.[175] Unless they were the sons of priests, however, their education was never entirely supervised by the Church.[176]

It is not until 527, in Spain, that we see the first signs of an official institution. We have observed that the Visigothic monarchy had been under the protection of Ostrogothic kings from 507.[177] Thus, obvious relations existed between Italy and Spain, particularly between Provence and the Tarraconaise. Important councils like those held in Provence during the same period also met at Tarragona in 516 under the presidency of Bishop John, at Gerona the next year, at Lerida and Valencia in 524, and at Toledo in 527.[178]

At this last council, over which Bishop Montanus presided, a decision was made to create an episcopal school. The bishops decided that young children destined by their parents for an ecclesiastical career would reside in the *domus ecclesiae* after they were tonsured. Here, under the supervision of the bishop, they were to be trained by a master specifically entrusted with this duty ("a preposito sibi debeant erudiri"). At age eighteen, they could choose between marriage or entrance into major orders.[179] In the latter case, they were to remain attached to the church

---

[173] Florianus, *Ep.* 6 (*MGH, Ep.*, III, 117, ll. 3–4): "Ipse igitur mihi Latinis elementis inposuit alfabetum sed et hunc pro famulo discipuloque suo inpetrare confido."

[174] Ennodius, *Vita Epifani, MGH, AA*, VII, 84ff., gave a detailed description of the spiritual and ascetical training Epiphanius received from Crispinus. For the latter's pedagogical talents, see ibid., p. 86, 36–40; for Epiphanius' asceticism, ibid., p. 87; and for his desire to read Scripture, ibid., p. 88.

[175] *Liber pont.*, I: 282. Felix recommended Boniface, his successor, for this reason.

[176] As in the case of Anastasius (496–98). See *ICR*, vol. 2, no. 126. For Agapitus, see *Liber pont.*, I: 288.

[177] See above, chap. I, sect. II.B.4.

[178] Councils of Tarragona, 516; Gerona, 517; Valencia, 524; Toledo, 527; Lerida, 524 and 546; and Barcelona, 540 (Mansi, VIII–IX). See the letters of Montanus of Toledo (*PL*, LXV, 57–58) and John of Tarragona's (496–519) epitaph (Vives, *Inscripciones*, no. 277: "Nitens eloquio rector doctorque praefuisti monacis et populis").

[179] Council of Toledo, c. 1 (Mansi, VIII, 785): "De his quos voluntas parentum a

where they had been educated.[180] This canon, especially because it goes so far in the direction of *stabilitas*, betrays unmistakable monastic influence.

Were the Fathers of Toledo, in fact, inspired by the example of Arles? Caesarius' work was known in Spain, especially in the eastern portion of the kingdom.[181] In fact, though, the decision taken at Toledo represented a response to the same need that was felt at Arles: thus, there need not have been any direct influence between the two centers. Complaints had been voiced about the intellectual and spiritual inertia of the Spanish clergy and the secular temptations which assailed them.[182] These conditions provided the impetus for the organization of communal residencies for young clerics.

Did this institution bear fruit? In the absence of texts, we are unable to judge for ourselves how effectively the canon of Toledo was applied. Let us simply note that, twenty years after this Council, the Spanish Church produced two great exegetes. Bishop Justus of Urgel—who came from an illustrious family which had given four brother-bishops, all writers, to the Church—wrote a commentary on the Canticle of Canticles.[183] Slightly later in Lusitania, at the other end of Spain, Bishop Apringius of Beja, "disertus lingua et scientia eruditus," was doing exegesis on the Apocalypse.[184] We should also note—without, however, arguing for a direct relationship between the creation of the episcopal school and these two works—that the Spanish Church, despite its quarrels (perhaps even because of them), seems more vibrant than the

---

primis infantiae annis clericatus officio emanciparit statuimus observandum ut mox cum detonsi vel ministerio lectorum contraditi fuerint in domo ecclesiae sub episcopali praesentia a praeposito sibi debeant erudiri. At ubi octavum decimum aetatis suae compleverint annum coram totius cleri plebisque conspectu voluntas eorum de expetendo conjugio ab episcopo perscrutetur."

[180] Ibid., 2: "Ne qui de his tali educatione imbuuntur . . . propriam relinquentes ecclesiam ad aliam transire praesumant."

[181] For the Arlesian origin of Spanish canonical collections, see José Tarré, "Sur les origines arlésiennes de la collection canonique dite 'Hispana,' " in *Mélanges Paul Fournier* (Paris, 1929), pp. 705–24. Caesarius' sermons were diffused in Spain (*Vita Caesarii*, I, 55 [Morin ed., p. 319]).

[182] Justus of Urgel, *Explicatio mystica in Cantica canticorum, prologus,* ed. Garcia Villada, *Historia eclesiástica*, 2, pt. 2, app. I: 265: "Cum nostris temporibus, tepescentibus studiis, rarus quisque reperiatur, qui sit vel ad legendum quae sancta sunt quotidiana intentione promptissimus."

[183] See Manuel C. Diaz y Diaz, "Juste d'Urgel," *DSp*, 8: 1620–21, and Schanz, IV-2, 629, for Justus of Urgel. Isidore of Seville, *De vir. ill.*, XXXIII–XXXIV, 43–44 (*PL*, LXXXIII, 1099–1100), listed the names of the four brothers: Justinian of Valenica, Justus of Urgel, Nebridius of Egara, and Helpidius of Huesca.

[184] See Schanz, IV-2, 629. Apringius lived under King Theudis, who died in 548.

Roman Church of the same period. The Spanish Church no doubt had a long tradition of learning behind it which the invasions did not interrupt, and it did remain in contact with Christian Africa.[185] Nevertheless, for this legacy to produce results, clerical training had to be carefully organized. The creation of the episcopal school by the Council of Toledo, in a city which was beginning to assume the role of a metropolitan see,[186] boded well for the future.

C. The First Parish Schools

The same undertaking, this time at the parish level, was attempted in the Ostrogothic kingdom. We have already noted that the evangelization of the countryside was one of the bishops' major concerns at the opening of the sixth century. This campaign, however, necessitated staffing new parishes at the same time that good priests were both scarce and inclined to live in cities. The solution to this problem was to train future parish priests in the presbyteral house itself.

We do not know how or where this institution was born.[187] It was so successful in Italy, however, that Caesarius of Arles introduced it to Provence. Caesarius, who continually visited parishes and authorized priests to preach in country churches,[188] could not help but be concerned with the training of rural clerics.

In 529, the Council of Vaison decided that each rural parish priest would take in lectors and teach them the Psalter, the holy texts, and divine law.[189] Like the canon of the Council of Toledo of 527, the canon of Vaison provided that young clerics incapable of celibacy would leave.[190] This famous canon is considered the birth certificate of parish schools. Although specializing at first in the training of clerics, these schools soon admitted even children destined for the life of laymen—an

---

185 See below, chap. 7, n. 199.

186 Duchesne, L'Eglise au VIe siècle, p. 557.

187 Gabriele Pepe, Le Moyen Age barbare en Italie (Paris, 1956), p. 44, supposes that Pope Zosimus (418) was behind this movement, but we have no proof that he was.

188 Vita Caesarii, I, 5 (Morin ed., p. 318).

189 Council of Vaison in S. Caesarii opera omnia, ed. Morin, 2: 86: "Hoc enim placuit ut omnes presbyteri qui sunt in parochiis constituti secundum consuetudinem quam per totam Italiam satis salubriter teneri cognovimus juniores lectores quantoscumque sine uxoribus habuerint secum in domo ubi ipsi habitare videntur recipiant, et eos quomodo boni patres spiritaliter nutrientes psalmos parare divinis lectionibus insistere et in lege Domini erudire contendant ut et sibi dignos successores provideant et a Domino praemia aeterna recipiant."

190 Ibid.: "Cum vero ad aetatem perfectam pervenerint si aliquis eorum pro carnis fragilitate uxorem habere voluerit potestas ei ducendi conjugium non negetur."

inevitable development in light of the disappearance of the Roman elementary schools. The canon of the Council of Vaison was probably put into effect immediately, since we already find an eight-year-old cleric in training for the subdiaconate in a parish Caesarius of Arles visited.[191]

Clerical schools were also established elsewhere in Gaul outside Provence. Shortly before the Council of Vaison, in the Burgundian kingdom, young Eptadus left his family to join children who were receiving a clerical education from a priest.[192] If the school Patroclus and his brother attended was a parish school (which is difficult to prove), then it existed around 506, twenty years before Vaison.[193] Without diminishing either the importance of the Council or of Caesarius' decision, it seems that the need for clerical schools had already been felt. By asking a council to take official action, Caesarius only favored the further development of the schools.

Thus, at the parish as well as at the episcopal level, the Church provided the means for clerics to obtain a true religious education. By requiring them to return to the source of Christianity through the study of Scriptures and the ascetic life, it was to influence all spiritual life to follow.

III. AN ATTEMPTED CHRISTIAN "UNIVERSITY"

Ascetic training did not satisfy all monks and clerics. In the institutions we have just studied, however, there was no opportunity for those who wished to deepen their understanding of the Scriptures to do so by appealing to profane disciplines. Thus a *via media* had to be found between Christian classical culture, which neglected the essentials of the Christian message, and ascetic culture. Biblical learning, as defined by the Church Fathers and especially by Augustine, had to be reestablished by the application of the research methods of the profane sciences to the sacred texts. The bishop of Hippo had precisely outlined his ideas

[191] *Vita Caesarii*, II, 20 (Morin ed., p. 333): "Cum in dioceses venissemus infans annorum circiter octo clericali habitu. . . ."

[192] *Vita Eptadi, MGH, SRM*, III, 186: "Cum est ergo annorum duodecim nesciente parente ejus ad disciplina fugit scolare ibique se ipse magistro infanciam aetatis suae tradidit sacris litteris edocandam. Ex quo facto pauca quidem tempora quae scolares sibi non tantum quoaequavit . . . scientiam litterarum . . . superavit." Eptadus was a contemporary of King Sigismund, who died in 523.

[193] Gregory of Tours, *Vitae patrum*, IX (*MGH, SRM*, I-2, 703).

on true Christian culture in a work written a century earlier, the *De doctrina christiana*. He argued that the Christian scholar had to borrow from the antique educational program in order to be able to interpret the Bible soundly. While this was not original, it was clearly formulated for the first time.[194]

Apparently, though, this particular work did not enjoy immediate success. Rather, it was Augustine's theological works that attracted the attention of fifth-century authors. At the opening of the next century, however, the *De doctrina christiana* was copied in its entirety[195] and in excerpts. When Abbot Eugippius collected *excerpta* from the Augustinian corpus for his monks, he gave an important place to the *De doctrina christiana*.[196] It is interesting to look at the passages he chose.

At first glance, Eugippius' selections seem rather arbitrary,[197] but one rapidly becomes persuaded that he made his choices in light of a well-defined goal. While he kept only five chapters from Book I, which deals with scriptural truths, and nothing of Book IV, which concerns Christian eloquence, he kept twelve chapters from Book II, on the definition of Christian culture, and ten chapters from Book III, on exegetical learning.

In the sections pertaining to Christian culture, after having cited several passages relative to *signa*, he repeated what Augustine said regarding the usefulness of profane culture (natural science, the science of numbers, music, dialectic, eloquence) and the uselessness of astrology. But he omitted the passages on Hebrew and Greek, languages which very few of his contemporaries had the opportunity to learn. Even more surprisingly, he left out passages on history, the physical sciences, and astronomy. However, he did not neglect to include the essential chapter on the legitimacy of profane studies, in which Augustine, following Origen, compared these studies to the riches the Hebrews stole from the Egyptians in order to put them to better use. The hermeneutic that Augustine developed in Book III was almost entirely reproduced, but

---

[194] See Marrou, *Saint Augustin*, pp. 331ff., for whom the *De doctrina* is "the fundamental charter of Christian culture" (p. 413). Pierre de Labriolle, "Saint Augustin," *Journal des Savants* (1938), pp. 149–50, holds a contrary opinion. Marrou, however, has ably defended his point of view in his *Retractatio*, in *Saint Augustine*, p. 638, n. 1.

[195] Our oldest manuscripts of the *De doctrina*—Leningrad, Q. v. 1–3 (from Corbie), and the Ambrosianus M 77 and 58—date from the end of the fifth century and from the sixth century. See E. A. Lowe, "The Oldest Extant Manuscripts of Saint Augustine," in Cassamassa, *Miscellanea agostiniana*, 2: 237, 240.

[196] Eugippius, *Opera, CSEL*, vol. 9, pt. 1. See Schanz, IV-2, 586.

[197] Chapter 250, in particular, is comprised of two very different passages.

the rules invented by Tychonius were attributed to Augustine in Eugippius' book.

In presenting these extracts, Eugippius had the training of the Christian scholar, particularly the exegete, in mind. Eugippius himself was, in the words of Cassiodorus, an exceptional exegete ("scripturarum divinarum lectione plenissimus").[198] He had founded an important monastic center of religious culture at Lucullanum, near the tomb of Saint Severinus outside Naples. We have already seen that Eugippius was in contact with the Roman ecclesiastical world.[199] Dionysius Exiguus had translated one of Gregory of Nyssa's works for him, more for an exegetical than for a philosophical purpose.[200] Lucullanum's reputation traveled as far as Africa: when Fulgentius of Ruspe organized a center of religious culture during his exile at Cagliari, in order to open to his monks the treasures of "spiritual learning,"[201] he asked Eugippius to have copied for him texts which he lacked.[202]

We know of no other center of biblical studies in Italy outside this Neapolitan center. Roman clerics at the beginning of the sixth century were no more interested in scriptural studies than they were in theology. Dionysius Exiguus, whose exegesis Cassiodorus praised,[203] left no work in this field or any disciples. Even if the Roman clergy had had the desire for a higher Christian culture, they would have had to possess the means: libraries with carefully revised texts and the various commentaries of the different Church Fathers. But ecclesiastical libraries in Rome hardly seem to have existed at this time. We do not know what became of the libraries Pope Hilary had built at the end of the fifth century at Saint Laurentius in Damaso.[204] It is doubtful that the Vatican

---

[198] Cassiodorus, *Inst.*, I, 23 (p. 62).

[199] For the rule that was followed at Lucullanum, see A. de Vogüé's hypothesis in "La Règle d'Eugippe retrouvée," *RAM* 47 (1971): 233–66.

[200] Courcelle, *LG*, p. 315.

[201] Ferrandus, *Vita Fulgentii*, XIX, XXIV (Lapeyre ed., pp. 95, 115). Fulgentius also organized a scriptorium from which one manuscript has come down to us; see André Wilmart, "L'odyssée du manuscrit de San Pietro qui renferme les oeuvres de saint Hilaire," in *Classical and Mediaeval Studies in Honor of Edward Kennard Rand*, ed. Leslie Webber Jones (New York, 1938), p. 293.

[202] Fulgentius, *Ep. ad Theodorum senatorem*, PL, LXV, 348: "Obsecro ut libros quos opus habemus servi tui describant de codicibus vestris." For contacts between Africa and Naples, where refugees had founded monasteries, see Germain Morin, *Etudes, textes, et découvertes* (Maredsous, 1913), p. 37.

[203] Cassiodorus, *Inst.*, I, 232 (Mynors ed., p. 62, l. 15): "Scripturas divinas tanta curiositate discusserat atque intellexerat ut undecumque interrogatus fuisset paratum haberet competens sine aliqua dilatione responsum."

[204] *Liber pont.*, 1: 245. According to A. Mundó, "*Bibliotheca*, Bible et lecture du Carême d'après saint Benoît," *RB* 60 (1950): 75, the phrase "fecit autem et bibliothecas II in

had a library separate from the *scrinium*, where papal archives were housed, before the seventh century.[205] The library of Saint Peter's basilica must also have been included with the scrinium of the basilica, since it was there and not in the Lateran, as some have said, that Arator's poem was deposited.[206] Presented to Pope Vigilius before the confession of Blessed Peter,[207] the poem could only have been conserved in the archives of this church, archives that other sources also describe.[208]

Even if these libraries had begun to be organized, Pope Agapitus' work shows that they cannot have been very rich. This pope, who, as a son of the priest Gordianus of Saint John and Saint Paul, was no doubt attached to the clergy of his father's church from his childhood and trained in ecclesiastical sciences,[209] saw the need for a library containing the works of the Church Fathers. He "had this beautiful place for books tastefully constructed" just opposite the family church, according to an inscription that decorated the hall.[210] If the first verse of

eodem loco" should be translated "he had two Bibles made." In fact, however, nowhere in the *Liber pontificalis* does *bibliotheca* have that meaning (see 1: 306 and 512). Even if this interpretation were accepted, it would point to the existence of a scriptorium at Saint Laurentius.

[205] J. B. de Rossi, "De origine, historia, indicibus et scriniis bibliothecae sedis apostolicae," in *Codices Palatini Latini bibliothecae vaticanae*, ed. B. Card. Pitra, H. Stevenson, I. B. de Rossi (Rome, 1886), 1: x ff. For the scrinium, see the old work by Pietro Luigi Galleti, *Del Primicerio della Santa Sede Apostolica e di altri uffiziali maggiori del sacro palagio laternanese* (Rome, 1776), and Henri Leclercq's article "Rome: Bibliothèque et archives pontificales," in *DACL*, XIV-2, 3100–3122. R. Bressie's study, "Early Church Libraries," in James Westfall Thompson, *The Medieval Library* (Chicago, 1939), pp. 14–29, has nothing new. The archives could house theological works, as in the case of Gelasius' books against Nestorius and Eutyches. The author of the notice on this pope in the *Liber pontificalis* expressly states the fact (1: 255): "Libri . . . qui hodie in bibliothecae ecclesiae archivo reconditi tenentur." Duchesne considered this sentence an interpolation despite the authority of five families of manuscripts.

[206] As de Rossi and, following him, Henri Leclercq ("La Bibliothèque apostolique," *DACL*, II-1, 865), have argued.

[207] Several manuscripts provide this information; A. P. McKinlay's edition of Arator's works in *CSEL*, 72: xxviii. Surgentius, "primicerius scholae notariorum," must have also directed the scrinium at Saint Peter's.

[208] Cassiodorus, *Var.*, XII, 20 (*MGH, AA*, XII, 337, l. 2). See de Rossi, "De origine," p. lii. Because of the Roman schism, Symmachus, who resided at Saint Peter's from 501 to 508, was able to organize the archives of that church.

[209] *Liber pont.*, 1: 287.

[210] The text of the inscription (*ICR*, vol. 2, no. 28) is as follows:

Sanctorum veneranda cohors sedet ordine [longo]
Divinae legis mystica dicta docens.
Hos inter residens Agapetus jure sacerdos
Codicibus pulchrum condidit arte locum.
Gratia par cunctis sanctus labor omnibus unus
Dissona verba quidem sed tamen una fides.

For the location of the library, see Marrou, "Autour de la bibliothèque," pp. 124–69.

this inscription is to be believed, the library was essentially ecclesiastical.[211] That is what drew Cassiodorus' attention to it when he became increasingly interested in religious matters and conceived the idea of founding a Christian "university" in Rome. He referred to this project in the preface of his *Institutiones*. While this is a well-known text, in view of its importance, it deserves to be reread:

> When I saw the great longing to study profane letters, so great that many men thought of attaining the wisdom of the world by them, I admit I was quite saddened to see that the Divine Scriptures were not publicly taught, whereas brilliant teaching made the profane authors celebrated. With the blessed Pope Agapitus, imitating what had formerly been done at Alexandria and what is now being accomplished at Nisibis . . . , I tried, after having obtained the necessary funds, to arrange that Christian rather than secular schools would receive professors in Rome, so that the souls of the faithful would be assured of eternal salvation and so that their tongues would speak a pure and correct language.[212]

Cassiodorus thus verifies, to his regret, that the highest level of religious training did not exist in Rome alongside profane instruction. He therefore attempted to organize a program on the model of the famous though ephemeral school at Alexandria and on the model of the Persian school begun at Nisibis in 457.[213] He undoubtedly used his political authority—he was prefect of the praetorium—to achieve his goal and to draw Pope Agapitus to his view.[214] Although Cassiodorus never mentioned it, the creation of the library of *Clivus Scauri* had been one of the determining elements of the common project. Cassiodorus alluded

---

[211] Marrou, "Autour de la bibliothèque," p. 169, and, after him, André van de Vyver, "Les *Institutiones* de Cassiodore et sa fondation à Vivarium," *RB* 53 (1941): 71, suppose that the revision of a Martianus Capella manuscript by the rhetor Felix was made for this library (see above, chap. 1, sect. II.B.2). The date and place do agree, but it is probably coincidental that they do.

[212] Cassiodorus, *Inst.*, preface (p. 3, ll. 1–13): "Cum studia saecularum litterarum magno desiderio fervere cognoscerem, ita ut multa pars hominum per ipsa se mundi prudentiam crederet adipisci, gravissimo, sum, fateor, dolore permotus ut Scripturis divinis magistri publici deessent cum mundani auctores celeberrima procul dubio traditione pollerent. Nisus sum cum beatissimo Agapito papa urbis Romae, ut, sicut apud Alexandriam multo tempore fuisse traditur institutum nunc etiam in Nisibi civitate Syrorum Hebreis sedulo fertur exponi, collatis expensis in urbe Romana professos doctores scholae potius acciperent Christianae unde et anima susciperet aeternam salutem et casto atque purissimo eloquio fidelium lingua comeretur."

[213] See Marrou, *Education*, pp. 432–33, for this school. For the school at Nisibis, see below, chap. 5, n. 163.

[214] Not the contrary, as van de Vyver thought ("Cassiodore et son oeuvre," p. 252). The preface to the *Institutiones* is clear on this point.

to his personal library in Rome in one of the passages of his *Institutiones*, but nothing suggests that he built it for his Christian "university".[215]

Did this "university" ever see the light of day? Some authors think so.[216] Circumstances, however, were hardly favorable for its success: no sooner had Agapitus mounted the throne of Saint Peter (May 535) than the Byzantine ambassador sent to Italy by Justinian declared war on King Theodahat. The Ostrogothic king occupied the environs of Rome when Belisarius' troops invaded Sicily (June–December).[217] After the capture of Syracuse, the king decided to send the pope on an embassy to Byzantium, where Agapitus suddenly died in May 536. It was scarcely possible, under these conditions between May and December 535, that the Christian "university" would actually be established. Cassiodorus' text is explicit on this point. He says further on in his text that "as a result of the furor of wars and the fighting which has extremely troubled the kingdom of Italy, my project could not be effected in any way."[218] We do not know what became of Agapitus' library.[219] Cassiodorus' library, which was partially destroyed, must have been transported to Vivarium, where, almost twenty years later, the former minister returned to his project of founding a Christian school, although this time, as we shall see, along monastic lines.[220]

The project to establish an advanced religious cultural center thus ran aground. But the history of this experiment is quite significant. It bears witness to the necessity for a school which organized its teaching around Holy Scripture while making use of the contribution of profane instruction. Also, and this fact deserves to be underscored, the creation of a new school was not made necessary by the disappearance of the profane

---

[215] Cassiodorus, *Inst.*, II, 5, 10 (p. 149, l. 15): "Librum . . . quem in bibliotheca Roma nos habuisse atque studiose legisse retinemus." For this library, see Cappuyns, "Cassiodore," *DHGE*, 11: 1389. I agree with Cappuyns that the two libraries should not be confused.

[216] See especially Courcelle, *LG*, p. 316.

[217] For these events, see Stein, 2: 338–47.

[218] Cassiodorus, *Inst.*, preface (p. 3, ll. 13–16); "Sed cum per bella ferventia et turbulenta nimis in Italico regno certamina desiderium meum nullatenus valuisset impleri."

[219] Courcelle, *LG*, p. 317, n. 1, has not retained Marrou's hypothesis ("Autour de la bibliothèque," p. 167) that this library constituted the first collection in the Lateran. Courcelle, however, confuses the library of Cassiodorus with that of Agapitus and thinks that they were both ransacked. If one distinguishes between them, Marrou's hypothesis remains valid.

[220] Cassiodorus, *Inst.*, 5, 10 (p. 149, l. 15), recommended a book from his library to his monks. He added, however, that "if by chance it has been stolen during the Barbarian attack, you have Gaudentius" ("qui si forte gentili incursione sublatus est, habetis Gaudentium"). It is curious that Cassiodorus was uncertain about the contents of his own library.

school. The antique school continued to enjoy success—and it was this success which led Cassiodorus to hope for a parallel institution for Christian teaching.

We have seen that Christian schools were being established at all levels, elementary as well as superior, while at the same time, profane instruction continued to be offered. It has too often been claimed that presbyteral, episcopal, and especially monastic schools were replacements for antique schools after their demise. The new schools, however, were born at the opening of the sixth century in order to give clerics what they could not find in the antique schools. They were essentially "seminaries." As such, young laymen did not have access to them. Only later, when they had no other means of education, would laymen enter clerical schools.

THE END OF ANTIQUE EDUCATION AND THE DEVELOPMENT OF CHRISTIAN SCHOOLS IN ITALY, GAUL, AND SPAIN FROM 533 THROUGH THE FIRST THIRD OF THE SEVENTH CENTURY

Part Two

In 533, Emperor Justinian undertook to rebuild the Roman Empire from Egypt to Spain by taking the West back from the Barbarians. His plan was partially successful: Africa, a part of Spain, and Italy became Byzantine possessions.[1] Justinian's reconquest had important consequences for the intellectual culture of the West. One of the Emperor's first acts was to restore the privileges and salaries of teachers. Antique culture thus gained a reprieve and a chance to survive in the reconquered countries. As a consequence, the independent kingdoms of Visigothic Spain and Merovingian Gaul, which were in contact with the Byzantine Empire, would also benefit from the revival of antique culture. But at the same time, Christian schools, whose birth we have observed at the beginning of the sixth century, had also been organized in Italy, Gaul, and Spain. Thus we shall see in these lands the coexistence of two types of education until the beginning of the seventh century.

[1] See Stein, 2: 339–68, 564–611, for the history of the Byzantine reconquest.

Education and
Culture in Byzantine Italy

T wenty years of war between Ostrogoths and Byzantines exhausted
Italy and dislocated economic and social structures that had survived until the wars. Many great Roman and provincial families were
decimated and ruined. Some aristocrats who had fled to Byzantium
remained there permanently, while others returned to Italy to rebuild
their fortunes. In Rome—which was taken, retaken, and for a time,
emptied of its population—the Senate no longer had any prestige; its
days were numbered. Yet antique Italy could have survived by trans-
forming itself if, three years after Justinian's death (568), a new invasion
had not once again devastated it. The Lombards quickly occupied the
Po River plain, then the region of Spoleto and Beneventum, and compartmentalized the Italian peninsula, which they intended to subdue
entirely.[1] Rome, which as a result could only barely communicate with
Ravenna, was once again besieged by the Barbarians. Well might Pope
Gregory (590–604) have lamented: "Where is the Senate, where are the
people? . . . Where are all those who once bathed in glory? Like an
eagle in mourning, Rome has lost all the feathers from her body."[2] In
the same sermon, the pope recalled the time when children and adolescents flocked to Rome to study.[3] Had the second half of the sixth
century thus witnessed the end of antique education?

---

[1] Lot, *Les destinées*, pp. 210ff.
[2] Gregory the Great, *Hom. in Ezech.*, II, 6, 22–24 (*PL*, LXXV, 1011).
[3] Ibid.: "Pueri, adolescentes, juvenes saeculares et saecularium filii huc undique con-
currebant, cum proficere in hoc mundo voluissent."

I. THE FATE OF ANTIQUE EDUCATION

The ruin of the great senatorial families, which, as we have seen, were the ones most interested in liberal studies, might have threatened to lead to the closing of the antique school. But the Byzantine State needed trained functionaries and thus was interested in maintaining schools. Consequently, Justinian tried to reorganize the schools of Rome in 554. He decreed in his *Pragmatic Sanction* that a salary would be paid, as it had been under Theodoric, to teachers of grammar, rhetoric, medicine, and law, "so that young men schooled in the liberal arts might abound in the State."[4]

Was this measure ever employed? At first glance, it might seem unlikely, judging from the other points in the program for the reconstruction of Italy which never saw the light of day.[5] But reasoning by analogy is too facile. In order to determine the situation properly, we must gather what little evidence we have by studying the four branches of learning cited in the *Pragmatic*.

One striking fact stands out above all—legal practice survived. Men trained in law continued to be consulted in Rome[6] and even in the provinces, as our evidence from Sardinia proves.[7] The *docti viri* of Cagliari mentioned by Gregory the Great were certainly similar to those notables who knew the law ("honorati qui legum possint habere notitiam") in Provence at the beginning of the century.[8] Although we cannot tell whether they performed official functions or maintained offices for consultation, the important point remains that they did exist.

In the realm of municipal administration, the offices continued to register acts, donations, and wills as custom required and as one of Justinian's *Novels* noted.[9] Thanks to the correspondence of Gregory,

---

[4] Justinian, *Novella pro petitione Vigilii* (*Corpus iuris civilis: Novellae, App.*, VII, 22 [Schöll ed., p. 802]): "Annonam etiam quam et Theodoricus dare solitus erat, et nos etiam Romanis indulsimus, in posterum etiam dari praecipimus, sicut etiam annonas, quae grammaticis vel oratoribus vel etiam medicis vel jurisperitis antea dari solitum erat et in posterum suam professionem scilicet exercentibus erogari praecipimus quatenus juvenes liberalibus studiis eruditi per nostram rempublicam floreant."

[5] Stein, 2: 615ff.

[6] Gregory the Great, *Dial.*, IV, 27 (Moricca ed., p. 265, l. 8) spoke of an "advocatus . . . curis saecularibus obligatus lucris terrenis inhiens."

[7] Gregory the Great, *Ep.* IX, 197 (*MGH, Ep.*, II, 186, l. 12), said, apropos of an abbess' right to make her will: "Necessarium visum est tam cum consilariis nostris quam cum aliis hujus civitatis doctis viris quid esset de lege, tractare."

[8] Cassiodorus, *Var.*, IV, 12 (*MGH, AA*, XII, 120, l. 10).

[9] De Boüard, *Acte privé*, p. 54.

we can also point to municipal offices in Sicily,[10] in several towns in Italy,[11] and in Rome.[12] The existence of these offices has been denied on the ground that the pope was repeating a meaningless formula when he referred to them.[13] But why did he not repeat the formula in reference to donations made in other places? Furthermore, papyri from Rome, Ravenna, and Rieti containing acts of donation from this period also use the same formulas.[14] Sometimes these texts bear the name of the *tabellion* who drew up the act and the location of his *statio*, as in the case of Theodosius in Rome "in porticum de Subora."[15] Corporations of court clerks could still be found in both Ravenna and Rome.[16]

Nevertheless, we must point out that what this all amounts to is the practice of law, and not legal culture. Did the Byzantine reconquest do anything to restore legal *studies* to honor? The *Pragmatic* does mention *jurisperiti*, but is there any proof of their teaching?[17] The imperial government must have been partial to legal instruction; one of Justinian's great achievements had been the reorganization of the law schools in the East. There is also the possibility that the introduction of a new code[18] in Italy might have revivified the schools of Ravenna and Rome. We do know that the texts of the *Institutes* and *Novels* were translated and commented on in Italy during Justinian's time,[19] but there is no evidence that Byzantine law was taught. A reading of the compilations of the sixth century—the *Summary of Perousia*, for example—reveals such depths of ignorance on the part of the lawyers that

[10] Gregory the Great, *Ep.* II, 9 and 15; IX, 180 (*MGH, Ep.*, I, 108, l. 5 and 113, l. 3; II, 174, l. 26): letters to Messina and Tyndaris.

[11] Ibid. II, 15 (I, 113, l. 3), to Rimini; IX, 58, and XIII, 18 (II, 81, l. 25 and 385, l. 16), to Fermo; VIII, 5 (II, 8, l. 20), to Luna.

[12] Ibid., Appendix I (II, 438, l. 21).

[13] DeBoüard, *Acte privé*, p. 127, n. 1.

[14] Marini, *I papiri*, nos. 89, 74, 90–92, 79; Tjäder, *Papyri*, nos. 4, 5, 16, 18–19, 7.

[15] Marini, no. 92: "Ego Theodosius v. h. tabell. urb. Rom. habens stationem in porticum de Subora reg. quarta scriptor hujus chartulae." (Tjäder, nos. 18–19; see Tjäder's comments in *Papyri*, p. 457).

[16] Marini, nos. 112, 113, 114, 88, 80 (Tjäder, nos. 25, 14–15, 8). There was a *statio* in Ravenna in 573 near the church of Saint John the Baptist (Marini, no. 75; Tjäder, no. 6). Another was located near the imperial palace in 572 (no. 20, p. 116). Some documents bore subscriptions in Tironian notes (Marini, nos. 15 [540], 88A [572], 75 [575]; Tjäder, nos. 6, 122 [591]). See Charles Diehl, *Etudes sur l'administration byzantine* (Paris, 1888), pp. 96–97.

[17] See n. 4 above.

[18] For this code, which weakened Theodosian law, see Astuti, *Storia di diritto*, pp. 57ff., and Francesco Calasso, *Medio evo del diritto* (Milan, 1954), pp. 279ff.

[19] For the *Epitome Juliani* of the mid-sixth century and the *Authenticum*, see Astuti, p. 66. Special attention is given to a glossed manuscript of the *Institutes* now conserved in Turin (ibid., pp. 321ff.).

one must wonder whether law schools existed.[20] If law were taught it was taught solely in the imperial offices. Young Gregory, the future pope, must have learned what he had to know for his future administrative career from jurists. It is not difficult to find traces of this training in his correspondence.[21]

The *Pragmatic* also mentioned the training of *medici*. We have much less information on them, however, than we do on the jurists. All we know is that there were some physicians who still practiced in Rome in Gregory the Great's time. Gregory tells the story in his *Dialogues* of two brothers, Copiosus and Justus, who were trained in the medical arts. One entered the monastery of Saint Andrew, while the other earned his living by caring for Romans.[22] The father of the future Pope Boniface IV practiced medicine in Rome.[23] When Gregory learned of the illness of his friend Marinian of Ravenna, he called upon all the physicians whose learning he knew, one by one, for consultation and passed the information on to Ravenna,[24] even though there were physicians, even Greek physicians, in the political capital of Italy.[25] Those in Rome, however, enjoyed greater prestige because of their proximity to the schools. Some Eastern physicians were to be found in Rome—one from Alexandria was a member of Gregory's entourage.[26] The pope, who was eternally ill, has scattered throughout his work scientific-sounding explanations of his problems[27] as well as medical terms borrowed from

[20] For this summary, see Max Conrat, *Geschichte der Quellen und der Litteratur des römischen Rechts im früheren Mittelalter* (Leipzig, 1891), pp. 182–87, and Astuti, pp. 331–32.

[21] Conrat, *Geschichte*, pp. 9–13, found more than fifty allusions to the *mundana lex*, most of which were borrowed from Justinian's Code and the *Novels*.

[22] Gregory the Great, *Dial.*, IV, 57 (p. 317): "Copiosus qui ipse quoque nunc in hac urbe per eamdem medicinae artem temporalis vitae stipendia sectatur." About his brother, Justus, Gregory wrote: "Medicina arte fuerat imbutus." Saint Samson, whose *Life* was written by Simeon Metaphrastus (*PG*, CXV, 279), began his career as a physician in Rome.

[23] *Liber pont.*, ed. Duchesne and Vogel, 1: 317.

[24] Gregory the Great, *Ep.* XI, 21 (*MGH, Ep.*, II, 282, ll. 12–13): "Singillatim eos quos hic doctus lectione novimus medicos fecimus requiri et, quid singuli senserint quidve dictaverint, sanctitati vestrae scriptum misimus."

[25] Marini, *I papiri*, no. 120 (from 572), concerning Greek physicians: "Eugenius . . . filius Leonti medici ab schola graeca."

[26] Gregory the Great, *Ep.* XIII, 44 (II, 406, l. 24): "Inter me atque familiares meos . . . quidam qui in magna civitate Alexandrina medicinale erat."

[27] See *Ep.* XI, 56 (II, 342, l. 18), on nocturnal emissions ("Cum vero ultra modum appetitus gulae in sumendis alimentis rapitur atque idcirco humorum receptacula gravantur") and *Reg. past.*, I, 11 (*PL*, LXXVII, 26), on hernia ("Vitium quippe est ponderis cum humor viscerum ad virilia labitur").

the Greek.[28] Greek medical works, at least in translation, still claimed readers, as the publication in Rome of the *Therapeutica* of Alexander of Tralles, a physician who was in Rome around 560, bears witness.[29]

The *Pragmatic* also mentioned *grammatici* and *oratores*. Here again, in the absence of inscriptions or of any other sources which would prove the existence of teachers in these disciplines, we must turn to indirect evidence.

The first of these is the epitaph of young Boethius, *clarissimus puer*, who died in 578, when eleven years old.[30] He had received a careful literary education, since his father, the notary Eugenius, praised the young boy's poetical precocity. Another example is Gregory, the future pope, who must not have been more than fifteen years old when the *Pragmatic Sanction* was promulgated. His education in the paternal house of Clivus Scauri conformed to the aristocratic tradition.[31] "He had learned," Gregory of Tours related, "grammar, dialectic, and rhetoric, and surpassed his fellow citizens with his culture."[32] The historian learned this bit of information directly from one of his deacons who had been sent to Rome in 590[33] and thus passed on an opinion which was generally held and, as we shall see, was quite justified.

A liberal education could also be had outside Rome. Fortunatus, who was born at Treviso, came to Ravenna to study around 550,[34] where he tells us that he and his friend Felix learned grammar, rhetoric, and even

[28] *Dial.*, III, 33 (p. 211, l. 6): "Quam molestiam greco eloquio sinconin vocant." Ibid., 35 (p. 215, l. 11): "Quem medicina graeco vocabulo friniticum." Ibid., IV, 16 (p. 252, l. 18): "Quam greco vocabulo medici paralysin vocant."

[29] For this physician, see Felix Brunet, *Les oeuvres médicales d'Alexandre de Tralles, le dernier auteur classique des grands médecins grecs de l'Antiquité* (Paris, 1933), 1: 193. For the translation of his work into Latin, see Schanz, IV-2, 295.

[30] *CIL*, VI, 8401 (*ICR*, vol. 1, no. 1122):

> . . . Te f(l)orale decus primo cum carmine coepto
> Doctorem doctor vidit et obstupuit . . .
> Annis parve quidem sed gravitate senex . . .
> Doctiloquum cupidus carminis ardor eras.

The inscription also tells us that he was the grandson of the city prefect. This prefect is not otherwise known. See Sundwall, *Abhandlungen*, p. 115.

[31] It is generally agreed that Gregory was born in 540; see Schanz, IV-2, 607. There is no information on his very early infancy except for the fact that he had a nurse (*Ep.* IV, 14 [*MGH, Ep.*, I, 279, l. 27]). She was settled in Constantinople in 594.

[32] Gregory of Tours, *HF*, X, 1 (*MGH, SRM*, I, 478): "Litteris grammaticis dialecticis ac rethoricis ita est institutus ut nulli in urbe ipse putaretur esse secundus."

[33] Ibid., p. 481, l. 16; *Glor. martyr.*, 82 (*MGH, SRM*, I-2, 544).

[34] For Fortunatus' youth, see Richard Koebner, *Venantius Fortunatus* (Leipzig and Berlin, 1915), pp. 11–12; Stein, 2: 695; and *Excursus*, p. 832.

law.[35] If in his own work there is little evidence of his legal background, there is, on the other hand, sufficient evidence in his work that the lessons of the grammarian and rhetor bore fruit. While almost all his literary work dates after his departure from Italy for Gaul (565), he nevertheless owed his literary talents to the training he received in Ravenna rather than to the reading he did on his own. In many respects, his work is reminiscent of that of Ennodius or Arator.

Except for these three names, we know of no other Italians who might still have benefited from instruction in the liberal arts during the second half of the sixth century.[36] Gregory the Great did make several passing references, however, to *mundi sapientes*,[37] *sapientes saeculi, eruditi*,[38] and to a *homo litteratus*.[39] Elsewhere, he spoke of the "worldly wisdom" that was being taught to children for a price.[40] In a letter to Venantius, the patricius of Sicily, he alluded to his learned friends (*clientes litterati*).[41] Thus we can divine a few individuals among the pope's contemporaries who had been trained in what he called "the sciences of the outside."[42]

Italy, especially Rome, maintained the tradition of profane instruction despite the misfortunes of the period. Rome, of course, did not enjoy the prestige it once claimed, but the wars nevertheless did not interrupt a basic cultural continuity which was to be so essential for the future.

---

[35] Fortunatus, *Vita Martini*, I, 29–33 (MGH, *AA*, IV-1, 296): "Parvula grammaticae lambens refluamina guttae / rhetorici exiguum praelibans gurgitis haustum / cote ex juridica qui vix rubigo recessit." See also Gregory of Tours, *Mir. Mart.*, I, 15 (MGH, SRM, I-2, 597), and the evidence of Paul the Deacon, HL, II, 13 (MGH, SRL, p. 79): "Ravennae nutritus et doctus in arte grammatica sive rhetorica seu etiam metrica clarissimus extitit."

[36] The *Vita Betharii*, MGH, SRM, III, 612, reports that this bishop of Chartres, who was born at the end of the sixth century and died in 623, was taught in Roman schools. This text, however, dates from the tenth century.

[37] Gregory the Great, *Moral.*, XV, 60, and XVII, 46 (PL, LXXV, 147), and X, 29 (ibid., col. 947), where the pope spoke at length on the *mundi sapientia*.

[38] *Moral.*, XXIV, 15 (PL, LXXVI, 309): "Sapientes ergo atque eruditi audite quod dico."

[39] *Ep.* IX, 6 (MGH, *Ep.*, II, 45), concerning *gloriosus* Bonitus, who was offered an administrative post: "Et inutile et valde laboriosum est hominem litteratum ratiociniorum causas adsumere." (In references to Gregory the Great, *Ep.*, hereafter, numbers in parentheses refer to volume and page of MGH, *Ep.*)

[40] *Moral.*, X, 29 (PL, LXXV, 947): "Haec . . . prudentia . . . a pueris pretio discitur."

[41] *Ep.* I, 33 (I, 47, l. 5). Venantius had abandoned his monastery to return to the world. Perhaps Venantius himself was a cultivated man—Gregory cited a phrase from Seneca to him.

[42] This expression, found twice in his works (*Dial.*, I, 1 and IV, 9), is the Latin equivalent of the Greek Fathers' οἱ ἔξω . See Basil, *Lettres aux jeunes gens*, II, 40; IV, 4 (Boulanger ed., pp. 43–44).

Gregory the Great's literary work, after all, cannot be explained in a land where all profane intellectual culture is supposed to have disappeared. Historians have too often portrayed Gregory as the first author of the Middle Ages while overlooking how much his thought owed to Antiquity. It is this aspect of Gregory's significance that I would now like to demonstrate.

II. GREGORY THE GREAT AND CLASSICAL CULTURE

We have already seen that Gregory received a liberal education in his youth. While fully acknowledging this fact, modern historians immediately add: "But he retained none of it and later condemned classical culture."[43] It has been fashionable since Edward Gibbon to accuse Gregory of obscurantism. Only his *Dialogues*, the most "popular" of his works, have been deemed worthy of remembrance.[44] Of course, we must also disagree with those historians who take John the Deacon's much later judgment[45] too literally and view Gregory as a protector of the liberal arts.[46] The reaction has been too brutal, however, and not entirely devoid of partisanship.

It is impossible, of course, to read Gregory's work and find any direct evidence of his years of study in Rome, because for Gregory the past was dead.[47] Gregory was, after all, "converted."[48] Destined from his

---

[43] See Schanz, IV-2, 622; Manitius, 1: 94; Roger, pp. 187–95; and A. Sepulcri, "Gregorio magno e la scienza profana," *Atti della Real Academia delle scienze di Torino* 39 (1903–11): 962–67.

[44] See Laistner, *Thought and Letters*, p. 108; E. Schneider, *Rom und Romgedanke* ("Gregor I als simplist"). Johannes Spörl challenged this definition of Gregory in "Gregor der Grosse und die Antike," in *Christliche Verwirklichung*, ed. Karlheinz Schmidthues (Rothenfels, 1935), p. 200; see especially, H. de Lubac, *L'exégèse médiévale* (Paris, 1961), II-1, 53–77 ("La 'barbarie' de saint Grégoire").

[45] John the Deacon, *Vita Gregorii*, II, 13 (*PL*, LXXV, 92).

[46] See especially Antoine Frédéric Ozanam, *La civilisation chrétienne chez les Francs*, 6th ed. (Paris, 1893), pp. 474–75, and Henri Joseph Leblanc's, *Utrum B. Gregorius Magnus litteras humaniores et ingenuas artes odio persecutus sit . . .* (Paris, 1852).

[47] We can find only one allusion—and a veiled one at that—to his past as a layman, in a passage on the resurrection of the body (*Hom. in Evang.*, II, 26 [*PL*, LXXVI, 1203]): "Multi etenim de resurrectione dubitant, sicut et nos aliquando fuimus, qui dum carnem in putredinem ossaque in pulverem redigi per sepulcra conspiciunt, reparari ex pulvere carnem et ossa diffidunt."

[48] For the meaning of *conversio* as used by Gregory, Jordanes, and Cassiodorus, see Schanz, IV-2, 118; Paul Galtier, "Conversi," *DSp*, 2: 2218; and C. Dagens, "La 'conversion' de saint Grégoire le Grand," *Revue des études augustiniennes* 15 (1969): 149–62.

youth for a worldly career, he was in charge of the prefecture of the city for about thirty years.[49] Shortly after, he broke with the world and retired to the family house, which had been transformed into a monastery.[50] We do not know the precise impetus for Gregory's conversion. He said that he "had long put off the grace of his conversion, that deeply rooted habits hindered him from abandoning the world."[51] Once his decision was made, however, the lifestyle he chose required that he excise all that was profane from his thought and that he deny himself every allusion to classical culture. Thus, we must uncover the influence of classical culture indirectly. We must investigate his intellectual past despite Gregory; may he pardon us this indiscretion.

Let us try to determine first of all what Gregory retained from the grammarian's and rhetor's lessons. One observation is immediate: compared with his contemporaries, Gregory wrote correct Latin.[52] Obviously, we cannot be sure whether the manuscripts have transmitted Gregory's orthography intact, but on the whole, his language remains fairly close to that of Late Antique authors.[53]

Gregory owed this relative correctness to his reading of classical Christian and profane authors. With but one exception, the pope never deliberately quoted directly from profane authors.[54] Perhaps when he compared himself and the Church to a sinking ship, he had Virgil's

---

[49] F. Homes Dudden, *Gregory the Great*, 2 vols. (London, 1905) 1: 101ff.; Pierre Battifol, *Saint Grégoire le Grand* (Paris, 1928), p. 17; and the old work by Coelestin Wolfsgruber, *Die vorpäpstliche Lebensperiode Gregors des Grossen nach seinen Briefen dargestellt* (Vienna, 1886).

[50] Battifol, *Saint Grégoire*, pp. 20–30.

[51] Gregory the Great, *Ep.* V, 53 (I, 354): "Diu longeque conversionis gratiam distuli . . . inolita me consuetudo devinxerat ne exteriorem cultum mutarem."

[52] For example, see the Latin of Antony of Piacenza, *Itinerarium CSEL*, 39: 159–218; and L. Bellanger, *In Antonii Placentini itinerarium grammatica disquisitio* (Paris, 1902). An example of vulgar Latin can be found in a list of saints dating from the seventh century; see Franz Steffens, *Lateinische Paläographie* (Trier, 1902), pl. 22.

[53] For Gregory's orthography, see L. M. Hartmann, "Ueber die Orthographie Papst Gregors I," *NA* 15 (1890): 527, and Dag Norberg's remarks, *In Registrum Gregorii Magni studia critica*, Uppsala Universitets Årsskrift, 4 (Uppsala, 1937), 6 (Uppsala, 1939). Norberg is preparing a new edition of Gregory's letters. For the vocabulary of the letters, see James Francis O'Donnell, *The Vocabulary of the Letters of Saint Gregory the Great: A Study in Late Latin Lexicography* (Washington, D.C., 1935). For the vocabulary of the *Moralia*, see R. M. Hauber, *The Late Latin Vocabulary of the "Moralia" of Saint Gregory the Great* (Washington, D.C., 1938).

[54] Gregory the Great, *Ep.* I, 33 (I, 47, l. 10): "Ut tibi aliquid saecularis auctoris loquar: cum amicis omnia tractanda sunt sed prius de ipsis." Compare this with Seneca's third letter to Lucilius: "Tu vero omnia cum amico delibera sed de ipso prius." These letters to Lucilius seem to have been read during the period; see Honorius Scholasticus' poem to the unknown Bishop Jordanes (*Anth. lat.*, p. 137, no. 666) and Schanz, IV-2, 269.

description of the tempest in mind;[55] the vocabulary is Virgilian, but the theme itself was quite common among ancient authors.[56] More precise were his allusions to "the empty tales of poets," in which he cited Hesiod, Aratus, and Callimachus.[57] Remembrances from his grammatical lessons are scattered throughout his works, especially in the dedicatory letters of the *Moralia*.[58] Writing to Leander of Seville that he did not observe grammatical rules, he developed this thought by listing technical grammatical terminology. This quite remarkable text can be compared to a passage from Cassiodorus' *Institutiones*.[59]

As he admitted several times, Gregory completely lacked any knowledge of Greek,[60] which is quite surprising for a former legate to Constantinople. Furthermore, the Byzantine restoration in Italy must have made the study of Greek important again. A Greek colony of monks and laymen had settled in Rome, but they seem to have lived by themselves.[61] Gregory was not the only one ignorant of Greek; he complained

---

[55] *Ep.* I, 41 (I, 56–57): "Nunc ex adverso fluctus inruunt, nunc ex latere cumuli spumosi maris intumescunt, nunc a tergo tempestas insequitur . . . putridae naufragium tabulae sonant." See Virgil, *Aeneid*, I, 100. Gregory's description of a tempest is found in *Dial.*, III, 36 (p. 216).

[56] For the fifth century, Maximus of Turin, *Homilia* LXXVII (*PL*, LVII, 419–20); for the sixth century, Ruricius of Limoges, *Ep.* I, 12–13; II, 3 (*MGH*, *AA*, VIII, 366, 390), and Arator's prefatory letter to Vigilius (*CSEL*, 72: 4). See Curtius, pp. 157ff., for nautical metaphors.

[57] Gregory the Great, *Ep.* V, 53a (I, 356): "Vanas fabulas poetarum sequitur ut mundi molem subvehi giganteo sudore suspicetur" (in reference to the legend of Atlas). See also the *Moral.*, IX, 11 (*PL*, LXXV, 865): "Vanas Hesiodi, Arati et Callimachi fabulas sequitur"; and Pierre Courcelle, "Grégoire le Grand à l'école de Juvenal," in *Studi in onore di Alberto Pincherle*, 2 vols. (Rome, 1967), 1: 170–74.

[58] *Ep.* V, 53 (I, 357). J. Fontaine has found several significant allusions; see *IS*, p. 36, n. 1.

[59] Cassiodorus, *Inst.*, I, 15, 9 (Mynors ed., p. 46): "In verbis quae accusativis et ablativis praepositionibus serviunt, situm motumque diligenter observa." For a comparison between the two texts, see R. Sabbadini, "Gregorio Magno et la grammatica," *Bolletino di filologia classica* 8 (1902): 204–6. See below, n. 101. Paul Ewald indicates in his edition of Gregory's letters (*Ep.* V, 53a [*MGH*, *Ep.*, I, 357]) that the manuscripts read "situs motusque," but he chose "situs modosque." Some philologists think that *situs* was taken for *hiatus*; see Norden, *Antike Kunstprosa*, 2: 531; Roger, p. 188, n. 3; Hartmann, "Ueber die Orthographie Papst Gregors I," *NA* 15 (1890): 544. This interpretation is hardly convincing.

[60] Gregory the Great, *Ep.* XI, 55 (II, 330, l. 6): "Nam nos nec graece novimus nec aliquod opus aliquando graece conscripsimus"; *Ep.* VII, 29 (I, 476): "Quamvis graecae linguae nescius." See Harold Steinacker, "Die römische Kirche und die griechischen Sprachkenntnisse des Frühmittelalters," *MIOEG* 62 (1954): 28–66 (also in *Festschrift Theodor Gomperz* [Vienna, 1902], pp. 324–41).

[61] For Greek elements in Rome, see Diehl, *Etudes sur l'administration byzantine*, pp. 247ff.; P. Battifol, "Les librairies byzantines à Rome," *MEFR* 8 (1888): 300ff.; idem, "Inscriptions byzantines de Saint Georges-du-Vélabre," *MEFR* 7 (1887): 419ff.; A. Michel, "Die griechische Klostersiedlungen zu Rom," *Ostkirchliche Studien* 1 (1952): 32–45.

that good translators were hard to find.[62] Latin and Greek culture were isolated from each other. One must await the seventh century to find again in Rome men who could understand both tongues.

Traces of Gregory's acquaintance with rhetoric can also be found in his work.[63] The style of his sermons has already been the subject of several major works: the pope employed the *cursus*, clausula, and rhymes, and remained faithful to certain classical figures.[64] He was aware of the deficiencies of false rhetoric and congratulated one of his correspondents for not cluttering his style with excess verbiage.[65] He was careful of form in his own letters, especially if they were sent to a learned lay or clerical correspondent. Those addressed to his friend Leander, a scholar like himself, were particularly carefully written.[66] Sometimes, like Ruricius or Ennodius, Gregory even wrote for the simple pleasure of writing or of celebrating a friendship.[67]

The pope was attentive to style in his great scriptural treatises—the dedicatory letter in the *Moralia* mentioned above should be reread with this point in mind. Here, Gregory related how he composed his work from the oral commentary he had given his monks: "When I had more

[62] Gregory the Great, *Ep.* X, 21 (II, 258, l. 27): "Indicamus praeterea quia gravem hic interpretum difficultatem patimur. Dum enim non sunt qui sensum de sensu exprimunt, sed transferre verborum semper proprietatem volunt omnem dictorum sensum confundunt." See what Courcelle has to say (*LG*, pp. 390–91). Even the translators at Vivarium were not very competent (ibid., pp. 319–20).

[63] Gregory the Great, *Hom. in Ezech.*, I, 11–12 (*PL*, LXXVI, 910): "Pensare etenim doctor debet quid loquatur, cui loquatur, quando loquatur, qualiter loquatur, et quantum loquatur." See *Reg. past.*, II, 2 (*PL*, LXXVII, 27), on the four premises of speech.

[64] H. M. Swank, *Gregor der Grosse als Prediger* (Berlin, 1934). P. V. S. Martic's *De genere dicendi S. Gregorii Magni I Papae in XL homiliis in Evangelia* (Freiburg, 1934) is a more rapid study. See Kathleen Brazzel, *The Clausulae in the Works of St. Gregory the Great* (Washington, D.C., 1939).

[65] Gregory the Great, *Moral.*, X, 29: "Hujus mundi sapientia est cor machinationibus tegere sensum verbis velare, quae falsa sunt verba ostendere quae vera sunt fallacia demonstrare." See ibid., XVIII, 46 (*PL*, LXXVI, 82); ibid., X, 2 (*PL*, LXXV, 919): "Nec fallacem quidem sophar sententiam protulit quod vir verbosus justificari nequaquam possit"; and *Ep.* IX, 147 (II, 142, l. 26), where Gregory wrote to Secundus of Trent, "Non in eis cultus eloquentiae non verborum typhus apparebant."

[66] See the beginning of the letter to Leander of Seville, *Ep.* IX, 227 (II, 218, l. 25): "Sanctitatis tuae suscepi epistulam solius caritatis calamo scriptam; ex corde enim lingua tinxerat quod in cartae pagina refondebat." See also letters to Empress Leontia (ibid., XIII, 42 [p. 404]), to Innocent, prefect of Africa (X, 16 [p. 251]), and to Bishop Dominicus of Carthage (VIII, 31 [p. 32]). Ildefonsus of Toledo, *De viris illustribus*, 1 (*PL*, XCVI, 199), had the following to say of Gregory's correspondence: "Extant epistolae . . . limato quidem et claro stylo digestae."

[67] Gregory the Great, *Ep.* XII, 1 (II, 347), to Dominicus of Carthage concerning his health; IX, 101 and 73 (II, 109 and 91), letters of consolation and congratulation; III, 65 (I, 226) and IX, 14 (II, 50), friendly notes.

leisure, I added a great deal, cut some, and left some things as they were. I amended the notes I made when I commented on the first reading in order to produce a well-composed work."[68] Nevertheless, he recognized its insufficiencies and begged Leander to excuse what was "insipid and careless" ("tepidum incultumque") in his work.[69] His state of health prevented him from doing better, and he compared himself to a musician whose instrument was out of tune.[70] We can find these scholar's scruples several times in the prefaces to his works. He complained, for example, of not having been able to correct the manuscript of his *Homilies on the Gospels* because his admirers had circulated it before he could stop them.[71] He also had some works sent back from Ravenna in order to amend texts he had previously dictated.[72]

Like scholars at the beginning of the century, Gregory also exhibited curiosity in the sciences. We saw earlier that he was interested in medicine.[73] He was also interested in the natural sciences. Like all accomplished exegetes, he used what he knew of the habits of animals and the qualities of minerals to draw moral considerations: he knew that mountain sheep (*ibices*), which he distinguished from the birds of the same name, reproduce in rocky areas and that they help each other descend from the heights much as deer help each other in crossing rivers; that crows make their young go hungry until they are certain their feathers are black; and that ostriches are unable to fly, despite their wings.[74] In passing, he gave tidbits of information on unicorns, centaurs,

[68] *Ep.* V, 53a (I, 355). See the translation of this letter in the edition of the *Moralia*, Books I and II, printed in *SC*, vol. 32 (Paris, 1950): 115–23. Elsewhere, Gregory defined *compositio* (*Hom. in Evang.*, II, 23, 1 [*PL*, LXXVI, 1282]). See Leclercq, *L'amour des lettres*, pp. 125–26.

[69] *Ep.* V, 53a (I, 357, ll. 15–17): "In qua quicquid tua sanctitas tepidum incultumque reppererit, tanto mihi celerrime indulgeat."

[70] Ibid., ll. 30–31: "Quassata organa proprie non resultant nec artem flatus exprimit, si scissa rimis fistula stridet." See Quintillian, *Inst. orat.*, XI, 3, 20 (Bornecque ed., 4: 192): "Ut tibiae . . . alium quassae sonum reddunt"; and similar images in Ennodius, *Carm.* I, 8, preface (*MGH, AA*, VII, 30, ll. 10–15).

[71] *Ep.* XII, 16 (II, 363, l. 5): "Notariorum schedas requirere studui easque . . . transcurrens . . . emendavi" (apropos of notes taken on his sermons on Ezechiel). For Gregory's stenographers, see Schmidt, "Die Evangelienhomilien Gregors der Grosse und die lateinische Tachygraphie," *Archiv für Stenographie* 52 (1900).

[72] *Ep.* XII, 6 (II, 352, ll. 15–23; p. 353, ll. 4–11).

[73] See sect. I of this chapter. I am not referring to images borrowed from the medical field, such as those found in *Reg. past.*, II, 2 and 14; *Moral.*, XXIV, 16; and *Hom. in Ezech.*, I, 11 (respectively, in *PL*, LXXVII, 27–28; LXXVI, 310, 913). Every sacred orator used these.

[74] *Moral.*, XXX, 10 (*PL*, LXXVI, 543–44); ibid., 9 (col. 542); ibid., XXXI, 8 (col. 578).

scorpions, and the asp.[75] He referred to the etymologies of *viper*[76] and *rhinoceros*,[77] and, passing to the mineral world, of *topaz*.[78] In denouncing the errors of the astrologers, he mentioned several constellations—the Pleiades, Boötes, the Bear, Orion and his sword[79]—and, in another passage, the signs of the zodiac.[80]

Did he acquire this information, which though superficial is nonetheless there, from his predecessors, the Church Fathers? Augustine, with whose works Gregory was thoroughly familiar, had an even more decided taste than Gregory for zoology and mineralogy.[81] I have not, however, found any obvious parallels between the two authors.[82] nor even between Gregory's work and Ambrose's *Hexameron*. Gregory certainly did not avail himself of the Latin translation of the *Physiologus*, which had been condemned at the beginning of the century by the Gelasian Decree.[83] Perhaps Gregory drew on some profane treatise, some ancestor of the bestiaries and lapidaries, for which he, in turn, would be a source in the Middle Ages.[84]

Gregory was also interested in Roman and contemporary history,[85]

---

[75] Ibid., XXXI, 15, 29 (col. 589); ibid., VII, 28 (PL, LXXV, 786); *Hom. in Ezech.*, I, 9, 21 (PL, LXXVI, 879); *Moral.*, XV, 15 (PL, LXXV, 1090).

[76] Ibid.: "Unde et vipera eo quod vi pariat nominatur."

[77] PL, LXXVI, 571: "Ejus . . . nomen latina lingua interpretatum sonat in nare cornu."

[78] Ibid., XVIII, 52 (PL, LXXVI, 89): "Topazium . . . et quia graeca lingua πάν omne dicitur pro eo quod omni colore resplendet."

[79] Ibid., XXIX, 31 (PL, LXXVI, 515): "Pleiades stellae ἀπὸ τοῦ πλείστου, id est a pluritate vocatae sunt. . . . Arcturus vero ita nocturna tempora illustra ut in caeli axe positus per diversa se vertat nec tamen occidat."

[80] *Hom. in Evang.*, I, 10 (PL, LXXVI, 1112), where he lays blame on astrologers (*mathematici*): "Fateri etiam mathematici solent quod quisquis in signo Aquarii nascitur in hac vita piscatoris ministerium sortiatur. Piscatores vero ut fertur Getulia non habet. Quis ergo dicat quia nemo illic in stella Aquarii nascitur ubi piscator omnimodo non habetur?"

[81] Marrou, *Saint Augustin*, pp. 136ff.

[82] But *Moral.*, XXX, 10 (PL, LXXVI, 543) is based on Cassiodorus, *In Psalm.*, 41, 4 (PL, LXX, 302), which in turn is from Pliny, *Hist. nat.*, VIII, 50. Likewise, *Moral.*, XXXI, 7 (PL, LXXVI, 576) is from Augustine, *Annotationes in Job*, 39, 13–18 (PL, XXXIV, 880). But Gregory does not seem to have known the *Annotationes*. Nor did he know the commentary on Job attributed to Jerome (PL, XXVI, 619–802).

[83] Friedrich Lauchert, *Geschichte des Physiologus* (Strasbourg, 1889), p. 88.

[84] See Alain de Boüard, *Une nouvelle encyclopédie médiévale: Le Compendium Philosophiae* (Paris, 1936).

[85] Gregory the Great, *Hom. in Evang.*, I, 3 (PL, LXXVI, 1088): "Fertur apud veteres mos fuisse ut quisquid consul existeret juxta ordinem temporum honoris sui locum teneret." See an allusion to an unknown law of Julian the Apostate in *Ep.* III, 64 (I, 225). Gregory seems to have had great admiration for Trajan; see the eighth-century *Vita Gregorii*, ed. Gasquet, p. 38. For the institutions of Gregory's times, see *Hom. in Ezech.*, I, 10 (PL, LXXVI, 1112): "In Persarum quoque Francorumque terra reges ex genere prodeunt."

arithmology,[86] and music. A *De musica* has been mistakenly attributed to him.[87] Gregory nevertheless must have had some theoretical acquaintance with music, since he spoke of musical instruments and the art of music more than once.[88] It could be that he perfected his knowledge of music at Constantinople and remembered enough about it to reform religious music at Rome.[89]

Gregory's works also bear several allusions to pagan philosophy. Some are literary allusions, such as the definition of friendship according to "the old philosophers."[90] Other allusions denounce errors, such as the skepticism of the Academicians, that is, of the New Academy, or the Stoics' philosophy of impassibility.[91] In general, Gregory was interested in philosophy only to combat it. When the Patriarch Eutychios of Constantinople discussed the physical status of the human body after the Resurrection by advancing neo-Aristotelian arguments, Gregory countered with a sentence from Scripture.[92] Without condemning reason outright, Gregory did think that knowledge of things divine took precedent: "Nec fides habet meritum, cui humana ratio praebet

---

[86] *Moral.*, XXXV, 8 (*PL*, LXXVI, 757–58): "Septenariusque numerus apud sapientes hujus saeculi quadam sua habetur ratione perfectus, quod ex primo pari et ex primo impari consummatur." See also ibid., I, 14, 18 (*PL*, LXXV, 534).

[87] Coelestin Vivell, *Vom Musik-Traktate Gregors des Grossen: Eine Untersuchung über Gregors Autorschaft und über den Inhalt der Schrift* (Leipzig, 1911). Guido of Arezzo was the first to attribute this treatise to Gregory; see Schanz, IV-2, 619.

[88] See the description of the citharist's art in *Reg. past.*, III (*PL*, LXXVII, 49).

[89] For Gregory's role in the reform of chant, see Amédée Gastoué, *Les origines du chant romain: L'antiphonaire grégorien* (Paris, 1907), and, more recently, Jacques Chailley, *Histoire musicale du Moyen Age* (Paris, 1950), pp. 48–51.

[90] Gregory the Great, *Ep.* III, 65 (I, 226): "Fuerunt quidam veteres philosophorum qui in duobus corporibus unam animam dicerent non affectu jungentes duos sed unam in duobus animae substantiam partientes." See Ruricius of Limoges, *Ep.* II, 1 (*MGH, AA*, VIII, 211, l. 6): "Antiqui sapientes amicos duos unam animam habere dixerunt"; and II, 10 (p. 318, l. 33): "Sapientes saeculi amicos duos unam animam habere dixerunt." See also the tripartite definition of philosophy in *Homiliae ii in Canticum canticorum*, ed. G. Heine, in *Bibliotheca anecdotarum*, 1 (Leipzig, 1848): 172. "Veteres tres vitae ordines esse dixerunt quas Graeci vitas ethicam, fisicam, theoricam nominaverunt." In the preface to the *Reg. past.*, I, 1, Gregory transposed the definition of philosophy and applied it to the governance of souls: "Ars est artium regimen animarum" (*PL*, LXXVII, 14). He alluded to Dionysius the Areopagite in the *Hom. in Evang.*, II, 34, 12 (*PL*, LXXVI, 1254).

[91] Gregory the Great, *Moral.*, XXXIII, 10, 19 (*PL*, LXXVI, 684): "Academicorum error qui certe conantur astruere certum nil esse, qui impudenti fronte assertionibus suis fidem ab auditoribus exigunt cum vera esse nulla testantur." *Moral.*, II, 16, 28 (*PL*, LXXV, 569): "Nonnulli magnae constantiae philosophiam putant si disciplinae asperitate correpti ictus verberum doloresque non sentiant."

[92] *Moral.*, XIV, 56–72 (*PL*, LXXV, 1078). See Battifol, *Saint Grégoire*, pp. 35–36. P. Courcelle shows, however, that the Gregorian doctrine of the eye of the soul comes indirectly from the mystical philosophy of Philo of Alexandria; see *Les Confessions de saint Augustin dans la tradition littéraire* (Paris, 1963), p. 54.

experimentum."[93] We point this sentence out because it will be repeated later in the Middle Ages by a philosopher incorrectly typed as a pre-rationalist: Abelard.[94]

There should be no misunderstanding our approach to Gregory. In assembling the above evidence, I have not tried to create an antithesis by making Gregory a humanist. Gregory was neither Augustine nor Cassiodorus. What we have tried to show is that Gregory, perhaps despite himself, shared in the same traditions as men of letters from the beginning of the century, even to the point of imitating their distaste for philosophy. Gregory's style, his thought, his taste for the exemplum and moralistic anecdote—all mark him as a man of Antiquity.[95] In this connection we have only to allude to his organizational abilities and to his talents as a statesman that earned him the title of "God's consul."

If these conclusions can be accepted, we should be astonished to learn that Gregory anathematized antique culture. It would be understandable if a man who knew this culture only from the outside condemned it; that Gregory would do so seems most extraordinary. Historians, though, have not really agreed on this point, so let us examine the subject as well as the texts usually cited.

III. GREGORY THE GREAT'S ATTITUDE TOWARD CLASSICAL CULTURE

I will leave aside the groundless legend from the twelfth century according to which Gregory had the Palatine library burned.[96] The legend was probably given a semblance of truth by the battle the pope led against astrological writings, which were still quite well known in Rome and elsewhere.[97] Let us look, rather, at two more germane texts,

[93] *Hom. in Evang.*, XXVI, 1 (*PL*, LXXVI, 1197): "Sciendum nobis est quod divina operatio si ratione comprehenditur non est admirabilis nec fides habet meritum, cui humana ratio praebet experimentum." See *Moral.*, VIII (*PL*, LXXV, 803).

[94] See Gérard Paré, Adrien Brunet, and Pierre Tremblay, *La Renaissance du XIIe siècle: Les écoles et l'enseignement* (Paris and Ottawa, 1933), pp. 298–99.

[95] This antique spirit has been treated by Spörl, "Gregor der Grosse und die Antike," and by R. Aigrain in Fliche-Martin, 5: 17ff., 543ff.

[96] See Dudden, *Gregory the Great*, 1: 290–91. John of Salisbury, *Policrat.*, II, 22 (ed. Clement C. J. Webb, 2 vols. [Oxford, 1909]) was responsible for this legend.

[97] J. Fontaine, "Isidore de Séville et l'astrologie," *REL* 31 (1953): 279. Bonnaud's thesis, according to which astrology "in its antique form had disappeared," is without foundation; see "Notes sur l'Astrologie latine au VIe siècle," *RBPh* 10 (1931): 562.

the dedicatory letter to Leander and the famous letter to Desiderius of Vienne. In the first, after apologizing for his style because of his health, Gregory came to what he thought was the essential point: if he refuses to submit to the rules of grammar, it is because "he regards it as highly improper to subject the words of the celestial oracle to the rules of Donatus." Then he immediately entrenched himself behind the authority of his exegetical forerunners: "None of the interpreters have observed these rules in regard to the authority of Holy Scripture."[98] The same statement can be found in all the Church Fathers.[99] It is even found in a true scholar, Cassiodorus: "The rules of Latin discourse are not to be followed everywhere; sometimes it is better to overlook the formulas of human discourse and preserve rather the measure of God's word."[100] This rapprochement between Gregory and Cassiodorus is all the more interesting for the analogous expressions and remarkable parallelisms one meets in their texts.[101] It is improbable that Gregory knew the *Institutiones,* even though he might have been in contact with the

---

[98] *Ep.* V, 53 (I, 357, ll. 40–41): "Quia indignum vehementer existimo ut verba caelestis oraculi restringam sub regulis Donati. Neque enim haec ab ullis interpretibus in scripturae sacrae auctoritate servata sunt."

[99] Ambrose, *Expositio evangelii secundam Lucam,* 2, 42 (*PL,* XV, 1568); Jerome, *Comm. in Ezech.,* V, prologue (*PL,* XXV, 141). For Augustine, see Wilhelm Suess, *Studien zur lateinischen Bibel, 1: Augustins Locutiones und das Problem der lateinischen Bibelsprache* (Tartu, 1932).

[100] Cassiodorus, *Inst.,* I, 15, 7 (p. 45): "Regulas igitur elocutionum Latinarum id est quadrigam Messii, omnimodis non sequaris ubi tamen priscorum codicum auctoritate convinceris. Expedit enim interdum praetermittere humanarum formulas dictionum et divini magis eloquii custodire mensuram."

[101] Roger, p. 188, noted but did not insist on the following parallels:

Cassiodorus, *Inst.,* I, 15, 7 (p. 45):	Gregory, *Ep.* V, 53a (I, 357):
"Regulas elocutionum latinarum . . . metacismos et hiatus vocalium omnino derelinque."	"Sub regulis Donati non metacismi collisionem fugio."
I, 15, 9 (p. 46):	Ibid.:
"In verbis quae accusativis et ablativis praepositionibus serviunt, situm motumque diligenter observa."	"Situs motusque et praepositionum casus servare contemno."

J. Fontaine, *IS,* p. 35, contrasts Gregory to Cassiodorus because the former, he says, "is speaking of his own prose, not of sacred texts." This is true. For Gregory, however, the language of the exegete falls under the same law as the text commented upon. As Fontaine remarks later in his book, Gregory knew the rules of grammar "but wanted especially to react against the excessive tendency to consider sacred texts solely from the point of view of grammar." See Henri de Lubac, "Saint Grégoire et la grammaire," *Recherches de science religieuse* 48 (1960): 185–226, and F. Weissengruber, "Zu Cassiodors Wertung der Grammatik," *WS* 3 (1969): 198–210, for a contrary view.

monks at Vivarium.[102] Their texts are so similar because, like Cassiodorus, Gregory was following a well-established tradition. The Middle Ages was to keep his counsel: exegetes would appeal to the authority of Gregory against the humanists who took Donatus as their authority.[103]

The second text, the letter to Desiderius of Vienne, is considered by many historians a veritable manifesto against classical culture.[104] Let us first describe its tenor. The pope had learned that Desiderius had taught grammar to certain individuals ("grammaticam quibusdam exponere") and that he had probably composed or read a poem on the pagan divinities.[105] Gregory was scandalized because it was impious for a bishop to utter the praises of both Jupiter and Christ. It was even forbidden for a "religious" layman to do so, he added.[106] The expressions with which Gregory reproached Desiderius for his teaching of grammar— and by grammar, we must understand profane literature in general— may seem very harsh. Gregory did not so much denounce the vanity or the falsity of literature as he did the fact that literature sullied one. He insisted on this several times: "Nefandum est . . . execrabile. . . . Cor vestrum maculari blasphemis . . . laudibus." Gregory's criticism was neither new nor more sweeping than that of his predecessors. He was simply following a well-established tradition in the Church that prohibited bishops from the teaching profession. That is what his letter was really all about. Desiderius of Vienne had first of all violated the *Statuta ecclesiae antiqua*, which, as we have seen, prohibited a bishop from reading profane texts, something that Desiderius was not alone in doing.[107] But what was even more serious was that he taught these texts in public. Any other pope, even a scholar-pope, would have reacted

---

102 *Ep.* VIII, 32 (II, 33–34).

103 Etienne Gilson, *La philosophie au Moyen Age* (Paris, 1944), p. 224.

104 Roger, pp. 156–57, 188; Ferdinand Lot, *La fin du monde antique et le début du Moyen Age* (Paris, 1951), p. 430; idem, *Les invasions germaniques* (Paris, 1945), p. 161 ("The holy pope hated antique, profane culture").

105 *Ep.* XI, 34 (II, 303): "Pervenit ad nos, quod sine verecundia memorare non possumus fraternitatem tuam grammaticam quibusdam exponere . . . quia in uno se ore cum Jovis laudibus Christi laudes non capiunt; et quam grave nefandumque sit episcopo canere." The use of the word *canere* proves that the passage concerns poems. Ibid. (p. 303, l. 21): "Neque vos nugis et saecularibus litteris studere constiterit." See the thesis cited above, n. 46, for this letter, and, more recently, M. Scivoletto, "I limite dell' ars grammatica in Gregorio Magno," *Giornale italiana di filologia* 17 (1964): 210–38.

106 "Laicus religiosus" undoubtedly means *conversus*: see elsewhere, *Ep.* VII, 27 (I, 472). When Cassiodorus was at Constantinople, the pope called him "religiosus vir" (*PL*, LXIX, 49). See Vogel, *La discipline pénitentielle*, p. 136, for the word *religiosus*.

107 See above, chap. 3, sect. III.

just as Gregory had. Gregory's reaction was more energetic because he had a very high concept of the sacerdotal function: the only art a bishop should learn was the art of caring for souls ("ars artium est regimen animarum").[108]

So, we should not attribute more to the letter to Desiderius than it actually says. At the time, it did not have the reputation it later developed. Only when a passage from the letter was incorporated in canon law would everyone begin to interpret it one way or another.[109]

Having reduced these two texts to their proper proportions, we must now turn to another text, which Gregory's advocates alone have cited in the controversy.[110] This passage is an excerpt from the *Commentary on the First Book of Kings*.[111] Gregory explicated several books of the Old Testament, among them this one, whose explications were later polished by one of Gregory's monks.[112] As a result, it was long held that this particular *Commentary* was not genuinely Gregory's work.[113] The authenticity of the work, however, has recently been upheld.[114] This attribution is important for us because the *Commentary* contains a passage of great interest in regard to Gregory's attitude vis à vis the liberal arts.

In explicating the verse in which the Philistines forbid the Israelites from working metal (1 Kings 13:19), Gregory transferred this episode to the intellectual plane. The arms the metal worker fabricates are secular letters—arms which are useless for the spiritual combat the Israelites must wage. Whosoever lives by God combats demonic spirits without the help of secular learning.[115] So far, Gregory was true to the ascetic

[108] *Reg. past.*, III, prologue (*PL*, LXXVII, 49). This definition is taken from Gregory Nazianzen.

[109] *Corp. Jur. Can.*, I, 86, 5: "Sacram scripturam non grammaticam licet exponere episcopus." This twists Gregory's thought in saying that Desiderius taught grammar instead of the Gospels ("pro lectione evangelica").

[110] See Viscardi, *Le origini*, p. 411, but also Gilson, *La philosophie au Moyen Age*, p. 154, and E. K. Rand, *The Founders of the Middle Ages* (Cambridge, Mass., 1928), p. 26.

[111] *PL*, LXXIX, 17ff.

[112] Gregory the Great, *Ep.* XII, 6 (II, 352, ll. 16–19): "Quae ego scripto tradere prae infirmitate non potui ipse [Claudius] ea suo sensu dictavit ne oblivione deperirent ut apto tempore haec eadem mihi inferret et emendatius dictarentur."

[113] Dudden, *Gregory the Great*, 1: x, n. 1, summarizes the principal objections. See Schanz, IV-2, 613.

[114] Patrick Verbraken, "Le commentaire de saint Grégoire sur le premier livre des Rois," *RB* 66 (1956): 159–217. B. Capelle, "Les homélies de saint Grégoire sur le Cantique," *RB* 41 (1929): 205, was already of this opinion.

[115] *In librum primum Regum expositionum libri vi*, V, 30 (*PL*, LXXIX, 355): "Ad

tradition. Then came a decisive sentence. According to Gregory, secular studies, which of themselves are not useful in the spiritual battles led by the saints, become useful when they are put to the service of a greater understanding of divine Scriptures: "In knowing the liberal arts, we understand divine words much better." But it is only in pursuit of this goal ("ad hoc quidem tantum") that the study of profane books is permitted.[116] Demons thwart the desire in some to educate themselves because they know that if men are ignorant of secular letters, they will not reach spiritual heights. They know quite well that spiritual understanding is facilitated by acquiring profane culture.[117] "Almighty God has placed secular learning here below so that we could mount the stages that would lead us to the heights of divine Scripture."[118] This is what Moses did when he mastered the learning of the Egyptians and what Isaiah, Jeremiah, and Saint Paul did after him.

There is no contradiction between this passage from the *Commentary on the First Book of Kings* and the first two texts discussed above. Gregory never overtly condemned secular culture; he simply assigned it a secondary level, "on the plain" and thought that it was useless for those who fought with spiritual weapons against the ambushes of evil. That is the essence of Gregory's thought. Gregory continuously contrasted worldly wisdom, which included profane studies, to God's wisdom.[119] Because of his monastic vocation and his belief that the end of the world was near,[120] he wanted to convert his fellow men to the su-

spiritualia bella non per saeculares litteras sed per divinas instruimur. Faber quippe ferrarius in Israël non invenitur quia fideles Domini viventes arte saecularis scientiae contra malignos spiritus nequaquam praeliantur."

[116] Ibid.: "Quae profecto saecularium librorum eruditio etsi per semetipsam ad spiritualem sanctorum conflictum non prodest, si divinae scripturae conjungitur ejusdem Scripturae scientia subtilius eruditur. Ad hoc quidem tantum liberales artes discendae sunt ut per instructionem illarum divina eloquia subtilius intelligantur."

[117] Ibid., 356: "A non nullorum cordibus discendi desiderium maligni spiritus tollunt, ut et saecularia nesciant, et ad sublimitatem spiritalium non pertingant. . . . Aperte quidem daemones sciunt quia dum saecularibus litteris instruimur, in spiritualibus adjuvamur. Cum ergo nos ea discere dissuadent, quid aliud quam ne lanceam aut gladium faciamus praecavent?"

[118] Ibid: "Hanc quippe saecularem scientiam omnipotens Deus in plano anteposuit ut nobis ascendendi gradum faceret qui nos ad divinae Scripturae altitudinem levare debuisset."

[119] See *Reg. past.*, II, 6 (*PL*, LXXVII, 34): "Ut sapientes stulti fiant stultam sapientiam deserant et sapientem Dei stultitiam discant"; *Moral.*, X, 29, 48 (*PL*, LXXV, 947); and *Dial.*, II, prologue (p. 72, l. 42). Studies were classed as external activities: "Alii bellorum titulis, alii altis aedificorum moenibus, alii disertis doctrinarum saecularium libris instanter elaborant" *Moral.*, XI, 30–42 (*PL*, LXXV, 972).

[120] *Ep.* IV, 23, 44 (I, 257, l. 29; p. 279, l. 24); III, 61 (I, 221, ll. 25–29). See G. Galligaris, "S. Gregorio Magno e la paura del prossimo finimundo nel medio evo," *Atti*

perior wisdom one acquired from the study of the sacred text. Gregory reminded clerics, monks, and even lay aristocrats of the urgency of studying the Bible,[121] which "transcends all learning and doctrine."[122]

But Gregory was conscious of the usefulness of profane training. Israel had to "descend," if only to learn to read and to write. As the pope said in a passage from the *Moralia*, the wise men of God take their language from the wise men of the world, just as God assumed the voice of men in order to save them.[123] In short, in order to pass into the world, God's word had to become incarnate and use in its service everything that human speech employs.

Gregory thus resembles Saint Paul, who also had been influenced by the learning of his native milieu and who also continually contrasted the two wisdoms.[124] Gregory the Great's attitude toward classical culture must be understood in this light without making him an enemy of all profane intellectual training.

If this interpretation is accepted, Gregory also resembles one of his models, Augustine, who tolerated profane studies only if appropriated to the study of the sacred text.[125] He also resembles another Christian scholar who remained equally faithful to the patristic tradition by subjecting profane wisdom to God's wisdom: Cassiodorus.

At the time Gregory the Great withdrew from the world, Cassiodorus had already spent twenty years in his monastery at Vivarium. Even though these two men were not of the same generation, they were contemporaries, since Cassiodorus died at an advanced age in 581 or 583. It is therefore proper to examine the principles of Cassiodorus' program of studies here.

---

della Real Academia delle scienze di Torino 31 (1895): vi, 264; Raoul Manselli, "L'escatologismo di Gregorio Magno," *Atti del I Congresso* (Spoleto, 1951), p. 383.

[121] *Ep.* V, 46 (I, 346), to the emperor's physician: "Stude quaeso et cotidie creatoris tui verba meditare"; XI, 59 (II, 346), to the daughters of the patricius Venantius: "Opto ut sanctam scripturam legere ametis ut quamdiu vos omnipotens Deus viris conjunxerit, sciatis et qualiter vivere et domum vestram quo modo disponere debeatis"; VII, 26 (I, 471), to a young man about to be married: "Sacris lectionibus vacare, celestia verba meditari." See also *Ep.* IX, 13, 15, 85; X, 16 (II, 50, 51, 99, 251).

[122] *Moral.*, XX, 1 (*PL*, LXXVI, 135): "Omnem scientiam atque doctrinam scriptura sacra sine aliqua comparatione transcendit."

[123] *Moral.*, IX, 11 (*PL*, LXXV, 865): "Scriptura sacra idcirco eisdem vocabulis utitur ut res quas insinuare appetit notitia usitatae appellationis exprimantur. . . . Sic igitur in sacro eloquio sapientes Dei sermonem trahunt a sapientibus saeculi sicut in pro utilitate hominis vocem in se humanae passionis ipse conditor hominum sumit Deus."

[124] 1 Cor. 1:19. Gregory often cited the "magister egregius Paulus" (*Reg. past.*, III, 6 [*PL*, LXXVII, 56–57]).

[125] Marrou, *Saint Augustin*, pt. 3, pp. 331ff.

IV. CENTERS OF SCRIPTURAL STUDIES

The creation at Vivarium of a monastery devoted to the organization of religious studies is considered by all historians of this period to be the great intellectual event of the second half of the sixth century. Cassiodorus, who in 537 had abandoned politics and had withdrawn from the world (what he, too, called his "conversion"), first studied the Psalms.[126] The war obliged him to leave Italy, and in 550, we find him at Constantinople.[127] Only after his return did he organize the monastic group at Vivarium on his property in Calabria.[128] This foundation, about which we shall have more to say, was not an exceptional event in Italy. Centers for scriptural studies, nonexistent at the beginning of the sixth century, were beginning to spring up almost everywhere. The horrors of war seemed to have impelled monks, bishops, and laymen to turn more attentively to the sacred text.

A. Centers of Christian Learning before Vivarium

Abbot Florianus of the monastery of Romanum in northern Italy in the diocese of Milan, [129] whom we have already met in the episcopal school at Arles,[130] was gifted with an extensive religious and profane education. He wrote to Nicetius of Trier in 551 that he was trained in Holy Scripture by his predecessor and master, Theodatus.[131] His two extant letters indicate that his Latin was quite elegant. Another text, however, gives us a better view of his religious culture. Arator probably

---

[126] Cassiodorus, *De orthographia*, preface (Keil ed., 7: 144): "Ubi . . . conversionis meae tempore primum studium laboris impendi." He had already been interested in *lectio divina* before his "conversion"; see *Var.*, IX, 25 (*MGH, AA*, XII, 292, l. 31).

[127] See van de Vyver, "Cassiodore et son oeuvre," pp. 253–59.

[128] Ibid. Van de Vyver's proof is convincing, and his point of view is shared by Paul Lehmann, "Cassiodorstudien," *Philologus* 171 (1912): 778; Leslie Webber Jones, *An Introduction to Divine and Human Readings by Cassiodorus Senator* (New York, 1946), p. 21; and Cappuyns, "Cassiodore," *DHGE*, 11: 1357. Laistner, *Thought and Letters*, p. 96, has kept 538 for the date of Vivarium's foundation.

[129] Florianus, *Ep.* 5–6 (*MGH, Ep.*, III, 116–18). The allusion to Bishop Datius ("domino meo Datio episcopo" [p. 117, l. 16]) localizes the letter to the diocese of Milan, perhaps to present-day Romano di Lombardia between Milan and Brescia, and provides the date, since Datius was held captive at Constantinople with Pope Vigilius at that time. See Stein, 2: 648.

[130] Gian Piero Bognetti, "Non l'isola Comacina ma l'isola di Lerins (a proposito della lettera di Floriano a Nicezio del 550)," *Archivio storico lombardo* (1944), pp. 129–35, thinks with the editor of the *Histoire littéraire de la France*, ed. Antoine Rivet de la Grange, 12 vols. (1865–69), 3: 319, that Florianus was abbot of Lérins. His proof is not convincing.

[131] *Ep.* 5 (*MGH, Ep.* III, 117, l. 8): "Qui mihi sacras exposuit scripturas et flores tenere lanuginis ipse suscepit."

sent his poem on the Acts of the Apostles to this Florianus in 544[132] and asked him to review the work, while at the same time praising his precocity, his natural talents, the size of his library, and his spiritual wisdom.[133]

At Ravenna during the same period, Bishop Maximian (546–56) had the Septuagint copied[134] and revised the Gospels with the help of the version Jerome had sent to Rome so that, as he explained in his subscription, "ignorant or incapable scribes might not corrupt the text."[135] Shortly afterwards, around 560, Angellus of Ravenna composed a treatise against the Arians.[136]

In southern Italy, around Capua and Naples, which were less ravaged by the war, clerics and laymen studied the Bible. Like his colleague at Ravenna, Bishop Victor of Capua carried out a revision of the text of the Gospels in 546 and 547.[137] Thanks to the Fulda manuscript, which perserves his amended text, we can see that this cultivated cleric still tried to respect the norms of classical orthography.[138] Victor

---

[132] Arator, *Ep. ad Florianum, CSEL*, 72: 1. Several clues point in Florianus' direction: the title *abbas*; the fact that Arator was the disciple of Ennodius, who, in turn, was the godfather of the abbot of Romanum; and, finally, the agreement of the dates.

[133] Ibid., pp. 9–12:

> Spiritaliter erudito Floriani abbati . . .
> . . . primaevus adhuc senibus documenta dedisti . . .
> Inter grandiloquos per mille volumina libros
> Maxima cum teneas et breviora lege
> Naturaeque modo quam rerum condidit Auctor
> Concordent studiis celsa vel ima tuis.

[134] Agnellus, *Liber pont. eccl. ravenn.*, 81 (*MGH, SRL*, p. 332): "Fecitque omnes ecclesiasticos libros id est septuaginta duo optime scribere . . . quibus usque hodie utimur."

[135] Ibid.: "Et ultimo, loco evangeliorum et apostolorum epistolarum si requirere vultis ipsius literas invenietis ita monentes: emendavi cautissime cum his quae Augustinus et secundum evangelia quae beatus Ieronimus Romam misit et parentibus suis direxit tantum ne ab idiotis vel malis scriptoribus vicientur."

Maximian was also responsible for a collection of masses, "edidit namque missales per totum circulum anni et sanctorum omnium," and perhaps also for a chronicle (see *Wattenbach-Levison*, 1: 56) which the Anonymous of Valois used. The famous ivory chair of Alexandrian origin has been attributed to Maximian too. See Carlo Cecchelli, *La cattedra di Massimiano ed altri avori romano-orientali* (Rome, 1935).

[136] Schanz, IV-2, 595.

[137] This is the *Codex Fuldensis*, edited by Ernst C. Ranke (Marburg, 1868) from the point of view of diplomatics. See the subscription in Ranke, p. 462: "Victor famulus Christi et ejus gratia episc. Capuae legi apud basilicam Consta[nt]ianam d. XIII Kal. maias. ind. nona, q. n. p. c. basili. I.c. cons.," for April 19, 546; and "Iterato legi ind. X. die prid. idium aprile," that is, April 12, 547. See F. Bolgiani, *Vittore di Capua e il Diatessaron*," Memorie dell'Accademia delle scienze di Turino, Classe di scienze morali, storiche e filologiche, ser. 4, no. 2 (Turin, 1962).

[138] For the orthographic correction of the text, see Ranke and, more recently, Corbett, "Prolégomènes," in Vanderhoven and Masai, *Regula Magistri*, pp. 45–46.

was also interested in Latin and even Greek exegesis and gathered together a volume of extracts from different Doctors.[139]

Eleven years later, in 558, another copy of the Gospels was revised by a reader in Eugippius' library who, like his colleagues at Ravenna and perhaps at Capua, used a Hieronymian text.[140] Thus, during this period we find evidence of activity once again in the scriptorium at Lucullanum for the first time since Eugippius' death. The monastery still existed, and its library continued to furnish manuscripts: a manuscript of Augustine's letters which a certain Facistus recopied and amended in 560[141] belonged to this library, as did two translations of Origen's works and one of Rufinus' works which the priest Donatus revised in 569.[142] In 582, while the Lombards were besieging Naples, the notary of the cathedral church, on his bishop's orders, was correcting a copy of Eugippius' Augustinian *Excerpta* that could only have come from Eugippius' library.[143] These few references are sufficient to show that the work Eugippius undertook at the beginning of the century lived on and already prefigured the accomplishments of Cassiodorus at Vivarium.

The presence of Lucullanum certainly had an impact on the clergy of Naples. If Bishop John's claim to the sermons that once were attributed to John Chrysostom can stand, he would be a case in point.[144] Monte Cassino, 110 kilometers (69 miles) from Naples, is also thought to have been affected by this center of sacred studies.[145] But what I have already said of Benedictine culture, coupled with the absence of any proof, makes this doubtful.

We do know for certain, though, that there was another center of Christian learning not far from Monte Cassino. A certain Dulcicius at Aquino corrected and partly punctuated a fragment of the *De Trinitate*

[139] Schanz, IV-2, 596; Gustav Bardy, "Victor de Capoue," *DTC*, 15, pt. 2:2874–75; van de Vyver, "Cassiodore et son oeuvre," p. 283, n. 1.

[140] See van de Vyver, "Cassiodore et son oeuvre," p. 282, who summarizes Dom Chapman's hypothesis attributing this revision to Cassiodorus and then rejects it.

[141] See the subscription in Paris, Bibliothèque Nationale, n. a. l. 1443.

[142] See van de Vyver, "Cassiodore et son oeuvre," p. 282. These were the translations of the Περὶ Ἀρχῶν, of the commentary on the Epistle to the Romans, and of Rufinus' *De adulteratione librorum Origenis*.

[143] See the subscription in Paris, Bibliothèque Nationale, lat. 11642, in the edition of the *Excerpta ex operibus s. Augustini* of Eugippius (*CSEL*, 9, pt. 1: xxv).

[144] For John "Mediocris," see *Clavis*, no. 915, and Germain Morin, "Etude sur une série de discours d'un évêque (de Naples?) du VIe siècle," *RB* 11 (1894): 386–91. In the *Gesta episcoporum Neapolitanorum*, 16, XXII (*MGH, SRL*, p. 410), John is portrayed as a great builder.

[145] A. Vaccari, "La Bibbia nell' ambiente di S. Benedetto," *Biblica* 29 (1948): 331ff.

of Saint Hilary now conserved at Vienna.[146] Even though some describe Dulcicius as a grammarian,[147] we really do not know who he was. His subscription simply says "Dulcicius Aquini legebam." If he corrected his text like a grammarian, it was because he took lessons from one.[148] It has been further argued that he revised his text in connection with a controversy with Barbarian Arians. If so, the controversy probably involved Goths rather than Lombards because Gothic Arianism still had adherents in Italy. Gothic Arianism was the target of a treatise Agnellus of Ravenna wrote around 560.[149] Augustine's *De Trinitate* was revised near Cumae in 559 by an important lay landowner[150] and provides yet more evidence that interest in doctrinal studies existed in southern Italy.

We can end our inquiry with the text from Cumae. Despite the paucity of evidence it is clear that the creation of Vivarium was part of a whole. Vivarium responded to a need, and without diminishing Cassiodorus' role, the way had been prepared for Vivarium.

B. Studies at Vivarium

In certain respects, the monastery of Vivarium recalls the foundations of the first half of the sixth century. Cassiodorus, like Cassian, thought that the cenobitic life was but a preparation for the anchoretic life.[151] For those whose "purified souls wished a more sublime life," he provided the "sweet retreats of Mount Castellum" on a height overlooking the site of Vivarium.[152] He was only following the example of the monks

---

[146] See Rudolf Beer, *Monumenta paleographica vindobonensia: Denkmäler der schreibkunst aus der handschriftensammlung des Habsburg-Lothringischen erzhauses . . .*, 2 vols. (Leipzig, 1910–13), 1: 26, and H. Klos, "Neue Fragmente des Hilarius-Papyruskodex," *MIOEG* 63 (1955): 47–52, for this papyrus.

[147] Beer was the first to do so; van de Vyver, "Cassiodore et son oeuvre," p. 281, followed him. A Dulcitius who lived in Campania appears in the correspondence of Pelagius I (558–66); see Samuel Lowenfeld, ed., *Epistolae pontificum romanorum ineditae* (Leipzig, 1885), p. 14, n. 25.

[148] See Beer, *Monumenta*, 1: 26, for the date of the papyrus.

[149] Schanz, IV-2, 595.

[150] Dijon, codex 141, bears the following subscription: "In provincia Campania, in territorio Cumano, in possessione nostra Acheruscio." Joseph Michael Heer, *Evangelium gatianum: Quattuor evangelia latine translata ex codice monasterii S. Gatiani Turonensis* (Freiburg, 1910), p. xli, identified this place name with the *Acherusia palus* near Cumae mentioned by Virgil (*Aeneid*, VI, 106) and Pliny (*Hist. nat.*, III, 61). Could this be present-day Lake Averno? See André Wilmart, "La tradition des grands ouvrages de saint Augustin," in *Miscellanea agostiniana*, ed. Antonio Cassamassa (Rome, 1931), 2: 27.

[151] Cassiodorus, *Inst.*, I, 29, 3 (p. 74): "Si vos in monasterio Vivariensi . . . coenobiorum consuetudo competenter erudiat, et aliquid sublimis defecatos animos optare contingat."

[152] For the location of these cells, see Pierre Courcelle, "Le site du monastère de Cassiodore," *MEFR* 55 (1938): 259–307.

of Lérins and Condat. Even at Vivarium there was a place for monks who were not cultured. Twice, Cassiodorus noted that such monks could attain perfect knowledge of God without intellectual training[153] by devoting themselves to work in the fields and to prayer, prayer which was organized just as at every other monastery of the period.[154] The monks had to know their Psalter in order to participate in the liturgy.[155] As at Arles or Monte Cassino, "purity of heart" was the essential condition for *lectio divina*. It was not sufficient, Cassiodorus said, that the ears hear but rather that the eyes of the soul see clearly.[156] Thus the founder was aware of the merits of the ascetical training which he hoped to apply in his monastery. But there is no indication, as some historians would have it, that he took the Benedictine rule for his model.[157] He was influenced, rather, by the spirit which inspired all monasticism during this period. What made his monastery original, however, was that he opened up a second current that some call "humanist."

No other monastery of the period was able to combine the two currents, which, as we have seen, were in complete opposition everywhere else. Cassiodorus took the precaution of establishing two monasteries, only one of which—Vivarium—he organized as a center of studies.

Vivarium consisted primarily of a library and a scriptorium. There are numerous studies of Cassiodorus' library that the reader may consult.[158] They have shown how rich the library was in Latin and Greek

---

[153] Cassiodorus, *Inst.*, preface, 7, and I, 28 (p. 7, ll. 1–5; p. 69): "Multi agrammati ad verum intellectum perveniant rectamque fidem percipiant caelitus aspiratam."

[154] Ibid., I, 28, 5 (p. 71, l. 18); Germain Morin, "L'ordre des heures canoniales dans les monastères de Cassiodore," *RB* 43 (1931): 145–52. For a contrary view, see Maieul Cappuyns, "Cassiodore," *DHGE*, 11: 1360, who believes that the *Regula Magistri* is the work of Cassiodorus. See also idem, "L'auteur de la *Regula Magistri*: Cassiodore," *RTAM* 15 (1948): 209–68.

[155] Cassiodorus, *Inst.*, preface, 4: "Ut primum tyrones Christi postquam psalmorum didicerint."

[156] Ibid., I, 24, 3 (p. 65): "Quapropter ad intentiones librorum generaliter semper animus erigatur, mentemque nostram in illa contemplatione defigamus, quae non tantum auribus sonat sed oculis interioribus elucescit." Also XVI, 2 (p. 52, ll. 9–10): "Quid enim in illis litteris utilitatis et suavitatis non invenies, si purissimo lumine mentis intendas?"

[157] See Herwegen's arguments for the supposed contacts between Benedict and Cassiodorus in *Saint Benoît*, p. 241, n. 23. John Chapman's hypotheses, which were presented in his *Saint Benedict and the Sixth Century* (London, 1929), pp. 93–110, continue to influence historians. Ensslin, *Theodorich*, p. 281, and P. Schmitz, "Benoît," *DHGE*, 7: 1062, think that Cassiodorus followed Benedict's rule. Van de Vyver, "Cassiodore et son oeuvre," p. 279, n. 4, did not express an opinion.

[158] See, above all, Courcelle, *LG*, pp. 313–88, and Cappuyns, "Cassiodore," *DHGE*, 11: 1388–99. Courcelle thinks that Cassiodorus did not have more than about a hundred

books and how the former minister tried to buy books he did not have, even from as far away as Africa.[159] The three versions of the *Institutiones,* correctly described as "an analytical bibliography," bear eloquent witness to the progressive enrichment of the library.[160] Commerce in books, even profane books, had not ceased. In fact, Vivarium's scriptorium was one of the sources of this commerce, as we learn from Cassiodorus' praise of copyists *(antiquarii),* in which he warned them not to work simply in hope of gain.[161]

Scribes, then, must have been trained at Vivarium. Cassiodorus reminded them of the rules of calligraphy. Obviously, specialists were needed for this difficult métier: to be a scribe was like being a physician.[162] Other monks, those with intellectual talents, were invited to study sacred literature according to a program, complete with bibliography, outlined by Cassiodorus.

Cassiodorus had long contemplated this program; he had it in mind in 535 when he proposed his Christian university. He had since been able to go to the East to observe the accomplishments of the school at Nisibis, where teachers fleeing from Edessa in the fifth century had gathered in order to insure public instruction in divine law.[163] While living in Constantinople in the middle of the sixth century, one of these masters, Paul of Nisibis, disseminated elementary manuals which had been prepared, if not for the pupils at Nisibis, at least for those of a neighboring school. According to the Latin adaptation of this treatise by the ex-quaestor Junilius,[164] Paul taught the rules of exegesis as well

---

codices ("Nouvelles recherches sur le monastère de Cassiodore," in *Actes du Ve Congrès international d'archéologie chrétienne* [Paris, 1957], p. 517).

159 *Inst.,* I, 8, 9; 29, 2 (p. 30, l. 18; p. 74, l. 12).

160 Pierre Courcelle, "Histoire d'un brouillon cassiodorien," *REA* 44 (1942): 65–86; L. Alfonsi, "Cassiodoro e le sue *Institutiones,*" *Klearchos* 6 (1964): 6–20.

161 Cassiodorus, *Inst.,* I, 30 (p. 75, l. 18): "Nequeo dicere vicissitudinem illum de tot bonis non posse percipere, si tamen non cupiditatis ambitu sed recto studio talia noscatur efficere."

162 Ibid., I, 30, *De antiquariis;* I, 31, *De medicis.*

163 Junilius, *Instituta regularia divinae legis,* ed. Heinrich Kihn (Freiburg-im-Breisgau, 1880): "Scola in Nisibi urbe . . . ubi divina lex per magistros publicos . . . ordine et regulariter traditur." See Schanz, IV-2, 583. For the school in Nisibis, see T. Hermann, "Die Schule von Nisibis," *Zeitschrift für die neutestamentliche Wissenschaft* 25 (1926): 89, 122; J. B. Chabot, "L'école de Nisibe, son histoire, ses statuts," *Journal asiatique,* 9th ser., 8 (1896): 43–93; and, more recently, Wanda Wolska-Conus, *La topographie chrétienne de Cosmas Indicopleustes* (Paris, 1961), pp. 67, 69.

164 This manual had no doubt been prepared for the students in the school at Abcadena. See the testimony of Měsiha-zkha in *Sources syriaques,* vol. 1, ed. and trans. Alphonse Mingana (Leipzig, 1907), p. 156; and of Thomas McNamara, *Iunilii Africani Instituta*

as those of theology.[165] Cassiodorus, in founding Vivarium, insisted especially on the first of these. As we have seen, he did not have a great taste for philosophy and theology. After he was converted, he hastily wrote an unoriginal treatise "on the soul" at the request of friends.[166] Philosophical treatises were rare in Vivarium's library, and the theological works of the Fathers were mentioned only insofar as they concerned the interpretation of Scripture.

Let us recall the outline of Cassiodorus' program. The first necessity was to work with well-established texts, which meant learning the rules of punctuation and orthography.

Punctuating a biblical text was a delicate operation because one had to choose between two methods: the classical punctuation of the grammarians[167] and that used by Jerome to make the text more readable "per cola et commata." Cassiodorus seemed to prefer the grammarians' rules and only grudgingly adopted the Hieronymian formula for certain parts of the Vulgate.[168] When he did, it was in Jerome's spirit: "for those who had not been taught by secular masters."[169] The conflict in Cassiodorus between the former student of grammarians and the exegete of sacred texts is apparent here as well as in matters pertaining to orthography. Cassiodorus entrusted orthographical work to the most learned monks,[170] whom he reminded of the grammarians' rules in his *Institutiones* and in the preface to his *De orthographia*. The rules could not be applied absolutely, however, because the Divine Word was not bound by human rules.[171] Cassiodorus followed the patristic tradition and, in that, reminds one of Gregory the Great. Cassiodorus, however,

---

regularia divinae legis: A Translation with an Introduction and Commentary (Washington, D.C., 1955).

[165] For his theology, see Heinrich Kihn, *Theodor von Mopsuestia und Junilius Africanus als Exegeten* (Freiburg-im-Breisgau, 1880). His exegesis has been studied by M. L. W. Laistner, "Antiochene Exegesis in Western Europe during the Middle Ages," *Harvard Theological Review* 40 (1947): 23ff.

[166] For this *Liber de anima*, see Schanz, IV-2, 100–101, and Cappuyns, "Cassiodore," *DHGE*, 11: 1368–69. Cassiodorus wrote this treatise around 538.

[167] For this punctuation, see J. Fontaine, *IS*, pp. 71ff.

[168] He praised classical punctuation (*Inst.*, I, 15, 12) but used Hieronymian punctuation for his *Codex grandior*. See van de Vyver, "Cassiodore et son oeuvre," pp. 266ff., and Courcelle, *LG*, p. 360.

[169] Cassiodorus, *Inst.*, preface, 9 (p. 8): "Propter eos qui distinctiones non didicerant apud magistros saecularium litterarum."

[170] Ibid., I, 15 (p. 42): "A paucis enim doctisque faciendum est quod simplici et minus eruditae congregationi noscitur esse praeparandum."

[171] Ibid., I, 15, 5 (p. 44, ll. 3–5; pp. 455ff.); Roger, pp. 179–81.

had more reservations than did Gregory about the patristic tradition: copyists must always refer to the authority of ancient and good manuscripts; they must not hesitate to correct basic mistakes;[172] lastly, everything outside the domain of scriptural authority—commentaries, letters, sermons—ought to be corrected without hesitation.[173] Cassiodorus demanded a thankless task while at the same time not allowing the corrector very much discretion: he had to have an excellent knowledge of orthographic usages (usages, because there had never been fixed rules ["orthographia saepe mutata est"]),[174] which he had to know how to apply without losing the slightest nuance of divine meaning.

The monk's second task, after the establishment of the text, was its interpretation. Here Cassiodorus had help from his predecessors, to whom he sent his disciples. He collected in his library the works of "Catholic masters" who were talented in unravelling obscure *quaestiones*[175] and the works of the *introductores* and *expositores*. He compiled the books of the "introducers"—Augustine's *De doctrina christiana*, Junilius' already mentioned *Instituta*, and Eucherius' *Liber formularum spiritalis*—into one volume.[176] He also had a second work by Eucherius, the *Liber instructionum*, a true biblical dictionary such as Augustine wanted.[177] As for the works of the *expositores*, that is, the biblical commentators, he cited them in his studies of the books of the Bible, especially mentioning those whom he thought were the "greats": Hilary, Cyprian, Ambrose, Jerome, and Augustine.[178]

---

172 *Inst.*, I, 15, 7 (p. 45): "Ubi tamen priscorum codicum auctoritate convinceris"; ibid., I, 15, 6 (p. 44, ll. 24–25): "Sed tamen . . . duorum vel trium priscorum emendatorumque codicum auctoritas inquiratur." See ibid., I, 15, 9 (p. 46, ll. 6ff.).

173 Ibid., I, 15, 14 (p. 49, l. 16): "Nunc quemadmodum extra auctoritatem reliquas lectiones debeamus emendare dicendum est. Commenta legis divinae, epistulas sermones librosque priscorum unus quis emendatur sic legat, ut correctiones eorum magistris consociet saecularium litterarum."

174 Quintillian, *Inst. orat.*, I, 7, 11 (Bornecque ed., 1: 110). For the rules of orthography—or, rather, for the lack of such rules—see Corbett, "Prolégomènes," in Vanderhoven and Masai, *Regula Magistri*, p. 72.

175 For the literature on the *Quaestiones*, see Gustave Bardy, "La littérature patristique des *quaestiones et responsiones* sur l'Ecriture sainte," *Revue biblique* 41 (1932): 210ff., 341ff., 515ff.; 42 (1933): 14ff., 211ff., 328ff.

176 Cassiodorus. *Inst.*, I, 10, 1 (p. 34, l. 12).

177 Cassiodorus did not cite this work, but he used it in his recension of the Epistles of Saint Paul (*Inst.*, I, 8 [p. 28]). See Augustine, *De doctrina christiana*, II, XXXIX, 59 (*PL*, XXXIV, 62).

178 Cassiodorus, *Inst.*, I, 18–22 (pp. 58–61). We should note that one of the monasteries at Vivarium was dedicated to Saint Hilary, who was known for his role in the anti-Arian struggle; see Courcelle, "Nouvelles recherches sur le monastère de Cassiodore," pp. 525ff.

It was in reference to this continual appeal to the teaching of the Fathers that Cassiodorus demanded that his monks consult profane books in their exegetical work. He discussed this subject four times, with an insistence that seems symptomatic to me. He must have had some monks at Vivarium who, faithful to the ascetic ideal, could not countenance reading profane writers. Cassiodorus repeatedly told them that they ought not to condemn secular studies,[179] that Abraham learned arithmetic and astronomy from the Egyptians,[180] that profane doctrines were very useful for understanding divine law.[181] Indeed, Cassiodorus even had misgivings that the monks would not like the second book of the *Institutiones*, which he devoted to the liberal arts. This book is truly a masterpiece of condensation: in but a few pages, Cassiodorus defined the seven arts by distinguishing literary studies from scientific studies—a new distinction in the West—while at the same time listing and summarizing the Greek and Latin manuals he had once read and had in his library. While the resulting work is of extreme interest for the historian of culture, the monk who had never attended an antique school must have found it repellent.

Cassiodorus' exegetical methods were not original: they were essentially those Augustine described in his *De doctrina christiana*, a work Cassiodorus knew well.[182] If the principles were the same, however, the results were different. One need only compare Augustine's *Enarrationes in Psalmos* with Cassiodorus' commentary on the same book, which he began in Ravenna and probably continued in Constantinople.[183] The ex-minister claimed to have followed Augustine's work closely, but in reality he commented on the Psalter in an entirely different spirit. If the habits of a former teacher often appear in the bishop of Hippo's exegesis, his exegesis nevertheless remains rich in spirituality.[184] But Cassiodorus' exegesis was primarily a literary exercise. He was interested in showing that the liberal arts existed before the profane masters studied them and that all kinds of stylistic figures could be found in

---

[179] *Inst.*, I, 28, 3 (p. 70): "Nec illud Patres sanctissimi decreverunt ut saecularium litterarum studia respuantur." Ibid., I, 27, 1 (p. 68, l. 15): "Patribus nostris visum est utilis et non refugienda cognitio."

[180] Ibid., II, 3, 22 (p. 132, ll. 1–2).

[181] Ibid., 7, 4 (p. 157, ll. 19–20).

[182] See the reference in Mynors' edition, p. 187.

[183] For this work, see Schanz, IV-2, 191–92, and Cappuyns, "Cassiodore," cols. 1369–70.

[184] Marrou, *Saint Augustin*, pp. 422ff.; Maurice Pontet, *L'exégèse de saint Augustin, prédicateur* (Paris, 1946), pp. 387ff.

the Bible,[185] a thesis which conforms to the Fathers' thought.[186] With this kind of approach, the meeting of the Bible and the scholar would bear fruit only if the scholar had an extensive profane culture. Cassiodorus studied all the rhetorical figures found in the Psalms: not only the syllogism, the anaphora, and the anastrophe,[187] but also the epidiothose, the syneresis, the synathroism, and others—about one hundred and twenty figures in all.[188] He appealed to the study of etymologies, as did other contemporary exegetes.[189] He appealed not only to grammar and rhetoric but even to arithmetic, and especially to geometry.[190] The commentary on Psalm 96:4 ("illuxerunt fulgura ejus orbi terrae") gave him the opportunity to define line and point and to discuss the difference between sense perception and rational knowledge in geometry so that in the end his commentary became a little treatise on elementary geometry.[191] We could go on and observe the same process with the other arts.[192]

Cassiodorus, while commenting on Holy Scripture according to the laws of the genre, remained in his exegesis an antique scholar. He con-

---

[185] Cassiodorus, *In Psalm.*, 23 (*PL*, LXX, 175): "Cognoscite magistri saecularium litterarum hinc schemata hinc diversi generis argumenta hinc definitiones hinc disciplinarum omnium profluxisse doctrinas quando in his litteris posita cognoscitis quae ante scholas vestras longe prius dicta fuisse sentitis."

[186] Curtius, p. 55, asks whether this theory is Cassiodorus'. But Jerome had already presented it (*Ep.* XXX, 1 [*PL*, XXII, 441–42]; *Comm. in Eccl.*, I [*PL*, XXIII, 1012]; *Comm. in Isaiam prophetam*, prologue [*PL*, XXIV, 19]), as did Augustine (*De doctrina christiana*, IV, 7 [*PL*, XXXIV, 92ff.]).

[187] Cassiodorus, *In Psalm.*, 41, 17; 43, 15; 61, 1 (*PL*, LXX, 306, 314, 428).

[188] Ibid., 61, 1; 34, 8; 22, 1. See Gustav Bardy, "Cassiodore et la fin du monde antique," *Année théologique* 6 (1945): 410; Beryl Smalley, *The Study of the Bible in the Middle Ages* (Oxford, 1952), p. 31; J. M. Courtes, "Figures et tropes dans le psautier de Cassiodore," *REL* 42 (1964): 361–75.

[189] Heinrich Erdbruegger, *Cassiodorus, unde etymologias in Psalterii commentario prolatas petivisse putandus sit* (Iena, 1912), pp. 34ff., has shown that Cassiodorus drew from Varro. See John of Naples' etymologies, perhaps from the same period, of *meridies*, *veritas*, and *semitae* in *Chrysostomus latinus, Sermones*, 19, 26, 30 (*PL: Supplementum*, ed. A. Hamman, 4, pt. 2 [Paris, 1968]: 787, 810, 827). See also G. Morin, *RB* 11 (1894): 386–91.

[190] Cassiodorus, *Expositio psalmorum*, 70 (*CCL*, 97: 640): "Meminisse autem debemus arithmeticam vel alias disciplinas Psalmos commemorare frequenter." (See also *Inst.*, II, 4, 8 [pp. 141–42].) *Expositio psalmorum*, 96 (p. 872): "Meminisse ergo debemus quod haec omnia sive punctum sive linea, sive circulus, sive trigonus . . . vel alia hujus modi theoremata quoties ad aspectum veniunt."

[191] Victor Mortet, "Notes sur le texte des *Institutiones* de Cassiodore, 3ᵉ article: Observations sur le caractère de la géometrie dans l'oeuvre de Cassiodore et sur l'enseignement de cette science dans les premiers siècles du Moyen Age," *RPh*, n.s. 27 (1903): 65–78.

[192] See *Expositio psalmorum*, 150 (pp. 1328–29) for a description of various musical instruments.

tinued as a scholar in his monastery, where he was, in essence, an untitled teacher of grammar and rhetoric. He worked for his monks until he was ninety-three years old; his treatise *On Orthography* was an intellectual testament addressed to them.[193]

How well did his monks receive the program Cassiodorus proposed? Our documentation here is very meager. We do not even know the origins of Vivarium's monks. Cassiodorus passed on the names of only two abbots, Chalcedonius and Gerontius.[194] His friends who did translations for him definitely were not members of the monastic community.[195] But here and there the founder did speak of the intellectual level of his monks. In comparing his *Institutiones* to the letter Jerome sent to Paulinus,[196] he realized that he was writing for monks who had not received a worldly education and who were "simplices et impoliti." He felt obliged to comment on Donatus in order to "make a clear author even more so."[197] In his *De orthographia*, he declared that he wanted to produce a few moderately cultivated men from among the mass of the ignorant.[198] Did he succeed? In another passage of the same treatise, he described some discouraged monks whom, he concluded, he had at least been able to teach orthography and punctuation.[199] To read Cassiodorus, we would think that Vivarium was only a publishing house. After Cassiodorus' time, the kind of men learned in the exegesis that the founder recommended for their erudite conversation must have been rare.[200] One fears that Cassiodorus' efforts did not long survive his death.[201] For one thing, conditions were not favorable. Around 590, Lombard armies got as far as Reggio Calabria,[202] and perhaps Vivarium

193 See Schanz, IV-2, 105–6, for this treatise.
194 Cassiodorus, *Inst.*, I, 32 (p. 79, l. 16).
195 For these translators, see Courcelle, *LG*, p. 320. Cappuyns correctly distinguishes them from the monks ("Cassiodore," col. 1360). See also André van der Vyver, "Les *Institutiones* de Cassiodore et sa fondation à Vivarium," *RB* 53 (1941): 88.
196 Cassiodorus, *Inst.*, I, 21, 2 (p. 60, ll. 15ff.): "Nobis vero fuit causa diversa, primum quod ad fratres simplices et impolitos scripsimus instruendos . . . ne aliquid eis deesse possit qui ad studia hujus saeculi non fuerunt." See ibid., II, 3, 20 (p. 130, l. 13).
197 *Inst.*, II, 1, 1 (p. 94, l. 12).
198 Cassiodorus, *De orthog.*, ed. Keil, 7: 144.
199 Ibid., prologue, p. 144, and conclusion: "Valete fratres . . . qui vos inter cetera et de orthographiae virtute et de distinctione ponenda quae nimis pretiosa cognoscitur."
200 *Inst.*, I, 10, 5 (p. 35): "Collocutio peritissimorum seniorum crebrius appetatur quorum confabulatione subito quod non opinabamur advertimus, dum nobis studiose referunt quod longis aetatibus suis discere potuerunt."
201 The *Institutiones* were revised again, however; see Courcelle, "Histoire d'un brouillon," *REA* 44 (1942): 85, where Martianus Capella's manual and Boethius' *De differentiis topicis* are mentioned.
202 Paul the Deacon, *HL*, III, 32 (*MGH, SRL*, p. 112).

suffered from these events. The monastery still existed eight years later, when Gregory the Great received a delegation of its monks engaged in a lawsuit with the bishop of Squillace,[203] but there is no indication that it was still a cultural center.

Cassiodorus' experiment was without immediate results. Perhaps his program was too ambitious for inadequately prepared monks. All that really remained of Vivarium was the library, which when later dispersed would contribute to the renewal of studies in the West.[204]

C. RELIGIOUS CULTURE OUTSIDE VIVARIUM

When Cassiodorus died, Italy already counted many monasteries. The accession to the papacy of Gregory (590), a former monk, could only have favored the further development of Italian monasticism. Through Gregory's correspondence, we know about a significant number of monasteries which would be interesting to study. Gregory personally established monasteries in Sicily, hoped for some in Corsica,[205] and while defending the rights of bishops, tried to protect monks from outside interference.[206] For him, the monastery was a place of complete retreat, designed for prayer and manual and spiritual work.[207]

What was studied in these monastic centers? Was the ascetic spiritual tradition followed, or was another formula for studies, closer to that of Vivarium, sought? While Gregory worried on several occasions about the kind of education children and adolescents were receiving in the monasteries,[208] he gave no precise information when he talked about monastic studies. One abbot was considered worthy of the episcopacy because he was nourished on scriptural learning;[209] another should read and pray more and teach his brothers God's law.[210] Gregory seemed to be satisfied with the minimum, which, though perhaps surprising

---

[203] Gregory the Great, *Ep.* VIII, 32 (II, 33). For the fate of the monastery after Cassiodorus, see Courcelle, "Le site," *MEFR* 55 (1938): 259–307; and idem, *LG*, p. 342, as well as Cappuyns, "Cassiodore," cols. 1358–59, and L. W. Jones, *An Introduction to Divine and Human Readings by Cassiodorus Senator*, p. 43.

[204] Courcelle, *LG*, pp. 342ff.

[205] Gregory the Great, *Ep.* V, 4 (I, 284, l. 18); Gregory of Tours, *HF*, X, 1 (p. 478). For Corsica, see Gregory the Great, *Ep.* I, 50 (I, 76).

[206] See Dudden, *Gregory the Great*, 2: 174ff., and Battifol, *Saint Grégoire*, p. 117.

[207] Gregory the Great, *Ep.* XI, 54 (II, 329, l. 3): "Opus Dei celebrare. . . ."

[208] *Ep.* I, 48 (I, 75, l. 8); VI, 10 (I, 389); X, 9 (II, 244). He requested a two-year probationary period: "Ut eos quos ad convertendum susceperint, priusquam biennum in conversatione compleant, nullo modo audeant tonsorare."

[209] *Ep.* XIII, 14 (II, 382, l. 4): "Divinae scripturae scientia . . . institutum."

[210] *Ep.* III, 3 (I, 161, l. 20): "Vos discere Dei mandata neglegatis."

to us, can be explained by the precarious situation of many of the monasteries.

The war that ruined Italy after the coming of the Lombards profoundly disturbed monastic life. Some monks became clerics without permission, lived without an abbot or a rule, purchased goods, cohabited with women, welcomed soldiers. The situation was no better in convents.[211] Furthermore, monasteries became centers where errant clerics and bishops were confined, a development that did not contribute to spiritual life. Studies were understandably neglected under these conditions. Gregory witnessed the effects of this negligence when he received some monks from Syracuse, was scandalized by them, and had to reprimand their abbot.[212]

In order to find an Italian monastery where studies were still in repute, one must go to Rome, to the monastery of Saint Andrew, founded by Gregory the Great. As at Vivarium, studies were undoubtedly one part of a variety of religious activities, including psalmody and the offices.[213] There was room in the monastic study program for learned monks as well as for simple monks such as Brother Antony, who "meditated on Holy Scripture with his tears and compunction more than with learned commentary."[214] Yet, under Gregory's guidance, exegetical learning occupied an important place at Saint Andrew, since Gregory knew the value of spiritual culture and discussions on Scripture.[215] He continually recommended study to his monks because, as he said, it was only a rare and privileged few who could profit without it. The case of Sanctutus, a priest from Nursia who led a holy life without benefit of instruction, was in Gregory's view, exceptional and miraculous.[216]

[211] See Dudden, *Gregory the Great*, 2: 174–75.

[212] *Ep.* III, 3 (I, 161, l. 18): "In ipsis autem fratribus monasterii tui quos video non invenio eos lectionem vacare."

[213] We know nothing about the internal organization of Saint Andrew's. Dudden, *Gregory the Great*, 2: 109, described it by using Benedict's rule. We do not know, however, whether Gregory followed this rule. See Kassius Hallinger, "Papst Gregor d. Grosse und der hl. Benedikt," *Studia Anselmiana* (1957), pp. 231–319, who is more prudent than Olegario M. Porcel, *La doctrina monástica de San Gregorio Magno y la Regula monachorum* (Madrid, 1950; Washington, D.C., 1951), pp. 129–55.

[214] *Dial.*, IV, 49 (p. 307): "Cum studiosissime et cum magno fervore desiderii sacra eloquia mediteratur non in eis verba scientiae sed fletum compunctionis inquirebat."

[215] See his letters to Jovinus of Catania (*Ep.* IX, 15 [II, 51, l. 18]), in which he expressed the wish that this layman would be his "[collega] in sacro eloquio"; and to the patriarch of Alexandria (*Ep.* VIII, 28 [II, 29]): "Utilis semper est docti viri allocutio."

[216] *Moral.*, XXII, 21 (*PL*, LXXVI, 245): "Sunt nonnulli qui nullo lectionis nullo exhortationis vomere proscissi quaedam bona quamvis minima tamen ex semetipsis proferunt." For Sanctutus, see *Dial.*, III, 37 (p. 223, l. 25).

Gregory provided his monks with a model of exegesis by explicating the Book of Job, a work which he began at Constantinople for his companions. He continued to work on it in Rome and finished it there about 596.[217] His method conformed to tradition: he commented verse by verse, giving historical or literal, moral, and allegorical explications. This tripartite plan was common to all exegetes of the time,[218] but whereas Cassiodorus, for example, insisted on the first point, Gregory was more interested in the allegorical and moral sense. On the other hand, here, as in all his other exegetical works, he displayed all the richness of his mystical theology. He took many of his explications from Augustine's and Origen's works, but many more came from his own spiritual experience.[219] Historians have not sufficiently insisted on the influence which the "mystical doctor" was to have on the spirituality of his time and on the entire Middle Ages.

Thus, Gregory did not organize as precise a program of studies in his monastery as did Cassiodorus at Vivarium. Study was part of the spiritual activities at Saint Andrew. But he did reserve deeper exegesis for a small group of initiated. "Whoever has penterated the profundity of doctrine in sacred teaching ought to unmask the sublime sense to those who do not understand," he wrote in a passage of the *Moralia.*[220] We can thus understand why he reproached his former disciple, Bishop Marinian of Ravenna, for publicly reading this difficult work in his cathedral.[221] Among those, other than Marinian,[222] who benefited from Gregory's teaching, we know the following names: Claudius, abbot of

---

[217] For the development of this book, see the dedicatory letter to Leander cited in sect. III of this chapter, and Battifol, *Saint Grégoire,* pp. 99ff.

[218] See Caesarius' *Expositio in Apocalypsim,* XII, in *S. Caesarii opera omnia,* ed. Morin, 2: 249, l. 15: "Triforme intellectum scripturarum intellegamus juxta historiam moralem et spiritualem." See also Arator, *Hist. Apos.,* II, 890, 1: "Historicum morale sonans typicumque volumen" (*CSEL,* 72: 127). For Gregory's exegetical method, see de Lubac, *L'exégèse médiévale,* passim, especially 1: 187ff., and Vincenzo Recchia, *L'esegesi di Gregorio Magno al Cantico dei Cantici* (Turin, 1967).

[219] For the spiritual doctrine of the *Moralia,* see Robert Gillet, preface to the French edition, *Morales sur Job, I–II,* in *SC,* 32 (Paris, 1950): 20; and Michael Frickel, *Deus totus ubique simul: Untersuchungen zur allgemeinen Gottgegenwart im Rahmen der Gotteslehre Gregors des Grossen* (Freiburg, 1956). For Origen's influence on Gregory, see de Lubac, *L'exégèse médiévale,* 1: 211. Gregory's "spiritual theology" is discussed by Leclercq, *L'amour des lettres,* pp. 30, 39, and by Robert Gillet, "Spiritualité et place du moine dans l'Eglise selon saint Grégoire le Grand," in *Théologie de la vie monastique: Etude sur la tradition patristique* (Paris, 1961), pp. 322–51.

[220] Gregory the Great, *Moral.,* XVII, 26 (*PL,* LXXVI, 28): "Qui in sacro eloquio jam alta intelligit sublimes sensus coram non sapientibus per silentium tegat."

[221] *Ep.* XII, 6 (II, 352, l. 27): "Quia non est illud opus populare et rudibus auditoribus impedimentum magis quam provectum generat."

[222] *Ep.* VI, 2 (I, 382): "A cunabulis in sanctae ecclesiae gremio nutritus."

Saint John and Saint Stephen in Classe, the port of Ravenna, who took notes from Gregory and put the lessons which Gregory gave on different books of the Bible in proper form;[223] Deacon Peter, who had studied with Gregory from his youth;[224] and lastly, Augustine, the future apostle of England, who, according to Gregory himself, "was full of the learning of holy Scripture."[225]

Except for Saint Andrew, we know nothing of monastic studies elsewhere in Rome. For example, we do not know how the monks of Monte Cassino organized their intellectual work after they took refuge in the Lateran around 580. They should have followed the program dictated by Saint Benedict. The settlement of Benedictine monks in an urban milieu, however, must have modified their way of living, perhaps giving more importance to studies than had been the case at Monte Cassino.[226] This is all merely supposition, since we have no Benedictine literary work before the eighth century.[227]

D. Gregory and Clerical Education

Did Gregory the Great propose monastic training for the secular clergy as had Caesarius at the opening of the century?[228] They both faced the same problems: clerics were too occupied with worldly affairs, and thus their intellectual and spiritual culture suffered. Gregory forbade ordination of unlettered priests on several occasions, complained that deacons were recruited at Rome more for their beautiful voices than for their knowledge,[229] and spoke of a priest who honored an idol in his home, of a cleric who preferred the life of weapons to that of the altar, and of simoniacs.[230] The higher we go in the hierarchy, the greater the evil. Bishops were conducting themselves like laymen: the bishop of Capua was too busy with trials; the bishop of Naples outfitted ships;

---

[223] Ep. XII, 66 (II, 353).

[224] Dial., preface (p. 13): "Petrus diaconus . . . mihi a primaevo juventutis flore amicitiis familiariter obstrictus atque ad sacri verbi indagationem socius."

[225] Ep. XI, 37 (II, 309, l. 12), to King Aethilbert "Augustinus . . . in monasterii regula edoctus sacrae scripturae scientia repletus."

[226] Gregory the Great, Dial., II, prologue (pp. 72–73), and Paul the Deacon, HL, IV, 17 (MGH, SRL, p. 122), are our only sources for the settlement of the monks of Monte Cassino in Rome.

[227] See below, chap. 9, sect. III.A.

[228] See above, chap. 4, sect. II.B.

[229] Gregory the Great, Ep. V, 57a (I, 363).

[230] Ep. X, 2 (II, 238, l. 3); IV, 37 (I, 274). For the practice of simony during this period, see Mueri Welcker, "Die Simonie im frühen Mittelalter," ZKG 64 (1952–53): 61–93.

the bishop of Salona was especially worried about the good meals he prepared for friends, and to excuse himself before the pope, he recalled that Abraham dined with angels. [231] The disorganization of the bishoprics in the aftermath of the Lombard invasion partially explains this situation. [232]

Except for those who came from a monastic environment, [233] cultivated bishops were quite rare. [234] Gregory recruited bishops from among former monks [235] and required that candidates for the episcopacy at least know the Psalter by heart, a requirement which was considered the elementary education of the monk. [236] In the treatise which he wrote for the edification of his fellow bishops and which he called a rule (*Regula pastoralis*), he continually insisted on study, much as would an abbot of a monastery. [237] He knew the difficulties that a former monk become bishop would encounter: temporal duties were heavy and one could not devote all one's time to reading and prayer. [238] Gregory himself had personal experience with this set of double demands; however, he still thought that monastic recruitment provided the best guarantee of a worthy episcopate.

Yet it does not appear that he was able or that he even wanted to transform the dwellings of Italian bishops into quasi-monastic communities, not even at the Lateran. [239] In a canon from the Roman council

---

[231] Gregory the Great, *Ep.* X, 4 (II, 239, l. 24); XIII, 29 (p. 394, l. 3); II, 20 and 50 (I, 116 and 152): "Pastorali cura derelicta solis e conviviis occupatum; . . . quia nequaquam lectioni studeas."

[232] See Louis Duchesne, "Les évêchés d'Italie et l'invasion lombarde," *MEFR* 23 (1903): 83ff.; Battifol, *Saint Grégoire*, pp. 113ff.

[233] Gregory the Great, *Ep.* X, 1 (II, 237), mentions the library of Trajan of Malta, a former monk. Maximian of Syracuse was the former abbot of Saint Andrew's (see Battifol, *Saint Grégoire*, p. 122). Marinian of Ravenna had also been a monk at the same monastery.

[234] The bishop of Taormina, to whom Gregory sent a copy of his *Homilies on the Gospels*, was an exception. See *Ep.* IV, 17 (I, 252).

[235] *Ep.* XIII, 14 (II, 382, l. 4), where Gregory proposed Abbot Urbicus for Palermo: "Divinae scripturae scientia . . . institutus."

[236] In *Ep.* V, 51 (I, 351, l. 4), he turned down a priest "psalmorum nescius"; see also *Ep.* XIV, 11 (II, 430, l. 9); X, 13 (II, 247). By these actions, Gregory reinforced the second canon of the Council of Nicaea (325), which forbade a man who did not know the Psalter from becoming a bishop.

[237] *Reg. past.*, II, 11 (*PL*, LXXVII, 48): "Studiose quotidie sacri eloquii praecepta meditetur . . . studere incessabiliter debet ut per eruditionis studium resurgat." See Battifol, *Saint Grégoire*, pp. 82ff., for the *Regula pastoralis*.

[238] In *Ep.* VI, 63 (I, 440), he reproached Marinian of Ravenna for neglecting his pastoral duties: "Non sibi credat solam lectionem et orationem sufficere."

[239] We know only a few cases of clerics educated in the bishop's residence (*Dial.*, I, 9 [p. 50]; III, 13 [p. 160]). Young Gregory was taught outside the episcopal quarters

of 595, the pope prohibited laymen from serving as valets (*cubicularii*) in his private apartments and decided to replace them with clerics and even with monks. He wanted, he said, to oblige bishops to lead lives worthy of imitation by their disciples.[240] But the reform never went further, and there was no talk of a larger community. The clerics of the Lateran church lived elsewhere. An *ordo Romanus* from the seventh century suggests that young lectors still lived with their parents.[241]

Gregory is sometimes credited with the creation of the *schola cantorum*. John the Deacon, a ninth-century author, was the first to report this event,[242] although the schola appears quite late in pontifical documents. The *Liber pontificalis* mentions it for the first time only at the end of the seventh century.[243] Even if the creation of the schola were due to Gregory, it would not have entailed any change in the religious education of Roman clerics. The object of the schola, it seems, was to train specialists in chant and thereby assure that clerics in higher orders would not be attracted to this function.[244] It is tempting to see the article of the council of 595 that prohibits deacons from becoming cantors as implying the creation of the schola, but additional evidence would be necessary to do so.

Gregory the Great did not change the organization of the Roman Church. His clergy, furthermore, were opposed to monastic life. Once the pope was dead, his successors replaced with secular clerics the monks who were in charge of certain churches.[245]

Gregory also supposedly intervened in another area pertinent to the training of clerics, the reorganization of the Lateran library, which, in fact, became well known during his pontificate. There was, of course,

---

at Agrigentum (*Vita Gregorii*, PG, XCVIII, 550). A verse from the epitaph of Pope Deusdedit (615–18) suggests that the future pope had been attached to the clergy of Saint Peter's in Rome at an early age: "Hic vir ab exortu Petri est nutritus ovili" (*ICR*, vol. 2, no. 127).

[240] *Ep.* V, 57a (I, 363, ll. 16–25): "Ut is qui in loco est regiminis testes tales habeat talesque viri ejus in secreto conversationem videant."

[241] *Ordines Romani*, ed. M. Andrieu, 4 vols. (Louvain, 1930–56), 4: 33. See below, chap. 8, n. 272.

[242] John the Deacon, *Vita Gregorii*, II, 6 (*PL*, LXXV, 90): "Scolam quoque cantorum . . . constituit." For the difficult question of the origin of the *scola*, see, most recently, Corbin, *L'Eglise à la conquête de sa musique*, pp. 172ff.

[243] See below, chap. 8, sect. IV.A.

[244] M. Andrieu, "Les ordres mineurs dans l'ancien rite romain," *Revue des sciences religieuses* 5 (1925): 234. During this period *cantores* were considered clerics; see Justinian's *Novel* cited by Gregory the Great (*Ep.* XIII, 50 [II, 415, l. 4]).

[245] Fliche-Martin, 5: 392, 394.

a collection of books at the Lateran before this.[246] Pelagius II, at the time of the quarrel of the *Three Chapters*, drew several works relative to this affair from his scrinium, among them the *Codex encyclius* translated by Cassiodorus.[247] The richness of the library during this period might be explained by the possibility that it received books from Vivarium. We know it was rich enough for the pope to send books east and west, to bishops, abbots, queens, and laymen.[248] These particular books contained texts of councils, extracts from the Bible, and saints' *Lives*.[249] Possibly the Church Fathers—in particular, Augustine—might have been represented in the Lateran library: the famous fresco fragment, depicting Augustine, discovered in the pontifical palace seems to have come from a library.[250] It is thought that Gregory had it executed when he wanted to transport the former library of Pope Agapitus from Clivus Scauri to the Lateran.[251] Although this hypothesis is seductive, nothing confirms it. Archaeologists, for one thing, are not agreed on the date of the Lateran fresco.[252] The *Liber pontificalis*, on the other hand, which on the whole carefully reported the building activities of the pontiffs, does not mention the construction of a new library in the notice devoted to Gregory.

It has also been thought that Gregory was the first to distinguish the scrinium, where the archives were kept, from the library, which was

[246] See above, chap. 4, sect. III.

[247] Courcelle, *LG*, p. 363. Courcelle has also shown that the translation Cassiodorus made of the *Tripartite History* was in the Lateran during the time of Gregory the Great (ibid., p. 381, n. 2).

[248] For bishops, see *Ep.* VIII, 28 (II, 29), to Eulogius of Alexandria; II, 49 (I, 151), to the bishops of Iberia; XII, 16a (II, 363), to Marinian of Ravenna. For abbots, *Ep.* V, 35 (I, 316, l. 7), to Abbot Helias of Isauria. For queens, *Ep.* VIII, 4 (II, 8), to Brunhilda; XIV, 12 (II, 431), to Theodelinda; also see Angelo Lipinsky, "Der Theodelindenschatz im Dom zu Monza," *Das Münster* 13 (1960): 146–74. For laymen, see *Ep.* VII, 33 (I, 482), to Dynamius and Aurelia of Marseille; X, 16 (II, 251), to Innocent, prefect of Africa.

[249] Specifically, synodal acts from the time of Justinian, the synod of Ephesus, Deacon Paschasius' treatise *On the Holy Spirit*, and Eusebius of Caesarea's *Deeds of the Martyrs*. Bishop Aetherius of Lyon asked the pope for the *gesta* of Saint Irenaeus (*Ep.* XI, 40 [II, 314]).

[250] Philippe Lauer, "Les fouilles du *sancta sanctorum* du Latran," *MEFR* 20 (1900): 250–87.

[251] Marrou, "Autour de la bibliothèque," pp. 124–69, has compared the distich written under Augustine's portrait ("Diversi diversa patres s[ed hic] Omnia dixit romano eloqu[io]") with the distichs from Agapitus' library.

[252] Lauer, "Les fouilles," dates it to the fifth or sixth century, while Joseph Wilpert, "Il piu antico rittrato di s. Agostino," in Cassamassa, *Miscellanea agostiniana*, 2: 1, believes that it is from Gregory's period.

reserved for books in the true sense.[253] In fact, however, Gregory generally used the words *scrinium* or *archivum* when referring to the place where ecclesiastical books were kept, while reserving the term *bibliotheca* for profane libraries.[254] Scribes worked in the scrinium recopying the pope's works, as well as other works, no doubt.[255] It was there that Paterius, one of Gregory's notaries, had the florilegium called the *Liber testimonium*, which was so widely diffused in the seventh and eighth centuries, made.[256]

Gregory the Great's work was immense in all domains. Let us recognize, however, that he was unable to change the educational conditions of the Italian clergy. His culture was a model for his own entourage, but Italian clerics did not immediately profit from it. This explains why the clergy was not particularly distinguished in the realm of sacred learning after the pope's death. Throughout nearly the entire seventh century, they could barely defend Catholic dogma and were unable to produce any great theological or exegetical work.

[253] G. Plessi, "La biblioteca della chiesa di Roma durante il pontificato di papa Gregorio Magno," *Archiginnasio* 35 (1940): 267.

[254] Gregory the Great, *Ep.* VIII, 28 (II, 29): "Nulla in archivo hujus nostrae ecclesiae vel in Romanae urbis bibliothecis esse cognovi."

[255] *Ep.* III, 49 and 54 (I, 206, l. 7; p. 212, l. 22). A study of ecclesiastical notaries would be useful. See Louis Halphen, *Etudes sur l'administration de Rome au Moyen Age* (Paris, 1907).

[256] Manitius, 1: 98.

CHAPTER SIX

The Education of
Laymen in Gaul and in Spain

I. THE CONTRAST BETWEEN ROMAN
AND BARBARIAN GAUL

Historians who specialize in the Merovingian period generally consider the Frankish kingdom as a whole when they speak of Merovingian political organization, Merovingian economy, Merovingian intellectual civilization, and so forth.[1] But what was perhaps true for political history when the same family ruled in Gaul for almost three centuries is certainly not true for the history either of society or of civilization. The Germans colonized only a small portion of Gaul, and while they tried to impose their authority throughout the *regnum*, they changed nothing of the administrative and social organization of the regions generally south of the Loire and of the Langres plateau. In these regions, Roman civilization and especially Roman culture survived. By using chronicles as well as extant diplomas or copies of those which have not survived, formularies, and inscriptions, we can make the case that an entire portion of Merovingian Gaul still participated in a civilization based on the written word.

The few authentic diplomas we have, whether royal or private charters, are only the debris of an important body of documents drawn up in royal, municipal, and ecclesiastical offices.[2] In three instances the formulary of Angers lists the *instrumenta*[3] that a layman could have drawn

---

[1] Lot, *Les destinées*, pp. 341ff.; Roger, pp. 89, 403; Salin.

[2] For royal diplomas, see Philippe Lauer and Charles Samaran, *Les diplômes originaux des rois mérovingiens* (Paris, 1908). For private documents, see J. M. Pardessus, ed., *Diplomata, chartae, epistolae, leges, aliaque instrumenta ad res Gallo-Francicas spectantia*, 2 vols. (Paris, 1843–49).

[3] *Form. Andecavenses*, 31, 32 (*MGH, Leg. sect. V*, pp. 14–15), and 33 (p. 15, ll. 26–28):

up and provides several models of these documents, as do other, similar collections.[4]

A written document was a necessary part of the transaction whenever property was sold or exchanged, a dowry or a will established,[5] a child adopted or a slave freed.[6] The right to property, payment of a fine, loans, and oaths were also witnessed by a document.[7] Such documents possessed great value in the eyes of sixth- and seventh-century men, and their literal formalism, already noticeable at the end of the Roman period, served only to reinforce this value.[8] Documents were carefully preserved in chests[9] and referred to in case of dispute.[10] There was a mechanism for their replacement in the event of theft, fire, or one of the frequent wars in the procedure known as *apennis*, or *plancturia*, according to which a poster was displayed in the forum for three days announcing the loss and listing the titles of the documents replaced.[11] Actual replacement of lost documents was easy enough, since the practice of registering documents in the *gesta municipalia* was still observed. As in Ostrogothic Italy,[12] registration gave way to a procedure that several formulas have preserved for us, in particular the formulary of Angers, which dates from the reign of King Childebert II.[13] The interested party who signed the document had it conveyed by a *prosecutor*

"Strumenta sua quam pluremas, vindicionis, dotis . . . convenencias, securitatis, vacuaturias, judiciis et noticias."

[4] *Formulae, MGH, Leg. sect. V*, pp. 1–220. See Buchner, *Die Rechtsquellen*, pp. 49–55, for these formularies.

[5] For property transactions, see *Form. And.*, 27; Marculf, *Form.*, II, 19ff. (*MGH, Leg. sect. V*, pp. 13, 89). For dowries, see *Form. And.*, 34; Marculf, *Form.*, II, 15; *Form. Turonenses*, 14 (ibid., pp. 16, 85, 142). See the wills of laymen and bishops in Pardessus, I, 81, 136; II, 422; and elsewhere. We have copies of more than twenty-five wills. For testamentary practices during the Merovingian period, see H. Auffroy, *Evolution du testament en France, des origines au XIIIe siècle* (Paris, 1899), pp. 175ff.

[6] For adoption, see *Form. Tur.*, 11 (*MGH, Leg. sect. V*, p. 141). For manumission, see *Form. Arvernenses*, 3; Marculf, *Form.*, II, 52 (ibid., pp. 30, 106).

[7] *Form. Tur.*, 41 (ibid., p. 157); *Carta compositionalis*, in *Form. And.*, 31 (ibid., p. 14); Gregory of Tours, *HF*, VII, 23 (p. 343: at Tours); ibid., IV, 46 (p. 182, l. 8).

[8] Marculf, *Form.*, II, 7 (*MGH, Leg. sect. V*, p. 79): "Scribturarum necesse est titulis alligari."

[9] Gregory of Tours, *HF*, IV, 46 (*MGH, SRM*, I, 181, l. 10): "In libellare, quo chartae abdi soleti sunt" (at Clermont).

[10] Pardessus, II, 233; Gregory of Tours, *HF*, IV, 12 (p. 142).

[11] *Form. Arvern.*, 1; *Form. Tur.*, 28; *Form. Bituricenses*, 7 (*MGH, Leg. sect. V*, pp. 28, 151, 171). See Emile Chenon, *Etude historique sur le "defensor civitatis"* (Paris, 1889); Jean Richard, "Le *defensor civitatis* et la curie municipale de Bourgogne au VIIIe siècle," *Mémoires de la Société pour l'histoire du droit et des institutions des ancient pays bourguignons* 21 (1960): 141–45.

[12] See above, chap. 1, sect. II.A.

[13] *Form. And.*, 1 (*MGH, Leg. sect. V*, pp. 4–5).

to the *curia publica* in the forum where the curiales, the *defensor*, and the court clerk variously known as the *amanuensis, notarius,* or *professor*[14] were all located. After having made his request, the prosecutor showed his order and then presented the document. The order to register it was then given. The *mandator* requested a copy of the minutes of the meeting, which was then followed by the signatures and the placement of the original document in the public archives.

As Henri Pirenne argued, there was still a great deal of writing in the Merovingian period.[15] The amount of papyrus imported from Egypt through Marseille must still have been considerable.[16] In this respect, Frankish Gaul resembled the Gothic and Burgundian kingdoms. Pirenne was mistaken, however, in extending the survival of written documents to Gaul as a whole. As Map 4 shows, the towns where written documents were prepared and used were situated either in Aquitaine (Poitiers,[17] Bourges, Clermont[18]), in the Rhône valley (Lyon,[19] Arles[20]), or between the Loire and the Seine (Le Mans,[21] Angers, Tours, Paris,[22] Orléans[23]). We find no trace of them elsewhere—a limitation of the greatest importance.[24]

Let us now compare these locations with the locations of Merovingian

[14] The term *amanuensis* appears in *Form. Tur.,* 3, and *Form. And.,* 1 (ibid., pp. 137, 4); and in *Actus pontificum Cenomannis,* ed. G. Busson and A. Ledru (Le Mans, 1901), p. 215. *Notarius* appears in *Form. Arvern.,* 2 (*MGH, Leg. sect. V,* p. 29). The word *professor* occurs in *Form. Bitur.,* 66, and Marculf, *Form.,* II, 38 (ibid., pp. 176, 98).

[15] Henri Pirenne, "De l'état de l'instruction des laiques à l'époque mérovingienne," *RB* 46 (1934): 170–71; idem, *Mahomet et Charlemagne* (Paris, 1937), pp. 118ff.

[16] Gregory of Tours, *HF,* V, 5 (p. 200, l. 2); see H. Pirenne, "Le commerce du papyrus dans la Gaule mérovingienne," *AcIB* (1928), p. 178, and E. Sabbé, "Papyrus et parchemin du haut Moyen Age," in *Miscellanea historica in honorem Leonis van der Essen,* 2 vols. (Louvain, 1947), 1: 97–106. A Bern papyrus manuscript was copied in Merovingian cursive (*ChLA,* II, no. 174). Is this a fragment from a letter?

[17] For Poitiers, see J. Tardif, "Les chartes mérovingiennes de Poitiers," *RHD* (1898), p. 763.

[18] *Form. Bitur.,* 3, and *Form. Arvern.,* 1–2 (*MGH, Leg. sect. V,* pp. 169, 28–29).

[19] Gregory of Tours, *Vitae patrum,* VIII (*MGH, SRM,* I-2, 695, l. 7), apropos of the opening of the will of Bishop Nicetius in 573.

[20] The *Vita Caesarii,* II, 39 (Morin ed., p. 341), mentions a *chartarius publicus.*

[21] *Actus pontificum Cenomannis,* ed. Busson and Ledru, p. 141 (an. 627), p. 162 (an. 643).

[22] *Form. And.,* 1; *Form. Tur.,* 3; *Form. Senonenses,* 39; Marculf, *Form.,* II, 38 (*MGH, Leg. sect. V,* pp. 4, 136, 202, 98).

[23] For Orléans, see Leodebodus' will (667), which was published by Maurice Prou and Alexandre Vidier in *Recueil des chartes de l'abbaye de Saint-Benoît-sur-Loire,* 2 vols. (Paris, 1907–32), 1: 1–19.

[24] The eighth chapter of the chronicle of Saint Wandrille mentions documents preserved in the "scrinia civitatum Rothomagenses Parisiacae et Baiocassae," but nothing indicates that registration offices existed in Rouen and Bayeux. See Fernand Vercauteren, *Les "Civitates" de la Belgique seconde* (Brussels, 1934), pp. 409–10.

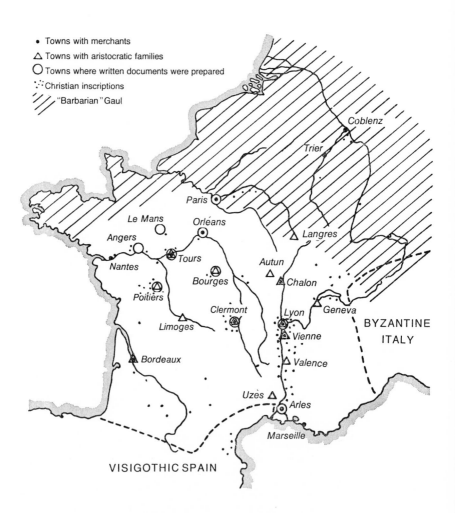

- Towns with merchants
△ Towns with aristocratic families
○ Towns where written documents were prepared
∴ Christian inscriptions
/// "Barbarian" Gaul

Coblenz

Trier

Paris

Le Mans   Orléans

Angers   Langres

Nantes   Tours   Autun

Poitiers   Bourges   Chalon

Clermont   Lyon   Geneva

Limoges   Vienne   BYZANTINE
                                          ITALY

Bordeaux   Valence

Uzès △

Arles

Marseille

VISIGOTHIC SPAIN

4. "Roman" Gaul and "Barbarian" Gaul

inscriptions, also shown on Map 4. An inscription is, in effect, the best manifestation of a written civilization: why would it have been engraved if not to be read? Of course, a map of inscriptions is difficult to interpret, since their discovery is often accidental. Moreover, it is not very easy to date these texts when the name of the consul or king is missing.[25] But such as it is, this map is significant, for it coincides with our map of administrative practice. Inscriptions are relatively quite numerous throughout the Rhône valley and especially between Arles and the region of Lyon (Lyon, Anse, Ambérieu, Belley). Stone engravers here kept their taste for beautiful Roman characters until the mid-seventh century, as a recent discovery in the Lyonnais quarter of Choulans shows.[26] In Aquitaine, the greatest number of inscriptions are found in the Auvergne and in Poitou. The valley of the Loire has a few, between Orléans and Nantes, as does the basin of the Seine, but they are poorly done and look like graffiti.[27] Quite astonishingly, we find a number of inscriptions in the Moselle and Rhine valleys between Mainz and Andernach. The map also indicates several blank spaces covering the regions of First and Second Belgium, Second Germany, and the Séquanaise. We can thus draw a line from Nantes to Geneva, bypassing Le Mans, Orléans, and Autun, which marks the northern frontier of written civilization. The Paris region forms a marginal zone and the Moselle valley an islet, at least so far as inscriptions are concerned. Now, with these two exceptions aside, we see a real contrast on Map 4 between southern and northern Gaul.

Urban civilization also survived in southern Gaul. The town, as I said earlier apropos of Ostrogothic Italy, was the normal setting for written civilization. Documents were rarely copied outside cities during the Roman period. The *defensor* and the *curator*, formerly municipal officials, were left only with the function of registering documents after the counts took over the cities in the sixth and seventh centuries. The defensors and curators were surrounded by curiales, sometimes called *boni homines* or *boni viri* in the texts.[28] These notables, whose exact

[25] See *CIL*, XIII, and especially, Le Blant, *IC*. Twenty-seven inscriptions have been dated to the second half of the fifth century, fifty-one to the first half of the sixth century, twenty to 700, and twenty to the eighth century.

[26] See below, n. 82.

[27] See, for example, Le Blant, *NR*, nos. 30 and 61. For inscriptions from Aquitaine, see L. Maurin, "Le cimetière mérovingien de Neuvicq-Montguyon (Charente-Maritime)," *Gallia* (1971), pp. 159–89, and the *Nouveau Le Blant*, the first volume of which has just been published (Paris, 1975), under the direction of Nancy Gautier.

[28] *Form. Tur.*, 2 and 20 (*MGH, Leg. sect. V*, pp. 136, 146).

social origins are unknown, must have been richer and more cultivated citizens than their neighbors and very much like the elites we met in Italy.

We also find merchants in these towns. The relative importance of economic life in Merovingian cities is a matter open for discussion,[29] but the presence of indigenous or foreign merchants cannot be denied. Furthermore, it is precisely in the cities just mentioned—Clermont, Bourges, Orléans, Tours, Bordeaux, Paris—that we find them.[30] Their activities, along with those of the bishop, prevented these cities from descending to the level of rural burgs.

In addition, city dwellers could harbor the allusion of still living under the Empire, since Roman décor was still evident. Even if the size of the towns decreased, gates, triumphal arches, and amphitheaters still stood, and baths and aqueducts were still in use.[31] Not until the eighth century would some Roman monuments be used for other ends and become chapels or residences.[32] Thus Rome survived and the psychology of city dwellers was certainly influenced by its survival. The towns of northern and eastern Gaul no doubt did not all disappear:[33] Roman monuments still decorate squares in Trier, Reims, and Metz. But they were often only façades without the same significance as Roman monuments south of the Loire, since they stood in a region whose atmosphere was no longer Roman.

On these three maps, we can superimpose a fourth, the map illustrating the origins of Gallo-Roman aristocratic families that Karl F. Stroheker prepared for his work.[34] This map coincides with the others: the known senatorial families of the sixth and seventh centuries issued from the regions south of the Loire and of the Langres plateau. These

[29] See Robert Latouche, *Les origines de l'économie occidentale, IVe–XIe siècle* (Paris, 1956), pp. 114ff., who disputes Pirenne's thesis.

[30] Pirenne, *Mahomet et Charlemagne*, pp. 65, 84.

[31] Lot, *La fin du monde antique*, p. 425; J. Hubert, "Evolution de la topographie et de l'aspect des villes de Gaule du Ve au Xe siècle," *Settimane*, 6: 529ff.; R. Rey, "La tradition gallo-romaine dans la civilisation méridionale jusqu'à l'invasion sarrasine," *Pallas* 2: (1954): 155–75.

[32] Vercauteren, *Les "Civitates,"* p. 384.

[33] Fernand Vercauteren, "La vie urbaine entre Meuse et Loire du VIe au IXe siècle," *Settimane*, 6: 446–71. It is somewhat paradoxical that Jan Dhondt can speak of "urban growth between the Meuse and the North Sea in Merovingian times" (*Studi in onore di A. Sapori* [Milan, 1957], 2: 53–78).

[34] See Stroheker, p. 234, Map III, and Franz Irsigler, *Untersuchungen zur Geschichte des frühfränkischen Adels*, Rheinisches Archiv, fasc. 70 (Bonn, 1969).

families preserved the kind of life their ancestors led under the Empire, and as we shall see, they still maintained their contacts with classical culture.

Obviously, given these conditions, we cannot study the education of laymen in Gaul without differentiating between two geographical zones: one embracing Aquitaine, Burgundy, and Provence, and the other including Neustria and Austrasia. Contemporaries were themselves aware of the differences between the two Gauls: Franks called Aquitainians *Romani* until the middle of the eighth century,[35] while Aquitainians were proud that they did not belong to the Barbarian world and made no attempt to understand Barbarian civilization. Gregory of Tours' work provides convincing evidence of this. This chronicler, so well informed on the deeds of kings and ever mindful of the least anecdote, was incapable of understanding the Germanic mentality. In his history, which was not a *History of the Franks* but the *Ecclesiastical History* of his time,[36] the portion devoted to the Barbarians is quite small. One looks in vain for a treatment of the Frankish people and their social customs and legislation. In one of the rare passages where Gregory described the system of composition, he reveals that he was completely ignorant of Salic law.[37]

Barbarian influence was predominant north of the Loire and of the Langres plateau. Even though they did not completely occupy these regions, the Franks eradicated the imprint of Roman civilization. Furthermore, this Gaul—which could be called Barbarian Gaul, in contrast to Roman Gaul in the south—was largely open to a new German infiltration from beyond the Rhine.[38] As a result, the Romano-Barbarian fusion of the sixth century was achieved at the expense of the Roman element.

[35] Eugen Ewig, "Volkstum und Volksbewusstsein im Frankenreich des 7. Jahrhunderts," *Settimane*, 5: 609ff.

[36] The title *Historia Francorum* is not that of Gregory of Tours; see *Wattenbach-Levison*, 1: 101. Bede called his history the *Historia ecclesiastica gentis Anglorum.*

[37] Gregory of Tours, *De virtut. Juliani*, 16 (*MGH, SRM*, 1-2, 571). See Brunner, *Deutsche Rechtsgeschichte*, 2: 11. Gregory was very much aware of the differences among people: by the word *barbarus*, he meant a German and not—as Godefroid Kurth would have it (*Etudes Franques* [Paris and Brussels, 1919], 2: 67–137)—warriors in general. See also Léon Levillain, review of *Etudes Franques* by Godefroid Kurth, in *BECh* 80 (1919): 248–64. We should note that Gregory only rarely used Germanic terms; see Max Bonnet, *Le latin de Grégoire de Tours* (Paris, 1890), p. 226.

[38] Franz Petri, *Germanische Volkserbe in Wallonien und Nordfrankreich*, 2 vols. (Bonn, 1937).

II. LAY EDUCATION IN ROMAN GAUL

If all the area south of the Loire and of the Langres plateau was part of the same cultural entity, it did not share the same historical character. We must distinguish Burgundy and Provence from Aquitaine. Aquitaine was conquered by the Franks in 507, while Burgundy and Provence were subjugated only in 536.[39] In the history of culture, especially during this period, a difference of thirty years is important. Aquitaine had been profoundly Romanized, but since it was farther from Italy and the Mediterranean and especially because it was more disrupted by the hazards of Merovingian politics, its civilization began slowly to pull away from that of the Rhône valley.

A. MEN OF LETTERS IN PROVENCE AND BURGUNDY

At the beginning of the sixth century, Provence and Burgundy still exhibited their Roman character: Burgundian nobles seduced by Rome soon fused with the Gallo-Roman aristocracy; Provence was never settled by Germans.[40] The Franks seem not to have wanted to change the political institutions of these two regions after they conquered them; *patricii* and *rectores*,[41] inscriptions dated according to consular years,[42] and money of a Roman type[43] could still be found. Contacts between Italy and southeastern Gaul partially explain these survivals: whether by land routes, the ancient Domitian and Aurelian ways, or by sea, travelers crossed the Alps from both sides.[44] Arles and Marseille were still major ports open to Italy, the East, and Spain. The Merovingians knew this and sharply contested possession of these towns.[45]

Given the evidence for the prolongation of Roman civilization in this region, it should come as no surprise that, as in Italy, men of letters

---

[39] Lot, *Les destinées*, pp. 201ff.

[40] See above, chapt. 1, sect. II.B.3.

[41] For the significance of these titles, see Paul Edmond Martin, *Etudes critiques sur la Suisse à l'époque mérovingienne, 554–715* (Geneva, 1910); Buchner, *Die Provence*, pp. 91–108.

[42] See the Lyonnaise epitaph of 601 (*CIL*, XII, 2391) and the one from 628 (*CIL*, XIII, 2097).

[43] Coins from Chalon and Autun were still of rather good manufacture; see Pierre Le Gentilhomme, *Mélanges de numismatique mérovingienne* (Paris, 1940), pp. 103, 106. The minters in Autun were Gallo-Romans.

[44] Buchner, *Die Provence*, pp. 32ff.

[45] E. Duprat, *La Provence dans le Haut Moyen Age*, vol. 1, *Le couloir austrasien du VIe siècle*, Mémoires de l'Institut historique de Provence, 20 (Marseille, 1923), pp. 36–45; Raoul Busquet and Régine Pernoud, *Histoire du commerce de Marseille* (Paris, 1949), 1: 115ff.

could be found in the king's entourage and rather soon after the
Frankish conquest. Asteriolus and Secundinus, whose classical culture
was remarked by Gregory of Tours, were counselors to Theodebert.[46]
One of them, perhaps because of his learning, was sent on several embassies to Byzantium, thereby arousing the jealousy of his colleague.
Even in poisoning himself, Secundinus remained faithful to antique
ways.

Parthenius, whom we have already met, was another counselor of
Theodebert who also met a tragic end. It was a strange twist of fate
that led this grandson of Ruricius from studies at Ravenna to the posts
of patricius and master of offices of Frankish kings. It is arguable
whether he was patricius of Provence or of Burgundy,[47] but it is certain
that Theodebert gave him the thankless task of collecting taxes, for
which the exasperated people of Trier massacred him after the king's
death.[48] The memory of his literary skills, however, lived on in Austrasian circles. Twenty years after his death, Gogo, mayor of the palace,
alluded to his rhetorical skills.[49] Lastly, we should mention one more
court counselor, Hesychius, whom an inscription titles "quaestor of the
kings" and who seems to have had a special acquaintance with arithmetic and *computus*.[50]

The scholars of Burgundy and Provence definitely influenced Theodebert's policy. Theoderic's son was, in fact, the Merovingian king who
tried most overtly to imitate the emperors. Procopius tells us that he
was the first Barbarian king to strike gold coins bearing his portrait—to
the scandal of Byzantium—and that he organized equestrian games in
the circus at Arles.[51] Gregory of Tours reported that he preferred a
noblewoman from Languedoc to his Lombard fiancée, a union which

---

[46] Gregory of Tours, *HF*, III, 33 (p. 129): "Erat autem uterque sapiens et retoricis
inbutus litteris."

[47] Stroheker, p. 199, no. 283; Buchner, *Die Provence*, p. 91.

[48] Gregory of Tours, *HF*, III, 36 (pp. 131–32). According to Stein, 2: 816, *excursus*
N, Parthenius would have died shortly after Theodebert, either in 546 or 547. The title
magister officiorum, which Arator gave him in a letter, is equivalent to *major domus*;
see Georg Waitz, *Deutsche Verfassungsgeschichte*, 8 vols. in 9 (Berlin and Kiel, 1874–85),
2, pt. 2: 192, 2.

[49] Gogo, *Ep.* 16 (*MGH, Ep.*, III, 130, ll. 23–24).

[50] Le Blant, *IC*, 2: 74–76 (no. 413): "Quisque mundanis titulis peractis / Quaestor et
regnum habilis benignus . . . / Temporum mensor numeros modosve / Calculo cernens
strenuusque doctor." This Hesychius became a bishop in 549 after the death of Pantagathus, who had been bishop of Vienne around 538. Hesychius thus could have been a
quaestor during the Frankish occupation; see Stroheker, pp. 181–82, no. 190.

[51] Procopius, *Bell. goth.*, III, 33 (Haury ed., p. 414). See Stein, 2: 525, for Theodebert
and his Italian ambitions.

produced Theodebald, who was to remain faithful to his father's Mediterranean policy after the latter's death and who continued to occupy territory in northern Italy.[52]

Gallo-Roman scholars continued to hold important positions close to the kings during the second half of the sixth century. Upon his accession in 561, Guntram replaced the patricius of Burgundy, Agricola, with Celsus, who came from a senatorial family and combined eloquence with a solid grasp of law.[53] The referendary Asclepiodotus—who, after Guntram's death in 592, entered the service of his heir, Childebert II of Austrasia—was equally skilled in rhetoric.[54] At the beginning of the seventh century, Queen Brunhilda chose as mayor of the palace a Claudius who was singled out as a man of letters by Pseudo-Fredegarius.[55]

A special place must be reserved for the Austrasian bureaucrats of Provence. We know about them through many channels, especially through Fortunatus, who corresponded with them. These cultivated aristocrats in the service of the Austrasian kings, all situated in the same region, can be described as an "Austraso-Provençal literary circle."[56] The most representative figure in this circle was the patricius Dynamius of Marseille, who corresponded with Fortunatus and sent him his poetic compositions.[57] Only one verse from his poems has survived,[58] but we do at least have several valuable letters from him which reveal that a Provençal aristocrat at the end of the sixth century wrote in the manner used by Ruricius and Ennodius at the beginning of the century. Dynamius exhibited the same taste for the "artful letter," for a convoluted style, and for the traditional metaphors,[59] and shared his pleasure in writing with those near him. The last antique example of the rhetorical theme of adynaton is preserved in a poem by his wife, Eucheria.[60] His

---

[52] Gregory of Tours, *HF*, IV, 9 (p. 140). See Stein, 2: 525ff., for Theodebald.

[53] Gregory of Tours, *HF*, IV, 24 (p. 156).

[54] Stroheker, p. 149, no. 38.

[55] Pseudo-Fredegarius, *Chron.*, IV, 28 (*MGH, SRM*, II, 132): "Majordomus genere romanus, litterum eruditus."

[56] Buchner, *Die Provence*, p. 77.

[57] Fortunatus, *Carm.* VI, X, v. 56 (*MGH, AA*, IV-1, 151): "Legi etiam missos alienos nomine versus / Quo quasi per speculum reddit imago virum."

[58] "Laeta sedens filomella fronde," in Keil, 5: 579, ll. 13–14.

[59] See the evidence of the letters contained in the *Ep.* 12 and 17 (*MGH, Ep.*, III, 127 and 131), which we will discuss in sect. II.C of this chapter. Dynamius corresponded with Gregory the Great; see Stroheker, pp. 164–65, no. 108.

[60] *Anth. lat.*, no. 390. The grammarian Julian of Toledo cited a verse from it. Eucheria's preciosity as well as her vocabulary prove that she was a contemporary of Fortunatus. See Max Manitius, "Zu Dynamius von Massilia," *MIOEG* 18 (1897): 229ff. Ernest

grandson was the author of his grandparents' metrical epitaph as well
as of a poem glorifying Lérins that is woven through with reminiscences
from Ovid, Virgil, Juvencus, and even Fortunatus.[61]

Among the mutual friends of Dynamius and Fortunatus was Senator
Felix, who perhaps belonged to the same family as Ennodius of Pavia.[62]
Gregory of Tours tells us that he studied classical literature at Marseille
and that he worked with a slave, which, we should note, was a common
antique practice.[63] The slave, who became learned in literature, law,
and calculation, also became ambitious, left his master for Duke Lupus,
and finally wound up in the service of Sigebert. So, he too is another
example of a scholar in the service of a Frankish king. The Provençal
circle of Duke Lupus[64] also included Jovinus, patricius of Provence and
poet,[65] and Bodisigelus, a former governor of Marseille whose eloquence
won over Fortunatus.[66]

Some aristocrats from Provence and Burgundy who left the lay state
to become bishops and abbots were also men of letters. Firminus, the
future bishop of Uzès whose talents were praised by Arator,[67] and his
nephew Ferreolus continued the tradition of a proud family. Ferreolus
received a good education: when he died in 581, he left a collection of
letters reminiscent of those of Sidonius as well as a monastic rule attributed to him.[68] In Burgundy, Attala, future abbot of Bobbio, was
trained in the liberal arts by his father.[69] Another Attala, count of Autun

---

Dutoit, *La thème de l'adynaton dans la poésie antique* (Paris, 1936), did not cite the
poetry of Eucheria.

[61] *Anth. lat.*, no. 786a, "De Lerine insula laus Dinamii." See Manitius, "Zu Dynamius
von Massilia," pp. 230ff. For Dynamius' epitaph, see Avitus, *Carm.* XXI (*MGH, AA,*
VI-2, 194).

[62] Fortunatus, *Carm.* VI, 10, v. 68 (*MGH, AA,* IV-1, 152).

[63] Gregory of Tours, *HF,* IV, 46 (p. 181): "Filices senatoris servus fuit, qui ad obsequium domini depotatus ad studia litterarum cum eo positus, bene institutus emicuit.
Nam de operibus Virgilii, legis Theodosianae libris artemque calculi adplene eruditus
est."

[64] Fortunatus, *Carm.* VII, 7 (p. 159).

[65] Ibid., 12, v. 111 (p. 168): "Scribe vacans animo refer alta poemata versu." For
Jovinus and his connections with Provence, see Stroheker, p. 186, no. 205.

[66] Fortunatus, *Carm.* VII, 5 (p. 158). This person married a Roman, Palatina, the
daughter of Gallus Magnus. His name does not necessarily indicate that he was a German.

[67] Arator, *Ep. ad Parthenium,* v. 93 (*CSEL,* 72: 153). According to the *Acta Firmini*
(*AS,* Oct., V, 646), he taught grammar to young Ferreolus.

[68] Gregory of Tours, *HF,* VI, 7 (p. 276): "Plenus sapientia et intellectu qui libros
aliquos epistularum quasi Sidonium secutus composuit." This collection has been lost.
For Ferreolus' rule, see Georg Holzherr, *Regula Ferioli* (Einsiedeln, 1961).

[69] Jonas, *Vita Attalae, MGH, SRM,* IV-1, 144: "Dum patri nobili liberalibus studiis
imbutus est." Attala descended from a Romanized Burgundian family.

and great-uncle of Gregory of Tours, ended his life as bishop of Langres and was "well trained in literature."[70]

We can add a cleric to this group, the famous Desiderius, an aristocrat perhaps born at Autun,[71] who became bishop of Vienne around 599. Even though he was fortunate enough to have a biographer almost his contemporary in the Visigothic king, Sisebut,[72] we are nevertheless poorly informed on his youth and intellectual training. We are told merely that "at an age when it is usual to learn, he devoted himself to literary studies, soon surpassing those who were learned, and developed a perfect knowledge of grammar."[73] We would know almost nothing of his intellectual activity if Gregory the Great had not criticized him for teaching grammar and for probably having read or written poetry. Perhaps Desiderius, as a cultivated individual, was upset that Vienne had no teachers and thus tried to fill the gap himself. Vienne had traditionally been open to intellectual culture and remained faithful to this tradition at least until the opening of the sixth century. At the end of the century, it could still boast an audience interested in classical studies, especially poetry.

Scholars had thus not disappeared in southeastern Gaul. It was not for nothing that the biographers of Caesarius of Arles worried about the severity of Provençal masters around 550.[74] Nor was it without reason that the abbot of Saint Laurentius in Paris around 561 refused the bishopric of Avignon in fear of the mockery of "high-minded senators and philosophical bureaucrats."[75] A seventh-century monk of Lérins was scandalized that pagan comedies and poems were still being

---

[70] Gregory of Tours, *Vitae patrum*, VII (*MGH, SRM*, I-2, 687): "Bene litteris institutus."

[71] This is according to the chronicler Ado of Vienne (*Chronicon, PL*, CXXIII, 111). For Desiderius, see W. J. McAuliffe, "Saint Desiderius of Vienne" (diss., Catholic University of America, Washington, D.C., 1942). I have not been able to consult this thesis.

[72] Sisebut, *Vita Desiderii episc. Viennensis, MGH, SRM*, III, 630. Sisebut could have gained information about Desiderius when Brunhilda sent the ex-fiancée of Theodoric II back to Spain; see Pseudo-Fredegarius, *Chron.*, IV, 30 (*MGH, SRM*, II, 132). This would explain Sisebut's hatred for Brunhilda; see J. Fontaine, *IS*, p. 841, n. 2.

[73] Sisebut, *Vita Desiderii episc. Viennensis, MGH, SRM*, III, 630: "Qui cum annos fas est doceri contigisset legitimos traditur ad studia literarum nec multa morula concrescente sensus sui vigore jam doctos transcendens plenissime grammatica edocatus."

[74] *Vita Caesarii*, ed. Morin, p. 297: "Ut si casu scholasticorum aures atque judicia nos simplices contigerit relatores attingere, non arguant quod stilus noster videtur pompa verborum et cautela artis grammatica destitutus."

[75] Gregory of Tours, *HF*, VI, 9 (p. 279): "Nec permittet simplicitatem illius inter senatores sophisticos ac judice philosophicos fatigari."

studied.[76] Inscriptions from this period bear witness to a taste for antique literature, especially for poetry. These metrical pieces—such as the magnificent epitaph of Abbot Florentinus of Arles, a sketch of which Peiresc left us;[77] or that of Guntram's children, which is the work of a polished poet;[78] or that of a deacon; or of a layman[79]—prove that Latin verse could still be written and that remembrances from pagan Antiquity were readily combined with Christian beliefs.[80]

Antique culture can be traced in southeastern Gaul at least until the mid-seventh century, when the Provençal priest, Florentius, was writing his skillfully composed *Vita Rusticulae*[81] and when, under Clovis II (650), stone engravers in Lyon were still capable of engraving inscriptions of remarkable formal elegance.[82] Classical culture, far from being destroyed by the Frankish conquest, had survived a century after the annexation of Burgundy and Provence.

B. Men of Letters in Aquitaine

Our sources of information for Aquitaine are much poorer. This region, stretching from the Loire to the Pyrenees and bounded on the east by the mountains between the Allier and Loire, definitely preserved antique traditions. The Barbarian presence here was negligible; in fact, the Franks were never really able to conquer their southern provinces.[83] One of the most rebellious regions and a region whose history we know

[76] *Vita Caprasii, AS*, June, I, 78: "Videmus quamplurimos homines gentilium libros studiose perlegere, fabulas poetarum comoedias et carmina perscrutare."

[77] Paris, Bibliothèque Nationale, lat. 6012, f. 80. This inscription, published by Le Blant, *IC*, 2: 246 (no. 512), dates perhaps from the seventh century. It merits study.

[78] See Avitus, *Carmina* XVI, XVII (*MGH, AA*, VI-2, 192). The editor notes that the poet imitated the epitaph of Vitalis the mime (*Anth. lat.*, p. 38, no. 487a).

[79] *CIL*, XII, 5862: "Eu nimium celere rapuit mors impia cursu." This epitaph was found at Andance; see Le Blant, *NR*, no. 130.

[80] *CIL*, XII, 2094, v. 5: "Phaebus nempe nitens merito producitur orto."

[81] P. Riché, "Note d'hagiographie mérovingienne: La *Vita S. Rusticulae*," *AB* 72 (1954): 369–77. Krusch thought that this text was too well written to be Merovingian and thus dated it to the ninth century.

[82] Pierre Wuilleumier, Amable Audin, and André Leroi-Gourhan, *L'eglise et la nécropole Saint-Laurent dans le quartier lyonnais de Choulans*, Institut des Etudes rhodaniennes de l'Université de Lyon, Mémoires et Documents, 4 (Lyon, 1949). See also the inscriptions from Briord (Ain) which N. Duval studied in *BSAF* (1964), pp. 77–84.

[83] There has been no general study of Merovingian Aquitaine since Claude Perroud's work, *Des origines du premier duché d'Aquitaine* (Paris, 1881). Maurice Broëns, in "Le peuplement germanique de la Gaule entre la Méditerranée et l'Océan," *AM* 68 (1956): 17–38, used toponymy to try to prove the existence of a large Frankish population (5–10 percent of the population of the Garonne valley). But he himself admits that Romans and Franks fused very rapidly.

quite well was Auvergne. Geographically isolated, it was a bastion of resistance to Germanic influences. Archaeology and toponymy both confirm that Auvergne was not settled by Germans.[84] It can claim more inscriptions than neighboring regions up to the mid-seventh century.[85] Furthermore, Auvergne was part of the same kingdom as Provence from 561, and Arvernians were sent to Marseille as bureaucrats.[86] These exchanges between the two regions could only encourage the survival of Roman customs.

Although not so near the Mediterranean as Auvergne, the other portions of Aquitaine remained in contact with Italy. Trips by Aquitainians to Rome were not rare. Italians reciprocated by coming to Aquitaine, if only to take the water cures at Aquae Bormiae (today, Bourbon-l'Archambault).[87]

The Franks were forced to accept the particularist situation in Aquitaine, and as in southeastern Gaul, they allowed Gallo-Romans to perform the duties of counts.[88] These individuals generally came from the important families, like the Apollinarii, the Leontii, the Sulpicii, and Gregory of Tours' ancestors. The lifestyle of these potentates in the cities or on their rural properties was still antique and was reflected in their intellectual training.[89]

We know almost nothing of the aristocrats' education during the first half of the sixth century. Sidonius' son undoubtedly transmitted to his son, Arcadius, the training he received from his father;[90] and we can suppose that the other Arcadius, whose premature death Fortunatus lamented, came from the same famous family. Fortunatus described this adolescent as overwhelming the most experienced with his elo-

---

[84] A. Dauzat, "Noms des domaines gallo-romaines en Auvergne et en Velay," *Zeitschrift für Ortsnamenforschung* 8 (1938): 206–37; ibid., 9 (1939): 10–45, 108–72; Joseph B. Delort, *Dix années de fouilles en Auvergne et dans la France centrale* (Lyon, 1901); Kurth, "Les Nationalités en Auvergne au VIᵉ siècle," in *Etudes franques*, 1: 226.

[85] They come from Clermont, Coudes, Artonne, Cusset, and Volvic; see Le Blant, *IC*, 2: 321–44 (nos. 556c–571), and Le Blant, *NR*, nos. 232–38. See also P. F. Fournier, "Fragment d'épitaphe du Haut Moyen Age découvert à Clermont," *Bulletin de la Société historique et scientifique de l'Auvergne* 60 (1940): 172.

[86] Gregory of Tours, *HF*, VIII, 43 (p. 409): "Nicetius arvernus rector Massiliensis provinciae" (587). See also the *Vita Boniti*, 3 (*MGH, SRM*, VI, 120, l. 23).

[87] See above, chap. 2, sect. III.A. The health resort at Néris may have been still active.

[88] Kurth, "Les comtes d'Auvergne" and "Les comtes de Tours," in *Etudes franques*, 1: 185, 226.

[89] See the descriptions of Leontius' villas in Fortunatus, *Carm.* I, 16 (*MGH, AA*, IV-1, 19–21).

[90] For this person, see Stroheker, p. 147, no. 29.

quence.[91] But for the latter half of the century, we have information on several types of scholars, thanks to Fortunatus and Gregory of Tours.

Bishop Sulpicius I of Bourges, who died in 591, was praised for his superiority in rhetoric and meter.[92] Felix, who was bishop of Nantes but came from an Aquitainian family,[93] was congratulated by Fortunatus for his poetry, several verses of which have survived.[94] Like their colleagues in Burgundy and Provence, these bishops came late to the episcopate and brought their lay education with them.

This was not the case with Gregory of Tours. When eight years old he learned the *notae litterarum*—that is, the alphabet—at home.[95] When his father became ill he entered the episcopal school at Clermont, which was under the direction of his uncle, Avitus; here, he applied himself to the study of the Psalms and other sacred texts.[96] The change was to influence Gregory. He received a uniquely ecclesiastical training at Clermont and did not have access to grammarians' works or to ancient authors. He seemed to regret more than once not having studied profane literature during his adolescence.[97] Later, when he wanted to fill these gaps, he read Virgil and other classics and as a consequence acquired intellectual habits comparable to those of the scholars of his time.[98] For this reason, he can rank with them.

Contrary to what one might think, the generation following Greg-

[91] Fortunatus, *Carm.* IV, 17 (p. 90): "Hic puer Arcadius veniens de prole senatus. Eloquio torrens, specie radiente venustus / Vincens artifices et puer arte rudis." This epitaph is obviously of the type that eulogized child prodigies. Mme. de Maillé, *Recherches sur les origines chrétiennes de Bordeaux* (Paris, 1960), p. 82, thought Arcadius was the son of Leontius II of Bordeaux.

[92] Gregory of Tours, *HF*, VI, 39 (p. 310): "Vir valde nobilis et de primis senatoribus Galliarum, in litteris bene eruditus rethoricis, in metricis vero artibus nulli secundus." Ozanam, *La civilisation chrétienne*, p. 491, believed that he could detect traces of hexameters in a letter from Sulpicius to Desiderius. Stroheker mentioned Sulpicius (p. 130) but omitted him from his prosopography.

[93] Fortunatus, *Carm.* III, 8, vv. 11–13 (p. 58). See Stroheker, pp. 172–73, no. 148.

[94] Fortunatus, *Carm.* III, 4 (p. 52, l. 10).

[95] Gregory of Tours, *Glor. confess.*, 39 (*MGH, SRM*, I-2, 772. ll. 10–11): "Nihil aliud litterarum praeter notas agnovi, in quorum nunc studio constrictus adfligo." See *Vitae patrum*, VIII, 2 (ibid., p. 692, l. 20): "Cum primum litterarum elementa coepissem agnoscere et essem quasi octavi anni aevo."

[96] *Vitae patrum*, II (p. 669, l. 1): "Qui me post Davitici carminis cannas ad illa evangelicae praedicationis dicta . . . perduxit."

[97] Ibid., p. 668: "Non enim me artis grammaticae studium imbuit neque auctorum saecularium polita lectio erudivit sed tantum. . . . Aviti . . . studium ad ecclesiastica sollicitavit scripta." See also, *Mir. Mart.*, IV (*MGH, SRM*, I-2, 586), and *Glor. confess.*, preface (ibid., p. 747): "Quia sum sine litteris rethoricis et arte grammatica."

[98] Gregory's erudition is discussed in sect. II.C of this chapter.

ory's did not decline. Sulpicius II of Bourges (ca. 630) was as learned as his predecessor and relative, as his letter to Desiderius of Cahors proves.[99] Desiderius himself, born about 590 in Albi, received a perfect literary education from his parents,[100] as perhaps did his two older brothers. In addition, the mother of these three boys was herself educated: three letters we have from her are written in relatively correct Latin.[101]

Bonitus, future bishop of Clermont, was born about 640 and thus represents the following generation. He received a literary and legal education envied by the scholars of his town.[102] His brother, Avitus, had also been trained in "exterior learning"—to borrow a phrase for profane literature from hagiography.[103] We should note also that Bonitus and Avitus, like Desiderius of Cahors[104] and perhaps Desiderius of Vienne,[105] belonged to the important Gallo-Roman family of the Syagrii. As in Ostrogothic Italy, classical culture remained the privilege of the high aristocracy.

Bonitus and Avitus end the list of known Aquitainian scholars. As in southeastern Gaul, the list does not go beyond the mid-seventh century. We will have to try to explain this coincidence later. We can conclude now, however, that in lands where written civilization survived, Gallo-Roman aristocrats, like those in Italy, remained loyal to belles-lettres. Of course, because our sources are so poor, we can give only a few names. But the relevant evidence is in sufficient agreement for us to say that there were still many cultivated laymen. It is not enough, however, to know that there were still men interested in classi-

---

99 *Ep.* II, 1 (*MGH, Ep.,* III, 203). See especially the beginning of the letter. See also, Paul of Verdun's letters, *Ep.* II, 11–12 (ibid., pp. 208–9) and that of Felix of Limoges, *Ep.* II, 21 (ibid., p. 214).

100 *Vita sancti Desiderii, MGH, SRM,* IV, 564: "Litterarum studia adplenum eruditus."

101 Ibid., pp. 569–70. The Germanic name Herchenfreda does not necessarily indicate that this woman was of Barbarian origin. Saint Eustadiola, abbess of Berry, who died around 680, was another woman who had received a literary education. See *AS,* June, II, 131: "Litteris sacris instituta exercitio disciplinarum."

102 *Vita Boniti, MGH, SRM,* VI, 119: "Grammaticorum imbutus initiis nec non Theodosii edoctus decretis . . . a sophistis probus atque praelatus est." *Sophistae* does not refer (as Pirenne thought in "De 'l'état de l'instruction") to teachers, but rather to men of letters or men of intelligence. See the references in my article, "L'instruction des laics en Gaule mérovingienne au VIIe siècle," *Settimane,* 5: 881.

103 *Vita Boniti,* ibid., p. 121: "Vir exterioribus studiis eruditus." The hagiographer perhaps was using Gregory the Great's expression; see above, chap. 5, n. 42.

104 Coville, pp. 18–19.

105 Desiderius could have been born in Autun, where members of the Syagrii family are known to have been; see Stroheker, pp. 221–22, no. 375. In addition, his name was a frequently used one in this family.

cal culture in southern Gaul. We must probe deeper to determine what
classical culture meant to them.

C. The Content of Classical Culture

We should state immediately that our inquiry will not be easy because, unlike the situation we discovered in Italy at the opening of the
sixth century, very few written works have come down to us except
for those of Gregory of Tours and Fortunatus. Fortunatus, of course,
was an Italian, but he wrote and lived in Gaul long enough to have
made many friends in the Frankish kingdom, and he may thus be used
as a source of information. But there is another difficulty: the literary
achievement of Merovingian Gaul has until recently attracted little
interest among philologists, who have been repulsed by the poverty of
the source material as well as by its incorrect form. There have been
a few studies on so-called Merovingian Latin here and there, but they
have not taken sufficient account of the historical circumstances of the
culture of this period. Without attempting a history of Merovingian
literature or a study of its different genres, let us try to reconstruct what
young aristocrats of the sixth and seventh centuries knew from the
works which have survived.

First of all, was the educational program still conceived as a whole?
Did the classical schema of the liberal arts still have any meaning?
Paradoxically, Gregory of Tours, who called himself the least polished
of men, gives us a definition of the seven liberal arts.[106] Although he
cited Martianus Capella's name ("Martianus noster"),[107] did Gregory
actually ever study his work? Some have thought so and have argued
that Gregory was quite cultivated.[108] That, however, is very uncertain.
Gregory knew practically nothing from the *De nuptiis Philologiae et
Mercurii*. In one sentence he gave a definition of each art which bears
only slight resemblance to reality: "Grammar teaches one to read, dialec-

---

[106] Gregory of Tours, *HF*, X, 21 (p. 536).

[107] How do we explain the familiar tone with which Gregory referred to Martianus?
Gabriel Monod, *Etudes critiques sur les sources de l'histoire mérovingienne*, pt. 1, *Grégoire
de Tours, Marius d'Avenches* (Paris, 1872), thought that the episcopal library contained
a copy of Martianus Capella's book. Gregory, however, also referred to the Christian
poet Prudentius as "Prudentius noster" (*Glor. martyr* 40 [*MGH, SRM*, I-2, 514]), and
called Sidonius "Sollius noster" (*De virtut. Juliani*, 2 [ibid., p. 585, l. 20]; *HF*, IV, 12
[p. 142, l. 26]), and Saint Martin, "Martinus noster." Gregory obviously thought that
Martianus was a Christian author.

[108] See Kurth, "Grégoire de Tours et les études classiques au VIe siècle," in *Etudes
franques*, 1: 129ff.

tic to answer propositions in discussion, rhetoric to know the different meters."[109] When he came to what Boethius called the quadrivium, Gregory wrote, "Geometry teaches one to calculate the area of land and the measure of distances, astrology to consider the course of stars, arithmetic to calculate the divisions of numbers, harmony to express modulation of smooth sounds in poems."[110]

Gregory's definitions call for a few remarks. Gregory, first of all, was not following the order of the arts which had been classic since Martianus and repeated by both Boethius and Cassiodorus. He placed dialectic before rhetoric (he does this elsewhere[111]), geometry before arithmetic, astrology—that is, astronomy—before music. Furthermore, he considerably impoverished some of the arts. According to Gregory, rhetoric only taught one how to write verse, dialectic was the science of the grammarian;[112] from the four branches of the quadrivium he kept only their practical applications.

Although Gregory did not know the arts very well, he at least cited them all and is our only source for them. Yet the priest Stephen of Auxerre, who wrote a *Life of Saint Amator* in the mid-sixth century, recalled that his hero was trained "in the doctrines of all the arts and in the subtleties of the disciplines."[113] At first glance, it might seem that Stephen was distinguishing what would later be called the trivium from the quadrivium. In fact, though, he meant only literary exercises, as is apparent from the examples he later gave: figures of poetical invention, rhetors' enthymemes, lawyers' difficulties and obscurities, and the syllogistic questions of the philosophers.[114] There is no mention of scientific disciplines. The same can be said for Fortunatus, who never spoke of the quadrivium.[115] Classical culture, then, was exclusively literary; the

---

109 Gregory of Tours, *HF*, X, 31 (p. 536): "In grammaticis [Martianus] docuit legere, in dialecticis altercationum propositiones advertere, in rhetoricis genera metrorum agnoscere."

110 Ibid.: "In geometricis terrarum linearumque mensuras colligere, in astrologiis cursus siderum contemplare, in arithmeticis numerorum partes colligere, in armoniis sonorum modulationes suavium accentum carminibus concrepare."

111 See his reference to Gregory the Great's culture in *HF*, X, 1 (p. 478, l. 8).

112 Ibid., preface (p. 1, l. 7): "Quisquam peritus dialectica in arte grammaticus."

113 Stephanus, *Vita Amatoris*, *AS*, May, I, p. 52: "Omnium artium doctrinam et disciplinarum subtilitatem est consecutum."

114 Ibid.: "Ut poeticarum adinventionum schemata, oratorum enthymemata jurisperitorum nodos atque aenigmata, philosophorum quoque syllogisticas questiones facili disputatione penitus enarraret."

115 Fortunatus, *Vita Martini*, I, 29–30 (*MGH*, *AA*, IV-1, 296); idem, *Carm.*, preface (ibid., p. 1).

sciences were interesting only for their applications. Our scholars' outlook thus is similar to that of the Italian scholars.

Let us now examine the various divisions of literary learning, beginning with grammar. Our authors mention "grammatical science" several times.[116] What did they mean exactly?

For Maurice Roger and Ferdinand Lot, the phrase means nothing. For these historians, the classical Latin of the sixth century was an artificial language understood only by those who had had advanced training. Since they believed they could show that this kind of teaching was no longer given, they concluded that Latin had already become a dead language.[117] Popular Latin on the other hand, freed from its tutelage to grammar and rapidly evolving in the direction of what was to become Romance, was alive. Utilizing literary, diplomatic, and epigraphic texts, Roger and Lot brought to bear as evidence all the innovations in spoken Latin: novelties in phonetics (confusion between $\bar{o}$ and $\breve{u}$, between $\bar{e}$ and $\breve{i}$, between long and short a, suppression of dipthongs), in morphology (greater use of the comparative, of the neuter, and of the adverb; confusion between active and passive voice; and so on), and lastly, in syntax (substitution of *suus* for *ejus*, placement of the demonstrative before the noun, innovations in the form of all three first conjugations, and so on). Gregory of Tours was aware of these transformations and confessed "to taking feminines for masculines, neuters for feminines, masculines for neuters."[118]

Roger's and Lot's overly categorical thesis has been refuted by some philologists, who argue that written and spoken Latin were not as far apart as has been thought and that grammatical innovations represented man's new attitude toward the universe. Merovingian Latin, we are told, should not be judged according to the laws of classical philology

116 "Eruditio grammaticae" (*Acta Firmini, AS*, Oct., V, 646); "cautela artis grammaticae" (*Vita Caesarii*, ed. Morin, p. 297); "grammaticorum initia" (*Vita Boniti, MGH, SRM, VI*, 119); "artis grammaticae studium, ars grammatica" (Gregory of Tours, passim).

117 See F. Lot, "A quelle époque a-t-on cessé de parler latin?" *ALMA* 6 (1931): 97–159; idem, *La fin du monde antique*, pp. 435ff.; Roger, p. 100. In his article, Lot refuted Henri F. Muller, "When Did Latin Cease to be a Spoken Language in France?" *Romanic Review* 12 (1921): 318–34. Einar Löfstedt, *Late Latin* (Oslo, 1959), p. 14, realized that it is difficult to fix a precise date but agreed with Muller that Latin was a dead language by the eighth century. For the evolution of Latin during this period, see Masai and Corbett, eds., *Regula Magistri*, pp. 77ff.; Dag Norberg, *Beiträge zur spätlateinischen Syntax* (Uppsala, 1944); idem, *Syntaktische Forschungen* . . . (Uppsala, 1943); Maria Corti, *Studi sulla latinità merovingica in testi agiografici minori* (Messina, 1939).

118 Gregory of Tours, *Glor. confess.*, preface (*MGH, SRM*, I-2, 748). See n. 127.

but rather should be placed in the social and psychological context in which it was born.[119]

In support of their opposing theses, each side envisions Merovingian Gaul as a whole. But what is true for the area north of the Loire is not so for the south. Let us limit ourselves for the moment to examining what Latin a polished aristocrat living in Roman Gaul knew.

We should note first that it is somewhat difficult to contrast literary language (*sermo scholasticus*) with vulgar Latin, since we do not know the spoken language of the period. Was it Latin, or one or another dialect that had issued from Latin? We have no way of knowing. We must distinguish, of course, between the language of the town and the language of the countryside, where Celtic had undoubtedly not completely disappeared.[120] Latin must have been spoken in towns with strong Roman traditions, but what Latin? It was hoped that Merovingian inscriptions might permit us to study the popular tongue, but those that have been examined show that stone engravers used formulas and stereotyped phrases.[121]

On the other hand, one cannot conclude, as did Lot, that literary Latin, whether profane or ecclesiastical, was no longer understood.[122] The faithful who heard the Epistles and the Gospels read could certainly still grasp their meaning. Witness a certain Celsus, a scholar to be sure, who was converted to a life of poverty after hearing a reading from Isaiah.[123] Preachers who gave their sermons in Latin in urban churches, as did Caesarius of Arles at the beginning of the sixth century, must have been understood by the aristocrats as well as by the people. But we can suppose that aristocratic families endeavored to

[119] See Henri François Muller, *L'époque mérovingienne: Essai de synthèse de philologie et d'histoire* (New York, 1945). Not all the opinions of this philologist, who was trained in the United States, have been accepted. See C. Mohrmann, "Transformations linguistiques et évolution sociale et spirituelle," *VChr* 1 (1947): 186–90. The controversy has been summarized by Mario Pei, *The Language of the Eighth-Century Texts in Northern France: A Study of the Original Documents in the Collections of Tardif and Other Sources* (New York, 1932), pp. 2ff. For Pei—as for his teacher, Muller—Merovingian Latin was a living language with its own laws.

[120] Bonnet, *Le latin*, pp. 25ff.; Paul Fournier, "La persistance du gaulois au VIᵉ siècle d'après Grégoire de Tours," in *Recueil de travaux offert à M. Clovis Brunel* (Paris, 1955), pp. 448–53. The expression *lingua rustica* can refer to vulgar Latin, but when a writer refers to a *sermo vulgaris* (see *MGH, Ep.*, III, 458, ll. 4–5: "Quia vulgari sermone ita dicitur qui cum pluribus consiliatur, solus non peccat"), he is speaking of a popular proverb.

[121] Jules Pirson, *La langue des inscriptions latines de la Gaule* (Brussels, 1901).

[122] Lot, "A quelle époque," pp. 97–159.

[123] Gregory of Tours, *HF*, IV, 24 (p. 156). For this passage, see Paul Tombeur, "*Audire* dans le thème hagiographique de la conversion," *Latomus* 26 (1965): 164–65.

speak differently from the masses. It is not necessary to exaggerate the process of linguistic leveling and think that the senator spoke like his slave. Gregory of Tours' contemporaries and Gregory himself still had sufficient culture and an ear to distinguish literary Latin from vulgar Latin. When Gregory heard a servant of the bishop of Tarbes speak, he judged him immediately: "He spoke in a vulgar manner, with a drawling, ugly, and indecent accent."[124] The circumstances surrounding this episode—the individual in question was praying before relics—lead one to believe that he was indeed speaking "Latin." Again, one day when Gregory was tired, he had a replacement say mass in his stead. His entourage, however, complained that the celebrant spoke in "I do not know what kind of *rustic* speech," and added that "it would be better to be silent than to speak so poorly."[125]

Thus, even when they expressed themselves orally, scholars had to watch out for their form. Their attention was sharper, of course, when they wrote: one never writes exactly the language he speaks, especially in a period of linguistic change—we have some good examples of this in our own day. Such was the case in the Merovingian period. In order to speak well—better yet, to write well—one had to refer to the authority of grammar.

Gregory mentioned grammatical studies several times in making the point that he had not been steeped in them. Nevertheless, he mentioned different stages in grammatical studies in passing: letters and syllables,[126] genders, cases, prepositions.[127] In Antiquity, letters were taught

---

[124] Gregory of Tours, *HF*, IX, 6 (p. 418, l. 17): "Erat enim ei et sermo rusticus et ipsius linguae latitudo turpis atque obscoena." See Cicero, *De orat.*, II, 91: "Latitudo verborum" ("a broad accent").

[125] Gregory of Tours, *Mir. Mart.*, II, 1 (*MGH, SRM*, I-2, 609, l. 24): "Sed cum presbiter ille nescio quid rustice festiva verba depromeret, multi eum de nostris inridere coeperunt, dicentes: 'Melius fuisset tacere quam sic inculte loqui.'" The clerics of Tours reacted much like the African men of letters who, according to Augustine, mocked priests who committed barbarisms; see *De catechizandis rudibus*, VIII, 13 (*PL*, XL, 205). See Helmut Beumann, "Gregor von Tours und der *Sermo rusticus*," in *Spiegel der Geschichte: Festgabe für Max Braubach zum 10. April 1964*, ed. Konrad Repgen and Stephan Skalweit (Münster, 1964), pp. 69–98.

[126] Gregory of Tours, *HF*, I, 1 (p. 3): "Si aut in litteris aut in sillabis grammaticam artem excessero."

[127] *Glor. confess.*, preface (*MGH, SRM*, I-2, 748, ll. 1–5): "Qui nullum argumentum utile in litteris habes qui nomina discernere nescis; saepius pro masculinis femina, pro femineis neutra et pro neutra masculina conmutas; qui ipsas quoque praepositiones quas nobilium dictatorum observari sanxit auctoritas loco debito plerumque non locas." Gregory was at least aware of what had to be done, which is saying a great deal. As Curtius (p. 185) remarked, following Traube, Gregory's complaints and apologies are really rhetorical artifices.

by the *magister ludi,* but this person no longer existed by the sixth century, when, as we shall see, parents taught the child how to read and write Latin. Primary and secondary instruction were now combined.

Did children use Latin grammatical manuals? Grammatical literature was important in Italy and Africa during this time, but was it so in southern Gaul? A few grammatical extracts have survived, but only in seventh- and eighth-century manuscripts.[128] The only sixth-century reference to a grammarian comes from Gregory of Tours, who was quite proud to show that he had filled the gaps in his education. He said in the preface to his *Vitae patrum* that he hesitated between *Vita* and *Vitae patrum* as his title because although Aulus Gellius and several "philosophers" used the plural, Pliny the Elder in his third book of grammar recommended the singular. Then followed Pliny's citation, the accuracy of which cannot be checked, since it comes from a work no longer extant.[129] Gregory must have found this information second-hand in a manual, no doubt one intended for the school.

Some have thought that southern Gaul could claim a grammarian in the person of a certain Virgil, who is supposed to have taught at Toulouse in the sixth century. Roger gave him an important place in his work even though he found his taste for the fantastic curious and his writings puerile. As Roger showed, the school of Toulousan grammar never existed.[130] Furthermore, Toulouse does not appear in any text as a center of culture even of the least magnitude. Virgil, on the other hand, seems to have known Isidore's work, which would place him in the second half of the seventh century. Perhaps he belonged, as is thought nowadays, to the lands of hisperic Latin—Wales or Ireland.[131]

Scholars found their models more in the literary works themselves than in theoretical treatises. Young children still learned fables, some

---

[128] For the seventh century we have only Bern, Burgerbibliothek 380 (Cledonius) Vienna, Oesterreichische Nationalbibliothek, lat. 16 (Eutyches); see Keil, 5: 3–6, and 7: 537. There are about fifteen eighth-century maunscripts containing grammatical fragments.

[129] Gregory of Tours, *Vitae patrum,* preface (*MGH, SRM,* I-2, 662).

[130] Roger, pp. 110–11.

[131] Heinrich Zimmer. "Der Gascogner Virgilius Maro Grammaticus in Irland," *Sitzungsberichte der preussischen Akademie der Wissenschaften zu Berlin, phil. hist. Klasse* (1910), p. 1031; Paul Grosjean, "Sur quelques exégètes irlandais du VIIe siècle, *SE* 7 (1955): 82; M. Esposito, "Latin Learning and Literature in Mediaeval Ireland: I–V," *Hermathena* 50 (1937): 151–53. Virgil could have had contacts with Hebrew circles. Dominique Tardi, *Les Epitomae de Virgile de Toulouse* (Paris, 1928), pp. 22–23, has correctly seen the influence of the doctrines of the Kabbala in the grammarian's work. Could Virgil have been a converted Jew?

of which are recounted by chroniclers.[132] Perhaps the *Disticha Catonis* were used as elementary school texts.[133] Later, the pupil read more serious authors. Gregory of Tours knew Sallust, Horace, and especially Virgil.[134]

Virgil was read in all lettered circles during the Merovingian period, even, as we shall see, in monasteries. He was still the model par excellence. Fortunatus, who was nourished on this poet from his childhood, continually cited him in his verse.[135] Even Gregory of Tours, despite his condemnation of the *fallaciae Virgilii*, did not hesitate to borrow about fifty times from Virgil in order to impart brilliance to his own work.[136] Virgil, then, was known, but how was he read? There must have been manuscripts of the *Aeneid* in Gaul during this period, but none have come down to us.[137] Virgil's commentators were also read.[138] Gregory himself consulted one of them.[139] It has been argued that Virgil was known especially through citations from his works in the Church Fathers. In fact, though, we find no citation from Jerome or Ambrose in the work of Gregory of Tours,[140] who, in any event, must not have read much in patristics.[141]

The seventy or so citations and Virgilian reminiscences found in pro-

---

[132] Gregory of Tours, *HF*, IV, 9 (p. 143), the fable of the serpent in the bottle; Pseudo-Fredegarius, *Chron.*, IV, 38 (*MGH, SRM*, II, 139), the wolf and his sons; ibid., II, 57 (p. 81), the lion and the deer.

[133] Fortunatus, *Carm.* II, 2, v. 8, and II, 9, v. 58 (*MGH, AA*, IV-1, 28 and 29) = *Disticha Catonis*, 8, 7, 7, and 1, 27, 2.

[134] For the classics Gregory used, see Kurth, "Grégoire de Tours et les études classiques," in *Etudes franques*, 1: 21ff. Some sixth-century manuscripts still preserve classical texts. See Autun, ms. 24, and Paris, Bibliothèque Nationale, n. a. l. 1629, which contain Pliny's *Natural History* covered over in the sixth century by Cassian's *Institutiones*. Sallust's preface, which Gregory cited, seems to have been a frequently used text; see Fulgentius the Mythographer, *Expositio virgilianae continentiae*, ed. Helm, p. 89, and Ennodius of Pavia, *Ep*. VI, 3 (*MGH, AA*, VII, 216).

[135] See the table of citations Max Manitius compiled for Fortunatus in *MGH, AA*, IV-2, 132ff.

[136] Kurth, "Grégoire de Tours et les études classiques," pp. 15–20, prepared a table of Gregory's Virgilian citations.

[137] The Autun library had a seventh-century copy, but it has been lost. See "Manuscrits de la bibliothèque du séminaire d'Autun," ed. G. Libri, in *Catalogue général des manuscrits des bibliothéques publiques des départements*, 7 vols. (Paris, 1849–85), 1: 4, n. 1.

[138] Sixth- and seventh-century manuscripts prove this; see *CLA*, IV, 498; V, 627; III, 297a.

[139] This would have been Servius' commentary, according to Max Manitius ("Zur Frankengeschichte Gregors von Tours," *NA* 21 [1896]: 553).

[140] It suffices to compare Gregory's citations to the patristic citations collected by Harald Hagendahl, *Latin Fathers and the Classics* (Göteborg, 1958), pp. 413–15. The variety of Merovingian citations proves that there was more than one Virgilian anthology.

[141] See below, chap. 7, sect. I.A.

fane and religious Merovingian works call for a few remarks. They are almost without exception from the *Aeneid*, especially from the first eight books. Gregory of Tours cited the *Eclogues* and *Georgics* only six times and nothing at all from the ninth book onward of the *Aeneid*. We can make the same observation for Paul of Verdun, for hagiographic texts where Virgil was cited,[142] for the Latin Fathers,[143] and for the schoolboys of Byzantine Egypt.[144] To study primarily the first books of the *Aeneid* is an educational tradition that has lasted to our own day.

Furthermore, the passages most cited by Merovingian writers are the episode of the tempest from Book One and those passages evoking the aurora, lightning, battles—anything that could give stories a poetic or epic coloring. Verses which became proverbs were inevitably repeated.[145] Thirdly, the citations were rarely textual and were more often adaptations.[146] Our authors seem to have remembered the sense of a verse they once read. Rarely did they mention Virgil by name but, rather, referred to him as the "poet," or as "a certain poet."[147] This custom was quite ancient and would be retained in the Carolingian period.

Virgil was more or less well known in Merovingian Gaul. The important point, however, is that he was known there at all. This fidelity to the "father of the West"[148] is a symbol of a more profound fidelity to classical culture.

Our scholars read the few classical texts available to them with profit. Gregory of Tours' Latin, which has been studied in a learned work,

---

[142] *Vita Genovefae* (13) = *Aeneid*, I, 118; (39) = *Aeneid*, III, 308; (6) = *Aeneid*, IV, 6. *Vita Dalmatii* (10) = *Aeneid*, I, 93; (7) = *Aeneid*, II, 794; (14) = *Aeneid*, VIII, 622. *Vita Boniti* (24) = *Aeneid*, VIII, 672. Paul of Verdun, *MGH, Epist.*, III, 209 = *Aeneid*, VI, 625.

[143] Hagendahl, *Latin Fathers*, found more than twenty citations from Book I, three from Book IX, and five from Book XII.

[144] See Paul Collart, "Les papyrus littéraires latins," *RPh*, 3rd ser. 15 (1941): 121.

[145] Gregory quoted the famous expression "auri sacra fames" (*Aeneid*, III, 56) seven times.

[146] "Et crebis micat ignibus aether" (*Aeneid.*, I, 90) became, in the hands of a cleric from Auxerre, "crebis micantibus ignibus ex aethere" (*AS*, July, VII, 206). "Par levibus ventis volucrique simillima somno" (*Aeneid*, II, 794) was transformed in the *Vita Dalmatii* into "par levibus ventis similisque somno volucri."

[147] "Ut quidam poeta ait," according to Paul of Verdun (*Ep.* II, 12 [*MGH, Ep.*, III, 209, l. 33]). See Columban's "ut ait quidam" in the same volume (p. 181, l. 12). Gregory of Tours cited Virgil's name only four times.

[148] This is what Newman called him. See Theodor Haecker, *Virgile, Père de l'Occident*, French trans. by Jean Chuzeville (Paris, 1935).

does show many infractions of grammatical rules,[149] but worse could be expected of a man who had not studied the classics as a child. The letters of his contemporaries bear witness to a relatively correct Latin.[150] The same is true fifty years later, during the first third of the seventh century. We can judge the Latin of this period rather precisely by an examination of Desiderius of Cahors' collection of letters, which contains fifteen letters from Desiderius and nineteen from his correspondents.[151] A study of the language of these texts would show that despite new spellings, due no doubt to the influence of pronunciation, and despite the solecisms that Carolingian scribes did not correct when they recopied the texts,[152] the important grammatical laws were known.

A study of poetry likewise shows that meter continued to be studied, or at least that an effort was made to follow metrical rules. Poetry was, in fact, very successful in Gaul. When he asked the priest Stephen to write the *Life of Saint Germanus* in verse and Amator's *Life* in prose, Bishop Aunarius of Auxerre reminded him that the tastes of the public were varied and that if "some liked to read prose, others confessed to being charmed by the numbers, rhythms, and sounds of verse."[153] Gregory of Tours enjoyed thinking that his *Ecclesiastical History* would be put into verse and said that his text prepared the way for someone more gifted than he to do so.[154] There were still many metrical epitaphs in southern Gaul, as we have seen. Fortunatus composed some for his friends,[155] to whom he even sent occasional poems, as did Ennodius of Pavia. Was he, as Roger and Lot claimed, not understood by his correspondents?[156] It is hardly probable, since his friends—Felix of Nantes,

---

[149] Max Bonnet, *Le latin de Grégoire de Tours* (Paris, 1890).

[150] These letters can be found in *MGH, Ep.*, III, 127–33.

[151] Ibid., pp. 193–214. To these, add three letters by Desiderius' mother, found in the *Vita sancti Desiderii, MGH, SRM*, IV, 569–70. Lot did not consider these letters, but they have just been treated in a scholarly edition (Dag Norberg, *Epistulae S. Desiderii Cadurcensis*, Studia Latina Stockholmiensia, VI [Stockholm, 1961]).

[152] These have been noted by Arndt, the editor of the letters (*MGH, Epist.*, III, 191–92). For example, *a* was used with the accusative, *ad* with the ablative, *per* also with the ablative, *cum* with the accusative. We should not forget, however, that these mistakes were already being made during the Roman period.

[153] *Ep.* 7 (*MGH, Ep.* III, 447, ll. 17–18): "Et quidam quidem prosaico oblectantur stilo, quidam autem numeris se rithmisve ac cantibus versuum delectari fatentur."

[154] Gregory of Tours, *HF*, X, 31 (p. 536, l. 15): "Si tibi in his quiddam placuerit, salvo opere nostro, te scribere versu non abnuo."

[155] Fortunatus, *Carm.* IV (*MGH, AA*, IV-1, 79–100) in its entirety. Some epitaphs were written in the name of friends; see ibid. IV, 9 (pp. 85–86) for Theudosius and ibid. IV, 23 (p. 98) for John.

[156] Roger, p. 100; Lot, "A quelle époque," p. 137.

Dynamius, Lupus, Bertechramnus of Bordeaux, and Sulpicius—were themselves poets. As far as we know, Gregory was not a poet, but he did appreciate poetry. He asked Fortunatus to write him some Sapphic verses[157] and even sent him a treatise on meter to enable him to do so.[158]

The poetry of this period is not without fault. Bishop Bertechramnus, according to Fortunatus, wrote lame verse. Fortunatus himself is not above reproach.[159] Perhaps their errors, though, were due to the development of rhythmic poetry. Our poets tried to respect the tradition of metrical poetry, all the while being influenced by accentual versification. This would explain the hesitations normal to a period of transition. Sixth- and seventh-century poetry struggled between two tendencies: on the one hand, it remained faithful to the traditions of the school, while on the other, it wanted to free verse from the too rigid yoke of meter.[160]

The study of poetry leads us naturally to rhetoric, since poetry is speech in verse.[161] We have to ask the same question here as we did for grammar. Were the figures which were supposed to embellish style —the *epichiremata, ellipsis, diaeresis,* the paradigms which Fortunatus quoted to Gregory of Tours in the prefatory letter to his works—still taught?[162] Were all these loci still familiar to our writers? Probably not.

Yet, the reading of antique authors did bear fruit. The rhetorical tradition survived especially in the epistolary style, which was transmitted from generation to generation. Dynamius of Marseille used

---

[157] Fortunatus, *Carm.* V, 5 (pp. 107–8), requesting of Fortunatus a poem on Avitus of Clermont; IX, 6, v. 9 (p. 211): "Hoc mandas etiam quo sapphica metra remittam." Gregory was capable of judging King Chilperic's verse; see *HF*, V, 44 (p. 254, l. 2), and below, sect. III.B.

[158] *Carm.* IX, 7, vv. 33ff. (p. 213). Wilhelm Meyer thought that the treatise in question was Terentianus' *De metris*; see *Der Gelegenheitsdichter Venantius Fortunatus,* Abhandlungen der königlichen Gesellschaft der Wissenschaft zu Göttingen, Phil. Hist. Klasse, n.s., vol. 4, no. 5 (Berlin, 1901), p. 127.

[159] For Fortunatus' versification, see Manitius, 1: 175, and Dominique Tardi, *Fortunat* (Paris, 1927), pp. 266–69, who repeats the conclusions of Hermann Elss, *Untersuchungen ueber den Stil und die Sprache des Venantius Fortunatus* (Heidelberg, 1907).

[160] See M. Nicolau, "Les deux sources de la versification accentuelle," *ALMA* 9 (1934): 54–87f., and especially Dag Norberg, *Introduction à l'étude de la versification latine médiévale* (Stockholm, 1958), pp. 87ff., for this development.

[161] Curtius, p. 182. Gregory of Tours himself said that rhetoric enables one to learn poetry. See above, n. 109.

[162] Fortunatus, *Carm,* preface (*MGH, AA,* IV-1, 1, l. 5): "Illi [the ancients] inventione providi, partitione serii distributione librati, epilogiorum calce jucundi, colae fonte proflui, commate succiso venusti, tropis, paradigmis, perihodis, epichirematibus coronati pariter et cothurnati tale sui canentes dederunt specimen." See also the *Vita Martini,* preface (ibid., p. 293).

figures in his letters that had previously been used by Ruricius and Ennodius, and he was quite worthy of his correspondent, Fortunatus.[163] Sulpicius of Bourges, Paul of Verdun, and Desiderius of Cahors, during the first half of the seventh century, also remained faithful to the "artful letter."[164] To write well undoubtedly meant for these scholars, as for those of Antiquity, to express oneself in a mannered style. Stephen's letter to the bishop of Auxerre is a good example of this mannerism: calling himself a modest writer, he wrote that "the stuttering tongue is paralysed by hideous neglect in the middle of a hoarse throat."[165] When he explained that one ought only to write with assurance, he used metaphors of the experienced hunter, of the soldier trained by the example of veterans, and of the bird, whose mother, *dux penniger*, helps him with his first flight. This is the last example of *tumor africanus* if it is true that Stephen was of African origin.[166] His letters of friendship, letters of consolation, and panegyrical letters were the last examples of good antique style. When a writer wrote more simply, as in Gregory of Tours' case, he did not abandon certain rhetorical forms altogether. Bonnet has revealed the use of chiasmus, hyperbates, word games, and alliteration, and a constant desire to avoid familiar language in the historian of the Franks.[167] Where did our writers find their examples? Perhaps in the rhetorical manuals which were still available in Gaul[168] but especially in their reading.

Their reading brought yet something else to our scholars. Here and there, they noted curious facts with which they could enrich their writing. We have already remarked that eruditio was still part of Italian

---

[163] One can judge from this passage taken from a letter to a friend (*Ep.* 12 [*MGH, Ep.*, III, 127]): "Quantum aestifero solis ardore defesso vel longinqui itineris vastitate quassato gelida limpha, dum ariditatem temperat, restinguit desideria sitientes, ita mihi vestrarum epistularum elocutio, cum incolomitatis vestrae indicia rettulit, gaudiorum incrementa nutrivit."

[164] I have given some examples in my "L'instruction des laics en Gaule," p. 879. See also Dag Norberg, "Remarques sur les lettres de saint Didier de Cahors," in *Classical, Medieval and Renaissance Studies in Honor of Berthold Louis Ullmann*, ed. Charles Henderson, Jr., 2 vols. (Rome, 1964), 1: 277–81.

[165] Stephanus, *Ep.* 8 (*MGH, Ep.*, III, 448, ll. 3–7): "Lingua balbutiens faucium inter raucidulos cursus squalido situ impedita non loquitur."

[166] René Louis, "L'église d'Auxerre et ses évêques avant saint Germain," in *Saint Germain d'Auxerre et son temps*, ed. Gabriel Le Bras (Auxerre, 1950), p. 49.

[167] Bonnet, *Le latin*, pp. 726, 743, 744. See, for example, Theodoric's speech to his troops in *HF*, III, 7 (pp. 103–4).

[168] Darmstadt, Hessische Landes- und Hochschulbibliothek, 166, contains the work of C. Chirius Fortunatianus; Paris, Bibliothèque Nationale, lat. 7530 (eighth century), contains the same work as well as a collection of *schemata dianoeas*. See Karl Halm, *Rhetorici latini minores* (Leipzig, 1863), preface and pp. 71, 81.

culture. The same was true for Gaul. The irreplaceable Gregory of Tours, especially, enables us to study this literary survival.

Gregory enumerated the several wonders of the world in the first part of his *De cursu stellarum*, as had Cassiodorus in the *Variae*, borrowing descriptions from Jerome, Orosius, and the Bible.[169] Then he presented the seven wonders of creation: the movement of oceans, germination, the phoenix (in connction with which he cited a poem attributed to *Lactantius*), Mount Etna, the boiling fountain at Grenoble of which Augustine had already spoken,[170] and lastly, the sun and the moon.[171] Like antique scholars, Gregory enjoyed giving geographic descriptions[172] and noting *mirabilia*: hundred-pound trout fished from Lake Leman, bloody bread, a ball of fire in the sky, and human monsters,[173] not to mention all the atmospheric or terrestrial prodigies presaging catastrophes.[174] All of this is more literary, of course, than scientific—it represents the taste for the marvelous which Antiquity bequeathed to the Middle Ages.[175]

Gregory had little interest in astronomy. For him, knowledge of the constellations and stars had a practical end: to fix the hours of the offices.[176] He did not use learned or poetical names for the stars but, rather, designated them according to popular usage.[177] Even though he called astronomy astrology, he kept from confusing the two sciences and denounced *mathesis* as diabolical.[178] We know, in fact, from councils and other sources that astrology always had its adherents.[179]

Medicine, on the other hand, interested Gregory. This art was still

---

[169] Gregory of Tours, *De cursu stellarum ratio*, 1–8 (MGH, SRM, I-2, 857–60).

[170] Marrou, *Saint Augustin*, p. 145.

[171] *De cursu stellarum ratio*, 9–16 (pp. 860–63).

[172] Gregory of Tours, *HF*, I, 10 (p. 11), on the Nile's floods and the pyramids; *Glor. martyr.*, 75 (MGH, SRM, I-2, 538), on Lake Geneva.

[173] *Glor. martyr.*, 75 (p. 539, l. 7); *HF*, VI, 21 (p. 289, l. 8), VI, 25 (p. 292, l. 17), VII, 41 (p. 363, l. 21).

[174] Torrential rains and earth tremors are mentioned in *HF*, VIII, 23 (p. 389), IX, 44 (p. 475); aurora borealis, in ibid., VI, 33 (p. 304), VII, 11 (p. 333), VIII, 8 (p. 376), VIII, 17 (p. 384), X, 23 (p. 514); premature blossoming, in ibid., VIII, 8 (p. 376); late blossoming, in ibid., VII, 11 (p. 333), IX, 5 (p. 416), IX, 44 (p. 475). These facts are found mostly in the last books of Gregory's *History*.

[175] E. Faral, "Les conditions générales de la production littéraire en Europe occidentale pendant les IXe et Xe siècles," *Settimane*, 2: 285.

[176] *De cursu stellarum ratio*, 12–15 (p. 863).

[177] Ibid., p. 863, ll. 10–12; "Sed nomina quae his vel Maro vel reliqui indiderunt poetae postpono, tantum ea vocabula nuncupans quae vel usitate rusticitas nostra vocat."

[178] Ibid.: "Quia non ego in his mathesim doceo neque futura perscrutare praemoneo."

[179] Elphège Vacandard, "L'idolâtrie en Gaule au VIe et au VIIe siècle," *RQH* 65 (1899): 443ff.

practiced in Merovingian Gaul: kings, abbeys, and hospitals all had physicians[180] and employed veterinarians.[181] In reading the works of the period—Anthimus' book and the medical calendars in use[182]—one realizes that Merovingian medical learning was limited to dietetics although some practitioners came from the East and applied the methods they learned there.[183] Furthermore, Graeco-Roman manuals that we have already mentioned were still being recopied.[184] Gregory of Tours definitely used them to describe certain illnesses. Thus, when he recounted the miracles that took place on the tomb of Saint Martin of Tours, he described the symptoms and effects of dysentery[185] and the troubles born of one of the bodily humors, melancholia,[186] and spoke of the operation for cataracts.[187] He liked to use technical words, sometimes giving both the learned and the popular word.[188] He must have borrowed the names of plants which cure the intestine (scammony),

[180] For Nicholas and Donatus, the physicians of Guntram, see Gregory of Tours, *HF*, V, 35 (p. 242), and Marius of Avenches, *Chron.*, anno 581 (*MGH, AA*, XI, 239). For Marileifus, the physician of Chilperic I, see *HF*, VII, 25 (p. 344); for Peter, the physician of Theodoric II, see Pseudo-Fredegarius, *Chron.*, IV, 27 (*MGH, SRM*, II, 131). The *Vita Praejecti* (*MGH, SRM*, V, 243) mentions physicians in a *xenodochium*: "Medicos vel strenuos viros qui hanc curam gererent ordinant." For the seal of a physician named Donobertus, see Maximin Deloche, *Etude historique et archéoloqique sur les anneaux sigillaires* (Paris, 1900), no. CCXIII (p. 239). Gregory mentioned Armentarius at Tours (*Mir. Mart.*, II, 1 [*MGH, SRM*, I-2, 609]), as well as a Jewish physician at Bourges (*HF*, V, 6 [p. 203]).

[181] *Vita Eligii*, II, 47 (*MGH, SRM*, IV, 726, l. 26): "Episcopus adhibito mulomedico jussit ei studium impendere quo scilicet sanari [equum] potuisset."

[182] *PL*, XC, 763. See Henri Leclercq, "Médecins," *DACL*, XI-1, 179, and Lynn Thorndike, *A History of Magic and Experimental Science*, 1 (New York, 1923): 676. There is some information on Merovingian medicine in Albert Marignan, *Etudes sur la civilisation française*, vol. 2, *Le culte des saints sous les Mérovingians* (Paris, 1899), pp. 184ff.

[183] Reovalis, the physician for Sainte-Croix in Poitiers, studied at Constantinople. See Gregory of Tours, *HF*, X, 15 (p. 504): "Adfuit Reovalis archiater dicens . . . sicut quondam apud urbem constantinopolitanam medicos agere conspexeram."

[184] See above, chap. 2, n. 121. Paris, Bibliothèque Nationale, lat. 10233, n. a. l. 1619, and Bern, misc. F. 219, are sixth- and seventh-century translations of Oribasius.

[185] Gregory of Tours, *Mir. Mart.*, II, 19 (p. 616). See also *HF*, V, 34 (p. 239). Bede, *Retractatio in Actus apost.*, in *Bedae venerabilis Expositio Actuum apostolorum et Retractatio*, ed. M. L. W. Laistner (Cambridge, Mass., 1939), p. 145, in defining this illness refers to Hippocrates *and* Gregory!

[186] *Mir. Mart.*, II, 58 (p. 628): "Melancoliam, id est decocti sanguinis fecem."

[187] Ibid., II, 19 (p. 616): "Quid umquam tale facere cum ferramentis medici, cum plus negotium doloris exserant, quam medellae, cum distentum transfixumque spiculis oculum." For quartanary fever, see *Vitae patrum*, IV, 5 (p. 677); for epilepsy, *Mir Mart.*, II, 18 (p. 615); for gout, *HF*, V, 42 (p. 248). Gregory was generally critical of physicians: see *HF*, III, 36 (p. 131), V, 6 (p. 203); *Mir. Mart.*, II, 18 (p. 613).

[188] See, for example, *Mir. Mart.*, II, 18 (p. 615, ll. 5–6): "Quod genus morbi ephilenticum peritorum medicorum vocitavit auctoritas; rustici vero cadivum dixere pro eo quod caderet." Bonnet, *Le latin*, p. 218, has listed twenty-eight medical expressions, mostly drawn from the Greek, found in Gregory's work.

THE EDUCATION OF LAYMEN IN GAUL AND IN SPAIN

lungs (hyssop), and head (pyrethrum) from pharmacopoeia.[189] Fortunatus exhibited the same taste for physiological descriptions. In his
poem "On Virginity," he painted a realistic picture of pregnancy and
delivery in order to dissuade young girls from marriage,[190] while in a
letter to Dynamius, he described the bloodletting he had just had, and
in the *Vita sancti Germani* he made many allusions to the medical
arts.[191]

Even though Gregory could cite Greek medical terms, he borrowed
them from Latin manuals, since it is evident that he and his contemporaries knew no Greek.[192] He asked an Easterner living in Tours to
translate the *Passion of the Seven Sleepers of Ephesus*.[193] Colonies of
Greeks, then known as Syrians, who continued to use their mother
tongue, resided in that town and in other centers in Gaul. Perhaps they
had some religious and artistic influence, but so far as we know, they
had no impact on intellectual culture.[194]

D. The Disappearance of Classical Culture in Roman Gaul during the Middle of the Seventh Century

The preceding pages have shown sufficiently that the scholars of
Roman Gaul were members of a cultivated aristocracy, just as were

---

[189] According to *Mir. Mart.*, III, 60 (p. 647, ll. 30–31), he had a medicine cabinet in
his home; see *Glor. martyr.*, 50 (*MGH, SRM*, I-2, 524, l. 3): "Vinum quod in apothecis
nostris habebatur."

[190] Fortunatus, "De virginitate," *Carm.* VIII, 3, vv. 355ff.; VI, 10 (*MGH, AA*, IV-1,
190, 150).

[191] The bloodletting is described in *Carm.* VI, 10 (p. 150). This was a very popular
remedy, as was the use of vesicants and suction cups. See Gregory of Tours, *HF*, VI, 15
(p. 285, l. 12); VII, 22 (p. 341). The allusions in Fortunatus' *Vita sancti Germani, MGH,
AA*, IV-2, 11, 17, 19, deserve study.

[192] See Courcelle, *LG*, pp. 249–53, on this question.

[193] Gregory of Tours, *Glor. martyr.*, 94 (p. 552, l. 11, and p. 847). Courcelle, *LG*, p.
249, thinks that the translator, John, translated from the Syriac. But this is only a hypothesis. Gregory was acquainted with Philostratus' *Life of Apollonius of Tyana* through
Nicomachus Flavius' translation as corrected by Sidonius. See Pierre Courcelle, "Philostrate et Grégoire de Tours," in *Mélanges Joseph de Ghellinck, S.J.*, 2 vols. (Gembloux,
1951), 1: 311–19; idem, "Les rapports possibles entre Philostrate et Grégoire de Tours,"
REL 28 (1950): 38–39.

[194] For these colonies, see L. Bréhier, "Les colonies d'orientaux en Occident au commencement du Moyen Age, V^e–VIIe siècles," *BZ* 12 (1903): 1–39, and Pirenne, *Mahomet
et Charlemagne*, pp. 62ff. For Jewish colonies, see Bernhard Blumenkranz, *Juifs et
Chrétiens dans le monde occidental, 430–1096* (Paris, 1960), pp. 14, 42. Jean Ebersolt
(*Orient et Occident: Recherches sur les influences byzantines et orientales en France avant
et pendant les Croisades*, 2 vols. [Paris and Brussels, 1928–29]), Pirenne (*Mahomet et
Charlemagne*, pp. 112ff.), and Emile Mâle (*La fin du paganisme en Gaule* [Paris, 1950])
have insisted on the influence of Easterners. Perhaps Eastern influence was really less
important than has been believed, however.

the scholars of Italy. They exhibited the same taste for poetry, for ornate speech, for erudition, even the same ignorance of science and Greek. But whereas in Italy, which was ruined by the Gothic and Lombardic wars, aristocrats began to "convert" their culture by orienting it toward religious questions, aristocrats in Gaul remained rather more faithful to the profane tradition, with grave consequences for the organization of sacred culture.[195]

This last characteristic of culture in Roman Gaul is why I think the theses of Roger and Lot, which attempt to prove complete ignorance of classical literature in Gaul, go too far. That is also why it seems to me incorrect to speak of Merovingian Latin at the end of the sixth century as liberated from the tutelage of the school and tending to become a purely spoken tongue.[196] Of course, Gallic scholars inherited the weaknesses of preceding generations, aggravated them, and present a picture of a very deformed culture. But their efforts to speak and write differently from their less polished contemporaries and the literary exchanges they fostered within their circle are proof enough that they were conscious of their role as the last defenders of the classical culture that distinguished them from the Barbarians. Gregory of Tours felt this strongly when in the preface of his *History* he showed that the decline of studies coincided with the progress of barbarism, a thesis familiar to ancient rhetors.[197] In order to remain Roman, one had to be lettered.[198]

This fidelity to classical literature expressed itself even outside the strictly literary arena. Latin names, for example, survived in Gaul during the sixth and seventh centuries.[199] More significantly, parents gave their children names borrowed from mythology and antique poetry:

[195] See below, chap. 7, sect. I.A.

[196] Christine Mohrmann, *Latin vulgaire, latin des chrétiens, latin médiéval* (Paris, 1955), p. 14, thinks that the decisive moment in the transformation of Latin was the beginning of the seventh century, not the beginning of the ninth century, as Muller and his school contend. See Henri F. Muller, "When Did Latin Cease to Be a Spoken Language in France?" *Romanic Review* 12 (1921): 318–34, and idem, "On the Use of the Expression *lingua Romana* from the First to the Ninth Centuries," *ZRPh* 43 (1923): 9–19. I opt for a mid-seventh-century date, as does D. Norberg, "A quelle époque a-t-on cessé de parler latin en Gaule?" *Annales* 21 (1966): 346–56.

[197] Gregory of Tours, *HF*, preface (p. 1): "Decedente atque immo potius pereunte ab urbibus gallicanis liberalium cultura litterarum cum . . . feretas gentium desaeviret; regum furor acueretur." See Libanios, *Ep.* 372, in *Libanii opera*, ed. Richard Foerster, 12 vols. in 13 (Leipzig, 1903–37), 10: 353: "If we lose eloquence, what will remain to distinguish us from the Barbarians?"

[198] Gregory of Tours, *HF*, VI, 39 (p. 310): "Vir . . . de primis senatoribus Galliarum in litteris bene eruditus rethoricis"; Pseudo-Fredegarius, *Chron.*, IV, 28 (*MGH*, *SRM*, II, 132): "Claudius . . . genere Romanus, litterum eruditus."

[199] Lot, *Les invasions germaniques*, p. 231.

Dido, Hector, Patroclus, Orestes, and Virgil, not to mention Plato and Cato.[200] This fashion was already evident in the fifth century and would reappear in the Carolingian period.[201] The same fidelity to the classical tradition is attested in an altogether different field: the minor arts. As in former times, rich aristocrats in Gaul owned plates and vases decorated with mythological scenes. We know about the collection that Bishop Desiderius left to his church at Auxerre in 621.[202] On some of the large plates (*missoria*), Mercury, Apollo and the serpent, Dionysus and Ariadne, wrestlers, animal fights, lovers, and beasts could be seen. The story of Aeneas is engraved on a plate which the Visigothic king Thorismund owned.[203] Certain profane vases so decorated were even used in worship after having been blessed and exorcised in some manner.[204] Aristocrats also owned rings and tablets of sculpted ivory bearing scenes of this nature.[205] Thus, it can be said that the aristocratic contemporaries of Chilperic and, later, of Dagobert still lived in an antique atmosphere.

Roman Gaul was still part of the Mediterranean cultural community. But with each year, the bonds that drew Gaul to the past weakened because Gaul was living on the remains of its patrimony and could not expect a "renaissance." Where could a renaissance come from? Since the closing of the public schools at the end of the fifth century, no agency or power was interested in rehabilitating studies. One searches

---

[200] There were bishops named Dido at both Albi and Tours in the sixth century and at both Poitiers and Châlons-sur-Marne during the seventh century. Hector was the name of a seventh-century patricius in Marseille. Patroclus was a seventh-century saint. A Bishop Orestes presided over the see of Bazas in 585, while another of the same name was bishop of Vaison. Arles had a Bishop Virgil during the sixth century. Cato was a priest at Clermont during the sixth century, the same period that saw a Bishop Plato at Poitiers. An Aquitainian aristocrat was named Socrates (*HF*, X, 8).

[201] Anchises was a popular name. Carolingian writers gave that name to Ansegisel, the son of Arnulf of Metz. See Paul the Deacon, *HL*, VI, 23 (*MGH, SRL*, p. 172), and *Pauli et Petri carm.* XX (*MGH, PAC*, I, 57). Aeneas was also a frequently used name.

[202] Heiric of Auxerre, *Gesta pontif. Autiss.*, 20 (*AS*, Oct., XII, 361). See Jean Adhémar, "Le trésor d'argenterie donné par saint Didier aux églises d'Auxerre," *RA* 4 (1934): 44–54; Jean Colin, "La plastique 'gréco-romaine' dans l'Empire carolingien," *CArch* 2 (1947): 93–96.

[203] *Gesta pontif. Autiss.*, 20: "Missorium argenteum qui Thorisomondi nomen scriptum habet; pensat libras XXXVII; habet se historiam Enae cum litteris grecis." The plates in the collection of Thorismond, king of the Visigoths in 451, were sought after. See Pseudo-Fredegarius, *Chron.*, IV, 73 (*MGH, SRM*, II, 158).

[204] See the ritual of Jumièges cited by Jean Adhémar, *Influences antiques dans l'art du Moyen Age français* (London, 1937), p. 132.

[205] See ibid., p. 108, for the tablets. See also Richard Delbrück, *Die Consulardiptychen und verwandt Denkmäler* (Berlin, 1929). Nicomachus Flavius' diptych was found near the tomb of Saint Bercharius, seventh-century abbot of Montierender; see Henri Leclerq, "Magie," *DACL*, X-1, 1090.

in vain for an official school still offering instruction in grammar and rhetoric in Gaul.[206] The only schools in existence were clerical schools, which trained future clerics and even some laymen.[207]

We must note, however, that the laymen who attended these elementary schools were not of aristocratic origin. Gregory of Tours was precise on this point.[208] When the municipal school disappeared, the sons of senators were taught at home in the antique tradition, since this was the only alternative available: parents took over teaching their children to read and to write without the help of a preceptor. The fathers of Nicetius in Geneva, Sequanus in Burgundy, and Gregory in Clermont gave their children their basic religious and profane education.[209] Others took their sons' education further: Attala of Bobbio, Desiderius of Cahors, and Bonitus of Clermont received their classical training at home.

Trained within the home and using the books they found in the library inherited from their ancestors, these young people were able to remain in contact with ancient authors. In the long run, however, the disappearance of scholarly institutions inevitably led to a slow degradation of learning. With each generation it weakened, and by the second half of the seventh century, it left no traces.[210] From then on, it is impossible to find men in Aquitaine, Provence, or Burgundy trained in the antique manner. The Barbarian influence seems to have been the reason for Roman resistance. By the second half of the seventh century though, southern Gaul was suffering from the anarchy that plagued the entire Merovingian kingdom: Provence, isolated, was no longer traversed by travelers on their way to Italy; Aquitaine was menaced by the advance of the Basques and was yet to undergo the devastation wreaked by the first Carolingians.[211] Senatorial families increasingly

---

[206] See my article, "L'instruction des laics en Gaule," pp. 873ff.

[207] See chap. 7, sect. II.A.

[208] In reference to the father of Patroclus, Gregory of Tours wrote (*Vitae patrum*, IX [*MGH*, *SRM*, I-2, 702]): "Non quidem nobilitate sublimes." Similarly, the father of Leobard, another student who attended an elementary school (ibid., XX [p. 741]), was "genere quidem non senatorio."

[209] Gregory of Tours, *Vitae patrum*, VIII (p. 691); *Vita Sequani*, *ASOB*, I, 263: "Christianis parentibus educatus."

[210] An example of the degradation of antique culture is provided by the *Cinq Epitres rimées dans l'appendice des formules de Sens*, which Gérard Walstra has re-edited (Leiden, 1962).

[211] Almost all the coins from the Bordeaux treasure of about 675 come from Aquitaine. This would indicate a break in north-south exchanges. For this treasure, see Le Gentilhomme, *Mélanges de numismatique mérovingienne*, pp. 5ff., and Jean Lafaurie, "A propos de la trouvaille de Bordeaux," *Revue numismatique* (1952), p. 229, who reduces the information that can be drawn from the discovery.

assimilated with Frankish families, adopted the Germanic way of life, and were more concerned with waging war than with educating themselves. Education, however, did not disappear completely, as we shall see, but took on a different character.

III. LAY EDUCATION IN BARBARIAN GAUL

A. The Conditions of Intellectual Culture

Barbarians and Gallo-Romans merged much earlier in northern and eastern Gaul,[212] with the consequence that young Franks and Germanized Gallo-Romans were educated differently than their compatriots in southern Gaul. As we have said already, Barbarian Gaul did not belong to the area of written civilization. Whatever impress Roman civilization had made on these regions was maintained with great difficulty after the third-century invasions. Urban schools, if they ever existed, disappeared quite early: Ausonius in the fourth century did not mention any teacher north of the Loire; Gratian's law of 376, which attempted to reorganize teaching in Gaul, was doubtless ineffectual.[213] The establishment of a capital at Trier might have paved the way for a renewal of Romanization in the country of the Moselle and the Rhine[214] if the Germans had not devastated these regions a century later.

Roman culture, however, did not disappear overnight and, in fact, survived longer in some areas than in others. Thanks to Sidonius Apollinaris, we know of scholars living in Barbarian Gaul around 470–80, the eve of the Frankish conquest. Among these were Bishop Remigius of Reims, whose declamationes, or oratorical exercises, Sidonius admired;[215] Bishop Auspicius of Toul, author of a famous rhythmic poem;[216] and Bishop Lupus of Troyes (425), who corresponded with

---

212 See Lot, *Les invasions germaniques*, pp. 191ff., for the progressive fusion of the two elements.

213 Roger, pp. 26–27; Marrou, *Education*, p. 408.

214 Albert Grenier, *Manuel d'archéologie gallo-romaine*, 4 tomes in 7 vols. (Paris, 1931–60), 2: 866; Fritz Fremersdorf, "Cologne gallo-romaine et chrétienne," in *Mémorial d'un voyage d'études de la Société nationale des antiquaires de France en Rhénanie, juillet 1951* (Paris, 1953), pp. 91–140.

215 Sidonius, *Ep.* IX, 7 (MGH, AA, VIII, 154–55). Remigius, born in the mid-fifth century near Laon (see Stroheker, pp. 207–8, no. 322), took lessons from a rhetor at home. See also R. Kaiser, *Untersuchungen zur Geschichte der Civitas und Dioceze Soissons im romisch- und merovingische Zeit* (Bonn, 1973).

216 Schanz, IV-2, 378–80; Norberg, *Introduction*, p. 106.

Sidonius and Ruricius.[217] Count Arbogast of Trier, who came from a family of Romanized Franks, still wrote remarkable Latin, especially when one considers that Latin was no longer spoken in Belgium and the Rhineland.[218]

Latin culture was thus preserved at the end of the fifth century in certain privileged regions. But then the Salian Franks to the north and the Alamanni to the east continued their advance. Clovis became king in 480, settled at Soissons six years later, and then imposed his authority throughout northern and eastern Gaul, thereby erecting a Barbarian monarchy that threatened to obliterate all traces of Roman influence. What we can gather from the texts and from archaeology does in fact seem to indicate that the western Germans were much more attached to their primitive way of life than the eastern Germans.[219] Arriving much later on the borders of the Roman empire, still living as pagans, the Franks were much less interested in preserving antique civilization than were the Goths and the Burgundians. A comparison between Salic law and the laws of the Burgundians and Visigoths is quite instructive: Salic law reflects a society of warriors and herdsmen little interested in Roman culture. Only Frankish chiefs, leaders who had for a long time served the Empire faithfully, could perhaps comprehend the value of Roman culture. Childeric, a federate and Clovis' father, had himself portrayed on the setting of his ring dressed as a Roman.[220] Clovis followed his example.[221]

The evils of the Frankish occupation should not be exaggerated. Northern Gaul, later to be called Neustria, was not entirely Germanized, since there were very few of Clovis' warriors south of the line that was later to become the linguistic frontier.[222] The Germanic popu-

---

[217] See the letter which Sidonius sent him upon the death of Lampridius the rhetor, around 480 (*Ep.* VIII, 10 [p. 138]), as well as the letter Ruricius sent him (*Ep.* I, 9 [p. 305]).

[218] Sidonius, *Ep.* IV, 17 (p. 68, ll. 9–11): "Quocirca sermonis pompa Romani, si qua adhuc uspiam est, Belgicis olim sive Rhenanis abolita terris in te resedit." For the Latin of the Rhenanian inscriptions, see Viatorinus' epitaph of about 430 (*CIL*, XIII, 8274), which J. Carcopino has studied ("Notes d'épigraphie rhénane," in *Mémorial d'un voyage*, p. 193).

[219] See the texts gathered by Salin, 1: 98, 2: 334ff.; and Lot, *Les invasions germaniques*, pp. 191ff.

[220] This ring has been lost, but we do have a galvano-plastic copy of it; see Ernest Babelon, *Le tombeau du roi Childéric et les origines de l'orfèvrerie cloisonnée*, Mémoires de la Société nationale de antiquaires de France, 76 (Paris, 1924).

[221] *Liber historiae Francorum*, MGH, SRM, II 257.

[222] Jan Dhondt, "Essai sur l'origine de la frontière linguistique," *L'Antiquité classique* 16 (1947): 278; Charles Verlinden, *Les origines de la frontière linguistique en Belgique*

lation steadily decreased the farther one went to the south. The archaeology and toponymy of the region between the Seine and the Loire agree on this point.[223] Thus, northern and northwestern Gaul, which had been only superficially Romanized and Christianized, returned to barbarism[224] without having been settled by Germans. The only region truly Germanized was eastern Gaul, later called Austrasia, extending from Reims to the Rhineland. Even in this region there were notable exceptions. Archaeology shows, for example, that Lorraine was a region where Barbarian and Roman influences competed, with the latter often prevailing.[225] Activity in towns devastated by the Barbarians was severely reduced, but towns, nevertheless, did manage to survive and were even occupied by the Barbarians.[226] Furthermore, Roman islands survived in the region around Trier and the confluence of the Moselle and the Rhine. While Latin inscriptions are almost nonexistent for northern Gaul, sixth-century inscriptions have been found in Trier, Coblenz, Andernach, Boppard, and Saint Goar.[227] It has also been shown recently that senatorial families in these regions maintained Latin traditions.[228] The abundance of Byzantine and Ostrogothic silver coins

---

et la colonisation franque (Brussels, 1955); Germaine Faider-Feytmans, *La Belgique à l'époque mérovingienne* (Brussels, 1964).

[223] Michel Roblin, *Etudes toponymique de la Civitas des Parisii: Le terroir de Paris aux époques gallo-romaine et franque* (Paris, 1951); Salin, 1: 377. For Touraine, see Jacques Boussard, "Essai sur le peuplement de la Touraine du Ier au VIIIe siècle," *MA* 60 (1954): 284ff. Boussard has exaggerated the size of the Frankish population; so-called Barbarian tombs are quite often really Gallo-Roman tombs. For an opposing view, see Kurth, "Les nationalités en Touraine," in *Etudes franques*, 1: 242ff., and Hans Zeiss, "Die germanischen Grabfunde des frühen Mittelalters zwischen mittlerer Seine und Loiremündung," *Berichte der römisch-germanischen Kommission* 31 (1942). See also Lucien Musset, *Les invasions* (Paris, 1965), pp. 171ff.

[224] We need a study of Barbarian Normandy, but in the absence of such a work, see Elphège Vacandard, *Vie de saint Ouen* (Paris, 1902), pp. 130ff. The Frankish tombs of northern Gaul are often actually Gallo-Roman tombs. See A. Bourgeois, "Le cimetière de Mazingheim," *Bulletin de la Société académique des antiquaires de la Morinie* 18 (1953): 332.

[225] Salin, 1: 328. For Alsace, see F. H. Himly, "Introduction à la toponymie alsacienne," *Revue d'Alsace* 95 (1956): 7–54.

[226] Vercauteren, "La vie urbaine entre Meuse et Loire du VIe au IXe siècle," *Settimane*, 6: 446–71. The Byzantine historian Agathias noted that the Franks did not live in the countryside as did other Barbarians (*PG*, LXXXVIII, 1282).

[227] R. Egger, "Rheinische Grabsteine der Merowingerzeit," in *Bonner Jahrbücher des Rheinischen Landesmuseum* (1954), pp. 146–58. The inscriptions from Trier have been assembled by Erich Gose, *Katalog der frühchristlichen Inschriften in Trier,* Trierer Grabungen und Forschungen, vol. 3 (Berlin, 1958). See H. Marrou's review of this work in *Germania* 37 (1959): 343–49.

[228] Eugen Ewig, *Trier im Merovingerreich* (Trier, 1954), pp. 69ff.; Kurt Böhner, *Die fränkischen Altertümer des Trierer Landes,* 2 vols. (Berlin, 1958).

found in these areas proves that relations with Italy had not been broken.[229]

Thus, little islands of *Romanitas* still dotted Barbarian Gaul when the sixth century opened, and more importantly, the region was actually to be reconquered culturally by southern influences during the next century and a half. Who would have thought that the advance of Clovis and his sons south of the Loire instead of entailing the Barbarization of all Gaul would have led to just the opposite result? The south helped in the "reconstruction" of the north. We can point to several examples taken from art and religion.

Pyrenean marble, quarried at Saint Béat and worked there, was transported by water or perhaps on the backs of camels to construction sites in the north. This was how the Church of the Holy Apostles in Paris acquired Aquitainian columns and capitals during the reign of Clovis. Later, Saint Vincent (Saint Germain-des-Prés) and Saint Denis in Paris and the churches of Reims, Duclair, Chartres, and Jouarre would likewise benefit from the south.[230] Sarcophagi from Aquitaine were used at Soissons and Paris.[231] The buckle badges which Barrière-Flavy thought were Visigothic but which are actually from a later period[232] were fabricated around Toulouse and exported to the north. Similarly, the so-called Burgundian buckles followed the route to northeastern Gaul.[233]

As for religious affairs, it was partially because of Aquitainians that the Church of northern and eastern Gaul was reorganized after the trauma of the invasions. King Theodoric, for example, brought some Arvernian clerics in 534 to serve the church of Trier.[234] Saint Goar and

---

[229] Joachim Werner, *Münzdatierte austrasische Grabfunde* (Berlin and Leipzig, 1935), pp. 79, 37 (map). This map is reproduced in Salin, 1: 170.

[230] Jean Hubert, *L'art pré-roman* (Paris, 1938), p. 94; Denise Fossard, "Les chapiteaux de marbre au VII⁰ siècle en Gaule: Style and évolution," *CArch* 2 (1947): 69–89.

[231] Hubert, *L'art pré-roman*, p. 95; Denise Fossard, "Répartition des sarcophages mérovingiens à décor en France," in *Etudes mérovingiennes*, pp. 117–26; idem, "La chronologie des sarcophages d'Aquitaine," in *Actes du V⁰ Congrès international d'archéologie chrétienne (1954)* (Vatican City and Paris, 1957), pp. 331–33.

[232] C. Barrière-Flavy, *Les arts industriels des peuples barbares de la Gaule du V⁰ au VIII⁰ siècle*, 3 vols. (Paris and Toulouse, 1901), corrected by Nils Åberg, *The Occident and the Orient in the Art of the Seventh Century*, vol. 3, *The Merovingian Empire* (Stockholm, 1947).

[233] Salin, 1: 344. For trade routes in Gaul, see Jean Hubert, "Les Grandes Voies de circulation à l'intérieur de la Gaule mérovingienne d'après l'archéologie," in *Actes du VI⁰ Congrès international d'études byzantines* (Paris, 1951), 2: 188.

[234] Gregory of Tours, *Vitae patrum*, VI, 2 (*MGH, SRM*, I-2, 681).

Saint Fridolin, founders of hermitages and monasteries in the Moselle region, were Aquitainians.[235] In the middle of the sixth century, Bishop Nicetius of Trier, perhaps originally from Limoges, called upon southerners to help him with his restoration program.[236] The churches of Reims, Metz, and Trier possessed property beyond the Loire, which in itself favored constant contact between eastern and southern Gaul. It would be impossible to forget, too, that the seventh-century Aquitainians Philibertus, Eligius, and Amandus were the great missionaries of the Dagobertian period.[237] Map 5 illustrates the influence of these Aquitainians outside their native region.

Provence also played an important role in the reconstruction of Barbarian Gaul and especially of Austrasia, of which Provence was a dependence.[238] If the kings of Metz were turning more and more to Byzantium than to their Neustrian colleagues, it was undoubtedly because of the influence of Provençal bureaucrats.[239]

Barbarian chiefs were thus inevitably affected by Roman influence. To the extent that they formed relationships with the southern aristocracy, they acquired new intellectual habits.

The Merovingian royalty had been forced from the very beginning to borrow from the Roman political system. Salian kings were acquainted with Roman administrative procedures from the time they settled in the former imperial fisc of Tournai. It could well be that Childeric's ring served to seal documents emanating from a modest office.[240] At least this would explain why the Latin inscription "Childirici regis" was engraved on the ring. Childeric's son, Clovis, most probably used personnel from the provincial administration of the conquered territories in his own service. Gallo-Romans, designated as *convivae regis* in

---

[235] Ewig, *Trier*, p. 86. Saint Fridolin, who founded a monastery at Säckingen, between Basel and Constance, was not an Irishman but an Aquitainian—he had been abbot of Saint-Hilaire in Poitiers before coming to Rhenania.

[236] Ibid., p. 90. Nicetius called in Italian artisans to reconstruct Trier. See the letter which Bishop Rufus of Turin wrote to him in *MGH, Ep.*, III, 133. Aredius, who was raised by Nicetius, also came from Aquitaine; see Gregory of Tours, *HF*, X, 29 (p. 522), and Ewig, *Trier*, p. 100.

[237] Fliche-Martin, 5: 526. Amandus was a Poitevin, Eligius a Limousin, and Philibertus came from Eauze.

[238] Buchner, *Die Provence*, pp. 6ff.

[239] For relations between Austrasia and Byzantium, see Paul Goubert, *Byzance avant l'Islam*, vol. 2, *L'Empire et les Francs*, (Paris, 1955), in particular the chapter devoted to "lettres austrasiennes." It is noteworthy that most of the ambassadors sent to the East were Gallo-Romans: Firminus, Evantius (Dynamius' son), Eusebius, Ennodius.

[240] See Babelon, *Le tombeau du roi Childéric*.

5. *The Cultural Reconquest of Northern Gaul*

the Salic law, helped to prepare a Latin edition of that law code.[241] The fact that no diploma from Clovis has come down to us, except for a rather late copy of one of them,[242] in no way proves that the king did not issue any.

The descendents of Clovis, who inherited the southern regions of Gaul and thus were in more direct contact with Italy and the Eastern Empire, perfected their predecessor's administration. Chilperic, a greedy prince, tried to reorganize the Roman financial system by having the tax rolls revised.[243] The Merovingians understood the importance of writing and the uses to which it could be put in government, at least in southern Gaul. A document signed by the king meant certain protection[244] or, on the other hand, an obligation to satisfy the whims of a Barbarian: when Chramm carried off the daughters of Arvernian senators, he made sure he had royal orders in his hands.[245]

The German aristocracy followed the example of their kings in adopting certain Roman legal practices. In 584, the nobles obliged to accompany the daughter of Chilperic to Spain prepared their wills before departing.[246] This practice, unknown to the Germans,[247] became current in Frankish society and was encouraged by the Church, the principal beneficiary of wills. We have several wills dictated in the seventh century by Franks, some of whom belonged to the royal family.[248] Likewise, the contracts, acts of sale, and donations preserved in the formularies were not drawn up exclusively for Gallo-Romans. Writ-

241 H. Dannenbauer, "Die Rechtstellung des Gallo-Römer in frankische Reich," *Welt als Geschichte* 7 (1941): 51–72.

242 See F. Lot, "Un diplôme de Clovis confirmatif d'une donation de patrice romain," *RBPh* 17 (1938): 906–11. For the circular to the bishops concerning the Council of Orléans, see De Clercq, *La législation religieuse*, pp. 7–8; for Clovis' chancellery, see Peter Classen's remarks, "Kaiserreskript und Konigsurkunde," *Archiv für Diplomatik* 1 (1955): 1–87; 2 (1956): 1–115.

243 Henri Pirenne, "Le trésor des rois mérovingiens," in *Festskrift til Halvdan Koht* (Oslo, 1933), p. 74, reprinted in Henri Pirenne, *Histoire économique de l'Occident médiéval* (Paris, 1957), p. 118.

244 See a formula for a *carta securitatis* in Marculf, *Form.*, II, 18 (*MGH, Leg. sect. V*, p. 88), and in *Form. Tur.*, 38 (ibid., p. 156). Gregory also mentioned one in *HF*, IX, 27 (p. 446).

245 Gregory of Tours, *HF*, IV, 13 (p. 144): "Ita ut filias senatorum, datis praeceptionibus eisdem vi detrahi iuberet."

246 *HF*, VI, 45 (p. 317, l. 12).

247 Tacitus, *Germania*, 20, 6.

248 Gregory of Tours, *HF*, IX, 26 (p. 445), contains the will of Ingoberga, Caribert's wife; *HF*, IX, 35 (p. 455), the will of Bertruda, Duke Laundebaudis' wife. See the texts of the wills of Irmina, Dagobert's daughter (Pardessus, 2: 251), of Erminentruda (Paris, Archives Nationales, K 4, no. 1; Pardessus, 2: 211), and of Iddana's son (Paris, Archives Nationales, K 3, no. 1; Pardessus, 2: 255).

ing also sanctioned oaths and payment of the *wergeld*.[249] I do not want to imply, however, that real contracts were no longer used. Non-Romanized Germans continued, as they had in the past, to exchange symbolic objects at sales and other kinds of contractual agreements. But now that they were influenced by the custom of writing, they reinforced this symbolic payment with a written notice.[250]

Royal agents, particularly counts, had to have a minimum of instruction in order to perform their duties:[251] the law of the Bavarians urged each judge to have a *liber legis* with him,[252] while the *rachinburgii* who surrounded the count as he performed his judicial functions seem to have had the same duties as the *boni homines* we mentioned earlier.[253]

In the seventh century writing made its appearance even in the lands of Germanic civilization. A comparison between Salic law and later Barbarian laws shows the progress made in this area. In Ripuarian law, a *cancellarius* was charged with drawing up procedural notices as well as private contracts established at a tribunal.[254] During the reign of Dagobert, public scribes were introduced in regions under Salic law. The establishment of a Frankish notariate in these areas is of capital importance and presages, two centuries in advance, Charlemagne's reforms and his attempt to restore the prestige of written documents.[255] Likewise, Bavarian law, which was written down in part during the same period, provided for the possibility of a sale *per cartam*, something that did not exist in Salic law.[256] It is true, of course, that the renaissance of written law was facilitated in the Danubian countries by the memory of Roman traditions.[257]

The Frankish aristocracy, like their Gothic and Burgundian counter-

---

[249] Marculf, *Form.*, II, 18 (*MGH, Leg. sect. V*, p. 88). See Jean Philippe Lévy, *La hiérarchie des preuves dans le droit savant du Moyen Age depuis la renaissance du droit romain jusqu'à la fin du XVe siècle* (Paris, 1939), p. 15.

[250] De Boüard, *Acte privé*, pp. 64–65.

[251] See Numa Denis Fustel de Coulanges, *La monarchie franque* (Paris, 1888), p. 213.

[252] *Lex Baiuvariorum*, II, 14 (in *Lex Baiuvariorum: Lichtdruckwiedergabe der Ingolstädter Handschrift des bayerischen Volksrechts . . .* , ed. Konrad Beyerle [Munich, 1926], p. 66): "Comis vero secum habeat judicem qui ubi constitutus est, judicare et lib[e]rum legis, ut semper rectum judicium judicent."

[253] For these individuals, see Brunner, *Deutsche Rechtsgeschichte*, 2: 295, 472; and Numa Denis Fustel de Coulanges, *Recherches sur quelques problèmes d'Histoire* (Paris, 1885), pp. 422ff.

[254] *Lex Ripuar.*, 41 (37), 61 (58), 62 (59) (ed. F. Beyerle and R. Buchner, *MGH, Leg. sect. I*, III-2, 95, 108, 114). See de Boüard, *Acte privé*, p. 129.

[255] See de Boüard, *Acte privé*, p. 129; and D. P. Blok, "Le notariat franc a-t-il existé?" *Revue du Nord* 42 (1960): 320–21.

[256] *Lex Baiuvariorum*, XVI, 2 and 15 (Beyerle ed., pp. 152, 160).

[257] See below, chap. 9, n. 497.

parts, recognized the utility of written documents but did not abolish the oral procedures and symbolic rites that accompanied each legal act among the Germans. The Franks remained illiterate and thus continued to give writing more of a religious than a legal value. Runes, which only a few privileged could comprehend, had long been regarded as magical characters in Germanic lands. Objects on which runes were engraved were thought to be protected by the characters and, consequently, capable of keeping those who possessed them from harm.[258] This belief spread in Gaul in the sixth and seventh centuries,[259] but by that time, Latin inscriptions increasingly replaced Barbarian characters. Barbarians also adopted a Roman custom and engraved the name of the owner, donor, or artisan on fibulae, rings, weapons, and ordinary objects;[260] even religious invocations were inscribed on these objects.[261] Inscriptions, however, no longer served a documentary function but, rather, served to charge the object with quasi-divine power. An inscription was a talisman. In like manner, a mysterious abracadabra was inscribed on the doors of tombs to protect them from robbers.[262] Christians adopted superstitions well known among primitive people. Sick people touched letters written by holy men to their bodies.[263] Merovingian texts are filled with such examples.[264] We are quite far from written civilization here.

B. ARISTOCRATIC EDUCATION IN BARBARIAN GAUL

Burgundian and Gothic aristocrats imitated the Roman way of life, but as we have seen, they were not won over to classical culture. Their own culture and the Arian religion they professed explain in part their

[258] See Hoops, IV, 15; Salin, 4: 136–39; and Lucien Musset and Fernand Mossé, *Introduction à la runologie* (Paris, 1965), for runes.

[259] Fortunatus, *Carm.* VII, 18, 19 (*MGH, AA*, IV-1, 172–73): "Barbara fraxineis pingatur rhuna tabellis." For a Rhenanian inscription combining runic characters and Latin letters, see Le Blant, *IC*, 1: 460 (no. 344); for the fibula from Charnay, see ibid., p. 216 (no. 146). See also J. A. Bizet, "Inscription runique d'Arguel," *Etudes germaniques* 3 (1948): 1–12, for the rune stone in the Besançon Museum, and Salin, 4: 117, n. 1, for a seventh-century pyxidia.

[260] See Le Blant, *NR*, nos. 54, 239, and 292 for rings; no. 90 for a shortsword. See the names of Barbarian goldsmiths in Salin, 3: 212.

[261] Le Blant, *NR*, no. 90A: "Emmanuel" on the tongue of a buckle.

[262] See the inscription from the hypogeum of Dunes ("grama. grumo . . ." [Henri Leclercq, "Mellébaude," *DACL*, XI-1, 253]).

[263] Gregory of Tours, *Vitae patrum*, VIII, 12 (*MGH, SRM*, I-2, 2); Fortunatus, *Vita Germani*, *MGH, AA*, IV-2, 23, l. 20; *Vita Eugendi*, *MGH, SRM*, III, 159ff.

[264] *Vitae patrum*, VII, 9 (p. 699); *Vita Austregesili*, *MGH, SRM*, IV, 188. Graffiti found on altars offer evidence of the same beliefs.

indifference. No such obstacle, however, stood in the way of the Franks, who had been officially Catholic since the baptism of Clovis. Would their aristocracy, which had adopted writing, deepen their culture and imitate the Gallo-Romans of southern Gaul? The question is difficult to answer because Gregory of Tours spoke only of the instruction of his compatriots in the south. We have to make do with other scattered and very poor sources. Furthermore, the same answer cannot be given for the entire Merovingian period: at least three periods must be distinguished.

We should note at the outset that we do not know how Gallo-Romans in the north taught their children at the beginning of the sixth century because we know nothing about the important aristocratic families of this region.[265] Perhaps they led a life identical to that of the Franks. Ecclesiastical circles alone preserved classical cultural traditions. Remigius, who was bishop of Reims until 530, may have kept alive a taste for literature among a small group. He was still remembered in Gregory of Tours' day for his talents as a rhetor.[266] Virgil was not totally forgotten. The author of the *Life* of Saint Genovefa, who perhaps came from Meaux, cites several of his verses.[267] This is all we can say.

The instruction of the Franks is hardly any better known. Let us first look at the kings. Were Clovis and his sons educated? The conqueror of Gaul has been traditionally cast as a brutal warrior whose crudity is contrasted with the culture of the Ostrogoth Theodoric, or even with that of Gundobad. Perhaps this is excessive. Remigius of Reims wrote letters to him, once consoling him on the death of his sister, another time praising him when he became master of Second Belgium.[268] The style and arguments of these letters remind one of the letters Avitus sent to Gundobad. Avitus himself wrote a very florid letter to the Frankish king congratulating him on his baptism.[269] Was Clovis unable to understand these letters? Because of his marriage to a Burgundian princess, his conversion, and the influence of Gallo-Roman bishops, he eventually was able to appreciate the value of Roman culture.

---

[265] See Stroheker, pp. 106ff.

[266] Gregory of Tours, *HF*, II, 31 (p. 77): "Erat autem sanctus Remegius episcopus egregiae scientiae et rethoricis adprimum imbutus studiis."

[267] This *Vita* was undoubtedly written about 530. See Kurth, "Etude critique sur la Vie de sainte Geneviève," in *Etudes franques*, 1: 1–96. For an opposing view, see Bruno Krusch, "Die neueste Wendung im Genovefa-Streit," *NA*, 40 (1915–16): 131–81.

[268] *Ep.* 1 and 2 (*MGH, Ep.*, III, 112–13).

[269] Avitus, *Ep.* XLVI (41) (*MGH, AA*, VI-2, 75).

We should not forget that he was also in contact with Theodoric's court and was jealous of his brother-in-law's splendor to the point that he asked Theodoric for an Italian citharist to entertain him during his meals.[270]

Like Theodoric, Clovis did not forget that he had taken the place of emperors. He chose Paris, a former residence for Roman princes, as his capital and wished to be interred there. Moreover, after his victory over the Arian Visigoths, for which he received a consul's diploma from Emperor Anastasius, he dressed himself in purple, wore a diadem, and had himself addressed as consul and Augustus. Some historians have refused to believe this information, which Gregory of Tours alone reports,[271] but we have no right to do so. Clovis' actions, of course, might have been a piece of propaganda aimed at rallying Gallo-Romans to his cause. Nevertheless, he would have had to have been quite aware of Roman grandeur in the first place in order to conceive the idea of organizing such a propaganda scheme.

Did Clovis educate his children, as did Theodoric? The texts do not tell us. Some historians have used a passage from Gregory of Tours as proof that instruction was traditional among Frankish kings, even though Gregory never specifically said that.[272] We can only hypothesize. Childebert's religious curiosity presupposed some profane learning, at least on an elementary level.[273] Theodoric must have had some interest in medicine for Anthimus to dedicate his treatise to him.[274] Theodoric's son Theodebert and grandson Theodebald, in turn, seem to have been sufficiently cultured to surround themselves with lettered counselors.[275] We know that Clodoaldus (Saint Cloud), Clodomir's son, was instructed in sacred literature.[276] We know nothing about the education

[270] Cassiodorus, Var., II, 40 (MGH, AA, XII, 70): "Cum rex Francorum convivii nostri fama pellectus a nobis citharoedum magnis precibus expetisset."

[271] Gregory of Tours, HF, II, 38 (p. 89). Although Gregory is the only source to report this episode, his testimony cannot be questioned; see Courcelle, "Clovis 'Auguste' à Tours," BSAF (1948–49), pp. 46–57.

[272] It suffices only to reread the passage from Gregory misunderstood by Pirenne, "De l'état de l'instruction des laïques," p. 167, no. 1; Bezzola, 1: 41; and Goubert, Byzance avant l'Islam, 2: 1. Gregory had the following to say about Gundovald (HF, VI, 24 [p. 291]): "Hic cum natus esset in Galliis et diligenti cura inutritus, ut regum istorum mos est crinium flagellis per terga dimissis, litteris eruditus." Mos est refers to the custom of wearing long hair.

[273] See the letters that Pope Pelagius I sent to him (MGH, Ep., III, 70, 75, 77).

[274] See above, chap. 2, n. 121.

[275] Gregory characterized Theodebert as elegans, a word which, like elegantia, connoted a certain culture; see above, chap. 2, n. 35. He accredited an antique fable in the style of Horace to Theodebald (HF, IV, 19 [p. 140]).

[276] The Vita Clodoaldi is quite late; see ASOB, I, 136.

of Clovis' last son, Chlothar, but we should note that he had Radegunda, his young spouse, and his bastard Gundovald carefully educated.[277]

Perhaps the companions of the first Merovingian kings imitated their princes. Since Gallo-Romans did not know the Frankish tongue, Franks had to learn to speak Latin, at the very least. Gregory of Tours, in fact, does not once mention the presence of an interpreter in Gaul.[278] It seems that the conquerors and the indigenous population were able to understand each other without difficulty, although the Barbarians must have spoken a very deformed kind of Latin such as that described by Caesarius' biographers. In portraying a scene in which a Frank requested a piece from Caesarius' habit, they have him say: "Da mihi de drapo sancti Caesarii propter frigoras, quia multis valet, volo bibere."[279] Is this not a specimen of the Latin the conquerors used?

Thanks to Fortunatus, we have better information on the education of the Franks during the second half of the sixth century. The poet made several trips into Austrasia and Neustria, where he made the acquaintance of Franks and formed friendships with them that were translated into epistolary exchanges. Without being absolutely certain of the nationalities of Fortunatus' correspondents, since many Gallo-Romans in the north took Germanic names, we are nevertheless led to believe from their functions or from the contexts of the letters that many of them were Barbarians.[280] It has been argued that they were unable to understand Fortunatus' missives,[281] but it is hardly likely that the poet would have written to them if he knew that they could not read. It could be objected that we do not have the replies of Sigoald, Berulf, Romulf, and others. Though true, this is not a valid argument, since we do have other clues which indicate that some Barbarian aristocrats were lettered: Bishop Bertechramnus of Bordeaux, who was linked to the royal family,[282] composed verses that he submitted to Fortunatus' judgment;[283] Dagaulf applied himself to the study of letters;[284] his wife, the Parisienne Vilihuta, though German by race was Roman by cul-

---

[277] Fortunatus, *Vita Radegundis*, II, 3 (*MGH, AA*, IV-2, 38, l. 13). For Gundovald, see above, n. 272.

[278] The only interpreter mentioned appears in an anecdote concerning the recluse Hospitius and the Lombards; see *HF*, VI, 6 (pp. 273–79).

[279] *Vita Caesarii*, II, 42 (Morin ed., p. 341, l. 29).

[280] See Bezzola, 1: 48.

[281] Roger, p. 100.

[282] Gregory of Tours, *HF*, VIII, 2 (p. 372, ll. 8–9).

[283] Fortunatus, *Carm.* III, 18 (*MGH, AA*, IV-1, 70).

[284] Ibid., IV, 26, v. 39 (p. 96): "Studiis ornata juventus / Quod natura nequit littera prompta dedit."

ture.[285] It could be that other young Frankish women wished to imitate Gallo-Romans and become "as skillful with the pen as with weaving."[286] Women played an important role in Merovingian life, and their culture was certainly less neglected than is usually thought.[287]

The lettered Barbarian we know best is Gogo, the mayor of the palace. Entering the service of Sigebert, king of Metz, about 565, he was sent to Spain for Princess Brunhilda. The king later entrusted him with the education of young Childebert II.[288] When Brunhilda was widowed, she brought Gogo into the royal chancellery, further proof that his culture was prized.[289] Fortunatus, in fact, compared the minister to Orpheus and Cicero; in other words, he liked his verse and rhetoric.[290] If his poems have been lost,[291] we still have four of his letters as witnesses to his education: he claimed that he wrote poorly, that he did not possess "eloquentia maroniana,"[292] and that he was not worthy of his correspondents or of his teacher, Parthenius.[293] Yet his letters compare well with those of his Gallo-Roman contemporaries.[294]

In a letter to a certain Traseric, Gogo alluded to a foreign poet who played the role of a teacher.[295] He was thinking of Fortunatus, who must have helped introduce aristocrats of Barbarian Gaul to classical literature. During the years he spent in Austrasia, then in Neustria,

---

285 Ibid., v. 15 (p. 95): "Romana studio, barbara prole fuit."

286 Eusebia's epitaph reads: "Docta tenens calamos, apices quoque figere filo / Quod tibi charta valet hoc sibi tela fuit" (Ibid., IV, 17, vv. 8–9 [p. 100]).

287 Bezzola, 1: 55ff.

288 Pseudo-Fredegarius, Chron., III, 59 (MGH, SRM, II, 109); Gregory of Tours, HF, V, 46, VI, 1 (pp. 256, 265).

289 We have a letter from him written in the name of the king to the Lombard Grasulf; see Ep. 48 (MGH, Ep., III, 152).

290 Fortunatus, Carm. VII, 1 and 2 (pp. 153ff.).

291 Gogo, Ep. 13 (MGH, Ep., III, 127–28): "Sed in his versiculis subter adnixis, quos amore solemni trepidantibus digitis exaravi et diligentis affectus ostenditur et ignorantis rusticitas propalatur."

292 Ibid.: "Et in cujus laudem vix sufficere poterat eloquentia Maroniana." In fact, he knew Virgil; see D. Norberg, "Ad epistulas varias merovingici aevi adnotationes," Eranos, 35 (1937): 111.

293 Gogo, Ep. 16 (p. 130): "Sed haec unda inrigua et inperitum ebromat sensum et componit barbarum dictatorem qui potius apud Dodorenum didicit gentium linguas discrepere, quam cum bone memoriae Parthenio obtinuisse rethorica dictione." We know nothing at all about the Doderenus mentioned here. Parthenius has been discussed earlier.

294 Roger called his style "pretentious and obscure" (p. 102). But this is a characteristic of the period which Gogo shared with Dynamius.

295 Gogo, Ep. 16 (p. 130): "Minime necessarium secundum quod scribitis, ad alienos requirere quod, per proprios vates aliis possumus fenerare, quonaim poetis datur indutia peregrinis prudentiam monstrari insignem, cum te incola regio nostra unicum meruit habere doctorem."

Fortunatus acted as an intellectual counselor in circles close to the court and at the court itself.

The Frankish kings of the second half of the sixth century seem more curious about matters of the mind than were their predecessors. According to Fortunatus, Caribert, a son of Chlothar I, spoke Latin as well as he did German and "triumphed over Romans with his eloquence"[296] —a courtier's flattery, no doubt, but still valuable evidence. Caribert's daughter, the wife of the king of Kent, was educated.[297] Fortunatus was less precise about Sigebert, the second son of Chlothar I; he portrayed him simply as a charming, wise young man.[298] He composed an epithalamium in the antique fashion for this prince's marriage, just as Cassiodorus had for the wedding of Vitigis.[299] The results of Fortunatus' relationships with Frankish princes suggest that his poetic composition enjoyed more success at Metz than did that of the Italian minister at Ravenna. Sigebert's wife, Brunhilda, a Visigothic princess, was definitely educated. After having confided her son to Gogo and then to a certain Wandelenus,[300] she took over his education herself. She did so well that Gregory the Great congratulated her in one of his letters.[301]

Guntram, king of Burgundy and Chlothar's third son, seems to have had a primarily religious culture. He liked to hear the Psalms chanted during his meals. His nephew Meroveus, Chilperic's son, shared the same tastes.[302]

Chlothar's last son, King Chilperic of Neustria, seems to have been the most learned member of his family—perhaps he owed his education to the special care of his father.[303] Certainly, we need not disguise all that was barbaric in Chilperic. Gregory of Tours has left us a sinister

---

[296] Fortunatus, *Carm.* VI, 2, vv. 97ff. (*MGH, AA,* IV-1, 133): "Cum sis progenitus clara de gente Sigamber / Floret in eloquio lingua latina tuo / Qualis est in propria docto sermone loquella / Qui nos Romanos vincis in eloquio?"

[297] Gregory the Great, *Ep.* XI, 35 (*MGH, Ep.,* II, 304, l. 24): "Litteris docta est."

[298] Fortunatus, *Carm.* VI, 1, v. 23 (p. 130): "Lingua, decus, virtus, bonitas, mens, gratia, pollent."

[299] Ibid. VI, 1 (pp. 124–29). See Bezzola, 1: 46 for this epithalamium. For Cassiodorus' epithalamium for Vitigis, see above, chap. 2, n. 47.

[300] Gregory of Tours, *HF,* VIII, 22 (p. 389): "Hoc tempore et Wandelenus nutritor Childeberti regis, obiit, sed in loco eius nullus est subrogatus, eo quod regina mater curam vellit propriam habere de filio."

[301] Gregory the Great, *Ep.* VI, 5 (*MGH, Ep.,* I, 383): "Excellentiae vestrae praedicandam ac Deo placitam bonitatem et gubernacula regni testantur et educatio filii manifestat."

[302] Gregory of Tours, *HF,* VIII, 3 (pp. 372–73); ibid., V, 14 (p. 209, l. 19): "Dum pariter sederemus, suppliciter petiit ad instructionem animae legi."

[303] Fortunatus, *Carm.* IX, 1, vv. 33–36 (p. 202): "In te dulce caput, patris omnis cura pependit. . . . Agnoscebat enim te jam meliore mereri / Unde magis coluit, praetulit inde pater."

portrait of him, which historians have generally accepted.[304] The reputation of his wife, Fredegunda, has weighed heavily in this verdict. But Gregory himself tells us that Chilperic was lettered, evidence which Fortunatus corroborates.[305]

The king of Neustria imitated the poet Sedulius in his own way and composed masses and hymns.[306] We have one of his hymns in honor of Saint Medard. While the form of the poem is far from classical and its vocabulary quite unusual, is it not significant, nevertheless, that its author imitated a metrical epitaph of the fourth century in one of its strophes?[307] Chilperic even undertook the study of theology and wrote a small treatise on the three persons of the Trinity, although the treatise was deemed slightly unorthodox by the bishops in his entourage.[308] Gregory of Tours reports that the king tried to convert his Jewish friend, Priscus, but realized that royal persuasion did not go far.[309] That a prince should play at being a theologian is not surprising: Chilperic was imitating the emperors in this respect—as he did on another occasion, when he sponsored games in the circuses at Soissons and Paris.[310]

According to Gregory of Tours, Chilperic even tried to reform the alphabet. The chronicler's sentence is quite obscure and deserves to be cited here: "Addit autem et litteras litteris nostris, id est, ω sicut Graeci habent, ae, the, uui, quarum caracteres hi sunt: ω (Θ) ae (Ψ) the (Z) uui (Δ)."[311] What did Gregory mean and what did Chilperic have in mind? It is improbable that Gregory invented this anecdote out of whole cloth. Could Chilperic have known that Emperor Claudius had

[304] Gregory of Tours, *HF*, VI, 46 (p. 319). See Lot, *Les destinées*, p. 315.

[305] *HF*, V, 44 (p. 254); Fortunatus, *Carm.* IX, 1, vv. 93, 99, 110 (pp. 203–4): "Discernens varias sub nullo interpres voces. . . . / Cui simul arma favent et littera constat amore. . . . / Praelia robor agit, carmina lima polit."

[306] Gregory of Tours, *HF*, VI, 46 (p. 320): "Conficitque duos libros quasi Sidulium meditatus quorum versiculi debilis nullis pedibus subsistere possunt . . . et alia opuscula vel ymnus."

[307] This hymn was published in *Rhythmi aevi merovingici et carolini*, I (*MGH, PAC*, IV-2, 455). See Dag Norberg, *La póesie latine rythmique du haut Moyen Age* (Stockholm, 1953), p. 131, for this poem. Chilperic was perhaps also the author of a verse in honor of Saint Germanus: see Aimoin, *De gestis Francorum*, XVI (*PL*, CXXXIX, 296), and Roger, p. 101, n. 9. On the fourth-century epitaph, see Norberg, p. 33. This epitaph was found in the church of Saint Agricola in Reims, where Chilperic could have read it.

[308] Gregory of Tours, *HF*, V, 44 (p. 252): "Chilpericus rex scripsit indicolum ut sancta Trinitas non in personarum distinctione sed tantum Deus nominaretur."

[309] Ibid., VI, 5 (p. 268).

[310] Ibid., V, 17 (p. 216).

[311] Ibid., V, 44 (p. 254).

added three letters to the alphabet,[312] and was he thus again imitating Roman sovereigns? Perhaps, but what was the motive for his choice? Bruno Krusch rightly saw that the matter had nothing to do with runes, arguing that the king borrowed Greek characters in order to represent new sounds, but he concluded that this reform was absurd.[313] Still, one might ask, as Lot suggested, whether the reform was an attempt to represent the new pronunciation of Latin by new letters.[314] We know, in fact, that during this period *a* became a nasal pronounced *ae*, that the intervocalic *t* was sounded like the English *th*, and that *o* was elongated in pronunciation. The remaining sound, *uui*, might indicate the pronunciation of the open *o* under the influence of *yod*. Perhaps Chilperic wanted to adapt orthography to the evolution in phonetics, which would indicate that he was aware of the increasing gap between written and spoken language. But this evolution was not limited to four phonemes. Although we might be able to explain the principles of the reform, we still cannot understand why these particular phonemes were chosen, no more than we can comprehend the choice of their capital equivalents.

Chilperic went further yet: Gregory tells us that he "sent letters to the different cities of the kingdom so that characters would be taught to children, and he prescribed that old manuscripts be erased with a pumice stone and rewritten from scratch."[315] Such a decision recalls the educational policy of the emperors. The Merovingian king wanted to apply a reform which emanated from on high. There was nothing improbable in that, since other Barbarian kings had similar pretensions. If such an order had been given, however, it was doubtless never applied. Schools, as we have said, were no longer in the hands of the State, if this word still had any meaning during the Merovingian period.

Frankish aristocrats and kings of the second half of the sixth century were more open to Roman literature than the Goths, Burgundians, or

---

[312] Suetonius, *Vies des douze Césars*, XLI, 6 (ed. Henri Ailloud, 2 vols. [Paris, 1931–32], 2: 146): "Novas etiam commentus est litteras tres ac numero veterum quasi maxime necessarias addidit."

[313] See the bibliography on the question in Krusch's edition, *MGH, SRM*, I, 254, n. 2. Buchner, the editor of the *Historia Francorum*, I, 365, believed that Chilperic was adapting the alphabet to the needs of the Germanic tongue.

[314] Lot, *Les invasions germaniques*, p. 239; idem, "Quels sont les dialectes romans que pouvaient connaître les Carolingiens?" *Romania*, 64 (1938): 435.

[315] Gregory of Tours, *HF*, V, 44 (p. 254): "Et misit epistulas in universis civitatibus regni sui ut sic pueri docerentur ac libri antiquitus scripti planati pomice rescriberentur."

even their Merovingian predecessors, if only because classical culture was, so to speak, brought down to their level. The Barbarians retained only the mundane aspects of classical culture—the poets' verbal jugglery entertained them. Furthermore, in honoring literature, the Franks could sustain the illusion that they were part of the great Roman tradition. Fortunatus, writing in Radegunda's name, did not hesitate to compare the conquest of Thuringia with the taking of Troy.[316] One could argue in this regard that the famous legend of the Trojan origin of the Franks, which Pseudo-Fredegarius reports, first appeared at this time.[317] The Franks thus provided themselves with a noble affiliation, as did all Barbarians who sought citizens' rights in the civilized world.[318]

We should note, however, that princes and aristocrats held religious culture in as much esteem as profane culture. King Guntram and King Chilperic, as well as Merovingian princesses, had a marked taste for chant and ecclesiastical literature. Their culture might have been limited to this domain were it not for Fortunatus, as we shall see in studying the education of their successors.

The education of Chilperic's son, Chlothar II, must have suffered from the conditions in which his youth was spent.[319] Bishop Pretextat criticized Fredegunda for neglecting the training of her son, a freedom which cost the bishop his life.[320] Pseudo-Fredegarius tells us that Chlothar was lettered but unfortunately nothing more.[321] We know nothing of the intellectual qualities of Dagobert, Chlothar's successor. Placed on the Austrasian throne when eleven years old and confided to Pepin of Landen and Arnulf,[322] Dagobert must have received a minimum of

---

[316] Fortunatus, *App. carminum*, I: *De excidio Thoringiae*, MGH, AA, IV-1, 271. On the authenticity of this poem, see E. Rey, "De l'authenticité des deux poèmes de Fortunat," *RPh*, n.s. 30 (1906): 124–38.

[317] Pseudo-Fredegarius, *Chron.*, II, 5 (*MGH, SRM*, II, 46). See Edmond Faral, *La légende arthurienne: Etudes et documents*, 1 (Paris, 1929): 262, and E. B. Atwood, "The *Excidium Troiae* and Medieval Troy Literature," *Modern Philology* 35 (1937): 115–28. Dares the Phrygian's work, *De excidio Troiae historici*, written at the beginning of the sixth century, was known in the Barbarian kingdoms; see Schanz, IV-2, 84–87.

[318] In the Ancient world, the Macedonian dynasty sought to attach itself to the Argeades; see Gustave Glotz and Robert Cohen, *La Grèce au IVᵉ siècle: La lutte pour l'hégémonie, 404–336*, vol. 3 of *Histoire grecque*, ed. G. Glotz (Paris, 1941), p. 215.

[319] Gregory of Tours, *HF*, VII, 19, VIII, 9 (pp. 339, l. 5 and 376, l. 10).

[320] Ibid., VIII, 31 (p. 397, l. 10); "Rectius enim erat tibi ut . . . parvolum quem genuisti perducere ad legitimam possis aetatem."

[321] Pseudo-Fredegarius, *Chron.*, IV, 42 (p. 142): "Patientiae deditus, litterum eruditus, timens Deus."

[322] *Vita Arnulfi*, 16 (*MGH, SRM*, II, 439): "Clotarius . . . [Arnulfo] regnum ad gubernandum et filium ad erudiendum in manu tradidisset."

instruction from them. The silence of the texts that discuss the most celebrated Merovingian king can be explained: the princes of this period received only the elementary culture necessary for their religious training. It was the same for the successors of Dagobert. We have their subscriptions on the bottom of diplomas[323]—proof that they had learned to write—but nothing else is known of their instruction. On the other hand, the bishop who addressed a short, edifying treatise to one of Dagobert's sons advised him to listen only to priests and to read the Scriptures frequently.[324]

The same observation can be made in regard to contemporary laymen. Although we know only a few important aristocratic families in Neustria and Austrasia through hagiography,[325] prudent use of this literature can help our inquiry. Let us take the family of Agneric, owner of a villa at the gates of Meaux, where the Irishman Columban was received when he traveled in Gaul. Agneric, a familiar of King Theudebert II, is presented to us as full of wisdom and as a model husband who gave his children good religious training. One of his sons, Chagnoald, became a monk at Luxeuil, while another, Faro, was bishop of Meaux. Their sister, Burgundofara, after refusing a marriage proposed by her parents, founded the monastery of Faremoutiers. There is no indication that these children received an extensive profane education.[326] We also know another family of the same region, with whom Columban also stayed—that of Autharius.[327] Autharius and his wife, Aiga, raised three children —Ado, Rado, and Dado—according to God's law. Dado, the future Saint Audoenus, has been described as having been "furnished with a quite extensive literary training for his time."[328] That is saying a bit too much. He must have had at least a care for correct form, as witnessed by a letter to Bishop Rodobertus.[329]

---

[323] Their subscriptions appear only on precepts, however—never on judgments. See Lauer and Samaran, *Les diplômes originaux*, p. vi. Princes who were too young to write said so; see a diploma of Childeric II (Pardessus, II, 118): "Propter imbecillam aetatem minime potui manu propria subtersignavi."

[324] *Ep.* 15 (*MGH, Ep.*, III, 460).

[325] For these families, see Rolf Sprandel, *Der merovingische Adel und die Gebiete östlich des Rheins*, Forschungen zur oberrheinischen Landesgeschichte, vol. 5 (Freiburg-im-Breisgau, 1957).

[326] Jonas, *Vita Columbani*, I, 26 (*MGH, SRM*, IV-1, 99) and II, 7 (p. 120). See also Sprandel, pp. 14ff., and Jean Guerout, "Faron," *DHGE*, 16: 643–65.

[327] *Vita Columbani*, I, 26 (pp. 209ff.); Sprandel, p. 16.

[328] Vacandard, *Vie de saint Ouen*, p. 22.

[329] He sent the letter to Rodobertus when he forwarded a copy of the *Life of Saint Eligius*; see *Vita Eligii, MGH, SRM*, IV, 663, and Rodobertus' response.

Young Wandregesilus, son of an Austrasian father and a Neustrian mother, is another case in point. His parents brought him up and trained him for a worldly career, but his biographer tells us nothing about his intellectual formation.[330] Is the *Life* of Saint Arnulf, whose parents were Austrasian, any more precise? Apparently so, since the *Life* relates that he was entrusted to a preceptor and that, thanks to his memory and intelligence, he stood out as the most gifted among his friends.[331] We would like to know more about him. The culture of Pepin I of Landen, who, with Arnulf, played a major political role in Austrasia, is equally unknown. Grimoaldus, his son and successor as mayor of the palace of Austrasia, must have been sufficiently educated to direct the education of young Sigebert III[332] and his son.[333] Gertrude, Grimoaldus' sister, like other young women of the time, received a good religious education, which at least presupposes elementary instruction. In the middle of the seventh century, Wulfram, future bishop of Sens, was confided by his father to *magistri catholici* and instructed in sacred literature.[334]

It is thus likely that most Frankish aristocrats received a minimum of instruction. The practice of writing—which they had adopted following the example of Gallo-Romans—in addition to their desire for a religious culture, required that they know how to read and to write. We possess material evidence of this instruction. Signet rings, which must have been used to seal correspondence, have been found in Barbarian tombs.[335] Writing styli have also been found. A distinction, no doubt, must be made between the very long styliform pins used to hold hair

[330] *Vita Wandregisili*, MGH, SRM, V, 13: "Ab ipsis [parentibus] juventutis suae rudimentis studiis juxta moris saecularium." Ansbert was confided to *magistri strenui*; see *Vita Ansberti*, 2 (*AB* 1 [1882]: 180).

[331] *Vita Arnulfi*, 3 (*MGH, SRM*, II, 433): "Jam tempus advenit ut litterarum studiis imbuendis daretur, mox itaque traditus praeceptori inter ceteros contubernales suo sagax ingenii et memoria capax." See Sprandel, *Der merovingische Adel*, p. 36 for Arnulf's origins.

[332] We can assume this much after what Fredegarius tells us of the rivalry between the king's first preceptor, Otto, and Grimoaldus, and then of Otto's subsequent assassination and replacement by Grimoaldus (Pseudo-Fredegarius, *Chron.*, IV, 86, 88 [*MGH, SRM*, II, 164–65]).

[333] See Louis Dupraz, *Le royaume des Francs et l'ascension politique des Maires du palais au déclin du VIIe siècle* (Freiburg, 1948), p. 109, who uses the late but well-informed *Life of Sigebert*. According to Dupraz (pp. 334ff.) Grimoaldus would have sent Dagobert II to Ireland to complete his education. This interpretation of the king's exile is interesting but hard to accept.

[334] Jonas of Fontenelle, *Vita Vulframni, MGH, SRM*, V, 606.

[335] Deloche, *Anneaux sigillaires*, nos. CXIX, CXX, CXXI (at Caranda); see also no. CXXIII, a ring fastened by a small chain. A bronze ring with monogram from Champigny-sur-Yonne is discussed in *RAE* 4 (1953): 37, and "L'anneau d'Arnegonde" is studied by Fleury in *BSAF* (1963), p. 34.

in place[336] and actual styli. Those found at Herpes,[337] in Aube,[338] in Normandy,[339] and in northern France[340] resemble Roman styli and could have been used to write on the tablets which were still in use during the Barbarian period and which would continue to be used for a long time.[341] Autograph subscriptions on private documents that have come down to us are yet another material proof of the education of Barbarian aristocrats, since to sign something with one's hand during this time was to demonstrate one's culture. In fact, in Merovingian Gaul, as in Antiquity, aristocrats wrote very little personally—letters were dictated to a secretary and authenticated with the author's signature and perhaps a few added words.[342] The evidence of autograph subscriptions allows us to conclude that the Frankish aristocracy remained faithful to these habits until the middle of the seventh century.

The Solignac charter of transfer, from the opening of the seventh century, bore six subscriptions and one hand-traced cross made by an illiterate.[343] Laymen from the region of Le Mans were still writing out their entire names on documents during the first half of the century.[344] In the diploma Clovis II granted in 654 for Saint Denis, Rodebert, the mayor of the palace, was the only one to use his monogram, while other laymen signed the document with their own hands.[345] Clotilda's charter of 673 is yet more interesting because it bears fourteen autograph signa-

---

[336] These have been found from the Bronze Age on; see *Germania* 28 (1944–50): 181.

[337] C. Barrière-Flavy, *Etudes sur les sépultres barbares du Midi et de l'Ouest de la France: Industrie wisigothique* (Toulouse and Paris, 1893), pp. 95, 171.

[338] J. Scapula, "Le cimetière mérovingien de Clérey (Aube)," *RAE* 5 (1954): 139; Pierre Tartat, "La civilisation dans l'Avallonnais aux temps des invasions d'après les fouilles de Vaux-Donjon," *Annales de Bourgogne* 21 (1949): 98.

[339] At Saint Pierre d'Autils; see Henri Leclercq, "Style," *DACL*, XV-2, 1697.

[340] At Mazinghem; see *Bulletin de la Société académique des antiquaires de la Morinie* 17 (1952): 560.

[341] Gregory of Tours, *HF*, VII, 30 (p. 350); Pseudo-Fredegarius, *Chron.*, IV, 40 (*MGH, SRM*, II, 140). For tablets, see below, chap. 10, sect. II.A.

[342] See Desiderius of Cahors, *Ep.* I, 2 (*MGH, Ep.*, III, 194): "Propria manu"; Sulpicius of Bourges, *Ep.* II, 1 (ibid., p. 203): "Istud manu propria fecit"; *Vita sancti Desiderii, MGH, SRM*, IV, 570 (letter from Herchenfreda): "manu propria. . . ." *Dictare* was still synonymous with *scribere*; see Gregory of Tours, *Glor. martyr.*, 63 (*MGH, SRM*, I-2, 531). In the eighth century, Ambrosius Autpertus in his commentary on the Apocalypse, *In sancti Ioannis apostoli et evangelistae Apocolypsim libri decem*, VI (in *Maxima Bibliotheca veterum patrum*, 13 [Lyon, 1677]: 536), wrote: "Et quia notariorum solatia deesse videntur ea quae dictavero, manu propria exarare contendo." For this practice during the patristic period, see Eligius Dekkers, "Les autographes des Pères latins," in *Colligere fragmenta, Festschift Alban Dold* (Beuron, 1952), pp. 127–39.

[343] *Vita Eligii, MGH, SRM*, IV, 748, l. 49.

[344] *Actus pontificum Cenomannis*, ed. Busson and Ledru, pp. 179, 190.

[345] Paris, Archives Nationales, K 2, no. 3. See Lauer and Samaran, *Les diplômes originaux*, p. 7 and plate 6bis.

tures and twelve *signa*. Two laymen, "shameful ignoramuses" in the words of the editor of the text, refused to trace a cross and instead made an effort to trace the first letter of their names.[346] After this point, autograph signatures became rarer. Laymen were satisfied simply to place a cross at the bottom of documents—they no longer knew how to write.[347]

Thus, up to about 650, as in southern Gaul, the Merovingian aristocracy received an intellectual training, but in contrast to what happened south of the Loire, their instruction was primarily religious. We are observing here the appearance of a lay culture which is already medieval.

C. FROM CHILDHOOD TO MARRIAGE

It might well seem foolhardy to attempt a study of the moral and physical training of young Merovingian aristocrats. If our sources for their education are quite poor, what will they be like for an inquiry into their upbringing in a larger sense? The Merovingian family has already been studied from a legal point of view, a study made easier by the survival of the texts of Barbarian laws.[348] I would like, however, to consider the question from a different angle. How did the child progress from the first years of infancy through adolescence and then on to marriage?

We know almost nothing about early infancy. All that we can do is to repeat the somewhat bald sentence from a Merovingian hagiographer: "Nascit puer, vagit in cunis, alitur in lacte, quid amplius?"[349] The child was nursed by his mother or a nurse until he was at least three years old.[350] Gregory of Tours sketched a few random pictures of

---

[346] Paris, Archives Nationales, K 2, no. 10, published by Léon Levillain, "Etudes mérovingiennes: La charte de Clotilde (10 mars 673)," *BECh* 105 (1944): 5–63. The donation of Bishop Reolus of Reims (686) during the same period provided for both subscriptions and manual *signa* (Pardessus, 2: 200): "Inlustris viris qui infra urbem commanere videntur quorum nomine vel signa subter tenentur inserta." Charters from Saint-Germain-des-Prés, which run from 682 to the end of the seventh century, continued to bear autograph subscriptions; see Poupardin, *Chartes de Saint-Germain-des-Prés* (Paris, 1909), pp. 14, 17–18. See also the documents registered in the curia at Poitiers during the reign of Dagobert II (677) (L. Maître, "Cunauld: Son prieuré et ses archives," *BECh*, 59 [1898]: 239ff.). Finally, we should note two autograph subscriptions preserved on papyrus at Basel; see C. Perrat, "Des Pères du Jura à l'humaniste Grynaeus: Le papyrus de Bâle 1B," *Bibl. HR* 12 (1950): 149–62.

[347] See below, chap. 9, sect. IV.B.

[348] Charles Galy, *La famille à l'époque mérovingienne* (Paris, 1901).

[349] *Vita Praejecti, MGH, SRM*, V, 227.

[350] Gregory of Tours, *Mir. Mart.*, II, 43; III, 51 (*MGH, SRM*, I-2, 624, l. 31; 644); *Glor. confess.*, 82 (ibid., p. 801, l. 3). Gregory the Great, *Ep.* XI, 569 (*MGH, Ep.*, II, 339) complained that mothers refused to nurse their children.

early childhood, but they are without historical interest.[351] It is likely that, in the sixth century, children played just as they had in the time of Sidonius Apollinaris:[352] Barbarian tombs have yielded figurines, clay birds, and ivory dolls, just as have Gallo-Roman tombs.[353] The toys of royal children were of gold.[354] Tops and balls were still favorite toys.[355] Older children and adults amused themselves playing dice, as Gallo-Romans had; this game delighted the leisure time of the Visigothic king Theodoric and of nuns in Poitiers.[356] Archaeologists in Spain discovered a gaming table, engraved on the forum at Barcelona, that undoubtedly dates from the Barbarian occupation.[357]

Outdoor games obviously prevailed. Gregory of Tours and hagiographers give us a few incidental examples.[358] If swimming and horse racing seem to have become less popular than in England,[359] the hunt remained in the sixth century as it had in the fifth century the favorite sport of aristocrats and kings. Whoever, like Saint Trudo, preferred visiting churches to the *ritus venandi* was regarded as odd by his friends.[360] In the course of the hunt, a really dangerous sport, more than one young man was killed:[361] crude designs carved on Barbarian sarcophagi show youngsters and their fathers hunting, in remembrance, no doubt, of some tragic accident.[362] Women do not seem to have

[351] See especially *Mir. Mart.*, III, 16 (p. 636).

[352] Sidonius, *Ep.* I, 2, 5; II, 9, 4; IV, 4, 1 (*MGH, AA*, VIII, 3, 31, 57). See Haarhoff, *Schools of Gaul*, pp. 97ff.

[353] Maurice Toussaint, *Répertoire archéologique du département des Ardennes, période gallo-romaine et époque franque* (Paris, 1955), p. 132; idem, *Répertoire archéologique du département de Meurthe-et-Moselle, période gallo-romaine* (Nancy, 1947), p. 36.

[354] *Vita Eligii*, II, 32 (*MGH, SRM*, IV, 727): "Quoddam opificium quod parvulo posset aptari fieri rogavit, atque ad usus ejus usque dum nasceretur custodiri jussit." Queen Bathilda placed this order. Was it for a teething ring?

[355] Fritz Roeder, "Ballspiel," in Hoops, 1: 160; Bede, *De orthographia*, ed. Keil, 7: 293: "Nam sive ventus sive quo ludunt pueri hic turbo dicitur."

[356] Sidonius, *Ep.* I, 2 (p. 4); Gregory of Tours, *HF*, X, 16 (p. 506, l. 9): "De tabula . . . etsi lusisset viventem domna Radegunde."

[357] A. Duran y Sampire, "Un antiguo juego de origen germanico en Barcelona," *Spanische Forschungen der Görresgesellschaft* 9 (1954): 30.

[358] Gregory of Tours, *Mir. Mart.*, IV, 17 and 18 (p. 654), mentioned children playing in the town square. The *Vita Pardulfi, MGH, SRM*, VII-2, 26, shows the saint and his friends at play burning down a tree. The *Vita Maximi, PL*, LXXX, 36, describes children playing on the walls of Riez.

[359] See below, chap. 8, sect. I.D.

[360] *Vita Trudonis, ASOB*, II, 1074: "Coeperunt praefati juvenes despuere eum et quasi degenerum aestimare." On hunting, see Samuel Dill, *Roman Society in Gaul in the Merovingian Age* (London, 1926), p. 252. *Lex Ripuar.*, XXXVI, ii (*MGH, Leg. sect. I*, III-2) mentions falconry.

[361] See *Actus pontificum Cenomannis*, ed. Busson and Ledru, p. 142.

[362] Henri Leclercq, "Langeais," *DACL*, VIII-1, 1266 (wild boar hunting). See additional hunting scenes in Salin, 2: 154–56. A Lombard sarcophagus portrays a similar

participated in this violent sport, although they must have at least learned how to ride a horse.[363]

Adolescence was a difficult period in the life of the child. In the Merovingian world as in Antiquity, childhood and adolescence were despised ages that one tried to put behind him as rapidly as possible. The best compliment one could give a young person was to tell him he had the maturity of an adult or the gravity of an old man (*cor senile gerens*), a commonplace which Fortunatus and the hagiographers never tired of repeating and which represented a genuine truth to them.[364] Every parent wished to make his child an adult as soon as possible.

The contents of children's tombs show that Merovingian girls wore jewels like their mothers: bronze bands, rings, bone bracelets, collars of glass pearls.[365] As for the young boy, he carried weapons adapted to his size[366] and must have been eager to accompany his father into war, the national sport of the Barbarians. Merovingian princes, in fact, participated in battles at quite a young age,[367] and the sons of aristocrats must have done so as well. To go to war for the first time was to attain one's majority.

There was no established age of majority, *aetas perfecta* or *legitima*, during this period. The Barbarians, who attached great significance to the number seven,[368] maintained the traditional divisions: childhood to age seven, adolescence to age fourteen. Majority came at age fourteen for the Visigoths, fifteen for the Burgundians, Ripuarians, and Anglo-

---

scene; see Julius Baum, *La sculpture figurale en Europe à l'époque mérovingienne* (Paris, 1937), p. 169, pl. LXIII.

[363] Gregory of Tours, *HF*, IX, 9 (p. 423, l. 4).

[364] See the *Vita Aredii*, 4 (*MGH, SRM*, III, 583), which repeats Gregory the Great, *Dial.*, II, preface; the *Vita Ansberti* (ibid., V, 620): "Dulcis infantia modestia pueritia gravis adolescentia"; the *Vita Lamberti* (ibid., VI, 353): "Aevum adolescentiae cum industria senectutis gerebat"; and Fortunatus, *Carm.* VII, 16, v. 30 (*MGH, AA*, IV-1, 171): "Ut juvenem regem redderes esse senem" (to Condan, Theodebald's preceptor). See above, Introduction, n. 37, for this classical commonplace.

[365] For children's rings, see Deloche, *Anneaux sigillaires*, nos. CXXXVI (p. 155), CXCVIII, CXCIX (p. 218). For other jewelry, see Toussaint, *Répertoire archéologique du département des Ardennes*, p. 132, and *Répertoire archéologique du département de Seine-et-Marne, période gallo-romaine et époque franque* (Paris, 1953), p. 127.

[366] *Vita Eligii*, II, 56, (*MGH, SRM*, IV, 730). Ebroin placed the *balteus* of his sick son on Saint Eligius' tomb. Paul the Deacon, *HL*, IV, 29, 37 (*MGH, SRL*, p. 130, l. 14), introduces us to a young prince who participated in battle with his little sword. See O. Doppelfeld, "Das Inventar des fränkischen Knabengrabes," *Kölner Domblatt* 21 (1963): 49–68.

[367] Pseudo-Fredegarius, *Chron.*, IV, 87 (*MGH, SRM*, II, 164).

[368] Eugen Mogk, "Sieben," in Hoops, 4: 172.

Saxons.[369] For the Franks, a first majority took place at twelve years, perhaps even at seven years for kings.[370] According to Salic law, when a youth reached the age of twelve, his hair was cut, an event perhaps corresponding to the Roman *capillaturia*.[371]

But he also had to have a second majority when he entered adulthood. Did he take up arms at this point, as in primitive German society?[372] For the Franks, we have no information. We see it with the Ostrogoths and Lombards, but it does not appear with the Franks before the Carolingian period.[373] Some historians have supposed that the practice of arming the young man was replaced in Merovingian Gaul by the *barbatoria*, the shaving of the first growth of beard.[374] Indeed, this ceremony, which was also known among Romans, was still in use in the sixth century, as a misunderstood text of Gregory of Tours proves. At the trial of some nuns at Poitiers in 590, the abbess was criticized at the sentencing for having had made "a golden band for her niece on the occasion of the celebration of a barbatoria in the monastery."[375] This passage has long been thought to refer to a masquerade in which a false beard was worn.[376] In reality, though, the passage definitely refers to the cutting of the first beard of a young man—a ceremony which, as the context of the passage indicates, coincided with the engagement of the abbess' niece. Texts from the eighth century, of course, also show that kings customarily celebrated the barbatoria of their sons.[377] Thus, Franks preferred a Roman practice that was still in use

---

369 *Leges Visigoth.*, II, 4, 10, and IV, 3, 3 (*MGH, Leg. sect. I*, I, 134); *Lex Burgundion.*, LXXXVII, 1 (ibid., II-1, 108); *Lex Ripuar.*, 84 (81) (ibid., III-2, 130). For the Anglo-Saxons, see *Theodore's Penitential*, XII, 36 (Haddan-Stubbs ed., 3: 201): "Puer usque ad XV annos sit in potestate patris sui."

370 L. Dupraz, *Le royaume des Francs*, pp. 153–54; Christian Courtois, "L'avènement de Clovis II et les règles d'accession au trône," in *Mélanges d'histoire du Moyen Age dediés à la mémoire de Louis Halphen* (Paris, 1951), p. 155.

371 *Lex Salica*, XXI (ed. Karl August Eckhardt [Weimar, 1953], p. 146), and XXXV (p. 148): "De puero tunsurato." See Brunner, *Deutsche Rechtsgeschichte*, 1: 104. See also the references in Paul Guilhiermoz, *Essai sur l'origine de la noblesse en France au Moyen Age* (Paris, 1902), p. 408, for the Roman *capillaturia*.

372 Tacitus, *Germania*, 13, 1. See Brunner, *Deutsche Rechtsgeschichte*, 1: 103.

373 Guilhiermoz, *Essai*, pp. 403ff.

374 Ibid., p. 406. The author does not mention the passage by Gregory of Tours cited in the following note.

375 Gregory of Tours, *HF*, X, 16 (p. 505, l. 18): "Vittam de auro exornatam idem neptae suae superfluae fecerit, barbaturias intus eo quod celebraverit."

376 See Henri Leclercq, "Barbe," *DACL*, II-1, 489. Charles Du Fresne Du Cange presented both interpretations in his *Vingt-deuxième dissertation sur l'histoire de saint Louis* (Paris, 1850), p. 88. See also *RE*, 3: 33.

377 *Lex Romana raetica curiensis*, VIII, 4 (*MGH, Leges*, V, 360): "Quando aliqua

to the Germanic custom of arming young men, which the Carolingians readopted after their contact with other Germanic peoples.

We can compare this evidence with what we know about Barbarian attitudes toward hair and beards. A sculpture from Rhenania shows a warrior touching his hair as if virile strength was located in one's hair.[378] Frankish kings who were shorn could no longer accede to the throne, while vanquished kings were scalped.[379] Reliquaries containing hair were attached to belts and worn to protect against evil.[380] Finally, adoptions were completed by touching the beard or cutting the hair.[381] We can conclude, then, that as with other peoples—Slavs, Hindus, and Aztecs—the offering up of the beard was part of the rite of passage from adolescence to adulthood.[382] We should note that the Church also adopted this rite for its clerics: the Visigothic *Liber ordinum* and the *Gelasian Sacramentary* have preserved the prayers recited when someone wished to offer his first beard to God.[383]

The second great event in the life of an adolescent, for boys as well as for girls, was marriage. Gallo-Roman and Frankish girls were married at a very young age. Eusebia was engaged when ten years old, Segolena at twelve; Vilihuta was married at thirteen and died three years later while pregnant.[384] The daughter of Pepin I, Gertrude, was sought in marriage before she was fourteen years old but was able to refuse be-

---

publica gaudia nunciantur hoc est aut elevatio regis aut nuptias, aut barbatoria." The epitome of Alaric's *Breviary* from Saint Gall indicates the same thing; see *Lex Romana Visigothorum*, ed. G. Hänel (Madrid, 1896), p. 157.

[378] This sculpture, from Niederdollendorf, is reproduced in *Mémorial d'un voyage*, p. 63.

[379] For the *rex crinitus*, see J. Hoyoux "Reges criniti, chevelures, tonsures et scalps chez les Mérovingiens," *RBPh* 26 (1948): 478–508.

[380] See A. France-Lanord, "La plaque-boucle de Saint-Quentin," *AclB* (1956), pp. 263–65. In the *Vita Eligii*, II, 68 (*MGH, SRM*, IV, 734), a woman took some of Eligius' hair and beard as a safeguard against evil.

[381] Pseudo-Fredegarius, *Chron.*, II, 58 (*MGH, SRM*, II, 82) apropos of Clovis and Alaric. See also Paul the Deacon, *HL*, IV, 38 (*MGH, SRL*, p. 132), and VI, 53 (p. 182). Liutprand adopted Pepin the Short this way.

[382] Hair was cut among the Aztecs at age ten (Jacques Soustelle, *La vie quotidienne chez les Aztèques à la veille de la conquête espagnole* [Paris, 1955], p. 69) and by the Slavs at age seven or fourteen (Lubor Niederle, *Manuel de l'antiquité slave*, 2 vols. [Paris, 1923–26], 2: 11). Hindus shaved the beard at sixteen years (Louis Renou, *L'Inde classique* [Paris, 1947], p. 363). For primitive peoples, see the examples given by Arnold van Gennep, *Les rites de passage* (Paris, 1909), pp. 93ff.

[383] *Liber ordinum*, ed. Ferotin, p. 43: "Ordo super eum qui barbam tongere cupit"; Antoine Chavasse, *Le sacramentaire gélasien* (*Vaticanus Reginensis 316*): *Sacramentaire presbytéral en usage dans les titres romains au VIIᵉ siècle* (Tournai, 1958), pp. 451–52: "Oratio pro eo qui prius barbam tondet."

[384] *Vita Segolenae* of Albi, *AS*, July, V, 630–37; Fortunatus, *Carm.* IV, 26 and 28 (*MGH, AA*, IV-1, 95, 100).

cause her father had just died.[385] Fathers could force their daughters
to marry, a fate young girls could escape only by flight.[386] Some men
made sure of their wives very early by carrying off young girls and
raising them for eventual marriage. The Burgundian noble who se-
questered little five-year-old Rusticula[387] was only imitating King
Chlothar I in his conduct toward Radegunda. Merovingian councils
condemned in vain the abduction of girls.[388]

Parents were also careful to marry their sons off quickly. Since the
sexual morality of young people was particularly relaxed during this
period,[389] adolescence was regarded as a dangerous age; hagiographers
loved to show their heroes resisting the snares which "the fervor of
the age excuses."[390] Mothers were disturbed by the prolonged celibacy
of their children and wished "to check adolescent license with the conjugal remedy."[391] Fathers viewed their sons' marriage as assurance
that their property would remain in the family. Gregory of Tours reported the speech that Leobard's father made to his reticent son: why
work if there is no one to inherit the fruits of one's labor, why not
continue the line and—a final argument from Scripture—sons should
obey their parents.[392] In several texts, we see that sons refused to marry
and fled,[393] or accepted but reached some sort of understanding with
their fiancée and led lives of perfect continence.[394] Other young people
were perfectly indifferent to the choices made for them. Young Austregesilus, finding himself at court, was forced to marry, but not knowing whom to marry, placed three notes containing the names of three
possible fathers-in-law on an altar. He hoped that after three nights of
prayer, God would show him which note to choose.[395]

[385] *Vita Geretrudis, MGH, SRM,* II, 447.
[386] See the case of Burgundofara in *Vita Columbani,* II, 7 (*MGH, SRM,* IV-1, 121).
[387] Florentius, *Vita Rusticulae, MGH, SRM,* IV, 344.
[388] Council of Tours (567), c. 21; Council of Paris (614), c. 15 (*MGH, Leg. sect. III,*
I, 130, l. 20, and 190).
[389] See Caesarius of Arles, *Sermones,* XLII–XLIII (Morin ed., pp. 185–89).
[390] *Vita Mauroni, AS,* May, II, 53.
[391] *Vita Eutropii,* in *Gallia christiana novissima,* ed. Albanés, 6: 11: "Cum licentiosam
adolescentiam conjugali remedio refrenisset."
[392] Gregory of Tours, *Vitae patrum,* XX (*MGH, SRM,* I-2, 741). In the case of an
only son, marriage was considered a state duty. See the *Vita Sequani, AS,* Sept., VI, 36–41.
Although this *Vita* is perhaps not contemporary, the information it furnishes is valid
for the period we are studying.
[393] *Vita Maximi, AS,* Jan., I, 91; *Vita Valentini, AS,* July, II, 41.
[394] *Vita Ansberti, MGH, SRM,* V, 620.
[395] *Vita Austregesili, MGH, SRM,* IV, 190. Krusch wrongly believed that this *Life*
was Carolingian. See Ferdinand Lot, *L'impôt foncier et la capitation personelle sous le
Bas-Empire et l'époque franque* (Paris, 1928), p. 94.

D. THE MEROVINGIAN COURT AS AN EDUCATIONAL CENTER

Merovingian aristocrats, like all parents, were concerned about the professional futures of their children. In order to assure their futures better, they tried to send their children as early as possible for a stay at court. The Merovingian court can thus be considered an educational center, and we shall study it from this point of view.[396]

There were no precise rules governing the recruitment of young aristocrats at the palace; as a rule, one gained entry through relatives. The king's friends—like Germer, who was allied to the royal family through his wife; Licinius' father; and Bishop Filibaudus, Philibertus' father[397]—normally sent their children to the court. Important aristocratic families, whether from Aquitaine (the families of Desiderius, Bonitus, Aredius), Neustria (Saint Audoenus' family), or Austrasia (the families of Leodegarius, Arnulf), also were accorded this privilege.[398] Thus, the court contributed to the "progressive fusion" of the Roman and German populations.

How old were children when they came to court? All the evidence agrees in fixing the age for arrival at court at puberty. The texts are explicit on this point: "roborata aetas" for Arnulf, "robutior aetas" for Austregesilus, "a pueritia" for Gundulf, "in pubentibus annis" for Bonitus.[399] Were these youths given a special title? The texts tell us that they were the *nutriti*, the *commendati* of the king, and that they entered into the *obsequium* of the king.[400] Should we take this term in its legal sense and regard the young palatines as *antrustiones*? Historians have not come to agreement on this point. For some, the German institution of the trust was composed of adult warriors, while the aristocrats at court more closely resembled the former Roman *comites*.[401] Others find this contrast too systematic and view the corps of antrus-

---

[396] For the court, see Waitz, *Deutsche Verfassungsgeschichte*, 1: 179–82, 2: 1ff.; and Fustel de Coulanges, *La monarchie franque*, pp. 135ff.

[397] *Vita Germeri, ASOB*, II, 818; *Vita Licini, AS*, Feb., II, 678; *Vita Philiberti, MGH, SRM*, V, 586.

[398] See the references in Guilhiermoz, *Essai*, p. 423.

[399] Let us add "puer adolescens" for Aredius. See also Desiderius' letter to Dagobert (*Ep.* I, 5 [*MGH, Ep.*, III, 195, l. 29]): "Dulcido auspicatae indolis pubertatis." Leodegarius' case provides the only reference to infancy: "A primi aetatis infantia" (*MGH, SRM*, V, 324, l. 16).

[400] For *nutriti*, see *Vita Sigiranni, AB* 3 (1884): 381; Desiderius, *Ep.* II, 13, and I, 3 (*MGH, SRM*, III, 210, l. 24 and 194, l. 27); for *commendati*, see *Vita Aredii, Philiberti, Austregesili, Licini*. Finally, see *Vita Austregesili, MGH, SRM*, IV, 190: "In obsequium gloriosi regis Gunthramni deputatur a patre."

[401] Guilhiermoz, *Essai*, p. 428.

tiones as comprised of men from different backgrounds and different peoples.[402] Even if this hypothesis is admitted, the most that can be said is that the young palatines might have been part of the royal antrustiones. If the texts indicate a strong bond between the king and the youths at court, it need not necessarily be the bond of *trustis*, which was sealed with an oath. Only the *Life of Saint Eligius* mentions an oath taken by a young man, although it does not specify the circumstances.[403] Moreover, this oath had nothing to do with the engagement formula of an antrustione, such as those Marculf included in his formulary.[404] Some texts say that the king's permission was necessary to leave court.[405] But this was an obligation of young men entering religious life and had nothing to do with breaking a contract. Although our young men would perhaps later be called to be antrustiones, they were not so yet.

This hypothesis is verified by the fact that young palatines never appear as part of a schola. Historians have followed blind alleys because the word *schola* bore several meanings in Merovingian times.[406] From Elphège Vacandard's work we know that *schola* did not mean "school" but, rather, signified "corps of antrustiones" when used in reference to the court.[407] Merovingian *scholares* bear close resemblance to the guards of the imperial court[408] and of many other courts.[409] Now,

---

[402] Joseph Calmette, "Le *comitatus* germanique et la vassalité," *Nouvelle revue historique de droit* (1904); Lot, *Les invasions germaniques*, p. 214.

[403] *Vita Eligii*, I, 6 (*MGH, SRM*, IV, 673): "Me presente, nescio quam ob causam nisi quod facile datur intelligi fidelitatis obtento dum apud regem puerolus habitarem . . . ut [Eligius] donaret sacramentum"

[404] Marculf, *Form.*, I, 18 (*MGH, Leg. sect. V*, p. 55). See Maximin Deloche, *Le trustis et l'antrustion royal sous les deux premières races* (Paris, 1873). The author was mistaken in neglecting the hagiographical texts we are using.

[405] *Vita Sulpitii, MGH, SRM*, IV, 371; *Vita Wandregisili*, 7 (*MGH, SRM*, V, 16). For the royal authorization, see Marculf, *Form.*, I, 19 (*MGH, Leg. sect. V*, p. 55): "Praeceptum de clericatum."

[406] *Schola* could designate a school, room, dormitory, group, or corporation. See above, chap. 4, n. 63.

[407] Elphège Vacandard, "La *scola* du palais mérovingien," *RQH* 61 (1897): 490–502; 62 (1898): 546–51; 75 (1904): 549–53. Roger, p. 97, repeats his conclusions. But Vacandard, like Lot (*Les invasions germaniques*, p. 214), gave a larger meaning to the word *schola* than any text warrants. The schola was not the court.

[408] Ernest C. Babut, *Recherches sur la garde impériale et sur le corps d'officiers de l'armée romaine aux IVe et Ve siècles* (Paris, 1914); Stein, 1: 123; O. Seek, "Scholae palatinae," *RE*, 2nd ser., 2: 621. Coins bearing the word *scola* were undoubtedly struck for Merovingian *scholares*; see August de Belfort, *Description générale des monnaies mérovingiennes par ordre alphabétique des ateliers*, 5 vols. (Paris, 1892–95), nos. 3490–96, 3504–06, 6342–48, etc.

[409] For example, the Slavic *druzina* (Niederle, *Manuel de l'antiquité slave*, 2: 268),

all our texts speak of the young men's service at the court or at the palace, never in the schola.[410] One phrase from Saint Ragnebertus' *Life* might be used to refer to the passage of these young men into the group of *scholares*,[411] but this *Life* is from the Carolingian period, when the word *schola* had a broader meaning synonymous with *aula*. Thus, the young palatines must be connected with the *convivae regis* rather than with the antrustiones. In welcoming them, the Merovingian court was imitating the Ostrogothic court.

Even though these young people were not part of a constituted body as such, they were not left without supervision. It has been correctly supposed that the mayor of the palace was responsible for their education, since parents in the sixth and seventh centuries addressed themselves to him.[412] The *major domus* had many tasks, among them the duty of organizing court life.[413] It has even been said that he directed the schola, but this is not very certain, since the one pertinent text is difficult to interpret.[414] In any event, he did concern himself with the education of Merovingian kings. When the princes left their nurses,[415] they were confided to a governor, who was often also the mayor of the palace. Thus, the major domus Condan raised Theodebald;[416] Gogo brought up the son of Sigebert I;[417] one of Dagobert's sons was entrusted to Otto, son of a *domesticus*, and then, after Otto's assassination, to the mayor of the palace, Grimoaldus.[418] I have no difficulty believing that

---

or the Mongol "antrusiones" (B. Vladimirtsov, *Le régime social des Mongols: Le féodalisme nomade*, trans. Michel Carsow [Paris, 1948], p. 110).

[410] "In regiam aulam" (*Vita Aredii, MGH, SRM*, III, 582; *Vita Hermelandi, ASOB*, III-1, 389); "in aula palatina" (Fortunatus, *Carm.* IV, 4 [*MGH, AA*, IV-1, 81–82], apropos of Saint Gall). See also *Vita Desiderii, Leodegardii, Nivardi.*

[411] *Vita Ragneberti, AS*, June, II, 695: "Scholastica ac dominico dogmate . . . eruditus."

[412] Gregory of Tours, *HF*, V, 46 (p. 256). A priest from Rodez confided his nephew to Gogo. Arnulf was entrusted to Gundulf *subregulus*; see *Vita Arnulfi*, 3 (*MGH, SRM*, II, 433). See also Guilhiermoz, *Essai*, p. 426, n. 24.

[413] See Lot, *Les destinées*, p. 323, for the *major palatii.*

[414] Fortunatus, *Carm.* VII, 4, vv. 25–26 (p. 156), presents Gogo applauded by the scola following behind him: "Sive palatina residet modo laetus in aula / Cui scola congrediens plaudit amore sequax." The word *scola* often simply meant entourage, however; see Gregory of Tours, *HF*, X, 26 (p. 519).

[415] Septimana, the nurse of the children of Childebert II, plotted with the preceptor Droctulf against Brunhilda; see Gregory of Tours, *HF*, IX, 38 (p. 458).

[416] Fortunatus, *Carm.* VII, 16 (p. 171).

[417] Gregory of Tours, *HF*, V, 46 (p. 256): "[Gogo] qui tunc regis erat nutricius." Vacandard translated *nutricius* as "nourri du roi," which is inexact; see "La scola du palais mérovingien," *RQH* 61 (1897): 498.

[418] Pseudo-Fredegarius, *Chron.*, IV, 86 (*MGH, SRM*, II, 164). According to Waitz (*Deutsche Verfassungsgeschichte*, 2, pt. 2: 93), *domesticus* and *major palatii* were sometimes synonymous.

the mayor of the palace assumed the duty of directing both young palatines and princes at the same time.

The familiarity between princes and youths confirms this opinion. In the sixth century, the Tourain Gundulf lived, from his childhood, with the son of Chlothar I.[419] In the following century, Desiderius of Cahors and his friends were raised with Dagobert. In a letter to Dagobert, Desiderius recalled "the memory of the camaraderie (*contubernium*) and the sweetness of a youth passed under a cloudless sky."[420] This community of princes and youths is a specific trait of the Merovingian period. Kings did not isolate themselves in their palaces like Roman emperors of the Late Empire but lived modestly with their warriors and *convivae*. The sons of kings shared the occupations of young palatines under the mayor's authority.

Their basic duty was their apprenticeship in their future métier. The court was not a school in the scholarly sense of the word, since it has already been proven that the young men received whatever little literary education they were ever to have from their families before they came to court.[421] The court was primarily a staff school which trained officers and bureaucrats.[422] Although we have little information on the military aspects of this training, the *Lives* of Arnulf and Austregesilus tell us that these youths quickly attracted attention by their courage with weapons.[423] Most often we see young palatines filling civil functions,[424] a sure indication that they did not belong to the corps of antrustiones. One of their most interesting duties from the viewpoint of the history of culture was their work in the chancellery. Young men from all over were admitted to the chancellery and could even direct it, as in the case of Aredius in the sixth century and Ansbert and Audoenus in the seventh century.[425]

---

[419] Gregory of Tours, *Mir. Mart.*, III, 15 (*MGH, SRM*, I-2, 636): "Gundulfus autem quidam ipsius urbis [Tours] civis ab infantia sua cum Gunthario Chlotari regis filio habitavit. In cujus dum haberetur servitio et ordinante rege ascendens in arbore matura decerperet poma." The reference is not to a slave, as the rest of the story makes clear, but to a playmate.

[420] Desiderius, *Ep.* I, 5 (*MGH, Ep.*, III, 195): "Recordatio contubernii et dulcedo auspicatae indolis pubertatis."

[421] Roger, pp. 96–97.

[422] The expressions used by hagiographers—"eruditio palatina" (*Vita Aredii, MGH, SRM*, III, 582); "militaribus gestis et aulicis disciplinis" (*Vita Wandregisili, ASOB*, II, 534)—prove this.

[423] *Vita Arnulfi*, 4 (*MGH, SRM*, II, 433): "Nam virtutem belligerandi seu potentiam illius deinceps in armis quis enarraret queat?" *Vita Austregesili, MGH, SRM*, IV, 191.

[424] See Guilhiermoz, *Essai*, pp. 426–27.

[425] Aredius: "Cancellarii fortiter officium"; Ansbertus: "Aulicus scriba doctus"; Au-

How were they prepared for such duties? Most likely, they began by acquainting themselves with the notariate before taking over the direction of this important service.[426] The royal notary had to have above all a certain amount of literary culture, but contrary to what has long been thought, the Latin which he wrote was not that which was ordinarily spoken. We can judge this from forty-seven original documents from 625 to 717 that have come down to us.[427] The language of these documents has been studied and attests that notaries, especially those of the first half of the seventh century, took great pains to bring themselves up to classical Latin.[428] A first reading of these documents leaves a deplorable impression, since the spelling is no longer classic. But, in fact, these texts do not contain more mistakes than other literary texts of the period. Philologists have even noticed in the texts a taste for mannerism, for rare and archaic words, and for learned etymologies.[429] Those who drew up the documents were still loyal to the rules of metrical prose[430] and rhetoric.[431] Thus, the influence of Parthenius, Asclepiodotus,[432] and of those Marculf called "eloquentissimos ac rhetores et ad dictandum peritos"[433] cannot be doubted.

Secondly, the notary had to learn how to prepare documents. From

---

doenus (Dado): "Annulum regis adeptus." We have the signature of Audoenus (Dado) on a charter (Paris, Archives Nationales, K 1, no. 5); see Lauer and Samaran, *Les diplômes originaux*, pl. 4.

426 See A. Giry, *Manuel de diplomatique* (Paris, 1894), pp. 708ff., for the referendary's duties; see also L. Levillain, "La souscription de chancellerie dans les diplômes mérovingiens," *MA* 15 (1911): 101ff.

427 Only the royal documents are available in a good edition (Lauer and Samaran, *Les diplômes originaux*).

428 Jeanne Vielliard, *Le latin des diplômes royaux et des chartes privées de l'époque mérovingienne* (Paris, 1927). A comparison of this learned work with that of P. Brillat, "La langue des inscriptions monétaires mérovingiennes," in *Positions des Thèses, Ecole de Chartes* (Paris, 1935), reveals that the language of the minters was closer to the spoken tongue.

429 Vielliard, *Le latin des diplômes royaux*, pp. 107, 119, 121, 122, 132; D. Norberg, "Erudition et spéculation dans la langue latine médiévale," *ALMA* 22 (1952): 5–16.

430 Julien Havet, *Oeuvres*, vol. 1, *Questions mérovingiennes* (Paris, 1896), pp. 313ff. Havet, while demonstrating this fact, refused to believe that the redactors were aware of what they were doing; this is difficult to prove.

431 Hartmann, *Geschichte*, 2: 70, had already noted this fact when he studied the letters the Merovingian kings sent to the emperors. See also A. Uddholm, "Les traits dialectaux de la langue des actes mérovingiens et le formulaire de Marculf," *ALMA* 25 (1955): 47ff.

432 Asclepiodotus, redactor of an edict of Guntram and of a decree of Childebert II (*MGH, Capit.* I, 10 and 15), had a style that was remarkable for the period. Karl August Eckhardt, the editor of the *Pactus legis salicae* (Göttingen, 1954), p. 171, attributes to this rhetor the brief prologue to the Salic law.

433 Marculf, *Form.*, preface (*MGH, Leg. sect. V*, p. 38).

some recent studies, we now know that the Merovingian chancellery inherited the customs of the provincial offices of the Empire.[434] The referendary probably had documents from the Roman period in his archives because the tone of some royal diplomas recalls that of imperial edicts.[435] The apprentice notary practiced with these models and, in addition, had collections of formulas at his disposal, as we have already indicated. The most famous Frankish formulary is that of Marculf, which contains ninety-two documents gathered together by a monk for a bishop named Landericus.[436] In his preface, the author remarked that he included documents originally intended only as models for teaching, thereby justifying the simplicity of his style.[437] His testimony is reinforced by a note added to three manuscripts of the formulary that takes us right into the schoolroom: a master complains of a young pupil who could not write well, was unable to fill the page in the specified time, and committed solecisms.[438] Marculf thus seems to have been the master of a notarial school. But where did he teach? Some have placed him at the head of an episcopal school that trained future notaries. Others have more correctly supposed that he taught in royal circles, since he seems to have known the usages of the Merovingian chancellery.[439] Perhaps he was a former royal notary who had retired

---

[434] Jean Mallon, *L'écriture de la chancellerie impériale romaine* (Salamanca, 1948); Classen, "Kaiserreskript und Königsurkunde," *Archiv für Diplomatik* 2 (1956): 23ff.

[435] The beginning of the edict of Chlothar II (died 629) (*MGH, Capit.*, I, 18) can be compared with *Novel* 26 of Valentinian III as it appears in Alaric's *Breviary* (in *Lex Romana Visigothorum*, ed. Hänel).

[436] Marculf, *Form.*, preface (p. 37). This Landericus was the bishop of Paris according to some or the bishop of Meaux according to others. See L. Levillain, "Le formulaire de Marculf et la critique moderne," *BECh* 84 (1923): 21–91; Buchner, *Die Rechtsquellen*, pp. 51ff.; and, more recently, Alf Uddholm, *Formulae Marculfi: Etudes sur la langue et le style* (Uppsala, 1953), and Franz Beyerle, "Das Formel-Schulbuch Markulfs," in *Aus Verfassungs- und Landesgeschichte: Festschrift zum 70. Geburtstag von Theodor Mayer*, ed. Heinrich Büttner, Otto Feger, and Bruno Meyer, 2 vols. (Lindau, 1954–55), 2: 365–89. Historians have not even been able to agree on a date for the formulary. Some date it 650, while others prefer a date around 720–30.

[437] Marculf, *Form.*, preface (p. 37): "Sed ego non talibus viris [men of letters and those skilled in the art of writing] . . . sed ad exercenda initia puerorum ut potui aperte et simpliciter scripsi."

[438] Ibid., p. 32: "Item alio dicatu ad jovenis nescientes scripturas: Miror prorsus tam prolixa tempora aut nullum me sermonem pagene consecutum, cujus aeloquia vestri velud ad verba dictantium polluti, mutuati caeras afferunt, currunt articolis falsitatis; sed ubi venitur ad revolvendum, delisse magis quam scripisse pro solicissimum solicissimo referet; quando sperabam capitola epistolae finisse, nec inciperat in primo." See Karl Zeumer, "Ueber die älteren fränkischen Formelsammlungen," *NA* 6 (1881): 21ff., for this text.

[439] W. John, "Formale Beziehungen der privaten Schenkungsurkunden Italiens und des Frankenreiches und die Wirksamkeit der Formulare," *AFU* 14 (1936): 1ff.

to a monastery—he said he was almost seventy years old[440]—and had provided a bishop with models of documents he had once drawn up for apprentice notaries.

Notaries and, to a greater extent, future referendaries also had to learn stenography. Originally, the *notarius* was one who mastered the *notae*, Tironian notes which are found in more than one Merovingian diploma and later in Carolingian documents.[441] We should note too that another method of abbreviation, syllabic tachygraphy, was used for new words not found in classical lexicons.[442]

It was not enough that the referendary know only administrative practices; he also had to know law, specifically Roman law. No traces of theoretical instruction in law have survived. The biographer of Desiderius noted that the young man learned Roman law when he came to court,[443] which would seem to imply that his knowledge was acquired by practical experience. A few hagiographic texts mention the skill of certain young men at unravelling suits,[444] but true lawyers never appeared at court. Nevertheless, Roman law was not forgotten— as royal diplomas and edicts,[445] bills of sale, and wills attest—at least until the beginning of the eighth century.[446] Authors of formularies cited Alaric's *Breviary* and the *Interpretatio*[447] and must have had at their disposal texts of the *Theodosian Code* or of the *Breviary*, of which several manuscripts from this period have come down to us.[448]

[440] Marculf, *Form.*, preface (pp. 36–37): "Cum fere septuaginta aut amplius annos expleam vivendi, et nec jam tremula ad scribendum manus est apta."

[441] Giry, *Manuel de diplomatique*, p. 522.

[442] See the following studies by Maurice Jusselin, a specialist on Tironian notes: "Notes tironiennes dans les diplômes mérovingiens," *BECh* 68 (1908): 481–508; "La transmission des ordres à la chancellerie mérovingienne d'après les souscriptions en notes tironiennes," ibid. 74 (1913): 67–73. See also A. Mentz, "Die tironischen Noten," *AFU* 17 (1941): 222ff.; Emile Chatelain, *Introduction à la lecture des notes tironiennes* (Paris, 1900); and Maurice Prou, *Manuel de paléographie* (Paris, 1924), pp. 123ff.

[443] *Vita sancti Desiderii*, 1 (MGH, SRM, IV, 564): "Contubernii regalis adulcicens se indedit dignatibus hac deinde legum romanarum indagatione studium dedit."

[444] *Vita Lifardi*, ASOB, I, 154: "Erat in causarum temporalium legibus discretor praecipuus"; *Vita Ebrulfi*, ibid., 354: "Oratoris facundia praeditus ad agendas causas inter aulicos residebat doctissimus."

[445] See J. Gaudemet, "Survivances romaines dans le droit de la monarchie franque du Ve au Xe siècle," *RHD* 23 (1955): 149–206.

[446] See Burgundofara's will of 632 (Pardessus, 2: 15), which has been studied by Jean Guérout, "Le testament de sainte Fare: Matériaux pour l'étude et l'édition critique de ce document," *RHE* 60 (1965): 761–821. See also Bertramnus of Le Mans' will of 614, in *Actus pontificum Cenomannis*, ed. Busson and Ledru, pp. 103–41.

[447] See *Form. Tur.*, 11 and 24 (MGH, *Leg. sect.* V, pp. 141, 149), and Louis Stouff, "L'interprétation de la loi romaine des Wisigoths dans les formules et les chartes du VIe au XIe siècles," in *Mélanges Fitting* (1907), 2: 165.

[448] Sixth- and seventh-century manuscripts conserved in Paris (Bibliotheque Nationale,

Certainly, notaries no longer understood the nuances of Roman legislation when they drew up this or that prescription adapting it to the usage of their times.[449] Perhaps, though, their ignorance has been exaggerated: studies of wills from Merovingian Gaul have shown that, despite a fatal obscurity, the redactors remained faithful to the essential principles of Roman law.[450]

The court provided a choice education for youngsters. By passing their tests, they could earn the esteem of the king and thus be entrusted with important duties in the central government or in a county.[451] Could they also acquire a certain *art de vivre* in this environment?

Perhaps a too serious reading of the hagiographers has resulted in a bad press for the Merovingian court. Hagiographers, in order to enhance the memories of their heroes, often showed them trying to flee from a court where they had been placed by their parents, sometimes against their wills.[452] They recalled all the dangers that lay in wait at court for the soul of a youth called to a more saintly life.[453] The Merovingian court, of course, was a reflection of the king who presided over it —brutality could reign there and debauchery sometimes must have been rife. Worried mothers, separated from their sons, thought the worst. In the letters Desiderius of Cahors' mother sent to him, she suggested the conduct he ought to maintain toward the king and his friends (*contubernales*) and begged him "to remain chaste above all."[454] Youth, eager to live and to enjoy itself, certainly had an important impact on

---

lat. 9643 and 4568) and in Berlin (Berl., 159) come from Lyon (see Mommsen and Meyer's edition of the *Theodosian Code, Theodosiani libri XVI*, 1: lxii). Cologne, ms. 212, from the seventh century, contains Valentinian's *Novels*; see Friedrich Maassen, *Geschichte der Quellen* . . . , 1 (Graz, 1870): 574.

[449] See Stouff, "L'interprétation de la loi romaine," p. 165, and Dirk Peter Blok, "Les formules de droit romain dans les actes privés du haut Moyen Age," in *Miscellanea mediaevalia in memoriam Jan Frederik Niermeyer* (Groningen, 1967), pp. 17–28.

[450] G. Chevrier, "Déclin et renaissance du testament en droit bourguignon du VIIᵉ au XIIᵉ siècle," *Mémoire de la Société pour l'histoire du droit des institutions des anciens pays bourguignons comtois et romands*, 9–10 (1943–44); idem, "Civilisation juridique de la Bourgogne mérovingienne," in *Etudes mérovingiennes* (Paris, 1953), pp. 23ff.

[451] Syagrius was sent as a *judex* to Marseille (*Vita sancti Desiderii, MGH, SRM*, IV, 564), as was Bonitus (*Vita Boniti, MGH, SRM*, VI, 121, l. 1).

[452] *Vita Ansberti*, pp. 179–91. This life is quite late but still useful. See the anonymous review note in *AB* 19 (1900): 234–35.

[453] *Vita Wandregisili*, 5 and 6 (*MGH, SRM*, V, 15–16).

[454] *Vita sancti Desiderii, MGH, SRM*, IV, 569–70: "Deum jugiter in mente habeas; mala opera quae Deus hodit nec consentias nec facias; regi sis fidelis, contubernales diligas." In a second letter, she wrote: "Caritatem circa omnes tenete, castitatem supra omnia custodite." In concluding, she offered to send him whatever he needed at court: "De speciebus vero quae vobis in palatio sunt necessariae, nobis per epistolam vestram significate et continuo in Dei nomine dirigemus."

the Merovingian court. Older counselors worried about this: Remigius of Reims had already warned sixteen-year-old King Clovis "to enjoy yourself with your friends but to discourse with the elders."[455] A century and a half later, the bishop who exhorted five-year-old King Clovis II or—more likely—Sigebert III, his older brother by four years, gave the same advice: be suspicious of those who please and consult instead your counselors "like a child who wisely wants to learn his letters." He should listen "to the one who, after him, directs the palace," the mayor, and in another useful bit of advice, "he should preserve chastity in marriage."[456]

In this lively atmosphere, there was room for diversions of a high quality. Games, stories, anything relaxing was welcome at court.[457] Fortunatus found a pleasant atmosphere in which to exercise his worldly talents when he came to Sigebert's court in 566. His poem to Childebert —from which the line "Florum flos florens, florea flore fluens" comes— was very much a kind of parlor game.[458] In some ways, Fortunatus was the Ennodius of the sixth century, since he too was an Italian, a cleric, and even a bishop, and he also delighted in the compliments of flatterers and the respect of the important and of kings. Read his verse on Queen Ultrogotha's garden.[459] Does it not bring to mind Ennodius' verse on Theodoric's garden?[460] In Fortunatus we see the reflection of a court that tried to be civilized.[461]

This ideal passed to the following generation, when the court still enjoyed brilliant splendor under Chlothar II and Dagobert.[462] The young men educated with Dagobert, as we have seen, retained a fond memory of this period. Later, they would allude to this time among

---

[455] Remigius, *Ep.* 2 (*MGH, Ep.*, III, 113, l. 29): "Cum juvenibus joca, cum sensibus tracta, si vis regnare nobilis judicare."

[456] *Ep.* 15 (*MGH, Ep.*, III, 458): "Juvenum quidem qui tibi proximi assistunt cauto ordine eorum verba recipe. Jocularis qui curiales sermones habet ad loquendum? Ne libenter eum audias; et quando tu cum sapientibus, locutus fueris aut cum tuis ministerialibus bonas fabulas habueris, joculares taceant." Ibid., p. 460: "Tu vero conserva unius thori castitatem."

[457] *Vita Aredii, ASOB*, I, 349: "Inutilia reputans, ut vere erant, palatina declinaret officia et jocas ac fabulas omniaque ludicra gesta quae in aula regia jugiter agebantur."

[458] Fortunatus, *App. carminum, Carm.* V (*MGH, AA*, IV-1, 279, v. 10).

[459] Ibid. VI, 6 (p. 146).

[460] Ennodius, *Carm.* 2, 111 (*MGH, AA*, VII, 214).

[461] Bezzola, 1: 53–54, following Koebner, *Venantius Fortunatus*, p. 33, speaks of *dulcedo* as the first form of "courtoisie." Curtius, p. 510, translated *dulcedo* as "eloquence," which is closer to the true sense of the expression.

[462] Fustel de Coulanges, *La monarchie franque*, p. 138, has already made this observation.

themselves: "How I would like, if time permitted me, to converse with you in the worldly manner we used to in the entourage of the most serene prince Chlothar, when we used to relax by discussing things of no great importance."[463] That is how Desiderius of Cahors evoked the happy days of youth to a friend who had also become a bishop. A poem, perhaps written at court, describes the *saeculares fabulae* which the courtiers told.[464] The mimes and players that can be observed around important families[465] certainly had their place among the princes—all the Barbarian courts had their players, the ancestors of medieval *jongleurs*.[466] The word *jocularis* itself appears at this time, perhaps with the meaning it was to have in the ninth century.[467]

In addition to trivial conversations, we must also mention the national epics, written more for the aristocracy than for the people. Fortunatus spoke offhandedly of the *leudos* Barbarian singers composed.[468] Pseudo-Fredegarius tells us that the reign of Guntram was so prosperous that neighboring peoples sung his praises.[469] Unfortunately, nothing has survived for us to reconstruct a "poetical history of the

---

[463] Desiderius, *Ep.* I, 9 (*MGH, Ep.*, III, 198): "Optarem frequenter si possibilitas adrideret, sacris vestris interesse conloquiis ut sicut nos sub saeculi habitu in contubernio serenissimi Flothari principis mutuis solebamus relevare fabellis." The last word is *fabellis* and not *tabellis*, as Vacandard would have it (*Vie de saint Ouen*, p. 40, following Migne's edition, *PL*, LXXXVII, 253).

[464] *Rhythmi aevi merovingici et carolini*, XLII (*MGH, PAC*, IV-2, 569): "Ymnorum sonus modulantur clerici / Ad aulam regis et potentes personae / Procul exclusit saeculares fabulas." See Norberg, *La poésie latine rythmique*, p. 51, for this poem.

[465] *Vita Audoeni* (*Vita* c), *AB* 5 (1887): 67.

[466] Sidonius mentioned mimes at the Visigothic court at the end of the fifth century (*Ep.* I, 2 [*MGH, AA*, VIII, 2]). See the representation of *jongleurs* on the diptych of the consul Anastasius (517) (Henri Leclercq, "Jongleurs," *DACL*, VII-2, 2641). See as well the *Vita Amandi*, 22 (*MGH, SRM*, V, 444): "quem vulgo mimilogum vocant"; and the *Vita Praejecti*, ibid., p. 245, l. 5. For the Suevian court, see Gregory of Tours, *Mir. Mart.*, V, 7 (*MGH, SRM*, I-2, 651).

[467] See n. 456. I say "perhaps" because, despite Lot's interpretation ("Quels sont les dialectes romans que pouvaient connaître les Carolingiens?" *Romania* 64 [1938]: 436), the word *jocularis*, as used in the text, can mean simply "someone who amuses." For the origin of the *jongleurs*, see Edmond Faral, *Les jongleurs en France au Moyen Age* (Paris, 1910).

[468] Fortunatus, *Carm.* VII, 8, v. 63 (*MGH, AA*, IV-1, 163):

> Romanusque lyra, plaudat tibi barbarus harpa . . .
> Nos tibi versiculos, dent barbara carmina leudos.

A capitulary of 789 (*MGH, Capit.*, I, 63) mentions the *winileodos*, who, according to the gloss, were *seculares cantilenae*.

[469] *Chron.*, IV, 1 (*MGH, SRM*, II, 124). This bit of evidence must be compared with a passage from Paul the Deacon, *HL*, I, 27 (*MGH, SRL*, p. 70, l. 4), devoted to the songs in honor of Alboin.

Merovingians."[470] These songs were accompanied by the harp or the cithara. Clovis asked Theodoric to send him a citharist.[471] A cantor and musicians were at Dagobert's court during the following century.[472] At least until the death of Dagobert, the Merovingian court was not yet the sinister place it has often been portrayed as. Rather, its reputation had gone even beyond the borders of Gaul. The widow of King Edwin of Northumbria sent her two children there for their education.[473] After 639, the court suffered from civil wars and recovered its prestige only with the first Carolingians.

IV. LAY EDUCATION IN VISIGOTHIC SPAIN

A. HISTORICAL CONDITIONS

More than one comparison can be made between Gaul and Spain during the sixth century and the first third of the seventh century. The Merovingian and Visigothic kingdoms at that time were the only Barbarian kingdoms which could boast a coherent political organization. The Lombards were still occupied with the difficult conquest of Byzantine Italy; the Anglo-Saxons, their paganism barely behind them, were to remain in a state of anarchy throughout the entire period. Of course, Gaul and Spain experienced various difficulties in the sixth century: the former suffered from the rivalry of princes and successive divisions, the second from the conflict between Arians and Catholics and from Byzantine interference.[474] At the opening of the seventh cen-

---

[470] Godefroid Kurth, *Histoire poétique des Mérovingiens* (Paris, 1893), tried to find epic themes in the chroniclers' tales; no one else has followed his lead. National songs did exist, and Charlemagne wanted to put them in writing; see Einhard, *Vita Caroli*, 29 (in *Eginhard: Vie de Charlemagne*, ed. and trans. Louis Halphen, 3rd rev. ed. [Paris, 1947], p. 82). For the birth of the epic, see René Louis, *De l'histoire à la légende: Girart, comte de Vienne, dans les chansons de geste*, 2 vols. (Auxerre, 1947); Italo Siciliano, *Les origines des chansons de geste: Théories et discussions*, French trans. P. Antonetti (Paris, 1951); and Ramón Menéndez Pidal, *La Chanson de Roland et la tradition épique des Francs*, French trans. Irénee-Marcel Cluzel, 2nd rev. ed. (Paris, 1960), pp. 3–50.

[471] See the texts of Cassiodorus and Fortunatus cited above, nn. 270 and 468. The tomb of a lyre player has been found in Cologne; see Fritz Fremersdorf, "Zwei wichtige Frankengräber aus Köln," *Jahrbuch für Prähistorische and Ethnographische Kunst* 15–16 (1941–42), p. 133, and Joachim Werner, "Leier und harpe im germanischen Frühmittelalter," *Festschrift P. Mayer*, 1 (1954): ix, 15.

[472] *Vita Eligii*, II, 6 (*MGH, SRM*, IV, 697): "Maurinus . . . cantor . . . in regis palatio laudatus." *Vita Ansberti*, p. 181: "Cum . . . diversa musicae artis in chordis et in tibiis instrumenta personantia audiret."

[473] Bede, *HE, II*, 20 (Plummer ed., p. 126): "Misit in Galliam nutriendos regi Daegoberecto qui erat amicus illius, ibique ambo in infantia defuncti."

[474] Menéndez Pidal, *HE*, 3: 95ff.

tury, however, both countries were calm. The reigns of Chlothar II and Dagobert I, from 613 to 639, led to a period of relative prosperity. In Spain, the annexation of the Suevian kingdom, the conversion of Reccared to Catholicism in 589, and then the reconquest of the Byzantines ushered in the "Isidorian" period—so called from the name of the most illustrious bishop of Spain.

Exchanges between the two countries were more frequent than is usually thought.[475] The political tension born of Frankish greed in Septimania did not stand in the way of numerous marriages between Visigothic and Frankish princes and princesses, each of which presented the opportunity for exchanges of embassies.[476] Merchants and pilgrims circulated by land and sea between the two kingdoms.[477] Only in the middle of the seventh century when Spain turned in on itself before the Arab conquest did contacts between the two countries diminish.

Thus, parallel study of the two countries does seem justified. We will see, in fact, that in the domain of the culture and education of laymen that the parallelism is striking, especially if one compares Spain and southern Gaul.

Spain, like Roman Gaul, preserved the impress of antique civilization. We have already seen that the Visigothic royalty had been under the political influence of Italy until the mid-sixth century. The troubles following the death of Theudis in 548 would have led to the disappearance of Roman survivals had not the Byzantine settlement in southern Spain helped preserve them. While continuously fighting the "Romans," the Visigothic kings of Toledo imitated them.[478] Towns had no doubt been unable to maintain all their institutions, but they were

---

[475] J. Fontaine, *IS*, pp. 835ff., rightly says that Gaul played no role in the development of Isidore's culture, but he contrasts the two kingdoms too absolutely. He admits that bonds existed only between southeastern Gaul and Spain. We have already seen the influence Provençals had in Austrasian circles, however.

[476] See Gregory of Tours, *HF*, VI, 33, 34; VII, 10 (pp. 304, 332); Pseudo-Fredegarius, *Chron.*, IV, 30 (ibid., II, 132).

[477] A. Lewis, "Le commerce et la navigation sur les côtes atlantiques de la Gaule du Ve au VIIe siècle," *MA* 59 (1953): 249–98. Thanks to Spanish pilgrims who came to venerate the tomb of Saint Martin, Gregory of Tours was particularly well informed on what was happening in Spain; see *HF*, V, 38; VI, 18; IX, 14 (pp. 243, 287, 428); *Mir. Mart.*, I, 11 (*MGH, SRM*, I-2, 594); *Glor. confess.*, 81 (ibid., p. 800).

[478] For these borrowings, see Menéndez Pidal, *HE*, 3: 212ff.; Eduardo Pérez-Pujol, *Historia de las instituciones sociales de la España Goda*, 4 vols. (Valencia, 1896), 2: 178; and Paul Goubert, *L'Espagne byzantine* (Paris, 1947), p. 139. Certain Roman institutions survived into the Middle Ages; see Claudio Sánchez-Albornoz, "El *Tributum quadragesimale*: Supervivencias fiscales romanas en Galicia," in *Mélanges Halphen*, pp. 645–58.

still important centers of social life. Some seventh-century texts still refer to the curiales and senators in the towns.[479] Roman monuments in Seville and Cordova, Tarragona, Barcelona, Segovia, and Merida—the Rome of Spain—and many other towns were still kept up and used. Visigothic kings even carried on the work of Rome and founded new towns like Reccopolis, Vitoria, and Olite.[480] Merchants in these urban centers were in contact with Mediterranean countries, especially with the Byzantine Empire. Byzantine ships came into two important ports in western Spain: Santarém on the Tagus and Merida on the Guadiana (Map 6). A Greek colony sprung up in the second of these towns, where Paul, a Greek physician, became bishop at the end of the sixth century and was succeeded by his nephew, who came to Spain with Greek merchants.[481] The eastern and southern shores of Spain were no different: Jews, Greeks, and Syrians formed a large part of the population of Narbonne in 589.[482] Greek inscriptions found in Lusitania prove that similar colonies existed in that province.[483] Greeks came to Spain to live until the end of the seventh century. King Erwig was even the son of one of them.[484]

Greek influences, whether they came directly from the East or through the intermediary of Byzantine Italy, were felt in the economic, artistic, and religious domains[485] and enabled Spain to remain tied to the antique tradition much longer. Spain's culture would be profoundly affected.

---

[479] See Claudio Sánchez-Albornoz, *Ruina y extinción del municipio romano en España y instituciones que le reemplazan* (Buenos Aires, 1943), pp. 44, 107; idem, "El gobierno de las ciudades en España del siglo V al X," *Settimane*, 6: 359ff.; J. M. Lacarra, "Panorama de la historia urbana en la peninsula ibérica desde el siglo V al X," ibid., 319ff. Braulio's *Vita Aemiliani* mentions senators several times (chaps. XI, XV, XVI, XVII [PL, LXXX, 707ff.]). See also Eugen Ewig, "Résidences et capitales pendant le Haut Moyen Age," *RH* 230 (1963): 31ff.

[480] Menéndez Pidal, *HE*, 3: 102, 115, 339.

[481] *Vitas sanctorum*, IV, 1 (Garvin ed., pp. 160, 168).

[482] Mansi, IX, 1013.

[483] Vives, *Inscripciones*, pp. 141–43. See J. Fontaine, *IS*, p. 848.

[484] *Adelfonsi Magni Chronicon*, chap. 3 (p. 479), cited by Roberto Grosse, *Las fuentes de la época visigoda y bizantinas* (Barcelona, 1947), p. 339. Erwig's father, Ardabastus, could have taken refuge at Toledo after having been expelled by the emperor.

[485] See Helmut Schlunk, "Relaciones entre la peninsula ibérica y Bizancio durante la época visigoda," *Archivo español de arqueologia* 18 (1945): 177–204; J. Fontaine, *IS*, pp. 846–48; Karl Friedrich Stroheker, "Das spanische Westgotenreich und Byzanz," in *Germanetum und Spätantike* (Zurich, 1965), pp. 205–45; J. N. Hillgarth, "Coins and Chronicles: Propaganda in Sixth-Century Spain and the Byzantine Background," *Historia* 15 (1966): 483–508.

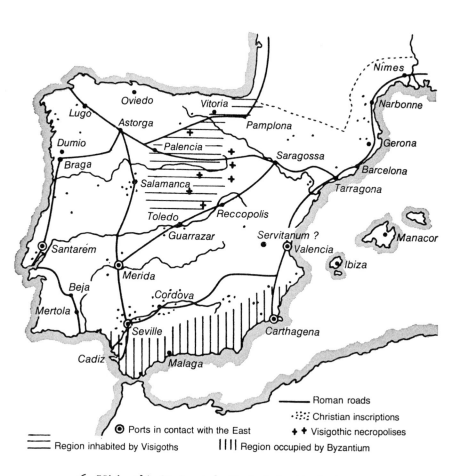

Roman roads
····· Christian inscriptions
◉ Ports in contact with the East
✦ ✚ Visigothic necropolises
═══ Region inhabited by Visigoths
||||| Region occupied by Byzantium

6. Visigothic Spain at the End of the Sixth Century

B. The Maintenance of Written Civilization

Opening the *Lex Visigothorum*, the twelve books Recceswinth had written in 654, we observe that the written document was still an intermediary of social relations, as it had been in Roman law. Let us take several examples. An entire chapter is devoted to wills, either those which a soldier or a traveler might draw up himself or those dictated to a notary and subscribed by witnesses.[486] There is a reference to sales made *per scripturam*, which were precisely defined by law. There is a reminder that proof by oath can be required only in the absence of written proof.[487] Judges summoned ligitants by means of letters.[488] By a letter, a slave was freed, a converted Jew made his profession of faith, and a widow took a vow of chastity.[489]

Bills of sale, donations, and wills were perhaps even registered in municipal offices, as in southern Gaul. We know of one such office at Cordova which housed the *principales*, the *magistri*, and a *curator*.[490] Documents were also kept in personal archives,[491] which allowed scripts to be compared (*contropatio*) as mentioned in the law.[492] Unfortunately, all documents, public as well as private, have been lost as a result of the fragility of papyrus, in addition to the disorganization following the Arab invasion, and are known today only through copies.[493] All we have left are models contained in the Visigothic formulary, which,

---

[486] *Leges Visigoth.*, II, 5 (*MGH, Leg. sect. I*, I, 105): "De scripturis valituris et infirmandis ac defunctorum volontatibus conscribendis." See also Isidore, *Origines*, V, xxiv (ed. Lindsay).

[487] *Leges Visigoth.*, X, 1, 19 (p. 390).

[488] Ibid., II, 1, 17 (p. 65): "De his admoniti judicis epistola vel sigillo ad judicem venire contemnunt."

[489] Ibid., II, 1, 22 (p. 71); II, 5 (pp. 105ff.); XII, 3, 14 (p. 442); Council of Toledo, X (656), c. 4 (Mansi, XI, 35).

[490] *Form. Visigoth.*, 25 (*MGH, Leg. sect. V*, p. 587). Sánchez-Albornoz, *Ruina y extinción*, p. 101, thinks that the formula reproduces a document of the fifth century, but his proof is not convincing. Isidore described municipal institutions in the present tense in his *Origines*, IX, iv, 25.

[491] *Leges Visigoth.*, II, 5, 17 (p. 116, l. 19): "Hec querenda ab utrisque partibus in scriniis domesticis instrumenta cartarum." The freedmen of the Church had to present their enfranchisement documents to the new bishop; see Council of Toledo, VI (638), c. 9 (Mansi, X, 666).

[492] *Leges Visigoth.*, II, 4, 3; II, 5, 17 (pp. 95, 116); for the *contropatio*, or comparison of scripts, see Karl Zeumer, "Zum westgothischen Urkundenwesen," *NA* 24 (1899): 38.

[493] One could read a diploma of Chindaswinth conserved at the monastery of Bierzo as late as the eighteenth century; see A. Millarès Carlo, *Tratado de paleografía española*, 2nd ed. (Madrid, 1932), p. 45. Possibly a fragment from a charter of the first half of the eighth century is still extant; see Bern palimpsest, Bern, Burgerbibliothek, AA, 90, 18, ed. Bruckner and Marichal, *ChLA*, I (1954), no. 2. But is this fragment from the Visigothic or the Asturian period?

like the formularies of Gaul and even influenced by one of them,[494] reproduces forty-six private documents. The dates of some of the documents show the formulary to have been composed by a notary of Cordova during Sisebut's time.[495]

The only original documents we possess are about a hundred sixth-
and seventh-century slates found between Salamanca and Avila and
covered with cursive script very reminiscent of the traditional Roman
cursive. The interpretation of these slates, which have not been studied
as a whole,[496] is quite difficult: one is thought to contain a note relating
to tolls; another bears a letter of an intendant to his lord concerning
problems of economic organization; a third concerns a legal action.
Christian formulas for prayers and incantations also appear on the
slates. All of this proves that writing was in current usage in this part
of Spain, as it must have been elsewhere, at least in the cities.[497]

Of course, not all laymen could write. The laws of the Visigoths,
like those of Justinian, provided for the fixing of a seal at the bottom
of documents in the place of autograph signatures.[498] In one formula,
a donor appealed to a lettered friend "because he did not know his
letters."[499] Such an avowal shows very well that this case was an individual one. Laymen who participated in the various councils at
Toledo left their signatures beside those of clerics.[500] This practice
lasted until the end of the Visigothic period, which, unlike the Mero-

---

494 For the influence of the Angers formulary on the Visigothic formulary, see Schwerin,
"Sobre las relaciones entre las formulas visigoticas y las Andecavas," *AHDE* 9 (1932).
Here is another proof of contacts between Gaul and Spain.
495 Formulas 19 and 25 date from Sisebut's reign. While Alvaro D'Ors ("La territorialidad del derecho de los Visigodos," *Settimane*, 3: 408) did not believe that these
formulas were authentic, M. C. Diaz y Diaz ("Un document privé de l'Espagne wisigothique sur ardoise," *SM*, 3rd ser. 1 [1960]: 52–71) has proven the contrary by comparing
the text of the formulas with the text of the slate which he dates to the reign of Reccared.
496 They have been partially published by Manuel Gómez-Moreno, *Documentación
goda en pizarra* (Madrid, 1966). See also A. G. Palacios, M. Diaz, and J. Maluquer de
Motes, "Excavaciones en la 'Lancha de Trigo' Diego Alvaro, Avila," *Zephyrus* 9 (1958):
59–78, and especially Diaz y Diaz's article cited in the previous note and his "Los
documentos hispano-visigóticos sobre pizarra," *SM*, 3rd ser. 7 (1966): 75–107.
497 One could also mention the graffiti from Tarrasa published by Vives (*Inscripciones*,
no. 322).
498 *Leges Visigoth.*, VI, 1, 6 (*MGH, Leg. sect. I*, I, 256, l. 8): "Eventibus signis aut
suscriptionibus." On the question of the *signa*, see Zeumer, *NA* 24 (1899): 13–28. See
also, *Fragmenta Gaudenzia*, 15 (*MGH, Leg. sect. I*, I, 471, l. 18): "Si autem ipse donator
et testes litteras nesciunt unusquisque signum faciat."
499 *Form. Visigoth.*, 7 (*MGH, Leg. sect. V*, p. 579): "Ill. rogitus a domino et fratre ill.
quia ipse literas ignorat, pro eum scriptor accessi et hanc oblationem . . . subscripsi."
500 There is but one *signum*—that of *vir. ill.* Gusin—by a layman among the several
subscriptions of the third council; see Mansi, IX, 986. The Visigothic slate which Diaz y
Diaz studied bears judges' subscriptions.

vingian period in Gaul, never saw the *signum* replace the subscription.

Lastly, we should note that, again unlike Gaul, there were no regions in Spain where writing was completely absent—Vives' map of Visigothic inscriptions is eloquent on this point.[501] In certain zones where Roman civilization penetrated more deeply and where towns were more numerous, there is a greater density of inscriptions: Betica, southern Lusitania, Galicia, the former Suevian kingdom, and the Mediterranean shoreline. Zones devoid of epigraphs correspond to the islets that were traditionally barren of inhabitants.

The survival of written civilization is the only proof of the existence of elementary instruction in Spain, but it is proof enough. As in Ostrogothic Italy, the schoolmaster appears nowhere in our texts, but that does not mean that he had disappeared. The study of letters (*litteratio*), which Isidore considered a *disciplina*,[502] could be given by private masters or parents. In addition, some clerics and monks placed themselves at the service of families whose children did not embrace a religious career. Clerical and monastic schools thus contributed to the maintenance of lay instruction.

C. INSTRUCTION IN MEDICINE AND LAW

The *Lex Visigothorum* is again our best source for the medical and legal culture of laymen, a culture which lasted longer in Spain than in Gaul.

One of the chapters of Visigothic law devoted to physicians and the sick mentions the fees due physicians.[503] If Isidore of Seville is to be believed, physicians were quite demanding[504]—the profession was so lucrative that clerics sought to practice it despite canons to the contrary.[505] At Merida, there was a dearth of surgeons even though the town claimed many physicians—among them a Reccared whose epitaph

---

[501] Vives, *Inscripciones*, unpaginated map.

[502] Isidore, *Origines*, I, iii, 1. J. Fontaine, *IS*, p. 58, thinks that this "promotion" can be explained by the growing number of illiterates. I do not think that Isidore wished to enroll elementary learning among the liberal arts. Elsewhere (*Sent.*, III, 13, 10 [*PL*, LXXXII, 688]) he made a fine distinction between "common letters"—that is, the alphabet —and "liberal letters," which Fontaine himself has noted (*IS*, p. 61). In the passage from the *Origines*, *disciplina* means learning in general.

[503] *Leges Visigoth.*, XI, 1 (p. 400): "De medicis et aegrotis"; ibid., XI, 1, 5: "Si quis medicus hipocisim de oculis abstulerit . . . V solidos pro suo beneficio consequatur."

[504] *Versus Isidori*, in *Isidor-Studien*, ed. Charles H. Beeson (Munich, 1913), p. 164: "Pauperis attende, medice, censum atque potentis / Dispar conditio dispari habenda modo est / Si fuerit dives, sit iusta occasio lucri; / Si pauper, merces sufficit una tibi."

[505] See Garcia Villada, *Historia eclesiástica*, 2, pt. 1: 265, and Joseph N. Garvin in the commentary of his edition of the *Vitas sanctorum*, pp. 367–68.

has come down to us.[506] A senator in the town had to appeal to Bishop Paul, a former Greek doctor, to deliver his wife by Caesarian section.[507] Medical learning passed from master to disciple. Visigothic law stipulated precisely the salary a physician could demand to teach his skill.[508] As with other kinds of instruction during this period, medical education was more practical than theoretical. Medical manuals, however, still circulated in Spain. Isidore of Seville, who devoted Book IV of the *Origines* to medicine, that "second philosophy,"[509] used the works of Caelius Aurelianus, Cassius Felix, and Pseudo-Soranus. Manuscripts of these African physicians, as well as African translations of Greek medical works,[510] helped to preserve the tradition of antique medicine in Spain. Perhaps the Arabs who were to come to Spain in the eighth century would benefit from this tradition.

Was instruction in the law here as in other Barbarian kingdoms also more practical than theoretical? This is not certain. The political and administrative organization of the Visigothic kingdom required more solid legal learning than was demanded elsewhere. Thanks to the *Lex Visigothorum*, which describes lay tribunals, we can see that judges and lawyers still functioned.[511] Counts were accompanied by *auditores*, who must have performed the same duty as Gallo-Roman *boni homines* in interpreting the law.[512] Roman law was applied in Spain, where, more than elsewhere, the conversion of the kings, the growing influence of the Church, and Byzantine influences[513] gave it new strength. Copies

---

[506] Vives, *Inscripciones*, no. 228.

[507] *Vitas sanctorum*, ed. Garvin, p. 162: "Cui cum multi medici diversa adhiberent." Ibid., p. 166: "Mira subilitate incisionem subtilissimam subtili cum ferramento fecit atque ipsum infantulum . . . abstraxit."

[508] *Leges Visigoth.*, XI, 1, 7 (*MGH, Leg. sect. I,* I, 402): "De mercede discipuli. Si quis medicus famulum in doctrina susceperit, pro beneficio suo duodecim solidos consequatur."

[509] Isidore of Seville, *Origines*, IV, xiii, 5. This definition was borrowed from Tertullian, *De anima*, II, 6 (*PL*, II, 650).

[510] See O. Probst, "Isidors Schrift De Medicina," *Archiv für Geschichte der Medizin* 8 (1916): 22–38, and J. Fontaine, *IS*, pp. 666ff.

[511] *Leges Visigoth.*, II, 1, 11 (*MGH, Leg. sect. I,* I, 60), describes the tribunals' recesses at Easter, in summer, and in autumn. See Isidore, *Sent.*, III, 56, "de Causidicis," for lawyers, and ibid., III, 52, 2, for the judges' learning (*PL*, LXXXIII, 724, 727, 728).

[512] *Leges Visigoth.*, II, 2, 2 (p. 80).

[513] Was Justinian's Code known in Visigothic Spain? The question has been debated: See Carlo Guido Mor, "Per la storia dei libri giustinianei nell'età preirneriana," in *Atti del Congresso internazionale di diritto romano e di storia del diritto (Verona, 27-28-29-IX-1948)*, ed. Guiscardo Moschetti, 4 vols. (Milan, 1951–53), 1: 281–94, and A. Larraona A. Tabea, "El derecho justinianeo en España," *Atti del Congresso internazionale di diritto romano (Bologna e Roma, XVII–XXVII aprile, MCMXXXIII)*, 4 vols. (Pavia, 1934–35), 2: 85–182. Isidore perhaps knew Justinian's *Pandects*; see J. Fontaine, *IS*, p. 82.

of private documents refer to major Roman laws and preserve the form of Roman documents.[514]

Judges and bureaucrats must have had access to manuals; even Isidore of Seville used books intended for law students when he wrote the chapters in his *Origines*.[515] Book V of his work, in turn, became a legal manual which passed into Italy and Gaul.[516] The *Lex Visigothorum* was a commercial publication whose maximum price was established by the king.[517] One studied law and meditated upon its significance. The first chapters of the *Lex Visigothorum*, a law code which Montesquieu judged so poorly in his disdain for the "Gothic" age, ought to be read.[518] They concern the legislator and the law, and we can read in them an effort to transcend the practical aspects of the law and to meditate on its nature that we find nowhere else in the West.

It has been thought that laws were drawn up by clerics rather than by laymen—Braulio of Saragrossa, for example, is supposed to have played an important role in the elaboration of Recceswinth's Code. This hypothesis is actually based on one passage in a letter from the king to Braulio, in which Braulio was asked to revise a manuscript full of mistakes.[519] It is not clear whether this *codex* is the Code. Saragossa's scriptorium received more than one book, and Recceswinth, a lettered king, could very well have sent Braulio something else. When kings wanted laws revised, they most often consulted laymen.[520] There undoubtedly was a growing tendency in Spain to confuse civil and canon law. Councils legislated religious discipline as well as political questions.[521] But this is still not enough evidence to reserve legal education to clerics alone. Would Isidore of Seville have been the canonist he was

---

[514] See the will of the bishop of Huesca (576) and the donation Deacon Vincent made to the abbot of Asan (551) in Fidel Fita, "Patrologia visigotica," *Boletin de la real academia de la Historia* 49 (1906): 152. See also P. Merea, "Estudios de derecho privado visigotico," *Anuario de historia del derecho español* 16 (1945): 45.

[515] Isidore of Seville, *Origines*, V. The chests in the Seville library contained law books; see *Versus in bibliotheca*, XV (Beeson ed., p. 162). See also H. Kubler, "Isidors Studien," *Hermes* 25 (1890): 505ff., for Isidore's legal sources.

[516] Joseph Tardif, "Un abrégé juridique des Etymologies," in *Mélanges J. Havet* (Paris, 1901), pp. 658–80.

[517] *Leges Visigoth.*, V, 4, 22 (p. 226): "Quo presens liber debeat pretio comparari."

[518] "De legislatore," *Leges Visigoth.*, pp. 38ff. Montesquieu's opinion is repeated and discussed in Lot, *Les invasions germaniques*, p. 183.

[519] Garcia Villada, *Historia eclesiástica*, 2, pt. 2: 187, based on Braulio, *Ep.* 38 and 39, in *El epistolario de San Braulio de Zaragoza*, ed. José Madoz (Madrid, 1941), pp. 172–73.

[520] See Recceswinth's "tomes" in *Leges Visigoth.*, suppl., pp. 472, 474; for Erwig, see ibid., p. 476. King Egica (ibid., p. 483) was the only one to address himself to clergy alone.

[521] Garcia Villada, *Historia eclesiástica*, 2, pt. 1: 107ff.

if knowledge of the law had disappeared from lay circles?[522] In this realm as in others, Isidore's work presupposes the existence of a cultivated lay milieu.

D. The Classical Culture of Aristocrats

It is relatively easy to learn about the culture of laymen in southern Gaul because of the variety of texts at our disposal. The same, however, does not hold for Spain. There are a very few saints' *Lives* and two epistolary collections but no history as well documented as that of Gregory of Tours: Isidore of Seville's immense work does not fulfill our expectations and informs us only very indirectly on lay culture. We can guess the reality but we remain unable to seize it.

For example, Braulio of Saragossa, in the middle of the seventh century, alluded to a book in the library of Count Laurentius, while another text tells us that this library was scattered upon the death of its owner.[523] About Laurentius himself, however, we know nothing. This one example, taken from among many, demonstrates the difficulty of the inquiry.

Until the conversion of Reccared in 589, the Arianism of the Goths was such an unbreakable obstacle between Roman and Visigothic families that there were no contacts between them. We can find some lettered people among Hispano-Romans—such as Duke Claudius, to whom Gregory the Great sent a carefully styled letter[524]—and among Goths converted to Catholicism—like John of Biclarum and Masona of Merida.[525] The fusion between the aristocrats was accomplished during the seventh century.[526] Important Visigothic families who were converted adopted the life style of *senatores*, took Roman names, and

---

[522] Paul Séjourné, *Le dernier Père de l'Eglise, saint Isidore de Séville* (Paris, 1929).

[523] Braulio, *Ep.* 25 (Madoz ed., p. 144): "Sane in tempore apud Laurentium comitem dudum eum fuisse novi"; ibid. 26 (p. 145): "Pro libris Laurentii solliciti fuimus sed quia illo tempore res sicut nostris in dispersionem venit nihil inde investigare postuimus." This Count Laurentius appears to have lived in Toledo. Braulio's correspondent, Abbot Emilian, wrote from that city.

[524] Gregory the Great, *Ep.* IX, 230 (*MGH, Ep.*, II, 226). See *Vitas sanctorum*, V, 10, 7 (Garvin ed., p. 234), for Duke Claudius. The letter which he is supposed to have written to Isidore is undoubtedly partially apocryphal; see Séjourné, *Le dernier Père de l'Eglise*, p. 73. For the Roman aristocracy, see Stroheker, "Spanische Senatoren . . . ," in *Germanentum*, p. 79.

[525] See Schanz, IV-2, 114, for John of Biclarum, and *Vitas sanctorum*, V, 2, 1 (pp. 190ff.), for Masona.

[526] Menéndez Pidal, *HE*, 3: 179: Ramón de Abadal y Vinyals, "A propos du legs visigothique en Espagne," *Settimane*, 5: 541ff.; J. Fontaine, "Conversion et culture chez les Wisigoths d'Espagne," *Settimane*, 14: 87–147.

opened themselves to literary culture. Count Laurentius, who was mentioned above, was not the only cultivated individual. Bishop Renovatus of Merida, a Goth of good family, had been trained in many branches of the arts, according to his biographer.[527] Teudisclus, who lived in Toledo during the mid-seventh century, was renowned for his profane culture.[528] Several important lettered bishops emerged from Gothic families.[529] While the process of fusion in Gaul led to the disappearance of classical culture, in Spain the reverse occurred; as Isidore of Seville wrote, the Barbarians discovered "the purity of the Latin tongue."[530] Several letters written by Count Bulgar, governor of Septimania under King Gundemar (died in 612), have survived.[531] They are very close to the elegant, mannered style of the "artful letters" that lay aristocrats in Gaul were writing at the same time. There is no indication, as some believe, that they were the work of a cleric in the count's entourage.[532] It is not at all surprising that a Visigoth might have written letters like these at the beginning of the seventh century. Braulio of Saragossa's correspondence with Gothic laymen permits us to think that it was the same during the middle of the century: the "honesti, prudentes maturique viri" whose criticism the bishop feared were his friends.[533]

All the lettered men we know, whether Barbarian or Hispano-Roman, gravitated to the court. The Visigothic court (*aula regia*) bears a closer resemblance to the Byzantine court than it does to the Merovingian court. Beginning with Athanagild's reign (554–58), the court was finally located at Toledo, where, thanks to its organization and pomp, it acquired great prestige.[534]

[527] *Vitas sanctorum*, V, 1, 4 (p. 254): "Vir natione gothus generoso stemmate procreatus . . . multis nimirum artium disciplinis existebat eruditus."
[528] *Vita Fructuosi*, 8 (Nock ed., p. 99): "Inter quos unus sophismae intelligentiaeque peritiam indeptus nomine Teudisclus."
[529] Ildefonsus in particular. Braulio could have come from a Roman or a Visigothic family. See C. H. Lynch, *Saint Braulio, Bishop of Saragossa* (Washington, D.C., 1938), pp. 4–5.
[530] Isidore, *Origines*, I, xxxii, 1: "Barbarismus a barbaris gentibus, dum latinae orationis integritatem nescirent."
[531] Count Bulgar, *Ep.* 11–16 (*MGH, Ep.*, III, 677–84).
[532] Bezzola, 1: 80, n. 2. On the other hand, this historian also cites (p. 34) a noble by the name of Wistremir who would have composed Antonina's epitaph, one of the loveliest poetical compositions of the period. In fact, though, this epitaph must have been the work either of Braulio or of an unknown poet. See Madoz, *El epistolario de San Braulio*, p. 8, and especially Diaz y Diaz, *AW*, pp. 36ff.
[533] Braulio, *Ep.* 28, 29, 30 (pp. 146–49); idem, *Vita Aemiliani*, preface (*PL*, LXXX, 699).
[534] For the court, see Claudio Sánchez-Albornoz, *El Aula regia y las asambleas politicas de los godos*, Cuadernos de historia de España, 5 (Buenos Aires, 1946), pp. 5–110.

Unlike the practice at other Barbarian courts, the daughters of aristocrats, as well as their sons, were sent to the Visigothic court. When Fortunatus described Galswintha's departure for Gaul, he mentioned the girls who accompanied the princess.[535] For the seventh century, other sources mention the *domicellae* who lived at the court of Toledo, among whom was the daughter of Count Julian, a victim, so the legend has it, of King Roderic's outrages.[536]

As at the Merovingian court, young aristocrats—the *filii primatum*—should not be confused with the antrustiones, who were called *gardingi* in Spain. These gardingi, whose history has been studied by Claudio Sanchez Albornoz,[537] were closely bound to the king by an oath and comprised the guard of *fideles*, who played an important role in the battle the Visigothic princes waged against the aristocracy. Their education was primarily athletic.[538] The young palatines, in contrast, were destined to fill administrative positions. Some of them could enter the royal chancery and become *comites notariorum*, while future referendaries probably went to a notarial school. A manuscript from Oviedo whose archetype was undoubtedly Visigothic served as a teaching manual for Tironian notes.[539] Thus, the activities of young Visigoths at Toledo must have been very similar to those of young aristocrats in Gaul.

Unfortunately we cannot say more than this because we do not have for Spain anything equivalent to the Merovingian saints' *Lives*. Spanish historians unhesitatingly use an educational treatise attributed to Isidore of Seville. The author, in addressing himself to a prince, describes the first education of a child, insisting on athletic training and on literary, religious, and moral instruction. Although it depends quite heavily on classical Latin writers, the treatise is not without interest—

[535] Fortunatus, *Carm.* VI, 5 (*MGH, AA*, IV-1, 136); Sánchez-Albornoz, *El Aula regia*, p. 70.

[536] Rodrigo Ximénez de Rada, *De Rebus Hispaniae*: "Mos erat tum temporis apud Gothos, ut domicelli et domicellae, magnatum filii, in regali curia nutrirentur" (cited by Sánchez-Albornoz, *El Aula regia*, p. 71).

[537] Claudio Sánchez-Albornoz, *En torno a los orígenes del feudalismo*, 3 vols. (Mendoza, 1942), I, pt. 1: 76ff.

[538] See the allusion to sports in Isidore of Seville, *Hist. Gothorum, Wandalorum, Sueborum*, 54 (*MGH, AA*, XI, 290): "Saepe etiam [Reccared] lacertos movit ubi non magis bella tractasse quam potius gentem quasi in palaestrae ludo pro usu certaminis videtur exercuisse." See also, ibid., *Recapitulatio* (p. 294): "Ludorum certamina usu quotodiano gerunt."

[539] "Incipiunt notas ob eruditione infantum editas ut fertur a Seneca cordubensis poeta" (Mentz, "Die Tironischen Noten," pp. 173–75). We should also note that the Visigothic formulary is also known through an Oviedo manuscript.

but does it belong to Isidore of Seville? So far, no answer is possible. While we await a critical study of the text, we must use it with great prudence.[540]

The originality of the court at Toledo lay in its position not only as a center of education but also as a place where intellectual culture was well received, at least in the seventh century. When the kings were still Arians, they did not appear interested in classical literature, resembling in that respect their predecessors at the end of the fifth century.[541] Leogivild, a warrior prince and dedicated Arian, does not seem to have had an extensive profane culture. At the same time, however, King Miro, a Suevian recently converted to Catholicism, corresponded with Martin of Braga and asked him for a treatise on "moral science."[542] Reccared, the son of Leogivild and the king who led the Visigoths to Catholicism, was perhaps more accessible to classical culture, but he did not have the means to make the court at Toledo an intellectual center. This would come with Sisebut, who became king in 612.

Visigothic kings during this period began to follow in the footsteps of Theodoric the Great by patronizing authors and requesting works from them. Isidore of Seville wrote his *De natura rerum* for Sisebut and his *History of the Goths* for Sisenand.[543] During the middle of the

[540] This text, edited by A. E. Anspach in *RhM* 67 (1912): 556–68, from a Carolingian manuscript, has been reedited by P. Pascal ("The *Institutionum disciplinae* of Isidore of Seville," *Traditio* 13 [1957]: 425–31). To Beeson's arguments in favor of the attribution to Isidore ("The *Institutionum disciplinae* and Pliny the Younger," *CPh* 8 [1913]: 93–98) we can add the contrast between *litterae communes* and the liberal arts, which was familiar to Isidore (see above, n. 502), and a comparison between an expression from this text ("de sanctarum scripturarum campis") and a passage from Sisebut ("per campos divinae legis testimonia," cited below in n. 572). Furthermore, the program proposed for the prince corresponds quite well with what we know of education at the Toledo court. Do the numerous borrowings from the *Panegyric* of Pliny the Younger, an author completely unknown to Isidore, warrant rejecting this work as inauthentic, as J. Fontaine, *IS*, p. 14, argues? A tighter argument is necessary, I think. The arguments I developed in "L'éducation à l'époque wisigothique: Les *Institutionum disciplinae*," *Anales Toledanos* 3 (1971): 171–80, have not convinced Jacques Fontaine: see "Quelques observations sur les *Institutionum disciplinae* pseudo-isidoriennes," in *La Ciudad de Dios* (1968), pp. 617–55.

[541] See above, chap. 2, sect. I.A. We know nothing about Athanagild's culture, but his daughters were educated. See Fortunatus' letter to Galswintha in *Carm.* VI, 5, v. 284 (*MGH, AA,* IV-1, 144).

[542] Martin of Braga, *Formula vitae honestae,* 1 (Barlow ed., p. 236): "Non ignoro clementissime rex flagrantissimam tui animi sitim sapientiae insatiabiliter poculis inhiare eaque te ardenter quibus moralis scientiae rivuli manant, fluenta requirere et ob hoc humilitatem meam tuis saepius litteris admoneri."

[543] J. Fontaine, ed., preface to *De natura rerum,* p. 46; *Dedicatio Historiarum Isidori ad Sisenandum (MGH, AA,* XI, 304). Isidore also dedicated his *Origines* to Sisebut.

seventh century, Chindaswinth and his son, Recceswinth, were friends with the great men of letters of their time, Braulio, Taio, and Eugenius.

The kings themselves wrote. They had a library in their palace, of which nothing remains, where they could find models to follow.[544] Sisebut was the most famous lettered prince. The *Life of Saint Desiderius of Vienne*, which is attributed to him, and the letters that he sent to laymen and clerics bear the mark of the rhetoric taught during the period.[545] The king was also a poet. He has left us several verses at the end of a letter to his son and, especially, an astronomical poem consisting of sixty-one hexameters in which he delighted in describing a lunar eclipse for Isidore of Seville.[546] Sisebut's poem was very much a diversion. The king complained at first of the political and military duties that overwhelmed him and left him no leisure for writing; then, in imitation of Lucretius, he gave a quite precise description of an atmospheric phenomenon. But far from imitating the sobriety of his model, he charged his own verses with rhetorical ornaments in the fashion of the times, to such an extent as to make the poem quite obscure. At least he could scan his verses well, which is more than can be said for the Frankish king, Chilperic.

Although Sisebut's successors did not exhibit his talents, they liked to write in verse and in prose: King Chintila (636) composed a welcoming poem to accompany a gift sent to Rome;[547] the letters of Chindaswinth and Recceswinth that were included in Braulio of Saragossa's correspondence do not detract from that collection.[548] While Merovingian kings of the period no longer knew how to sign their names and had only an elementary education, Visigothic princes still maintained the classical Roman cultural tradition.

The content of this culture remained the same. In a letter to young Adaloald, son of the Lombard king Agilulf, Sisebut incidentally slipped

[544] Emilian, Braulio's correspondent, alluded to the royal library in discussing a book Braulio was seeking (Braulio, *Ep.* 26 [p. 145]): "Domino nostro suggessi et ipse inter libros suos inquirere jussit." Bezzola, 1: 34, cites the contents of this library, but his reference is a work without any scholarly value.

[545] *Vita Desiderii episc. Viennensis, MGH, SRM*, III, 621–23; Sisebut, *Ep.* 2, 4, 7, 8, 9 (*MGH, Ep.*, III, 662–71).

[546] See Jacques Fontaine, "La culture littéraire du roi wisigoth Sisebut," in *Actes du Congrès de l'Association Guillaume Budé* (Grenoble, 1949), pp. 156–58, and the reedition and translation of the royal poem at the end of Fontaine's edition of the *De natura rerum*, pp. 151–61, 328–35.

[547] Vives, *Inscripciones*, no. 389.

[548] Braulio, *Ep.* 32, 39, 41 (pp. 154, 173, 175).

in a definition of what was to become the trivium, those three branches of learning which were judged essential.[549] In actuality, however, it was grammar and rhetoric that especially interested lettered Visigoths, whose Latin, which was superior to Merovingian Latin, can only be explained as resulting from a serious study of the grammarians.[550] The manuals of Donatus and Pompey, which were the ones most familiar to Isidore, might have had lay readers before Isidore provided them with a grammatical compendium in his *Origines*. As a result, the evolution of spoken Latin, which was never influenced by the Gothic tongue, was halted. Romance dialects, the ancestors of Spanish, appear only much later.[551]

Laymen could write in prose and verse. If José Vives proves anything, it is that metrical inscriptions were very numerous in Visigothic Spain. They can be found on tombs as well as on religious and profane buildings[552] and were not only the work of clerics. Kings loved to versify; laymen must also have done so. A *promissio dotis* is presented in the Visigothic formulary in the form of a poem of ninety-two hexameters.[553] Perhaps a notary wrote it or even a young fiancé who wanted to transpose a notarial document into verse, as was done several times in the Middle Ages.[554]

There is nothing we can say in particular about rhetoric. It is preserved primarily in the letters of the period. Count Bulgar's letter of consolation to King Gundemar[555] and the letters of Visigothic princes can easily be compared to the epistolary literature we have already mentioned. But in Spain, rhetoric was applied to other fields, in par-

---

[549] Sisebut, *Ep.* 9 (*MGH, Ep.*, III, 673, ll. 27ff.): "Ergo quod splendor artis mensurate grammaticae, quod facundia adclamationis rethoricae, minus quod argumentatio defuerit dialecticae disciplinae, non dicendi copiam indigentia denegavit."

[550] Except for several articles by Manuel C. Diaz y Diaz, there have been few studies of Visigothic Latinity: see Diaz y Diaz, "Notes lexicographiques wisigothiques," *ALMA* 26 (1952): 77–85; "Rasgos lingüisticos del latin hispanico," *Enciclopedia lingüistica Hispanica*, vol. 1 (Madrid, 1959), as announced in Diaz y Diaz's 1956 paper, "El latin medieval español," published in *Actas del Primer congreso español de Estudios clásicos* (Madrid, 1958), pp. 559ff. See also Paul Joel Cooper's Columbia University thesis, "The Language of the Forum Judicum," summarized in *DA* 14 (1954): 138, and the introduction to Fontaine's edition of *De natura rerum*, pp. 85ff.

[551] Ramón Menéndez Pidal, *Origines del español: Estado lingüistico de la peninsula ibérica hasta el siglo XI*, 3rd ed. (Madrid, 1950).

[552] Vives, *Inscripciones*, nos. 272, 300, 313–15, 340, 341, 348–53, 356, 361–63.

[553] *Form. Visigoth.*, 20 (*MGH, Leg. sect. V*, p. 583). The first two lines are "Insigni merito et Geticae de stirpe senatus / Illius sponsae nimis dilectae ille." The date is indicated in v. 88: "Gloriosi merito Sisebuti tempore regis."

[554] Giry, *Manuel de diplomatique*, pp. 450ff.

[555] Count Bulgar, *Ep.* 16 (*MGH, Ep.* III, 684).

ticular, to judicial eloquence. In his definition of rhetoric, Isidore of Seville wrote that this branch of learning "is a rational method of expression, a lawyer's skill to which orators are devoted."[556] Elsewhere, in one of the chapters of his *Sentences*, he addressed himself to judges and lawyers—lawyers who, according to a classic image repeated by King Sisebut, "bayed at the tribunals."[557] No doubt the writer of the *Lex Visigothorum* had their verbal excesses in mind when he warned legislators that whoever undertakes to write law ought not to use subtleties in his text but, rather, should present valid precepts simply; he ought to deal with customs rather than with speeches; he ought not to play at orator but should indicate the rights of those who govern.[558] In the middle of the seventh century, Roman rhetoric was still so much alive that its defects were still being condemned.[559]

Grammar and rhetoric did not comprise the only intellectual baggage of the Visigothic aristocracy. The Visigothic aristocrat, like the lettered Italian of the sixth century, enjoyed history. Isidore and later Julian recounted the exploits of the Goths at the demand of kings who wished thereby to stimulate the courage of young men.[560] History thus abandoned the realm of grammar and reasserted its moral role. Alongside the national epics, which were certainly already being sung at court,[561] history contributed, as Isidore remarked, "to train men of today."[562]

Laymen were likewise impressed by the history of the physical world, by descriptions of natural phenomena, and by the search for their causes. We have already mentioned that King Sisebut asked Isidore of

[556] Isidore, *Differentiarum*, II, 39, 153 (*PL*, LXXXIII, 94): "Rhetorica est ratio dicendi, jurisperitorum scientia quam oratores sequuntur."

[557] *Sent.*, III, 56 (*PL*, LXXXIII, 724, 727, 728). See J. Fontaine, *IS*, pp. 334–35.

[558] *Leges Visigoth.*, I, 1 (*MGH, Leg. sect. I*, I, 38): "Neque sillogismorum acumine figuras inprimat disputationis sed puris honestisque preceptis modeste statuat articulos legis." Ibid., p. 39: "Unde nos melius mores quam eloquia ordinantes non personam oratoris inducimus sed rectoris jura disponimus." We should note that when the redactor "eulogized the law" (see above, n. 518), he sacrificed himself to a rhetorical commonplace.

[559] In *Origines*, II, xx, Isidore criticized the obscure style of his contemporaries. See J. Fontaine, *IS*, pp. 281, 288.

[560] See the preface to Julian of Toledo's *Historia de Wambae regis Gothorum Toletani expeditione*, *MGH, SRM*, V, 501: "Solet virtutis esse praesidio triumphorum relata narratio animosque juvenum ad virtutis adtollere signum, quidquid gloriae de praeteritis fuerit praedicatum." For Isidore's concept of history and time, see A. Borst, "Das Bild der Geschichte in der Enzyklopädie des Isidor von Sevilla," *Deutsches Archiv für Erforschung des Mittelalters* 22 (1966): 1–62, and M. Reydellet, "Les intentions politiques et idéologiques dans la *Chronique* d'Isidore de Séville," *MEFR* 82 (1970): 363–400.

[561] For the Visigothic epic, see Ramón Menéndez Pidal, "Los godos y el origen de la epopeya española," *Settimane*, 3: 285–322.

[562] Isidore, *Origines*, I, xliii. For Isidore's conception of history, see J. Fontaine, *IS*, pp. 180ff.

Seville for a *De natura rerum*, for which the king thanked him with a poem on astronomy. Later, Isidore gave a résumé of his work in one of the books of the *Origines*. He may have intended to publish this book separately, since it is the only book of the *Origines* bearing a preface to the reader.[563]

In his study of the world Isidore gave a large place to astronomy. As in Italy and Byzantium, so in Spain too, this science excited laymen. What they retained from their study, however, was less the description of the map of the heavens than the power of the stars over different human activities: to their minds astronomy and astrology were always one. Civil and ecclesiastical laws denounced astrological superstitions in vain. It was undoubtedly to help the Church and the Monarchy that Isidore accepted Sisebut's request to summarize what science taught him about the course of the stars and planets. This appeal to reason could have helped to purify the religious beliefs of his contemporaries.[564]

E. THE RELIGIOUS CULTURE OF THE VISIGOTHIC ARISTOCRACY

Laymen in the Ostrogothic kingdom and in the Empire played an important role in religious matters: they can be observed attending councils, taking part in doctrinal quarrels, and putting their pens to the service of the Church.[565] We find the same situation in the Visigothic kingdom during the sixth and seventh centuries. While in Gaul only bishops or their delegates attended councils,[566] in Spain magnates took their place beside the king in religious assemblies, especially in the national councils at Toledo, and affixed their signatures to the bottom of promulgated canons. By the end of the seventh century, so many aristocrats were participating in Church councils that the Church moved to limit their intervention.

The role of the councils of Toledo in political affairs explains this lay

---

[563] Isidore, *Origines*, XIII, preface: "De mundo et partibus. In hoc vero libello quasi in quadam brevi tabella quasdam caeli causas situsque terrarum et maris spatia adnotavimus, ut in modico lector ea percurrat et conpendiosa brevitate etymologias eorum causasque cognoscat."

[564] See Fontaine, "Isidore de Séville et l'astrologie," pp. 293ff., and *IS*, pp. 454ff., as well as A. Benito Duran, "Valor catéquetico de la obra De natura rerum de San Isidoro de Sevilla," *Atenas* 78 (1938): 41–51.

[565] See above, chap. 3, sect. I. Séjourné, *Le dernier Père de l'Eglise*, pp. 123–24, thought that the attendance of laymen at councils was due to Provençal influence. Actually, it was an imperial tradition still in observance at Byzantium.

[566] There was one exception. Duke Lupus and other nobles were present at the Council of Bordeaux (663/675) (*MGH, Leg. sect. III*, I, 215–16). But this was a period during which Aquitaine was more oriented toward Spain than toward Gaul.

participation.[567] We should not think, however, that the laymen present were interested only in royal succession, revisions of laws, and measures concerning Jews, since religious problems were not foreign to them. When Count Bulgar wrote to laymen and bishops, he bejeweled his letters with scriptural citations in the manner of an ecclesiastic.[568] Braulio of Saragossa corresponded with laymen interested in exegesis. An aristocratic woman asked him for a manuscript containing the books of Tobias and Judith;[569] when he sent them to her, Braulio included a letter explaining the figures that were to be found in the books. When he wrote to other laymen, especially consoling them for the loss of a dear one, he consistently appealed to scriptural texts known to his correspondents.[570] Let us note, finally, that the book Braulio searched for in the library of Count Laurentius was Apringius of Beja's *Commentary on the Apocalypse*.[571]

The library of the king was probably just as rich in ecclesiastical as in profane works. Sisebut's letter to young Adaloald is a veritable treatise of anti-Arian scholarship. He does not appeal to theological concepts but, as he said himself, offers "a florilegium gathered in the fields of Divine Scripture."[572] All that he was able to find in the Scriptures concerning the Trinity was carefully noted and filed. He had not really needed the advice of Isidore and Helladius, a former count of the patrimony who later became bishop of Toledo, to do this: indeed, he pillaged the Bible just as he pillaged Lucretius for his astronomical poem. Without denying the influence lettered bishops had on laymen, we need not believe that bishops had to guide their pens. According to some historians, for instance, King Chindaswinth's letter to Braulio reveals ecclesiastical influence because of its tone and its scriptural citations.[573] But why not attribute it to Chindaswinth himself? He certainly had a personal religious culture, since it was at his request that Taio, later bishop of Saragossa, went to Rome to seek out the works of

[567] See Garcia Villada, *Historia eclesiástica*, 2, pt. 1: 107, and Etienne Magnin, *L'Eglise wisigothique au VIIe siècle* (Paris, 1912), 1: 59–61.

[568] Count Bulgar, *Ep.* 11–16 (*MGH, Ep.*, III, 677–84). The editor found citations from the Gospels, the Psalter (most were from this source), Genesis, Proverbs, Ecclesiastes, and the Apocalypse.

[569] Braulio, *Ep.* 16 (p. 112).

[570] Ibid. 15, 19, 20, 28–30 (pp. 109–49).

[571] Ibid. 25 (p. 143).

[572] Sisebut, *Ep.* 9 (*MGH, Ep.*, III, 674): "Patent et alia per campos divinae legis testimonia copiose florigera."

[573] Braulio, *Ep.* 32 (p. 154). Madoz, the editor, repeats Lynch's hypothesis (*Saint Braulio*, p. 81) that Abbot Emilian was responsible for this letter.

Gregory the Great that were unavailable in Spain.[574] It was also he who asked Eugenius of Toledo to revise the works of the African poet Dracontius.[575]

Kings, of course, had greater need of advice when they dealt with theology. Consecrated by the metropolitan of Toledo, they asked councils that met in that town to take part in the quarrels dividing the Churches.[576] A chronicler reported that King Recceswinth would seek out men of letters, who conferred before him on articles of faith, and that he himself enjoyed reading Scripture.[577] The distinction made by the chronicler confirms what we have already said: the religious culture of kings, like that of laymen, was above all scriptural.

Laymen continued to have a liking for sacred literature until the end of the Visigothic period. Here is how one chronicler defined the culture of Duke Theudemer, a subject of King Egica (687–702): "Fuit enim scripturarum amator, eloquentia mirificus, in praeliis expeditus."[578] This expresses very well the triple nature of a Visigothic laymen's training, a training which was religious, literary, and military.

The religious culture of the Visigoths calls to mind that of Byzantines in Italy, Africa, and the East, who with their knowledge of the Bible could, as Gregory the Great said, "walk dry amidst the waters which submerged all worldly men."[579] The Byzantine patricius Caesarius and his correspondent King Sisebut were equally concerned with religious questions.[580] At Byzantium, laymen were so taken with their own learning and so eager to replace clerics in discussions that the Council in Trullo of 692 had to intervene.[581] Two years later, the Council of Toledo decided to exclude laymen from their deliberations on the faith

---

574 The *Anonyme de Cordoue* reports this fact. See Lynch, *Saint Braulio*, p. 157, n. 35, and Madoz, *El epistolario de San Braulio*, p. 184.

575 See Eugenius' dedicatory letter to Chindaswinth in *MGH, AA*, XIV, 27. The revision is discussed by Schanz, IV-2, 60–61.

576 Garcia Villada, *Historia eclesiástica*, 2, pt. 1: 111ff. According to this historian, kings had been consecrated from Reccared's time; for others, evidence of consecration can only be found from Wamba's reign. See M. David, "Le serment du sacre," *RMAL* 6 (1950): 39.

577 Luca Tudensis, *Chronicon mundi*, III, 55, 11–18, cited by Grosse, *Las fuentes*, p. 322: "Hic fidem catholicam in tantum dilexit, ut semper perquireret viros litteratos qui frequenter coram ipso conferrent de articulis fidei. Delectabatur in divinis scripturis." Although this evidence is from a very late historian, there is no reason to reject it.

578 *Continuationes Isidorianae byzantina, arabica et hispana, MGH, AA*, XI, 354.

579 Gregory the Great, *Ep.* VII, 26 (*MGH, Ep.*, I, 472, I, l. 2). For Italian laymen, see above, chap. 5, n. 121.

580 *Ep.* 3–6 (*MGH, Ep.*, III, 663–68).

581 Mansi, XIII, 219, c. 64.

and morals of the clergy.[582] This similarity between texts and dates is astonishing and almost makes one believe that Visigothic Spain was still in contact with the Byzantine Empire—at least, the problems which concerned the culture of laymen were the same in both countries. Spain and the Empire were still Roman while Gaul was becoming more and more Barbarian.

[582] Ibid., c. 1.

CHAPTER SEVEN

The Education of Clerics and
Monks in Gaul and in Spain

W e have just argued that no Pyrenees divided the culture of a
Gallic senator from that of a Spanish aristocrat. But a barrier
does present itself when one compares the ecclesiastical cultures of the
two kingdoms. The intellectual mediocrity of the Merovingian clergy is
usually contrasted to the astonishing renaissance of the Spanish Church.
Before trying to explain the reasons for this contrast, it would be useful
to reduce the disparity to just proportions.

I. ECCLESIASTICAL CULTURE
IN GAUL AND IN SPAIN

A. Gaul

"Decadence of thought," "intellectual crisis," and "poetical and theological sterility" are some of the phrases used by authors who have
studied Merovingian ecclesiastical culture.[1] Yet the Church of Gaul was
very active in the sixth and seventh centuries: bishops participated in
political and economic developments in the kingdom, helped counts to
govern their cities, and undertook building projects.[2] Apparently, however, there is a difference between action and thought. Did the literary
works of the Church of Gaul disappear like the monuments mentioned

---

[1] Lot, *Les destinées*, pp. 371ff.; Fliche-Martin, 5: 368ff.; von Schubert, *Geschichte*, pp.
146ff.

[2] For ecclesiastical building activity, see Raymond Lantier and Jean Hubert, *Les origines
de l'art français* (Paris, 1947), pp. 139ff.

by Fortunatus and Gregory of Tours? Or, perhaps, was the Church stricken with intellectual paralysis to the point where it could produce nothing?

Certainly, our first impression is of a disaster. We are unable to find clerics trained in sacred learning not only in Barbarian Gaul but also in a large part of Roman Gaul. Except for Nicetius of Trier, who was from Aquitaine, no names can be cited in the dioceses dependent on the metropolitan sees of Reims, Rouen, Trier, and Besançon; the same poverty can be observed in the provinces of Bordeaux and Eauze. Fortunatus introduces us to the sixth-century bishops of Bordeaux, who emanated from an illustrious Roman family, the Leontii. While they were great landowners, administrators, and builders who graced Bordeaux, Saintes, and Agen with monuments, the Leontii produced no ecclesiastical writers. As has been recently pointed out, the epitaph of Leontius II is "more that of a sovereign than of a bishop."[3] Desiderius of Cahors, although an active prelate, remained a man of letters after the antique fashion without any particular taste for religious study.[4] The only bishops to exhibit an ecclesiastical culture were Dido of Albi, to whom a cleric dedicated a canonical collection,[5] and Maurillus of Cahors, of whose exegesis Gregory of Tours gave a curious example, as we shall see. The situation worsens when we pass into Provence. After the generation of the disciples of Caesarius of Arles (died 546)— Cyprian of Toulon, Aurelian of Arles, and Ferreolus of Uzès—we find no other lettered bishops. While, as we saw, lay culture survived until the mid-seventh century, ecclesiastical culture virtually ceased to exist. The Provençal Church no longer played the role it had had from the middle of the fifth century and entered a period of decadence that lasted for centuries.[6]

The peripheral regions of Gaul remained on the margin of the intellectual life of the Church. Centers of ecclesiastical studies were located only in central Gaul in a zone limited by the valley of the Seine

---

[3] De Maillé, *Les origines*, p. 96.

[4] His biographer, who is usually well informed on Desiderius' work, gives only a very vague indication of Desiderius' interest in religious studies by citing Saint Jerome in paragraph 21 ("Sermo ejus ad omne suum erat convivium de scripturis aliquid proponere" [*MGH, SRM*, IV, 579]).

[5] Gabriel Le Bras, "Notes pour servir à l'histoire des collections canoniques," *RHDE* 8 (1929): 767ff. This canonical collection was undoubtedly more influenced by the Visigothic example than by that of Arles. Albi was very near Visigothic Septimania.

[6] For the halt in canonical activity at Arles, see Fournier and Le Bras, *Histoire des collections canoniques*, 1: 44; for the disorganization of the Provençal Church, see Buchner, *Die Provence*, p. 28.

268. THE EDUCATION OF CLERICS AND MONKS

in the north and the Massif Central in the south. This zone coincides with the location of Merovingian councils as shown on Map. 7. In fact, in checking the names of the cities where national councils met in the sixth and seventh centuries, it is striking to note that they were all situated on one side of a line that passes through Paris, Chalon, Lyon and Clermont.[7] Furthermore, the bishops who met in the councils came primarily from the provinces of Sens, Bourges, and Lyon.[8]

Quartered in a well-defined district, ecclesiastical culture in Gaul was also limited to certain genres. Neither theology nor exegesis seems to have interested Merovingian clerics. Although Gaul had known heresies[9] and had felt the effects of the quarrel of the *Three Chapters*,[10] councils defended Catholic orthodoxy without breeding the controversies that arose in Italy and Spain. The indifference of the bishops cannot be explained by their ignorance of the Fathers. Patristic works were, in fact, recopied in ecclesiastical scriptoria: manuscripts of the works of Jerome, Augustine, Origen, Hilary, Eucherius, and others emerged from the episcopal workshop of Lyon. Yet the bishops of this city did not devote themselves to the study of dogma or Scripture.[11] The ones we know were administrators and builders, not scholars. Nicetius himself, whose life Gregory of Tours recounted, appears not to have been a lettered cleric.[12] Were the bishops of Lyon, then, simply collectors of beautiful manuscripts? Did their workshop of copyists bear no relation to the Church? This apparent discordance is disturbing, not for the future of sacred literature, because a day would come when the manuscripts would be used, but very much for the sixth and seventh centuries.

Northwest of Lyon in Burgundy, Bishop Syagrius and his disciple

[7] For Merovingian councils, see De Clercq, *La législation religieuse*, in addition to the texts published by Maassen (*MGH, Leg. sect. III*, I).

[8] The bishops of the provinces of Trier, Arles, and Vienne were represented on only three occasions. The bishops of Toulouse attended two councils. In the province of Bordeaux, the bishop of that city was generally the only one to attend councils.

[9] The Council of Orléans of 538 (c. 34) and the Council of Clichy of 626 (c. 5) condemned the Bonosian heresy; see also the *Vita Columbani*, II, 8 (*MGH, SRM*, IV-1, 122). The Council of Tours of 567 (c. 20) was concerned with Nicolaism.

[10] Duchesne, *L'Eglise au VIe siècle*, p. 191, and Stein, 2: 833, suppose that Fortunatus informed Nicetius of Trier on Eastern dogmatical quarrels. Judging from Nicetius' letter to Justinian (*MGH, Ep.*, III, 118), the bishop was poorly taught.

[11] E. A. Lowe studied this scriptorium in his *Codices lugdunenses antiquissimi*. In his *CLA*, VI, xiii ff., Lowe again took up the question and revised some of his earlier hypotheses. See also Célestin Charlier, "Les manuscrits personnels de Florus," in *Mélanges E. Podechard: Etudes de sciences religieuses offertes pour son émeritat* (Lyon, 1945), p. 73.

[12] See Coville, pp. 469ff., for these bishops.

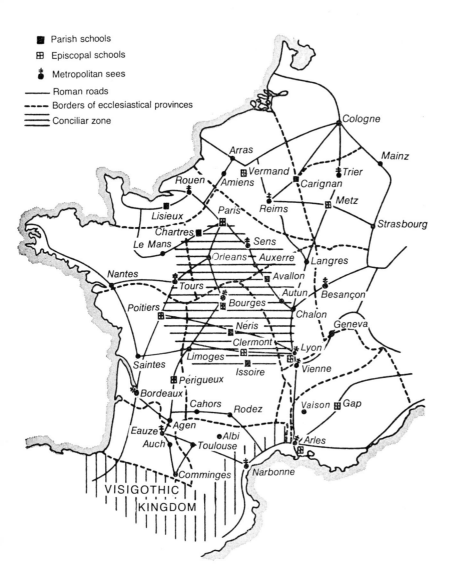

Parish schools
Episcopal schools
Metropolitan sees
——— Roman roads
- - - - Borders of ecclesiastical provinces
≡≡≡ Conciliar zone

Cologne
Arras
Mainz
Vermand
Rouen   Amiens   Trier
Carignan
Metz
Lisieux
Paris   Reims
Strasbourg
Chartres
Le Mans   Sens
Orleans   Auxerre   Langres
Nantes   Avallon
Tours   Autun   Besançon
Poitiers   Bourges   Chalon
Néris   Geneva
Clermont   Lyon
Saintes   Limoges   Vienne
Issoire
Périgueux
Bordeaux
Cahors   Rodez   Vaison   Gap
Eauze   Agen   Albi
Auch   Toulouse   Arles
Comminges   Narbonne

VISIGOTHIC
KINGDOM

7. *Centers of Ecclesiastical Studies in Gaul in the Sixth Century
and at the Beginning of the Seventh Century*

Aunarius were responsible for making Autun and Auxerre centers of religious study at the end of the sixth century. They were the only Merovingian bishops to maintain consistent relations with the popes.[13] They were also in contact with Spain and Byzantine Africa.[14] Despite these advantages, the ecclesiastical production of Burgundian towns was limited to hagiography in verse and prose and to the development of canonical collections.[15] The bishops of Gaul were jurists, poets, and hagiographers. Their social origins and education explain these emphases.

Most bishops came to the episcopate after having been royal bureaucrats. Gregory of Tours noted with some bitterness that clerics rarely acceded to episcopal power.[16] Kings preferred to choose men who were able to administer the diocese and to collaborate with the counts;[17] bishops, as a result, behaved like judges and legislators. Conciliar canons made more than one allusion to the *lex romana*[18] and preserved the severe and succinct style of antique juridical works.[19] Furthermore, as members of the aristocracy, these bishops had received a literary training that emphasized erudition, poetry, and rhetoric.

The Bible was read in the Merovingian Church; at least, certain of

---

[13] See the letter of Pope Pelagius II to Aunarius in Maximilien Quantin, ed., *Cartulaire général de l'Yonne*, 2 vols. (Auxerre, 1854–60), vol. 1, nos. 2–3, and Gregory the Great's letter to Syagrius (*MGH, Ep.*, II, 200–201 [no. 3]).

[14] Syagrius of Autun was the protégé of Brunhilda the Visigoth. Gregory the Great sent Abbot Cyriacus to Autun, then to Spain in the summer of 599; see *Ep.* IX, 208 and 230 (II, 195, 227). Aunarius of Auxerre and Stephanus, an African, were in contact.

[15] See G. Le Bras, "L'organisation du diocèse d'Auxerre à l'époque mérovingienne," *Mémoires de la Société pour l'histoire du droit et des institutions des anciens pays bourguignons, comtois et romands* 5 (1938): 307–30. Was the Hieronymian martyrology revised at Auxerre? Historians have not come to agreement on this point. See *AS, Prop.* (1931), p. xv. For hagiography at Auxerre, see René Louis, "L'église d'Auxerre et ses évêques avant saint Germain," in *Saint Germain d'Auxerre et son temps*, ed. Gabriel Le Bras (Auxerre, 1950), pp. 62ff. Some authors think that the *Missale gothicum* came from Auxerre; see von Schubert, *Geschichte*, pp. 638, 645.

[16] Gregory of Tours, *HF*, VI, 46 (p. 320). He gave several examples of functionaries who became bishops (*HF*, IV, 3; V, 36, 45; VI, 7, 9, 37; VIII, 22, 39; IX, 23).

[17] See von Schubert, *Geschichte*, p. 161. Marculf's diplomas nominating bishops (*Form.*, I, 5 and 7) speak only of the nobility and morality of the bishop, never of his intellectual qualities. Gregory the Great complained several times about the hasty promotion of laymen to the clerical state; see *Ep.* V, 59–60; IX, 218 (*MGH, Ep.*, I, 371–74; II, 208).

[18] Gaudemet, "Survivances romaines," pp. 164–67, states that these references were especially numerous in the sixth century. But a seventh-century Cologne manuscript (Col. 212) contains imperial letters in the midst of conciliar acts. See Maassen, *Geschichte der Quellen*, p. 574. Alaric's *Breviary* and the *Theodosian Code* were among the manuscripts from the scriptorium of Lyon.

[19] One can only hope with Gabriel Le Bras (*Mémorial des Etudes latines* [Paris, 1943], pp. 423, 428) that a study of the style of the conciliar texts will be undertaken.

its books were known.[20] The sacred text, however, was considered but one classic among others, all of which were used to nourish the memory more than the mind or heart. When Gregory of Tours praised Bishop Maurillus of Cahors, he wrote: "He was remarkably nourished on the Scriptures, so much so that he could recite by heart the series of different generations in the Old Testament, something quite difficult to remember."[21] That was what was remembered from scriptural studies—a genealogical table of the royal families of Israel. When Gregory of Tours tells us that one of his clerics from Tours was "eruditus in spiritualibus scripturis,"[22] we can conclude that he possessed biblical erudition rather than exegetical learning. Although Gregory had received a clerical education, he displayed a culture that was more literary than ecclesiastical. The sole exegetical treatise he composed was a commentary on the Psalms, of which only the headings have survived.[23] Should we regret this loss after learning that Gregory was better acquainted with Sulpicius Severus and Prudentius than with Jerome and Augustine?[24] When he tried to demonstrate the truth of the Catholic faith in the face of a heresy, all he could do was to accumulate biblical citations.[25] Like his colleague Nicetius of Trier, Gregory believed more in the power of miracles than in the success of an extended proof.[26] The Bible was considered a reservoir from which one drew citations more or less adapted to the case in question.

Lettered clerics, moreover, must have agreed with Fortunatus that the text of the Bible was too common,[27] preferring instead the poetic version by Juvencus and his continuators. Arator's work made its way

[20] The Bible still circulated as separate books in a version which was obviously not the Vulgate; see Gregory of Tours, *HF*, IV, 16 (p. 149), and Bonnet, *Le latin*, p. 55.

[21] Gregory of Tours, *HF*, V, 42 (p. 249): "Fuit . . . in scripturis ecclesiasticis valde instructus ita ut seriem diversarum generationum quae in libris Veteris Testamenti describitur, quod a multis difficile retinetur, hic plerumque memoriter recensiret."

[22] *Mir. Mart.*, I, 33 (*MGH, SRM*, I-2, 604): "Ex clericis meis Armentarius nomine bene eruditus in spiritualibus scripturis."

[23] *In psalterii tractatus*, MGH, SRM, II, 873. A fifteenth-century Canterbury manuscript mentions a work by Gregory on "the passion and resurrection of the Lord"; see Manitius, 1: 219, n. 4. Undoubtedly the passage in *HF*, X, 13 (p. 496), in which Gregory debated with a priest who denied the Resurrection, gave rise to this legend.

[24] Gregory's ecclesiastical sources were studied by Bonnet, *Le latin*, pp. 55ff. See also P. Antin, "Note sur le style de saint Grégoire de Tours," *Latomus* 22 (1963): 273–84.

[25] *HF*, V, 43; VI, 40 (pp. 249 and 310). See also the letter of Chrodobertus to Abbess Bobba (*Ep.* 16 [*MGH, Ep.*, III, 461–64]) with its thirty-one scriptural citations bearing on the problem of a nun guilty of adultery.

[26] See the letter of Nicetius to the granddaughter of Clovis, in which Nicetius tried to convert her husband, the king of the Lombards (*MGH, SRM*, III, 119).

[27] Fortunatus, *Vita Martini*, I, 10 (*MGH, AA*, IV-1, 295).

into Gaul; Prudentius and Sedulius were still being read there. King Chilperic, as we have seen, imitated Sedulius when he composed his own hymns. Fortunatus' poems, which mixed pagan and Christian themes,[28] were not only well received but even imitated by Bishops Felix of Nantes, Bertechramnus of Bordeaux, and Sulpicius of Bourges. To present Christian truth in an agreeable form was one of the great concerns of clerics in the sixth and seventh centuries.[29]

Bishops displayed their literary talents and erudition whenever they gathered at councils. Gregory of Tours, for example, reported that during the Council of Mâcon (585), Bishop Pretextat read to his colleagues *orationes* composed during his exile;[30] some, Gregory said, liked these works, while others were critical of their lack of art.[31] This council transformed itself into an academy of men of letters, where the literary quality of a text was judged as much as its religious merit. During the course of this same meeting, one bishop, who no doubt had a taste for *quaestiones*, presented the bishops with a problem that had troubled other men of letters before him: could woman, created by God, be called *homo*?[32] The Merovingian cleric was still the erudite scholar he had been in his youth and loved to display his learning. In another conciliar meeting, a reader of Seneca slipped an expression attributed to the Roman moralist into a canon.[33]

Loyal to the traditions of profane literary culture, Merovingian clerics excelled in the saint's *Life*, the "period's best-seller."[34] The author of a good *Vita* had to obey the rhetorical laws of the panegyric genre, mak-

---

[28] See Bezzola, 1: 65ff., on the equivocal character of these poems.

[29] *Rhythmi aevi merovingici et carolini*, MGH, *PAC*, IV-2, 495, 564. For didactic poems by Merovingian clerics, see Norberg, *Introduction*, pp. 148–50. See also the priest Felix's metrical epitaph from Briord in Le Blant, *IC*, 2: 12 (no. 377).

[30] *HF*, VIII, 20 (p. 387). We are uncertain as to the meaning of *orationes*. Koebner, *Venantius Fortunatus*, p. 74, translates it as *sermons*. But in another passage (*HF*, IX, 6) Gregory used *oratio* to mean "prayer." Pretextat could have composed some hymns.

[31] *HF*, VIII, 20 (p. 387): "A quibusdam vero quia artem secutus minime fuerat repraehendebantur; stilus tamen per loca aeclesiasticus et rationabilis erat."

[32] For this *quaestio*, see Marrou, *Saint Augustin*, p. 471. This episode gave rise to the legend of the woman created without a soul. See Elphège Vacandard, "La question de l'âme des femmes et le Concile de Mâcon," *Etudes de critique et d'histoire religieuses*, 2nd ser. (1910), pp. 171–75, and M. Pribilla, "Frauenseele und Kirche," *Stimmen der Zeit* 127 (1934): 418–21.

[33] *MGH, Leg. sect. III*, I, 125, ll. 27–28: "Sicut ait Senica: 'Pessimum in eum vitium esse, qui in id, quod insanit, ceteros putat furere?'" This text seems to have come from a work attributed to Martin of Braga, *Liber de moribus* (PL, LXXII, 29). Claude W. Barlow has described the contacts which existed between Tours and Braga in *Martini episcopi Bracarensis opera omnia* (New Haven, 1950), p. 276.

[34] Maurice Wilmotte, *Origines du roman en France: L'évolution du sentiment romanesque jusqu'en 1240* (Brussels and Liège, 1941), pp. 110ff.

ing sure to include a study of the milieu in which the hero lived, his education, his spiritual qualities, his deeds, and his renown.[35] Careful attention was given to the style of the eulogy, which was checked by another person.[36] Authors had to obey yet another rule of the hagiographic genre, simplicity of form. In their prefaces, they contrasted their *rusticus et plebeius sermo* to the beautiful style of the learned (*scolastici*).[37] When Fortunatus wrote the *Life of Saint Albinus*, he obediently accepted this requirement in order to be understood by the people.[38] One senses that he made a real effort to combat his usual style. Gregory of Tours had a less difficult time writing simply. Nevertheless, he was constantly preoccupied with the criticisms the learned would direct toward his work. He defended himself against their attacks by arguing that he had not gone to school, that he gathered material which others would use with greater profit,[39] and—the decisive, final argument—that an angel had ordered him to write despite his rusticity because, for God, "innocent simplicity is worth more than philosophers' arguments."[40] When it came to style, clerics always took into account the judgment of men of letters and tried not to disappoint them. Even in the seventh century, an anonymous writer asked a preacher not to be obscure for the sake of the people but also not to offend the lettered with too rustic language.[41] We are far from the rigorist position of Caesarius of Arles and his disciples.

[35] For the rules of the hagiographical genre, see Hippolyte Delehaye, *Passions des martyrs* (Brussels, 1921), and Leonid Arbusow, *Colores Rhetorici* (Göttingen, 1948), pp. 117ff. Hagiographers were specialists who filled orders for saints' *Lives*. Fortunatus worked for the bishops of Angers, Paris, and Poitiers as well as for the abbot of Saint Pair. Warnecarius worked for Bishop Ceraunus of Paris: see the prefatory letter in *MGH, Ep.*, III, 457.

[36] See the letter from Audoenus to Rodobertus in *MGH, SRM*, IV, 741: "Si quid forte aut mea aut notariorum incuria in verbis vel syllabis incompositum aut minus aptum depraehenderis . . . studiose emendes nobisque demum emendata restaures."

[37] Louis Furman Sas, "Changing Linguistic Attitudes in the Merovingian Period," *Word: Journal of the Linguistic Society of New York* 5 (1949): 131–35, has collected some of these statements.

[38] *Vita Albini*, II (*MGH, AA*, IV-2, 28–29): "Et ne mihi videlicet in hoc opere ad aures populi minus aliquid intelligibile proferatur."

[39] *Glor. confess.*, preface (*MGH, SRM*, I-2, 748): "Opus vestrum facio et per meam rusticitatem vestram prudentiam exercebo." See also *Mir. Mart.*, preface (ibid., p. 586, ll. 1–7).

[40] *Mir. Mart.*, II, 1 (p. 609): "Apud Dei maiestatem magis simplicitas pura quam philosophorum valet argutia."

[41] *PL*, LXXII, 83: "Ita arte temperans ut nec rusticitas sapientes offendat nec honesta loquacitas obscura rusticis fiat." This passage can be compared with the preface of the *Vita Eligii, MGH, SRM*, IV, 664: "Ita stylum placet corrigere, ut nec simplicibus quibusque grammaticorum sectando fumus discpliceat, nec scolasticos etiam nimia contentos rusticitate offendat."

Merovingian clerics, unlike the rigorists, did not renounce the classical culture they had received while they were still laymen and did not "convert" themselves to a uniquely religious culture. No canonical text contrasts the two kinds of training. Gregory of Tours, as we saw earlier, even sought to fill the gaps in his earlier education, since he thought it desirable that a bishop possess a good profane education. He criticized a cleric from Clermont "for knowing neither ecclesiastical nor secular literature."[42] He thought it normal that his successors would study the liberal arts: "If you, bishop of God, have studied the seven arts of Martianus Capella . . ." he wrote in the conclusion to his *History*.[43]

The religious culture of the Merovingian clergy was thus less poor than is usually thought. It was, however, a uniquely literary culture that brings to mind that of Italian clerics at the opening of the sixth century. Faithful to the tradition of Christian classical culture, they did not see the urgency of adopting a new type of training whose principles had been defined by the monks. We will see later that this conservative attitude influenced the organization of ecclesiastical schools.

B. SPAIN

From the middle of the sixth century to the first third of the seventh century, the religious culture of Spanish clerics was in full flower. During almost the entire sixth century the Church suffered from Arian persecution, persecution which was undoubtedly more or less violent and which inevitably impeded ecclesiastical life. But from 589, the date of the Arian King Reccared's official conversion, the Catholic Church had civil rights. This important historical event freed the Church and allowed it to organize itself temporally and politically. Religious thought from that time took on new strength. Therefore, contrary to what is usually done, we must examine the characteristics of Spanish religious culture before and after 589.[44]

We have seen that the ecclesiastical culture of mid-sixth-century Spain was superior to that of other Western kingdoms.[45] The Arian heresy, however, was a live issue in Spain. The kings wanted to complement the political unity of the kingdom with religious unity and

---

[42] *HF*, IV, 12 (p. 144), in reference to Cautinus of Clermont: "De omnibus enim scripturis tam ecclesiasticis quam saecularibus ad plena immunis fuit."

[43] *HF*, X, 18 (p. 536): "Quod si te, o sacerdos Dei, quicumque es, Martianus noster septem disciplinis erudiit . . . si in his omnibus, ita fueris exercitatus."

[44] The best work on the religious culture of Visigothic Spain is Garcia Villada's *Historia eclesiástica*, vol. 2, pt. 2.

[45] See above, chap. 4, sect. II.B.

hoped that Catholic clerics would abjure. In 580, Leovigild called a conference at Toledo, where Catholic and Arian bishops opposed each other, but he was not able to impose the heresy on the entire realm. Central Spain seems to have been the bastion of Arianism. Unfortunately, even though we can discern the activities of Arian bishops and the culture of Visigothic laymen,[46] we cannot pursue our research much farther, since all the texts concerning Arianism have been destroyed.[47]

The strongholds of Catholic resistance were in the peripheral regions of the kingdom. In the east, the cities on the Mediterranean shoreline could boast bishops who were outstanding authors, such as Eutropius of Valencia (died 589), Severus of Malaga, and Licinianus of Carthagena (died 603). Leander, one of the architects of King Reccared's conversion, came from this last town. He made Seville an important religious center after he moved there, first as abbot and then as bishop (584). Merida, in the west, was a theater of controversies between Arians and Catholics. Lastly, Braga, in the northwest, became the religious metropolis of Lusitania under Bishop Martin, the apostle of the Suevians (566).

Thus, there were two churches in Spain—one might even say three, since beginning in 555, the Byzantines occupied the south of the peninsula from Dianium to Lacobriga.[48] Licinianus of Carthagena, a Byzantine bishop, died in Constantinople about 603. Leander was in Constantinople around 580 and established a friendship there with the future Pope Gregory the Great. As we have already seen, Greek influence in Spain extended beyond the frontiers of Byzantine possessions.[49] The Greeks Paul and Fidelis became bishops of Merida[50] and young John of Biclarum left his native city of Santarém to study at Constantinople.[51] Braga, despite its more northerly position, had long welcomed Easterners, one of whom had converted the Suevians to Arianism

---

[46] We can list the following Arian bishops: Uldida at Toledo (John of Biclarum, *Chron.*, *MGH*, *AA*, XI, 218), Sunna at Merida (*Vitas sanctorum*, IX [Garvin ed., p. 284]), and Athalocus at Narbonne (Gregory of Tours, *HF*, IX, 15 [p. 430]). The bishop of Saragossa was a convert to Arianism; see Isidore, *De vir. ill.*, 43, 61 (*PL*, LXXXIII, 1105). Agila and Oppila, the two laymen Leovigild sent to Gaul, held their own with ease against the arguments of Gregory of Tours; see *HF*, V, 43; VI, 40 (pp. 249, 310). See also Stroheker, "Leovigild," in *Germanentum*, pp. 178–91.

[47] Pseudo-Fredegarius, *Chron.*, IV, 8 (*MGH*, *SRM*, II, 125).

[48] For the Byzantine occupation, see Paul Goubert, "Byzance et l'Espagne wisigothique," *Revue des études byzantines* 2 (1945): 24ff.

[49] See above, chap. 6, sect. IV.A.

[50] *Vitas sanctorum*, V, 12 (Garvin ed., p. 168), and, in the editor's commentary, p. 377.

[51] Isidore of Seville, *De vir. ill.*, 44 (*PL*, LXXXIII, 102): "Joannes . . . nativitate gothus provinciae Lusitaniae Scalabi natus. . . . Cum esset adolescens Constantinopolim perrexit."

in the fifth century; in the sixth century, Martin, a Pannonian and former monk from Palestine, led them back to Catholicism. Martin brought with him a collection of Greek canons, which he had one of his disciples translate into Latin.[52] Perhaps he even brought artists with him who worked at Braga and in his abbey at Dumio.[53] Thus, Byzantine influence helped to enrich the religious culture of the Spanish Church.

During this period, clerics devoted long works to apologetics, since it was necessary to defend Catholic dogma. The Arian heresy—which Leander, Masona of Merida, Licinianus of Carthagena, and Severus of Malaga[54] fought—was not the only danger. The Bonosians in Betica and the Neopriscillianists in Galicia continued to have their followers.[55] In the Levant, Licinianus and Severus combatted clerics who supported the materiality of the soul, a position also found in Provence at the end of the fifth century.[56] Licinianus' treatise De anima, which was patterned on the classic work of Claudian Mamertus, shows that the bishop of Carthagena had a respectable philosophical training, rare for his period. As in sixth-century Italy, acquisition of a philosophical education was not without risk. Licinianus, who was perhaps openly interested in the astrological beliefs revived by Neopriscillianists, was accused of believing that stars were rational spirits and had to defend himself before Gregory the Great.[57]

Since the clerics we have just cited remained in contact with antique literature, it is not difficult to find reminiscences from classical authors in their works. Bishop Martin of Braga compiled the works of Seneca to teach the Suevian King Miro or the bishop of Orense the principles of Stoic morality.[58] Leander of Seville's speech at the conclusion of the

---

[52] Fournier and Le Bras, Histoire des collections canoniques, 1: 65–66; Barlow, preface, Martini episc. Bracarensis, pp. 84–85.

[53] G. Gaillard, "Une sculpture funéraire préromane conservée au musée de Braga," BSAF (1951), pp. 191–95.

[54] We no longer have the treatises of Leander and of Severus of Malaga which Isidore mentioned in De vir. ill., 41, 43 (PL, LXXXIII, 1103–5).

[55] See Garcia Villada, Historia eclesiástica, 2, pt. 2: 142ff.

[56] José Madoz, "Un caso de materialismo en España en el siglo VI," Revista española de teologia 8 (1948): 203–30. See also Madoz's introduction to the letters of Licinianus (Liciniano de Cartagena y sus cartas, Estudios Onienses, vol. 1, pt. 4 [Madrid, 1948], pp. 53–55).

[57] Licinianus, Ep. I, 41a (MGH, Ep., I, 58–61): "Mihi . . . nullo pacto suaderi potest, ut credam astra caeli spiritus habere rationales."

[58] Martin of Braga, Formula vitae honestae, and De ira, ed. Barlow, p. 146.

Third Council of Toledo in 589 contained many features borrowed from classical rhetoric.[59]

This great council, which dealt with the conversion of the Visigoths, closed a period of Spanish history. It made of the Church militant a Church triumphant, with the result that the character of religious culture itself was modified.

We note, first of all, a relocation of centers of culture. They are no longer found on the Mediterreanean littoral but in the interior of Spain. As the Visigoths pushed the Byzantines into the sea, the former Byzantine possessions declined in importance. Sisebut destroyed Carthagena.[60] Merida in the west was eclipsed,[61] while Braga was to emerge from the shadows only in the second half of the seventh century, during the episcopate of Fructuosus.[62] The major towns—Seville, Toledo, and Saragossa—were now all located on an axis which traversed central Spain from south to north, as shown in Map. 8. Seville remained an important intellectual center until Isidore's death in 636, while Toledo replaced Carthagena as a metropolitan see and became the seat of the monarchy and of national councils. Saragossa boasted a succession of lettered bishops—Maximus (died in 619), Braulio (died in 656), and Taio— during the second half of the century.

While the centers of culture in Spain were being relocated, the content of religious thought was also changing. Literature, after the victory of Catholicism, was much less *engagée*. Of course, not all Arians were converted at once—Isidore of Seville took it upon himself to prove the validity of the Trinitarian faith several times.[63] The Jewish problem, on the other hand, became increasingly acute. Isidore composed a *Contra Judaeos* in refutation of Jewish propaganda.[64] But the literature of combat was reduced to the level of propaganda exchanges.

---

[59] See Mansi, IX, 977, for Leander's speech. See also F. Görres, "Leander, Bischof von Sevilla und Metropolit der Kirchenprovinz Bätica," *Zeitschrift für wissenschaftliche Theologie* 29 (1886): 36–80.

[60] Menéndez Pidal, *HE*, 3: 113. The only known literary work from this region is a poem by Bishop Suintaricus of Valencia; see Norberg, *Introduction*, p. 149.

[61] Sixth-century inscriptions are much more numerous than those of the following century; see Vives, *Inscripciones*, nos. 24ff.

[62] See below, chap. 8, sect. IV.B.

[63] Menéndez Pidal, *HE*, 3: 112, discusses the Arian resistance of the seventh century. Garcia Villada, *Historia eclesiástica*, 2, pt. 2, app. VI: 282–89, published Isidore of Seville's treatise against the Arians. At the Second Council of Seville, Isidore opposed the "acephalite" heresy of an Eastern bishop. See Séjourné, *Le dernier Père de l'Eglise*, p. 97.

[64] Séjourné, *Le dernier Père de l'Eglise*, p. 32.

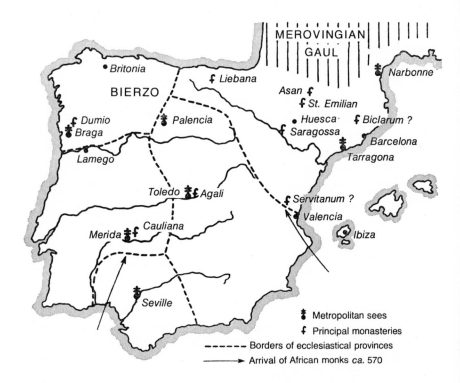

8. *Centers of Ecclesiastical Culture in Seventh-Century Spain*

"Isidore's work surprises us with its serenity and its optimism," wrote the scholar who best knows Isidore's work.[65] Lettered Visigoths contributed to the general stabilization of Spain and rekindled a humanism which the years of war had not permitted. The diversity of the work of Isidore, Braulio, and their disciples brings to mind the writers of the fourth century. The Spaniards were exegetes, theologians, and moralists, as well as poets, letter writers, and musicians. In the history of the culture of Barbarian times, the "Isidorian" period shines as a truly privileged moment.[66]

How do we explain this success? By the influence of lay culture? If lay culture alone had nourished ecclesiastical thought, we would have seen in Spain a predominantly literary religious culture such as developed in Gaul. Moreover, the lettered clerics of Spain were rarely former laymen. The renewal of scriptural and theological studies was tied to the development of ecclesiastical schools.

II. PARISH AND EPISCOPAL SCHOOLS IN GAUL AND IN SPAIN

A. Parish Schools in Gaul

We have seen, in Chapter 4, how the presbyteral school was established during the first half of the sixth century. This type of school, although differing according to local circumstances, spread rapidly in Roman as well as in Barbarian Gaul.

Shortly after the Council of Vaison (529), the hermit Patroclus opened a school at Néris. In this center, known for its hot springs and very prosperous in Roman times, the public school disappeared with the decline of the city. Patroclus was not, we should note, the pastor of the parish but a monk who placed himself at the disposal of children who wanted an education.[67] At the same time, Germanus, future bishop of Paris, went off with a cousin to Avallon to receive instruction from one of his relatives, who was a cleric teaching in a presbyteral school in a

---

[65] J. Fontaine, *IS*, p. 9.

[66] Manitius, 1: 1–242, has studied the literature of this period. See also M. Ruffini, *Le origini*. For the expression "Isidorian Renaissance," see Fontaine, *IS*, pp. 863ff.

[67] Gregory of Tours, *Vitae patrum*, IX (*MGH, SRM*, I-2, 703): "Pueros erudire coepit in studiis litterarum." Patroclus died in 579 when eighty years old; he must have opened his school around 535.

castrum.[68] Leobard attended the parish school at Clermont.[69] Early in the seventh century the young Praejectus was sent to school at Issoire and took a pension for his meals with a deacon of the city.[70] These two schools in Auvergne were not simply the "seminaries" proposed by the Council of Vaison but day-schools where children could go every day and where laymen were admitted alongside future clerics. Let us go on to northern Gaul. At Chartres, if the late *Life of Saint Launomar* can be believed, a priest named Chirmirus ran a school during the first half of the sixth century.[71] Saint Gaugericus and other children received their first clerical training around 550 at the *castrum Ebosium* (Carignan).[72] A priest opened a school at Lisieux at the request of the bishop, but because of the master's bad conduct, it did not last long.[73] Even though the bishop created this school, it was not an episcopal school because, as in Auvergne, the students came from the outside. All the schools just cited, we should note, were in very important centers, situated on former Roman roads (see Map 7), where small Roman schools could have existed previously.

As we observed at Lisieux, priests who taught were controlled by bishops. When the school was outside the episcopal city, the bishop would visit it during his circuits through the parishes. Gaugericus' hagiographer describes the bishop of Trier's inspection at Carignan. The priest presented the children intended for the clerical state to the bishop for questioning. When Gaugericus was asked where he was in his reading of Scriptures, the young boy replied with a verse from Psalm 2. The bishop, in leaving, promised to make him a deacon if he knew the Psalter by heart by the time he returned:[74] in an area where clerics were rare, the bishop liked to encourage the best elements.

---

[68] Fortunatus, *Vita Germani*, II, 5 and III, 8 (*MGH, AA*, IV-2, 12): "Deinde cum Avallone castro cum Stratidio propinquo puer scolis excurreret. . . . Hinc ad parentem suum sanctum Scupilionem Lausea se conferens moribus honestis alitus et institutus est."

[69] Gregory of Tours, *Vitae patrum*, XX (p. 741).

[70] *Vita Praejecti, MGH, SRM*, V, 224: "Paladius innuit puero [Praejecto] ad quemdam diaconem vocitantem Bobonem sibi rogatum prandii causa secum accessurum."

[71] *Vita Launomaris, AOSB*, I, 335: "Parentis . . . cuidam venerabili presbytero Chirmiro sacris imbuendum litteris ac conversatione tradiderunt. Beatus autem Chirmirus intra urbem Carnotum fulgebat doctrina." An inscription now lost mentioned the name of one of Chirmirus' students, the priest Lancegesilus: "Hic jacet Lancegesilus presbiter disciplus Chirimi." (The inscription was noted in Jean-Baptiste Souchet's seventeenth-century work, *Histoire du diocèse et de la ville de Chartres*, Société archéologique d'Eure-et-Loir, 4 vols. [Chartres, 1866–73], 1: 446.)

[72] See below, n. 74.

[73] Gregory of Tours, *HF*, VI, 36 (p. 307).

[74] *Vita Gaugerici, MGH, SRM*, III, 652: "Veniens in memorato castro Ebosio, inter-

As this text shows, studies began with the Psalter, which the children probably memorized by singing, thus gaining some idea of music in the process. Praejectus was at the head of his class at Issoire in his knowledge of sounds and antiphons.[75] Study of Scriptures and hagiographic texts then followed. Probably only future clerics devoted themselves to chant and reading of the holy texts. This is what the *Vitae sanctorum* tell us about the program of elementary schools in Gaul.

B. Parish Schools in Spain

Unfortunately, we do not have any such source with which to study the elementary school in Spain, which consequently remains practically unknown to us.

The sole text which mentions Spanish elementary school is a conciliar canon from Merida of 666.[76] It is much less precise, however, than the text of the Council of Vaison. The Merida canon permitted parish priests to train certain freedmen for the clerical state by educating them for holy office. This decision, which must have been in response to a need for clerics in the parishes of the diocese, cannot be considered the birth certificate of the parish school. A canon from the Sixth Council of Toledo in 638 had already required freedmen to enroll their children in the church to which they belonged so that they might be instructed (*causa eruditionis*).[77] From the sixth century, schools opened whenever rural parishes were established, and bishops regularly visited their churches to inquire about the condition of the buildings and the intellectual level of the priests.[78] It is quite likely that they also checked on the school, although the texts are silent on this point.

---

rogans sacerdotem cujus sollicitudinem de ipso castro commiserat, quos haberet ad officium praeparatos, illi ita respondens ait. . . . Abemus, domine pontifex, officialibus inter quos quidam puerolus nomine Gaugericus adhuc in scolis ad magisterium eruditionibus commendatus. . . .

"Interrogatus ab ipso pontifice qualem lectionem de divinis scripturis quas usitare videbatur haberet, in ordine ei patifecere deberit."

[75] *Vita Praejecti, MGH, SRM,* V, 227: "Coaeteneos suos de grammaticorum sonis antiphonisque praehiret." The expression "grammaticorum sonis" is surprising. The hagiographer seems to be calling the authors of the works that were used "grammarians."

[76] Council of Merida, c. 18 (Mansi, XI, 85): "Ut omnes parochitani presbyteri . . . de ecclesiae suae familia clericos sibi faciant; quos per bonam volontatem ita nutriant ut et officium sanctum digne peragant et ad servitium suum aptos eos habeant."

[77] Council of Toledo, 638, c. 10 (Mansi, X, 666): "Et enim decet ut hi quorum parentes titulum libertatis de familiis ecclesiae perceperunt, intra ecclesiam cui obsequium debent, causa eruditionis enutriantur."

[78] See Alonso, *La cura pastoral,* p. 396, for the development of rural churches.

The program of studies, as in Gaul, must have been based on the study of the Psalter and chant. An inscription from Mertola speaks of the "princeps cantorum" of the church.[79] If we compare this expression with a definition from Isidore of Seville,[80] we learn that it referred to a cleric who directed psalmody and undoubtedly taught it to children.

Also as in Gaul, the opening of an elementary school depended on the presence of a lettered cleric or monk. Unfortunately, we cannot cite any names until the second half of the seventh century, when the monk Valerius taught children in his hermitage at Bierzo (Asturia). These children went up to him in the summer, coming back down again in the winter to their families, who lived in the valley. Some of them, in what must have been a *tour de force*, learned the Psalter by heart in six months. Valerius exchanged the books he wrote for the children's instruction for the necessities with which their families provided him.[81]

Instruction in the presbyteral schools of Gaul and Spain was, as we can see, very modest. Children who wished to pursue their clerical studies had to go to the bishop and enter the episcopal school.

C. Episcopal Schools in Gaul

The episcopal schools, whose origins we observed in Gaul and Spain, became much more important in the sixth and seventh centuries. Episcopal schools could be found in about twenty towns in Gaul, in the north (Vermand, Reims, Paris, Metz, Tongres, and others) as well as in the south (Bourges, Poitiers, Clermont, Lyon, and Périgueux, among others). Our texts do not describe a scholarly institution in the strict sense of the word, as they would in later centuries; but they do speak of groups of young men gathered around the bishop or the archdeacon, both of whom served as teachers. We must, therefore, study the genesis of the school.

The school itself was located in the episcopal buildings (*domus ecclesiae*), where, according to canonical rule,[82] clerics were to live in a community with the bishop. The "crowd of young clerics"[83] which

---

[79] Vives, *Inscripciones*, no. 93.

[80] Isidore, *De eccl. off.*, II, 12 (*PL*, LXXXIII, 792): "Psalmistarum id est cantorum principes."

[81] Valerius, *Ordo querimoniae*, PL, LXXXVII, 448ff.

[82] See the councils of Tours (567), c. 13 and 20, and Orléans (533), c. 9 (*MGH, Leg. sect. III*, I, 125, 127, 63).

[83] Council of Tours (567), c. 13 (*MGH, Leg. sect. III*, I, 125): "Clericorum turba juniorum"; Council of Paris (614), c. 6 (ibid., 187): "Juniores ecclesiae."

gravitated around the bishop was composed of his nephews, who some-times became bishops in their turn;[84] sons of priests;[85] orphans;[86] children confided to the Church;[87] some who experienced miracles and thanked their patron saint by entering his service;[88] and lastly, young children who came from the parish school.[89] They generally entered the bishop's service at about the age of ten because the younger they were the better chance they had for a solid education.

Some began their careers as lectors, which, as we have seen, was an ancient tradition in the Church.[90] They were directed by the *primicerius lectorum*, who taught them how to read the sacred text.[91] To *lectio* was added *modulatio davitica*—that is, the chanting of Psalms and hymns[92] —which was taught by the cantor.[93] The episcopal school thus repeated and perfected the training already given in the presbyteral school.

When he enumerated the dignitaries of the *domus ecclesiae* in Metz, Gogo, the mayor of the palace, listed the archdeacon, the head of the lectors, the cantor, and the notary.[94] Certain youths were, in fact, trained in the episcopal school to assist the bishop with his administrative duties. The episcopal bureaucracy was sizable, since bishops delivered titles of ordination and letters for traveling clerics, for the poor and for former captives, in addition to preparing bills of sale and wills. The bishop generally kept a copy of the letters he received by putting them into Tironian notes and depositing them in his archives.[95] We know of some episcopal notaries, such as those of Caesarius of Arles, who must have been secretaries since their youth.[96]

---

84 Such was the case of Nicetius of Lyon, Constantius of Albi, and Ebbo of Sens. For the effort of Felix of Nantes' nephew, see Gregory of Tours, *HF*, VI, 15 (p. 285).

85 This was mentioned at the Council of Orléans (511), c. 4 (*MGH, Leg. sect. III*, I, 4).

86 See Le Blant, *IC*, 2: 207–10 (no. 483) for an instance at Viviers.

87 Magnodobus of Angers and Attala of Bobbio are cases in point.

88 Gregory of Tours, *Mir. Mart.*, I, 7 (*MGH, SRM*, I-2, 593), related that Theodemondus, a cured deaf-mute, "a Chrodigilde regina collectus est et ad scolam positus."

89 As was the case of both Gaugericus and Praejectus.

90 See above, chap. 4, sect. II.A. An inscription from Viviers mentions a thirteen-year-old lector; see Le Blant, *IC*, 2: 210–11 (no. 484). Cato of Clermont was a lector at age ten; see Gregory of Tours, *HF*, IV, 6 (p. 139).

91 A *primicerius lectorum* was mentioned at the school in Tongres before 533. See Remigius, *Ep.* 4 (*MGH, Ep.*, III, 155, l. 12), and Edouard de Moreau, *Histoire de l'Eglise en Belgique*, 5 vols. (Brussels, 1945–52), 1: 54.

92 According to the author of the *Vita Aredii*, *AS*, May I, 111.

93 *Vita Praejecti*, *MGH, SRM*, V, 228.

94 Gogo's letter is found in *MGH, Ep.*, III, 134–35.

95 Gregory of Tours, *HF*, X, 19 (p. 511).

96 *Vita Caesarii*, I, 40 (Morin ed., p. 300).

Beyond this strictly professional training, the youngsters were introduced to "sacred literature." The texts speak vaguely of "sacrae litterae," "divina scientiae," "doctrina ecclesiastica," "spiritualis scriptura" —expressions which undoubtedly refer to the Scriptures, the *Acts* of the martyrs, and saints' *Lives*. We do not know how these texts were explicated, since everything depended on the teacher's learning. The bishop generally confided the charge of *clericorum doctor* to the archdeacon, as was the case at Poitiers, Nîmes, Rodez, Bourges, Paris, and Clermont.[97] Sometimes the bishop directed the school, as did Aredius of Gap, who closely concerned himself with the education of those entrusted to him.[98] Occasionally the bishop would attract a renowned layman to the school. Sulpicius, who came to Bourges from the royal court, was such a successful teacher that the bishop asked the king's permission to make him a cleric.[99]

The instruction these masters dispensed was uniquely religious, since no bishop taught the liberal arts.[100] Those clerics whose profane culture we have noted acquired it outside the episcopal school either, like young Attala, before they were confided to a bishop[101] or, as in Gregory of Tours' case, after they left the clerical school.

An education received at an episcopal school was, as far as we can tell, hardly any different from that given by a presbyteral school. Lettered bishops did not attempt to introduce a program of literary studies

[97] Archdeacon Leodegarius was a "clericorum doctor egregius" at Poitiers (*Vita Leodegarii*, 1 [MGH, SRM, V, 283–84]). At Nîmes, the archdeacon had the "studium docendi parvulos" (Gregory of Tours, *Glor. martyr.*, 77 [MGH, SRM, I-2, 540]); for Rodez, see Gregory of Tours, *HF*, X, 8 (p. 490); for Bourges, Gregory of Tours, *Vitae patrum*, IX (p. 703); for Paris, Fortunatus, *Vita Marcelli*, 6 (MGH, AA, IV-2, 51); for Clermont, *Vita Praejecti*, 3 (MGH, SRM, V, 228). For the duties of the archdeacon in the sixth and seventh centuries, see A. Amanieu, "Archidiacre," DDC, 1: 953ff.

[98] *Vita Aredii*, AS, May, I, 111. Nicetius of Trier confided Aredius, a fellow Aquitainian, to a priest; see Gregory of Tours, *HF*, X, 29 (p. 522).

[99] *Vita Sulpicii*, 8, *vita long.* (PL, LXXX, 577): "Poscente Austregesilo Bituricae urbis episcopo a Theodorico principe ut sibi licentia daretur participationem docendi ei in ecclesia tradere eo quod ad ipsum doctrinae gratia multitudines convolarent; nec mora, regia defertur auctoritas, ut decisa caesarie, clericatus suspiceret onus." Sulpicius soon became an archdeacon (*Vita Amandi*, 5 [MGH, SRM, V, 433]). See Maurice de Laugardière, *L'Eglise de Bourges avant Charlemagne* (Paris, 1951), pp. 148ff., for Sulpicius of Bourges.

[100] Only one text indicates an exception: "Cum esset infantulus traditus est beato Modoaldo qui . . . litteris liberalibus eum erudire coepit" (*Vita sancti Germani*, 1 [MGH, SRM, V, 33]). But this instruction took place outside the episcopal school. Also, the author, Bobulenus, was paraphrasing Jonas' *Vita Attalae*.

[101] *Vita Attalae*, MGH, SRM, IV-1, 113: "Itaque dum patri nobili liberalibus litteris imbutus fuisset, Arigii quondam a genitore commendatus est."

into the clerical school. Consequently, those clergy who did not belong
to the aristocratic class had a limited and quite mediocre culture.[102] The
need for clerics made bishops less and less demanding. As we have
already noted, Caesarius of Arles had future deacons read the Bible
four times, while the bishop of Trier was happy if they knew the
Psalter by heart.

D. Episcopal Schools in Spain

We would expect to find flourishing episcopal schools and extensive
religious instruction in Spain. For one thing, councils in this kingdom
were concerned with establishing schools. It was the Council of Toledo
of 527 that decided to organize schools for clerics in the *domus ecclesiae*.[103]
Succeeding councils required clerics to abandon secular occupations and
devote themselves to study under the direction of the bishop.[104] Parents
were invited to present their children to the cathedral church quite early
so that early training would accustom clerics to life away from the
world. The *Liber ordinum* preserves the prayers which were said over
the child who was tonsured when he entered the church and the child
who was admitted to the episcopal school.[105] This distinction suggests
that very young children became clerics even before attaining school
age. In fact, the *Life of the Fathers of Merida* refers to *pueruli* who still
did not even know their letters but who performed liturgical services
under the direction of a *prepositus*.[106] They were educated when older
and climbed more or less rapidly the various echelons of ecclesiastical
orders. As adolescents, they were more strictly supervised, and as the
Fourth Council of Toledo (633) ordained, they were entrusted to and
lived with an older cleric.[107] Those who proved themselves were later
given individual cells, as in a monastery: as a young cleric at Palencia,

---

[102] That is, if they had any culture at all. For examples of ignorant priests, see
Gregory of Tours, *HF*, X, 13; X, 14; X, 25 (pp. 496, 500, 518). The Council of Orléans
(533), c. 16 (*MGH, Leg. sect. III*, I, 63), forbade the ordination of illiterate priests.

[103] See above, chap. 4, sect. II.B.

[104] See Alonso, *La cura pastoral*, pp. 173–77.

[105] *Liber ordinum*, no. 38: "Oratio super parvulum quem parentes ad doctrinam
offerunt"; ibid., no. 39: "Benedictio super parvulum qui in ecclesia ad ministerium
detonditur."

[106] *Vitas sanctorum*, I, 1 (Garvin ed., p. 139). See Alonso, *La cura pastoral*, p. 77.

[107] Council of Toledo (632), c. 24 (Mansi ed., X, 626): "Qui in clero puberes aut
adolescentes existunt, omnes in uno conclavi atrii commorentur, ut lubricae aetatis annos
non in luxuria, sed in disciplinis ecclesiasticis agant deputati probatissimo seniori, quem
et magistrum doctrinam et testem vitae habeant."

Fructuosus, future bishop of Braga, had lodgings (*habitaculum*) and youths in his service.[108]

As in Gaul, the archdeacon added the direction of young clerics to his other responsibilities. When he assumed his duties, the bishop gave him a rod and reminded him that he ought to be prudent in speech and rich in learning.[109] He had the *prepositi* and the *seniores* we spoke of earlier under his orders and was seconded by the *primiclericus*, or *primicerius*, who "taught the group of clerics by word."[110]

What exactly do we know about this teaching? According to a hagiographer already cited, the bishop of Merida had the entire ecclesiastical office taught to his nephew over several years as well as the entire "library of divine Scripture."[11] Thus, again, as in Gaul, studies were of two kinds, practical and theoretical.

One first learned how to read and chant liturgical texts. Isidore of Seville gives us a few details on the instruction of young lectors: they had to know grammar sufficiently "to understand, without punctuation, where a group of words ended, where a sentence was incomplete, and where the sentence's meaning was complete."[112] The lector had to have a clear, natural voice and sober gestures so as to speak, not to the eyes, but to the heart and ears.[113]

We know very little about how chant was taught. An inscription from Seville, perhaps from the top of the door of the schola of the cathedral, invited those who "wanted to meditate on the praises and canticles of Christ to undertake good studies."[114] In the work already cited, Isidore gave advice on the diet of the *cantores*, hoping that their voices would be "lilting, sweet, limpid, piercing, and of melody appropriate for holy religion."[115] Still, he tells us nothing about how music was taught.

---

108 *Vita Fructuosi*, 2 (Nock ed., p. 91): "Quidam de sumptoribus scolae ipsius adveniens interrogavit dicens: Quis hunc occupavit habitaculum?"

109 *Liber ordinum*, no. 15 (Férotin ed., p. 51): "Sit baculum nobis et virga indisciplinatis . . . ; sit sermone cautus et scientia providus."

110 Ibid., no. 16 (p. 53): "Commissum cleri gregem et verbo instruat et moribus ad meliora componat."

111 *Vitas sanctorum*, IV, 1 (Garvin ed., p. 172): "Omne officium ecclesiasticarum omnemque bibliothecam scripturarum divinarum . . . docuit."

112 Isidore of Seville, *De eccl. off.*, II, 11 (*PL*, LXXXIII, 791): "De Lectoribus. Iste erit doctrina et libris imbutus, sensuumque ac verborum scientia perornatus, ita ut in distinctionibus sententiarum intelligat ubi finiatur junctura, ubi adhuc pendet oratio, ubi sententia extrema claudatur."

113 Ibid., II, 11 (col. 792).

114 Vives, *Inscripciones*, p. 121, no. 352: "Qui meditari vis laudes et cantica Christi / Hic promtos animos subde bonis studiis."

115 Isidore of Seville, *De eccl. off.*, II, 12, 2 (*PL*, LXXXIII, 792): "Psalmistarum id est

Music during this period played an important role in the liturgy. Leander of Seville, John of Saragossa, and Conantius of Palencia wrote sacred melodies[116] and helped to form the bases of Visigothic music—music which is lost to us today because, as Isidore said, "sounds perished because they could not be written down."[117] Greek musical notation, in fact, had not yet been replaced by a new technique. The theoretical study of music was abandoned in favor of an apprenticeship to a musical art in which chant held the primary place.[118]

Alongside lectors and cantors, we find, as in Gaul, young notaries who worked in the episcopal offices under the direction of the *senior scribarum*.[119] The stenography mentioned by Isidore in his *Origines* was still a familiar technique to those clerics, who wrote down the deliberations of councils.[120]

More yet was demanded of the cleric who passed beyond the minor orders and headed for the priesthood. The Eighth Council of Toledo (653) stipulated that he had to know the entire Psalter, the canticles and hymns, and the baptismal rite.[121] In order to assure that they would not forget their training, rural priests were given a small book (*libellus officialis*) at their ordination so that "they would not bring any harm to the divine sacraments through ignorance," for "ignorance is the mother of all errors and ought to be eliminated especially in a priest of God."[122]

---

cantorum principes . . . ; ex hoc veteri more ecclesia sumpsit exemplum nutriendi psalmistas."

[116] Ildefonsus, *De vir. ill.*, 11 (*PL*, XCVI, 203): "Conantius . . . melodias soni multas noviter edidit." Ibid., 6 (col. 201): "Johannes in ecclesiasticis officiis quaedam eleganter et sono et oratione composuit." Isidore, *De vir. ill.*, PL, LXXXIII, 1104: "Leander . . . in sacrificio quoque laudibus atque psalmis multa dulci sono composuit."

[117] Isidore, *Origines*, III, xv, 2: "Nisi enim ab homine memoria teneantur soni, pereunt, quia scribi non possunt." This passage definitely proves that neumatic notation was unknown at this period. For the origin of neumes, see Solange Corbin, "La notation musicale neumatique dans les quatres provinces lyonnaises," (thesis, Paris, 1957).

[118] J. Fontaine, *IS*, pp. 417ff.; W. Gurlitt, "Zur Bedeutungsgeschichte von Musicus und Cantor bei Isidor von Sevilla," *Akademie der Wissenschaften und der Literatur* 7 (1950): 543–58.

[119] *Liber ordinum*, no. 21 (Férotin ed., p. 43): "Ordo in ordinatione ejus cui cura librorum et senior scriborum committitur. . . . Esto custos librorum et senior scribarum."

[120] Mansi, IX, 978, and X, 763; *Continuationes Isidorianae byzantina arabica et hispana*, MGH, AA, XI, 341, l. 36: "Notariis, quos ad recitandum vel ad excipiendum ordo requirit." See J. Fontaine, *IS*, pp. 8off., for stenography in Spain.

[121] Council of Toledo (653), c. 8 (Mansi, X, 1218).

[122] Fourth Council of Toledo (633), c. 26 (Mansi, X, 627): "Quando presbyteri in parochiis ordinantur, libellum officialem a sacerdote sui accipiant ut ad ecclesias sibi deputatas instructi succedant, ne per ignorantiam etiam ipsis divinis sacramentis offendant." Ibid., c. 25: "Ignorantia mater cunctorum errorum maxime in sacerdotibus Dei vitanda est." The *Liber ordinum*, no. 17 (Férotin ed., p. 55), also mentioned this *libellum* but as a *manualis*.

This manual no doubt contained a resumé of the episcopal *Ordo*.[123] The priest was not to separate himself from it—indeed, upon his death, it was placed on his coffin.[124]

Doctrinal training, of which we know almost nothing, accompanied the cleric's professional training. Priests who, like Fidelis of Merida, had learned the entire Bible were quite rare.[125] A trained deacon, the author of the *Vitas sanctorum patrum emeritensium*, knew only the Psalms, although he did cite hagiographic texts several times.[126] The *Lives of the Saints* and *Deeds of the Martyrs* that were used in the liturgy complemented the study of the Bible.[127] Spanish councils were more concerned than those in Gaul to establish schools;[128] however, they left each bishop to care for the instruction of his clerics as he saw fit.

It could be that Spanish clergy were more educated than those in Gaul and that unlettered priests were punished more severely. The Council of Narbonne (589) decided to cut them off from their livings until they had learned their letters and to lock them up in a monastery if they refused.[129] We ought not, nevertheless, to delude ourselves about the educational level of the clerics, since the councils of Toledo and Braga asked bishops to supervise closely their priests' ministry, including their manner of administering baptism.[130]

There was never any mention of secular studies in the training that clerics received at the episcopal school. Isidore hoped that his readers would study grammar, but this was a wish he expressed while commenting on their grammatical mistakes. The deacon of Merida we mentioned earlier had not read classical authors; the elegance of his style derives from his use of metric clausulae, a usage common to ecclesiastical authors. The liberal arts were not included in the "curricu-

---

[123] Garcia Villada, *Historia eclesiástica*, 2, pt. I: 262.

[124] *Liber ordinum*, Férotin ed., p. 112, l. 10.

[125] See n. 111 above.

[126] See the references in the preface to Garvin's edition, pp. 30–31. The deacon of Merida knew Gregory the Great's *Dialogues*, the *Vita Desiderii*, the *Vita Martini*, and the *Vita Fructuosi*.

[127] See Baudouin de Gaiffier, "La lecture des Actes des Martyrs dans la prière liturgique en Occident," *AB* 72 (1954): 153ff.

[128] Council of Toledo (633), c. 25 (Mansi, X, 627): "Ut sacerdotes scripturarum et canonum cognitionem habeant." This canon passed into Gratian's *Decretum*.

[129] Council of Narbonne (589), c. 11 (Mansi, IX, 1017). The Council of Toledo (633), c. 19 (Mansi, X, 625) forbade clerics "inscii litterarum" from becoming bishops. The Second Council of Seville, c. 7, condemned Bishop Agapius of Cordova: "Virum ecclesiasticis disciplinis ignarum" (Mansi, X, 559).

[130] Council of Toledo (633), c. 26 (Mansi, X, 627): "Ita ut quando ad litanias vel ad concilium venerint, rationem episcopo suo reddant qualiter susceptum officium celebrant vel baptizant."

lum" of episcopal schools in Spain any more than they were in Gaul. The optimistic opinion of Spanish historians, even recent ones, on this point is without foundation.[131]

The clerical schools of Gaul and Spain were thus organized on the same principles and followed the same program. The training they gave to clerics was primarily practical. How, then, can we explain the culture of those lettered bishops Leander, Isidore, Braulio, and their disciples who were the pride of the Visigothic Church? To do so, we must study the school which educated them, which was not the school organized by the cathedral but rather the monastic school. Most of the great Spanish bishops were, in fact, former monks: for the sixth century we can cite Martin, who directed the abbey of Dumio, "the Lérins of Galicia";[132] Vincent of Huesca (576), who was raised in the monastery of Asan;[133] John of Biclarum, abbot of Gerona before becoming bishop of that city;[134] Eutropius of Valencia, a disciple of Donatus, abbot of Servitanum;[135] and Leander, abbot at Seville. For the end of the sixth century, we have Isidore, who was undoubtedly trained in the monastery his brother Leander directed. For the beginning of the seventh century, we can mention Bishop Renovatus of Merida, who came from the monastery of Cauliana.[136]

It became customary for those who wished to become bishops to spend a period in a monastery, although no rule ever explicitly required it. Former laymen who were promoted to a bishopric, as were Helladius and Ildefonsus of Toledo and Teudisclus of Lamego, passed through the cloister before they were invested with the episcopal honor.[137] When monastic candidates and candidates from the secular clergy vied for a bishopric, the former had greater chance of success.[138] Important monasteries (Honoriacense, Agali, Cauliana, Santa Engracia) were established in the environs of the four major cities of Seville, Toledo, Merida,

---

[131] Garcia Villada, *Historia eclesiástica*, 2, pt. 1: 269, repeated by Madoz, *Epistolario de S. Braulio de Zaragoza*, p. 14.

[132] This, according to Fortunatus, *Carm.* V, 1 (*MGH, AA*, IV-1, 101).

[133] Vincent mentioned this fact in his will: "Ubi me dominus a pueritia mea vestra eruditione nutrivit" (Fidel Fita, "Patrologia visigotica," *Boletin de la real Academia de la historia* 49 [1906]: 152).

[134] Isidore of Seville, *De vir. ill.*, XLIV (*PL*, LXXXIII, 1105).

[135] Ibid., XLV. Licinianus of Carthagena may also have been a former monk from Servitanum; see Madoz, *Liciniano de Cartagena y sus cartas*, p. 15.

[136] *Vitas sanctorum*, V, 14-6 (Garvin ed., p. 256).

[137] For Helladius, see Ildefonsus, *De vir. ill.*, 8 (*PL*, XCVI, 202). For Teudisclus, see *Vita Fructuosi*, 8 (Nock ed., p. 99).

[138] J. F. Rivera Reico, "Cisma episcopal en la iglesia toledana visigoda," *HS* 1 (1948): 269–98.

and Saragossa, and thus maintained close contacts with cathedral churches.

Thus, what Gregory the Great, at the end of the sixth century, had hoped for Italy[139] came true in Spain; monasticism produced an elite secular clergy. In order to understand the success of the Isidorian period, we must next study the monastic school.

III. MONASTIC EDUCATION
IN GAUL AND IN SPAIN

A comparison between the two kingdoms will enable us to appreciate better the richness of monastic culture in Spain. While the intellectual activities of monasticism in Gaul had very limited objectives before the arrival of the Irishmen, true centers of religious culture flourished in Spain.

A. GAUL

The sixth century was a very fruitful period for monasticism in Gaul, since at least two hundred monasteries were in existence around 600.[140] Of course, not all these monasteries were asylums of sanctity and culture: exiles, political prisoners, and children without real vocations were forcibly consigned to monasteries, a practice which could only have been detrimental to the intellectual and spiritual development of the monks.[141] On the other hand, not all monastic establishments experienced these abuses, or at least, their rules were strong enough to neutralize the impact of pseudo-monks.

We have seen how the spirit of Lérins animated the monasteries of southern Gaul at the beginning of the sixth century. Afterwards, Caesarius' disciples, Ferreolus and Bishop Aurelian of Arles, were influenced by Caesarius' rules when they founded monasteries, as was the un-

---

139 See above, chap. 5, sect. IV. D.

140 Christian Courtois, "L'évolution du monachisme en Gaule de St. Martin à St. Colomban," *Settimane*, 4: 52; Friedrich Prinz, *Frühes Mönchtum im Frankenreich* (Munich, 1965); H. Atsma, *Klöster in Gallien bis zum ausgehenden 6. Jahrhundert: Untersuchungen zur Forschungssituation und zur Quellenlage, mit kritischem Klosterkatalog* (Munich, 1973).

141 Courtois, "Evolution du monachisme," pp. 69ff. Courtois uses canons from Merovingian councils to paint a rather dark picture of Merovingian monasticism. We should not forget that the councils denounced only those abuses which had to be suppressed.

known author of the *Rule of Paul and Stephen*.[142] The Provençal monastic tradition was spread in central Gaul by monastic founders of the
second half of the sixth century. When Aredius made a monastery out
of his family home, he followed the rules of Basil and Cassian.[143] At
Moutier-Saint-Jean, the Lérinian spirit introduced by John of Réomé
(died 450), a former monk of Lérins, survived until young Sequanus
read the *Collationes* and the *Institutiones*, that is, Cassian's work.[144] At
Autun, monks followed the rules of Antony and Basil.[145] Droctoveus
transplanted these customs to Saint Vincent in Paris when he became
abbot there.[146] Given these circumstances, monastic education in Gaul
was not very different from what we have already observed. Provençal
rules subsequent to Caesarius required that a monk know and be able
to read his Psalter[147] and provided for reading the rule and the Deeds
of the Martyrs at table or in private.[148] In Ferreolus' monastery, monks
who did not work the land copied and decorated manuscripts in the
scriptorium.[149] The *Rule of Paul and Stephen*, more precise than the
others, gives us entry into the monastic school, where we can observe
small groups of children under the care of a *dictator* (one who dictates)
who was responsible for their education.[150]

At Tours, or rather at Marmoutier, on the other side of the Loire, the
monks remained faithful to the precepts of Saint Martin. Leobard, for
example, made parchment and recopied manuscripts to ward off evil
thoughts.[151] In addition, he meditated on the Psalms and had Gregory

---

[142] For this rule, see U. Berlière, "La règle des Etienne et Paul," in *Mélanges Paul
Thomas* (Gand and New York, 1930), pp. 39–53, and J. Evangelista M. Vilanova's
edition in the series Scripta et Documenta, 11 (Abadía de Montserrat, 1959).

[143] *Vita Aredii*, 10 (*MGH, SRM*, III, 586); Fliche-Martin, 5: 508.

[144] Jonas, *Vita Ioannis abbatis, MGH, SRM*, III, 507–8; *Vita Sequani, AS*, Sept., VI, 36–
41. Roger, p. 166, translates "Patrum Collationes et Institutiones" as "works of the
Fathers," but there is no doubt that the hagiographer was referring to Cassian's works.

[145] *Vita Droctovei*, 8 (*MGH, SRM*, III, 539). This ninth-century *Life* incorporates
elements of a Merovingian *Life*.

[146] Saint Vincent, later known as Saint-Germain-des-Prés, was more a basilica than
an abbey. For this distinction, see L. Levillain, "Etudes sur l'abbaye de Saint-Denis à
l'époque mérovingienne," *BECh* 86 (1925): 44ff.

[147] Ferreolus, *Regula*, 11 (*PL*, LXVI, 963); Aurelian, *Regula*, 18, 25–26 (*PL*, LXVIII,
390). See also the advice of Abbess Caesaria of Arles to Radegunda (*Ep.* 11 [*MGH, Ep.*,
III, 451, l. 40]): "Nulla sit de intrantibus quae non litteras discat. Omnes psalterium
memoriter teneant."

[148] Aurelian, *Regula*, 32, 55 (*PL*, LXVIII, 391). See also de Gaiffier's article cited
above, n. 127.

[149] Ferreolus, *Regula*, 28 (*PL*, LXVI, 969): "Paginam pinguant digiti."

[150] See below, chap. 10, sect. II.A.

[151] Gregory of Tours, *Vitae patrum*, XX, 2 (*MGH, SRM*, I-2, 742): "Scribebat interdum ut se a cogitationibus noxiis discuteret."

of Tours furnish him with the *Lives of the Fathers*, Cassian's *Institutiones*, and "all that ought to be in the cell of a recluse."[152] The *Life of Saint Martin* was also a favorite text of monks, who even kept it under their pallets in order to meditate on it during the night.[153]

We know little about the monasteries of northern Gaul before the arrival of the Irish; however, the few bits of evidence available show that their culture was ascetic. After a stay at Lérins and Arles, Leobinus (died 556) founded a monastery in Perche. His biographer describes him as an indefatigable reader who studied day and night.[154] Monks at Saint-Loup-de-Troyes and in Maine were "trained in sacred letters and monastic disciplines."[155] Even those who imitated the Eastern ascetics in their most extraordinary manifestations maintained an elementary culture. The Lombard stylite Vulfilaic, who lived on a column at Carignan in the Ardennes, and the recluses whom Gregory of Tours mentioned meditated on sacred texts.[156]

Whether they followed the Lérinian tradition or sought to observe an Eastern way of life, the monks of Merovingian Gaul had a minimum of ecclesiastical training. While reading of Holy Scripture was recommended by the rules and councils, we can wager that the monk went no further.

The only monastery open to a more literary and humanistic culture was Sainte Croix in Poitiers, but this was an exceptional case. Radegunda's monastery followed a relaxed version of Caesarius' *Rule*: the nuns played dice, took baths, and admitted men into the cloister.[157] This liberalism explains in part the troubles which followed Radegunda's death. The presence of the poet Fortunatus at Poitiers brought worldly culture into the monastery; Radegunda and Abbess Agnes enjoyed receiving Fortunatus' poems, and Radegunda herself wrote poems.[158] Ab-

---

[152] Ibid., p. 742, ll. 29–30.

[153] Gregory of Tours, *Mir. Mart.*, III, 42 (*MGH, SRM*, I-2, 642): "Pro salute animae et vitae correctione librum vitae beati antestis secum detulit."

[154] Fortunatus, *Vita Leobini, MGH, AA*, IV-2, 74: "Qua occupatione detentus, per diem se lectioni vacare non posse comperiens declinantibus ad dormiendum monachis, pernoctabat intente ut disceret normam justitiae." So that his monks would not see him, "velum opposuit . . . et ipse lectionis caperet incrementum."

[155] *Vita Winebaudi, AS*, April, I, 573; *Vita Ernei, AS*, Aug., II, 426.

[156] Gregory of Tours, *HF*, VIII, 15 (p. 581). The Arvernian Galuppa also knew the Scriptures (Gregory of Tours, *Vitae patrum*, XI [p. 710, l. 30]).

[157] Gregory of Tours, *HF*, IX, 40 (p. 464). Caesaria of Arles was disturbed by the reports from Poitiers (*MGH, Ep.*, III, 452, l. 32): "Familiaritates virorum omnino quantum potestis rarius habete."

[158] Fortunatus, *App. carminum*, Carm. XXXI, v. 1 (*MGH, AA*, IV-1, 290): "In brevi-

bess Caesaria of Arles, perhaps aware of these courtly exchanges, expressed her fear in a letter to Radegunda that the study of Scripture was forgotten at Poitiers and recommended the reading of sacred texts, "true ornaments of the soul."[159]

Nuns from royal or aristocratic backgrounds were generally more educated. One of them, Baudinivia, author of a *Vita Radegundis*, wrote correct Latin and knew how to draw from hagiographical models.[160] Perhaps we can attribute to the monastery of Sainte Croix a nun's letter that has come down to us without a name or date. The authoress' mannered style is close to that of Fortunatus and his contemporaries. After having praised the biblical learning of her correspondent, another nun, she concluded: "I desire that the roots of my senses be frequently watered with baskets of droppings, that is, by the fecundity of your words."[161] The intellectual life of those at Sainte Croix in Poitiers recalls that of the Merovingian clerics we have described above. This monastery was not a center of sacred studies such as those in Italy during the same time and those we find in Spain.

B. Spain

Spanish monasticism was also affected by Eastern influences: In Galicia, in Asturia, and on the Balearic Islands, monks lived like desert ascetics.[162] In addition to these isolated monastic establishments, however, near the large cities there were also important monasteries, from which the great lettered bishops came.[163] Thanks to the rules and biographies of certain monks, we can piece together the intellectual life of these monasteries.

Sacred culture here appears to have been much more profound than

---

bus tabulis mihi carmina magna dedisti." See Bezzola, 1: 55ff., for the relations between Radegunda and Fortunatus.

[159] *MGH, Ep.*, III, 452: "Lectiones divinas iugiter aut legite aut audite, quia ipsae sunt ornamenta animae."

[160] For Baudinivia's Latin, see Bonnet, *Le latin*, p. 85, and Krusch's preface to his edition of the *Vita Radegundis, MGH, SRM*, II, 362.

[161] *MGH, Ep.*, III, 716 and 718: "Tui cordis, in qua omnis librorum biblioteca congesta est . . . ; rogo, ut aridas radices sensus mei cophinum stercoris, hoc est ubertatem verborum tuorum frequenter effundas."

[162] Anscari Mundó, "Il monachesimo nella penisola iberica fino al sec. VII," *Settimane*, 4: 85ff.; M. C. Diaz y Diaz, "El eremitismo en la España visigótica," *Revista portuguesa de historia* 6 (1964): 221–37.

[163] See above, sect. II.D. The *De monachis perfectis* (Diaz y Diaz, *AW*, pp. 80–87) is a treatise intended for urban monks. For the recent bibliography on Isidore's spirituality, see Jacques Fontaine, "Isidore de Séville," *DSp*, 7, pt. 2: 2104–16.

in Gaul. In the rule written for his sister Florentine, Leander of Seville made prayer and reading obligatory for the nuns. They were to avoid carnal readings in the Old Testament in order to "extract the sense of spiritual meaning from the truth of history."[164] It could be that the *Moralia in Job* which Gregory the Great had sent to Leander was studied in this monastery. Florentine asked her brother Isidore for his treatise *De fide catholica contra Judeos* in order to deepen her understanding of the Old Testament.[165]

Isidore was more precise than his brother Leander when it came to the intellectual duties of monks: monks, he said, following Saint Augustine, lived by praying, reading, and discussing among themselves.[166] In the rule that was undoubtedly written for the monastery of Seville, he provided for three hours of reading every day and for a period when the assembled brothers would meditate or discuss questions concerning the sacred text.[167] The abbot, in response to questions from his monks, was to explain the meaning of difficult passages before everyone.[168] Monks were to borrow books every day at the first hour and return them after vespers to the *sacrarius*, who kept them and distributed them with the sacred vases and wax.[169]

The culture of the Spanish monk thus brings to mind a more developed version of the culture of sixth-century Italian monasteries. But a new element appeared in Spain, which Isidore singled out when he spoke of the kinds of books a monk could borrow: "The monk should refrain from reading the books of pagans or heretics. It would be better, in fact, to ignore their pernicious teachings than to fall, from knowing them, into error."[170] No rule up to this point had mentioned pagan

---

[164] Leander, *Reg. ad virgines*, 6 (*PL*, LXXII, 883–84): "Ut jugiter virgo oret et legat"; Ibid., 7: "Ut carnaliter non legi debeat Vetus Testamentum . . . de historiae veritate intelligentiae spiritalis sensum cape."

[165] Isidore of Seville, *Contra Judeos*, preface (*PL*, LXXXIII, 449): "Haec sancta soror te petente ob aedificationem studii tui tibi dicavi."

[166] Isidore, *De eccl. off.*, II, 16, 11 (*PL*, LXXXIII, 799): "Viventes in orationibus, in lectionibus, in disputationibus."

[167] *Reg. mon.*, VI, 3 (*PL*, LXXXIII, 876): "Post vespertinum congregatis fratribus oportet vel aliquid meditare vel de aliquibus divinae lectionis quaestionibus disputare."

[168] Ibid., VIII, 1 (col. 877): "De his autem quaestionibus quae leguntur nec forte intelliguntur unusquisque fratrum aut in collatione aut post vesperam abbatem interroget et recitata in loco lectione ab eo expositionem suscipiat ita ut dum uni exponitur caeteri audiant."

[169] Ibid.: "Omnes codices custos sacrarii habeat deputatos a quo singulos singuli fratres accipiant, quos prudenter lectos vel habitos semper post vesperam reddant." The books were distributed at a fixed hour in the morning. Those who abused books were punished: "Qui codicem negligenter usus fuerit" (XVII, 1 [col. 885]).

[170] Ibid., VIII, 3 (col. 877): "Gentilium libros vel haereticorum volumina monachus

books; obviously, it was forbidden to read them. In Isidore's monastery, though, profane books were placed beside sacred books. This calls for reflection.

That Isidore was aware of the dangers of reading pagan authors and made his feelings known in the passage just cited and in others[171] does not mean, as has long been believed, that he had no taste for antique literature. All his work indicates just the opposite.[172] If he put his monks on guard, it was because he knew the dangers readers with un-proven minds would face. The danger was much more serious in Spain, where paganism was stronger than elsewhere.

Although paganism is thought to have survived primarily in popular forms,[173] can its hold on aristocrats be underestimated? During Isidore's time, the theater, with its equivocal plays, still attracted spectators, among whom bishops could be found.[174] Public baths were still open, and the pleasure of the bath supported the cult of the body.[175] Leander of Seville had to explain to his nuns that one should love men not be-cause of their physical beauty but because they were creatures of God.[176] The poetry lettered men read in anthologies, such as the *Latin Anthol-ogy* that circulated in Spain, could still trouble the hearts of clerics and monks and "through the enchantments of silly tales excite the mind by spurring on passions."[177] It has been noted that Isidore rarely cited antique poets other than Virgil.[178] An inscription on the door of his library invited those who were scandalized by the poets to turn to the Christian poets Avitus and Sedulius.[179] The reading of pagan literature also kept alive astrological beliefs, which continued to draw adherents,

legere caveat; melius est enim eorum perniciosa dogmata ignorare quam per experientiam in aliquem laqueum erroris incurrere."

[171] *Sent.*, III, 13 (*PL*, LXXXIII, 685): "Ideo prohibetur Christianus figmenta legere poetarum quia per oblectamenta inanium fabularum mentem excitant ad incentiva libidinum." See his other warnings in *In Lev.*, 17, 1 (*PL*, LXXXIII, 335); *In Exod.*, 14, 3 (ibid., 292). *In Jos.*, 8, 2 (ibid., 375).

[172] Fontaine has dealt with some of these judgments of Isidore's work in *IS*, p. 806, n. 2. He brilliantly proves that such opinions have little foundation.

[173] J. Fontaine, "Isidore de Séville et l'astrologie," pp. 271–300; idem, *IS*, p. 789.

[174] See Sisebut's letter to Bishop Eusebius of Tarragona (*MGH, Ep.*, III, 668): "Quod de ludis teatriis, faunorum scilicet ministerio."

[175] Leander, *Reg. ad virgines*, 10 (*PL*, LXXII, 880): "Balneo non pro studio vel nitore utaris corporis sed tantum pro remedio." See also Isidore, *Reg. mon.*, XXI (*PL*, LXXXIII, 892).

[176] Leander, *Reg. ad virgines*, 3 (*PL*, LXXII, 882): "Amandi sunt certe viri ut opus Dei, sed absentes . . . propter Deum qui eos fecit non propter pulchritudinem corporis."

[177] See above, n. 171.

[178] J. Fontaine, *IS*, pp. 793–94.

[179] Isidore, *Versus in bibliotheca*, X (Beeson ed., p. 160).

especially in Betica. Urban monasteries were not sheltered from the side effects of this late paganism, especially when their libraries contained pagan works.

Isidore, in the passage noted above, forewarned ("legere caveat") those who could not tolerate this reading. The rule was made for all monks, adults as well as children, lettered as well as *simplices*.[180] It was to the last group that Isidore addressed himself. Profane books were reserved for more experienced monks, who used them to deepen their sacred culture.

In fact, even though he did not speak of it in his rule, Isidore's true opinion was that "it would be better to be a grammarian than a heretic because the knowledge of the grammarians can be profitable for our way of life as long as one nourishes himself from it for a better end."[181] Elsewhere, he repeated the classic image of the captive shorn by the Israelites to refer to the Christian use of the liberal arts.[182] Isidore in this respect joined himself to the tradition of the Church Fathers from Tertullian to Augustine, as well as to Cassiodorus and even Gregory the Great. We can easily prove that the principles of this tradition were applied in the major Spanish monasteries. At the end of the sixth century Martin of Braga introduced his monks at Dumio to the works of Seneca and had a reputation as a great rhetor.[183] Around 578, Isidore acquired his first literary and scientific learning in his brother Leander's monastic library.[184] Under his brother's direction, Braulio undertook

---

[180] The presence of children in Spanish monasteries is often noted in the sources. For Cauliana, see *Vitas sanctorum*, II, 14 (Garvin ed., p. 152): "Pueri parvuli qui sub pedagogum disciplinis in scholis litteris studebant." The Council of Toledo of 633, c. 60 and 63 (Mansi, X, 634), obliged the children of baptized Jews to be brought up in monasteries.

[181] Isidore, *Sent.*, III, 13 (*PL*, LXXXIII, 688): "Meliores esse grammaticos quam haereticos. Haeretici enim haustum lethiferi succi hominibus persuadendo propinant, grammaticorum autem doctrina potest etiam proficere, ad vitam, dum fuerit in meliores usu assumpta." By *grammatici*, Isidore definitely meant the authors studied in class, as had Gregory the Great. See above, chap. III.

[182] Isidore, *In Deuteronomium*, 18, 6, 71 (*PL*, LXXXIII, 368).

[183] For Martin's classical culture, see Barlow, *Martini episc. Bracarensis*, pp. 5, 205; for his rhetoric, see Fortunatus, *Carm.* V, 1 (*MGH, AA*, IV-1, 102, ll. 19ff.): "Quid loquar de perihodis, epichirematibus, enthymemis, syllogismisque perplexis? Quo laborat quadrus Maro, quo rotondus Cicero?"

[184] Dom Séjourné, *Le dernier Père de l'Eglise*, pp. 27–29, suggests that Isidore succeeded Leander as abbot when the latter became bishop of Seville. It could well be: Isidore is called an abbot in one manuscript; see Férotin, "Deux manuscrits wisigothiques de la bibliothèque de Ferdinand Ier," *BECh* 62 (1901): 377. See J. Fontaine, *IS*, pp. 7–8, for the various conjectures on Isidore's education. What we have said about the establishment of episcopal schools reinforces the hypothesis that Isidore was educated in a monastery.

"the study of secular disciplines" at the monastery of Saragossa.[185] Around 620, the abbot of this monastery greeted a cleric eager for "wisdom," who was later to become Bishop Eugenius II of Toledo.[186] At the monastery of Agali near Toledo, the monk Eugenius, who was also bishop of Toledo, was taught by Abbot Helladius and later amazed his friends with his scientific learning.[187] Medical studies perhaps were particularly honored in this monastery dedicated to Cosmas and Damian. Finally, around 620, young Ildefonsus of Toledo found in Agali's library all that he needed to fashion a surprising culture.[188]

The monastic education of the important bishops of Visigothic Spain explains the character of their literary work, since it was in monasteries and not elsewhere that they had access to the authors of Antiquity. When they became bishops, they wanted the same working conditions in their *domus ecclesiae*. When he moved from the monastery of Seville to the episcopal see, Leander organized the study center that his brother later developed. Isidore, regrettably, never spoke of his episcopal school; thus, we must reconstruct the contents of its library with great difficulty.[189] The verses which decorated the walls of his scriptorium are a precious source of information on the contents of the chests, but they tell us nothing abut the organization of work. It hardly helps to know that the gossip was expelled from the library and that the lazy were punished.[190] It is in Isidore's work itself, then, that we must seek the richness of his library. When Braulio became bishop at Saragossa, he maintained close

---

[185] Braulio, *Vita Aemiliani*, preface (*PL*, LXXX, 699): "Quamobrem disciplinarum saecularium studium etsi ex parte attigi." For Braulio's youth, see Madoz's preface to his edition of Braulio's letters, *El epistolario de San Braulio*, pp. 11ff.

[186] Ildefonsus, *De vir. ill.*, 14 (*PL*, XCVI, 204): "Hic cum ecclesiae regiae clericus esset egregius, vita monachi delectatus est. Qui sagaci fuga urbem Caesaraugustaniam petens, illic martyrum sepulcris inhaesit, ibique studia sapientiae et propositum monachi decenter incoluit."

[187] Ibid., 13: "Eugenius ab Helladio . . . sacris in monasterio institutionibus eruditus. . . . Nam numeros, statum, incrementa, decrementaque cursus recursusque lunarum tanta peritia novit, ut considerationes disputationis ejus auditorem et in stuporem verterent et in desiderabilem doctrinam inducerent."

[188] Julianus, *Vita Ildlefonsi*, PL, XCVI, 43: "Hic igitur sub rudimentis adhuc infantiae degens . . . Agaliense monasterium petit." See Manitius, 1: 234.

[189] On this subject read Fontaine's chapter in *IS*, pp. 738ff., which happily supersedes Julius Tailhan's "Les bibliothèques espagnoles au Moyen Age," appendix to *Nouveaux mélanges d'archéologie, de littérature, et d'histoire sur le Haut Moyen Age*, published by Charles Cahier and Arthur Martin, 3rd ser., vol. 4 (Paris, 1877), pp. 217–346, and Joseph Christian Ernest Bourret's mediocre work, *L'école chrétienne de Séville sous la monarchie des Visigoths: Recherches pour servir à l'histoire de la civilisation chrétienne chez les barbares* (Paris, 1855).

[190] Isidore, *Versus in bibliotheca*, XXV, XXVI, XXVII (Beeson ed., p. 166).

contact with his former monastery. Consequently, the scriptoria of both establishments provided each other with mutual service. Thanks to Braulio's correspondence, we can gain an idea of the size of the episcopal library, which was famous both in Toledo and in Braga.[191] Whenever the bishop was questioned on a liturgical or dogmatical point he was sure to provide the pertinent bibliographical information.

The major monasteries of Spain and the episcopal centers that adopted their cultural life were unique institutions in the West of the early seventh century. Nothing like them existed in Gaul, as we have seen, or in northern Italy or England, as we shall see. They remind us of the sixth-century study centers we encountered in Africa and in southern Italy at Lucullanum and Vivarium.

One wonders whether the Spaniards were influenced by Cassiodorus' foundation. Isidore knew the *Institutiones* but seems not to have known of Vivarium; there is no evidence that Campanian or Calabresian monks came to Betica. On the other hand, we do know that, about 570, African monks fleeing the devastations of the Berbers and the persecutions of the Byzantines came to Spain. Some settled in the province of Merida,[192] others around Valencia at Servitanum. The foundation of this monastery, which chroniclers thought was an important event,[193] bears directly on the history of culture. The monks, led by their abbot, Donatus, brought with them a large number of books and made Servitanum an important center of studies.[194] We can appraise its significance through the work of Eutropius—Donatus' disciple, successor, and later bishop of Valencia—and of Licinianus of Carthagena.[195]

Donatus and his monks must have tried to reconstruct an African center of studies in Spain, and thus, if we knew about monastic culture in Africa, we might have an element of comparison for our present study. Unfortunately, our information on Africa is practically nonexistent after Fulgentius' time. We know of several lettered abbots during the course of the battles the African Church led against the political

---

[191] See Braulio, *Ep.* 43–44 (Madoz ed., pp. 188, 195).

[192] *Vitas sanctorum*, II, 2 (Garvin ed., p. 156).

[193] Ildefonsus, *De vir. ill.*, 4 (*PL*, XCVI, 200): "Ferme cum septuaginta monachis copiosisque librorum codicibus." John of Biclarum also mentioned this event in his *Chronica* (*MGH*, *AA*, XI, 212, 217).

[194] For the significance of their arrival, see Garcia Villada, *Historia eclesiástica*, 2, pt. 1: 282, and C. J. Bishko, review of *Liciniano de Cartagena y sus cartas* by José Madoz, *Traditio* 7 (1949–51): 499.

[195] For Eutropius' literary work, see Diaz y Diaz, "La producción literaria de Eutropio de Valencia," in *AW*, pp. 9–27. There is reason to think that Licinianus also passed through Servitanum; see Madoz, *Liciniano de Cartagena y sus cartas*, p. 16.

policy of the emperors: Abbot Peter was one of the great powers in the Councils of Carthage in 525 and 534;[196] in the seventh century, we find Abbot Thalassius, to whom Maximus the Confessor dedicated his *Questions on Scripture* and who was himself a writer.[197] When Maximus, fleeing Monothelite persecution, came to Africa to settle at Carthage, he was welcomed warmly by African monks. Among them perhaps was the young Hadrian, who was later to be abbot of Nisida near Naples before becoming one of the founders of Anglo-Saxon culture.[198]

The arrival of African monks in Spain, which is only one example of the relations which always existed between Africa and the Iberian peninsula,[199] certainly played an important role in the establishment of Spanish centers of monastic culture.

Furthermore, were not the intellectual principles of Isidore and the lettered bishops of Spain those which Augustine proposed in the *De doctrina christiana?* Certainly, there were shades of difference between Augustine's attitude toward classical culture and that of Isidore, but they are differences that we can attribute to the character of the two writers and to the time in which each lived. Isidore is said to have been much more timid than Augustine in the christianization of profane culture, preferring to affirm the autonomous value of this culture in his own work.[200] Yet, like Augustine, the bishop of Seville thought it necessary to place the profane disciplines in the service of Christian learning. His chapter on diacritical marks, knowledge of which was indispensable in establishing the sacred text, and his remarks on the tropes found in the Bible remain very Augustinian.[201] In giving a word and its etymology a sacred value, he reunited with the Judeo-Christian tradition and opened up a vast field of research to the exegete.[202] Again, fulfilling Augustine's wish and completing Eucherius of Lyon's

---

[196] Mansi, VIII, 635 and 841. These councils were concerned with monastic exemptions. In 616, a certain Abbot Felix of Gilita continued Dionysius' paschal computation; see Courcelle, *LG*, p. 344, n. 2.

[197] *PG*, XC, 243. Thalassius' four hundred sentences "On Charity" have been published in *PG*, XCI, 1427. Maximus had perhaps settled in the monastery of Mandracium.

[198] Hadrian died in 704 at an advanced age. He must have been born in the first half of the seventh century.

[199] See R. Lantier, "Les arts chrétiens de la péninsule ibérique et de l'Afrique du Nord," *Anuario del cuerpo facultativo de archiveros, bibliotecarios y arqueólogos* 3 (1935): 257–72, and the works listed in J. Fontaine, *IS*, p. 854, n. 3. A. Mundó commented on the African influence on Spanish monasticism in "Il monachesimo nella penisola iberica," *Settimane*, 4: 83–84.

[200] J. Fontaine, *IS*, pp. 794ff.

[201] Ibid., pp. 75, 143, 210.

[202] Ibid., pp. 43–44.

sketch,[203] Isidore composed a *Liber numerorum*, a veritable treatise on the art of arithmology.[204] Without going so far as to say that Isidore founded this art, let us at least claim that he was the first, to our knowledge, to place a manual at the disposal of exegetes. He united the Christian and profane traditions and gave the Middle Ages formulas which were to enjoy great success. Isidore wrote his *De natura rerum* in the same spirit: drawing from the works of learned Christians and pagans, he gave the lettered cleric a practical manual that was greatly diffused after his time.[205]

Isidore did not work for the exegete alone. The Christian orator, thanks to Isidore, could develop a style that, while abandoning the obscurities of profane rhetoric, remained faithful to beautiful language. Lettered clerics in Spain, as elsewhere, condemned the affected style of their contemporaries: Martin of Braga, Braulio of Saragossa, and the deacon of Merida denounced "the pretentious froth of rhetors," "the fictions painted over with eloquence," the "ostentatious and overbearing speeches."[206] These clerics reacted against excesses which were quite familiar to them even while using classical commonplaces. Isidore of Seville, like the others, preferred *res* to *verba* and feared that "puffed-up style reflects a soul puffed up with conceit."[207] In his desire for the pure, the natural, and the true,[208] he reiterated the requirements of Cicero and Quintillian while criticizing the excesses of Fronto. Thus, like Augustine in the fourth book of his *De doctrina christiana*, he placed in the service of Christian eloquence—thinking especially of bishops[209]

---

[203] Augustine, *De doctrina christiana*, II, 39–59 (*PL*, XXXIV, 62); Eucherius, *De numeris, CSEL*, 31: 59.

[204] Isidore of Seville, *Liber numerorum qui in sanctis scripturis occurrunt, PL*, LXXXIII, 179–200. See J. Fontaine, *IS*, pp. 370ff.

[205] For this treatise, see the preface and notes to Fontaine's edition.

[206] Martin of Braga, ed. Barlow, p. 74: "Nec pomposas in ea spumas rhetorum quaeres quia humilitatis virtus non verborum elatione sed mentis puritate requiritur." Braulio, *Vita Aemiliani*, preface (*PL*, LXXX, 699); in a letter to Fructuosus, (*Ep.* 44 [Madoz ed., p. 202]), Braulio contrasted evangelical simplicity to the "spumas gentilium eloquiorum." *Vitas sanctorum*, IV, preface (Garvin ed., p. 160): "Omittentes phaleratas verborum pompas."

[207] Isidore, *Sent.*, III, 13, 6 and 9 (*PL*, LXXXIII, 687–88): "Omnis saecularis doctrina spumantibus verbis resonas, ac se per eloquentiae tumorem attollens . . . ; quanto majora fuerint litteraturae studia, tanto animus arrogantiae fastu inflatus majore intumescit jactantia." Ibid., II, 29, 12 (col. 630): "Horret sapientia spumeum verborum ambitum ac fucum mundialis eloquentiae inflatis sermonibus perornatum."

[208] *De eccl. off.*, II, 5, 17 (*PL*, LXXXIII, 785): "Sermo purus, simplex, apertus." For Isidore's style, see J. Fontaine, "Théorie et pratique du style chez Isidore de Séville," *VChr* 14 (1960): 65–101.

[209] *Sent.*, III, 36, 2; 37, 7 (*PL*, LXXXIII, 707–8).

—a classical tradition that had too often been betrayed. For Isidore, as for his contemporaries, it would not do to speak or write carelessly, because stylistic beauty very often was a guarantee of truth. When Licinianus of Carthagena wanted to prove to the bishop of Ibiza the fraudulence of a letter supposedly fallen from heaven, he criticized both the impropriety of the style of the letter and the falsity of its doctrine.[210] One would think that Cassiodorus was speaking.

In one domain, however, Christian learning in Spain did not fulfill the Augustinian program. The study of Greek and Hebrew, indispensable for the interpretation of the sacred text, was not undertaken. This is a surprising gap, especially for Spain, which had long been under Byzantine influence and which counted many Jews among its population.

Greek was still spoken in southern Spain, but few clerics knew it. At Braga, Martin taught Greek to one monk and translated some Eastern *Vitae patrum*.[211] John of Biclarum, who spent his youth at Constantinople, likewise knew Greek. But Licinianus of Carthagena and Leander of Seville, who had also lived in the Byzantine capital, remained ignorant of the language.[212] Isidore's work shows that he too did not know Greek.[213] This distaste for Greek has been viewed as a manifestation of the Visigothic battle against the Byzantines. Is it not, rather, a case of intellectual impoverishment, with clerics being content with the translations they had?

Nor did they seek to learn Hebrew, even though sizable Jewish communities in Spain had resisted Sisebut's persecutions.[214] Synagogues were still centers of study in the major towns.[215] Even without contacts

---

[210] Licinianus, *Ep.*, ed. Madoz, p. 126: "Ubi nec sermo elegans nec doctrina sana praebent."

[211] For Greek at Braga, see M. Martins, "Pascasio Dumiense traductor," *Brotéria* 51 (1950): 294.

[212] See what Madoz has to say in *Liciniano de Cartagena y sus cartas*, pp. 61ff. Licinianus knew Origen through Hilary of Poitiers' translation (*Ep.* I [Madoz ed., p. 94]).

[213] J. Fontaine, *IS*, pp. 849ff.; José Madoz, *La literatura patristica española continuadora de la estética de los clásicos* (Saragossa, 1950), pp. 20–24.

[214] For the Jews in Spain, see Solomon Katz, *The Jews in the Visigothic and Frankish Kingdoms of Spain and Gaul* (Cambridge, Mass., 1937); and Bernhard Blumenkranz, *Juifs et Chrétiens dans le monde occidental, 430–1096* (Paris, 1960), pp. 105ff. Tarragona was called the "city of Jews" by Arabs. See J. M. Millas, "Una nueva inscripcíon judaica bilingue en Tarragona," *Sefarad* 17 (1957): 3–10. The story of the "letter fallen from heaven" from Ibiza may have come from Jewish circles; see Madoz, *Liciniano de Cartagena y sus cartas*, p. 72.

[215] See Katz, *The Jews*, pp. 75–76, who uses the *Leges Visigoth.*, XII, 3, 11 (*MGH, Leg. sect. I*, I, 438) and the Toledo councils. Isidore, *De eccl. off.*, I, 10, 1 (*PL*, LXXXIII, 745) alluded to lectors in the synagogues.

with Jewish exegetes,[216] clerics might have worked with Hebrew manuscripts. But this was never done.[217]

The Christian learning of Spanish monks was not comparable to that of the Africans. Although their basic principles were identical, the Spaniards' results were quite inferior. No major piece of exegesis or theology saw the light of day in Spain. Isidore's great contribution to Christian culture lay in the composition of practical manuals that assembled diverse information on onomastics, biblical toponomastics, arithmology, and Church institutions.[218] Similarly, he planned his *Origines* as a compendium of classical culture for his public. In his manuals he presented the Christian researcher with the essentials of what he had to know in order to read the Bible with profit.[219]

Isidore, in effect, was very much aware of his contemporaries' talents.[220] He was sufficiently perceptive to realize that profane and sacred letters were harbored only within a very restricted circle. Not every bishop in Spain shared the curiosity of Isidore, Braulio, and their disciples: they were more often men of action than scholars.[221]

Isidore certainly tried to reawaken a taste for study in the clergy. The Council of Toledo of 633, which he guided, concerned itself, as we have seen, with the establishment of episcopal schools.[222] Surprisingly, though, the man called "the most famous pedagogue of the Middle Ages"[223] never spoke of his pupils or of his teaching. When he does speak of the clerics of Seville, he tells us that they laughed at him for

[216] For relations between Jews and Christians, see Blumenkranz, *Juifs et Chrétiens*, pp. 46ff.

[217] Isidore of Seville could only reproduce the Hebrew names he found in Jerome.

[218] For these various works, see Manitius, 1: 54ff., and Menéndez Pidal, *HE*, 3: 397ff.

[219] Isidore knew that his work was only an introduction to the Ancients; see the preface to his *De eccl. off.*, *PL*, LXXXIII, 737. For the sources of this work, see A. C. Lawson's article, "Sources of the *De ecclesiasticis officiis* of S. Isidore of Seville," *RB* 50 (1938): 26–36.

[220] *Quaestiones in vetus Testamentum*, preface (*PL*, LXXXIII, 207): "Offerimus non solum studiosis sed etiam fastidiosis lectoribus qui nimiam longitudinem sermonis abhorrent."

[221] Ildefonsus, *De vir. ill.*, *PL*, XCVI, 199–201; (2) Asturius and Aurasius of Toledo, "plus exemplo vivendi quam calamo scribentis"; (6) John of Tarragona, "Plus verbis intendens docere quam scriptis; (7) Helladius of Toledo, "scribere renuit quia quod scribendum fuit quotidianae operationis pagina demonstravit."

[222] Isidore, *De eccl. off.*, II, 5, 16 (*PL*, LXXXIII, 785); Council of Toledo (633), c. 19 and 25 (Mansi, X, 625, 627). See above, sect. II.D., and Séjourné, *Le dernier Père de l'Eglise*, p. 61.

[223] There has been a vain attempt to study Isidore's pedagogy in the absence of texts. Rosario Seijas's article "San Isidoro en la Pedagogía," *Revista española de Pedagogía* 6 (1948), is based primarily on the *Institutionum disciplinae*, which may not be Isidore's work. See above, chap. 6, sect. IV.D.

trying to restore proper Latin pronunciation.[224] Only his friends and disciples Braulio and Ildefonsus have left us information on his teaching.[225]

Thus, the "Isidorian renaissance" touched but a few clerics. The manuals Isidore composed were intended only for an elite, and it is therefore impossible to think that they found readers in all monastic and episcopal schools. Later, thanks to the diffusion of Isidorian manuscripts, this renaissance would bear fruit.[226]

[224] Isidore, *De eccl. off.*, II, 11, 4 (*PL*, LXXXIII, 791): "Plerumque enim imperiti lectores in verborum accentibus errant et solent irridere nos imperitiae hi qui videntur habere notitiam detrahentes et jurantes penitus nescire quod dicimus."

[225] Braulio, *Renotatio librorum Isidori*, ed. Lynch, in *Saint Braulio*, p. 358: "Nostrum tempus antiquitatis in eo scientiam imaginavit." Ildefonsus, *De vir. ill.*, *PL*, XCVI, 202: "Nam tantae juncunditatis affluentem copiam in eloquendo promerint ut ubertus admiranda dicendi ex eo in stuporem verteret audientes."

[226] See the Conclusion, n. 12.

THE BEGINNINGS OF
MEDIEVAL EDUCATION

Part Three

Although the former ROMANIA *still maintained an antique appearance in the aftermath of the great invasions, during the seventh century and the first half of the eighth century the West was profoundly transformed. The Arab invasion, which swallowed up part of the Byzantine Empire and reached Europe in 711, was not the only reason for the change. The triumph of the aristocracy in Gaul, the conversion and organization of the Anglo-Saxon and Lombard kingdoms, the arrival of Irish missionaries on the Continent, and the political emancipation of the papacy—all contributed to give the West a medieval appearance.*

These events modified the way Westerners thought. Gradually, a new civilization that would replace antique culture evolved. The seventh century was a time of preparation. The last two decades of that century and the first half of the following century saw the new civilization firmly in place.

CHAPTER EIGHT

The New Elements of the Seventh Century

I. THE FIRST CHRISTIAN SCHOOLS IN ENGLAND

A. Culture in England and the Celtic Lands
at the End of the Sixth Century

The Roman armies began to evacuate Britain at the beginning of the fifth century. During the second half of this century, the Angles, Jutes, and Saxons moved in in their place. For the next two hundred years, the Barbarians made slow progress in pushing the Celts to the west. At the end of the sixth century they tried to break the Celtic front by separating the Britons of Dumnonia (Devonshire) from those of Wales, and the Welsh from their brothers in Lancashire.[1] During these two centuries—which are the most obscure in English history—traces of Roman civilization gradually disappeared. Only the highway system, which the invaders used, and a few monuments in London, Lincoln, and York, survived from the Roman period.[2] Abandoned Roman forts were occupied by monks. People who had forgotten how to use stone in building looked in astonishment at the ruins of the "ancient dwellings of giants," left to the mercy of time and man.[3] All that drew other Barbarian kingdoms to the Roman past had disappeared here.

The Germans who occupied Britain, unlike the Goths, Vandals, and Burgundians, did not care to save Roman civilization. It is not very

[1] For this invasion, see F. M. Stenton, *Anglo-Saxon England*, 2nd ed. (Oxford, 1947), p. 131; Peter Hunter Blair, *An Introduction to Anglo-Saxon England* (Cambridge, 1956); L. Musset, *Les invasions*, pp. 150ff.; and H. Anson, *Christianity in Britain, 300–700* (Leicester, 1968).

[2] See R. G. Collingwood and J. L. Myres, *Roman Britain and the English Settlements* (Oxford, 1936), for the fate of Roman monuments.

[3] See the *Vita Cuthberti*, VIII, ed. Bertram Colgrave (Cambridge, 1940), p. 122, and the Anglo-Saxon poem "The Ruins," in *Anglo-Saxon and Norse Poems*, ed. N. Kerslaw (Cambridge, 1922). The ruins were often used as quarries; see Bede, *HE*, IV, 17 (Plummer ed., p. 245).

surprising that they preserved their Germanic way of life: they had had only superficial contacts with the Roman Empire before they moved into a land that had hardly been Romanized. They do not seem to have fused with the Celtic population during the period of occupation. Whether they absorbed the Celts or pushed them back, they borrowed neither their language nor their religion.[4] It is precisely this which accounts for the originality and significance of these people: for the first time in our investigations we come upon Barbarians untouched by Roman culture. Under these circumstances, however, we are condemned to ignorance or near ignorance of their civilization before their conversion to Christianity. In the absence of written sources, we must be satisfied to learn about them through archaeological discoveries[5] and traditions collected much later.

Roman influence had not entirely disappeared from ancient Britain. It found refuge to the west of a line which ran from Portland to Chester, passing through Bath and Gloucester, in the British kingdoms that resisted the Germanic advance.[6] It is difficult to judge the level of culture in all the small Celtic kingdoms at the end of the sixth century, but we do know something about the intellectual life in Wales, thanks to epigraphy and hagiography.[7] Latin was still used in this region, and quite correctly, as bilingual inscriptions in Latin and ogamic characters and inscriptions in Latin alone show.[8] Roman traditions might have been especially maintained at the court of King Cadfan of Gwynedd, who died in 625.[9]

[4] For the relationship between the Germans and Celts in England, see the introduction to Kenneth H. Jackson, *Language and History in Early Britain* (Edinburgh and London, 1953).

[5] The old work by Gerald Baldwin Brown, *The Arts in Early England*, 6 vols. (London, 1903–37), can still be used. See also E. T. Leeds, *Early Anglo-Saxon Art and Archaeology* (Oxford, 1936). For the civilization of the Jutes in Kent, see C. F. C. Hawkes, "The Jutes of Kent," in *Dark Age Britain: Studies Presented to E. T. Leeds*, ed. D. B. Harden (London, 1956), pp. 91–111.

[6] Nora K. Chadwick, "The Foundations of the Early British Kingdoms," in *Studies in Early British History*, ed. Nora K. Chadwick (Cambridge, 1954), pp. 147ff.; John Edward Lloyd, *A History of Wales*, 2 vols. (London, 1939), 1: 92ff.

[7] Victor Erle Nash-Williams, *The Early Christian Monuments of Wales* (Cardiff, 1950); Arthur W. Wade-Evans, *Vitae sanctorum Britanniae et genealogiae* (Cardiff, 1944).

[8] Nash-Williams (*Early Christian Monuments*) counted twenty-six bilingual inscriptions, nine in ogamic characters, and one hundred and four in Latin. Numbers 103, 92, 104, and 138 mention a *protector*, a *medicus*, and a *magistrat(us)*. One inscription (see p. 93) is dated from the consular years. For the survival of Roman culture, see Jackson, *Language and History*, pp. 118–20, and Lloyd, *History of Wales*, 1: 155.

[9] Caramanus' epitaph was influenced by antique inscriptions: "Rex sapienti[s]imus opinati[s]imus omnium regum." For contacts between Gwynedd and the Continent, see

But it was essentially in the Celtic Church that Latin culture found refuge. This Church, created in the fourth century, resisted the crisis of the following century and was even able to keep its liturgical practices different from those of Rome for quite some time.[10] Ecclesiastical institutions were established around monasteries in this land devoid of towns. As in Ireland during the same period, monasteries were veritable cities directed by an abbot who could be simultaneously a bishop (save for exceptions), a clan chief, and a great landowner. He directed monks in a life of asceticism reminiscent of that of the East: perpetual fasting, prayers accompanied by multiple genuflections or crossed arms, and immersion in cold water, among other practices.[11] The discipline, such as we can perceive it in the penitentials that have come down to us, was rigorous.[12] Monasteries were thus primarily schools of asceticism. In the great sixth-century Welsh centers—the monastery founded by Saint Illtyd on the island of Caldey and, in the north, that of Bangor Iscoed— monks studied the sacred texts in conformity with the principles of ascetic culture followed by the monks of Lérins and their imitators.[13]

What made Welsh monasteries original, however, was the place they gave to profane studies. The biographies of Saints Illtyd, Cadoc, and Samson note that these abbots had studied the various disciplines of the liberal arts[14] and taught them to their pupils. How did these Celtic monasteries come by Roman educational tradition? This question has been answered in various ways, although the lack of sources permits only hypotheses. According to some, continental rhetors fleeing before the Barbarian invasions trained the Celts,[15] while others speculate that

---

Nora K. Chadwick, "Early Culture and Learning in North Wales," in *Studies in the Early British Church,* ed. Nora K. Chadwick et al. (Cambridge, 1958), p. 93.

[10] Fliche-Martin, 5: 301ff.

[11] For the organization of Celtic monasteries, see Lloyd, *History of Wales,* 1: 103ff., and Louis Gougaud, *Les chrétientés celtiques* (Paris, 1911). For the beginnings of Irish monasticism, see Walter Delius, *Geschichte der irischen Kirche von ihren Anfängen bis zum 12. Jahrhundert* (Munich, 1954), pp. 155ff.

[12] For the Celtic penitentials, see Gabriel Le Bras, "Pénitentiels," *DTC,* 12, pt. 1: 1160– 72, and idem, "Les pénitentiels irlandais," in *Le miracle irlandais,* ed. H. Daniel-Rops (Paris, 1956), pp. 172–90.

[13] There have been attempts to trace Celtic monasticism to the customs of Lérins. Saint Patrick's visit to Lérins is not established fact, however. We can only suppose that, like Saint Martin, he spent some time on the islands of the Tyrrhennian Sea where anchorites had settled. See Paul Grosjean, "Notes chronologiques sur le séjour de saint Patrick en Gaule," *AB* 63 (1945): 89ff.

[14] See the references in Roger, p. 228.

[15] Heinrich Zimmer and Kuno Meyer accepted this hypothesis; see James F. Kenney, *The Sources for the Early History of Ireland* (New York, 1966), p. 142, no. 19. Roger, p. 269, and Maieul Cappuyns, *Jean Scot Erigène* (Paris, 1933), pp. 15ff., had reservations.

9. *Cultural Centers in England and in the
Celtic Lands in the Seventh Century*

cultural exchanges between the Continent and Britain in the fifth century led to the development of studies in Celtic lands.[16] Lastly, some have supposed that Irish monks were the masters of the Welsh.[17]

Sixth-century Irish monasteries were important study centers, at least according to the Latin sources at our disposal.[18] At Clonard, founded by Finian (died 549); at Bangor, founded by Congall (died 601); and at Derry and its filial, Iona, founded by Columba, monks read the Scriptures and studied computus. Thanks to Columban, who had been a monk at Bangor before coming to Gaul, we can reconstruct the study program of this monastery. He wrote a commentary on the Psalms under the direction of his master, Sinilis, who was renowned for his knowledge of the Scriptures.[19] He also learned, no doubt by means of Latin grammars he studied, several passages from profane authors, the traces of which are easily enough found in his works.[20] Lastly, he knew men learned in the science of computus whom he praised in a letter to Gregory the Great.[21] Among them we can cite Monino Mocan

---

[16] Chadwick, "Intellectual Contacts between Britain and Gaul in the Fifth Century," in *Studies in Early British History*, pp. 189ff.

[17] See Heinrich Zimmer, "Keltische Kirche," *Realencyklopädie für protestantische Theologie und Kirche*, ed. Albert Hauck, 10 (Leipzig, 1901): 224, whose arguments are summarized by Roger, pp. 232ff. For a contrary view, see Eoin MacNeill, "The Beginnings of Latin Culture in Ireland," *Studies: An Irish Quarterly* 20 (1931): 39–48, 449. See also Ludwig Bieler's rapid overview, "The Island of Scholars," *RMAL* 8 (1952): 213–34, and E. Cocchia, "La cultura irlandese pre-carolingia: Miracolo o mito?" *SM*, 3rd ser. 8 (1967): 257–420.

[18] There is no serious work on the culture of sixth-century Irish monasteries. John Ryan's passages in *Irish Monasticism: Origins and Early Development* (Dublin, 1931; with new introduction and bibliography, Ithaca, 1972), pp. 200–216, 360–83, are not sufficiently critical. W. G. Hanson's *The Early Monastic Schools in Ireland: Their Missionaries, Saints, and Scholars* (Cambridge, 1927) is useless. So too is John Healy's *Insula sanctorum et doctorum; or, Ireland's Ancient Schools and Scholars* (Dublin, 1890).

[19] Jonas, *Vita Columbani*, I, 3 (*MGH, SRM*, IV-1, 69): "Ut intra adulescentiae aetatem detentus psalmorum librum eliminato sermone exponeret." For this commentary, see Manitius, 1: 183, and Germain Morin, "Le *Liber S. Columbani in Psalmos* et le Ms. Ambros. C 301 inf.," *RB* 38 (1926): 164–77. See also Walker's edition, *S. Columbani opera*, p. lxiv. Jonas tells us that Columban's master, Sinilis, "scripturarum sacrarum scientiae flore inter suos pollebat" (*Vita Columbani, MGH, SRM*, IV-1, 70, l. 4). Jonas also mentioned instruction in chant at Bangor ("Multa alias quae vel ad cantum digna vel docendum utilia condidit dicta").

[20] For Columban's "humanism," see Ludwig Bieler, "The Humanism of St. Colombanus," *Mélanges colombaniens* (Paris, 1951), pp. 95–102. Did Columban acquire his "classical" culture on the Continent as Ludwig Traube thought (*Vorlesungen und Abhandlungen*, ed. F. Boll [Munich, 1911], 2: 174)? Probably not. Perhaps he did, however, perfect it on the Continent. Alfred Cordoliani thinks that Columban became acquainted with Fortunatus' works in Gaul ("Fortunat, l'Irlande et les Irlandais," *Etudes mérovingiennes*, p. 39). See also Johannes Wilhelmus Smit, *Studies on the Language and Style of Columba the Younger (Columbanus)* (Amsterdam, 1971).

[21] Columban, *Ep.* 1 (*MGH, Ep.*, III, 157, l. 31): "Scias namque, nostris magistris et

(died 610), who could have tried to introduce Dionysius' computus to Ireland.[22] We know very little about Columban's studies at Derry and then Iona under Columba (Columcille), a former monk of Clonard. Columba's biographer, Adamnan, simply tells us that he spent many hours reading and writing.[23] If the hymn "Altus prosator" is really Columba's, it bears witness to a very extensive Latin education.[24]

To suppose, however, that Irish masters influenced Welsh monasteries is only to push the problem back one step, because we now must ask how culture penetrated to Ireland in the sixth century.

For the present, we are reduced to a few basic assertions. In the important sixth-century Welsh and Irish monasteries, we see that the study of the sciences was limited to work on ecclesiastical computus,[25] while literary studies were limited to grammar and rhetoric. The few writings dating from this period allow us at least to say that the monks had learned Latin, a language foreign to them, and that antique authors were known to them. Not having to combat the dangers of Graeco-Roman paganism, they could use profane authors with less reticence than could monks on the Continent. Not having to adapt their style to the level of the Christian people who spoke only the national tongue, they did not react against the excesses of the oratorical art. They undertook the study of Latin primarily to learn the Bible and thus were led to study hymnic poetry, history, and rhetoric.[26]

Everyone who has studied the famous *Hisperica famina*, the most celebrated Celtic literary production in Latin of the period,[27] has been

---

Hibernicis antiquis philosophis et sapientissimis componendi calculi computariis Victorium non fuisse receptum."

[22] For this person, see Paul Grosjean, "Recherches sur les débuts de la controverse pascale chez les Celtes," *AB* 64 (1946): 231ff. A ninth-century manuscript reports that he learned computus from a Greek. The reference, as Father Grosjean saw, is undoubtedly to the works of Dionysius Exiguus.

[23] Adamnan, *Vita Columbae*, I, 1, 23; II, 8, 14 (Fowler ed., pp. 13, 16).

[24] Roger, p. 230.

[25] See A. Cordoliani, "Les computistes insulaires et les écrits pseudo-alexandrins," *BECh* 106 (1945–46): 5–34, and Grosjean's article cited in n. 22 above.

[26] Roger, pp. 236–37.

[27] For these texts, which F. J. H. Jenkinson edited (Cambridge, 1908), see Roger, pp. 238–56; Manitius, 1: 156–58; Kenney, *Sources*, p. 257; and P. W. Damon, "The Meaning of the *Hisperica famina*," *American Journal of Philology* 74 (1953): 398–406. Some scholars, such as R. A. S. Macalister (*The Secret Languages of Ireland* [Cambridge, 1937], p. 83), view the *Hisperica famina* as academic parodies. Paul Grosjean summarized the various theories in his "*Confusa caligo*: Remarques sur les *Hisperica famina*," *Celtica* 3 (1956): 35–85. The problem remains to be clarified. See the remarks of de Bruyne, *Etudes d'esthétique*, 1: 115ff., and of Michael Winterbottom, "On the *Hisperica famina*," *Celtica* 8 (1968): 126–39.

struck by their strange, mannered style. The vocabulary is formed from words borrowed from ecclesiastical Latin, Greek,[28] Hebrew, and especially from terms created from classical words. These neologisms bring to mind the twelve Latinites Virgil the Grammarian exposed in his *Epitomae.*[29] As for the style itself, consisting of amazing periphrases and decorated with multiple epithets, it seems very close to the rhetorical exercises so dear to Ennodius of Pavia and to the author of the preface to the *Latin Anthology.*[30] The hisperic style that marked the Celtic literature of the period should thus be attached to a well-known current in Latin literature, "asianism," which was developed primarily in Africa. It found favorable ground in Celtic milieux because the genius of these people enjoyed the complicated and the mannered. The design of miniatures and of gold work provides a good example of this in the artistic sphere: the eye strains to follow the complex spirals and interlaces; everything is fluid, abstract; the human and animal shapes are almost caricaturized.[31]

We must not forget, however, the influence of the national Celtic literature, which the superficial Romanization of Britain did not eradicate. It could be that the departure of the Romans coincided with a renewal of Celticism. Welsh bards and Irish *filids* continued to ply their trade as official poets in the entourages of kings and competed among themselves in relating the exploits of warriors, the adventures and loves of demi-gods, and sea voyages in search of marvelous islands in the other worlds.[32] They, too, had an astonishingly colored and varied language and could invent daring metaphors. There were no barriers be-

---

[28] We still have no precise knowledge of Greek studies in Celtic monasteries, despite many studies of the subject: see Roger, pp. 268ff.; M. Esposito, "The Knowledge of Greek in Ireland," *Studies: An Irish Quarterly* 1 (1912): 665; J. Vendryes, "La connaissance du grec en Irlande au début du Moyen Age," *Revue celtique* 34 (1913): 220; and, more recently, B. Bischoff, "Das griechische Element in der abendländischen Bildung des Mittelalters," *BZ,* 44 (1951): 39–48 (reprinted in *Mittelalterliche Studien,* 2: 246–75). G. S. M. Walker's "On the Use of Greek Words in the Writings of St. Columbanus of Luxeuil," *ALMA* 21 (1949–50): 117–31, is open to question.

[29] This connection has been made many times. See Jenkinson's edition, p. 5; Tardi, *Les Epitomae de Virgile de Toulouse,* pp. 31–32; and Paul Grosjean, "Quelques remarques sur Virgile le grammairien," in *Medieval Studies Presented to Aubrey Gwynn, S. J.,* ed. J. A. Watt et al. (Dublin, 1961), pp. 393–406.

[30] *Anth. lat.,* pp. 82–84.

[31] Françoise Henry, *La sculpture irlandaise pendant les douze premiers siècles de l'ère chrétienne,* 2 vols. (Paris, 1933), 1: 193–96; idem, *Art irlandais* (Dublin, 1954), pp. 56–57.

[32] For Celtic vernacular literature, see James Carney, *Studies in Irish Literature and History* (Dublin, 1955); Ifor Williams, *Lectures on Early Welsh Poetry* (Dublin, 1944); and Bezzola, 2, pt. 1: 140ff.

tween the lay and monastic world, and thus Celtic and Latin literature reciprocally influenced each other—young Irishmen could move from the school of the *filid* to that of the abbot and thus benefit from a double culture.[33]

In order to become thoroughly acquainted with the teaching dispensed in Celtic monastic schools, it would be necessary to make a parallel study of Latin and national literature. This study is now underway and cannot be attempted here. Still, this question had to be mentioned because Celtic influence was to affect the schools of England and even those of the Continent after the sixth century.

B. The Beginnings of Christian Schools in Southern England

In Barbarian Britain, which now can be called England, the first schools did not appear before the beginning of the seventh century—that is, not before the coming of Roman missionaries to the south and of Irish monks to the north.

When Pope Gregory decided to send a mission to England, he chose the kingdom of Kent as the first site of the apostolate. The nearest kingdom to the Continent, Kent—more than the other Anglo-Saxon kingdoms—had retained the imprint of Roman civilization.[34] Furthermore, in the sixth century, Kent maintained close contact with Neustria after King Aethilbert's marriage to a Frankish princess.[35] In 597, this king established the missionaries, Prior Augustine and his companions, at Canterbury,[36] where Augustine became bishop and, shortly afterwards, founded the monastery of Saint Peter and Saint Paul.

While clerics in the episcopal quarters led a quasi-monastic life, the monks in the monastery no doubt continued the way of life they had known in Rome at Saint Andrew's, inspired perhaps by the Benedictine

[33] On the schools of the *filids* and the bards, see Henri Hubert, *Les Celtes et l'expansion celtique jusqu'à l'époque de la Tène* (Paris, 1932), pp. 320ff., and H. d'Arbois de Jubainville, *Cours de littérature celtique*, vol. 1, *Introduction à l'étude de la littérature celtique* (Paris, 1883), pp. 334–89. For more recent treatments, see Chadwick, "Intellectual Contacts," and R. Bromwich, "The Character of the Early Welsh Tradition," both in Chadwick, *Studies in Early British History*, pp. 194ff., 98–99; and the remarks of Paul Grosjean, "*Confusa caligo*," *Celtica* 3 (1956): 57, n. 2.

[34] See Blair, *Introduction*, p. 278, and Thomas Downing Kendrick, *Anglo-Saxon Art to A.D. 900* (London, 1938), pp. 63–65.

[35] M. Deanesly, "Canterbury and Paris in the Reign of Aethelbert," *History* 26 (1941): 97–104; J. M. Wallace-Hadrill, *Early Germanic Kingship in England and on the Continent* (Oxford, 1971).

[36] For the establishment of the Roman mission, see Fliche-Martin, 5: 279ff. For Augustine, see Henry H. Howorth, *Saint Augustine of Canterbury* (London, 1913).

rule.[37] Both establishments, however, must have stressed sacred study. The first elements of a library supporting such study had been brought together: Gregory the Great is known to have sent several manuscripts to the missionaries, although we do not know which ones.[38] Some historians, nevertheless, have not hesitated to identify these manuscripts as copies of profane works, thus arguing that classical literature was studied at Canterbury.[39] There is certainly nothing to this. In order to train missionaries, Augustine the monk needed only holy books, the Bible and its commentaries. Perhaps the evangeliary preserved at Cambridge is one of the books the pope sent.[40] The iconography of this manuscript—a series of tableaux portraying scenes from Christ's life—could have helped the monks to catechize their first Anglo-Saxon lay or clerical disciples. Religious instruction through images was, as we shall see in Chapter 10, often practiced in England.

There is even some doubt that Canterbury was a center for sacred studies—at least, we have no proof on that point. Augustine received a solid biblical culture at Saint Andrew's, but he must have adapted his learning to the necessities of the moment.[41] The only extensive teaching organized at Canterbury was in religious chant: several times, Bede mentions the success Roman chant had among the pagans and notes that it was called the "chant of Kent."[42] Gregory the Great's disciples taught it to their Anglo-Saxon pupils,[43] with the consequence that the latter credited the great pope as the inventor of the *modulatio romana*. The legend of the origin of Gregorian chant was certainly born in English ecclesiastical circles.[44]

[37] See above, chap. 5, sect. IV.C.

[38] Bede, *HE*, I, 29 (Plummer ed., p. 63): "Sanctorum reliquas nec non et codices plurimos." Thomas of Elmham, a medieval chronicler (*Historia monasterii sancti Augustini Cantauriensis* ed. Charles Hardwick [London. 1858]), thought he had the list of Augustine's books, but this source cannot be trusted.

[39] Arthur F. Leach, *The Schools of Medieval England*, 2nd ed. (London, 1916); J. W. Adamson, *The "Illiterate Anglo-Saxon"* (Cambridge, 1946), pp. 7–8. For a contrary view, see P. F. Jones, "The Gregorian Mission and English Education," *Speculum* 3 (1928): 335–48.

[40] *CLA*, II, 126. Francis Wormald has studied this manuscript in *The Miniatures of the Gospels of Saint Augustine (Corpus Christi College ms. 286)* (Cambridge, 1954).

[41] Gregory the Great, *Ep.* XI, 37 (*MGH, Ep.*, II, 309, ll. 12–13): "In monasterii regula edoctus, sacrae scripturae scientia repletus."

[42] Bede, *HE*, II, 20 (Plummer ed., p. 126), in reference to Deacon James, Paulinus of York's companion: "Qui quoniam cantandi in ecclesia erat peritissimus. Magister ecclesiasticae cantionis juxta morem Romanorum seu Cantuariorum."

[43] Ibid., IV, 2 (p. 206): "Putta maxime autem modulandi in ecclesia more Romanorum quam a discipulis beati papae Gregorii didicerat peritum."

[44] See Corbin, "La notation musicale," pp. 552ff. For a different view, see H. Ashworth, "Did Saint Augustine Bring the 'Gregorianum' to England?" *EL* 72 (1958): 39–43.

It would take about thirty years for the teaching at Canterbury to begin to bear fruit. Among the Anglo-Saxon clerics trained in this school, Bede singled out Ithamar, bishop of Rochester in 644, whose life and culture put him on a par with his Roman predecessors.[45] At this time, Canterbury furnished masters for the other Anglo-Saxon kingdoms of Essex, East Anglia, and Wessex.

Christianity took hold in East Anglia with greater difficulty than in Kent,[46] but, remarkably, one of the first manifestations of Christianity in East Anglia was the creation of a school. Around 630, King Sigebert, who had been baptized in Gaul, decided to open a school in his kingdom for the training of young clerics.[47] Bede, who reported this, tells us that Sigebert "wanted to imitate what he had seen organized so well in Gaul." This praise of Gaul's schools is surprising in light of what we know of them in Dagobert's time.[48] But the modest schools we spoke of in Gaul were adequate models for a land that had barely emerged from paganism. In addition, the king was helped by a Burgundian cleric named Felix, who did not come directly from Gaul but had been in the service of Honorius, metropolitan of Canterbury.[49] Soon named bishop of Dunwich, Felix called in teachers trained "according to the customs of Kent,"[50] which means that they also came from Canterbury. The instruction provided at Dunwich was thus the same as that at Canterbury: reading of sacred texts and training in chant.

Thus, Sigebert's school was born under a double influence: the idea had come from Gaul, but the program was that of the Roman monks of Kent. Let us add a third influence that began to appear. Sigebert had received offers from the Irishman Fursa, an ascetic who settled near Yarmouth. Can this be seen as competition between Roman and Celtic missions? It is not improbable. Irish monks, who had earlier come to northern England, as we shall see, began to penetrate the south. In fact, Fursa hardly tarried in East Anglia but instead quickly moved on to Gaul.[51]

---

[45] Bede, *HE*, III, 14 (p. 54): "Ithamar, oriundum quidem de gente Cantuariorum, sed vita et eruditione antecessoribus suis aequandum."

[46] Fliche-Martin, 5: 294ff.

[47] Bede, *HE*, III, 18 (p. 162): "Sigberct . . . mox ea, quae in Galliis bene disposita vidit, imitare cupiens, instituit scolam, in qua pueri literis erudirentur."

[48] See above, chapt. 7, sect. II.C.

[49] Bede, *HE*, III, 18, II, 15 (pp. 162, 116).

[50] Ibid., III, 18 (p. 162): "Juvante se episcopo Felice quem de Cantia acceperat eisque paedagogos ac magistros juxta morem Cantuariorum praebente."

[51] Ibid., III, 19 (p. 163). Fursa, founded Lagny and died at Péronne.

The same situation obtained in Wessex: here too, Italian, Frankish, and Irish currents converged. Wessex was first converted by Birinus, an Italian bishop, around 625 but then returned to paganism, only to be evangelized once again, but this time by the Frank Agilbert. Agilbert came from Ireland where he had been educated and because of his erudition—an erudition uniquely ecclesiastical—was installed as bishop of Dorchester.

Christian culture thus began to establish itself in southern England around 640 but only very slowly. Schools opened with the first cathedrals at Canterbury, London, Rochester, Dunwich, and Dorchester. Monasteries took root too but still in such small numbers that, according to Bede, many Anglo-Saxons went to seek the way to sanctity in Gaul.[52] Threatened by frequent recurrences of paganism and constant warfare among the princes, these schools could not yet really get under way. Their distance from Rome also made it difficult to equip them with books. Conditions in the religious centers of northern England were much more favorable.

C. MONASTIC SCHOOLS IN NORTHERN ENGLAND

The Roman missionaries Gregory the Great sent to Kent also tried to convert the northern kingdoms and restore the former Roman bishopric of York.[53] Paulinus, who came to England shortly after Augustine, built a cathedral at York and churches at Lincoln and Campodonum near Leeds. With the help of Deacon James, a compatriot, he evangelized Bernicia and Deira and converted King Edwin. But this young, already prosperous church was destroyed after Edwin's defeat in 633. Paganism was restored, and Paulinus was forced to retire to Kent. Subsequent political events drove Roman missionaries out of these regions for almost a half century, to the profit of the Irish. As a result, the history of Christian culture in England took a different turn. Map 9 shows the zones affected by both groups.

In 635, King Oswald—who had been raised among Celts—called Aidan, a monk of Iona, to his kingdom and installed him on the island of Lindisfarne as bishop and abbot.[54] This new monastery, built "more

---

[52] Ibid., III, 8 (p. 142): "Nam eo tempore necdum multis in regione Anglorum monasteriis constructis, multi de Brittania monachicae conversationis gratia Francorum vel Galliarum monasteria adire solebant."

[53] See Fliche-Martin, 5: 292, and Peter Hunter Blair, "The Bernician and the Northern Frontier," in *Studies in the Early British Church* (Cambridge, 1958), pp. 137ff.

[54] Bede, *HE*, III, 3 (p. 131). See A. Hamilton Thompson, "Northumbrian Monasticism," in *Bede, His Life, Times, and Writings* (Oxford, 1935), pp. 60–101.

Scottorum"[55]—that is, in wood—became the center for the re-evangelization of England as well as an important cultural and educational center. Did Aidan try to transplant the program of studies he knew at Iona to Lindisfarne? When Bede, in rather general terms, sketched religious life under Aidan, he did note that the abbot's scriptural culture was great and that laymen as well as clerics "meditated"—that is, "they studied Scriptures and learned the Psalter."[56] He tells us, finally, that ransomed Angle slaves received an extensive education at Lindisfarne in preparation for the priesthood. There is no question here of classical education, as Roger thought. Bede simply tells us that "young Angles along with older monks took courses from Irish teachers and learned to observe the rule."[57] Instead of making Lindisfarne a new Iona,[58] Aidan adapted his teaching to his public, molding it especially in view of the apostolate, as had Augustine before him at Canterbury.

After Aidan's death in 651, his disciples established religious centers more to the south. The first bishops in Mercia after King Peada's baptism were disciples of Irishmen.[59] Anglo-Saxon princesses helped the monks in their task of evangelization and education. In southern Northumbria, Hilda, grandniece of Edwin, was designated in 657 to found a double monastery for men and women at Whitby, after having directed the monastery of Hartepool.[60] Hilda received her education from Aidan and transmitted it to the monks and nuns of Whitby and even to laymen.[61]

[55] Bede, HE, III, 25 (p. 181).

[56] Ibid., III, 5 and 17 (pp. 136, 161): "Nil ex omnibus quae in evangelicis vel apostolicis sive propheticis litteris facienda cognoverat praetermittere . . . curabat"; ibid., III, 5 (p. 136): "Ut omnes qui cum eo incedebant . . . seu laici, meditari deberent, id est aut legendis scripturis aut psalmis discendis operam dare."

[57] Ibid., III, 3 (p. 132): "Imbuebantur praeceptoribus Scottis parvuli Anglorum una cum majoribus studiis et observatione disciplinae regularis." Roger, p. 277, misunderstood the sentence when he wrote about "majora studia." It is clear that "cum majoribus" modifies "parvuli," not "studiis."

[58] For education at Iona, see Roger, p. 228, who used the only sources we have on the subject—Adamnan's Vita Columbae and the hymn "Altus prosator," attributed to Columba.

[59] Fliche-Martin, 5: 297, 313; Thompson, "Northumbrian Monasticism," in Bede, pp. 79ff.

[60] Bede, HE, IV, 21 (23) (p. 253). For the many Irish as well as Eastern double monasteries, see Henri Leclercq and J. Pargoire, "Monastère double," DACL, XI-2, 2182, and Stephanus Hilpisch, Die Doppelklöster: Entstehung und Organisation, Beiträge zur Geschichte des alten Mönchtums und des Benediktinerordens, vol. 15 (Münster, 1928), p. 44.

[61] Bede, HE, IV, 21 (23) (p. 253): "Nam et episcopus Aidan et quique noverant eam

Thanks to Bede and to archaeological excavations,[62] we know that this monastery was a major center of religious culture. Hilda, who was called "the mother," directed studies.[63] She also brought Caedmon into the monastery, educated him, encouraged his work, and later introduced the poet who put sacred history into Anglo-Saxon verse to the "savants" gathered round her.[64] She likewise trained her successor from infancy,[65] as well as priests who later became bishops.[66] We should note, though, that instruction at Whitby did not go beyond the limits of scriptural studies.

Lindisfarne, Whitby, and their daughter houses introduced northern England to a culture close to that of the Irish, without, however, always becoming study centers comparable to those in Ireland. The Irish centers, whose beginnings we mentioned earlier in this chapter, appear to have been much better organized in the seventh century and more receptive to literary culture. Since the appearance of Roger's work, which had already acknowledged this superiority, the importance of Irish learning—which emphasized grammar, poetry, computus, and exegesis—has been underscored.[67] Bangor, Armagh, and a monastic group in the south of the island produced works whose significance is just now being discovered.[68] Irish monks knew the work of Gregory

---

religiosi . . . diligenter erudire solebant"; ibid.: "Etiam reges ac principes nonnunquam ab ea quarerent consilium et invenirent."

[62] See the report on the digs by C. Peers and C. A. Ralegh-Radford in *Archaelogia* 89 (1943): 27–89. The monastic cells were localized by the discovery of numerous bronze and bone writing styli. See ibid., pp. 64–65 and plate XXVII.

[63] Bede, *HE*, IV, 21 (23) (p. 254): "Tantum lectioni divinarum scripturarum suos vacare subditos . . . ut facillime viderentur ibidem qui ecclesiasticum gradum, hoc est, altaris officium apte plurimi posse reperiri."

[64] Ibid., 22 (24) (p. 260): "Ad abbatissam perductus, jussus est multis doctioribus viris praesentibus . . . dicere carmen."

[65] Ibid., III, 24 (p. 179): "Aelfleda discipula vitae regularis deinde magistra exstitit." This text can be compared to the abbess' epitaph, which was found at Whitby: "Ael-[fleoda] quae ab infanti[a] concilia trixque vas." See Peers and Ralegh-Radford, *Archaeologia* 89 (1943): 27–89.

[66] Bishops Bosa of York, Aetla of Dorchester, and John of Beverley came from Whitby.

[67] See Roger, pp. 257–61; John Ryan, "Irish Learning in the Seventh Century," *Journal of the Royal Society of Antiquaries of Ireland* 80 (1950): 164–71; B. Bischoff, "Il monachesimo irlandese nei suoi rapporti col continente," *Settimane*, 4: 121–38; Kathleen Hughes, "Irish Monks and Learning," in *Los mofijes y los estudios* (Abadia de Poblet, 1963), pp. 61–86; and, especially, Grosjean, "Sur quelques exégètes," pp. 67–97.

[68] "Aileranus sapiens" (died 665) worked at Clonard; see Kenney, *Sources*, p. 279, no. 107. The *De mirabilibus sacrae scripturae*, falsely attributed to Augustine, is a product of the southern monasteries. This work by itself merits study. Adamnan, the future abbot of Iona who died in 704, was a monk there during this period. For him, see Manitius, 1:

the Great[69] and, what is even more surprising, were also acquainted with that of Isidore of Seville.[70] We know that there were contacts between Ireland and Rome; we have to suppose that they also existed during this period between Ireland and Spain.[71]

At the same time, a new type of script, of which the famous *Cathach* is one of the first examples, was invented in the scriptoria of Irish monasteries.[72] The monks also began to decorate their manuscripts by combining Celtic decorative motifs with motifs that came to them indirectly from the East.[73]

The reputation of Irish culture was such that many foreign monks wished to spend some time on the island where "learning flourished."[74] Bede tells us that in the middle of the seventh century, young Anglo-

---

236–39. Miuchu wrote the *Life* of Saint Patrick at Armagh. Bernhard Bischoff is preparing an edition of a mid-seventh-century commentary on *Donatus major*. See his "Eine verschollene Einteilung der Wissenschaften," *AHMA* 25 (1958): 14 (reprinted in *Mittelalterliche Studien*, 1: 273–88).

[69] Lathcen (died 661), a monk of Clúain-ferta-Molua (Cloyne), commented on the *Moralia in Job* (Kenney, *Sources*, p. 278, no. 106). See Grosjean, "Sur quelques exégètes," pp. 67–97, and Delius, *Geschichte der irischen Kirche*, p. 83. Lathcen's commentary has been published in *CCL*, vol. 145 (1969).

[70] See M. C. Diaz y Diaz, "Isidoriana II: Sobre el *Liber de ordine creaturarum*," *SE* 5 (1953): 147–66, and Grosjean, "Sur quelques exégètes," p. 95.

[71] The contacts between Ireland and Rome developed as a result of the controversy concerning the date of Easter; see Fliche-Martin, 5: 310–11. Bede, *HE*, III, 25 (p. 181), wrote thus of the Irishman Ronan: "Natione quidem Scottus, sed in Galliae vel Italiae partibus regulam ecclesiasticae veritatis edoctus." Ronan defended the Roman reckoning of Easter.

No information has come to light yet on navigation between Spain and Ireland. Mediterranean ships had been to Cornwall during our period: see C. A. Ralegh-Radford, "Imported Pottery Found at Tintagel, Cornwall," in Harden, *Dark Age Britain*, pp. 68–70. They could have gone on as far as southern Ireland. For Latin Visigothic works in Ireland, see L. Bieler, "Hibernian Latin and Patristics," *Studia Patristica* 1 (1957): 182; and J. N. Hillgarth, "The East, Visigothic Spain and the Irish," ibid. 4 (1961): 442–56. See also Hillgarth's "Visigothic Spain and Early Christian Ireland," *Proceedings of the Royal Irish Academy* 62 (1962): 167–94. So-called "Spanish symptoms" in insular manuscripts are yet another indication of contacts between Spain and Ireland. On this point, see Edmund Bishop, *Liturgica historica: Papers on the Liturgy and Religious Life of the Western Church* (Oxford, 1918), chap. VIII, "Spanish Symptoms," pp. 164–210.

[72] L. Bieler, "Insular Paleography: Present State and Problems," *Scriptorium* 3 (1949): 276–94.

[73] Françoise Henry, "Les débuts de la miniature irlandaise," *Gazette des Beaux-Arts* (1950), p. 5; Carl Nordenfalk, "Before the Book of Durrow," *Acta archaeologica* 18 (1947): 141. Masai, in his work *Essai sur les origines de la miniature dite irlandaise* (Brussels, 1947), pp. 35ff., denies the existence of Irish culture in the seventh century. For a contrary view, see F. Henry, "Irish Culture in the Seventh Century," *Studies: An Irish Quarterly* 37 (1948): 267ff.

[74] "Floret multa sapientia," wrote the author of the *Versus de Asia et de universi mundi rota*, 47 (*MGH, PAC*, IV-2, 59).

Saxons were welcomed in the cells of Irish monks, where they received food and the books they needed at no expense.[75] Young Egbert, who settled around 660 at Rathellsigi and later drew other Anglo-Saxons to him, and Ceadda, future bishop of York, were Bede's examples.[76] He also mentioned young Wilfrid, an Anglo-Saxon noble who entered the monastery of Lindisfarne when thirteen years old and could have gone on to Ireland had he not elected to complete his studies in Rome.[77]

During Wilfrid's period, in fact, the "Romans" once again tried to penetrate into northern England. The liturgical controversy that set them apart from the disciples of the Irish hindered their progress, but the conflict itself, and the discussions on the reckoning of Easter in particular, led to several meetings between the adversaries. Some Irishmen, like Ronan, had already rallied to the Roman tradition; while Italians—like Deacon James, Paulinus' former companion—and Franks—like Agilbert, the ex-bishop of Dorchester who became bishop of Paris—tried to win over other monks. Anglo-Saxons in the north next began to look beyond their southern frontiers and to take the road for Rome.

Wilfrid was the most famous of these travelers. Although he had learned the Psalms by heart and read many books at Lindisfarne,[78] he was still unsatisfied. At nineteen years of age, he moved to Canterbury, despite the liturgical quarrels that divided Celts and Romans.[79] Under the influence of Bishop Honorius, a disciple of Gregory the Great, he read a great deal and studied a new version of the Psalms.[80] Finally, in

---

[75] Bede, *HE*, III, 27 (p. 192): "Et quidam quidem mox se monasticae conversationi fideliter mancipaverunt alii magis circumeundo per cellas magistrorum, lectioni operam dare gaudebant; quos omnes Scotti libentissime suscipientes victum eis quotidianum sine pretio libros quoque ad legendum et magisterium gratuitum praebere curabant."

[76] Ibid.: "Erant inter hos duo iuvenes . . . de nobilibus Anglorum, Edilhun et Ecgberct"; ibid., IV, 3 (p. 211): "Cum eodem Ceadda adulescente et ipse adulescens in Hibernia monachicam in orationibus et continentia et meditatione divinarum scripturarum vitam sedulus agebat."

[77] Ibid., V, 19 (p. 323): "Animadvertit paulatim adulescens animi sagacis, minime perfectam esse virtutis viam quae tradebatur a Scottis, proposuitque animo venire Romam et qui ad sedem apostolicam ritus ecclesiastici sive monasteriales servarentur videre." Wilfrid obviously was not the first "Scot" to go to Rome. Bertuinus lived there for two years before settling in Gaul; see *MGH*, *SRM*, VII-1, 180.

[78] Eddius, *Vita Wilfridi*, II (Colgrave ed., p. 6): "Omnem psalmorum seriem memoraliter et aliquantos libros didicit." The same evidence is given by Bede (*HE*, V, 19 [p. 323]): "Et quia acris erat ingenii, didicit citissime psalmos, et aliquot codices."

[79] Eddius, *Vita Wilfridi*, II (p. 8).

[80] Ibid.: "Psalmos nam qui quos prius secundum Hieronymi emendationem legerat, more Romanorum, juxta quintam editionem memoraliter transmetuit." Some manuscripts carry the more probable "antiquam" in place of "quintam." See Colgave's edition, p. 152.

653, he decided to leave for Rome in the company of another Anglo-Saxon, Biscop Baducing, the future Benedict Biscop.[81]

We shall see later what Wilfrid found at Rome. Let us note for the moment the fact and its consequences. Upon his return from Italy, Wilfrid took part in the synod of Whitby, which met in 664 to discuss the paschal question once more. He succeeded in convincing his adversaries to put an end to Celtic dissidence, at least in northern England.[82]

Thus, Northumbria little by little entered the cultural sphere of Rome; a new period was dawning in the history of English schools.

D. LAYMEN IN THE MONASTIC SCHOOL

The Anglo-Saxon aristocracy had been closely associated with the evangelization of England and had contributed to the organization of religious culture. But it would take a century before the aristocracy would truly rally itself to the cause and, as a result, a century for all England to be evangelized. Was it that the Barbarians' pagan culture was strong enough to enable them to resist the Catholic Church? Our information on the culture of the first Anglo-Saxons is quite poor, but in comparing the few clues given by Christian writers (especially Bede) with what we know of contemporary Scandinavian culture, we can gain some idea of it.[83] The chief, surrounded by his companions and "sages," led a warrior's life. Priests wielded great authority.[84] They maintained idols in the temples, established the calendar,[85] and were the only ones who knew the magical runic characters and the incantations. *Beowulf*, an epic poem which dates from the eighth century but which sought to revive ancient times, depicted the life of a chief from his infancy to his death in combat.[86] It shows the prince as a young man battling sea creatures, practicing with the bow, and going on daring missions at a very early age. It takes us into the banquet hall, where the

[81] Eddius, *Vita Wilfridi*, X (pp. 20–22).

[82] The problem would not be resolved in northern Ireland until the beginning of the eighth century; see Fliche-Martin, 5: 316.

[83] On Anglo-Saxon pagan culture, see Stenton, *Anglo-Saxon England*, pp. 96–102, and F. Peabody Magoun, "On Some Survivals of Pagan Belief in Anglo-Saxon England," *Harvard Theological Review* 40 (1947): 33–46. Fritz Roeder undertook a study of the Anglo-Saxon family in his *Die Familie bei den Angelsachsen*, but only the first part, *Mann und Frau*, appeared (see the Bibliography).

[84] For pagan religion, see Blair, *Introduction*, pp. 120ff.; for the priesthood, see E. A. Philippson, *Germanisches Heidentum bei den Angelsachsen* (Leipzig, 1929).

[85] Bede, *De temporum ratione*, in *Bedae Opera de temporibus*, ed. Charles W. Jones (Cambridge, Mass., 1943), pp. 211–12, preserved the names of the Anglo-Saxon months.

[86] This poem is discussed further in chap. 9, sect. II.B.2.

scop, "the man of sublime thought whose memory is full of songs," tells how the earth was born, describes the shining plain surrounded by water, heroes' adventures, Sigmund's combat, and the guardian dragon of the treasure. *Beowulf* itself must have been one of those poems the aristocracy loved to hear sung.

When they became Christians, the aristocrats did not abandon their sporting and warrior education, nor did they forget their national epics. Bede tells us that clergy and laymen participated in horse racing.[87] Cuthbert's biographers tell us how the future abbot of Lindisfarne as a young man was unbeatable in fighting, jumping, and racing, and provide examples of his acrobatics: thanks to his physical training he entered the king's service when fifteen years old.[88]

The education of young Anglo-Saxons is thus reminiscent of that of aristocrats' sons in Gaul and Spain but with one exception: literary instruction was not given in the family. Princely courts did not know the preceptorate as it had been established at the Merovingian court.[89] Whenever English princes and aristocrats wanted their children educated, they confided them to monasteries, without intending them to become monks. The daughter of Earcombert of Kent was sent to Faremoutiers around 640;[90] King Oswy of Northumbria was raised by Irish monks;[91] Wilfrid was taught at Lindisfarne, even though he remained a layman.[92] When Wilfrid became abbot of Ripon, the children of the aristocracy were entrusted to him only when they reached adolescence. After a period in the monastery, they could choose between monastic life and the active life of a soldier.[93]

This system of education for laymen was an innovation in the West. Until this time, children of the powerful were entrusted to preceptors or governors according to the antique tradition. Those who were raised in monasteries did not generally return to the world. We are seeing in England the birth of a type of education that is already medieval.

---

[87] *HE*, V, 6 (p. 289).

[88] *Vita Cuthberti*, ed. Colgrave, p. 64: "Alii stantes nudi versis capitibus contra naturam deorsum ad terram et expansis cruribus erecti pedes ad caelos sursum prominebant."

[89] See above, chap. 6, sect. III.D.

[90] Bede, *HE*, III, 8 (p. 142).

[91] Ibid., III, 25 (p. 182): "Osuiu a Scottis edoctus et baptizatus."

[92] Eddius, *Vita Wilfridi*, II (Colgrave ed., p. 6): "Adhuc enim laicus capite."

[93] Ibid., XXI (p. 44): "Principes quoque seculares viri nobiles filios suos ad erudiendum sibi dederunt ut aut Deo servirent si eligerent aut adultos si maluissent regi armatos commendaret." Alchfrid, Oswy's son, had been Wilfrid's disciple; see Bede, *HE*, III, 25 (p. 182): "Porro Alchfrid magistrum habens eruditionis Christianae Vilfridum."

II. IRISH MONKS AND CULTURE IN GAUL

As we have already seen, the Christian schools of Gaul that had been established in bishoprics, monasteries, and parishes in the sixth century dispensed a very elementary training. At the beginning of the seventh century, however, a thrust came from the outside that was to give new impetus to religious culture. At the origin of this renewal, we find the Irish.

About seven years before the arrival of Roman monks in England, twelve Irishmen, led by Columban, left Bangor for Gaul and eventually settled near Luxeuil in Burgundy.[94] They certainly were not the first Irishmen to come to the Continent.[95] But until Columban's time the Celts were content either to pass through without stopping or to settle in deserted places without making any impact on the Church of Gaul.[96] The arrival of Columban and his monks, however, was to have important consequences. It has long been thought that the Irishmen brought with them a tradition of intellectual culture and that they instilled a taste for classical studies in the Merovingian Church. Roger has shown that there is nothing to this idea,[97] but as was often the case in his book, he was more critical than constructive. Let us then take up this question and try first to determine how education was organized at Luxeuil.

From the beginning of his foundation, Columban attracted young people drawn to asceticism: vocations, most of which came from the aristocratic classes, increased during his travels in Gaul. The new monks were young adolescents,[98] those *juvenculi* mentioned in the Columbanian *Rule*,[99] and even children offered at a very young age by their parents.[100]

---

[94] For this foundation, see Fliche-Martin, 5: 512ff.; Besse, *Les moines de l'ancienne France*, pp. 269ff.; and *Mélanges colombaniens*.

[95] For sixth-century recluses, see Cordoliani, "Fortunat, l'Irlande et les Irlandais," in *Etudes mérovingiennes*, p. 37.

[96] The *Vita Samsoni*, 37 (R. Fawtier ed., p. 133), undoubtedly written at the end of the eighth century, mentions Irishmen passing through Gaul on the way back from Rome.

[97] Roger, pp. 403ff.

[98] Jonas, *Vita Columbani*, I, 10 (*MGH, SRM*, IV-1, 76): "Ibi nobilium liberi undique concurrere." *Vita Agili, AS*, Aug., VI, 5: "Cum aliis nobilium virorum filiis."

[99] *Regula coenob.*, 8 (Walker ed., p. 154): "Juvenculi quibus imponitur terminus, ut non se appellent invicem, si transgressi fuerint, tribus superpositionibus."

[100] Donatus, son of Duke Waldelenus, entered Luxeuil as an infant; see Jonas, *Vita Columbani*, I (p. 79). Agilus was offered to the monastery as a seven-year-old child (*AS,*

In order to find out what instruction they received, we must interrogate the texts, especially Columban's rule. It is surprising that there is so little information in it. Columban insisted above all on ascetical training; study was not considered essential. He made no provision for periods devoted to reading as had Benedict—in fact, he even criticized the monk who preferred intellectual work to manual tasks.[101] He devoted but a few sentences to the monastic school.[102] Here and there throughout his writings Columban alluded to the education given in the monastery: in one sermon, he spoke of false learning by way of contrasting it to the learning the monk was to acquire;[103] in another place he was more precise—the monastery was the school where the discipline of disciplines was taught, the one which led to eternal joy. By comparison, music, medicine, and philosophy, which were difficult to learn, counted for very little.[104] For Columban, study, which he called "delectatio litterarum," allowed one to resolve conflicts of the soul and to conquer carnal desires.[105]

By "delectatio litterarum" Columban meant primarily study of the Bible. Jonas, Columban's biographer, tells us that the saint never left the

---

Aug., VI, 304). Domoaldus and Bobolenus were designated as *pueruli* (Jonas, *Vita Columbani*, I, 9 and 15 [pp. 75, 81]).

[101] *Reg. mon.*, 3 (Walker ed., p. 126): "Cotidieque est legendum." This is the only allusion to reading. See also ibid., 10.

[102] *Reg. coenob.*, 10 (Walker ed., p. 152): "Qui consanguineum docet aliquam discentem artem aut aliud quidlibet a senioribus impositum ut melius lectionem discat tribus superpositionibus." The *Reg. mon.*, 7 (Walker, ed., p. 128) alludes to the study of the Psalter.

[103] *Instructio*, I (Walker ed., p. 64): "Quaere ergo scientiam summam non verborum disputatione sed morum bonorum perfectione"; ibid., XI (p. 108): "Sicut enim falsa scientia legitur sic falsa etiam imago umbrata deprehenditur."

[104] Ibid., IV (p. 78): "Si vero temporalia disciplinarum genera praesentis gaudii suavitatem adimunt, quid de hac nostrae scholae disciplina sperandum est? Quae etiam disciplina disciplinarum est quaeque aeterni temporis jucunditatem et aeterni gaudii amoenitatem praesenti maerore comparat?"

"Quantis verberibus, quibus doloribus musicarum discentes imbuuntur? Quantisve fatigationibus vel quantis maeroribus medicorum discipuli vexantur? Qualibus vero inquietudinibus sapientiae amatores vel quantis paupertatis angustiis philosophici coarctantur?"

Farther on, Columban returns to this theme: "Temporalia ergo, ut diximus, studia . . . maerores ac tristitias . . . tolerant, nostrae scholae disciplina . . . fugienda putabitur." Seebass attributed this sermon to Faustus of Riez ("Ueber die sogenannten Instructiones Columbani," *ZKG* 13 [1892]: 513–34), but G. S. M. Walker has restored it to the Irishman. See also Jean Laporte, "Etude d'authenticité des oeuvres attribuées à saint Colomban," *Revue Mabillon* 45 (1955): 15.

[105] Columban, *Ep.* 7 (*MGH, Ep.*, III, 181, ll. 3–5): "Frequenter docendi sunt ac inbuendi fili dulcissimi ut per quasdam delectationes litterarum suas vincere possint de intestino amaritudinis bello."

sacred text.[106] One biographer wrote that he explicated it to monks.[107] Columban sought out exegetical works at Luxeuil: when Gregory the Great's reputation reached Burgundy, Columban acquired the *Regula pastoralis* and wrote to the pope asking him for his *Commentary on Ezechiel* and the end of his *Commentary on the Canticle of Canticles*, and questioned him on the significance of Zacharias' prophecies.[108]

Did Columban want his monks to acquire a profane culture as well? The point has been argued, especially in light of the fact that he himself had a classical culture quite superior to that of his contemporaries.[109] Moreover, he wrote a letter to a certain Sethum advising him to study the ancient poets. After recommending that Sethum know the dogmas of the law and the exemplary *Lives* of the Fathers, he spoke about the "songs of the poets."[110] But we must try to understand what he meant by *vates*. Did he mean Virgil and Horace, whose expressions he cites without giving the authors? Or did he mean the Christian poets he knew: Prudentius, Sedulius, Dracontius?[111] One quite properly hesitates to answer. It could very well be that Sethum was not a monk; at least, there is nothing in the poem to indicate that he was.[112] Columban probably was writing to a lettered layman whom he was trying to

---

[106] Jonas, *Vita Columbani*, I, 8 (p. 74, l. 16): "Librum humero ferens de scripturis sacris secum disputaret"; ibid., I, 20 (p. 90, l. 23), upon his arrest by soldiers: "Residebat ille in atrio ecclesiae librumque legebat."

[107] *Vita Walarici*, 8 (*MGH, SRM*, IV, 163): "Dum pater ad instruendos fratres divinae lectione insisteret." This *Vita* dates from the Carolingian period.

[108] *Ep.* I, 9 (Walker ed., p. 10): "Mihi idcirco sitiendi tua largire per Christum precor opuscula quae in Ezechielem miro, ut audivi elaborasti ingenio. . . . Transmitte et cantica canticorum . . . et ut totam exponas obscuritatem Zachariae."

[109] Georg Heinrich Hörle, *Frümittelalterliche Mönchs- und Klerikerbildung in Italien* (Freiburg-im-Breisgau, 1914), p. 56. See above, n. 20, for Columban's classical culture.

[110] *Ep. ad Sethum*, ed. Walker, p. 186:

> Sint tibi divitiae divinae dogmata legis
> Sanctorumque patrum casta moderamina vitae
> Omnia quae dociles scripserunt ante magistri
> Vel quae doctiloqui cecinerunt carmina vates.

[111] He wrote "ut ait quidam" when citing Virgil; see *Ep.* 7 (*MGH, Ep.*, III, 181, l. 1). One wonders whether Columban was aware of what he was doing when he enriched his prose with reminiscences from antique authors. The citations he used no doubt had come from the Latin grammarians he read and thus were anonymous.

He called Dracontius *vates* in this same letter and cited the *Latin Anthology* eleven times. Elsewhere, he applied the same title to Sappho (*Carm.*, ed. Walker, p. 194): "Inclyta vates nomine Saffo."

[112] The principal theme of the poem was the abandonment of Sethum's riches and the fragility of the things of this world. Walker supposes that Sethum was a pupil of Congall (*S. Columbani opera*, p. xviii). But I tend to agree with Gundlach, who dates these poems to 612–15; see *Ep.* 8 and 9 (*MGH, Ep.*, III, 182–83).

convert. I would say as much about another of his correspondents, Fidelius, to whom Columban, after preaching on the abandonment of worldly goods, gave advice on how to write Adonic verse. Fidelius certainly was not a monk but rather, as the tone of the poem suggests, a rich layman who hesitated about entering the cloister.[113] We should not forget that Columban's prestige went beyond the monastery, and that in Gaul and later in Italy, at Milan, he had literary relationships with several laymen. The poem to Fidelius dates from the time he was in Italy.[114]

When Columban spoke to his monks, whether in his instructions or in letters, he never spoke of the acquisition of profane culture. The only possible reference to profane culture is an allusion to an antique philosopher who was imprisoned for having maintained that there was but one God.[115] But even in evoking Socrates, Columban probably had a passage from the *City of God* in mind.[116]

Furthermore, an examination of Columban's disciples reveals that the training he gave them was religious. Eustasius, who directed Luxeuil after the master left for Italy, trained many bishops, thanks to his ecclesiastical learning.[117] According to his biographer, Amatus of Remiremont was a master of the sacred sciences.[118] At Faremoutiers, a monastery founded by Burgundofara, another disciple of Columban, scriptural studies were the only studies prescribed.[119] None of the Co-

---

[113] *Carm.*, ed. Walker, p. 194:

Inclyte parva	Pascere pingui
Litterolarum	Farre caballos
Munera mittens	Lucraque lucris
Suggero vanas	Accumulando
Linquere curas	Desine nummis
Desine quaeso	Addere nummos.
Nunc animosos	

See Ludwig Bieler, "Versus Sancti Columbani: A Problem Re-Stated," *Irish Ecclesiastical Records* 76 (1951): 376–82, for these poems.

[114] Columban said so himself: "Nunc ad olympiadis ter senos venimus annos." Walker correctly thinks that this poem was written in Milan (*S. Columbani opera*, p. lix).

[115] *Ep.* IV, 6 (Walker ed., p. 30): "Quidam philosophus olim sapientior caeteris eo quod contra omnium opinionem unum Deum esse dixerit in carcerem trusus est."

[116] Augustine, *De civitate Dei*, VIII, 3 (*CSEL*, 40, pt. 1: 356).

[117] Jonas, *Vita Columbani*, I, 30 (*MGH, SRM*, IV-1, 108): "Cohortem fratrum disciplinae habenis erudiret." See also ibid., II, 8 (p. 123): "Fuit ejus studii ut multos sua facundia erudiret." We cannot cite the *Vita Agili* for Agilus' studies, since the relevant passage in the *Life* comes from Jonas' *Vita Eustasii*. See Roger, p. 409.

[118] *Vita Amati*, 12 (*MGH, SRM*, IV, 220). While he was dying he made himself reread Pope Leo's letter to Flavian.

[119] Jonas, *Vita Columbani*, II, 11–12 (pp. 130–31).

lumbanian monasteries of the first half of the seventh century can compare to contemporary Spanish study centers.

One wonders why this was so. Roger thought that the Irish asceticism implanted in Gaul was incompatible with the cult of belles-lettres.[120] Certainly these monks renounced material comfort; their way of life brings to mind that of the Easterners in the desert. When Jonas described Annegray and Luxeuil, he mentioned the huts of wood or stone grouped around the monastic chapel, a description which corresponds to what we know of the little Irish monastic centers of the same period.[121] The monk's life was divided among manual work, personal and collective prayer, and mortifications. Since Irish monks had practiced such a life in Ireland without any hindrance to their literary studies,[122] another reason must be found. Columban found young men in Gaul who were semiliterate but who knew enough Latin to read the sacred text and thus did not need to study the grammarians as had the Irish. In fact, we have already said that in northern Gaul—the only region touched by Columban's preaching—lay culture had not entirely disappeared. Columban was content with what he found because this minimum was all he needed to train his disciples for the task for which he intended them.

In fact, away from his birthplace, in *peregrinus*, Columban became a missionary despite himself. He said this himself in a letter written after his forced departure from Luxeuil: "My goal was to visit the pagans so that the Gospel could be preached to them through us."[123] When he left for the East, it was in order to convert the Alamanni,[124] work his disciples Gall and Eustasius continued.[125] Luxeuil, located in the midst of a forest, was like a seminary for these new missionaries,[126] its way of life closer to that of Anglo-Saxon monasteries than to Irish

---

[120] Roger, p. 412.

[121] Jonas, *Vita Columbani*, I, 13 (p. 78); F. Henry, "Early Monasteries, Beehive Huts, and Dry Stone Houses in the Neighbourhood of Cahirciveen and Waterville, Co. Kerry," *Proceedings of the Royal Irish Academy* 58 (1957): 45–166. See the same author's "Habitat irlandias du Haut Moyen Age," *RA* 28 (1947): 167–76. See also the plan of Scelj Mhichel (Kerry) in Máire and Liam De Paor, *Early Christian Ireland* (London, 1958), p. 53.

[122] See sect. I.A. of this chapter.

[123] *Ep.* IV, 5 (Walker ed., p. 30): "Mei voti fuit gentes visitare et evangelium eis a nobis praedicari."

[124] Jonas, *Vita Columbani*, I, 27 (p. 102).

[125] For Eustasius' missionary work in Bavaria, see ibid., II, 8 (pp. 121–22).

[126] Ibid., I, 27; II, 8 (pp. 102, 121).

study centers. Columban, like Aidan at Lindisfarne, renounced studies in order to devote himself to his new vocation.

Let us not view Columban as the restorer of literary culture in Gaul. All he did was to reawaken abruptly the religious conscience of his contemporaries and to implant in them the desire to meditate on Scripture. It was on this basis that intellectual culture was gradually to be reborn. But we are only at the beginning of this renewal, which still touched but very few.

What kind of audience did Columban have outside the monastery he founded? It certainly did not include clerics. From the beginning, bishops mistrusted this Irishman, who stood for a disturbing nonconformity and spirit of independence and who, in particular, did not celebrate Easter in the Roman fashion.[127] When called to a council, Columban responded with an impertinent letter reminding the bishops of their duties as pastors and affirming the legitimacy of Celtic usages.[128] Priests, with few exceptions, had no contact with Columban and thus would have adopted the hostile attitude of bishops. It could be argued that the important decisions of the Council of Paris of 614 owed nothing to the Columbanian spirit.

Columban enjoyed great success, however, with laymen. During his travels from Luxeuil to Nantes and from Nantes to Coblenz, he converted the men and women he met to a more demanding Christian life. He invited them to practice rigorous penance and provided them with a penitential that was addressed to them as well as to clerics.[129] Women, especially, were seduced by the rigors of Columban's teachings, and the number of convents increased throughout Gaul. Such convents had already existed, as we have seen, but in the seventh century Columban's arrival spurred a renewal of female monasticism. As in Ireland and England, women participated with men in spiritual and intellectual life. Not all lay converts entered the monastery, though. Many remained in the world, adopting a new way of life that was reflected in the way they educated their children.[130]

---

[127] See Grosjean, "Recherches sur les débuts de la controverse pascale chez les Celtes," *AB* 64 (1946): 231ff.

[128] *Ep.* II (Walker ed., p. 14): "Haec idcirco breviter tetigi ut, si volueritis nos [quasi] inferiores, vos patres docere, hanc vocem veri pastoris et in opere et in ore semper habeatis."

[129] *De paenitentia,* XXVI (Walker ed., p. 178).

[130] See the quality of education in Autharius' family (*Vita Audoini, MGH, SRM,* V, 534). See also above, chap. 6, sect. III.B.

Apparently aristocrats in Gaul did not want to entrust the education of their sons and daughters to monks as was done in England and Ireland. Only one text, the *Visio Baronti*, leads us to this hypothesis. The author recounts that Abbot Francard, who directed the monastery of Longoretus, had received goods because "he had brought up and taught some nobles' sons."[131] It is not precisely stated whether these sons ever returned to the world. Aristocrats in Gaul still observed the Roman tradition of family teaching. When children were confided to monks, they went as oblates who were to remain forever in the monastery.

The laymen Columban met in Burgundy, Neustria, and Austrasia belonged to important families well placed at court. Thus, the Merovingian court was also to feel the effect of the Luxovian reform. Following the example of the Columbanians, important officials in Austrasia as well as in Neustria adopted an ascetic life and eventually abandoned the world. Arnulf, the former political counselor of young Dagobert, left his episcopal seat at Metz for the monastery of Habend;[132] in the court of Chlothar II, Dado, the referendary and future Saint Audoenus, had not forgotten Columban's stay with his parents and could speak of this prestigious man to his friends Eligius and Desiderius, who were also employed at court. This small group of palatines, of whom we spoke earlier, led a monastic life while still remaining in the world.

Eligius, in particular, surprised his contemporaries by his religious wisdom. In order to perfect the studies he began in the Limousin,[133] he read while performing manual labor, taking from all his books whatever "made his honey," and shared his scriptural learning with his friends.[134] At the same time, he founded monasteries, which he endowed with sacred books.[135] When he established Solignac, he stipu-

---

[131] *Visio Baronti*, MGH, SRM, V, 385, l. 8: "Ipse [abbas] enutrivit me ab infantia. Erat in Dei timore devotus et de sacra lectione instructus. . . . Erat enim nutritor et doctor filiorum nobilium." The monastery of Longoretus (Lonrey) had been founded during Dagobert's reign by Siranus.

[132] *Vita Arnulfi*, MGH, SRM, II, 426. He rejoined Romaricus, another Austrasian aristocrat (*Vita Romarici*, ibid., IV, 222).

[133] *Vita Eligii*, I, 3 (MGH, SRM, IV, 671).

[134] Ibid., I, 10 (p. 676): "Codicem sibimet prae oculis praeparabat apertum ut quoquo genere laborans divinum perciperet madatum"; ibid., I, 12 (p. 679): "Libros . . . post psalmodiam et orationem revolvens et quasi apis prudentissima diversas ex diversis flores legens." This entire chapter is devoted to Eligius' studies. Eligius' religious culture was to be useful to him when he became bishop of Noyon in 641. See the *Vita Eligii*, I, 33 and 55.

[135] For Paris, see ibid., I, 17 (p. 683): "Vasa simul et vestimenta nec non et sacra volumina aliaque quam plurima ornamenta." For Solignac, see ibid., I, 15: "Volumina sacrarum scripturarum quam plurima."

lated that the customs of Luxeuil were to be followed there.[136] Dado, for his part, helped to found Rebais, whose first abbot was a Luxovian, and also enriched this monastery with books.[137] Desiderius, after having been at court "a soldier of Christ in a secular habit" (to use Dagobert's phrase),[138] was named bishop of Cahors. He too introduced the customs of Luxeuil to his diocese.[139]

With Eligius and Desiderius, the Columbanian spirit penetrated southern Gaul for the first time. If we take a look at the monastic map of Gaul at the time Dagobert came to the throne (629), we see that the known Columbanian monasteries were situated in areas traversed by Columban: Burgundy, Neustria, and Austrasia. Under Luxeuil's second abbot, Eustasius, who died in 629, a few monasteries were founded in Berry and the Nivernais but never again in the south.[140] Likewise, former Columbanian monks who became bishops occupied sees limited to northern and eastern Gaul, as Map 10 shows.[141]

The court thus served as a staging point for the diffusion of Columbanian asceticism throughout the entire Frankish kingdom.

Aquitainians were also attracted to this kind of monasticism. Philibertus, born at Eauze, spent some time at court before shutting himself away in the monastery of Rebais.[142] Amandus, after having lived in Bourges for fifteen years, felt a missionary vocation: he moved to northern Gaul, adopted Columban's rule of life, and, encouraged by Dagobert, converted the pagans of the Gantois;[143] he also ransomed slaves, taught them, and made them priests whose religious worth was superior to that of the secular clergy in his entourage.[144] Remaclus, another

136 Ibid., I, 21: "Praeter Lussedio ergo qui solus dictum est districtionem regulae tenebat."
137 *Vita Agili*, AS, Aug., VI, 584.
138 See the *Vita sancti Desiderii*, MGH, SRM, IV, 571: "Cognovimus religionis observantiam ab ipso pueritiae suae tempore in omnibus custodire et sub habitu saeculi Christi militem gerere."
139 In ibid., 23 (p. 580) he pointedly says that Columban's "sect" was introduced to his diocese. Further on, he writes of the good relations between Desiderius and the "Scot" Arnanus (ibid., 32 [p. 589]).
140 *Vita Columbani*, II, 10 (MGH, SRM, IV-1, 128–29). See Maurice de Laugardière, *L'Eglise de Bourges avant Charlemagne* (Paris, 1951), pp. 169ff.
141 Acharius became bishop of Tournai and Vermand; Omer was bishop of Thérouanne. See the *Vita Columbani*, II, 8 (p. 123), and Louis M. Duchesne, *Fastes épiscopaux de l'ancienne Gaule*, 3 vols. (Paris, 1907–15), 3: 103.
142 *Vita Philiberti*, MGH, SRM, V, 585.
143 *Vita Amandi*, MGH, SRM, V, 428. For Amandus' missions, see Edouard de Moreau, *Saint Amand, apôtre de la Belgique et du Nord de la France* (Louvain, 1927), and E. de Moreau, "Belgique (VIe–VIIIe siècle)," DHGE, 7: 530.
144 *Vita Amandi*, I, 9 (MGH, SRM, V, 480): "Redimebat puerus transmarinos . . .

10. *Centers of Columbanian Culture in Gaul*

Aquitainian and founder of Stavelot and Malmédy in the Ardennes forest, likewise made these centers into seminaries for missionaries.[145]

By 640, then, northern and southern Gaul began to be won over to the Columbanian movement. A monastic network had been created which was to revivify the kingdom when the religious culture of the secular clergy became anemic.

In order that the new spirituality itself not weaken, it would have to be receptive to exterior influences. The establishment of monasteries promoted exchanges between different Western countries. Irishmen remained in contact with their native land and at Rebais met their compatriots.[146] Columban's establishment of the Italian monastery of Bobbio in 614 led to the renewal of contacts between Ireland and Italy via England and Gaul. Bobbio received monks who came to venerate the tomb of the founder and soon became a stop for those on their way to Rome. If we add the fact that Anglo-Saxons in turn came to the Continent around 650–60,[147] we can see that Merovingian Gaul would greatly benefit from these different currents.

Let us look at several examples important to the history of culture. The Frank Agilbert left before 640 to study in Ireland and later, after having been bishop of Dorchester, as we have already seen, became bishop of Paris.[148] His nephew replaced him at Dorchester, while Agilbert himself maintained sufficient contact with the Anglo-Saxons to participate in the synod of Whitby. In 656 Bishop Dido of Poitiers was charged with leading young Dagobert II to Ireland,[149] where he remained long enough to discover Irish learning. It could be that his disciple and nephew Leodegarius, the future bishop of Autun, profited from Dido's experience. In return, Irishmen came to Austrasia, some

---

litteris affatim imbui praecipiebat." Amandus complained to Martin I about the "duritia sacerdotum gentis illius" (*PL*, LXXXVII, 1356).

[145] *Vita Remacli, MGH, SRM*, V, 104. For Stavelot, see Cottineau, 2: 3085, and F. Baix, "Saint Remacle et les abbayes de Solignac et de Stavelot-Malmédy," *RB* 61 (1951): 167–207.

[146] *Vita Agili*, 21 (*AS*, Aug., VI, 587); *Vita Fursei, MGH, SRM*, IV, 423. In the middle of the seventh century, Ronan went to Gaul and Italy to study; see Bede, *HE*, III, 25 (p. 181). For the Irishmen on the Continent, see L. Gougaud, "L'oeuvre des Scotti dans l'Europe continentale," *RHE* 9 (1908): 21–37, 255–77.

[147] See above, sect. I.C.

[148] There is a short biography of Agilbert by M. Besson in *DHGE*, 1: 956–57.

[149] *Liber historiae Francorum, MGH, SRM*, II, 316. See Louis Dupraz, *Le royaume des Francs et l'ascension politique des maires du palais au déclin du VIIᵉ siècle* (Freiburg, 1948), p. 313.

of them loaded with books.[150] When Gertrude, the daughter of Pepin of Landen, was made abbess of Nivelles by Amandus, she called in scholars from overseas—that is, Ireland—to help her with her religious studies.[151]

Neustrians had become more oriented toward England ever since Bathilda, an Anglo-Saxon, had married Clovis II (639–57).[152] Young princesses from the other side of the Channel were sent to Jouarre for a monastic education.[153] The abbess of Chelles, Bertilla, a former nun of Jouarre, sent books to Anglo-Saxons.[154] In 653, Wilfrid, on the way to Rome, stopped at Lyon, a customary resting place for Anglo-Saxon pilgrims, but the bishop of the city tried to detain the intelligent young man there.[155]

Let us now look to the south. The Italian monk Jonas, to whom we shall return later, came to Gaul from Bobbio around 641 and spent three years with Amandus at Elnone before going on to Saint Vaast in Arras, Faremoutiers, and finally, Moutier-Saint-Jean in Burgundy.[156] In the opposite direction, Wandregisilus and Philibertus spent some time at Bobbio before founding their monastery in Normandy.[157] Others went as far as Rome. Amandus made two trips there, maintaining good relations with the papacy.

Amandus wrote to Pope Martin I and asked him to send some books to Gaul.[158] Rome, in fact, had been a source of manuscripts for the West, especially since the time of Gregory the Great, but in the middle of the seventh century, the requests became more and more pressing, with consequences to which we shall return. Gertrude of Nivelles also

---

[150] As in the case of Foillan, Fursa's brother (*Additamentum Nivialense, MGH, SRM*, IV, 449): "Sanctis inventis reliquiis . . . et libris in navi oneratis."

[151] *Vita Geretrudis, MGH, SRM*, II, 458: "Per suos nuntios . . . de transmarinis regionibus gignaros homines ad docendum divini legis carmina . . . meruisset habere." For the ties between Pepin's family and the Irishmen, see Dupraz, *Le royaume des Francs*, p. 313.

[152] Bathilda founded the monastery of Corbie and then that of Chelles, where she died in 680; see *Vita Bathildis, MGH, SRM*, II, 482.

[153] Bede, *HE*, III, 8 (p. 142).

[154] *Vita Bertilae, MGH, SRM*, VI, 106.

[155] Bede, *HE*, V, 19 (p. 324): "Delectabatur enim antistes [Dalfinus] prudentia verborum juvenis gratia venusti vultis, alacritate actionis et constantia ac maturitate cogitationis."

[156] For Jonas' travels, see *Wattenbach-Levison*, I: 133–34.

[157] *Vita Philiberti*, 5 (*MGH, SRM*, V, 587); *Gesta sanctorum patrum fontanellensis coenobii (Gesta abbatum fontanellensium)*, I, 5–6 (Lohier and Laporte ed., p. 3; hereafter cited as *Gesta abb. font.*).

[158] The letter is lost, but we do have the pope's reply; see below, n. 274.

had books sent from Rome,[159] while Wandregisilus' nephew and Audoenus went to Rome themselves in search of precious volumes.[160] Among the books brought back was one text which until this time had not been read very much in Gaul, Benedict's *Rule*. In fact, the oldest Benedictine monastery known in Gaul was Altaripa in the diocese of Albi, which dates from 620–30.[161] Eligius was acquainted with the rule, since he combined it with Luxeuil's rule for his monastery at Solignac.[162] The Benedictine rule was also adopted shortly afterwards at Fleury-sur-Loire[163] and at Chamalières (Puy-de-Dôme).[164] During the second half of the century it gradually made its way into the northern regions of Gaul, always along with, significantly, Columban's rule. Wandregisilus around 649, Philibertus around 654, and Bishop Donatus of Besançon about the same time paired the two rules for their monasteries.[165] Even at Luxeuil, Abbot Waldebert adopted the compromise: "Benedict's rule in the fashion of Luxeuil."[166] Thus, the most important consequence of the exchanges we have just talked about was the diffusion of the Benedictine rule throughout Gaul by Columbanian monks.

[159] *Vita Geretrudis, MGH, SRM,* II, 458: "Sancta volumina de urbe Roma . . . meruisset habere."

[160] *Gesta abb. font.,* I, 6 (Lohier and Laporte ed., p. 10). Among these works were those of Gregory the Great.

[161] L. Traube, *Textgeschichte der Regula S. Benedicti* (Munich, 1910), pp. 55, 87 (= *CCL,* 117: 502). This monastery, founded by Venerandus, has not been precisely located (perhaps Hauterive, commune of Labruguière, south of Castres).

[162] *Vita Eligii, MGH, SRM,* IV, 747. Krusch, the editor, thought that this document was authentic, but Malnory rejected it (*Quid luxovienses monachi discipuli sancti Columbani ad regulam monasteriorum atque ad communem ecclesiae profectum contulerint* [Paris, 1894], pp. 28, 83).

[163] See Leodebodus' will in favor of Fleury in Maurice Prou and Alexandre Vidier, eds., *Recueil des chartes de l'abbaye de Saint-Benoît-sur-Loire,* 2 vols. (Paris, 1907–32), 1: 1–19.

[164] Praejectus (died 674) combined the rules of Benedict, Caesarius, and Columban; see *Vita Praejecti, MGH, SRM,* V, 235.

[165] *Vita Philiberti,* 5 (MGH, SRM, V, 587): "Benedicti decreta, Columbani instituta sanctissima lectione frequentabat assidua"; Donatus of Besançon, *Reg. ad virgines, PL,* LXXXVII, 273.

[166] *Vita Sadalbergae,* 8 (*MGH, SRM,* V, 54) and Faro's charter in Pardessus, II, 275: "Regula Benedicti ad normam luxoviensis coenobii." See Malnory, *Quid luxovienses,* pp. 26ff. Waldebert may have been the author of the female rule of Faremoutiers (*PL,* LXXXVIII, 1051), which owes much to Benedict; see Louis Gougaud, "Inventaire des règles monastiques irlandaises," *RB* 25 (1908): 329–31; Jean Gaudemet, "Les aspects canoniques de la règle de saint Colomban," in *Mélanges colombaniens,* p. 175; and James O'Carroll, "Sainte Fare et les origines," in *Sainte Fare et Faremoutiers* (Abbey of Sainte-Fare, 1956).

It has been rightly said that the adoption of this rule permitted the disciples of the Irishmen to stabilize the monastic institution.[167] From the point of view of culture, it seems to me that it also served to re-emphasize the importance of sacred study at a time when monks were devoting themselves particularly to missionary activity and to clearing uncultivated land. A comparison between the rule of Columban, which is so discreet on this point, and the rules of Donatus or Waldebert is instructive. The rules of Donatus and Waldebert lay down the times devoted to personal and common reading,[168] require that children be taught, and devote an entire chapter to their education.[169]

With the adoption of the Benedictine rule, a new period began in the history of Gaul's monasteries. They grew larger in the middle of the seventh century, acquired books, and would soon be ready to become true centers of study.

III. THE BEGINNINGS OF CHRISTIAN CULTURE IN THE LOMBARD KINGDOM

The arrival of the Goths in Italy, as we have seen, did not result in the disappearance of the tradition of antique culture. It survived, although with some difficulty, even after the Byzantine reconquest. In 568, new Barbarians, the Lombards, invaded northern Italy and tried to occupy the entire peninsula. The seventh century was completely dominated by this drama, on which hung not only the maintenance of Byzantine possessions in Italy but the fate of antique and Christian culture as well.

When Gregory the Great died in 604, the Lombards were solidly established in the plain of the Po, where they had founded a kingdom, and in peninsular Italy around the duchies of Spoleto, Tuscany, and Beneventum.[170] The Lombard conquest had been brutal; all sources

---

[167] See R. Aigrain in Fliche-Martin, 5: 516.

[168] Waldebert, *Reg. ad virgines*, 9, 12, 24 (*PL*, LXXXVIII, 1053ff.); Donatus of Besançon, *Reg. ad virgines*, 6, 8, 20, 33, 62 (*PL*, LXXXVII, 273ff.).

[169] Waldebert, *Reg. ad virgines*, 24 (*PL*, LXXXVIII, 1070): "De nutriendis infantibus."

[170] On the Lombard conquest of Italy, see Lot, *Les destinées*, pp. 210ff.; Schmidt, *Die Ostgermanen*, pp. 565ff.; Besta, *Storia del diritto italiano*, 1: 225; Gian Piero Bognetti, "S. Maria *foris portas* di Castelseprio e la storia religiosa dei Longobardi," in Bognetti, Gino Chierici, and Alberto De Capitani d'Arzago, *Santa Maria di Castelseprio* (Milan, 1948), pp. 24ff., 385; and *Problemi della civiltà e dell'economia longobarda*, ed. A. Tagliaferri, Biblioteca della revista *Economia e Storia* (Milan, 1964).

agree on that. Even Paul the Deacon, a Lombard who wrote the history of his people in the eighth century, recalled the destruction of property and the executions ordered by Alboin and his successors.[171] These semi-nomadic people remained pagan—the aristocracy alone had been converted to Arianism—and, long isolated from the Mediterranean world, they preserved a purely Germanic way of life. The education of young Lombards, as described by Paul the Deacon, conformed to the Barbarian tradition. They were raised at court[172] and accompanied the king on the hunt or into war.[173] At an early age they were trained to mount horses and to fight,[174] ample occasion for which was provided by the wars against the Slavs, Avars, and Byzantines.[175] At puberty, the sons of princes had to receive their weapons from a foreign king in order to be admitted to their father's table. As with other Barbarians, important military deeds were transmitted orally, by writing, and by poems.[176]

Lombard education can be compared with Anglo-Saxon education. Furthermore, the Lombards and the Anglo-Saxons were interrelated through their laws and customs.[177] Like the Anglo-Saxons, the Lombards had not been prepared to appreciate Roman civilization; however, unlike the Anglo-Saxons, the Lombards occupied a land that was still very Romanized—despite themselves, they were going to be won over to Roman civilization.

After a period of adaptation, Lombard kings tried to pass for heirs of the Romans, as had Ostrogothic princes.[178] Settled in Theodoric's

---

[171] Gregory the Great, *Ep.* V, 42; VI, 58; VII, 23 (*MGH, Ep.*, I, 336, 432, 466); Paul the Deacon, *HL*, II, 32 (*MGH, SRL*, p. 90).

[172] Paul the Deacon, *HL*, V, 40 (p. 160, ll. 4–5). They were part of the "gasindi qui palacio regis custodiunt" (*Glossarium cavense et vaticanum*, 32 [*MGH, Leges*, IV, 653]).

[173] Paul the Deacon, *HL*, V, 39 (p. 158, l. 25). See the hunting scene on a sarcophagus from Civita Castellana in Julius Baum, *La sculpture figurale en Europe à l'époque mérovingienne* (Paris, 1937), p. 169, pl. LXIII.

[174] *Consularia italica: Auctarii Haviensis extrema*, 22 (*MGH, AA*, IX, 339): "Sundrarius . . . qui apud Agilulfum bellicis rebus instructus erat." See Paul the Deacon, *HL*, IV, 37 (p. 131) for the story of young Grimoaldus, the son of the duke of Friuli.

[175] Paul the Deacon, *HL*, I, 23 (p. 61).

[176] Ibid., I, 27 (p. 70): "Virtus in eorum carminibus celebratur."

[177] Ibid., IV, 22 (p. 124): "Vestimenta vero eis erant laxa et maxime linea qualia Anglisaxones habere solent." See Thomas Hodgkin, "Sulla relazione ethnologica fra i Longobardi e gli Angli," *XI centenario di Paolo Diacono: Atti e memorie del Congresso storico tenuto in Cividale nei giorni 3, 4, 5 settembre 1899* (Cividale, 1900), and Brunner, *Deutsche Rechtsgeschichte*, 1: 536ff.

[178] We should note that Alboin married Theodoric's granddaughter (see Stein, 2: 528) and thus could have pretended to the Ostrogothic succession.

palace in Pavia, they adopted the habits of Roman life.[179] In 584, Authari even took the name Flavius; his successor, Agilulf, had himself portrayed on a throne surrounded by warriors and victories of Roman or Byzantine type.[180] As in the previous century, Romans placed themselves in the service of the kings and helped them administer their state.[181] Under their influence, Agilulf adopted a Byzantine ceremonial and restored monuments.[182]

Agilulf had definitely been influenced by his wife, the Bavarian Theodelinda, to continue the Roman work. The Bavarian dynasty, which had early been converted to Catholicism, settled in ancient Noricum, which, while politically attached to the Frankish kingdom, remained in the Italian sphere of influence.[183] In the seventh century, the two regions were in constant contact by means of the ancient Via Claudia Augusta.[184]

Theodelinda had received a good education in Bavaria. Word of her intellectual excellence traveled to distant Spain, where King Sisebut painted a flattering portrait of the Lombard queen.[185] Gregory the Great sent her an evangeliary and his book of *Dialogues*, thus making known the *Life of Saint Benedict* in northern Italy.[186] The queen had a

---

[179] See Paul the Deacon, HL, II, 31; III, 19 (pp. 90, 102), for the epitaph of a Romanized Lombard. For Pavia during the Lombard period, see the few lines in Pietro Vaccari, "Pavia nell'alto medioevo," *Settimane*, 6: 151. See also Gian Piero Bognetti, "L'influsso delle istituzioni militari romane sulle istituzioni longobarde del sec. VI e la natura delle 'fara,'" *Atti del Congresso internazionale di diritto romano e di storia del diritto: Verona 27–28–29 IX–1948*, ed. Guiscardo Moschetti, 4 vols. (Milan, 1951–53), 4: 167–210.

[180] This is the famous gilt copper band preserved in the museum at Bargello; see Emmerich Schaffran, *Die Kunst der Langobarden in Italien* (Jena, 1941), p. 85.

[181] Paul the Deacon, HL, IV, 35 (p. 128) named Agilulf's notary: Stabilicianus. Gregory of Tours, HF, X, 3 (p. 486) and Honorius, *Ep.* 2 (MGH, *Ep.*, III, 694, l. 11), refer to a Peter and a Paul. For these individuals, see Gian Piero Bognetti, "Ministri romani di re longobardi," *Archivio storico lombardo* (1949), p. 10.

[182] When Agilulf associated his son with him in the exercise of royal power, he presented him at the circus in Milan just as the Byzantine emperors were presented at the hippodrome (Paul the Deacon, HL, IV, 30 [p. 127]). Agilulf and Adaloald restored a monument in Milan. See the plate in Ugo Monneret de Villard, *Catalogo delle iscrizioni cristiane anteriori al secolo XI* (Milan, 1915), p. 48. See also Ewig, "Résidences et capitales," pp. 36ff.

[183] See N. Jorga, "La 'Romania' danubienne et les Barbares au VIe siècle," *RBPh* 3 (1924): 35–51; for Bavaria in the seventh century, see Ignaz Zibermayr, *Noricum, Baiern, und Oesterreich: Lorch als Hauptstadt und die Einführung des Christentums*, 2nd ed. (Horn, 1956).

[184] Joachim Werner, "Longobardischer Einfluss in Süddeutschland während des 7. Jahrhunderts im Lichte archäologischer Funde," *Atti del I Congresso*, pp. 521–24.

[185] Sisebut to Adaloald in MGH, *Ep.*, III, 673, ll. 5–8: "Oratione compunctam, almis studiis deditam . . . suavem eloquio, acrem ingenio."

[186] Gregory the Great, *Ep.* XIV, 12 (MGH, *Ep.*, II, 431).

church and a palace built at Monza, welcomed artists,[187] had frescoes painted depicting the deeds of the Lombards,[188] and at the same time asked the monk Secundus of Trent to write a history of her people.[189] Perhaps she knew that a century earlier another Barbarian prince, Theodoric, asked a Roman to perform the same task.[190] Secundus, the monk-historian, was the queen's counselor and soon the godfather of young Adaloald, the first Lombard king to be baptized in the Catholic rite.[191]

Theodelinda was keenly interested in religious questions. One can divine a small group of clerics around her excited by the prospect of converting the Arian Lombards or by the affair of the *Three Chapters*.[192] Some bishops, among whom were Agrippinus of Como and the bishop of Brescia, tried to persuade the queen to refuse communion from the metropolitan of Milan, Constantius, who was loyal to the pope. The monk Secundus served as intermediary between the queen and Pope Gregory. When the Irishman Columban arrived in Italy in 614, the bishops and the king tried to get him to side with the group favorable to the *Three Chapters* and hostile to the papacy, which had approved their condemnation.[193] But Columban was really thinking about the conversion of the Arians and their king and during his stay in Milan wrote a little work against Arianism, which has unfortunately been lost.[194] Thus the intellectual preoccupations of the Lombard court at the opening of the seventh century were exclusively religious. No great literary work was ever produced: the metrical inscriptions composed by semiliterate clerics cannot be called great literature.[195]

During the course of the seventh century, after an initial period of

---

[187] E. Sturms, "Die Funde aus dem Sarcophage des kön. Theodolind im Monza," *Germania* 30 (1952): 368–79. The binding on Theodelinda's evangeliary is undoubtedly Byzantine work; see Pietro Toesca, *Storia dell'arte italiana* (Turin, 1927), 1: 332, and Fernanda Wittgens, "Art primitif de Lombardie," *Cahiers d'Art* 24 (1949): 202.

[188] Paul the Deacon, *HL*, IV, 22 (p. 124).

[189] Ibid., IV, 40 (p. 133). For this person and his role, see Bognetti, "S. Maria *foris portas* di Castelseprio," p. 155.

[190] See above, chap. 2, n. 40.

[191] Paul the Deacon, *HL*, IV, 27 (p. 125).

[192] See Duchesne, *L'Eglise au VIe siècle*, pp. 150ff., and Fliche-Martin, 5: 43ff., for this affair.

[193] Columban, *Ep.*, 5 (Walker ed., pp. 37ff.). See Bognetti, "S. Maria *foris portas* di Castelseprio," pp. 163ff.

[194] Jonas, *Vita Columbani*, I, 34 (*MGH, SRM*, IV-1, 107).

[195] For Pavia, see Gaetano Pannaza, "Catalogo delle iscrizioni e sculture paleo-cristiane e pre-romaniche di Pavia," *Arte del primo millenio: Atti del II Congresso per lo studio sul'arte dell'alto medio evo tenuto presso l'Università di Pavia, 1950* (Turin, 1952), pp. 225ff.

hostile coexistence,[196] the Lombards opened themselves more to Roman culture. The people themselves dressed as Romans.[197] The great Lombard necropolises at Nocera Umbra and Castel Trosino have yielded ordinary Roman objects and even a fibula bearing a Latin inscription.[198] The occupiers began to comprehend and speak Latin. Paul the Deacon conveys the surprising note that during his own time—the eighth century—a small group of Bulgars who had settled in the duchy of Beneventum were still bilingual.[199] It is likely that the Lombards had been Latinized before this date; at least they spoke the popular tongue.[200]

During Rothari's reign (636–43), the Lombard people were sufficiently Romanized to want their customs drawn up in Latin.[201] The king wanted the law understood in both the Lombard and Roman communities and took care to provide equivalent popular and Germanic terms for the Latin terms in his *Edict*.[202] The Lombard *Edict* reveals to us a people who were still very much attached to Barbarian ways, but here and there we can see that written documents began to be used, thus marking the passage toward another kind of civilization.[203]

The redaction of this *Edict* poses some problems. Under what conditions had it been elaborated and by whom? Historians of law have uncovered Bavarian, Alamannic, Visigothic, and even Byzantine influences in this text.[204] It is certain that a small group of jurists was brought together to make this compilation; this does not imply, how-

---

[196] For relations between Lombards and Italians, see Bognetti, "S. Maria *foris portas* di Castelseprio," pp. 56ff.

[197] Paul the Deacon, *HL*, IV, 22 (p. 124).

[198] U. Pasqui and Roberto Paribeni, "Necropoli barbarica di Nocera Umbra," *Monumenti antichi* 25 (1918): 254. The fibula bears the phrase "Si deus pro nus qui contra nus." The same device has been found on silver phalera from Reggio Emilia; see J. Werner, "Langobardische Grabfunde aus Reggio Emilia," *Germania* 30 (1952): 190. For the inscriptions on fibulae from Castel Trosino, see Siegfried Fuchs, *Die Langobardischen Goldblattkreuze aus der Zone südwärts der Alpen* (Berlin, 1938).

[199] Paul the Deacon, *HL*, V, 29 (p. 154): "Qui usque hodie in his ut diximus locis habitantes quamquam et latine loquantur, linguae tamen propriae usum minime amiserunt."

[200] E. Sestan, "La composizione etnica della società in rapporto allo svolgimento della civiltà in Italia nel secolo VII," *Settimane*, 5: 674ff.

[201] See Franz Beyerle, *Die Gesetze der Longobarden* (Weimar, 1947).

[202] *Edictus, MGH, Leges*, IV, 17–59ff.; Bengt Löfstedt, *Studien über die Sprache der langobardischen Gesetze: Beiträge zur frühmittelalterlichen Latinität* (Stockholm, 1961).

[203] *Edictus, MGH, Leges*, IV (243): "De cartola falsa aut quolibet membranum"; (224): "Necesse est propter futuri temporis memoriam ut ipse manumissio in cartolam libertatis commoretur"; (227): "Libellus scriptus" for a sale; (178 and 182): reference to the use of a *carta* for the "traditio nuptiarum."

[204] See the bibliographies in Buchner, *Die Rechtsquellen*, pp. 33–34, and in Gian Piero Bognetti, "L'Editio di Rotari," in *Studi in onore di Pietro de Francisci*, 4 vols. (Milan, 1956), 2: 235–56.

ever, that there was a school at Pavia, as Mengozzi and his disciples believe.[205] No such law school, which has vainly been linked to the past,[206] appears in any of our texts. What did exist was an embryonic bureaucracy which employed Romans. Rothari, like his successors, must have had Roman notaries.[207] He said in the preface to his law that he received advice from nobles, judges (*judices*), and the people.[208] In addition, he certainly consulted local and foreign jurists.

As Arianism waned, Roman influence was increasingly felt at court. The princes who succeeded Adaloald, Theodelinda's son, were convinced Arians, but their spouses were Catholics who built churches at Pavia and elsewhere.[209] Columban's monks at Bobbio contributed to the progress of Catholicism by maintaining their contacts at court.[210] Finally, in 653, a Bavarian dynasty moved into Pavia under Aripert and put an end to Arianism, at least at court. A new period was beginning for the Lombard dynasty.

Under the first Catholic kings, there were no known centers of culture outside the court. In the absence of any written texts, we have only a few inscriptions to give us any information on the life in the bishoprics.[211] Monasteries likewise remained in the shadows. Yet we know that Lombard kings and queens founded monastic establishments at Monza, Milan, and Pavia,[212] although we do not know which rule these monasteries adopted and what their religious and cultural life was like. Bobbio alone is known because of the great impact it exerted in the beginning—an impact which was limited to the spiritual realm. Contrary to what some would believe, Bobbio was not a place of refuge

[205] Guido Mengozzi, *Ricerche sull'attività della scuola di Pavia nell'alto medio evo* (Pavia, 1924), repeated by Viscardi, *Le origini*, p. 198.

[206] See above, chap. 2, n. 154.

[207] It was one of these Romans, no doubt, who composed a chronicle around 625 which has been published in the *MGH, AA*, IX, 266–339. See *Wattenbach-Levison*, 1: 205.

[208] See the epilogue of Rothari's edict, *MGH, Leges*, IV, 89–90.

[209] Paul the Deacon, *HL*, IV, 47; V, 34 (pp. 136, 156).

[210] Jonas, *Vita Columbani*, II, 24 (*MGH, SRM*, IV-1, 147).

[211] We should mention the metrical epitaph of Bishop Celsus of Vercelli (died 665), which was composed by Deacon Gratianus ("Gratianus suus caro et levita ornavit amando sepulchrum" [*CIL*, no. 6725]) and the epitaph of Agrippinus of Como (Carlo Troya, *Codice diplomatico longobardo dal DLXVIII al DCCLXXIV con note storiche, osservazioni e dissertazioni*, 5 vols. in 6 [Naples, 1852–56], 1: 318). See Bognetti's commentary in "S. Maria *foris portas* di Castelseprio," pp. 141ff.

[212] Paul the Deacon, *HL*, IV, 42, 48; V, 33–34 (pp. 134, 136, 155–56). The disorganization of Italian monasticism in the seventh century has been greatly exaggerated. See Tommasso Leccisotti, "Le conseguenze dell'invasione longobarda per l'antico monachesimo italico," *Atti del I Congresso*, pp. 369–76, and idem, "Aspetti e problemi del monachesimo in Italia," *Settimane*, 4: 319ff.

for antique culture during this period, a point which must be stressed.

Columban settled in a "desert" in 614. He restored a half-destroyed church and erected monastic buildings. During his brief stay in Italy, as I have already indicated, he had dealings with lettered men in Milan and Pavia. One would like to imagine a meeting of those Irishmen and Italians who were still capable of appreciating belles-lettres. But Columban, who was already an old man, died a year after he came to Bobbio and did not have the opportunity to make his small monastery a center for studies. Attala, his successor, was a Burgundian aristocrat who had received a classical education before entering Luxeuil.[213] Did he remember his education afterwards? His biographer, Jonas, does not breathe a word about it. During Attala's abbacy, the monks seem to have been primarily peasants and missionaries.[214] The conversion of neighboring pagans and Arian Lombards still had to be accomplished—a task to which the Irish could not remain indifferent. The presence of Arian manuscripts in Bobbio's library perhaps proves that the monastery was active at this time in the fight against heresies.[215] Attala, in fact, followed the example of his master Columban and placed his learning at the service of missionary work because he was, according to Jonas, "skilled in elucidating questions and stalwart in the face of heretics' storms."[216] Attala's successor, Bertulf (627–40), who was also brought up at Luxeuil, was encouraged by Pope Honorius to battle against Arianism.[217] The intellectual activity of Bobbio thus seems rather limited; the studies done there were exclusively religious. There was a library, of course, but it was still rather modest. Shortly before his death, Attala initiated several important projects, among which were the restoration of the books' bindings.[218] A book believed to have come down to us from Attala still survives. It is a palimpsest bearing a commentary on Isaiah over an earlier Arian text.[219] This manuscript represents one

213 See above, chap. 6, n. 69.

214 Jonas, *Vita Columbani*, II, 25 (pp. 149–50). The monk Agibodus worked in a mill; Baudacharius tended vines; Meroveus burned down a tree venerated by the pagans.

215 For the Arian palimpsests from Bobbio, see *CLA*, III, 20. M. Van der Hout, "Gothic Palimpsests of Bobbio," *Scriptorium* 6 (1952): 91–93, does not believe that they were at Bobbio in the seventh century but supplies no proof for this contention.

216 Jonas, *Vita Columbani*, II, 4 (p. 117): "In solvendis ac opponendis quaestionibus sagax, adversus haereticorum procellas vigens ac solidus."

217 Ibid., II, 23 (p. 145): "Et arianae pestis perfidiam evangelico mucrone ferire non abnuerit." Honorius' letter to Bertulf spoke only of monastic life (*PL*, LXXX, 483).

218 Jonas, *Vita Columbani*, II, 5 (p. 117): "Vehicula quoque fovet, libros ligaminibus firmat."

219 *CLA*, III, 365: "Liber de arca domno Atalani." François Masai, in Vanderhoven and

of the earliest moments in the history of a library whose prestige was to grow so great. There is no evidence anywhere, however, that Bobbio acquired manuscripts from other libraries. The famous hypothesis according to which Bobbio was the heir of Vivarium is groundless.[220] Even contacts with Rome were rare. The abbot of Bobbio and Jonas, his secretary, visited Honorius, but Bobbio did not participate in the theological quarrels which divided Rome and Constantinople.[221]

Nevertheless, one monk during this period distinguished himself from the others by his culture: Jonas, the biographer of the abbots of Bobbio and Luxeuil. A monk of Bobbio from 618 to 640, Jonas undertook to tell the life of Columban at the request of Bertulf, the abbot whose secretary he was.[222] He finished his work around 643 in France, where he settled at Elnone with Amandus. Jonas was a good writer for the period; he knew both Christian and pagan poets and was acquainted with details from the Roman past.[223] He had read Gregory the Great's *Dialogues*, which he imitated in his *Miracles of Saint John of Réomé*. Of course, like a good hagiographer, he accused himself of clumsiness and contrasted his style with that of the learned, who were "completely impregnated with the dew of eloquence."[224] But in the preface, as in the work itself, the complicated turns of speech he loved to use link him to the Italian rhetors of the sixth century.[225] Jonas was,

---

Masai, *Regula Magistri*, p. 49, n. 1, hesitates to read *Atalani*, but he is the only one to do so.

[220] Courcelle, *LG*, pp. 343ff. For the history of Bobbio's library, see Giovanni, cardinal Mercati, *M. Tulli Ciceronis De re publica libri e codice rescripto vaticano latino 5757 phototypice expressi. Prolegomena de fatis bibliothecae monasterii s. Columbani Bobiensis et de codice ipso Vat. lat., 5757* (Rome, 1934), pp. 15–19.

[221] Abbot Bertulf's visit to Honorius is the only evidence of contacts between Bobbio and Rome. See Jonas, *Vita Columbani*, II (*MGH, SRM*, IV, 145). It could be that the monastery was placed under the direct dependence of the pope during this period; see Terence Patrick McLaughlin, *Le très ancien droit monastique de l'Occident: Etude sur le développement general du monachisme* (Paris and Ligugé, 1935), pp. 187–88.

[222] For Jonas, see *Wattenbach-Levison*, 1: 133–34.

[223] Paul Lehmann, "Panorama der literarischen Kultur des Abendlandes im 7. Jahrhundert," *Settimane*, 5: 857–58.

[224] Jonas, *Vita Columbani*, preface (pp. 62–63): "Plerosque musicorum omnium, organi scilicet, psalterii, cytharae melos aures oppletas, mollis saepe avenae, modulamini auditum accomodare. . . . Praesertim si doctorum facundia fultus . . . nobis ex Hibernia vix butyrum pinguescit."

[225] Edward Kennard Rand, "The Irish Flavor of the *Hisperica famina*," in *Studien zur lateinischen Dichtung des Mittelalters: Ehrengable für Karl Strecker*, ed. W. Stach and H. Walther (Dresden, 1931), p. 134, supposes that Jonas had been influenced by Celtic works. Asianism, however, was not the privilege of the Celts alone. For Jonas's style, see D. Norberg, "Le développement du latin en Italie de Saint Grégoire le Grand à Paul Diacre," *Settimane*, 5: 490ff.

in fact, an Italian who had been born in the "noble town" of Susa and had come from a good family.[226] He was converted when he entered Bobbio, undoubtedly after having received secondary instruction from teachers at Susa. What we know of Bobbio during this time does not indicate that the abbey could have provided the monks with anything more than a religious culture.

In the middle of the seventh century, Bobbio left the heroic age behind and was affected by influences other than those emanating from Luxeuil. In circumstances which escape us, but certainly under the influence of Rome, the monastery adopted Benedict's rule. While some are suspicious of the document that records this event,[227] the fact itself cannot be denied. It was probably through the intermediary of Bobbio that the Benedictine rule was welcomed shortly afterwards in the Columbanian monasteries of Gaul. Abbot Bobolenus (641–54) was in charge of the monastery at that time. The son of a priest-friend of Columban, he had been raised at Luxeuil[228] and had then followed the master into Italy. One unknown poet celebrated his learning and pedagogical skills.[229] The library began to grow during his abbacy. Lowe has tried to reconstruct its contents by studying the common features of a whole series of manuscripts that seem to have come from Bobbio's scriptorium during the second half of the seventh century. These manuscripts consist of biblical texts, the acts of councils, Church Fathers (Augustine, Hilary, Origen, Jerome), Christian poets,[230] and, among the more recent authors, Gregory the Great.[231] Almost all of these manuscripts are palimpsests, ecclesiastical texts having replaced those of Latin writers or Arians.[232] Their presentation is not too careful and

---

[226] He mentioned his family when he spoke of his trip to Susa (*Vita Columbani*, II [p. 118]). The allusion to Ireland cited above (n. 224) referred to Bobbio and not to Jonas' native land.

[227] See the letter of Pope Theodore, *PL*, LXXX, 99: "Sub regula sanctae memoriae Benedicti vel reverendissimi Columbani." Some think this text is apocryphal; see McLauglin, *Le très ancien droit monastique*, p. 189, n. 2.

[228] Jonas, *Vita Columbani*, I, 15 (p. 81).

[229] *Versus de Bobuleno, MGH, SRM*, IV, 154–55, vv. 5 and 17: "Edoctus a sancto Dei Columbano praesule . . . parvulorum pedagogos." See Norberg, "Le développement du latin en Italie," *Settimane*, 5: 498–500, for this poem.

[230] *CLA*, I, 36, bears the note, "De arca dom. Bobuleni," and contains works by Jerome, Augustine, and Lactantius. *CLA*, IV, 438, "De arca dom. Vorgusti ab.," bears works by Lactantius, Hilary, and Origen. See P. Engelbert, "Zur Frühgeschichte des Bobbieser Skriptoriums," *RB* 78 (1968): 220–60.

[231] Book III of Gregory the Great's *Dialogues* was copied around 650 at Bobbio; see A. Dold, "Zwei Doppelblätter in Unziale des 7. Jahrhundert mit Text aus den Dialogs Gregor der Grosse," *Zentralblatt für Bibliothekswesen* 55 (1938): 253–58.

[232] *CLA*, III, 351 (the text of the Gospels on Ulfila); ibid., no. 344b (the Book of

seems to indicate that the scriptorium was still poor and badly organized. The monks of Bobbio acquired manuscripts of Livy, Cicero, and Plautus and, for reasons of economy, erased them in order to recopy ecclesiastical authors who seemed to them more relevant and more worthy of study. Only in the eighth century would Bobbio undertake the study of profane authors.

IV. THE MAINTENANCE OF TRADITIONAL CULTURE IN ROME AND SPAIN

While England, Gaul, and Lombard Italy were developing a new kind of religious culture, in the Mediterranean regions the cultivated circles in Rome and in Spain remained faithful to their own intellectual traditions.

A. Culture in Seventh-Century Rome

Rome was a Byzantine city in the seventh century. The imperial representative ensconced in the Palatine considered the pope a bureaucrat.[233] Byzantine artists worked to decorate the churches of Saint Agnes and Saint Stephen (Rotondo) and the oratory of Saint Venantius in the Lateran, among others.[234] Greek monasteries were established on the Aventine and Esquiline hills and near Saint Paul Outside the Walls.[235] Three popes during the first half of the seventh century had previously served as apocrisiaries at Constantinople; one had come from Jerusalem, and another, Theodore, was Greek.[236] Lettered Byzantines also settled in Rome: they included John Moschus (who was in Rome in 619); the mathematician Ananias of Chirak; Sophronius, a former sophist from Damascus; and Maximus the Confessor.[237]

Kings on Plautus); ibid., no. 362 (Sedulius' *Carmen Paschale* on Cicero); ibid., no. 364 (Gregory the Great's *Commentary on Ezechiel* on Ulfilas).

[233] See Diehl, *Etudes sur l'administration byzantine*, pp. 368ff.

[234] Ernst Kitzinger, *Römische Malerei von Beginn des 7. bis zur Mitte des 8. Jahrhunderts* (Munich, 1936); Carlo Cecchelli, "Modi orientali e occidentali nell'arte del VII secolo in Italia," *Settimane*, 5: 383–87.

[235] F. Antonelli, "I primi monasterii di monaci orientali in Roma," *Rivista di archeologia cristiana* 5 (1928): 105–21; Hörle, *Frühmittelalterliche Mönchs- und Klerikerbildung in Italien*, p. 29; A. Michel, "Die griechische Klostersiedlungen zu Rom," *Ostkirchliche Studien* 1 (1952).

[236] J. Gay, "Remarques sur les papes grecs et syriens avant l'Iconoclastie," in *Mélanges offerts à M. Gustave Schlumberger*, 2 vols. (Paris, 1924), 1: 40.

[237] For Ananias, see F. Tournebize, "Ananie de Chirak," *DHGE*, 2: 1432–33; for

At the same time, Rome served as a refuge for those who fled invasions and religious persecutions. Refugees came from the East, either fleeing before the Persians and Arabs or escaping from the religious persecutions of the Byzantine emperor.[238] From the south came Africans, also in flight from the partisans of Monothelitism. To these were added Dalmatians fleeing before the Slavs.[239] Finally, beginning in 650, Anglo-Saxon pilgrims also took the road to Rome.

As a result of the arrival of all these foreigners, cultural conditions were good, and they should have been favorable for the intellectual development of Roman Latin circles. In fact, though, we find no writers among the laity or among the clergy. The only evidence of literary activity outside of a few letters sent by the Lateran chancellery consists of epitaphs which bear a distinct antique cast.[240] Pope Honorius, a disciple of Gregory the Great, was himself a poet—a rather poor one according to some critics.[241] The discussions on the will and energy of Christ that divided Latin and Byzantine clerics throughout the seventh century did not provoke new theological work at Rome.[242] Quite to the contrary, innovations were condemned, and "philosophic" studies were blamed as the origin of doctrinal deviations.

Pope Honorius or his secretary, John (the future Pope John IV), repeated an image familiar to the Fathers by comparing philosophers to croaking frogs.[243] Honorius left it to the grammarians, those "vendors of words," to discuss the differences between Christ's functioning as man and as God.[244] Christ, he said, spoke to sinners, and all philosophical reflection was in vain—an attitude that did not serve the Church. Poorly advised by his entourage, Honorius did not see the trap laid

---

Sophronius, see Gustav Bardy, "Sophrone de Jérusalem," *DTC*, 14, pt. 2: 2379–83; for Maximus, see n. 247, below.

238 G. Schreiber, "Levantinische Wanderungen zum Western," *BZ* 44 (1951): 521.

239 Pope John IV was among them; see *Liber pont.*, ed. Duchesne and Vogel, 1: 330.

240 The letters sent by the chancellery are listed in *Clavis*, nos. 1724–40. For the epitaphs, see *ICR*, vol. 2, nos. 128 and 208.

241 See his poem on the Ascension in *PL*, LXXX, 483; de Rossi (*ICR*, 2: xliv) judges him rather harshly.

242 For these questions, see Duchesne, *L'Eglise au VIe siècle*, p. 407, and Fliche-Martin, 5: 121, 165ff.

243 Honorius, *Ep. ad Sergium*, *PL*, LXXX, 474: "Ut vani naturarum pondatores, otiose negotiantes, et turgidi adversus nos insonent vocibus ranarum philosophi."

244 Ibid., 473: "Utrum autem propter opera divinitatis et humanitatis una an geminae operationes debeant derivatae dici vel intelligi, ad nos ista pertinere non debent relinquentes ea grammaticis qui solent parvulis exquisita derivando nomina venditare." Did the pope know that Augustine had already portrayed teachers as "venditores verborum" (*Confess.*, IX, 5, 13 [de Labriolle ed., p. 218])?

by Patriarch Sergius and accepted the theological definitions of Byzantium.[245]

His successors were more perspicacious. Under Martin I (649–53), it seemed for a time as if the Romans tried to answer the Byzantines on their own ground. Martin's long letters to the emperor and to the Eastern Churches and the various sessions of the Lateran Council of 649, during the course of which dossiers prepared by Lateran notaries were presented, would seem to indicate quite a new thrust.[246] In reality, however, this council was led primarily by African and Eastern refugees in Rome. The theological learning of Maximus the Confessor helped the Romans.[247] Martin even asked the sons of Dagobert—King Sigebert of Austrasia and King Clovis II of Neustria—to send him competent bishops to reinforce the delegation that was leaving for Constantinople.[248] But Martin's pontificate ended tragically when the pope and Maximus were deported and died in the East.

Martin's successors and the Roman clergy did not pursue these attempts at theological confrontation. They had other, more urgent worries. The famous letter of Pope Agatho (679–81) to the emperor is quite revealing on this point. In excusing Latin bishops for their lack of learning, he wrote: "How can men, placed in the midst of Barbarians and required to work with great difficulty for their daily nourishment, be expected to acquire more sacred learning in addition to that defined by the saints, the apostolic predecessors, and the five councils?"[249] The pope went on to contrast worldly eloquence with the apostolic faith. The Credo and the Scriptures were the basis for all belief, so why search elsewhere? Throughout the seventh century, the Church of Rome,

---

[245] See Duchesne, *L'Eglise au VIe siècle*, pp. 407–12, and Fliche-Martin, 5: 121ff.

[246] Fliche-Martin, 5: 166ff. The speeches of Martin I and of the bishops were published in Mansi, X, 883ff. Theophylactus, the *primicerius notariorum*, presented the dossier, but we do not know what role he played in its preparation.

[247] W. M. Peitz, "Martin I und Maximus Confessor: Beiträge z. Geschichte des Monothelitenstreites in Jahren 645–668," *HJ* 30 (1917): 213–36, 429–58. See, more recently, J. Pierres, *S. Maximus confessor princeps apologetarum synodi Lateranensis 649* (Rome, 1940). Abbot Thalassius from the Armenian monastery of the Renati (Mansi, X, 903–4) also played an important role in the debate.

[248] *MGH, SRM*, V, 452; Mansi, X, 1183. Eligius of Noyon and Audoenus of Rouen were the bishops chosen—a real acknowledgment of their religious learning. See Vacandard, *Vie de saint Ouen*, pp. 73–74.

[249] *PL*, LXXXVII, 1164: "Nam apud homines in medio gentium positos et de labore corporis quotidianum victum cum summa hesitatione conquirentes, quomodo ad plenum poterit invenire Scripturarum scientia, nisi quod quae regulariter a sanctis atque apostolicis praedecessoribus et quinque conciliis definita sunt?" See ibid., 1217 and 1220, for the profession of faith of the bishops gathered in the Lateran: "Licet parvi et simplices scientiae." See also Damian of Pavia's letter, ibid., 1261, and below, chap. 9, n. 317.

depository of Catholic doctrine, would thus remain on theological matters very conservative, in the full sense of that term.

The timidity of Roman thought can be explained in part by political circumstances, especially the Lombard war. Then, too, as we saw in the sixth century, the pontifical milieu had never been very inclined to theological discussion.[250] The arrival of Eastern refugees in the seventh century could have contributed to a renaissance of theological studies. But for this to occur, it would have been necessary that these Easterners not seem foreigners in Rome and that their language not act as a barrier between them and Roman clerics. In fact, however, ignorance of the Greek tongue prevented pontifical circles from combatting Byzantium with equal weapons. A "translation bureau," with official interpreters, was established in the Lateran, but the translations were not perfect.[251] Popes who had been apocrisiaries or who were of Sicilian origin seem to have forgotten their Greek.[252] The presence of Byzantine officials did nothing to diffuse Greek in Rome; in fact, Latin seems to have been the only language used in administration.[253]

There were other centers of Greek culture in Italy, especially in Ravenna, where Greek was not completely unknown.[254] The so-called *Ravenna Cosmography* was written around 700 by an anonymous cleric.[255] But even so, bilinguists must have been rare. During Theodore's episcopate (677–91), in order to have a notary, the exarch had to recruit a young cleric trained in Greek whom he took into his service only after the notary passed an examination.[256] The almost total absence of Greek

---

[250] See above. chap. 3, sect. I.

[251] Steinacker, "Die römische Kirche und die griechischen Sprachkenntnisse des Frühmittelalters," *MIOEG* 62 (1954): 28–66. This article is the completion of a study which the author had published under the same title in his *Festschrift Theodor Gomperz* (Vienna, 1902), pp. 324–41. For knowledge of Greek during the pontificate of Martin I, see Siegmund, *Die Ueberlieferung*, pp. 174–75.

[252] I do not share Diehl's opinions on this point (*Etudes sur l'administration byzantine*, pp. 284ff.).

[253] See the dialogue between the pope and a Byzantine official in *PL*, LXXX, 190. The epitaph of the Byzantine Theodore is in Latin (Henri Leclercq, "Cécile," *DACL*, II-2, 2738). Diehl, who insists on the significance of the Greeks in Rome, admits that the Greek tongue was not used; see *Etudes sur l'administration byzantine*, p. 283.

[254] See the epitaph of the patricius Isaac (died 643), *CIG*, IV, 1177, no. 9869, p. 574. The bilingual Verona Psalter (*CLA*, IV, 472) may date from this period.

[255] The *Ravenna Cosmography* was written at the beginning of the seventh century and shortly afterwards translated from Greek to Latin. See Joseph Schnetz's edition, *Ravennatis anonymi Cosmographia*, Arkiv för germansk namnforsking, 10 (Uppsala, 1951).

[256] Agnellus, *Liber pont. eccl. Ravenn.*, 120 (*MGH, SRL*, p. 356): "Hic adolescens unus Johanicius nomine scriba peritissimus, in scriptura doctus, graecis et latinisque eruditus est."

inscriptions is likewise indicative of the ignorance of that tongue.[257] Northern Italy, poorly defended by the Byzantines, could not become a center of Hellenism.[258]

In fact, the realm of Greek culture during this period was limited to the extreme south of the peninsula, especially to Sicily.[259] At Agrigentum, Syracuse, and Palermo, where a colony of Alexandrians settled, Greek won out over Latin.[260] In Sicily, Cosmas, John Damascene's master, undoubtedly studied rhetoric, dialectic, the ethics of Aristotle and Plato, and the four disciplines of the quadrivium.[261] Theophanes, a theologian and polemicist who became patriarch of Antioch in 681, came from the monastery of Baias in Syracuse. Conversely, the future bishop of Syracuse, George, studied at Constantinople.[262] When Emperor Constantius dreamed about transferring the capital of the Byzantine Empire to the West in 660, it was not Rome or even Ravenna that he chose but Syracuse.[263] His choice was not dictated simply by the strategic reasons imposed on him by the war with the Arabs. Syracuse, more than Rome, represented a center of culture and of civilization.

Even the papacy recognized the superiority of Eastern clerics. When

[257] See the inscription from Bologna, *CIL*, XI, 764. The Greek inscription from Saint Radegunda in Milan (Monneret de Villard, *Catalogo*, p. 32) is perhaps from the ninth century.

[258] In 671 the bishop of Ravenna tried in vain to free himself from Roman tutelage. See Fliche-Martin, 5: 403–4. Justinian's Code did not penetrate to Ravenna. See Pier Silverio Leicht, "Ravenna e Bologna," in *Atti del Congresso internazionale di diritto romano (Bologna e Roma, XVII–XXVII aprile, MCMXXXIII)*, 4 vols. (Pavia, 1934–35), 1: 281; and R. Trifone, "Il diritto giustinianeo nel mezzogiorno d'Italia," in ibid., pp. 3ff.

[259] For Hellenism in Naples, see N. Tamassia, "L'ellenismo nei documenti napoletani del medioevo," *Atti della real istituto veneto* 66 (1906–7): 79. There have been numerous studies of Hellenism in Sicily since Gerhard Rohlfs' work, *Griechen und Romanen in Unteritalien: Ein Beitrag zur Geschichte der unteritalienischen Gräzität* (Geneva, 1924). See Ignazio Scatturo, *Storia di Sicilia*, 2 vols. (Rome, 1950–51), 2: 307ff.; R. Weiss, "The Greek Culture of South Italy in the Later Middle Ages," *Proceedings of the British Academy* 37 (1951): 23–50; P. F. Russo, "Attività artistico-culturale del monachismo calabro-greco anteriormente all'età normanna," in *Atti del'VIII Congresso internazionale di Studi bizantini, Palermo, 3–10 aprile 1951*, 2 vols. (Rome, 1953), 1: 463; and E. Sestan, "La composizione etnica della società in rapporto alla svolgimento della civiltà in Italia nel secolo VII," *Settimane*, 5: 651–53.

[260] There are a great many more Greek inscriptions. G. Agnello, *La Scilia sotterana cristiana e la Sicilia byzantina* (Rome, 1935), found 417 Greek inscriptions as against 44 Latin inscriptions in Syracuse. See Nunzio Maccarone, *La vita del latino in Sicilia fino all'età normanna* (Florence, 1915), pp. 58ff.

[261] *Vita S. Joannis Damasceni*, *PG*, XCIV, 442.

[262] Ottavio Gaetani, *Vitae sanctorum siculorum*, 2 vols. in 1 (Palermo, 1657), I, 143, 227; II, 6, 193–229.

[263] O. Bertolini, *Roma di fronte a Bisanzio e ai longobardi* (Bologna, 1941), pp. 358–59.

Anglo-Saxon princes requested a new bishop for the see of Canterbury, the pope called upon Theodore, a monk from Tarsus and a refugee in Rome. To accompany him to England and ensure his orthodoxy, the pope designated another monk, Hadrian, an African who was also abbot of a Neapolitan monastery.[264] That these men were chosen in preference to Romans tellingly indicates the mediocrity of the clergy of this city.

What, then, was the source of Rome's prestige among clerics in the West—be they Celts, Anglo-Saxons, or Franks? We can find out by studying the case of Wilfrid, the former monk of Lindisfarne who left Canterbury in 653, as we have already seen, and moved to Rome. He was not simply making a pilgrimage to the tombs of the Apostles. His biographers tell us that he had formed a friendship with Archdeacon Boniface, a papal counselor, and that under Boniface he had read the four Gospels, studied the paschal computus, and learned what the ecclesiastical disciplines in his own country had not taught him.[265] Bede tells us that Wilfrid wanted to become acquainted with the rites clerics and monks followed in Rome.[266] For Wilfrid, then, it was primarily a matter of studying the Roman liturgy, which at that time he knew only indirectly through the school of Canterbury. Working with Archdeacon Boniface, he had access to the schola cantorum that the archdeacon of the Lateran directed.[267]

The young clerics he met in Rome had been trained from their childhood in Roman chant in this schola. According to the Ordines Romani of the seventh century, children who knew the Psalms were admitted to the schola as interns and became part of the Ordo cantorum.[268] They

---

[264] Bede, *HE*, IV, 1 (p. 202); see Fliche-Martin, 5: 318.

[265] Bede, *HE*, V, 19 (p. 324): "Pervenit ad amiticiam viri doctissimi ac sanctissimi Bonifacii videlicet archidiaconi qui etiam consiliarius erat apostolici papae; cujus magisterio quattuor Evangeliorum libros ex ordine didicit, computum paschae rationabilem et alia multaque in patria nequiverat ecclesiasticis disciplinis accomoda."

Eddius, *Vita Wilfridi*, V (Colgrave ed., p. 12): "A quo quattuor Evangelia Christi perfecte didicit et pascalem rationem quam scismati Brittaniae et Hiberniae non cognoverunt et alias multas ecclesiasticas disciplinae regulas Bonifacius archidiaconus quasi proprio filio suo diligenter dictavit."

We may have Boniface's seal: see Levison, *England*, p. 17.

[266] Bede, *HE*, V, 19 (p. 323): "Proposuit animo venire Romam et qui ad sedem apostolicam ritus ecclesiastici sive monasteriales servarentur."

[267] *Ordines Romani*, XXXVI (Andrieu ed., 4: 195ff.): "De gradibus Romanae ecclesiae." Except for Andrieu's article "Les ordres mineurs dans l'ancien rite romain," *Revue des sciences religieuses* 5 (1925): 232–74, there is no study of the schola cantorum.

[268] *Ordines Romani*, XXXVI (Andrieu ed., 4: 195): "Primum in qualicumque scola reperti fuerint pueri bene psallentes tolluntur unde et nutrientur in scola cantorum." The schola had property with which it provided for the needs of the clerics. See *Liber diurnus*,

learned chant, and even though we have no information on this subject, they must undoubtedly have received an elementary ecclesiastical culture in order to be admitted to the first degrees of the clericature. As a young man, Pope Benedict II (684-85) served in the Roman church and had learned the Scriptures and chant (*cantilena*).[269] Sergius (687-701), his successor, had also received this training at an early age.[270] The schola thus became a nursery for important pontifical officials.[271]

Not all young clerics went to the schola. Lectors were trained by individual masters, according to what an ordo tells us: when a child confided to a teacher by his parents had been trained in divine Scriptures and, having reached his majority, was made a cleric, then, after he had learned to "read," he was to be taken before the pope by his father or a relative to make his request in good and proper form. Having accepted it, the pope put him to the test during an office before the clergy and people.[272] The development of the Roman liturgy required extensive training on the part of cantors and lectors: the *Ordo I* gives us an echo of the grandiose ceremonies celebrated in Roman basilicas, word of which traveled as far as ecclesiastical circles in England.[273]

Rome's renown in the seventh century came also from its wealth of manuscripts—one could almost certainly find whatever texts one needed in Rome. The abbess of Nivelles and Amandus, we have already seen, sent for codices from Rome. Pope Martin wrote to Amandus on that occasion, complaining that his library was continually pillaged by lovers of manuscripts.[274] The fact is that since Gregory the Great popes had generously distributed books without having either the time or the means to replace them with copies. The Lateran scriptorium, further-

---

in *Liber diurnus romanorum pontificum*, ed. Theodor von Sickel (Vienna, 1889), p. 97: "Frequentia cessavit infantium quibus deerant expensae providenti . . . ne cantorum deficiret ordo."

[269] *Liber pont.*, 1: 363: "Ab ineunte aetate sua ecclesiae militavit atque sic se in divinis Scripturis et cantilena a puerili aetate et in presbiterii dignitate exhibuit."

[270] Ibid., p. 374. Sergius used the term *nutritor* when speaking of Saint Peter.

[271] See Bertolini, *Roma*, p. 373.

[272] *Ordines Romani*, XXXV (Andrieu ed., 4: 33): "Ordo quomodo in sancta romana ecclesiae lector ordinatur. Dum infans traditus a parentibus magistro sacris apicibus fuerit edoctus atque clericus jam legitima aetate adultus, et ad legendum prudenter instructus, si patrem habet et per semetipsum valet, suggerat de eo ad domnum apostolicam sic . . . : Domine filium habeo . . . jam imbutum lectione sancta et arbitror quod condigne in conspectu vestro ad legendum."

[273] Ibid., 2: 39–48. See Josef Andreas Jungmann, *Missarum sollemnia*, 1 (Paris, 1951): 97–106.

[274] The letter is in Mansi, X, 1186, and in *MGH, SRM*, V, 542: "Nam codices jam exinaniti sunt a nostra bibliotheca et unde ei dare nullatenus habuimus."

more, does not seem to have been very active in the seventh century. Since we have no manuscript which might have come from this scriptorium, it seems that the Romans were living on their capital.[275] Their library was rich because, as has now been proven, it had inherited some of the books from the monastery of Vivarium.[276] The acts of the Lateran Council of 649 give us an outline of its contents as far as works by the Fathers and even by heretics are concerned.[277] In the absence of a complete catalogue, however, it is difficult to estimate the number of volumes the library held.

Seekers of books came to the Lateran from all over the West. Around 642, Taio of Saragossa was sent to find Gregory the Great's *Moralia in Job* in the scrinium of the Roman library. He tells us that he had a hard time finding it because of the multitude of other books.[278] Under Pope Vitalian (657), Wandregisilus' nephew brought back from Rome biblical texts and the works of Gregory the Great.[279] Wilfrid's traveling companion, Benedict Biscop, made six trips to Rome and each time came back loaded down with books. In this way, the treasures which had found refuge in the Lateran began to be dispersed all over the West.

B. HUMANIST AND ASCETIC CULTURES IN SPAIN

In the politically and culturally evolving West, Spain seems mired in formulas of a bygone age. The kings, with the support of the Church, succeeded in checkmating the aristocracy, which tried to exercise power in Spain, as it did in Gaul. The *Forum judiciorum*, a new legal code

[275] The *Capitulare evangeliorum* of Würzburg was in Rome in 640, but was it written there? See Germain Morin, "Liturgie et basiliques de Rome au milieu du VIIIe siècle, d'après la liste d'Evangiles de Würzburg," *RB* 28 (1911): 319.

[276] Courcelle, *LG*, pp. 373ff.

[277] The *primicerius* of the notaries brought the Fathers the books they requested: "Necesse est ut codex praedicti doctoris afferatur. . . . Omnis generis cartae et codices quamplurimi sumpti e scrinio et bibliotheca statim tanquam e loco proximo." See J. B. de Rossi, "De origine, historia, indicibus et scriniis bibliothecae sedis apostolicae," in *Codices Palatini Latini bibliothecae vaticanae*, ed. B. Card. Pitra, H. Stevenson, I. B. de Rossi (Rome, 1886), 1: lxiv.

[278] Taio, *Ep.* IV (*MGH, AA*, XIV, 288) "In arcivo domnae nostrae sanctae Romanae ecclesiae, scilicet in sacro Lateranensi scrinio quia in scrinio Romanae ecclesiae at adfirmant scrinarii cum ceteris exemplaribus supra dicti quanti non inveniebantur." For this trip and the legends attached to it, see José Madoz, "Tajon de Zaragoza y su viaje a Rome," in *Mélanges Joseph de Ghellinck S.J.*, 2 vols. (Gembloux, 1951), 1: 345–61. Gregory's works were still in the scrinium in the middle of the eighth century; see Bede, *HE*, preface (p. 6), and Boniface, *Ep.* 33 (*MGH, Ep.*, III, 284).

[279] *Gesta abb. font.*, ed. Lohier and Laporte, 1: "Qui Romam adiit Vitaliano papa eodem tempore . . . nec non et volumina sacrarum scripturarum diversa veteris et Novi Testamenti maxime ingenii beatissimi atque apostolici gloriossimi papae Gregorii."

promulgated by Recceswinth (654–72), sought to achieve legal unity in an apparently cohesive kingdom. Thus, the Isidorian renaissance went on.[280]

Isidore of Seville's work dominated the entire second half of the century: the Council of Toledo of 653 proclaimed him the most learned man of "these last times"; Ildefonsus of Toledo imitated him in his own works; at the end of the century, the author of the *Vita Fructuosi* saw the bishop of Seville as one "who made the principles of Roman wisdom come alive again."[281]

But Seville was no longer the center of the Isidorian renaissance.[282] Under Bishop Braulio, Saragossa became the great intellectual center of Spain. Then, in the second half of the century, thanks to a remarkable series of bishops, Toledo developed as the capital of studies. The bishops of Saragossa and Toledo were more in contact with the bishops of Narbonne than they were with their colleagues in the south.[283] This displacement of intellectual life to the north, which had already begun during the first half of the seventh century, was accompanied by a like displacement of artistic centers. The known churches of this period— San Juan de Baños (begun by Recceswinth), Quintanilla de las Viñas, and the crypt of Palencia (ca. 672), among others—were built primarily north of the Tagus.[284] This shift can be explained by the new political conditions in the kingdom: Spain was by now definitely liberated from Byzantine tutelage and, consequently, could turn once more to the Continent. As the Barbaro-Roman fusion was progressively realized, cultural centers developed in central and northern Spain, where the Gothic Barbarians had settled. In addition, around 670, the first Arab incursions had begun to threaten the south.[285] The importance of Se-

---

[280] See Menéndez Pidal, *HE*, 3: 118ff., for the political history of this period.

[281] Council of Toledo (653), c. 2 (Mansi, X, 1215); Séjourné, *Le dernier Père de l'Eglise*, p. 372; *Vita Fructuosi*, 1 (Nock ed., p. 87): "Ille autem oris nitore clarens, insignis industriae, sophistae artis indeptus praemicans, dogmata reciprocavit Romanorum."

[282] The only literary work mentioned for Seville after Isidore is Bishop Honoratus' (died 641) metrical epitaph (Vives, *Inscripciones*, no. 273). See J. Fontaine, *IS*, p. 560.

[283] See the letters exchanged between Quiricus and Idalius of Barcelona and Taio, Ildefonsus, and Julian (*PL*, XCVI, 193ff.). See also the letters of Sunifridus of Narbonne, Protasius of Tarragona, and Eugenius of Toledo (ibid., 818ff.).

[284] For construction activity during this period, see Menéndez Pidal, *HE*, 3: 504ff., and E. Lambert, "L'église wisigothique de Quintanilla de Las Viñas," *AcIB* (1955), pp. 483–93.

[285] The first important attack took place during the reign of Wamba (672–80). See Menéndez Pidal, *HE*, 3: 125–26. We should mention that Wamba came from the north and retired to enter a monastery near Burgos.

ville and Merida declined, to the advantage of the northern ports at Barcelona and Narbonne.

We can best study the effects of the Isidorian renaissance at the episcopal school of Toledo, which the bishops directed and worked for.[286] Eugenius of Toledo, who died in 657, left a charming series of poems on illness, the approach of old age, summer, the wind, the nightingale, and other subjects.[287] This, however, was no rediscovery of the sentiment for nature. Eugenius, who was acquainted with rhetorical manuals, especially the *Praeexercitamina* of Priscian, knew that certain themes were particularly appropriate to the study of scholarly rhetoric.[288] Similarly, Eugenius' acrostic poem composed in the manner of Lucilius, which he dedicated to a certain John,[289] is reminiscent of traditional verbal skills. It is not difficult to imagine the disciples of Eugenius— among whom was his successor, Ildefonsus—repeating the bishop's didactic poems on the six plagues of Egypt, the seven sentences, and the invention of letters, or even learning the *Disticha* written in the manner of Cato.[290] Julian of Toledo (died in 690) either composed or had composed a grammar for his students which borrowed from Donatus and took examples from works Isidore knew.[291] When he composed his history of the "Expedition of Wamba," Julian had in mind the youths who would draw lessons from reading it and who, at the same time, would develop a taste for historical discourse.[292] All the works of this period were written primarily for students who wished to learn to speak and to write well. "He spoke well, he argued eloquently" is a praise read constantly, but never "He thought well."

Thus we find ourselves back in the time of Ennodius and Avitus. But, unlike them, Visigothic bishops did not scruple to study and teach profane literature. It seemed completely legitimate to them to write

---

[286] A scribe from Toledo wrote that a scriptorium was attached to this school: "Longum est scribere quia rare nobis pergamena largiuntur a principe." See Charles H. Beeson, "The *Ars grammatica* of Julian of Toledo," in *Miscellanea Francesco Ehrle* (Rome, 1924), p. 51, and B. Bischoff, "Ein Brief Julians von Toledo über Rhythmen, metrische Dichtung und Prose," *Hermes* 87 (1959): 247–56 (reprinted in *Mittelalterliche Studien*, 1: 288–98).

[287] *MGH, AA*, XIV, 267ff.

[288] Curtius, p. 195.

[289] *MGH, AA*, XIV, 262: "JO versiculos nixos quia despicis ANNES."

[290] See F. J. E. Raby, *A History of Christian Latin Poetry* (Oxford, 1953), p. 149, and Ruffini, *Le origini*, 1: 159ff., for Eugenius' poems. Ildefonsus also wrote some enigmas, which unfortunately have not survived; see *PL*, XCVI, 44.

[291] J. Fontaine, *IS*, p. 95; Beeson, "The *Ars grammatica* of Julian of Toledo."

[292] Julian of Toledo, *Historia de Wambae regis Gothorum Toletani expeditione, MGH, SRM*, V, 500: "Solet virtutis esse praesidio triumphorum relata narratio, animosque juvenum ad virtutis attolere signum"; ibid., 8, 9 (Wamba's speech).

pleasant poems, epigrams, and grammatical treatises. In fact, thanks to the men of letters at the beginning of the century—Isidore of Seville especially—peace was concluded between Christianity and pagan litera-ture and the synthesis of the two cultures accomplished. In his gram-mar, Julian took examples from pagan and from Christian sources.[293] The culture which Eugenius and Taio acquired at the monastery of Saragossa and which Ildefonsus received at Agali was not really a double culture because they drew from Christian as well as from pagan classics, as had Isidore.[294] They put Christian and pagan authori-ties on the same plane. Unfortunately, we have no Spanish library cata-logues from this period.[295] Nevertheless, an analysis of the contents of an eighth-century manuscript from a scriptorium in northern Spain[296] or a study of the *Liber glossarum* of the same date[297] gives some idea of the variety of works consulted.

Lettered Visigoths of the seventh century drew more from classical works than from those of the Church Fathers. The many exegetical and theological works which we owe to them lack originality. If Spanish clergymen deeply venerated Gregory the Great, it was not only because they recognized how much of the antique was in the great pope's style, but also because they admired the sacred learning they were far from possessing.[298]

If they did perform a service for Christian thought, it was more for-mal than fundamental. Eugenius of Toledo placed his poetical and musical talents in the service of the liturgy by correcting chants that

[293] *De vitiis et figuris*, ed. W. M. Lindsay (Oxford, 1922), p. 38.

[294] On the education of these clerics, see above, chap. 7, sect. III.B.

[295] It is difficult to understand how Lot could state that the episcopal library at Toledo contained only one classical author (Cicero) at the end of the seventh century (*La fin du monde antique*, p. 431). Lot was actually repeating worthless information from H. Leclercq's *L'Espagne chrétienne* (Paris, 1906), p. 319.

[296] This is the Albi manuscript (see *CLA*, VI, 705), which contains Cicero's *Synonyms*, works by Eucherius and Isidore, grammatical works, works on natural science, and a mappemonde. (On the mappemonde, see below, chap. 10, n. 174.)

[297] For the *Liber glossarum*, also known as the *Glossarium Ansileubi*, see Manitius, 1: 133–34, and especially W. M. Lindsay, *Glossaria latina* (Paris, 1926), vol. 1. This glossary contains extracts from Fulgentius, Junilius, Cicero, Orosius, Julian, the Physiologus, and others.

[298] Ildefonsus, *Liber de cognitione baptismi*, preface (*PL*, XCVI, 112), realized this: "Non nostris novitatibus incognita proponentes, sed antiquorum monita vel intelligentiae reserantes vel memoriae adnotantes." Julian of Toledo's *Prognosticum* is a cento of patristic sentences; see Idalius of Barcelona's letter to Julian, *PL*, XCVI, 815. Taio of Saragossa collected a series of extracts from Gregory's works in his *Liber sententiarum*, *PL*, LXXX, 727–990. See L. Serrano, "La obra morales de San Gregorio en la literatura hispanogoda," *Revista de archivos, bibliotecas, y museos* (Madrid) 24 (1911): 484–97. See also Ildefonsus of Toledo's praise of Gregory (*De vir. ill.*, 1 [*PL*, XCVI, 195]).

had become deformed through misuse;[299] his disciple Ildefonsus composed masses and hymns, which have unfortunately been lost.[300] The hymns of this period that have come down to us are generally elegant in style.[301] The Visigothic *Orational*, composed at the beginning of the eighth century for the cathedral of Tarragona, still had an antique flavor.[302] Lastly, the language of sermons and councils remained polished until the end of the Visigothic period.[303] Julian's and Ildefonsus' treatises were written in a fluent, fluid, and lyrical style.

Thus, we find again in seventh-century Spain the contradictions we analyzed in regard to classical culture at the beginning of the preceding century.[304] Loyalty to an antique tradition that could no longer produce original work stunted the development of a religious culture based on profound personal study of the sacred text. Moreover, lettered Visigoths, so proud of the superiority of their culture,[305] did not take account of the fact that they were but a handful who had access to it. Literary exchanges and loans of manuscripts took place within the confines of a small circle. Only a few privileged individuals benefited from the teaching of the schools of Toledo and Saragossa. The canons of the councils of the second half of the seventh century, in fact, denounced several times the ignorance of clerics and even of bishops.[306] Without going so far as some, who say that the Visigothic Church was plainly decadent on the eve of the Arab conquest, we should admit that Isidore

[299] Ildefonsus, *De vir. ill.*, 14 (*PL*, XCVI, 204): "Cantus pessimis usibus vitiatos melodiae cognitione correxit."

[300] For Ildefonsus, see Sister Athanasius Braegelmann, *The Life and Writings of Saint Ildefonsus of Toledo* (Washington, D.C., 1942), and, better, Madoz's article, "San Ildefonso de Toledo," *Estudios eclesiásticos* 26 (1952): 473.

[301] A. S. Walpole, *Early Latin Hymns* (Cambridge, 1922), pp. 398–401; R. Messenger, "The Mozarabic Hymn," *Trans. of the Amer. Philol. Assoc.* 75 (1944): 183–36.

[302] See Vives' edition in *Monumenta hispaniae sacra*, vol. 1 (Barcelona, 1946). For the style of this work, see Michel Andrieu, review of *Oracional visigotico* by José Vives, *RMAL*, 5 (1949): 60. See also B. de Gaiffier, "Les oraisons de l'office de saint Hippolyte, dans le *Libellus orationum* de Vérone," *RAM* 25 (1949): 219–24, who notes an allusion to Theseus' son.

[303] We need a study of the language of the Spanish councils. See Manuel C. Diaz y Diaz, "La cultura de la España visigotica del siglo VII," *Settimane*, 5: 840. Much work has been done on the dogmatic content of the councils; see *Clavis*, no. 1790. See also José Madoz, *Le Symbole du XIe Concile de Tolède: Ses sources, sa date, sa valeur* (Louvain, 1938).

[304] See chap. 3.

[305] Eugenius of Toledo, *Ep. ad Protasium*, PL, LXXXVII, 412: "In hac patria tam accurati sermones habentur atque sententiae ut simile non possim excudere."

[306] See the Eighth Council of Toledo (653), c. 1; the Eleventh Council (675), c. 2; the Thirteenth Council (683), c. 7; the Sixteenth Council (693), c. 3 and c. 10; and the Seventeenth Council (694), c. 4 (Mansi, X, 1210; XI, 137, 1069; XII, 71, 78, 98).

of Seville's effort to develop clerical training did not have the desired results. Visigothic clerics and even monks in the major cities were too much engaged in worldly affairs to have time to devote to studies.[307] In order for the Visigothic Church to regenerate itself and rediscover its mission, it would have had to spend some time in the "desert."

Some clerics had already felt this necessity and, in the mountainous regions of northern Spain, gathered in isolated outposts that offered the possibility of an ascetic life to whomever desired it. One of the promoters of this movement was a Visigothic noble, Fructuosus (died 667), who founded monastic establishments in Bierzo near Astorga and in Galicia.[308] In the fifth and sixth centuries these regions had already witnessed an intense religious life and an Eastern form of monasticism; however, the monastic movements organized in the seventh century were more reminiscent of those in Ireland and England. One wonders whether the establishment of a Celtic population in Galicia contributed to this revival.[309] In fact, veritable monastic clusters sprouted (see Map 11), as in the British Isles and later in Gaul; even double monasteries were organized.[310]

As in Ireland, England, and Gaul, these monasteries were centers of religious culture.[311] Fructuosus was educated: he had received the training available to an aristocrat of this period and could write poems and well-turned letters;[312] later, he attended the episcopal school in Palen-

---

[307] During Wamba's reign, clergymen were subject to military service; see *Leges Visigoth.*, IX, II, 8 (*MGH, Leg. sect. I*, I, 371).

[308] For Fructuosus of Braga, see Manuel C. Diaz y Diaz, "Fructueux de Braga," *DSp*, 5: 1541–46, and Garcia Villada, *Historia eclesiástica*, 2, pt. 1: 326. Frances Clare Nock has translated and studied the *Vita Fructuosi* (*The Vita Sancti Fructuosi: Text with a Translation, Introduction, and Commentary* [Washington, D.C., 1946]). For the authorship of the *Vita*, generally attributed to Valerius of Bierzo, see Diaz y Diaz's review of Nock's edition (*HS* 2 [1949]: 248–50). For Bierzo, see A. Lambert's article in *DHGE* 8: 1440–42. A more recent discussion appears in *Actas do Congresso de estudos da commemoração do XIII centenário da morte de S. Frutuoso, I–II*, Bracara Augusta, vols. 21–22 (Braga, 1967–68).

[309] For the diocese of Britonia and the Celtic population of Galicia, see Pierre David, *Etudes historiques sur la Galice et le Portugal du VIe au XIIe siècle* (Paris, 1940), p. 60. Charles J. Bishko, "The Date and Nature of the Spanish *Consensoria monachorum*," *American Journal of Philology* 69 (1948): 377–95, assumes that the Galician penitential system was influenced by Irish penitentials. This is one argument which allows him to date this text to the seventh rather than to the fifth century.

[310] Fructuosus, *Reg. mon. comm.*, 6 (*PL*, LXXXVII, 1151). See Hilpisch, *Die Doppelklöster*, pp. 52–55.

[311] See P. Martins, "Vida cultural de San Frutuoso e seus monjeus," *Brotéria* 45 (1947): 58–69.

[312] Until Diaz y Diaz's promised edition of Fructuosus' poems comes out, see the *Carmina Fructuoso* in *PL*, LXXXVII, 1129–39. See A. C. Vega, "Una carta autentica de S. Fructuoso," *La Ciudad de Dios* 153 (1941): 335–44, for the letter to Recceswinth.

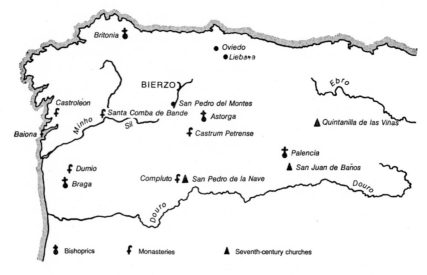

11. Monastic Centers in Northwestern Spain in the Seventh Century

cia, where Bishop Conantius, who had been trained in literature and music,[313] taught him ecclesiastical literature. When he abandoned the world, Fructuosus did not break completely with culture. He brought manuscripts along with him whenever he traveled, and his monastic rules provided for periods of personal reading and for teaching.[314] This program essentially involved the "spiritual disciplines"—reading the Bible and religious texts.[315] Fructuosus recommended that those who came to join him renounce their former habits. Addressing himself to those who had already received a worldly education, he told them not to concern themselves with "empty tales," which seems to mean that they should not read pagan authors.[316] From a letter he wrote to Braulio of Saragossa, we know what Fructuosus read: Cassian's *Collationes*; the *Life* of Honoratus, the founder of Lérins; the *Life* of Saint Germanus; and the *Life* of Saint Emilian, which Braulio had just written.[317] The author of the *Vita Fructuosi* clearly saw the contrast between Isidore of Seville and Fructuosus of Braga: one represented humanistic culture, the other represented ascetic culture.[318]

This ascetic culture was taken up at the end of the seventh century by Valerius of Bierzo (died 695), a monk with an attractive personality. Like Fructuosus, he had studied hard, but desiring to flee the "empty wisdom of the world,"[319] he became an anchorite in the environs of

[313] Ildefonsus, *De vir. ill.*, 11 (*PL*, XCVI, 203): "Ecclesiasticorum officiorum ordinibus intentus et providus, nam melodias soni multas noviter edidit. Orationum quoque libellum de omnium decenter conscripsit proprietate psalmorum." *Vita Fructuosi*, 2 (Nock ed., pp. 90–91): "Tradidit se erudiendum spiritualibus disciplinis sanctissimo viro Conantio episcopo."

[314] *Vita Fructuosi*, 20 (p. 109): "Cum caballo qui codices ipsius viri Dei gestabat"; *Reg. mon.*, 3, 6 (*PL*, LXXXVII, 1102): "Juniores . . . lectione vel recitatione vacent." See also *Reg. mon. comm.*, 5 (ibid., 1114).

[315] *Vita Fructuosi*, 15 (p. 119): "Haec nempe spiritualibus studiis diligente indepta." This passage concerns Benedicta, a young aristocrat who came to join Fructuosus and to live in a cell. The young monks and the abbot introduced her to sacred literature ("litteras ostendere").

[316] *Reg. mon. comm.*, 8 (*PL*, LXXXVII, 1116): "Habent enim et ipsi consuetudinem mores pristinos nunquam abhorrere et ut olim fuerunt docti, vanis fabulis evagari."

[317] Braulio, *Ep.* 43–44 (Madoz ed., pp. 186–87).

[318] *Vita Fructuosi*, 1 (p. 87): "Ille . . . sophistae artis indeptus praemicans dogmata reciprocavit Romanorum. . . . Ille activae vitae industria universam extrinsecus erudivit Spaniam; hic autem contemplativae vitae peritia vibranti fulgore micans intima cordium inluminavit arcana."

[319] Valerius, *Ordo querimoniae*, *PL*, LXXXVII, 439: "Intra adolescentiae tempora . . . vanis disciplinis intentus." One of his works is entitled *De vana saeculi sapientia* (ibid., 425). For Valerius, see C. M. Aherne, *Valerio of Bierzo: An Ascetic of the Late Visigothic Period* (Washington, D.C., 1949). Until we have Diaz y Diaz's new edition, see Ramón Fernández Pousa, *San Valerio Obras* (Madrid, 1942).

his home town, Astorga, before entering the monastery of Compluto, which Fructuosus had founded. There Abbot Donadeus put his literary talents to use.[320] Then Valerius was made master of a rural school,[321] finally ending his life as abbot of San Pedro del Montes, where he had gathered many disciples. Valerius wrote a number of works for his students, among which were a florilegium of hagiographical works and a beginner's commentary on the Psalms.[322]

Even though Valerius' literary culture was great,[323] it was quite far from that of his contemporary Julian of Toledo. Valerius was a demanding ascetic, a tormented mind who lacked the balance and optimism of the Isidorian men of letters: his combats with the devil, his visions and trips to the beyond that he loved to report,[324] link him more to contemporary Irish and Anglo-Saxon monks.[325]

Thus, Spain, although isolated from the rest of the West, did not completely escape the religious culture of its time. In addition, the creation of monastic centers in the north was an important event for the future because they were to serve as refuges for Visigothic clerics and monks fleeing the Arab invasion of 711. These modest schools with their scriptoria were the centers where Mozarabic culture was to be established.

[320] He composed a *De genere monachorum* for Donadeus (see Diaz y Diaz, *AW*, pp. 49ff.). In the *Dicta ad beatum Donadeum*, *PL*, LXXXVII, 431, Valerius mentioned one of the scribes of the scriptorium: "Quidam frater . . . librorum scriptor, psalmodiae meditator."

[321] See above, chap. 7, sect. II.B.

[322] Among the hagiographical works, we should note the *Lives* of the Eastern Fathers and the *Life of Saint Martin*. See Diaz y Diaz, "Sobre la compilación hagiográfica de Valerio del Bierzo," *HS* 4 (1951): 3–25. The commentary on the Psalms is *Caput opusculorum quinquagenis numeris psalmorum* (edited by Diaz y Diaz, *AW*, p. 115). The last verse of the preface reveals the goal of the work: "Ingens lectio si fastidium ingerit imperito haec eum placavit brevitatio."

[323] Valerius' poems have been published by Diaz y Diaz, *AW*, p. 144. They bear witness to an astonishing taste for acrostics and verbal acrobatics. In thirteen of the poems every word begins with the same letter. Unlike his compatriots, Valerius preferred rhythmic poetry to the classical meters.

[324] Valerius of Bierzo, *De caelesti revelatione*, *PL*, LXXXVII, 433.

[325] For example, see the *Visio Baronti*, *MGH*, *SRM*, V, 368, from the end of the seventh century. See also Boniface's letter to Eadburg, *Ep.* 10 (*MGH*, *Ep.*, III, 252–57).

The Renaissances: The End of the Seventh Century to the Middle of the Eighth Century

I. THE DECISIVE YEARS

B y the mid-seventh century the monastic and episcopal schools of England, Gaul, and Italy, which were still primarily centers for ascetic and missionary training, began to emerge from their isolation and to become conscious of the new culture they were fashioning for the West. By the end of the century they had transformed themselves into intellectual and artistic centers. Thanks to them, the first elements of a renaissance began to appear, the forerunner of the great Carolingian renewal. Surprisingly, this movement began in all the Barbarian kingdoms almost simultaneously, during the period from 680 to 700.

Archaeologists, in fact, date the construction of the hypogeum of Abbot Mellebaudus at Poitiers and the tombs of Jouarre,[1] and the decoration of the sarcophagi of Dicetius at Delle, Drausius at Soissons, and Theodata at Pavia[2] to this period. Furthermore, they have also been able to establish relationships between the décor of the hypogeum

---

[1] For the hypogeum at Poitiers, see Mâle, *La fin du paganisme*, pp. 178, 181. The tombs of Jouarre are discussed in Hubert, *L'art pré-roman*, p. 18, and Geneviève Aliette (de Rohan-Chabot), marquise de Maillé, *Les cryptes de Jouarre* (Paris, 1971). Bishop Agilbertus, whom we have already met, was interred at Jouarre in 680 / 691. He built the crypt of Saint Paul for his own tomb and that of his sister, Abbess Theodechilda (died 662).

[2] See Jean Hubert, "Les monuments funéraires de l'église de Saint-Dizier en Alsace," *Bulletin Monumental* (1935), p. 215, for Dicetius' tomb (*MGH, SRM*, VI, 55). The sarcophagus of Bishop Drausius (died 680) can be compared with that of Leudalus of Auch (end of the seventh century) and that of Theodata (died 720). See Geza De Francovich, "Il problema della scultura cosidetta 'longobarda,'" *Atti del I Congresso*, pp. 255–56, and Hubert, *Art pré-roman*, p. 95.

at Poitiers and the décor of Cuthbert's sarcophagus at Durham (698)[3] and between the cross at Ruthwell in Northumbria and Lombard sculpture.[4]

The renaissance in sculpture is contemporary with the artistic activity of monastic scriptoria in England and Gaul. We can establish a more exact chronology here, thanks to the manuscripts which have come down to us. The first two known illustrated manuscripts decorated at Lindisfarne and Jarrow date between 689 and 721,[5] while Luxeuil's lectionary was illustrated around 700,[6] and manuscripts were being illustrated at Corbie before 704.[7] A manuscript of Pseudo-Fredegarius' chronicle was illustrated about the same time in a scriptorium in eastern Gaul.[8] We can add to this list the famous evangeliary which was at Echternach around 690.[9] Even though we have no work from Jouarre's scriptorium, the engraver who was responsible for the magnificent inscription that adorns the tomb of Theodechilda must have had a manuscript model before him.[10]

The abbots and bishops who employed sculptors and illustrators also encouraged scribes in the scriptoria and monks who had literary talent. Religious leaders were like so many foremen who organized their houses as cultural centers for the greater glory of God. At the end of the seventh century, one can observe the activity of scribes and illustra-

[3] See Ernst Kitzinger, The Coffin of St. Cuthbert (Oxford, 1950), and idem, "The Coffin of St. Cuthbert," in The Relics of St. Cuthbert, ed. C. F. Battiscombe (Oxford and London, 1956), pp. 202–304.

[4] For the relationship between Anglo-Saxon and Mediterranean art, see Åberg, The Occident and the Orient, vol. 1, The British Isles (Stockholm, 1943), and Lawrence Stone, Sculpture in Britain: The Middle Ages (London, 1955). For Lombard and Merovingian art, see Salin, 2: 136.

[5] See CLA, II, 187, for the Lindisfarne Evangeliary. For the Amiatinus from Jarrow, see CLA, III, 299. Both manuscripts are discussed below, sect. II.A.4.

[6] See Pierre Salmon, Le lectionnaire de Luxeuil, 2 vols. (Rome, 1944–53), and CLA, V, 579. Célestin Charlier, "Note sur les origines de l'écriture dite de Luxeuil à propos d'une étude récente," RB 58 (1948): 149–57, thinks that the lectionary came from a southeastern scriptorium, perhaps from Lyon. For this controversy, see Robert Marichal, review of Le lectionnaire de Luxeuil by Pierre Salmon, BECh 63 (1955): 283–91. We should note that the manuscript of Ivrea, which came from Luxeuil, dates from 680; see CLA, VI, lvi.

[7] See E. H. Zimmermann, Vorkarolingische Miniaturen (Berlin, 1916), pp. 189–90; CLA, IV, 433. The first manuscript contains a poem dedicated to Basinus of Trier (died 705).

[8] Paris, Bibliothèque Nationale, lat. 10910. See Zimmermann, Miniaturen, pl. 74.

[9] It is still debated whether this manuscript was made there or whether it was brought there for Willibrord. See CLA, V, 578, and Carl Nordenfalk, "On the Age of the Earliest Echternach Manuscripts," Acta archaeologica 3 (1932): 57–62.

[10] Marquise de Maillé, Les cryptes de Jouarre, p. 237, dates this inscription to the middle of the seventh century.

tors at Corbie, Luxeuil, and Soissons,[11] and of writers at Corbie, Nivelles, Rebais, Fontenelle, Remiremont, and Laon.[12] In the farthest reaches of Normandy, a region which until this time had not produced any great literary work, Bishop Frodomundus of Coutances found a poet around 677 to write (in septenary trochaic tetrameters) the inscription engraved on the altar of Ham.[13]

Burgundy, where important study centers were organized, experienced an auspicious period for intellectual culture. While the monks of Luxeuil were recopying manuscripts, the bishops of Autun and Auxerre contributed to the renaissance of canon law.[14] Bishop Leodegarius of Autun (660–78) was one of the most remarkable clerics of the period. He spent his early years at court, before he was admitted to the clergy of Poitiers—who were under the direction of his uncle, Bishop Dido. He became archdeacon and master of the episcopal school,[15] then abbot of Saint Maixent around 653, before obtaining the bishopric of Autun with the help of Queen Bathilda. Leodegarius has been viewed primarily as a man of action, a representative of the aristocracy in per-

---

[11] For Corbie, see *CLA*, VI, xxiii. The first known Luxeuil manuscript dates from 669; see ibid., pp. xvi–xvii. Abbot Numidius (695–97) had Caesarius of Arles' homilies copied at Saint Médard in Soissons. See Léopold Victor Delisle, "Notice sur un manuscrit mérovingien de la Bibliothèque royale de Belgique, no. 9850–9852," *Notices et extraits des manuscrits* 31, pt. 1 (1881): 34–35. For all these manuscripts, see Jean Porcher, in Jean Hubert, Jean Porcher, and Wolfgang Fritz Volbach, *L'Europe des Invasions* (Paris, 1968), pt. 2, and idem, *Le catalogue de l'Exposition Charlemagne* (Aix-la-Chapelle, 1965), pp. 227ff.

[12] For Corbie, we can cite the poems of Abbot Theofridus, who died sometime after 681. See Manitius, 1: 200–203, and Norberg, *La poésie latine rythmique*, pp. 49ff., for these poems. From Nivelles, we have the *Life of Saint Gertrude*, written after 669 (see Paul Grosjean, "Notes d'hagiographie celtique," *AB* 75 [1957]: 382, and *Clavis*, no. 2109); from Rebais, the *Life of Saint Agilus* (Auguste Molinier, *Les sources de l'histoire de France des origines aux guerres d'Italie (1494)*, vol. 1 [Paris, 1901], no. 474); from Fontenelle, the *Life of Saint Wandregisilus*, written before 688, and the first *Life of Saint Ansbertus*, before 702 (*Clavis*, nos. 2146, 2089; A. Legris, "Les vies interpolées des saints de Fontenelle," *AB* 17 [1898]: 305); from Remiremont, the *Life of Saint Amatus*, around 670 (*Clavis*, no. 2111); from Laon, the *Life of Saint Sadalberga*, before 707 (Molinier, *Sources*, vol. 1, no. 501, and Krusch, *MGH, SRM*, V, 40).

[13] *Rhythmi aevi merovingici et carolini, MGH, PAC*, IV-2, 652. For this altar, see L. Musset, "Recherches sur l'art préroman et la très ancienne histoire monastique de la Basse-Normandie," *Bulletin historique de la Société des antiquaires de Normandie* 53 (1955–56). This inscription can be compared to Bishop Ansbert's acrostic poem which dates from 679–84; see *MGH, SRM*, V, 542.

[14] Gabriel Le Bras, "Auxerre dans l'histoire du droit canon," *Mémories de la Société eduenne* 48 (1937), and idem, "Notes pour servir à l'histoire des collections canoniques," *RHDE* 8 (1929): 273.

[15] *Vita Leodegarii*, 1 (*MGH, SRM*, V, 283): "Ad diversis studiis quae saeculi potentes studire solent . . . esset politus . . . ; praesertim cum mundanae legis censuram non ignoraret, saecularium terribilis judex fuit, et dum canonicis dogmatibus esset repletus, extitit clericorum doctor egregius."

petual conflict with the Neustrian mayor of the palace, Ebroin. Certainly, Leodegarius made his city a minor political capital, but he was also a pastor who carefully superintended the life of the secular and regular clergy. The influence of his uncle Dido, who had lived in Ireland, as well as his own stay at Luxeuil perhaps inclined him to use the Luxovian model when he reorganized the monasteries of his diocese.[16]

To the south of Burgundy in Lyon, where the episcopal library continued to grow,[17] Wilfrid encountered on his return from Rome "learned scholars" (doctores eruditi) who completed his education during his three-year stay with them.[18] At Vienne, a neighboring town, Benedict Biscop collected the books he brought back to England.[19] We should note, finally, that Bonitus, formerly bishop of Clermont and one of the last men of letters in Aquitaine, died in Lyon at the beginning of the eighth century.[20]

Aquitaine also participated in the intellectual renewal. As in northern Gaul, the style of the hagiographic texts which issued from monasteries bears witness to a greater concern for form. At Méobec, in the diocese of Bourges, a monk who knew Gregory the Great's Homilies and Irish literature composed the strange Vision of Barontius around 678.[21] At Saint Maixent, the monk Ursinus, at the request of Bishop Ansoald of Poitiers, wrote a Life of Saint Leodegarius shortly after the death of the bishop of Autun (678).[22] Around the same time, an Arvernian monk from Volvic wrote the Life of Saint Praejectus, who died in 674; at the beginning of the eighth century, a monk of Manglieu wrote the Life of Saint Bonitus. These last two hagiographers knew not only ecclesiasti-

---

[16] There is no general study of Leodegarius. Jean-Baptiste Pitra's biography, Histoire de saint Léger évêque d'Autun et martyr, et de l'Eglise des Francs au septième siècle (Paris, 1846), is worthless, while Richard Du Moulin-Eckart's Leudegar, Bischof von Autun: Ein Beitrag zur fränkischen Geschichte des 7. Jahrhunderts (Breslau, 1890) is quite partisan. See Fliche-Martin, 5: 351ff., and especially the Vita Leodegarii, which was written shortly after the saint's death (see below, n. 22).

[17] See the list of manuscripts from the end of the seventh century and the beginning of the eighth century in Lowe, Codices lugdunenses antiquissimi, pp. 47ff.

[18] Eddius, Vita Wilfridi, VI (Colgrave ed., p. 12): "Nam per tres annos simul cum eo mansit et a doctoribus valde eruditis multa didicit." This took place during the episcopacy of Aunemundus (658).

[19] Bede, Vita abb., 4 (Plummer ed., p. 367): "Rediens autem ubi Viennam pervenit emptitios ibi quos apud amicos commendaverat, recepit."

[20] Vita Boniti, 31 (MGH, SRM, VI, 136).

[21] MGH, SRM, V, 368. This text deserves further study. See Maurice de Laugardière, L'Eglise de Bourges avant Charlemagne (Paris and Bourges, 1951), pp. 188–98.

[22] MGH, SRM, V, 323–56. Krusch could not believe that this Life was from the seventh century because its style was so correct. His arguments are not convincing, however; see AB 11 (1892): 104–10. Perhaps Ursinus was the same individual as Defensor's teacher (see the text below).

cal authors like Jerome, Sulpicius Severus, Gregory the Great, and Jonas of Bobbio but, what is more surprising, were also acquainted with classical authors such as Caesar and Virgil. In imitation of the latter, the two hagiographers introduced into their stories poetic images and even transcribed verses from the *Aeneid*[23]—clumsy efforts, no doubt, but still proof of a conscious effort for good style. The same observation can be made about two vitae emerging from the clerical milieu of Rodez, since the authors of the *Lives* of Dalmatius and Amandus had read extracts of Virgil, Ovid, and Ennius and remembered them.[24] We can conclude, then, that at the end of the seventh century, classical works were being read in the monasteries of Gaul, a fact which troubled certain monastic rigorists.

Defensor, a monk of Ligugé, was among the troubled monks. Around 700, at the request of his master, Ursinus, he composed his *Liber scintillarum*, in which he collected patristic thoughts on a variety of different moral subjects, such as abstinence, boasting, silence, and virginity.[25] His chapter titles amply indicate that he wrote for monks, undoubtedly for young monks, who were training for an ascetic life. Now, in the chapter on reading, he borrowed his text almost entirely from Isidore of Seville and specifically reproduced the warning directed to monks inclined to read the "lies of the poets."[26] We have already seen how we should interpret this advice.[27] Here, isolated from its context, it amounts to an interdiction. Would Defensor have realized the relevance of

[23] *Passio Praejecti*, 26 (*MGH, SRM*, V, 241, l. 7): "Sed cum jam aurora diei daret initium et jubar solis jam emineret terris." See ibid., p. 234. The description of Clermont contains borrowings from Caesar's *Gallic Wars* (*Vita Boniti*, 24 [*MGH, SRM*, VI, 119]). The architecture and décor of the monastery of Manglieu were still quite antique; see J. Hubert, "Les églises et les bâtiments monastiques de l'abbaye de Manglieu au début du VIIIe siècle," *BSAF* (1958), pp. 91–96.

[24] *Vita Dalmatii*, 7 (*MGH, SRM*, III, 545): "Par levibus ventis similisque sompno volucri"; ibid., 8: "Ac roseum aurora jubar adduxerat" (= *Aeneid.*, VI, 535); "Cum primum radiis suis mundum Titan parat" (= *Aeneid*, IV, 118); "Illic sirenica lintri cantis opponitur" (= *Aeneid*, V, 864). *Vita Amantii, MGH, AA*, IV-2, 55: "Horror omnium quatit membra" (= *Aeneid*, III, 29); "Terribilique sono tubae" (= *Aeneid*, IX, 503). Krusch thought that the *Vita Dalmatii* was from the ninth century, since it contains expressions from the *Life of Saint Genofeva*. We now know, however, that the latter dates from the sixth century: see Charles Kohler, *Etude critique sur le texte de la vie latine de Sainte-Geneviève de Paris, avec deux textes de cette vie* (Paris, 1881). Krusch could not bring himself to admit that a Merovingian hagiographer could have known Virgil.

[25] The *Liber scintillarum* has been reedited by H. M. Rochais (*CCL*, vol. 117 [1957]). For the author, see Rochais, "Le *Liber scintillarum* attribué à Défensor de Ligugé," *RB* 58 (1948): 77–83.

[26] Chapter LXXXI, 35 (p. 234): "Prohibetur christianus figmenta legere poetarum."

[27] See above, chap. 7, sect. III.B.

this passage if profane authors were no longer read in his period?

In northern Gaul, we can detect a new trend in the allusions to pagan literature in the prefaces of certain saints' *Lives*.[28] Furthermore, we know that during this period manuscripts of classical authors began to be recopied in the monasteries of Gaul.[29] Ascetic culture, revivified by Columbanian monks, was thus evolving at the end of the seventh century toward a more humanistic culture.

Italy and England also shared in the renewal. At Pavia, for the first time in many years, a grammarian was welcomed and showered with honors at the court of the Lombard king Cunincpert (died 700).[30] At Bobbio, monks who customarily studied only ecclesiastical works now began to read grammars. At both Pavia and Bobbio, clerics and monks tried their hands at poetry, more or less successfully. Rome, lastly, experienced a renaissance of Hellenism.

English monks and clerics at the end of the seventh century manifested the same desire for learning. Thanks to the arrival at Canterbury in 669 of an African, Hadrian, and of a Greek, Theodore, ecclesiastical schools were reorganized and began to form a new generation of lettered men.[31]

We shall return to the Italian and Anglo-Saxon renaissances. They had to be mentioned here in order to prove the concurrence of these revivals. Whether in the artistic realm or in the realm of sacred and profane intellectual matters, this period was very decisive. It is not sufficient, of course, to acknowledge the renaissances; we must also try to explain them.

By the end of the seventh century the West had begun to emerge from the political anarchy that had characterized its history for several decades. A period of relative stability settled over all the kingdoms. In Gaul, Pepin of Herstal had reunited the two mayoralties of the palaces of Neustria and Austrasia with his victory at Tertry and consolidated the position of his family before he died in 714.[32] Three events in Italy

---

[28] See the preface to the *Vita Eligii*, MGH, SRM, IV, 663. The author, who was partially influenced by Jerome (*Ep.* XLVIII, 4 [*CSEL*, vol. 54] enumerated Latin and Greek writers in order to condemn the reading of them. See the preface to the *Vita Sadalbergae*, MGH, SRM, V, 40, and even the preface to the *Vita Praejecti*, ibid., p. 225 ("Unde lectorem obsecro . . . non quaerat in his Tullianum eloquentiam non philosophorum flosculis et his storicorum diversas assertationes").

[29] The Latin manuscript of Bern, 611 (see *CLA*, VII, 604), which contains grammatical works, dates from this period.

[30] Paul the Deacon, *HL*, VI, 7 (MGH, SRL, p. 167); see below, sect. III.B.

[31] Bede, *HE*, IV, 2 (Plummer ed., pp. 204–5).

[32] See Lot, *Les destinées*, pp. 289ff.; Pirenne, *Mahomet et Charlemagne*, pp. 176ff.; and

contributed to a détente there: the victory of the papacy over Monothelitism at the Council *in Trullo* (681); the peace concluded between the Lombards and the Byzantines in 680; and the end of the schism of Aquilea in 698.[33] In England, the kings of Mercia imposed their authority on neighboring kingdoms.[34] Thus, new lines of force were appearing in Europe when northern Africa fell into the hands of the Arabs (Carthage was first captured in 695) and Spain began to be dangerously threatened.[35] In this almost "Carolingian" setting, a new civilization could be established.

In the monastic world, a new generation of rich and lettered monks succeeded the generation of missionaries and peasants. Huts gave way to better-built structures. At Jumièges, for example, an imposing group of two churches and buildings protected by a wall flanked with towers was built.[36] Monastic complexes such as those in Ireland and Spain were organized, and their material richness enabled them to establish scriptoria and libraries and to specialize their tasks. Freed from material servitude, some monks devoted themselves completely to study. In England, the clergy underwent a profound renewal for other reasons: the plague of 664 had decimated the clerical and monastic population.[37] It was to reorganize this weakened church that the pope sent Theodore and Hadrian to England in 669, and they were thus able to reconstruct the Church of England on new bases.

The fact that a Greek and an African were sent to the Anglo-Saxons proves clearly that political borders no longer hindered contacts. Movement across borders, already underway during the second half of the seventh century, accelerated at the end of the century. Anglo-Saxons and Irishmen passed through Gaul to get to Italy via the Alpine passes. Auxerre, Langres, and especially Lyon were way stations for Anglo-Saxon pilgrims, since Provence was no longer the route to Italy.[38] Bene-

---

H. E. Bonnell, *Die Anfänge des karolingischen Hauses* (Berlin, 1866), a work which has not been superseded.

[33] See Fliche-Martin, 5: 183ff., for these events.

[34] F. M. Stenton, "The Supremacy of the Mercian Kings," *English Historical Review* 33 (1918): 433–52.

[35] Pirenne, *Mahomet et Charlemagne*, p. 134.

[36] Hubert, Porcher, and Volbach, *L'Europe des Invasions*, p. 64.

[37] On this plague, which affected the entire West, see J. N. Biraden and J. Le Goff, "La Peste dans le Haut Moyen Age," *Annales* 24 (1969): 1484–1510.

[38] The father of Bishop Quintillian of Auxerre (died 735) founded a *xenodochium* for Anglo-Saxons; see Rainogala and Alagus, *Gesta episc. Autisiod.*, 29 (*MGH, SS*, XIII, 395). Ceolfrid of Jarrow was buried at Langres; see Bede, *Vita abb.*, 21 (p. 385). At Lyon, Bishop Goduinus (or Godwin, perhaps an Anglo-Saxon) consecrated Bishop Berthwald

dict Biscop traveled back and forth to Rome until 684. Wilfrid was there again in 704. Willibrord was in Rome in 692 and 695. Two Anglo-Saxon kings ended their lives in a Roman monastery.[39] Very close political and familial ties were established between the Lombard and Anglo-Saxon courts.[40] Pavia was a meeting place for Anglo-Saxons, Romans, and Easterners. Bishop Cummean, an Irishman, chose Bobbio as a place to retire around 720.

Some travelers remained on the Continent: Irishmen and Anglo-Saxons settled in northern Gaul at Péronne (Perrona Scottorum), which was founded by Cellanus in 706 and served as a way station for the "Scots";[41] Pepin of Herstal established a monastery for Willibrord at Echternach;[42] Austrasian princes welcomed the Irish and Anglo-Saxon missionaries who began to evangelize Germany.[43]

Such travels and exchanges could only favor intellectual and artistic renewal. As the treasures of each country found whatever was needed to fructify them in foreign lands, the Christian West began to realize its cultural unity. We should add that the Arab conquest of Spain in 711 provoked a flood of refugees not only to the north of the Iberian peninsula but beyond the Pyrenees as well. Clerics and monks bearing manuscripts came as far as Burgundy, northern Italy, and Rome. Thus, Spanish culture, which until this period had been quite isolated, was spread, and Spanish literary works were imitated.[44]

---

of Canterbury; see Bede, *HE*, V, 8 (p. 295), and Levison, *England*, p. 242. For the establishment of the route to Italy via Lyon, see Buchner, *Die Provence*, pp. 37, 40. It could be that the "Franks Casket" found at Brioude, which has one panel representing Romulus and Remus and another the Emperor Titus, was made for a Northumbrian pilgrim on his way to Rome (see Karl Hauck, *Das Katschen von Auzon* [Munich, 1970]). The casket from Mortain undoubtedly came from Northumbria to Gaul in the same manner; see Hubert, "Le coffret de Mortain," *BSAF* (1958), pp. 98–102.

[39] Wilfrid J. Moore, *The Saxon Pilgrims to Rome and the Schola Saxonum* (Freiburg, 1937); Levison, *England*, pp. 37–38.

[40] Levison, pp. 13–14.

[41] Traube, "Perrona Scottorum," in *Vorlesungen und Abhandlungen*, 3: 100–112. For contacts between Ireland and Gaul, see H. Zimmer, "Ueber direkte Handelsbeziehungen zwischen Gallien und Irland im Altertum und frühen Mittelalter," *Sitzungsberichte der preussischen Akademie der Wissenschaften zu Berlin: Phil. hist. Klasse* 49 (1908–09): 363–401, 430–78, 543–618.

[42] Levison, *England*, p. 64. For Willibrord, see Camille Wampach, *Sankt Willibrord: Sein Leben und Lebenswerk* (Luxembourg, 1953).

[43] Fliche-Martin, 5: 531ff. For the cultural work of these missionaries, see below, sect. IV.C.2.

[44] Visigothic manuscripts found their way to Albi (*CLA*, VI, 705), and to Autun (R. P. Robinson, "Manuscripts 27 and 107, Autun: A Study of Spanish Half-Uncial and Early Wisigothic Minuscule and Cursive Scripts," *Memoirs of the American Academy*

The West thus was in the midst of a complete intellectual transformation. We must now study the different aspects of this renewal in the Anglo-Saxon kingdoms, Italy, and Gaul.

II. THE FLOWERING OF MONASTIC AND EPISCOPAL SCHOOLS IN ENGLAND

Between Theodore's arrival in England in 669 and Alcuin's departure for the Continent in 778, four generations of students filled the benches of English schools: that of Aldhelm, who benefited from the lessons of Theodore and Hadrian; that of Bede and of Boniface, born around 673–76; that of their disciples, Lull, Cuthbert, and Egbert; and finally, Alcuin's generation, born around 730, just after Bede had died. We can thus study the evolution of studies for an entire century. In addition, these schools were spread throughout England (see Map 12), the most important being in the kingdoms of Kent, Wessex, and Northumbria. Their geographical positions and the origin of the masters who animated them gave each a particular character.

A. Diversity of Schools
1. the schools of kent

The kingdom of Kent, which, as we have seen, had been the first evangelized, had the privilege of welcoming Theodore and Hadrian, the monks the pope sent to reorganize the Church of England. Bede emphasized the arrival of these two men, who were as skilled in secular literature as they were in ecclesiastical literature, when he remarked that England had never known such a happy period.[45] Even though Theodore did not found the episcopal school at Canterbury, he did give it new life. Around this old man there gathered a crowd of clerics and monks, some of whom came from Whitby,[46] while others received their

---

in Rome 16 [1939]), and to Italy (*CLA*, IV, xviii). Manuscript 490 from Lucca could have been copied from a Visigothic manuscript; see John Miller Burnam, *A Classical Technology Edited from Codex Lucensis 490* (Boston, 1920), and sect. III.B below. The metropolitan of Toledo was in Rome in 721 (Mansi, XII, 264). For the diffusion of Isidore of Seville's manuscripts, especially those of the *De natura rerum*, see the preface to Fontaine's edition, *Isidore de Séville: Traité de la nature*, pp. 71–83. For the contacts between Spain and Ireland, see J. N. Hillgarth, "Visigothic Spain and Early Christian Ireland," *Proceedings of the Royal Irish Academy* 62 (1962): 167–94.

[45] Bede, *HE*, IV, 2 (p. 204): "Et quia literis sacris simul et saecularibus . . . abundanter ambo erant instructi . . . ; neque unquam prorsus ex quo Brittaniam petierunt Angli, feliciora fuere tempora." See Laistner, *Thought and Letters*, p. 151, for the culture of Theodore and Hadrian.

[46] Bede, *HE*, IV, 2 (p. 204): "Congregata discipulorum caterva scientia salutaris

Bishoprics   Principal monasteries   – – – Borders of dioceses

12. Episcopal and Monastic Cultural Centers in Eighth-Century England

entire education from Theodore. The books he brought with him and those which he had produced in the episcopal scriptorium[47] permitted him to organize instruction around several disciplines. Bede was quite exact about the program the bishop proposed to his students: metrics, astronomy, and "ecclesiastical arithmetic" (that is, computus).[48] To this list, we must add medicine (if one of Theodore's disciples is to be believed),[49] exegesis,[50] and even Greek.

Greek was taught in an ecclesiastical school for the first time in England, an event which distinguished the schools of Kent,[51] although it is difficult for us to know the extent of Greek studies. Theodore must have brought Greek books with him for his disciples' use, and perhaps he maintained his contacts with the Greek world in the East.[52] The discovery of Coptic and Syrian vases and Byzantine jewels in Kent proves that there were exchanges between England and the East during this period.[53] But, as we shall see later, the implantation of Hellenic culture in Kent was neither profound nor durable.[54]

---

quotidie flumina irrigandis eorum cordibus emanabant." Among these disciples, we can name Oftfor, who, after a stay in Rome, became a bishop in Mercia (*HE*, IV, 23), and John of Beverley. Both had formerly been monks at Whitby (*HE*, V, 3). The Irishmen who were also at Canterbury appear to have been more critics than disciples; see Aldhelm, *Ep.* 5 (*MGH, AA*, XV, 492).

[47] The Vespasian Psalter, the *Codex aureus*, and other manuscripts came from Canterbury's library. See Carl Nordenfalk, in André Grabar and Carl Nordenfalk, *Le haut Moyen Age du quatrième au onzième siècle* (Geneva, 1957), p. 124.

[48] Bede, *HE*, IV, 2 (p. 204): "Ita ut etiam metricae artis, astronomiae et arithmeticae ecclesiasticae disciplinam inter sacrorum apicum volumina suis auditoribus contraderent."

[49] In ibid., V, 3 (p. 285), John of Beverly recalled: "Memini enim beatae memoriae Theodorum archiepiscopum dicere, quia periculosa sit satis illius temporis phlebotomia, quando et lumen lunae, et rheuma oceani in cremento est."

[50] *Quaest. liber*, III (*PL*, XCIII, 456): "Quosdam audivi astruentes quod beatae memoriae Theodorus ... exposuerit."

[51] *HE*, IV, 2 (p. 205): "Usque hodie supersunt de eorum discipulis qui latinam graecamque linguam aeque ut propriam in qua nati sunt norunt." Bede cited the cases of Albinus and Tobias (*HE*, V, 23 [p. 348]).

[52] For Theodore's problematic stay in Athens and the importation of Greek books to England, see A. S. Cook's questionable article, "Theodore of Tarsus and Gislenus of Athens," *PhQ* 2 (1923): 1–25. Pope Zachary in 748 was the first to mention Theodore's education "in Athens" in a letter to Boniface: "Theodorus graeco-latinus ante philosophus et Athenis eruditus Romae ordinatus" (*Ep.* 80 [*MGH, Ep.*, III, 357, l. 17]). Did not Zachary mean simply that Theodore had a Greek culture?

[53] Thomas Downing Kendrick, *Anglo-Saxon Art to A.D. 900* (London, 1938), pp. 62–68. For the Coptic vases found in the Sutton Hoo treasure, see R. Bruce-Mitford, "The Sutton Hoo Ship Burial," *Proceedings of the Royal Society of Suffolk* 25 (1949): 83–94. For the jewels and Byzantine objects, see Nils Åberg, *The Anglo-Saxons in England* (Uppsala, 1926), pp. 102–6. For contacts between England and the East, see the article by R. S. Lopez, "Le problème des relations anglo-byzantines du VIIe au Xe siècle," *Byzantion* 18 (1948): 147–54.

[54] See below, sect. II.B.1.

When Theodore died in 690, Berthwald, a former abbot endowed with a good ecclesiastical education, replaced him.[55] In 731, Tatwin, a monk from a monastery near Wales, became bishop of Canterbury. His little grammatical treatise and his *Enigmas* in hexameter form made him famous.[56] Nothelm (734–39) and Cuthbert (740–58), his successors, were also lettered bishops.[57] Thus, for almost a century, the episcopal school at Canterbury was an important study center.

The monastic school of Saints Peter and Paul in Canterbury was just as famous. At first under the leadership of Benedict Biscop, this school was later directed, from 669, by Theodore's companion, the African Hadrian, who in turn was succeeded by his own disciple Albinus (709–31).[58] The program of the school must have matched closely that of the cathedral school. Aldhelm, Hadrian's pupil,[59] recalled in a letter to Bishop Leutherius that he had learned meter, chant, calculation, astronomy, and even Roman law at Canterbury.[60] The correspondence between the two kinds of training becomes obvious when we note that former monks studied under the bishop, while secular clerics became monks. In England, as we shall observe on several occasions, the two orders were not so compartmentalized as in Gaul.

2. THE SCHOOLS OF WESSEX

The abbey of Malmesbury in Wessex, which had been founded by an Irishman in the middle of the seventh century, was directed by Aldhelm, Hadrian's former student.[61] Aldhelm, who is considered the first English writer, studied at this monastery. When he became abbot, he

---

[55] Bede, *HE*, V, 8 (p. 295): "Vir et ipse scientia scripturarum imbutus sed et ecclesiasticis ac monasterialibus disciplinis summe instructus tametsi praedecessori sua minime comparandus."

[56] Ibid., 23 (p. 350). For Tatwin's work, see Manitius, 1: 203.

[57] Nothelm collaborated on Bede's *Historia*; see Bede's preface (p. 6). Cuthbert corresponded with Lull; see *Ep.* 111 (*MGH, Ep.*, III, 397).

[58] Bede, *Vita abb.*, 3 (p. 367); *HE*, V, 20 (p. 331): "In tantum studiis scripturarum institutus est ut graecam quidem linguam non parva ex parte latinam vero non minus quam Anglorum quae sibi naturalis noverit." Albinus also helped Bede gather the documents for his *Historia*; see *HE*, preface (p. 6).

[59] See Aldhelm's letter to Hadrian, *Ep.* 2 (*MGH, AA*, XV, 478): "Reverendissimo patri meaeque rudis infantiae venerando praeceptori Hadriano."

[60] Aldhelm, *Ep.* 1 (ibid., pp. 476–77): "Legum Romanarum jura medullitus . . . centena scilicet metrorum genera pedestri regula . . . ad musica cantilenae modulamina recto sillabarum tramite . . . de ratione vero calculationis . . . de zodiaco XII signorum circulo."

[61] On Aldhelm, in addition to L. Bönhoff's old book, *Aldhelm von Malmesbury* (Dresden, 1894), see Roger, pp. 290–301; Manitius, 1: 134–41; and Rudolf Ehwald's preface to Aldhelm's works (*MGH, AA*, XV, ix–xxv). There is very little in Eleanor Shipley Duckett's *Anglo-Saxon Saints and Scholars* (New York, 1948), pp. 3–100.

collected a large library, part of which survived until the twelfth century.[62] He was named first bishop of Sherborne in 705 and continued his intellectual work there. Forther, his successor as bishop, maintained a taste for scholarship in this city.[63] Not far from Sherborne, at Winchester, which also had just been made an episcopal city, Daniel, a former monk, was named bishop. According to Bede, his education was comparable to Aldhelm's.[64] In southwestern Wessex at Exeter, the monk Winfrid, the future Boniface, received his first education around 687[65] but was unable to find a master there who could help him pursue his studies.[66] He moved to Nursling, which was directed by Abbot Windrecht; there, he found a good library[67] and completed his education in such a fashion that he became master in the monastery. Until 716, the date of his departure for the Continent, his learning continued to attract numerous disciples for whom he wrote two grammatical treatises.[68] Among the monasteries favorable to studies, we must also mention Glastonbury, which was in contact with Malmesbury and Waltham,[69] as well as a number of convents that we shall discuss later.

Thanks to the work of Aldhelm and Boniface, we know that studies in Wessex were organized in a very original spirit. The style of Aldhelm's letters and treatises is so obscure, mannered, and convoluted that they surprise and often repulse one.[70] This is because he was influenced by hisperic literature[71]—despite Rome's triumph, Wessex had always been under the literary influence of neighboring Celtic lands. In fact,

---

[62] M. R. James, *Two Ancient English Scholars: St. Aldhelm and William of Malmesbury*, Glasgow University Publications, vol. 22 (Glasgow, 1931).

[63] Bede, *HE*, V, 18 (p. 321): "Vir et ipse in scripturis sanctis multum eruditus."

[64] Ibid. (p. 320): "Ambo in rebus ecclesiasticis et in scientia scripturarum sufficienter instructi." Daniel perhaps ended his life as abbot of Malmesbury. See Plummer, *Venerabilis Baedae* . . . , 2: 308.

[65] Willibald, *Vita Bonifatii*, 1 (Levison ed., pp. 6–7). See Manitius, 1: 142, and Levison, *England*, pp. 70ff.

[66] *Vita Bonifatii*, ed. Levison, p. 8, l. 30: "Ad finitima quoque monasteria magisteriali lectionis provocatus penuria . . . perveniret."

[67] He alluded to this library in a letter to Daniel of Winchester (*Ep.* 63 [*MGH, Ep.*, III, 329]).

[68] *Vita Bonifatii*, 2 (Levison ed., p. 9). He prepared one of these treatises with the help of his pupil, Duddo. See *Carm.* II (*MGH, PAC*, I, 16): "Vynfreth priscorum Duddo congesserat artem. Viribus ille jugit juvavit in arte magistrum." See below, sect. II.B.1, for these treatises.

[69] Clark H. Slover, "Glastonbury Abbey and the Fusing of English Literary Culture," *Speculum* 10 (1935): 147–49; Hugeburc, *Vita Willibaldi, MGH, SS*, XV-1, 69. (This Willibald, the future bishop of Eichstädt, should not be confused with the biographer of Boniface.)

[70] See the opinions of Traube, Laistner, and Roger as reported by Curtius, p. 560.

[71] Ozanam made this comparison in *La civilisation chrétienne*, pp. 517–19.

before he became Hadrian's pupil, Aldhelm was the student of an Irishman, Mailduib.[72] Young Anglo-Saxons were still attracted by the reputation of Irish schools at the end of the seventh century.[73]

In the enthusiasm of the intellectual revival in England, Aldhelm wanted to prove that one did not have to go to Ireland to become a man of letters. That was why around 686–90 he wrote to young Ehfrid, who had just spent six years in Ireland, "clinging to the breasts of wisdom,"[74] to deplore the fact that young people were going away to study grammar, geometry, physics, and the science of Scripture:[75] "Why should Ireland, where students are flocking in droves, have this privilege as if this green and fertile Britain were lacking Greek and Roman masters to explain the difficult problems of the celestial library to those who question them?"[76] He then mentioned his masters, Hadrian and Theodore, whom he compared to two shining stars. Elsewhere, in a letter to the king of Northumbria, he showed that the Anglo-Saxons could themselves be teachers and basked in the fact that he was the first to teach meter to the Germans—he even compared himself to Virgil, who introduced Greek pastoral poetry to the Romans.[77]

His effort was successful. The Irish themselves acknowledged his

[72] "A quodam sancto viro de nostro genere nutritus es," one of Aldhelm's correspondents reminded him (Aldhelm, *Ep.* I (6) [*MGH*, *AA*, XV, 494]).

[73] Effrid, son of the king of Northumbria, was sent to Iona "ob studium litterarum" (Bede, *Vita Cuthberti*, XXIV [Colgrave ed., p. 236]). Abbot Adamnan presided over Iona from 674 to 704; for his culture, see Manitius, 1: 236, and Roger, p. 261. Roger thinks that Adamnan profited from Theodore's arrival. But how? We should remember that Irish learning had already begun to bear fruit before Theodore's time; see above, chap. 8, sect. I.A.

[74] Aldhelm, *Ep.* 5 (*MGH*, *AA*, XV, 489): "Ubi ter bino circiter annorum circulo uber sofiae sugens metabatur." Ehfrid's identity is still a matter for discussion. According to A. S. Cook, he was a former monk of Glastonbury ("Bishop Cuthwini of Leicester [680–691], Amateur of Illustrated Manuscripts," *Speculum* 2 [1927]: 253–57). For Colgrave, though, he was the friend of Wilfrid mentioned by Eddius in chapter LVIII (p. 124) of Colgrave's edition of Eddius' *Vita Wilfridi* ("Pontifex noster electos nuntios Baldwinum presbyterum et abbatem magistrumque Alfrithum ad Aldfrithum regem . . . emisit").

[75] Aldhelm, *Ep.* 5 (*MGH*, *AA*, XV, 490, l. 17): "Non solum artes grammaticas atque geometricas bisterasque omissas fisicae artis machinas, quin immo allegoricae potiora ac tropologicae disputationis bipertita bis oracula aethralibus opacorum mellita in aenigmatibus problematum siticulose sumentes carpunt et in alveariis sofiae jugi meditatione letotenus servanda condentes abdunt."

[76] Ibid. (p. 492): "Cur inquam Hibernia, quo catervatim istinc lectitantes classibus advecti confluunt, ineffabili quodam privilegio efferatur, acsi istic fecundo Britanniae in cespite dedasculi Argivi Romanive Quirites reperiri minime queant, qui caelestis tetrica enodantes bibliothecae problemata sciolis reserare se sciscitantibus valeant?"

[77] Aldhelm, *De metris*, *MGH*, *AA*, XV, 202: "Quanto constat neminem nostrae stirpis prosapia gentium et Germanicae gentis cunabulis confotum, in hujuscemodi negotio ante nostram mediocritatem tantopere desudasse."

literary merits.[78] They discovered in the letter to Ehfrid and in the treatise *De septenario* (or *De metris*) the "luster" of the hisperic style.[79] To judge from the poems of young Aethilwald, who along with others had been introduced to the "mysteries of the liberal arts" and the world of letters,[80] Aldhelm's disciples were worthy of him.[81] The works of Virgil the Grammarian and other Celtic works were read at Malmesbury and Sherborne. Repertories of rare words that had been newly created or drawn from Greek were used.[82] The poems of the *Latin Anthology* and Symphosius' enigmas were imitated.[83] Literary pieces were stuffed with all the mythological allusions dear to sixth-century Italian and African writers.[84] Perhaps Aldhelm's disciples even played at composing apocryphal writings.[85] The atmosphere of Aldhelm's school reminds us of what we have said about Ennodius and his disciples: the master, like Ennodius or Fortunatus, displayed his learning to whomever wished to listen by amassing technical terms which smelled of the school, even Virgil the Grammarian's school. For example, he described "his bark which slides between the Scylla of solecism and the barathra of barbarism, avoiding the collisions which the rocks of iotacism reserve for him and the abysses of myotacism."[86]

Aldhelm's work cannot be discussed in terms of one period—a barren

---

[78] See the letters of Cellanus and of an Irishman in *Ep.* III (9) and I (6) (*MGH, AA,* XV, 498, 494).

[79] Bede described him in these words in *HE,* V, 18 (p. 321): "Nam et sermone nitidus et scripturarum . . . tam liberalium quam ecclesiasticarum erat eruditione mirandus."

[80] Aldhelm, *Ep.* II (7) (*MGH, AA,* XV, 495): "Arcana liberalium litterarum studia, opacis dumtaxat misteriorum secretis."

[81] See Manitius, 1: 141, for Aethilwald. His poems have been published in *MGH, AA,* XV, 528–37. Other disciples of Aldhelm include Deacon Pecthelm, who died in 735 as bishop of Candida Casa (Whitherne) (see Bede, *HE,* V, 18 and 23 [pp. 320, 351]), and an anonymous cleric who wrote a poem to Aldhelm (*MGH, AA,* XV, 523). For the influence of Aldhelm's writings on the biographer of Guthlac, see the preface to Colgrave's edition of the *Vita Guthlachi,* pp. 17–18.

[82] For Aldhelm's sources, see Max Manitius, "Zu Aldhelm und Beda," *Sitzungsberichte der Oesterreichischen Akademie der Wissenschaften zu Wien: Phil. hist. Klasse* 112 (1886): 535–634, and Roger, pp. 291ff.

[83] See Aldhelm, *De metris, MGH, AA,* XV, 75, 97.

[84] Read the letter to Wilfrid, *Ep.* 3 (*MGH, AA,* XV, 479).

[85] Paul Grosjean thinks that the *De excidio* was partly written at Malmesbury ("Remarques sur le *De excidio* attribué à Gildas," *ALMA* 25 [1955]: 155–87; idem, "Le *De excidio* à Malmesbury à la fin du VIIe siècle," *AB* 75 [1957]: 212–22).

[86] Aldhelm, *De virginitate (prosa),* LIX (*MGH, AA,* XV, 320–21): "Quasi inter Scillam, soloecismi et barbarismi barathrum indisruptis rudentibus feliciter transfretaverint, scopulosas quoque labdacismi collisiones et myotacismi voragines, incautos quosque sine grammaticorum gubernaculo repertos ad erroris naufragia truciter trudentes minime perhorruerint."
See Ennodius, *Ep.* I, 1 (*MGH, AA,* VII, 8, l. 7): "Sermonum cymbam inter loquelae scopulos frenare."

period as some would have it[87]—in Anglo-Saxon literature. Rather, we must see Aldhelm's work as the expression of a tendency in Latin culture which found favorable soil in Wessex for its rebirth. The succeeding generation, raised in schools near Celtic lands, remained faithful to this tradition: we need only read Tatwin's enigmas[88] or Boniface's letter to Nithard to be convinced of this. Boniface's letter can be compared to certain of Aldhelm's pages: Boniface, too, sprinkled his letter with rare words and mixed Greek expressions with Latin[89] and decorated his poems, particularly his enigmas and acrostic poems, with mannered phrases.[90] Porfyrius, the inventor of the *Carmina figurata*, was rediscovered and imitated during Boniface's lifetime.[91] Boniface transmitted the literary heritage he received to his disciple Lull and to those he trained on the Continent.[92] Lettered Carolingians, in turn, would be further tributaries of this heritage. The welcome Aldhelm's works received in the ninth and tenth centuries is, thus, not difficult to explain.[93]

Irish influence marked the schools of Wessex in yet another way: lettered monks were also missionaries. It is noteworthy that the Anglo-Saxons who left their country to evangelize Gaul and Germany were all trained in Irish schools or in schools influenced by Irishmen. The "peregrinatio pro Christo" that impelled Columban and his disciples to travel inspired Anglo-Saxons also: Egbert, Weitbert, and Willibrord were trained in Ireland;[94] Boniface rejoined Willibrord in Frisia in 719.[95] When he could have become the "Bede of Wessex," Boniface abandoned everything for the mission. Collaborators like his disciple

---

[87] Roger, p. 300.

[88] Tatwin, the author of the *Enigmas* (see Manitius, 1: 203), came from western Mercia; see Bede, *HE*, V, 23 (p. 350): "De provincia Merciorum cum fuisset presbyter in monasterio quod vocatur Briudun." Briadon, or Breedon, is located near Leicester.

[89] Take, for example, the following passage: "Et hac de re universi aurilegi Ambrones apo ton grammaton agiis frustatis adflicti, inservire excubiis et fragilia aranearum in cassum—ceu flatum tenuem sive pulverem captantia—tetendisse retia dinoscuntur; quia kata psalmistam" (Boniface, *Ep.* 9 [*MGH, Ep.*, III, 249–50]).

[90] His poems have been published in *MGH, PAC*, I, 3–20. For the *Aenigmata*, see ibid., pp. 20–23. In the *Aenigmata de virtutibus*, he presented faith, hope, and justice as Ennodius had beauty, faith, chastity, and the liberal arts; see *Paraenesis didascalica*, Schanz, IV-2, 139. Martianus Capella had also used prosopopoeia. See above, n. 68, for the acrostic poem to Duddo.

[91] Milret, *Ep.* 112 (*MGH, Ep.*, III, 401, l. 40). Cuthbert of Canterbury borrowed this work from Milret of Worcester. See Elsa Kluge, "Studien zu Publilius Optatianus Porfyrius," *Münchener Museum für Philologie des Mittelalters und der Renaissance* 4 (1924): 323–48, and Levison, *England*, p. 145.

[92] Lull, *Ep.* 98 (*MGH, Ep.*, III, 385, l. 12).

[93] Manitius, 1: 141.

[94] Bede, *HE*, V, 9–10 (pp. 298ff.)

[95] See Fliche-Martin, 5: 534ff.

Lull; Weethbert, a monk of Glastonbury; and Willibald, a monk of Waltham, soon came from his native country. Finally, Boniface appealed to educated women in the monasteries of Wessex.

The culture of nuns was, in fact, more developed in Wessex than elsewhere—another mark of Irish influence. In Ireland and in all monasteries affected by the Irish spirit, the education of women found favorable ground in the seventh century. Aldhelm corresponded with the nuns from Barking and Wimborne and addressed two works in verse and prose on virginity to lettered nuns, who would have to have been quite literate to understand the author's subtleties.[96] Boniface was also a literary counselor of nuns: of Lioba, a nun from Wimborne;[97] of Eadburg, who taught poetry to Lioba[98] and who furnished Boniface with books;[99] of Egburg, a former pupil of Boniface;[100] and of Eangyth and her daughter, Bugga.[101] The letters they exchanged reveal the profound friendship between the missionary and his compatriots, friendship comparable to that of Fortunatus for Radegunda but on a less mundane and more spiritual level.[102]

3. STUDIES IN THE CENTRAL KINGDOMS

Between the kingdoms of southern England and Northumbria stretched Mercia and its dependencies, Essex and East Anglia. Monasteries had been founded there, but none of them were important centers of studies. Yet, we should mention Briadon, near Leicester, from which Tatwin came; Lichfield, started by Bishop Chad;[103] and Crowland, where the monk Felix wrote the *Vita Guthlachi* around 730.[104] The

---

[96] Aldhelm, *De virginitate*, II (*MGH, AA*, XV, 230, l. 4): "Velut sagaces gimnosofistas sub peritissimo quodam agonitheta palestricis disciplinis et gimnicis artibus in gimnaso exerceri." Further on, he called them "alumniae scholasticae" and noted their "discipulatus industria" (pp. 230, l. 25, and 323, l. 4).

[97] Lioba, *Ep.* 29 (*MGH, Ep.*, III, 280–81). In the ninth century, Rudolfus of Fulda wrote a *Vita Leobae* (*MGH, SS*, XV-1, 121–31), incorporating information on studies in a convent.

[98] Lioba, *Ep.* 29 (p. 281): "Istos autem subter scriptos versiculos conponere nitebar secundum poeticae traditionis disciplinam. . . . Istam artem ab Eadburge magisterio didici."

[99] *Ep.* 10, 30, 35 (pp. 252, 281, 286); Lull, *Ep.* 70 (ibid., p. 337).

[100] Egburg, *Ep.* 13 (*MGH, Ep.*, III, 258–60).

[101] Eangyth, *Ep.* 14 (ibid., pp. 260–64); Bugga, *Ep.* 15 (ibid., pp. 264–65). Bugga was the sister of King Centwin of Wessex, who died in 751. For Boniface's correspondents, see Heinrich Hahn, *Bonifaz und Lul: Ihre angelsächsische Korrespondenten* (Leipzig, 1883).

[102] See J. Leclercq, "L'amitié dans les lettres au Moyen Age," *RMAL* 1 (1945): 391–410.

[103] Bede, *HE*, IV, 3 (p. 209).

[104] *Vita Guthlachi*, preface (Colgrave ed., p. 60).

monastery of Ely, which was to become one of the great religious centers of medieval England, was not distinguished for its intellectual activity during this period.[105] Among the bishops of these kingdoms, we
can cite only two lettered men: Tatfrid of Worcester, a former monk of
Whitby,[106] and Cuthwin of Dunwich (716–21), which had a very active
scriptorium.[107] Mercia—whose political power would only begin to
grow in the mid-seventh century, reaching its height in the following
century—thus could not boast any schools comparable to those of
Wessex.

4. THE SCHOOLS OF NORTHUMBRIA

In the kingdom of Northumbria, on the other hand, where political
decadence was the norm, we find the most famous schools in England.

When Benedict Biscop, himself a Northumbrian, returned from
Rome, he established the great abbeys of Saint Paul and Saint Peter
at Wearmouth and Jarrow (674–85) at the mouths of the Wear and the
Tyne.[108] The foundation of these two abbeys made the eastern coast of
Northumbria from Lindisfarne to Whitby a veritable monastic Riviera.
The new abbeys, however, were quickly to supersede the Irish founda-
dations, thanks to the work of Abbot Benedict and Abbot Ceolfrid.[109]

During his many trips to the Continent, Benedict studied different
monastic *statuta* in Gaul and in Italy. At the end of his inquiry, he decided to introduce the Benedictine *Rule* to Northumbria.[110] In 678,
when he was in Rome with his friend Ceolfrid, he obtained a privilege

---

105 Bede, *HE*, IV, 17 (19) (p. 244), described religious life at the royal monastery of
Ely but said nothing about intellectual culture there.

106 Ibid., 21 (23) (p. 255): "Tatfrid vir strenuissimus et doctissimus."

107 Bede, *Quaest. liber*, VI (*PL*, XCIII, 459). See A. S. Cook, "Bishop Cuthwini of
Leicester," *Speculum* 2 (1927): 253–57. Levison, *England*, p. 133, thinks, however, that
the reference is to the bishop of Dunwich rather than Leicester. An Antwerp manuscript
(Mus. Plant. Moretus 126) bearing Sedulius' *Carmen paschale* reproduces the following
notice from an insular archetype: "Finit fines fines [*sic*] Cudwini." See C. Caesar, "Die
Antwerpener Handschrift des Sedulius," *RhM* 56 (1901): 264.

108 See Thompson, "Northumbrian Monasteries" in *Bede*, pp. 84ff.

109 As we have already noted, Benedict had been Wilfrid's traveling companion. For
Benedict Biscop, see T. Bucheler, *Benedict Biscop als Pionier römisch-christlicher Kultur
bei den Angelsachsen* (Heidelberg, 1923). For Ceolfrid, see the anonymous *Vita sanctissimi Ceolfridi abbatis* in Plummer's edition of *Venerabilis Baedae*, 1: 388–404.

110 Levison, *England*, pp. 22ff. The introduction of the Benedictine *Rule* to these
monasteries, although certain, has been the subject of much discussion. Bede devoted
only two lines to Saint Benedict in his martyrology ("XX, Kal., april."). He does tell
us, however, that Benedict Biscop applied Benedict's rule for the election of the abbot;
see *Vita abb.*, 11 (p. 375): "Juxta quod regula magni quondam abbatis Benedicti." The
Oxford manuscript of the *Regula* comes no doubt from Worcester; see *CLA*, II, 240, and
E. A. Lowe, *Regula S. Benedicti: Specimina selecta e codice antiquissimo Oxoniensi elegit
. . .* (Oxford, 1929).

of exemption for Wearmouth from Pope Agatho.[111] He also was able to persuade the archcantor of Saint Peter to come to teach Roman chant to his monks and to anyone else who wished to learn from him.[112] Finally, he built a large library with the books he brought back from his six trips to Gaul and Rome.[113] In this way some of the books from Vivarium that had been conserved in Rome came eventually to Wearmouth and Jarrow.[114] In addition to books, Benedict brought back paintings to decorate the walls of his monastery.[115] He brought over masons and glassmakers who could build "in the Roman style."[116] Perhaps he even imported the engravers who cut the inscriptions of which we still possess a fragment.[117] When Ceolfrid had the famous *Amiatinus* manuscript copied as an offering to the pope, he asked an Italian scribe to undertake the project.[118] With the *Amiatinus*, whose organization and miniatures were based on one of Cassiodorus' manuscripts, and with the establishment of a major library, Wearmouth and Jarrow emerged as the heirs of Vivarium. Italian humanism made its reappearance in Northumbria.

The significance of these events appears even greater if we compare Benedict's monasteries to the old monastery of Lindisfarne eighty kilometers (fifty miles) to the north. In the eighth century this monastery remained faithful to the tradition of sacred studies developed in the seventh century and, indeed, even seemed somewhat reactionary because of its greater emphasis on asceticism than on study.[119] When Benedict

---

[111] Bede, *Vita abb.*, 6 (p. 369).

[112] Bede, *HE*, IV, 16 (18) (p. 241): "Non solum autem idem Johannes ipsius monasterii fratres docebat, verum de omnibus pene ejusdem provinciae monasteriis ad audiendum eum qui cantandi erant periti confluebant."

[113] For these trips, see Bede, *Vita abb.*, 6 (p. 369). Benedict was not the only one during this period to bring books back from Rome. See an allusion in Aethilwald's poem (*MGH, AA*, XV, 531).

[114] See Courcelle, *LG*, pp. 374–75.

[115] *Vita abb.*, 6 (p. 369): "Picturas imaginum sanctarum quas ad ornandum ecclesiam beati Petri apostoli quam construxerat detulit."

[116] Ibid., 5 (p. 368): "Caementarios qui lapideam sibi ecclesiam juxta Romanorum quem semper amabat morem facerent, postulavit, accepit, attulit." Two monuments, the tower at Jarrow and the little church at Escomb in the diocese of Durham, still bear witness to this new practice. See Blair, *Introduction*, p. 157. The king of the Picts asked Ceolfrid for workers: "Sed et architecturos sibi mitti petiit qui juxta morem Romanorum ecclesiam de lapide in gente ipsius facerent" (*HE*, V, 21 [p. 333]).

[117] Blair, *Introduction*, pp. 156–57.

[118] For the history of this manuscript, see Courcelle, *LG*, pp. 356ff.; Vanderhoven and Masai, *Regula Magistri*, p. 58; and idem, "Il monachesimo irlandese nei suoi rapporti col continente (arte)," *Settimane*, 4: 151. The scriptorium at Jarrow also produced the Leningrad manuscript, whose very oriental decoration has been described by M. Schapiro, "The Decoration of the Leningrad Manuscript of Bede," *Scriptorium* 12 (1958): 191–207.

[119] See above, chap. 8, sect. I.C.

Biscop was founding Wearmouth, Lindisfarne was guided by an abbot whose way of life reminds one of the Eastern anchorites. Cuthbert, who often liked to retire to a hut on a small island, imposed on his community at Lindisfarne psalmodies, vigils, manual labor, and scriptural readings, all of which are reminiscent of the Eastern monastic tradition.[120] Lindisfarne maintained an ascetical culture even after Cuthbert's death, after which, except for a *Life* of Cuthbert which Abbot Eadfrid (698–721) judged unworthy of the saint and asked Bede to redo,[121] Lindisfarne produced no great literary work.

It was during Eadfrid's abbacy that the Lindisfarne Evangeliary was written. As this manuscript is almost contemporary with the *Amiatinus*, art historians have compared the two masterpieces.[122] Those who, with François Masai, hold that Northumbrian painting on the whole was influenced by Italian currents have found several Mediterranean themes in the evangeliary. The contrast between the two manuscripts is obvious, however: the *Book of Lindisfarne* preserves "insular" decoration of either Irish or Northumbrian origin and is closer to the *Book of Durrow*.[123] The carpet pages of these two manuscripts reveal an esthetic which contrasts at every point with that of Greco-Roman works.

The originality of Benedict's foundations must be stressed in order to understand the work of Bede the Venerable, which bears the stamp of the "Roman" atmosphere into which he was born. After he entered Wearmouth at the age of seven, Bede studied first under Benedict and other lettered men. In 685 he accompanied Ceolfrid to the new monastery at Jarrow, where he wrote his first works at the beginning of the eighth century.[124] Bede remained in this monastery for fifty years, devoting his life to study: "While observing the discipline of the rule and the daily chanting of the offices in the church, my chief pleasure

[120] *Vita Cuthberti*, ed. Colgrave, p. 61; ibid., XVI (pp. 206–13); idem, *HE*, IV, 25 (27)–27 (29) (pp. 268–76).

[121] Bede, *Vita Cuthberti*, preface (Colgrave ed., p. 143).

[122] Masai, "Il monachesimo irlandese," p. 154; Carl Nordenfalk, "Before the Book of Durrow," *Acta archaeologica* 18 (1947): 141–74: Grabar and Nordenfalk, *Le haut Moyen Age*, pp. 121–22; E. A. Lowe, "A Key to Bede's Scriptorium: Some Observations on the Leningrad Manuscript of the *Historia Ecclesiastica Gentis Anglorum*," *Scriptorium* 12 (1958): 182–90.

[123] F. Henry, "Les débuts de la miniature irlandaise," *Gazette des Beaux-Arts* (1950), pp. 5–34; Grabar and Nordenfalk, *Le haut Moyen Age*, p. 118.

[124] Bede, *HE*, V, 24 (p. 357). For Bede's youth, see C. F. Whiting, "The Life of the Venerable Bede," in Thompson, *Bede*, pp. 5ff. R. Davis, "Bede's Early Reading," *Speculum* 8 (1933): 179–95, has tried to reconstruct Bede's early reading program. He thinks that the books Bede used had been purchased in Ireland (p. 185), although he offers no proof.

has been to learn, to teach, and to write."[125] This great worker was faithful to this program until his last moments.[126] He had at his disposition the books that Benedict had brought back from Rome, and from his contact with these profane and sacred classics, he acquired the clear and measured style which contrasts him so happily with Aldhelm.[127] He had no taste for enigmas or complicated poetical figures but, rather, used the Latin language as a useful tool in the service of historical, scientific, and scriptural work.[128] With Bede, Roman *gravitas* overcame literary mannerism. We shall have to return to Bede's work when we try to determine whether this great lettered monk in the new Vivarium was a new Cassiodorus.

The Roman spirit could also be found in the schools of the two Northumbrian bishoprics of Hexham and York. Created in 678 at the expense of Lindisfarne, the see of Hexham was occupied for a time by Wilfrid, after whose death Acca (706–40), one of his study and travel companions, succeeded him. In his childhood Acca had been educated by Bosa,[129] a former monk of Whitby and bishop of York, and then had become a disciple of Wilfrid.[130] It was with Wilfrid that he traveled to Rome on a journey that would mark his life. At Hexham, Acca was a great builder who brought together a large library composed mainly of hagiographical and ecclesiastical works.[131] He also excelled in chant and established a school for Roman chant in his church. To this end he brought in a certain Maban from Canterbury, who, for twelve years,

---

[125] Bede, *HE*, V, 24 (p. 357): "Cunctum ex eo tempus vitae in ejusdem monasterii habitatione peragens omnem meditandis Scripturis operam dedi atque inter observantiam disciplinae regularis et quotidianam cantandi in ecclesia curam, semper aut discere aut docere aut scribere dulce habui." He spoke elsewhere of the pleasure of writing ("meditandi vel scribandi voluptas" [*In Samuel*, IV (*PL*, XCI, 603)]). Bede rarely left his monastery. His trip to Rome is pure legend; see Whiting, "The Life of the Venerable Bede," pp. 12–13.

[126] Cuthbert, his disciple, related Bede's last moments in a famous letter, *De obitu Baedae*, published in *Venerabilis Baedae* . . . , ed. Plummer, 1: clx–clxiv. See also Roger, pp. 306–7.

[127] See Roger, p. 305.

[128] Bede disdained Porfyrius' *carmina figurata*: "Quae quia pagana erant nos tangere non libuit" (*De arte metrica*, ed. Keil, 7: 258). But could not another reason for his distaste be his failure to appreciate literary virtuosity?

[129] Bede, *HE*, V, 20 (p. 332): "Qui in pueritia in clero sanctissimi . . . Boza nutritus atque eruditus est." For Acca, see V. Ermoni, in *DHGE*, 1: 259, and A. S. Cook, "The Old English *Andreas* and Bishop Acca of Hexham," *Connecticut Academy of Arts and Sciences* 26 (1925): 245–332.

[130] Bede, *HE*, V, 20 (pp. 331–32).

[131] Ibid., p. 331: "Historias passionis eorum [martyrum] una cum ceteris ecclesiasticis voluminibus summa industria congregans, amplissimam ibi ac nobilissimam bibliothecam fecit." Acca requested the *Vita Wilfridi* from Eddius (Colgrave ed., p. 2) and a series of exegetical treatises from Bede (*Hexam.*, PL, XCI, 9; *In Samuel*, ibid., 500; *De templo*

taught new chants and corrected those which had become corrupt through the negligence of the clergy.[132]

In this project, Acca was imitating Wilfrid, who also had a master of chant at his Benedictine monastery at Ripon and his bishopric at York[133] and who had undertaken great architectural projects,[134] created a library at York, and established a scriptorium from which perhaps one work has come down to us.[135] At Ripon, he had the four Gospels written in golden letters, a new technique no doubt imported from Rome.[136]

Wilfrid's successors at York, all former monks of Whitby, did not let the school perish. Bishop John of Beverley (686–721), a disciple of Theodore of Canterbury, is depicted by Bede as surrounded by clerics who had come to him to learn to read and to chant.[137] Egbert, a pupil of Bede and brother of the king of Northumbria, became bishop of York in 732. During Egbert's episcopacy York was elevated to the status of a metropolitan see, a rank it had lost since the Roman period; and its episcopal school was at its apogee.[138] Egbert, who was primarily an organizer, confided the direction of the school to his relative Aelbert just at the time that young Alcuin entered the clergy of York.[139]

Alcuin was born about 730 and remained in England until 778, thus spending his youth and adulthood at York.[140] When his former master

---

Salomonis, ibid., 738; *In Esdram*, ibid., 807; *Super Apost.*, ibid., XCII, 937; *In Luc.*, ibid., 301).

[132] Bede, *HE*, V, 20 (p. 331): "Per annos duodecim tenuit, quatenus et quae illi non noverant carmina ecclesiastica doceret et ea quae quondam cognita longo usu vel negligentia inveterare coeperunt, hujus doctrina priscum renovarentur in statum."

[133] Ibid., IV, 2 (p. 205). This was Eddius Stephanus, who was to become the biographer of Wilfrid; see Colgrave ed., *Vita Wilfridi*, p. x.

[134] Eddius, *Vita Wilfridi*, XVI, XVII (Colgrave ed., pp. 32–37); XXII (pp. 44–46).

[135] This would be the Maeseyck Gospels, according to Nordenfalk's hypothesis (Grabar and Nordenfalk, *Le haut Moyen Age*, p. 122).

[136] Eddius, *Vita Wilfridi*, XVII (Colgrave ed., p. 36).

[137] Bede, *HE*, V, 6 (p. 289). One of them, Abbot Heribaldus of Tynemouth, told Bede: "Nam cum primaevo adolescentiae tempore in clero illius degentem legendi quidem canendique studiis traditius."

[138] For Egbert, see the *Vita Alcuini*, 4 (*MGH, SS*, XV-1, 186), a vita from the beginning of the ninth century: "Beati gentis Anglorum Bedae doctissimi discipulo Hechberto traditus." See Roger, pp. 314ff. Bede spent some time in Egbert's monastery; see *Ep. ad Ecgbertum*, ed. Plummer, 1: 405: "Cum tecum aliquot diebus legendi gratia in monasterio tuo demorarer."

[139] Alcuin, *Versus de sanctis Euboricensis eccl.*, ll. 1431–48. Aelbert brought books back from Rome (ibid., ll. 1453–56 [*MGH, PAC*, I, 201]). See also Roger, p. 315, and Emile Lesne, *Les écoles de la fin du VIIIᵉ siècle à la fin du XIIᵉ siècle* (Lille, 1940), pp. 10–12.

[140] For Alcuin's youth, see Arthur Jean Kleinclausz, *Alcuin* (Paris, 1948), p. 22; Manitius, 1: 275; and *Wattenbach-Levison*, 2: 225ff.

Aelbert became bishop, Alcuin took charge of the school, whose fame had spread to the Continent.[141] In a poem which he dedicated to the bishops of York, Alcuin recalled the material that was taught and the authors that were studied in the episcopal school.[142] Roger used this poem to reconstruct the program of the school at York.[143] Perhaps, however, Roger did not see that this work, written in 781–82, was primarily intended to encourage Carolingian men of letters, who at that time were reorganizing Frankish schools. The poem, it seems to me, represents less Alcuin's remembrances than it does a model for a school —thus, this source must be exploited prudently. The library at York was rich: after Alcuin became abbot of Saint Martin of Tours, he wrote to his compatriots that he regretted no longer having the books he knew in his youth.[144] The training he received at the episcopal school determined in great part his literary work. Yet, it would be misleading to make all of Alcuin's learning dependent upon his stay at York. He completed his education during the course of his travels on the Continent to Murbach, Rome, and Pavia.[145] We have already remarked that the lettered men of this period, no matter what their age, were eternal students. Alcuin's travels outside England enabled him to enlarge the framework in which his masters had established the program of their studies.

B. THE CHARACTERISTICS AND LIMITATIONS OF THE ANGLO-SAXON RENAISSANCE

Whether they were influenced by Ireland or Rome, the schoolmasters we have just mentioned all eagerly hoped for a rebirth of studies in their monasteries or bishoprics. What did they accomplish? It has often

---

[141] *Vita Liudgeri*, I, 11 (Diekamp ed., p. 17), notes that young Liudger spent three years at York: "Et mansit ibi annis tribus et mensibus sex proficiens in doctrinae studio."

[142] Alcuin, *Versus*, ll. 1433–1545 (*MGH, PAC*, I, 201–4). For this poem, see Margaret Lee Hargrove, "Alcuin's 'Poem on York,'" *Cornell University Abstracts of Theses . . . 1937* (Ithaca, 1938), pp 20–23.

[143] Roger, pp. 314–15. Instruction at York was geared toward the study of Scripture; see *Versus*, l. 1445 ("Maxime scripturae pandens mysteria sacrae"), and Alcuin, *Ep.* 42 (*MGH, Ep.*, IV, 85: "Vos fragiles infantiae meae annos materno fovistis affectu et lascivum pueritiae tempus pia sustinuistis patientia, et paternae castigationis disciplinis ad perfectam viri edocuistis aetatem et sacrarum eruditione disciplinarum roborastis").

[144] Alcuin, *Ep.* 121 (*MGH, Ep.*, IV, 177, l. 4): "Sed ex parte desunt mihi . . . exquisitiores eruditionis scholasticae libelli, quos habui in patria per bonam et devotissimam magistri mei industriam [vel] etiam mei ipsius qualemcumque sudorem."

[145] Kleinclausz, *Alcuin*, p. 35, dates the trip to 766. Although thirty-six years old at the time, Alcuin said that he was still an *adolescens*: "Dum ego adolescens Romam perrexi et aliquantos dies in Papia regali civitate demorarer" (*MGH, Ep.*, IV, 285).

been said that the Anglo-Saxon renaissance led to the rediscovery of the liberal arts program and that it had revived antique education.[146] We shall see that it did nothing like this.

1. A NEW CONCEPT OF CHRISTIAN CULTURE:
ANGLO-SAXON MASTERS AND THE LIBERAL ARTS

We should note first of all that Aldhelm alone enumerated the liberal arts. Yet he did not follow the order that had been classic since Cassiodorus and Martianus Capella. Rather, under the influence of Irishmen no doubt, he added astrology, mechanics, and medicine to the quadrivium.[147] Whatever Bede might have had to say about the subject,[148] he never spoke of the traditional classification, and his contemporary Boniface also ignored it.[149]

In fact, the scientific knowledge of the Anglo-Saxons was limited to certain well-determined domains. They knew a little arithmetic. Aldhelm tells us that he learned fractions with a great deal of difficulty.[150] The only treatise that bears witness to Bede's taste for calculation is on digital computation.[151] There is no echo in his own work of Boethius or even of Isidore. The Anglo-Saxons were interested only in what Theodore taught at Canterbury: "ecclesiastical arithmetic."[152] But was this arithmology? Actually, except for Aldhelm's *De septenario*—a study of the qualities of the number seven—and a few remarks Bede borrowed from the Fathers,[153] no real research was undertaken in this

---

[146] Louis Halphen, *Les Barbares: Des grandes invasions aux conquêtes turques du XIᵉ siècle*, 3rd rev. ed. (Paris, 1936), p. 236; Gilson, *La philosophie au Moyen Age*, p. 181.

[147] Aldhelm, *De virginitate*, XXXV (*MGH, AA*, XV, 277): "Igitur consummatis grammaticorum studiis et philosophorum disciplinis quae VII speciebus dirimuntur, id est arithmetica, geometrica, musica, astronomia, astrologia, mechanica, medicina." Ibid., LIX (p. 320): "Omnes philosophorum disciplinas hoc est." *De metris*, ibid., p. 71, l. 22: "Saeculares quoque et forasticae philosophorum disciplinae totidem supputationum partibus calculari cernuntur, arithmetica scilicet, geometrica." For the Irish origin of this classification, see B. Bischoff, "Eine verschollene Einteilung der Wissenschaften," *AHMA* 25 (1958): 5–20 (reprinted in idem, *Mittelalterliche Studien*, 1: 273–88).

[148] Roger, p. 320, refers to the *De computo*, which has been wrongly attributed to Bede. See Charles W. Jones, *Bedae pseudepigrapha: Scientific Writings Falsely Attributed to Bede* (Ithaca, 1939), pp. 5–20.

[149] Alcuin defined the seven liberal arts in his *Grammatica*, but this was written much later and on the Continent; see *PL*, CI, 853.

[150] Aldhelm, *Ep.* I (*MGH, AA*, XV, 477): "De ratione vero calculationis quid commemorandum? . . . Difficillima rerum argumenta et calculi supputatione, quas partes numeri appellant, lectionis instantia repperi."

[151] This is incorporated in the *De temporum ratione*, ed. Jones, p. 174.

[152] See above, n. 48.

[153] Aldhelm, *De metris, MGH, AA*, XV, 61ff.; Egbert, *De institutione catholica dialogus*, XVI (*PL*, LXXXIX, 441). For Bede, see the references given by Plummer, *Venerabilis Baedae* . . . , 2: lx–lxi, n. 8.

field. "Ecclesiastical arithmetic" was really the computus used to determine the dates of religious holy days, especially Easter.

The Anglo-Saxons outdid themselves in this discipline. Their manuals (especially Bede's), benefiting from the research that had resulted from the controversy with the Irish, became classics.[154] Bede continued his work even after he wrote his *De temporibus liber* in 703 at the request of his students.[155] For his study of computus, he returned to some ideas he had already touched on in another work, the *De natura rerum*,[156] and considered astronomy and cosmography. The precision with which Bede described meridians, parallels, terrestrial zones, the revolutions of the stars, and especially the mechanism of tides astonished men in the Middle Ages and still surprises us. Unlike his predecessors, he neglected anecdotes concerning plants, beasts, and stars and chose from his authorities—primarily Pliny the Elder—that which appeared to him to be worthy of the science.[157] The erudition dear to men of letters did not tempt Bede. Consequently, his field of view remained quite limited; computus, astronomy, and cosmography comprised the only scientific baggage of the Anglo-Saxons. There was nothing of geometry and very little of medicine.

Of course, medicine was practiced in monasteries but in an empirical fashion.[158] Bede had some medical knowledge which he drew from Pliny and other "naturalium scriptores rerum."[159] Aldhelm too knew certain medical terms.[160] Even if monastic and episcopal libraries still

[154] A. Cordoliani, "Les traités de comput ecclésiastique de 525 à 990" (thesis, University of Paris, 1942). See *Positions de Thèses de l'Ecole Nationale des Chartes* (1942), p. 52; Jones, *Bedae opera*, pp. 165–66; and van de Vyver, "Les étapes," p. 436.

[155] See Bede's preface, ed. Jones, pp. 135–36.

[156] *PL*, XC, 187–278.

[157] K. Welzhöfer, "Beda's Zitate aus der *Naturalis Historia* des Plinius," in *Abhandlungen aus dem Gebiet der klassischen Altertums-Wissenschaft Wilhelm von Christ zum sechzigsten Geburtstag dargebracht* (Munich, 1891), pp. 25–41. Bede described Pliny as "orator et philosophus, solertissimus naturalium inquisitor."

[158] Physicians are mentioned at Lindisfarne (Bede, *Vita Cuthberti*, IV, 7, XXX, XXXII [Colgrave ed., pp. 136, 254, 258]), as well as at Hexham (Eddius, *Vita Wilfridi*, XXIII [Colgrave ed., p. 46]).

[159] The definition of dysentery in the *Retractatio in Actus apost.*, ed. Laistner, p. 145, is taken from Cassius Felix (*Cassii Felicis De medicina*, ed. Valentin Rose [Leipzig, 1879], p. 122). See the discussions of the properties of aloe salt in *In cantica*, IV, 14 (*PL*, XCI, 1148), and of mustard in *In Luc.*, V, 17 (*PL*, XCII, 540). For the development of the embryo, Bede reported what the "naturalium scriptores rerum" had to say: see *Homel.*, II, 1 (*CCL*, 122: 189, l. 193), which is derived from Augustine, *De divers. quaest.*, PL, XL, 39.

[160] See J. D. A. Ogilvy, *Books Known to Anglo-Saxon Writers from Aldhelm to Alcuin* (Cambridge, Mass., 1936), p. 63. Joseph F. Payne has studied Anglo-Saxon medicine (*English Medicine in the Anglo-Saxon Times* [Oxford, 1904]).

contained medical works, they were nevertheless difficult to use. Cyneardus of Winchester wrote to Bishop Lull of Mainz about 760 asking him for medical treatises. He said that they already had some treatises but the medical recipes prescribed by scholars from overseas were unknown to him and difficult to prepare.[161] The learning of foreign physicians—Greeks undoubtedly—could not be applied in England.

Music might have been the subject of individual works, at least the music intended to sing God's glory.[162] Roman chant, as we have seen, had been adopted at Canterbury, Jarrow, York, and Hexham.[163] But no English treatise on musical theory has come down to us. Whenever an abbot or bishop wanted to introduce the study of chant to his school, he did not send for manuscripts but rather for masters who would teach through practice. The sole allusion to a musical work comes from Bede: he related that the archcantor of Saint Peter's in Rome was not content to teach *viva voce* at Jarrow but also left some writings that were later kept in the monastic library.[164] Some think that this might be the *De musica* attributed to Bede, but that hypothesis is difficult to verify.[165]

Passing to the strictly literary realm, we see that the Anglo-Saxons let slip the study of rhetoric and dialectic, retaining only the study of Latin grammar. Aldhelm himself designated the arts of the future trivium with the expression *grammaticorum studia*.[166]

Ancient Latin grammarians such as Donatus, Dositheus, Charisius, and Phocas, as well as their more modern counterparts, Audax, Julian of Toledo, Virgil the Grammarian, and Isidore of Seville, were well represented in monastic and episcopal libraries.[167] But Anglo-Saxons were not content to recopy their works: Aldhelm, Bede, Boniface, and

---

161 Cyneardus of Winchester, *Ep.* 114 (*MGH, Ep.*, III, 403, ll. 16–18): "Si quos saecularis scientiae libros nobis ignotos adepturi sitis—ut sunt de medicinalibus, quorum copia est aliqua apud nos, sed tamen sigmenta ultramarina, quae in eis scripta conperimus, ignota nobis sunt et difficilia ad adipiscendum."

162 Bede, *Hexam.*, II (*PL*, XCI, 74): "Utebantur psalmistae cithara et organo, sed ad laudandum in eis Dominum et e contra arguit propheta eos qui cithara, tympano et lyra in conviviis personabant."

163 See above, sect. II.A.4.

164 Bede, *Vita abb.*, 6 (p. 369): "Qui illo perveniens non solum viva voce quae Romae didicit ecclesiastica discentibus tradidit sed et non pauca etiam litteris mandata reliquit quae hactenus in ejusdem monasterii bibliotheca memoriae gratia servantur."

165 Ogilvy, *Books Known to Anglo-Saxon Writers*, p. 55. According to U. Pizzani, the *De musica theorica* would be a glossed commentary of Boethius' *De institutione musica* ("Uno pseudo trattato dello Pseudo Beda," *Maia* 9 [1957]: 36–48).

166 Aldhelm, *De virginitate (prosa)*, XXXV (*MGH, AA*, XV, 277): "Igitur consummatis grammaticorum studiis et philosophorum disciplinis."

167 Roger, pp. 328–29.

Tatwin all composed their own grammatical treatises. Roger has studied in detail the object of these grammatical investigations: the eight parts of speech, orthography, prosody, metrics, tropes.[168]

This surprising interest in grammar is easily explained. The Anglo-Saxons had to learn Latin as a foreign language, since their own national tongue bore no relation to Latin. In this circumstance, they attached greater importance to practical applications than to speculative questions. Comparing Cassiodorus' *De orthographia* to that of Bede, we notice that the Anglo-Saxon gave his monks a glossary of rare words and synonyms but completely left aside the theories of antique authors on the use of the *h*, doubled letters, the distinction between *v* and *b*, and other such problems.[169] Similarly, Anglo-Saxon masters thought that the works of the fourth and fifth centuries were too complicated and thus adapted their own works to their public.

The study of Greek occupied a very modest place in Anglo-Saxon schools. Bede's enthusiasm for the double culture of the students of Theodore and Hadrian came from a man who could appraise the Hellenism of his contemporaries only with difficulty.[170] Still, Bede was not completely ignorant of Greek: he said that he reviewed and corrected the text of a *Life of Saint Anastasius* that had been badly translated from Greek, which would suggest that he could read a text whose translation he already knew.[171] He also consulted the bilingual copy of the Acts of the Apostles, the *Codex Laudianus* of Oxford,[172] for which he had to use the Greek-Latin glossaries in his library.[173] It could be that he progressed in his study of Greek over the years, but whenever he cited Origen, Basil, or Clement, it was in translation.[174] Aldhelm, Hadrian's student, apparently had a more profound knowledge of

---

[168] Ibid., pp. 319ff. See, more recently, George John Gebauer, *Prolegomena to the Ars grammatica Bonifatii* (Chicago, 1942).

[169] Bede, *De orthographia*, ed. Keil, 7: 261–94.

[170] See above, sect. II.A.1.

[171] Bede, *HE*, V, 24 (p. 359): "Librum vitae et passionis sancti Anastasii male de graeco translatum et pejus a quodam imperito emendatum, prout potui ad sensum correxi."

[172] See M. L. W. Laistner, "The Library of the Venerable Bede," in Thompson, *Bede*, p. 257, and Claude Jenkins, "Bede as Exegete and Theologian," in ibid., pp. 162–63. See *CLA*, II, 251, for this sixth-century manuscript, which undoubtedly came to England at the end of the seventh century.

[173] We still have one of these glossaries; see L. Delaruelle, "Dictionnaire grec-latin de Crastone," *Studi di filologia classica*, n.s. 8 (1931): 228.

[174] Laistner, "The Library," p. 256. We should note an invocation to the Virgin in Greek in a manuscript from Jarrow; see E. A. Lowe, "The Uncial Gospel Leaves Attached to the Utrecht Psalter," *The Art Bulletin* 34 (1952): 237.

Greek. It has been proven that he had the texts of Greek grammarians in his hands.[175] But he could no more penetrate the culture of ancient Greece than could Bede. When he defined the philosophical schools, he repeated expressions that undoubtedly meant little to him: "the sect of Epicurus," "the *taciturnitas* of the Stoics," "Aristotle's categories."[176] These were the pretensions of a man of letters who wished to impose himself on his more ignorant readers. Boniface exhibited the same reflex when he slipped some Greek words into a letter to Nithard.[177] When Alcuin tells us that Athanasius, Basil, and John Chrysostom were studied at York, he certainly had in mind Latin translations that had been circulating in England since Aldhelm's time.[178]

Most of the liberal arts, then, were consciously ignored by educated Anglo-Saxon men. The arts were strangers to them, as Aldhelm expressed it so clearly.[179] We have already said that Jarrow could have become a new Vivarium. Here, we must argue that Bede did not follow Cassiodorus' program.

In his commentary on Esdras, Bede incidentally mentioned Cassiodorus, "formerly a senator, then a doctor of the Church." It is *that* Cassiodorus, the exegete of the Psalms, who alone interested Bede.[180] Thus, Bede placed himself outside the tradition of the Fathers, who had hoped that the liberal arts would be used in the service of Christian thought. He even separated himself from the man the Anglo-Saxons called their "father" and their "pedagogue," Gregory the Great.

[175] Roger, pp. 361–62, 387–90; Ogilvy, *Books Known to Anglo-Saxon Writers*, p. 336. A correspondent of Aldhelm wrote: "Te prestantem ingenio facundia qui Romana etiam Graecorum more" (*MGH, AA*, XV, 237).

[176] In *De virginitate*, XLIV (*MGH, AA*, XV, 296), Aldhelm spoke of the education of Eugenia in the following terms: "Omnes filosoforum sillogismos et Epicuri sectas atque Aristotelis argumenta simulque quinquennem Stoicorum taciturnitatem perfecte juxta sofismatum disciplinas didicisset." Apropos of Chrysantus of Alexandria, he wrote: "Cuncta Stoicorum argumenta et Aristotelicas categorias quae X praedicamentorum generibus distinguuntur" (ibid., XXXV [p. 277]). Bede alluded to the Stoics and Epicureans (see *Expositio Actuum apost.*, XVII, 18 [Laistner ed., p. 65]) and mentioned Plato and Diogenes in his homily for the feast of Saint Benedict (I, 13 [*CCL*, 122: 87]).

[177] See above, n. 89.

[178] Aldhelm, *De virginitate (prosa)*, XXV, XXXII, XXVIII (*MGH, AA*, XV, 257, 273, 265). One of these translations is preserved in London, British Museum, Cotton, Vesp., A, 1 (see *CLA*, II, 193).

[179] Aldhelm, *De metris, MGH, AA*, XV, 71, l. 22: "Saeculare quoque et forasticae philosophorum disciplinae." In his preface to the *De virginitate (carmen)*, Aldhelm repudiated the Muse in the name of rigorism; see *MGH, AA*, XV, 353, vv. 23ff.

[180] Bede, *In Esdram*, II, 6 (*PL*, XCI, 849): "Qualis fuit Cassiodorus quondam senator, repente ecclesiae doctor, qui dum in expositione psalmorum quam egregiam fecit." There is a manuscript of this work at Durham (*CLA*, II, 152).

In his *Commentary on the First Book of Kings,* Gregory legitimized the study of the liberal arts as a propaedeutic.[181] Bede knew this commentary and repeated Gregory's allegory when he did his own exegesis on the Book of Kings. Bede, however, gave the allegory an entirely different meaning. In fact, he condemned Christians who, under the influence of the demon, descended from the heights of God's Word to secular sciences.[182] He did not speak of an inverse movement leading from the liberal arts to God. This should not be surprising in light of Bede's several reminders to his readers that secular literature was noxious. He compared secular letters to the thorns that surround a rose and to the poisonous stinger of bees that one could not study with impunity.[183] Bede recalled that the masters of the Church had incurred the reproach that they were more Ciceronian than Christian.[184] A Christian must not follow the example of Jonathan, who, despite the interdiction of his father, tasted the honey of the forest: these sweets were useless and deceptive.[185]

The disciplines that seemed most dangerous to Bede, as well as to Aldhelm, were rhetoric and dialectic because they were the diabolical weapons used by heretics and philosophers, those "patriarchs of heretics."[186]

It might seem surprising that eighth-century men were still troubled

[181] See above, chap. 5, sect. III.
[182] *In Samuel*, VIII (*PL*, XCI, 583): "Descendunt et hodie nonnulli, relicta altitudine verbi Dei, ad quod audiendum ascendere debuerant, auscultantque fabulis saecularibus, ac doctrinis daemoniorum, et legendo dialecticos, rhetores poetasque gentilium, ad excercendum ingenium terrestre." Bede never cited Gregory.
[183] Ibid., IX (*PL*, XCI, 588): "Ab appetenda saecularis eloquentiae dulcedine abstinere."
[184] Ibid., (*PL*, XCI, 589): "Et nobiles saepe magistri Ecclesiae magnorumque victores certaminum ardentiore quam decet oblectatione libros gentilium lectantes, culpam quam non praevidere contrahebant." He alluded, in a later passage, to Jerome's dream without naming Jerome.
[185] Ibid., II, 9 (*PL*, XCI, 589–90).
[186] *Sup. parab. Salom.*, I, 7 (ibid., 963): "Ornatus eloquentiae et versutia dialecticae artis"; *In Esdram*, ibid., 842: "Sal in palatio comedunt Samarithani cum haeretici sapore mundanae philosophiae cum suavitate rhetoricae, cum versutia dialectae artis instituunt"; *In Samuel*, IV, 10 (ibid., 710): "Unde pulchre quidam nostrorum ait philosophi patriarchae haereticum ecclesiae puritatem perversa maculare doctrina" (Tertullian was obviously meant here; see chap. 3, n. 53). See also *In liber Nehemiae*, III, 28 (ibid., 923), on the vanity of philosophical research; *In cantica*, III, 3, 11 (ibid., 1118); *In Samuel*, IV, 9 (ibid., 706), where he mentioned the controversy between the philosophers and the Fathers at Nicaea, which he found recounted in Socrates' *Ecclesiastical History*, I, 8. Aldhelm alluded to Basil the Great in the following terms: "Rhetoricis sofismatum edoctus disciplinis" (*De virginitate* [*prosa*], XXVII [*MGH, AA*, XV, 263]). Concerning Daria, he wrote: "Dialecticis artibus imbuta et captiosis syllogismi conclusionibus instructa" (ibid., p. 278).

by the errors of philosophy, when the study of philosophy had been practically abandoned in the West. Neither Bede nor Aldhelm had any philosophical culture, and yet they feared philosophy and its daughter, heresy, as real dangers. Did they share the reasons of the seventh-century popes? The theological innovations of the Greeks did not have great repercussions in England, and the arrival of an Easterner to the see of Canterbury did not provoke a revival of philosophical thought.[187] If Theodore received the surname of "philosopher" from his contemporaries, it was primarily because of his great learning and his knowledge of Greek.[188] What preoccupied Bede more was a resurgence of Pelagianism in ecclesiastical circles. He inserted in his *History* a letter that Pope John IV wrote to the Celtic clergy in 640 on this subject.[189] This heresy must still have been in existence a century later because Bede denounced it several times[190] and thought it necessary to respond to Pelagius' *De amore* in a work called *De gratia Dei*.[191]

Lettered Anglo-Saxons were just as condemnatory when it came to natural philosophy because they feared pagan mythographical and astrological deviations which might result from the study of the "nature of things."[192] Even Isidore of Seville's scientific works were suspect. Bede redid a *De natura rerum* under the influence of Isidore's work, but he wanted to write a treatise which was more descriptive than explicative. Toward the end of his life, Bede returned once again to Isidore's treatise to draw extracts from it, "so that his disciples would not read lies and would not work without profit."[193] This is a clear expres-

---

[187] Bede, *HE*, IV, 15 (17)–16 (18) (pp. 238–42), simply noted without comment the Council of Heathfield of 680.

[188] Aldhelm, *Ep.* 5 (*MGH, AA*, XV, 492): "Id est Theodoro . . . ab ipso tirocinio rudimentorum in flore philosophiae artis adulto." Bede, *Vita abb.*, 3 (p. 366): "Theodorum videlicet saeculari simul et ecclesiastica philosophia praeditum virum." Pope Agatho accorded him the same title; see *PL*, LXXXVII, 1224.

[189] Bede, *HE*, II, 19 (p. 123).

[190] Bede, *In primam epistolam sancti Joannis*, PL, XCIII, 119; *In Esdram*, II, 8 (*PL*, XCI, 855).

[191] Bede, *In cantica*, PL, XCI, 1066ff. Bede thought that Julian of Eclanum was responsible for the *De amore*. For this treatise, see Jenkins, "Bede as Exegete and Theologian," in Thompson, *Bede*, pp. 184–85.

[192] Bede was openly hostile toward astrology; see *De temporum ratione*, ed. Jones, p. 183. The *De planetarum et signorum ratione*, which has been wrongly attributed to Bede, perhaps issued from a Northumbrian school; see Jones, *Bedae pseudepigrapha*, p. 86.

[193] Cuthbert, *De obitu Baedae*, ed. Plummer, *Venerabilis Baedae . . .* , 1: clxii: "Et de libris [rotarum] Isidori episcopi excerptiones quasdam dicens: Nolo ut discipuli mei mendacium legant et in hoc post obitum meum sine fructu laborent." As Fontaine proved in his edition of Isidore's *De natura rerum* (pp. 79–80), a chapter was added to Isidore's work in the eighth century. Fontaine thinks that it is more probable that the addition

sion of Bede's criticism of the Sevillian for what Bede thought was an abuse of the allegorical genre and for digressions that were still too close to the cosmic system of the pagans. We should note, however, that except for the *De natura rerum* and *Origines*,[194] Isidore's work was almost entirely unknown to Bede. At one point, apropos of the calendar, he even affirmed that he preferred the Roman interpretation to that of the Spaniard.[195]

Bede, unlike certain Eastern and Irish exegetes, did not try to bring his scientific learning to bear on the clarification of the sacred text. For him the sole explanation for the miracles recounted in the Bible was the direct intervention of God. For example, having explained the passage in the Epistle in which Saint Paul recalls his stay in the depths of the sea, he remarked that Theodore of Canterbury compared this text to the chasm of Cyzicus into which criminals were pitched. But he refused to embellish this scientific interpretation and compared Paul at the bottom of the sea to Peter who walked on the waters.[196]

We can now better define the principles that inspired the program of Anglo-Saxon masters. They affirmed even more strongly than their predecessors that the Bible was superior to all other texts, "not only by authority, since it is divine, or because of its usefulness, since it leads to eternal life, but even more by its antiquity and its form."[197] Since it contains all literary genres, it was necessary to study grammar, the only liberal art worthy of interest, in order to appreciate all its richness. "Especially apply yourself unceasingly to the reading of the Bible and sacred texts," Aldhelm wrote to his disciple Aethilwald. "If in addition you want to know something about secular literature, do so with the following goal in mind: since in the Scriptures all or nearly all the sequence of words rests on grammar, you will comprehend all the more

---

was made by Irishmen than by Anglo-Saxons. I must disagree, however, with his argument that Cuthbert alluded to a translation of the *De natura rerum* (p. 79). The allusion is to extracts of the work.

[194] Although Bede used these works, he never cited their author's name. A manuscript of the *Origines* was recopied in Northumbria; see *CLA*, II, 559. Laistner, "The Library of Venerable Bede," in Thompson, *Bede*, p. 256, has already noted that Bede treated Isidore "with more freedom or less respect than his other authorities."

[195] Bede, *De temporum ratione*, XXXV (Jones ed., p. 247): "Romani, quorum in hujus modi disciplinis potius quam hispanorum auctoritatem sequi consuevit."

[196] Bede, *Quaest. liber*, II (*PL*, XCIII, 456). Paul Lehmann noted this passage in his *Wert und Echtheit einer Beda abgesprochenen Schrift*, Sitz. der Bayerischen Akad. der Wissenschaften, Ph. Hist. Klasse, 4 (Munich, 1919), pp. 4ff. For the "rationalist" interpretation of the Irish, see Beryl Smalley, *The Study of the Bible*, p. 35.

[197] Bede, *Liber de schematibus et tropis*, in *Rhetorici latini minores*, ed. Karl Halm (Leipzig, 1863), p. 607 (also in *PL*, XC, 175).

easily the deeper and more sacred sense of this divine language when you have learned the very diverse rules of the art of forming its thread."[198] This famous text can be joined to the statements of Bede and Boniface underscoring the importance of grammatical studies for the study of the sacred text.[199]

Detached from the other branches of the future trivium, grammar was now Christianized. The examples from classical authors that had to be known, isolated from their contexts, were no longer noxious for the monk, who only retained the mechanics of their construction. The verses of pagan poets, which were still feared as dangerous,[200] were neutralized in grammatical treatises when used to illustrate the mechanism of the language.[201] Bede read the classics but did not experience them as literary works. He borrowed only their clarity and correctness of style. He was a poet, but he placed his talent in the service of God and the saints. Far from plagiarizing the pagans, as had the representatives of Christian classical culture,[202] he created a new Christian religious poetry, as had the Irishmen before him.[203]

The interest the Anglo-Saxons had in scientific research was also dictated by religious preoccupations. They left aside theoretical concerns, retaining only the sciences useful in fixing the time and the calendar: astronomy, cosmography, and computus. But as a result, they reconstructed a scientific program around the *ratio temporum*, which no longer existed in the antique school.

---

[198] Aldhelm, *Ep.* 8 (11) (*MGH, AA*, XV, 500): "Sed multo magis . . . vel lectionibus divinis vel orationibus sacris semper invigila! Si quid vero praeterea saecularium litterarum nosse laboras ea tantummodo causa id facias ut, quoniam in lege divina vel omnis vel paene omnis verborum textus artis omnino grammaticae ratione consistit, tanto ejusdem eloquii divini profundissimos atque sacratissimos sensus facilius legendo intelligas, quanto illius rationis qua contexitur diversissimas regulas plenius ante didiceris."

I cannot follow Roger's translation, p. 300. *Lectio divina* refers to the Bible and not to "divine readings"; *oratio* does not mean "prayer." *Lex divina*, which Roger does not translate, could refer to the Scriptures; see Aldhelm, *Ep.*, ibid., pp. 73, 78, 157, 311, etc.

[199] Bede, *De arte metrica*, ed. Keil, 7: 260, preface: "Parvum subicere libellum non incongruum duxi, tuamque dilectionem sedulus exoro ut lectioni operam impendas illarum maxime litterarum in quibus nos vitam habere credimus sempiternam." Boniface, *Ep.* 9 (*MGH, Ep.*, III, 250, ll. 14ff.); preface to the *Ars grammatica, MGH, Ep.*, IV, 564–65: "Quia peritia grammaticae artis in sacro sancto scrutinio laborantibus ad subtiliorem intellectum."

[200] Aldhelm warned one of his correspondents about the evils of mythological tables (*MGH, AA*, XV, 479).

[201] See Bede, *Hexam.*, I (*PL*, XCI, 29). Laistner, "Bede as a Classical and Patristic Scholar," *Transactions of the Royal Historical Society* 16 (1933): 73, has collected Bede's Virgilian references.

[202] See above, chap. 3, sect. I.

[203] For Bede's poems, see Raby, *A History of Christian Latin Poetry*, p. 148.

It cannot be said that the Anglo-Saxons had "passed on a mutilated Antiquity," for they did not wish to be the heirs of the Ancients.[204] What Gregory the Great called the *exteriora studia*, that is, the program of the liberal arts, had no meaning for them. As Boniface said in the preface to his grammatical treatise, no knowledge can exist outside the circle of the faith.[205] The only culture worthy of existence was religious culture.

In organizing their studies by abandoning an entire portion of the antique program, the Anglo-Saxon masters freed themselves from the equivocacy that we have noted in studying the culture of Cassiodorus and Isidore. The conditions under which they lived facilitated this break. Cassiodorus, Isidore, and Gregory the Great lived in an atmosphere charged completely with Roman civilization. They were monks and clerics, but first of all, they were Romans. The men of letters in England, on the contrary, were cut off from this milieu. The evangelization of England recreated the bonds between Rome and the island, but the *Romanitas* that the Anglo-Saxons knew was artificial: a civilization cannot be reconstructed on the basis of books and works of art.

Also, educated Anglo-Saxon men were as far from the ascetic culture of Eastern monasticism as they were from the humanistic culture of Cassiodorus and Isidore. They organized a new kind of Christian studies and offered their contemporaries and successors a formula that would contribute to the building of medieval culture.

2. THE LIMITED INFLUENCE OF EDUCATED ANGLO-SAXONS

As was true everywhere else during the period, the Anglo-Saxon intellectual renewal touched only an elite. We know of only about twenty episcopal and monastic centers where culture was favored. Furthermore, not all clerics and monks in these centers were lettered. Bede certainly did not teach all the six hundred monks who comprised the community at Jarrow.[206] He spoke of the "simplices fratres" whom lettered monks should not scorn and of the "illitterati" who could be taught by the pictures in church.[207] One must imagine Bede at work

[204] Roger, p. 309. The *Vita Leobae*, although written in the ninth century, leads to the same conclusion. The nun used the grammatical learning she acquired as a child in order to penetrate better the sacred text.

[205] The preface was published by Paul Lehmann in *Hist. Vierteljahrschrift* 26 (1931): 755, and analyzed by Leclercq in his *L'amour des lettres*, pp. 42–43. W. A. Eckhardt has studied an eighth-century manuscript of Boniface's *Ars grammatica* ("Das Kaufinger Fragment der Bonifatius-Grammatik," *Scriptorium* 23 [1969]: 280–97).

[206] Roger, p. 306.

[207] Bede, *Sup. parab. Salom.*, II, 20 (PL, XCI, 997): "Nemo cum scripturarum se

in his cell in the midst of a few disciples and even then sometimes having difficulty finding help.[208] If it was like this at Jarrow, the situation must have been worse elsewhere. Bede complained about his compatriots' lack of zeal.[209] Every time he mentioned a learned person, he did not neglect to insist on his intellectual qualities. Whenever he described a monastery without stating exactly what kinds of studies the monks there pursued, we can conclude that they were content with the daily office and the simple reading of the Bible.[210]

But is not that itself a sign of vitality? We should not forget that England, like Gaul during the same period, had experienced a serious religious crisis. Many Anglo-Saxon monasteries were family possessions and suffered from lay interference—Bede complained of this in 734 in his famous letter to Egbert of York.[211] Thirteen years later Boniface drew a dark picture of monasticism and of the Church of England in general and asked Cuthbert of Canterbury to imitate the Frankish clergy's efforts at reform.[212] Reading the acts of the Council of Cloveshoe in 747, we can see just how far the intellectual and moral decadence of the English clergy extended. Bishops and monks forgot their responsibilities as pastors and led the life of laymen: they fought, married, and took in poets and musicians.[213]

The reformers demanded very little of the clerics: it sufficed that they know how to preach, baptize, and give penance.[214] They did not even require them to know Latin. Bede spoke of priests who knew only their mother tongue and was not scandalized by the fact.[215] Some monks

---

scientiae institutum et ad dicendum verbum Dei viderit idoneum, despiciat simplicitatem fratris"; *Vita abb.*, 6 (pp. 369–70): "Quatenus intrantes ecclesiam omnes etiam litterarum ignari . . . contemplarentur aspectum."

[208] Bede, *Ep. ad Accam*, PL, XCII, 304, noted that he had to fulfill the obligations of a *dictator, notarius,* and *librarius* all at the same time.

[209] Bede, *Explanatio Apocalypsis*, PL, XCIII, 134: "Nostrae siquidem id est Anglorum gentis, inertiae consulendum ratus . . . et idem quantum ad lectionem tepide satis excoluit."

[210] As in the case of Ely (*HE*, IV, 17 [19] [p. 244]) and Tunnacaestir (ibid., 20 [22] [p. 250]).

[211] Bede, *Ep. ad Ecgbertum*, 11–17 (Plummer ed., pp. 414–18). See T. Allison, *English Religious Life in the Eighth Century* (London, 1929).

[212] *MGH, Ep.*, III, 350ff.

[213] Allison, *English Religious Life*, pp. 104ff. See the Council of Cloveshoe, ed. Haddan-Stubbs, 3: 364, c. 7 ("De lectionis studio per singula monasteria") and c. 12 (against priests who "saecularium poetarum modo in ecclesia garriant").

[214] Council of Cloveshoe, 6 (Haddan-Stubbs ed., 3: 364): "Qua . . . potest ratione aliis integritatem fidei praedicare, sermonis scientiam conferre, peccantibus discretionem poenitentiae indicare."

[215] Bede, *Ep. ad Ecgbertum*, ed. Plummer, p. 409: "Sed idiotas, hoc est eos qui

recited the Psalms even though ignorant of Latin.[216] Priests were to explain the Credo and the text of the mass in the vulgar tongue.[217] Thus, the Anglo-Saxon clergy could be content with a very superficial Latin culture or practically none at all. In this respect, they were as uncultured as the majority of laymen.

We must, indeed, distinguish two categories of laymen. One, a very small group, had been raised as in the previous century, in monasteries and episcopal schools.[218] There, they learned enough Latin to read hagiographical and historical works and to exchange letters with abbots and bishops.[219]

King Ceolwulf, to whom Bede sent the rough draft of his *Ecclesiastical History*, was interested in Holy Scripture and in the Deeds of the Ancients.[220] King Aelfwald of East Anglia requested the monk Felix to write the *Life of Saint Guthlac*, and Aethilbert II of Kent corresponded with Boniface.[221] Certain princes even wanted to compete in learning with the most lettered monks. We know of the cases of Aelfred of Northumbria and Aethilwald of Mercia. The former, raised at first in Ireland, had spent some time with Aldhelm[222] and was especially interested in exegesis and geography. In exchange for a few parcels of land, he obtained from Abbot Ceolfrid a magnificent cosmographical

---

propriae tantum linguae notitiam habent. . . . Propter quod et . . . multis saepe sacerdotibus idiotis."

[216] Council of Cloveshoe, 10 (Haddan-Stubbs ed., 3: 366): "Quamvis psallendo latina quis nesciat verba . . . ; et lingua latina vel qui eam non didicerunt sua saxonica dicunt."

[217] Ibid.: "Ut presbyteri quoque symbolum et missarum verba in sua lingua discant scire: Interpretari atque exponere posse propria lingua qui nesciant, discant."

[218] As at York in Alcuin's time: "Erat siquidem ei ex nobilium filiis grex scholasticorum quorum quidam artis grammaticae rudimentis, alii disciplinis erudiebantur artium jam liberalium, nonnulli divinarum Scripturarum" (*Vita Alcuini*, 2 [*PL*, C, 93]). The same was true in John of Beverley's time; see Bede, *HE*, V, 6 (p. 289): "Coeperuntque juvenes, qui cum ipso erant, maxime laici."

[219] Bede wrote his *Historia* for laymen. *HE*, V, 13 (p. 313), bears an allusion to a lettered layman: "Hanc historiam . . . simpliciter ob salutem legentium sive audientium narrandam esse putavi." The story concerned a layman who had not corrected the errors of his youth.

[220] Bede, *HE*, preface (p. 5): "Et prius ad legendum ac probandum transmisi et nunc ad transcribendum ac plenius ex tempore meditandum retransmitto: satisque studium tuae sinceritas amplector quo non solum audiendes Scripturae sanctae verbis aurem sedulus accommodas, verum etiam noscendis priorum gestis sive dictis et maxime nostrae gentis virorum illustrium, curam vigilanter impendis."

[221] Felix, *Vita Guthlachi*, preface (Colgrave ed., p. 60); Aethilbert II, *Ep.* 105 (*MGH*, *Ep.*, III, 391).

[222] Bede, *Vita Cuthberti*, XXIV (Colgrave ed., p. 236); *HE*, IV, 24 (26) (p. 268): "Vir in scripturis doctissimus"; Aldhelm, *De metris, pref. ad. Acircium* [Aelfred], *MGH*, *AA*, XV, 61–62. See V. H. Galbraith, "The Literacy of the Medieval English Kings," *Proceedings of the British Academy* 21 (1935): 207ff.

manuscript that Benedict had bought in Rome.[223] When his first teach-er, Adamnan of Iona, paid him a visit, the master gave him a copy of his *De locis sanctis*.[224] King Aethilwald of Mercia, another student of Aldhelm, took great pleasure in the poetry and verbal prowess so dear to the Malmesbury school.[225] These princes were not cultural patrons in the mold of Maecenas. On the contrary, they were good students of clerics and monks who would have become, if circumstances had per-mitted, monks and abbots themselves.[226]

Beyond this minority, consisting primarily of princes, other laymen were strangers to Latin literature.[227] The only culture they could ac-quire came from the old national sources, which in Celtic and Anglo-Saxon lands were not relegated to the background, as they were in the continental kingdoms. The magical, incantorial, moral, and epic poems that have come down to us presuppose a quite varied public.[228] Princely courts welcomed poets, the scops, to whom credit must be given for perpetuating these literary traditions.[229] During the first half of the eighth century, *Beowulf* was composed in Northumbria, perhaps in Aelfred's court, for the education of a young prince.[230] In this context

[223] Bede, *Vita abb.*, 15 (p. 380): "Dato quoque cosmographorum codice mirandi operis quem Romae Benedictus emerat, terram octo familiarum . . . ab Aldfrido rege in scripturis doctissimo in possessionem monasterii beati Pauli apostoli comparavit."

[224] *HE*, V, 15 (p. 317). Aelfred gave it to the young people in his entourage as a gift: "Porrexit autem librum hunc Adamnan Aldfrido regi ac per ejus est largitionem etiam minoribus ad legendum contraditus."

[225] See above, sect. II.A.2., and Ingeborg Schröbler, "Zu den *Carmina rhythmica* in der Wiener Handschrift der Bonifatiusbriefe (*Monum. Germ. AA* XV, 517ff.): Oder über den Strabreim in der lateinischen Poesie der Angelsachsen," *Beiträge zur Geschichte der deutschen Sprache und Literatur* 79 (1957): 2.

[226] Some princes, in fact, retired to monasteries: Ceolwulf (died 737) went to Lindis-farne; Caedwalla of Mercia and Offa of Essex went to Rome. See Bede, *HE*, V, 7 and 19 (pp. 292, 322).

[227] Some were illiterate. Frithuwold, a chieftain from Surrey, signed a document with a cross "pro ignorantia litterarum" (see Walter de Gray Birch, *Cartularium saxonicum* [London, 1885], I, no. 34). We have only copies of charters from this period; see Levison, *England*, pp. 174–233, and F. M. Stenton, *The Latin Charters of the Anglo-Saxon Period* (Oxford, 1955).

[228] For the national literature, see Alois L. Brandl, *Geschichte der altenglischen Literatur* (Strasbourg, 1908), and H. Munro Chadwick and N. Kershaw Chadwick, *The Growth of Literature*, 3 vols. (Cambridge, 1932–40), I: 445. For magical poems, see Felix Grendon, "The Anglo-Saxon Charms," *Journal of American Folklore* 22 (1909): 105–237, and *CBEL*, I: 898.

[229] Lewis F. Anderson, *The Anglo-Saxon Scop*, University of Toronto Studies, Phil-ological Series, no. 1 (Toronto, 1903); R. L. Reynolds, "Le poème anglo-saxon Widsith: Réalité et fiction," *MA* 59 (1953): 302.

[230] Raymond W. Chambers, *Beowulf: An Introduction to the Study of the Poem, with a Discussion of the Stories of Offa and Finn*, with a supplement by C. L. Wrenn, 3rd ed.

the scops filled the role of pedagogue. The *Exeter Book* has even preserved "instructions of a father to his son," a kind of "mirror for princes" like those known in Ireland during the same period.[231]

The national literature was transmitted orally until the seventh century.[232] In the eighth century, it began to be collected in written form, a process in which clerics most likely played an important role. Latin and vernacular literature did, in fact, have more than one point in common: the enigmas of the *Exeter Book* seem to have been adaptations of Latin enigmas.[233] Moral and biblical poems were inspired by clerical themes.[234] *Beowulf* itself was perhaps the product of a cleric who knew the ancient epic as well as Latin teratological literature.[235] In fact, the metaphors of *Beowulf* bring to mind those of hisperic literature.[236] Finally, Bede himself saw a connection between the meter of Anglo-Saxon poems and that of clerics who adapted Latin to rhythmic verse.[237]

Anglo-Saxon clerics, then, like their Irish colleagues,[238] helped to develop a national culture. In the middle of the eighth century, some priests were so excited about profane poetry that they had it recited in

---

(Cambridge, 1959), p. 489. See Ritchie Girvan, *Beowulf and the Seventh Century: Language and Content* (London, 1935), and A. Bonjour, "Beowulf et l'épopée anglo-saxonne," *La Table Ronde: l'Epopée vivante* 132 (1958): 140ff.

[231] *Exeter Book*, VIII, 10, in *The Exeter Book: An Anthology of Anglo-Saxon Poetry Presented to Exeter Cathedral by Leofric, First Bishop of Exeter (1050–1071)* . . . , 2 vols., Early English Text Society, original ser., 104, 194, ed. and trans. Israel Gollancz (London, 1895–1934), 1: 301–5. For gnomic poetry, see H. M. Chadwick and N. K. Chadwick, *The Growth of Literature*, 1: 377ff.; for Irish gnomic literature, see R. I. Best, *Bibliography of Irish Philology and of Printed Irish Literature* (Dublin, 1913), p. 263.

[232] Francis P. Magoun, Jr., "The Oral-Formulaic Character of Anglo-Saxon Narrative Poetry," *Speculum* 28 (1953): 446ff.

[233] See *CBEL,* 1: 81; trans. in R. K. Gordon, comp. and trans., *Anglo-Saxon Poetry* (London, 1927), pp. 320–40. The same Leiden manuscript, *Voss.* 106, contains the enigmas of Aldhelm and Symphosius as well as some Anglo-Saxon enigmas.

[234] One of the passages in Cynewulf's poem "The Christ" borrows from a sermon of Caesarius of Arles; see *The Christ of Cynewulf: A Poem in Three Parts (The Advent, The Ascension, and the Last Judgment)*, ed. Albert S. Cook (Boston, 1900), vv. 1380–1515.

[235] For the relationship between *Beowulf* and ancient epic poetry, see J. R. Hulbert, "Beowulf and the Classical Epic," *Modern Philology* 44 (1946): 65–67. The author may have known the eighth-century *Liber monstrorum de diversis generibus*, which perhaps came from Ireland; see Manitius, 1: 114–18.

[236] For the metaphors in *Beowulf*, see Fernand Mossé, *Manuel de l'anglais au Moyen Age des origines au XIVᵉ siècle*, vol. 1, *Vieil-anglais* (Paris, 1945), p. 176.

[237] Bede, *De arte metrica*, ed. Keil, 7: 258: "Videtur autem rhythmis metris esse consimilis, quae est verborum modulata compositio, non metrica ratione sed numero syllaborum ad judicium aurium examinate, ut sunt carmina vulgarium poetarum."

[238] James Carney, *Studies in Irish Literature and History* (Dublin, 1955).

the churches. Poets and musicians were quite welcome in monasteries. Councils had to intervene in order to stop these abuses.[239]

The Anglo-Saxon Church, in addition, went beyond prohibitions and encouraged the creation of poetry in the vulgar tongue to turn clerics and laymen from certain pagan poems. Bede reported how the shepherd Caedmon was patronized by the abbess of Whitby. She had him admitted among the monks to be taught Divine Scripture so that he could transcribe it poetically into Anglo-Saxon.[240] In relating this episode, Bede contrasted this sacred poet to those who acquired the *ars cantandi* but used it only for profane songs.[241] Bede himself recited poems to his monks in Anglo-Saxon.[242] According to William of Malmesbury, Aldhelm gained the esteem of his diocesans by singing popular songs which he gradually Christianized.[243] From this period on, further advances were made, and even holy texts were literally translated. Shortly before his death, Bede had begun the translation of the Gospel of John, thus beginning an enterprise that others were to take up after him.[244]

We can now place the "Anglo-Saxon renewal" in proper perspective. An elite of monks and clerics defined the principles of a new Christian

[239] Council of Cloveshoe, 12 (Haddan-Stubbs ed., 3: 366): "Presbyteri saecularium poetarum modo in ecclesia . . . garriant [et] tragico sono sacrorum verborum compositionem ac distinctionem corrumpant vel confundant." See ibid., 20 (p. 369), against the "poetae, citharistae, musici," who populated the monasteries. The Roman synod of 680 had already denounced bishops for having citharists and players and had forbidden the practice; see Mansi, XI, 279. The taste for music and profane poetry was introduced to Jarrow during the abbacy of Cuthbert, who, embarrassed, asked Lull for a citharist (*PL*, XCVI, 839). See Alcuin's letter to Hygebald of Lindisfarne, *MGH, Ep.*, IV, 183, l. 12.

[240] For Caedmon's poems, see *CBEL*, 1: 73, and Charles L. Wrenn, *The Poetry of Caedmon* (London, 1947). The only poem to come down to us from Caedmon is the hymn published by A. H. Smith in *Three Northumbrian Poems: Caedmon's Hymn, Bede's Death Song, and the Leiden Riddle* (London, 1933; New York, 1968), pp. 38–41. For Caedmon, see M. M. Larès, "Echos d'un rite hiérosolymitain dans un manuscrit du haut moyen âge anglais," *Revue de l'histoire des religions* 165 (1964): 15.

[241] Bede, *HE*, IV, 22 (24) (p. 259): "Unde nihil unquam frivoli et supervacui poematis facere potuit, sed ea tantummodo quae ad religionem pertinent, religiosam ejus linguam decebant."

[242] Cuthbert, *De obitu Baedae*, ed. Plummer, *Venerabilis Baedae* . . . , 1: clxi: "In nostra quoque lingua, ut erat doctus in nostris carminibus dicens." It is thought that Bede composed five verses before his death. See Smith, *Three Northumbrian Poems*, pp. 42–43, and Elliott van Kirk Dobbie, *The Manuscripts of Caedmon's Hymn and Bede's Death Song, With a Critical Text of the "Epistola Cuthberti de obitu Bedae,"* Columbia University Studies in English and Comparative Literature, no. 128 (New York, 1937).

[243] William of Malmesbury, *De gestis pontificum Anglorum libri quinque*, V, 191, ed. N. E. S. A. Hamilton (London, 1870).

[244] Cuthbert, *De obitu Baedae*, ed. Plummer, *Venerabilis Baedae* . . . , 1: clxii: "Evangelium sancti Johannis in nostram linguam ad utilitatem ecclesiae Dei convertit." See Lancelot Minor Harris, *Studies in the Anglo-Saxon Version of the Gospels, Part I: The Form of the Latin Original and Mistaken Renderings* (Baltimore, 1901), and *CBEL*, 1: 95.

culture but were followed by only a few lay princes. The great mass of the regular and secular clergy did not have access to Latin culture and thus shared the culture of the majority of laymen. We are already witnessing a very medieval ambiance.

III. ITALIAN SCHOOLS IN THE EIGHTH CENTURY

A. Ascetic Culture in Italian Monasteries

Contrary to what we might have expected, Italian monastic culture of the first half of the eighth century did not attain the high level of Anglo-Saxon culture. The Italian monasteries, which had contributed so much to the West, were thwarted in their development by the Lombard invasion. At the end of the seventh century, Lombard princes piously strove to restore or found monastic centers (see Map 13), but these were still only centers of ascetic culture.

Duke Abbo, son of the bishop of Turin, founded the monastery of Novaliciensum in 726 near Susa in the Lombard kingdom on the border of the Frankish kingdom;[245] King Liutprand encouraged the creation of monasteries; Guidoald, his physician, established monks at Pistoia;[246] a certain Angelpert founded the monastery of Civate on Lake Como;[247] in 735 Duke Anselm of Friuli founded Nonantola;[248] in the duchy of Spoleto at the end of the seventh century, Faraoald II restored Ferentillo;[249] and Thomas of Maurienne settled at Farfa.[250] Three young monks left Farfa to establish a religious center among the still pagan Bulgarians and organized a monastery at the mouth of the Volturno in the duchy of Beneventum.[251]

---

[245] See *Monumenta novaliciensia vetustiora: Raccolta degli atti e delle cronache riguardanti l'abbazia della Novalesa*, ed. Carlo Cipolla, Fonti per la storia d'Italia, vols. 31–32 (Rome, 1898–1901). According to Luciano Gulli, this monastery was founded quite a bit later ("A proposito della più antica tradizione novalicense," *Archivio storico italiano* 117 [1959]: 306–18).

[246] *CDL*, II, no. 206, year 767.

[247] For Civate, see Cottineau, 1: 791–92, and Carlo Marcora, *L'abbazia benedittina di Civate* (Civate, 1947).

[248] *De fundatione monasterii Nonantulani*, MGH, SRL, p. 570.

[249] Cottineau, 1: 1124. Faraoald was buried there in an antique third-century sacrophagus; see Carlo Pietrangeli, "I sarcofagi romani dell'abbazia longobarda di Ferentillo," *Atti del I Congresso*, p. 451.

[250] *Il Chronicon farfense di Gregorio di Catino: Precedono la Constructio farfensis e gli scritti di Ugo di Farfa*, ed. Ugo Balzani, Fonti per la storia d'Italia pub. dall'Istituto storico italiano: Scrittori secoli IX–XII, nos. 33–34, 2 vols. (Rome, 1903), 1: 122.

[251] Vincenzo D'Amico, "Importanza della immigrazione dei bulgari nell'Italia meridionale al tempo dei longobardi e dei bizantini," *Atti del III Congresso*, p. 370; *Chroni-*

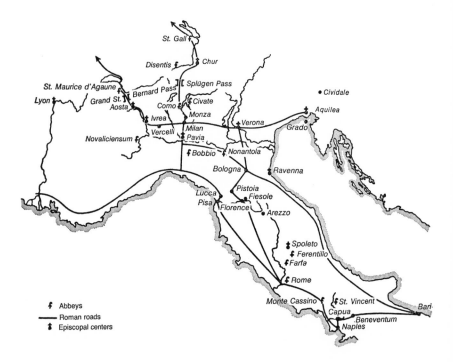

13. Cultural Centers in Northern and Central Italy in the Eighth Century

These monasteries all followed the Benedictine *Rule* and adopted a way of life very close to that of sixth-century abbeys.[252] The education which the abbots provided for children entrusted to them is reminiscent of that the *pueri* received at Monte Cassino under Benedict. Lucerius, the second abbot of Farfa, learned "sacred literature" from his master, Abbot Thomas.[253] Frodoin, son of a Lombard aristocrat and future abbot of Novaliciensum, was introduced to *scientia litterarum* in this monastery.[254] Farfa would have to await the arrival of Alan (761–70), an Aquitainian, before its scriptorium would produce beautiful manuscripts, such as its collection of homilies, which rapidly gained wide acceptance.[255] Saint Vincent (Volturno) would also emerge as a cultural center only with the abbacy of Ambrosius Autpertus (died 784), a Frank.[256] Nonantola, whose scriptorium would be active at the end of the eighth century, was culturally insignificant.[257]

The restoration, around 720, of Benedict's Monte Cassino, which had been abandoned after the Lombard invasion of 580, provided the new monasteries with a model of monastic observance. Petronax, a Lombard from Brescia, and Pope Gregory II were responsible for the restoration.[258] Gregory II, like his illustrious homonym, was a pope-monk: he converted his home into a monastery, surrounded himself with monks

---

con *vulturnense,* I, 133, in *Chronicon vulturnense del monaco Giovanni,* ed. Vincenzo Federici, Fonti per la storia d'Italia, vol. 58 (Rome, 1925).

[252] See the foundation charter of Novaliciensum in *Monumenta novaliciensia vetustiora,* ed. Cipolla, 1: 7ff. For the establishment of the monastery of Pistoia, see the foundation diploma in *CDL,* II, no. 206.

[253] *Il Chronicon farfense,* ed. Balzani, 1: 16ff.: "Lucerius quem ipse sanctae recordationis Thomas puerum enutrivit ac sacris litteris erudire curavit." See *Il regesto di Farfa compilato da Gregorio di Catino,* ed. Ignazio Giorgi and Ugo Balzani, 5 vols. (Rome, 1879–1914), no. 25: "Ita ut filii nostri ibi tenderent, et in ejus traderentur servitio, et ad discendum litteras."

[254] *Monumenta novaliciensia vetustiora,* ed. Cipolla, 2: 171: "Filio quem tradidit monastico ordini erudiendum nutritis vero idem puer, hoc eruditus in omnia scientia litterarum, sive in cunctis in quibus doceri cum oportuerat factusque juvenis."

[255] *Il Chronicon farfense,* ed. Balzani, 1: 31–36: "Qui tam spiritualis philosophiae quam etiam saeculariter astutiae prudentissimus fuit . . . multa etiam mirifice exaravit codices." For the Farfa Homilary, see E. Hops, "Il sermonario de Alano di Farfa," *EL* 50 (1936): 375–83; 51 (1937): 210–40.

[256] Ambrosius was born in Gaul, perhaps in Provence. See Jacques Winandy, *Ambroise Autpert, moine et théologien* (Paris, 1953), and C. Leonardi, "Spiritualità di Ambrogio Autperto," *SM,* 3rd ser. 9 (1968): 1–131. Abbot Atto (736–60), Ambrosius' predecessor, had an evangeliary copied (*CLA,* I, 162).

[257] Some paleographers consider Nonantola one of the centers that evolved pre-Carolingian script in Italy; see G. Cencetti, "Scriptoria e scritture nel monachesimo benedettino," *Settimane,* 4: 200ff. But this center developed only toward the end of the eighth century.

[258] *Liber pont.,* ed. Duchesne and Vogel, 1: 397, 401.

to run the administration of the Lateran,[259] and in 719 charged an Anglo-Saxon monk, Boniface, with the task of converting the Germans.[260] He encouraged Petronax to organize several ascetics who had settled in the ruins of Benedict's ancient monastery and to become their *senior*.[261] Foreigners soon came to Monte Cassino, among them a Spanish priest about whom we know absolutely nothing,[262] and an Anglo-Saxon, Willibald. Willibald, who had been trained in the monastery of Waltham (Wessex), stopped at the newly restored Monte Cassino on his return from a pilgrimage to the Holy Land and remained there for ten years, from 729 to 739. Willibald's activities at Monte Cassino were more limited than historians, especially English historians, usually imply.[263] There is nothing to suggest that he transplanted the program of studies he knew in Wessex to this Benedictine monastery. His *Vita* tells us simply that he trained monks in the *Rule* by his exhortations and example.[264] Furthermore, Monte Cassino could not have been transformed into an intellectual center overnight. Its library was modest —so modest, in fact, that sometime before 747 Pope Zachary sent Petronax several books of Holy Scripture and the manuscript of the *Regula*, which, according to tradition, would have been Benedict's own copy.[265] A school existed at Monte Cassino, but we must wait for Paul the Deacon and the commentary on the *Rule* attributed to him before we can glean any information on the education of monks.[266] A mid-eighth century customary mentions young monks reading, but the notice is even more vague than the Benedictine rule.[267]

---

259 Theodore, his notary, was a monk (Gregory II, *Ep.* X [*PL*, LXXXIX, 511]).

260 Fliche-Martin, 5: 537.

261 Paul the Deacon, *HL*, VI, 40 (*MGH, SRL*, p. 178): "Hortatu tunc Gregorii." See J. Chapman, "La restauration du Mont-Cassin par l'abbé Petronax," *RB* 21 (1904): 74–80.

262 Hugeburc, *Vita Willibaldi, MGH, SS*, XV-1, 102.

263 See Tommasso Leccisotti, "Le conseguenze dell'invasione longobarda per l'antico monachesimo italico," *Atti del I Congresso*, pp. 372ff. On the negligible historical value of Leo of Ostia as a source, see Suso Brechter, "Die Frühgeschichte von Monte Cassino nach der chron. Leos von Ostia," in *Liber Floridus: Mittellateinische Studien Paul Lehmann gewidmet* (St. Ottilien, 1950), pp. 271–86.

264 Hugeburc, *Vita Willibaldi, MGH, SS*, XV-1, 102: "Statim illi magno mentis moderamine et dogmatum ingenio felicem fratrum contuberniam sedulis disputationibus admonens . . . rectae constitutionis formam et cenobialis vitae normam praebebat."

265 Paul the Deacon, *HL*, VI, 40 (*MGH, SRL*, p. 179): "Libros scilicet sanctae Scripturae et alia quoque quae ad utilitatem monasterii pertinent, insuper et regulam quam beatus Pater Benedictus suis sanctis manibus conscripsit, paternae pietate concessit." On the question of the autograph *Rule*, see Ezio Franceschini, "Regula Benedicti, neoterici magistri, Regula magistri," in *Liber Floridus*, pp. 95–119.

266 See below, chap. 10, sect. I.

267 Bruno Albers, ed. *Consuetudines monasticae*, 5 vols. (Stuttgart, 1900–1912), 3: 14:

Monte Cassino's influence at this period, then, was not on the intellectual order. The monastery was a school for monastic life, just as the Lateran was a school for the liturgy. One came to Monte Cassino to learn the observance of the Benedictine rule. Sturm, Boniface's disciple, spent a year at Monte Cassino; Liudger, a disciple of Abbot Gregory of Utrecht, also spent some time there.[268] When Willibald moved on to Eichstädt, he tried to transplant the kind of life he led at Monte Cassino to Bavaria.[269] In the middle of the century, princes who abandoned the world, such as the Lombard Ratchis and the Frank Carloman, would choose Monte Cassino as a place of retreat.[270]

Only then would Monte Cassino begin to organize a scriptorium. In 750, the future abbot of Nonantola spent some time at Monte Cassino. The manuscripts he acquired there constituted the first resources of the library of his new monastery.[271] But twenty years would have to pass before studies at Monte Cassino were no longer exclusively religious.[272] Paul the Deacon, who came to Monte Cassino in 774, was the first lettered monk at the abbey. The history of Monte Cassino as a center of studies thus belongs to the Carolingian renaissance.

We must conclude, then, that the only monastery that was truly an intellectual center during the first half of the eighth century was the Irish foundation at Bobbio, whose beginnings we have already observed. At the end of the seventh century, Bobbio's scriptorium, which until that time had produced only ecclesiastical works, began to develop

---

"Post opus et tertiam . . . pleniter conveniant ad lectionem in locum deputatum . . . custodito summo silentio in intentione lectionis nisi jubeat prior alicui doctiori minus doctus fratribus vel doctrinam indigentibus lectionem tradere, de cujus moribus securus sit."

[268] Eigil, *Vita Sturmi*, 14 (*MGH, SS*, II, 372); *Vita Liudgeri*, ed. W. Diekamp, p. 50.

[269] Hugeburc, *Vita Willibaldi*, p. 105.

[270] *Liber pont.*, 1: 433; Einhard, *Vita Caroli*, 2 (in *Eginhard: Vie de Charlemagne*, ed. Halphen, p. 12).

[271] *Catalogi abbatum Nonantulanorum*, II (*MGH, SRL*, p. 571): "Apud praefatum locum Cassinum beate vixit et multa codices adquisivit."

[272] Hörle, *Frühmittelalterliche Mönchs- und Klerikerbildung in Italien*, pp. 47–51, believes without sufficient reason that grammar, medicine, and poetry were studied at Monte Cassino before the time of Paul the Deacon. For the first manuscripts to issue from Monte Cassino, see E. A. Lowe, *The Beneventan Script: A History of the South Italian Minuscule* (Oxford, 1914), p. 6. The first manuscript from the middle of the eighth century would be Monte Cassino 753 (*CLA*, III, 381), which contains the *Sentences* of Isidore of Seville. The famous Bamberg manuscript (B 61), which bears works by Cassiodorus, Isidore, and Gregory of Tours, was copied between 779 and 797. The Vivarian medical corpus preserved at Monte Cassino in a ninth-century manuscript must have come to the abbey much later; see Courcelle, *LG*, pp. 382ff. The only literary work that might have come from Monte Cassino before the arrival of Paul the Deacon is Marcus' poem on Benedict; see Brechter, "Marcus Poeta von Monte Cassino," in *Benedictus, der Vater des Abendlandes*, pp. 341–59.

an interest in profane works. During the first half of the next century, the monks recopied grammars, metrical treatises, glossaries, and extracts from profane historians and philologists.[273] They even erased manuscripts bearing biblical texts in order to write grammatical treatises.[274] Thus, the monks of Bobbio, rather than those of Monte Cassino, deserve the title of "Benedictine humanists" during this period.

How can Bobbio's peculiar place in Italian monastic culture be explained? One must, of course, consider the bonds that linked the monastery to the British Isles and to Gaul.[275] But there was more. Early in the eighth century, an Irish bishop, Cummean, came to Bobbio to finish his days. A monk-poet composed an epitaph in rhythmic verse for his tomb, while a sculptor, Master John, decorated the tombstone.[276] Now the poem and John's sculpture bring to mind the work that was being done in Pavia at the same time.[277] Close contacts had always existed between the abbey and the Lombard capital. When literary studies and art reappeared at Pavia, Bobbio also opened itself to profane and artistic culture. Thus, we must look primarily to the Lombard schools to explain the cultural development of Bobbio.

B. Urban Schools in Northern Italy

Urban civilization had never totally disappeared in Italy, either in the regions under Byzantine control or even in the Lombard kingdom.[278] The activity of the towns revived at the end of the seventh century and the beginning of the eighth century. There was much building: Rothari's edict has already provided us with information on the work of builders; in a famous text, Liutprand, whose reign began in 713,

---

[273] The grammars included those of Charisius, Servius (*CLA*, III, 400), and Probus (*CLA*, III, 388); the historians, Julius Valerius' *Res gestae Alexandri* (*CLA*, III, 349). For the glossaries, see *CLA*, III, 308, 340, and 397b (extracts from Macrobius). The *Questiones enigmatum retoricae artis* (*MGH*, *PAC*, V-2, 737–59) were undoubtedly composed during this period at Bobbio. The *Corpus gromaticorum* was preserved at Bobbio (see above, chap. 2, n. 110).

[274] See *CLA*, III, 368–9, for Kings, and ibid., nos. 396–97, for the Acts of the Apostles.

[275] The script of Merovingian scriptoria influenced the scribes at Bobbio. See A. R. Natale, "Influenze merovingiche e studi calligrafici nello scriptorium di Bobbio (secoli VIII–IX)," in *Miscellanea Giovanni Galbiati*, 3 vols. (Milan, 1951), I: 209–52.

[276] *MGH*, *PAC*, IV-2, 723. See Marcello Remondini, *Memoria interno alle iscrizioni antiche di Bobbio* (Genoa, 1806), pp. 34–40.

[277] See below, sect. III.B.

[278] Guido Mengozzi, *La città italiana nell'alto medio evo: Il periodo langobardo-franco*, 2nd ed., rev. Arrigo Solmi (Florence, 1931). Not all of Mengozzi's theses on the origins of urban institutions have been accepted. See Besta, *Storia del diritto italiano*, pp. 329ff.

stipulated the salaries builders were to receive.[279] *Negotiatores*, trading with Commachio and Venice, reappeared during this period.[280] Although the city was not a legal entity and still remained closely attached to its rural surroundings, it did have an embryonic administration. Texts mention the *peraequator*, the *curator* or the *procurator rei publicae*, and the *judex*. Urban projects and the fight against epidemics were discussed in the popular assembly, no doubt composed of the city notables.[281]

Town administration and commercial practice demanded, as in the sixth century, a minimum of instruction. The notables knew how to write, or at least how to sign the documents which they had the notaries draw up. In leafing through the series of Lombard diplomas edited by Luigi Schiaparelli, we can attest that autograph signatures were still in use. Among the lettered signatories we can count merchants, physicians, goldsmiths, and minters.[282] In Milan, at least, this last group seems to have formed a very cultivated category of citizens.[283] As in previous circumstances, those who did not know how to write said so and sketched a cross at the bottom of documents.[284] Contrary to the trend in Gaul at this time, however, these manual *signa* do not outnumber autograph subscriptions.

The preparation of documents presupposes the existence of a public notariate. Several diplomas mention *notarii* entitled *clarissimi* or *magnificii*. Were they simply *tabelliones*, or did they belong to an official urban notariate? Opinions are divided. When the texts, however, speak of the *exceptor civitatis* or the *scriba publicus*, there is no reason to doubt

---

279 *Memoratorium de mercedibus commacinorum, MGH, Leges*, IV, 96. For the *magistri commacini*, see Bognetti, "Santa Maria *foris portas* di Castelseprio," p. 289, who traces their name to the town of Comagena.

280 Ludo Moritz Hartmann, *Zur Wirtschaftsgeschichte Italiens in Frühenmittelalter* (Gotha, 1904), pp. 74–90; G. Fasoli, "Aspetti di vita economica e sociale nell'Italia del secolo VII," *Settimane*, 5: 138ff.

281 Besta, *Storia del diritto italiano*, pp. 329–30.

282 *CDL*, I, no. 18 (charter from Senator to Pavia in 714 with the signatures of a *vir illuster* and a *vir magnificus*); II, no. 155 (Pavia, 761, three *viri magnifici*); II, no. 130 (Piacenza, 758, *vir illuster*); II, no. 231 (Monza, 769, signatures of a physician and of a goldsmith); II, no. 177 (Milan, signature of a minter); I, no. 82 (Monza, 745, "vir magnificus . . . subscripsi"). See also *Il regesto di Farfa*, ed. Giorgi and Balzani, 2: 65, 69, 70.

283 R. S. Lopez, "An Aristocracy of Money in the Early Middle Ages," *Speculum* 28 (1953): 33. According to Lopez, the majority of counts and high officials were illiterate. But this remains to be proven. Lombards who went on pilgrimages to Rome left their names on walls; see O. Marucchi, "La cripta storica dei SS. Pietro e Marcellino," *Nuovo bollettino di archeologia cristiana* 3–4 (1898): 160.

284 *Il regesto di Farfa*, ed. Giorgi and Balzani, 2: 81: "In hoc testamento pro ignorantia litterarum signum sancta + feci"; ibid., p. 71.

that these eighth-century municipal officials fulfilled the same role as the functionaries in the antique curia.[285] Of course, the latter had disappeared, but the survival of the written document necessitated professional scribes endowed with a certain amount of authority.

The presence of educated notables and of a notarial apparatus presupposes, in turn, the existence of schools. Thus, we are faced with the question of elementary education in Lombard towns. Historians have long admitted the existence of such education, but the results of their research seem to me open to criticism. Some, of a neo-Ghibbeline tendency, have argued that only the lay school could have transmitted the tradition of antique culture.[286] Others have acknowledged that clerical schools existed alongside lay schools but have insisted that there was no break in continuity between the fifth and eighth centuries.[287] Actually, the texts at our disposal that mention schools do not permit such an interpretation. Antique educational institutions had disappeared between the sixth and eighth centuries—the only centers of study known from inscriptions and diplomas were organized by the Church.

There are only a few relevant texts: a cleric from Monza recalled that he had been raised in the church of Saint John;[288] another made a donation to Saint Zeno of Verona, where he had spent his childhood;[289] Bishop Theodore of Pavia recalled that his predecessor, Peter, who died in 745, had taught him his letters when he was still a child;[290] in Tuscany, Bishop Theoaldus of Fiesole remembered having been raised for several years in the church of Saint Donatus of Arezzo,

---

[285] Besta, *Storia del diritto italiano*, p. 330; De Boüard, *Acte privé*, p. 158. For the Lombard notariate, see L. Schiaparelli's study, "Note diplomatiche sulle carte longobarde," *Archivio storico italiano*, 7th ser. 17 (1932): 5ff.

[286] Wilhelm von Giesebrecht, *De litterarum studiis apud Italos primis Medii Aevi saeculis* (Berlin, 1845); Italian trans. C. Pascal, Florence, 1895). See A. F. Ozanam's response, "Des écoles et de l'instruction publique en Italie aux temps barbares," in *La civilisation au cinquième siècle* (Paris, 1873), 2: 401–94. Giesebrecht painted a portrait of intellectual ignorance on the part of the clergy during the Lombard period, while Ozanam, hoping to rehabilitate ecclesiastical studies, went too far in the other direction.

[287] Giuseppe Salvioli, *L'istruzione pubblica in Italia nei secoli VIII, IX, e X* (Florence, 1898); Giuseppe Manacorda, *Storia della scuola in Italia*, vol. 1, pt. 1, *Storia del diritto scolastico*, vol. 1, pt. 2, *Storia interna della scuola medioevale italiana e dizionario geografico delle scuole italiane nel medio evo* (Milan, 1913). These historians have tried to show that the Carolingian influence was negligible in the formation of Italian schools and that, in fact, these schools were in operation even before the Lombard period. For these various theses, see Viscardi, *Le origini*, pp. 392ff.

[288] *CDL*, II, no. 218 (768): "In ecclesia sancti Johanni notritoris mei." See ibid., II, no. 231 (769).

[289] Ibid., I, no. 83 (745): "sancti Zenonis nutritoris nostri."

[290] *Tituli saeculi octavi*, I (*MGH, PAC*, I, 101–2): "Me sibi praeclarus doctor nutrivit alumnum . . . / Litterulas ex quo primaevo tempore sumpsi."

where he was also educated;[291] an archdeacon in Lucca left his books to the church that had welcomed him as a child.[292] The texts from Lucca seem to be more exact in that they mention *magistri* and even a *presbyter mag. scolae*.[293] In addition, a charter of 767 gives the precise location of the schola: "near the portico of the cathedral."[294]

The terms *magister* and *schola*, however, are not as easy to interpret as it might first seem. Many historians have been misled by the word *magistri*, which does not always mean "schoolmaster." There were master goldsmiths, master sculptors,[295] master booksellers,[296] and even master cobblers,[297] not to mention the famous *magistri commacini*. When we have a *magister scholae*, we are much closer to the real thing. Still, we would have to know what kind of schola was meant: a schola for lectors, cantors, notaries, or scribes? One sees what kind of interpretive difficulties we run into. The charter of Lucca of 746 was drawn up by Master Gaudentius, a priest who had under his orders a disciple, the cleric Perterad. Also, in 762 Master Osprand had his disciple Philip prepare a document. Here, the references seem to be to a school of ecclesiastical notaries.[298]

Instruction was not highly specialized, however; the same cleric could direct several schools. At the end of the eighth century, a certain Giselpertus, *decanus* and *portarius*, was in charge of the schola of cantors and scribes.[299] Whoever directed the episcopal notariate could be

---

[291] *CDL*, I, no. 19 (715): "Per annos pluris in eclesia Sancti Donati notritus et litteras edoctus sum."

[292] *CDL*, I, no. 73 (740).

[293] Ibid., I, no. 62 (737): "Teudualdus magister"; I, no. 86 (746): "Gaudentio magistro meo"; II, no. 165 (762): "Philippo cl. ex dictato magistri meo." See also Carlo Troya, *Codice diplomatico longobardo* . . . (Naples, 1852–56), 4: 331: "Deusdeditus presb. mag. scole."

[294] *CDL*, II, no. 207: "Offerimus Deo . . . casam . . . quae est prope porticalem ejusdem basilicae, ubi est scola."

[295] "Ursus magister cum discipulis suis . . . aedificavit hanc civorium" is written in the church of Saint George in Valpolicella. The name Ursus *magister* is again found in Ferentillo; see E. Herzog, "Die Longobardischen Fragmente in der Abtei s. Pietro di Ferentillo," *Römische Quartalschrift für christliche Altertumskunde und Kirchengeschichte* (1906), pp. 41–81.

[296] "Confectus codex in statione magistri Viliaric antiquarii." This is a seventh-century Orosius manuscript; see Wilhelm Wattenbach, *Das Schriftwesen im Mittelalter* (Leipzig, 1896), p. 450, and *CLA*, III, 298.

[297] *CDL*, II, no. 278 (773).

[298] This is Luigi Schiaparelli's interpretation (*Il codice 490 della Bibliotheca Capitulare di Lucca, ST* 36 [1924]: 57ff.). For a contrary opinion, see Manacorda, *Storia della scuola in Italia*, 1: 14.

[299] *MGH, Leg. sect. III*, II, 791: "Giselpertus decanus et portarius quem schola cantorum et scribarum magistrum ordinavimus."

employed not only in the scriptorium but also in the clerics' school, as was the case in the ninth century at Saint Martin of Tours.[300] In Verona in 763, the name of a notary is found at the end of a manuscript from the scriptorium.[301] In addition, works recopied in Verona's scriptorium were used in the school, as the contents of some of the manuscripts indicate.[302] One of the most celebrated manuscripts to come out of Lucca's scriptorium in the eighth century, manuscript 490, had been written in part by two scribes whose names are mentioned in diplomas of the period. This manuscript contains works which must have figured in the study program of young clerics:[303] historical works (the chronicles of Isidore and Jerome, the *De viris* of Jerome and Gennadius, the *Liber pontificalis*); treatises pertaining to ecclesiastical institutions (Isidore's *De officiis* and a fragment of Book VIII of the *Origines, De ecclesia et sectis*); treatises on computus (Pythagoras' *Ars numeri*, a fragment from Pliny's *Historia naturalis* on the division of time, a work on paschal computus); and, lastly, some recipes for goldsmiths and painters which could have been intended for artists employed by the bishop.

The notariate, the scriptorium, and the clerical school were closely connected. As was often the case in the Middle Ages, children could spend some time in each of the various sections that made up the episcopal school. Such an arrangement must have been absolutely necessary, given the small number of educated clerics. In several diplomas from Farfa, Lucca, and Florence, clerics confessed when they were asked to sign the document that they had not learned how to write.[304]

The only urban schools mentioned in the sources, thus, were clerical schools. The same can be said for the countryside. We are fortunate to

[300] Emile Lesne, *Les livres, scriptoria et bibliothèques du commencement du VIIIe siècle à la fin du XIIe siècle* (Lille, 1938), p. 339.

[301] L. Schiaparelli, "Sulla data e provenienza del codice LXXXIX della biblioteca capitolare di Verona," *Archivio storico italiano*, 7th ser. 9 (1924): 106–17. For the scriptorium at Verona, see Viscardi, *Le origini*, pp. 160–61. An eighth-century manuscript from Autun (107, fol. 93) has as a *probatio pennae* the beginning of a formula for the sale of property; see Robinson, "Manuscripts 27 and 107, Autun," *Memoirs of the American Academy in Rome*, 16: 419, n. 48.

[302] Manuscript CLXIII, 150, from the middle of the eighth century (see *CLA*, IV, 516) contains the *Disticha Catonis* and Claudian's poetry.

[303] Schiaparelli, *Il codice 490*; Burnam, *A Classical Technology Edited from Codex Lucensis 490*.

[304] *Il regesto di Farfa*, ed. Giorgi and Balzani, 2: 73: "Ego Aderisius clericus pro ignorantia litterarum" (768); "Pietro clerici nescientis litteras" (775). *CDL*, II, no. 131: "Ariprand cleris propter neglegentia usui sui manibus suis propriis menime potuit subscrivere" (Lucca, 758). *Chartes de Florence*, XXXVI (32), 793; XLVI (53), 798, in *Codice diplomatico toscano*, ed. Filippo Brunetti, 3 vols. (Florence, 1806–33).

have a diploma from 715 concerning a conflict between the bishop of Arezzo and the bishop of Siena over a rural church in which the judges appealed to the memories of the children of the church in question. One of them said that he had served in the church from his infancy.[305] Children who had been baptized in the church and who had undoubtedly received their first instruction there were also questioned. In the case of rural schools, then, we can assume that there was continuity between the sixth and eighth centuries.

The laymen who received an elementary education had benefited from the lessons which clerics gave them outside the episcopal and rural school. One such priest took charge of a child and gave him his basic education.[306] Lay notaries might also have received their early training from their ecclesiastical colleagues. The *excerptor civitatis* in Piacenza was a deacon, which suggests that clerics and laymen shared the duties of notaries.[307]

Can evidence of lay education be found in Pavia, the capital of the kingdom? During the reign of Cunincpert (688–700) and those of his successors, grammatical and legal education is supposed to have flourished.[308] Cunincpert, in fact, was a cultivated prince—*vir elegans*[309]—who employed artists and poets to decorate the churches he built with metrical inscriptions.[310] He asked a certain Stephen of Pavia to write a poem in celebration of the end of the schism of Aquilea. Stephen's verses are not excellent: the poet preferred to compose a rhythmic poem because of his admitted ignorance of classical meters.[311] Nevertheless,

---

[305] *CDL*, I, no. 19: "Bonefatius presbiter . . . qui interrogatus dixit: . . . quia ab infantia in ista ecclesia Sancti Valentini militavi."

[306] *CDL*, II, no. 218: "Illum puerum quem ergo nutrivi" (Monza, 768).

[307] Troya, *Codice diplomatico longobardo*, no. 431: "Vitalis subdiaconus exceptor civitatis" (721). See also no. 479 from 729.

[308] Mengozzi, *Ricerche*; Maria M. Bassi Costa, *Le origini dello studio di Pavia: Formazione della scuola di Pavia nell'alto medio evo*, Annali della biblioteca governativa e libreria civica di Cremona, vol. 4, fasc. 1 (Cremona, 1951).

[309] Paul the Deacon, *HL*, VI, 17 (*MGH*, *SRL*, p. 170).

[310] *Epitaphia* CXL–CXLI, CXLIII–CXLIV (*MGH*, *PAC*, IV-2, 724–27). The first inscription concerns the king's mistress, Theodata, who came from an illustrious Roman family. See Paul the Deacon, *HL*, V, 37 (p. 157).

[311] Ibid., CXLV, 18 (p. 731):

> Mihi ignosce, rex, quaeso, piissime
> Tua qui jussa nequivi; ut condecet
> Pangere ore styloque contexere
> Recte ut valent edissere medrici
> Scripsi per prosa ut oratiunculam.

For this poem, see Norberg, *Introduction*, pp. 92, 111. Manitius, 1: 199, thought that v. 46 was a reminiscence from the *Aeneid*, II, 6–8.

we should hail the reemergence of the court poet. We should also note that Stephen was not a layman but most probably a monk, perhaps a monk of Bobbio[312]—new proof of the bonds between the court and the great abbey. During the same period, a grammarian named Felix received from the king a staff decorated with silver and gold as a symbol of his magisterial authority.[313] Cunincpert may have remembered that Theodoric, two centuries earlier, had showered teachers with presents and had hoped to revive the Roman and Ostrogothic tradition.[314] But Felix, too, was not a layman but a deacon, attached most probably to the clergy of Pavia.[315]

We know, in fact, that the episcopal school in Pavia was a center of literary studies. According to Paul the Deacon, Bishop Damian, one of the king's intimates, was acquainted with the liberal arts.[316] In a letter to the Byzantine emperor, Damian provides us with a glimpse of a literary style reminiscent of that of Ennodius, his sixth-century predecessor.[317] Other lettered deacons—such as Thomas,[318] and Sinodus, who "expressed maxims like the philosophers"—gravitated around him.[319]

In all likelihood, it was these clerics who composed a series of epitaphs which were thought to be Carolingian but which actually date from the

---

312 Paul Lehmann, "Stefanus magister?" *Deutsches Archiv für Erforschung des Mittelalters* 14 (1958): 469–71. The acrostic "Stephanus mg" had previously been misinterpreted.

313 Paul the Deacon, *HL*, VI, 7 (p. 167): "Eoque tempore floruit in arte grammatica Felix patruus Flaviani praeceptoris mei quem in tantum rex dilexit, ut ei baculum argento auroque decoratum inter reliqua suae largitatis munera condonaret."

314 An architect under Theodoric received an *aurea virga* as recompense; see Cassiodorus, *Var.*, VII, 5 (*MGH*, *AA*, XII, 205).

315 Chapter 7 of Paul the Deacon's *Historia Langobardorum* is entitled "De Felice diacono grammatico" (*MGH*, *SRL*, p. 162).

316 Paul the Deacon, *HL*, V, 38 (p. 157): "Liberalibus artibus sufficienter instructus."

317 *PL*, LXXXVII, 1264. Repeating the arguments of seventh-century popes, Damian contrasted evangelical simplicity to the artifices of dialecticians: "Nam si sunt qui audacia dialecticae artis inflati cothurnata cervice, buccis tumescentibus sinuosis circumitionibus et flexuosis ambagibus, phaleris verborum pompisque sermonum, sua ferali calliditate simplicem fidei rationem convellere . . . voluerint. . . . Nam si [regulas fidei] relegas, insignissime imperator non cum dialecticis, non cum rhetoricis, non cum grammaticis, sed cum ruricolis et piscatoribus Dominus posuit rationem." J. B. Bognetti deduced from a phrase in Damian's epitaph—"Quos sinus enutrit Ligurie et gignunt Athenae rura" (*ICR*, 2: 170, no. 26, v. 12)—that Damian was born in Greece; see "S. Maria *foris portas* di Castelseprio," pp. 237ff. See as well Enrico Cattaneo, "Missionari orientali a Milano nell' età longobarda," *Archivio storico lombardo* (1963), pp. 216–45.

318 Paul the Deacon, *HL*, V, 38 (p. 157): "Thomam diaconum . . . sapientem scilicet et religiosum virum."

319 *ICR*, 2, pt. 1: 171, no. 28: "Ore spirabas dogmati philosophorum more." Bognetti, "S. Maria *foris portas* di Castelseprio," pp. 265–66, supposes that this Sinodus was the Deacon Zeno of Saint John the Baptist whom Paul the Deacon mentioned in *HL*, V, 40 (p. 160).

beginning of the eighth century.[320] Cunincpert's court at Pavia thus more closely resembles the court at Toledo in the seventh century than it does the court at Ravenna in the sixth century. It had become a cultural center, thanks to monks and to the cathedral clergy.

Liutprand (713–44) continued to welcome lettered clergymen. Liutprand had been raised with Cunincpert's son, since his father had been the governor of the royal heir.[321] In an epitaph Liutprand commissioned in memory of his father, he recalled his father's eloquence and wisdom.[322] The king evidently did not inherit his father's intellectual qualities. In fact, Paul the Deacon, who was generally quite generous to the prince, tells us that he was unlettered but adds that his wisdom was equal to that of the philosophers.[323] Thus Liutprand would seem to resemble Theodoric if it is true that the Ostrogothic king could not write. He reminds one of Theodoric in many other ways. Like him, Liutprand wanted to imitate the Romans by completing the Lombard code and by building churches and inviting poets to decorate them with metrical inscriptions.[324] Perhaps it was at his request that an historian wrote the *Origo gentis Longobardorum*, which recalled the relationship between the Lombards and the Greeks of Troy.[325] One act during his reign proves his piety as well as his admiration for Christian culture. Having learned that the relics of Saint Augustine that had been transferred to Sardinia in the sixth century were threatened by the Arabs, he transferred them and deposited them in the church of Saint Peter in Pavia, where Boethius' remains were also later deposited.[326] It is likely that

[320] For the style of these inscriptions, see Viscardi, *Le origini*, pp. 326ff. The epitaph of Columba, the wife of an important royal official, is noteworthy (see *ICR*, 2, pt. 1: 166, no. 15).

[321] Paul the Deacon, *HL*, VI, 18, 21, 35 (pp. 171–72).

[322] *Epitaphium* CXLII (*MGH, PAC*, IV-2, 726):

> Sapiens, modestus, patiens, sermone facundus
> Adstantibus qui dulcia flavi mellis ad instar
> Singulis . . . promebat de pectore verba.

See Paul the Deacon's opinion (*HL*, VI, 35 [p. 177]): "Vir egregius et cujus sapientiae rari aequandi sunt."

[323] *HL*, VI, 58 (p. 189): "Fuit vir multae sapientiae . . . litterarum quidem ignarus sed philosophis aequandus."

[324] See *Tituli saeculi octavi*, *MGH, PAC*, I, 105, for an inscription from the church of Olonna.

[325] Opinions are divided on the date of the *Origo*; see *Wattenbach-Levison*, 2: 207.

[326] Paul the Deacon, *HL*, VI, 48 (p. 181): "[Liutprandus] quoque audiens quod Sarracenis depopulata Sardinia . . . misit et dato magno pretio accepit et transtulit ea in urbem Ticinensiem ibique cum debito sancto patri honore recondedit." Bede had already noted the event; see *Chronica*, *MGH, AA*, XIII, 321. For this transfer, see Henri Leclercq, "Pavie," *DACL*, XIII-2, 2769–70, and, more recently, Marrou, "La Basilique chrétienne

when this transfer was being made, African and Spanish manuscripts sheltered on Sardinia were also transported to Italy.[327] We know that the Visigothic *Orational*, which was composed at Tarragona around 700, came to Verona before 733, after having been kept on Sardinia.[328] As in the sixth century, the great island was a way station among the various Mediterranean kingdoms.

African clerics were not the only foreigners at Liutprand's court. Boniface enjoyed the king's hospitality when he returned from Rome in 719 and again in 739.[329] Charles Martel sent his son Pepin to the king in 735 on the occasion of his barbatoria[330] and asked Liutprand to "adopt" the young man. Pepin's first stay in the Lombard capital—where he found poets, architects, and physicians—helped to enrich his education.[331] Did he meet the grammarian Flavian, nephew of the Deacon Felix we mentioned above and later Paul the Deacon's teacher? We cannot say. It is even difficult to know when Paul the Deacon himself arrived at the court in Pavia: there is no way to tell whether it was during the last years of Liutprand's reign or during the beginning of the reign of his successor Ratchis (744-49).[332] In any event, even if the meeting never took place, it is important to note that Charlemagne's father and the future artisan of the Carolingian renaissance found Pavia a vibrant cultural center enlivened by clerics—a presage of Carolingian achievements.

The Frankish prince could also have observed and learned from the smooth operation of the Lombard administration. In fact, it is probable

---

d'Hippone d'après le résultat des dernières fouilles," *Revue des études augustiniennes* 6 (1960): 134-35. Liutprand founded the church of Saint Peter, where later, at some unknown date, Boethius' body was interred; see Maieul Cappuyns, "Boèce," *DHGE*, 9: 357.

[327] As Traube has already conjectured (*Vorlesungen und Abhandlungen*, 2: 131).

[328] For the travels of this manuscript, see *CLA*, IV, 515, and André Wilmart, "L'odyssée du manuscrit de San Pietro," in *Classical and Mediaeval Studies in Honor of E. K. Rand*, ed. Leslie Webber Jones (New York, 1938), p. 304. The manuscript was copied at Cagliari in the sixth century, and then, after having been brought to Africa and Spain, was brought to Italy in the eighth century.

[329] Willibald, *Vita Bonifatii*, 5, 7 (Levison ed., pp. 20, 22, 27).

[330] Paul the Deacon, *HL*, VI, 53 (p. 183): "Ut ejus juxta morem capillum susciperet; qui ejus caesariem incidens, ei pater effectus est, multisque eum dilatum regiis muneribus genitori remisit." See above, chap. 6, sect. III.C., for this ceremony, which here accompanied the adoption.

[331] Ibid., V, 33 (p. 155): "Gaiduald vir magnificus medicus regiae potestatis." See *CDL*, II, no. 38 (726).

[332] Paul was certainly at the court during Ratchis' reign. See his epitaph in Karl Neff, ed., *Die Gedichte des Paulus Diaconus* (Munich, 1908), p. 155. If he was born around 720-25, he then spent about twenty years under Liutprand and thus could have been taught by Flavian. For Paul's chronology, see Manitius, 1: 257-58, and *Wattenbach-Levison*, 2: 212ff.

that the Carolingians imitated the techniques of the Lombard notariate when they reorganized their own administration.[333] We know from the texts of the Lombard laws and the documents that came out of the royal chancellery that the Lombard princes and dukes had organized their offices according to Roman tradition.[334] But we cannot really speak, as does Mengozzi, of "instruction in law at Pavia" which later would be transferred to Bologna.[335] No text supports such a hypothesis nor is there any trace whatsoever of legal instruction at Bologna before the eleventh century.[336] Was there even a notarial school at Pavia? Contrary to what some historians think, the invention of a new type of stenography, syllabic tachygraphy, cannot be attributed to the activity of the offices in Pavia.[337] If the documents were formally more elegant, was it not because of the intellectual renewal we have already discussed?[338]

Pavia has occupied our attention for several pages. We should not forget, however, the other northern Italian towns that also established study centers in competition with the capital. Bishop Benedict of Milan (died 725) wished to restore the former glory of his city. He claimed for a time the privilege of consecrating the bishops of Pavia.[339] The pope asked Benedict, who was a poet, to compose the epitaph of the Anglo-Saxon king Caedwalla, who died in Rome shortly after having been baptized.[340] Another poem concerned with medical questions has long been attributed to the bishop, but it is now certain that if this work is of the seventh century, it belongs to a Milanese cleric.[341] Under Bene-

[333] De Boüard, *Acte privé*, pp. 159ff.

[334] Besta, *Storia del diritto italiano*, pp. 296–99, 310.

[335] See Viscardi, *Le origini*, p. 216, who repeats Mengozzi's theses (*Ricerche*, p. 19).

[336] See Hermann H. Fitting, *Die Anfänge der Rechtsschule zu Bologna* (Berlin, 1888), and Albano Sorbelli and Luigi Simeoni, *Storia della Università di Bologna*, 2 vols. (Bologna, 1944–47), 1: 11ff. There was no relationship between Pavia and Bologna during the period we are considering; see Pietro Vaccari, "Pavie e Bologna," *Atti del I Congresso*, pp. 293–312.

[337] Giorgio Costamagna, "La pretesa formazione di un nuovo tipo di scrittura tachigrafica sillabica nell'epoca longobarda," *Atti del I Congresso*, pp. 228ff.

[338] That is, rather than because of the survival of lay education, as some still think. See Christine Mohrmann, *Latin vulgaire, latin des chrétiens, latin médiéval* (Paris, 1955), p. 14.

[339] See his letter to Pope Constantine (*PL*, LXXXIX, 364), in which he praised the town.

[340] Paul the Deacon, *HL*, VI, 15 (*MGH, SRL*, p. 169). Jacob Hammer published a new version in "An Unrecorded *Epitaphium Caedwallae*," *Speculum* 6 (1931): 607. Bede admired this poem and included it in his *Ecclesiastical History* (V, 7 [pp. 293–94]). For Benedict, see *Wattenbach-Levison*, 2: 208.

[341] *PL*, LXXXIX, 369. See Manitius, 1: 198, for this poem. F. Brunhölzl thinks that

dict's successor, Theodore (725–31), another cleric wrote a remarkable poem in praise of Milan in which the poet used all the resources of classical rhetoric and demonstrated real mastery of rhythmic verse.[342]

Ravenna, although a Byzantine city, more and more entered the Lombard sphere of influence. Occupied for a time in 732 by the Barbarians, it owed its salvation only to the pope. The Ravennates, who increasingly detested the Byzantines, turned willingly toward Rome, so much so that beginning in 709 Justinian II ordered reprisals against the town—in which Bishop Felix was one of the most illustrious victims.[343] The *Liber pontificalis* of Ravenna described him as a remarkable orator and a prolific writer who had composed several works, including a commentary on Saint Matthew and a treatise on the Last Judgment. But, blinded on the emperor's orders, he was unable to revise his works and ordered them burned.[344]

Paul the Deacon received his education in a clerical school in Cividale in the duchy of Friuli. Unfortunately, he never spoke of his education except for a short passage in which he stated that he forgot the rudimentary Greek he had learned "in scolis."[345] The court at Friuli tried to imitate the court of Pavia as an artistic and cultural center.[346] Arichis,

---

the poem dates from the thirteenth or fourteenth century ("Benedetto di Milano ed il 'carmen medicinale' di Crispo," *Aevum* 33 [1959]: 25–49).

[342] *Versum de Mediolano civitate*, MGH, PAC, I, 24. See Norberg, "Le développement du latin en Italie," *Settimane*, 5: 501–2, for the style of the poem. The Milanese cleric congratulated Theodore for his liturgical reforms:

> Pollens ordo lectionum cantilene organum
> Modolata psalmorumque conlaudatur. Regula
> Artiusque adimpletur in ea cotidie.

[343] *Liber pont.*, 1: 390–91. See Diehl, *Etudes sur l'administration byzantine*, p. 274.
[344] Agnellus, *Liber pont. eccl. Ravenn.*, 136 (MGH, SRL, p. 366): "Egregius praedicator multorum conditor voluminum."
[345] *Pauli et Petri carm.* XII (MGH, PAC, I, 49–50):

> Graiam nescio loquellam, ignoro Hebraicam
> Tres aut quattuor in scolis quas didici syllabas
> Ex his mihi est ferendus maniplus ad aream . . .
> Sed omnino ne linguarum dicam esse nescius
> Pauca mihi quae fuerunt tradita puerulo
> Dicam; cetera fugerunt jam gravante senio:
> De puero qui in glacie extinctus est.

The word *puerulo* in conjunction with the phrase *in scolis* offers sufficient proof that this education was not received in Ravenna, as Manitius, 1: 257, and Hörle, *Frühmittelalterliche Mönchs- und Klerikerbildung in Italien*, p. 406, thought. See Viscardi's hypothesis (*Le origini*, p. 23) on Paul's stay in Cividale. The poem that follows the verses cited above is a translation of a Greek epigram often taught in the schools; see Curtius, pp. 355–56, and Norberg, *La poésie latine rythmique*, pp. 98ff.

[346] Patriarch Callixtus' baptistery was built in 737; the ivory of Duke Orso was sculpted

originally from Friuli but later duke of Beneventum, was noted for his love of "wisdom." When Paul the Deacon praised his compatriot and protector in those terms, perhaps he wanted to evoke Arichis' philosophical culture. In the epitaph he composed for Arichis, he noted, in fact, that the prince was acquainted with logic, physics, and ethics.[347] Combining this text with Paul's allusion to schools where Greek was taught, we can conclude that Friuli was one of the few regions in northern Italy where Hellenic culture had not totally disappeared. This is not at all unlikely, since Hellenic culture reemerged in Rome at the same time.

C. CLERICAL EDUCATION IN ROME

Romans were not very well disposed to studies throughout the period of the Monothelite crisis, as we saw in chapter 8. But with the defeat of the Byzantine heresy a new era opened for the papacy. In addition, political conditions were favorable for the popes because the anarchy that reigned at Constantinople freed them from imperial tutelage. By defending the population against the excesses of Byzantine officials, the popes increasingly became the chief temporal power in Italy.[348] The pontiffs who succeeded after 680 were veritable sovereigns in the duchy of Rome. John VII (705-7), son of a high Byzantine bureaucrat in Rome, went so far as to establish his home on the Palatine and to transform the church of Santa Maria Antiqua into a family mausoleum.[349] Like other popes of the period, he restored and built churches and called in Eastern artists to decorate them.[350] Surer of its strength, the papacy could confront the new crisis that broke out in 726 when Leo the Isaurian attempted to apply his iconoclastic policy to Italy.

The popes were better armed intellectually for this conflict than they had been for the Monothelite controversy. Natives of Sicily and of the

---

around 749. See Carlo Cecchelli, *I monumenti del Friuli dal secolo IV al XI*, vol. 1, *Cividale* (Milan and Rome, 1943).

[347] In Neff, *Die Gedichte des Paulus Diaconus*, p. 12: "Cum ad imitationem excellentissimi comparis, qui nostra aetate solus paene principium sapientiae palmam tenet." Paul wrote to Adelperga, the daughter of the Lombard king Desiderius (757-74) and wife of Arichis; see Bezzola, 1: 26-27. See also Paul the Deacon, *HL*, V, 9 (*MGH, SRL*, p. 146): "Quod logos et physis, moderansque quod ethica pangit: / Omnia condiderat mentis in arcae suae." See Bezzola, pp. 27-28, for this poem.

[348] Bertolini, *Roma*, pp. 369ff.

[349] *Liber pont.*, 1: 385, 3: 98; Stein, 2: 742, n. 2; W. de Grüneisen, *Sainte-Marie-Antique*, 2 vols. (Rome, 1911).

[350] Per Jonas Nordhagen, "Nuove constatazioni sui rapporti artistici tra Roma e Bisanzio sotto il pontificato di Giovanni VII (705-707)," *Atti del III Congresso*, pp. 445-52.

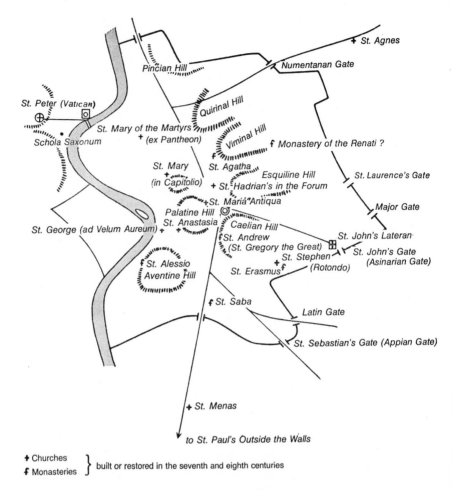

St. Agnes

Pincian Hill

Numentanan Gate

St. Peter (Vatican)

Quirinal Hill

Schola Saxonum

St. Mary of the Martyrs
+ (ex Pantheon)

Viminal Hill

f Monastery of the Renati ?

St. Mary
+ (in Capitolio)

St. Agatha

Esquiline Hill

St. Laurence's Gate

+ St. Hadrian's in the Forum

+ St. Mariá Antiqua

Major Gate

Palatine Hill

St. Anastasia

Caelian Hill

St. George (ad Velum Aureum) +   + St. Andrew
(St. Gregory the Great)

St. John's Lateran

St. John's Gate
(Asinarian Gate)

+ St. Stephen
+ f (Rotondo)

f St. Alessio
Aventine Hill

St. Erasmus f

f St. Saba

Latin Gate

St. Sebastian's Gate (Appian Gate)

+ St. Menas

to St. Paul's Outside the Walls

+ Churches   }
f Monasteries } built or restored in the seventh and eighth centuries

14. Rome in the Eighth Century

East,[351] they began to restore Hellenic culture to an honored position at the end of the seventh century. The *Liber pontificalis* attests for the first time that popes knew Greek: Leo II (682–83) was learned in Scriptures and chant and eloquent in Greek as well as in Latin;[352] Boniface, counselor of Benedict II (684–85), translated the *Miracles of Saint Cyr and Saint John* into Latin;[353] at the Council of 704, presided over by John VI—a pope of Eastern origin—the Anglo-Saxon Wilfrid remarked that several bishops spoke Greek among themselves.[354] The last popes of this period were still reputed Hellenists: during the pontificate of the Syrian Gregory III (731–41), whose culture seems to have been as great as that of Leo II,[355] a *Life* of Pope Martin I was composed in Greek.[356] Around 740 a work influenced by John Malalas' chronicle appeared in Rome.[357] Zachary (741–52) himself translated Gregory the Great's *Dialogues* for the clerics and monks who did not know Latin.[358]

There were more Greek clerics and monks ignorant of Latin in the eighth century than there had been in the previous century. The colony of Greek monks on the Aventine and Palatine hills was augmented by new arrivals.[359] Pope Paul I welcomed the monks driven from Constantinople in 761 and built a monastery for them where they could

[351] Leo (682–83) and Conon (686–87) were Sicilians; John V (685–86), Sergius (687–701), John VI (701–5), John VII (705–7), Sisinnius (708), and Constantine (708–15) were Greeks. See J. Gay, "Remarques sur les papes grecs et syriens avant l'Iconoclastie," in *Mélanges offerts à M. Gustave Schlumberger* (Paris, 1924), vol. 1.

[352] *Liber pont.*, 1: 359: "Vir eloquentissimus in divinis Scripturis sufficienter instructus, Greca Latinaque lingua eruditus, cantelena ac psalmodia praecipuus et in earum sensibus subtilissima exercitatione limatus; lingua quoque scolasticus et eloquendi majore lectione politam, exortator omnium bonorum operum plebique florentissime ingerebat scientiam."

[353] Siegmund, *Die Ueberlieferung*, p. 261. For the Greek culture of eighth-century popes, see Steinacker, "Die römische Kirche," *MIOEG* 62 (1954): 28–66.

[354] Eddius, *Vita Wilfridi*, LIII (Colgrave ed., p. 112): "Tunc inter se grecizantes et subridentes nos autem celantes, multa loqui coeperunt." Bilingual inscriptions cover the walls of Santa Maria Antiqua; see *Liber pont.*, 3: 99.

[355] In *Liber pont.*, 1: 145, the biographer repeated expressions applied to Leo II. Through Bede we learn that Gregory loved exegetical discussions; see *Retractatio in Actus apost.*, XIX, 12 (Laistner ed., p. 139).

[356] P. Peeters, "Une vie grecque du pape Martin I," *AB* 51 (1933): 253–62.

[357] *Laterculus imperatorum romanorum Malalianus*, MGH, *AA*, XIII, 424. See Siegmund, *Die Ueberlieferung*, p. 172.

[358] *Liber pont.*, 1: 435: "Quattuor Dialogorum libros de latino in greco translatavit eloquio et plures qui latinam ignorant lectionem per eorum inluminavit lectionum historiam." The oldest manuscript of this translation is Vat. grec., 1666, which dates from the end of the eighth century and comes from Rome; see Battifol, "Les librairies byzantines à Rome," *MEFR* 8 (1888): 300ff.

[359] For this colony, see Hörle, *Frühmittelalterliche Mönchs- und Klerikerbildung in Italien*, p. 29; Battifol, "Inscriptions byzantines de Saint-Georges-du-Vélabre," *MEFR* 7 (1887): 419ff.; and, more recently, E. Patlagean, "Les moines grecs d'Italie et l'apologie des thèses pontificales, VIIIe–IXe siècles," *SM*, 3rd ser. 5 (1964): 579–603.

celebrate the office in the Greek tongue.[360] It is likely that the refugees brought manuscripts with them and that they organized scriptoria.[361] Perhaps it was through them that Paul I acquired the grammatical and geometrical works he was to send to Pepin the Short.[362]

Except for the renewal of Greek culture, especially at the Lateran, there were no innovations in Roman clerical education. The institutions already functioning in the seventh century continued to provide education, just as the schola cantorum remained the nursery of clergymen and popes.[363] Perhaps the schola increasingly approximated the Byzantine *orphanotrophium*. Perhaps also, as in the Byzantine institution, the study of sacred poetry occupied as important a place as chant.[364] More precise knowledge of eighth-century educational institutions in Byzantium would perhaps help us understand what was happening in Rome. The reputation of the Roman schola went beyond the walls of the City: in the middle of the eighth century (766–67), Bishop Stephen of Naples sent three of his clerics there,[365] and a future abbot of Farfa was raised there.[366] Foreigners also sought masters from the schola. In 760 Simeon, the *secundus* of the schola, left with the bishop of Rouen (Pepin the Short's brother) to introduce the monks of Neustria "to the modulations of Roman psalmody."[367] By 754, the Church of Metz had adopted Roman usages, and shortly afterwards Pepin sought to diffuse them throughout his kingdom.[368]

Early in the eighth century the schola was complemented by another center for religious and administrative training, the *cubiculum*, which was located in the Lateran after Pope Zachary's reorganization of the

---

[360] *Liber pont.*, 1: 465.

[361] We can cite a Greek manuscript copied in Rome in 759 (Paris, Bibliothèque Natonale, grec, 111, 5).

[362] See below, n. 382.

[363] *Liber pont.*, 1: 371 (Sergius): "Quia studiosus erat et capax in officio cantilenae priori cantorum pro doctrina est traditus."

[364] A tenth-century text made this comparison: "Scola cantorum quae appellatur orphanotropio" (*Register of Subiaco*, 919). We are well informed on the *orphanotrophium* at Byzantium around 700, thanks to the work of Andrew of Crete; see the articles on him, by L. Petit in *DACL*, I-2, 2034–41, and by S. Vailhé in *DHGE*, 2: 1659–61.

[365] John the Deacon, *Gesta episcoporum Neapolitanorum*, 42 (*MGH, SRL*, p. 425): "Hic etenim Roman direxit tres clericos qui in scola cantorum optime edocti omni sacro Romanarum ordine imbuti ad propria redierunt."

[366] *Il Chronicon farfense*, ed. Balzani, 1: 524: "Maxima vero sanctae Romane ecclesiae cantu a pueritia plene eruditus."

[367] Paul I, *Ep.* VII (*PL*, LXXXIX, 1151). When Simeon returned to Rome, the bishop of Rouen sent monks to the schola there (*Ep.* IX [ibid., col. 1187]).

[368] Paul the Deacon, *Gesta episcoporum Mettensium*, PL, XCV, 709; Duchesne, *Origines du culte chrétien*, p. 106.

palace. It was open to the best students of the schola and to sons of noble Romans.[369] The future Gregory II, as well as Leo and the two brothers Stephen and Paul—all three, future popes—came out of the *cubiculum*.[370] Zachary I called the monk Stephen, the future Stephen III, there.[371]

Young clerics raised in the entourage of the pontiffs received a strictly religious education. Papal biographers, in fact, repeated the classic formula, "divinis scripturis eruditus, pro eruditione ecclesiasticae disciplinae," and never alluded to profane instruction. The *Liber pontificalis* relates that Stephen II called together the clerics and priests of the Lateran to encourage them to scrutinize Divine Scriptures so that they could answer the Church's adversaries.[372] The only literary works that permit us to judge the level of studies at the Lateran are the letters of the popes, the biographical notices of the *Liber pontificalis*, and certain *ordines Romani*. Their Latin is correct[373] but devoid of stylistic mannerisms or anything that might indicate contact with classical writers. The style of several eighth-century Roman inscriptions is quite inferior to that of the northern Italian inscriptions we mentioned earlier.[374]

A glance at the contents of Roman libraries confirms the predominantly religious nature of eighth-century clerical education. After the pillage of the preceding century, libraries had to be reorganized at the beginning of the eighth century. The future Gregory II as *sacellarius*

---

[369] *Ordines Romani*, XXXVI (Andrieu ed., 4: 195): "De gradibus Romanae ecclesiae. Primum in qualicumque scola reperti fuerint pueri bene psallentes, tolluntur unde, et nutriuntur in scola cantorum, et postea fiunt cubicularii. Si autem nobilium filii fuerunt statim in cubiculo nutrientur." The text is from the ninth century, according to Andrieu (ibid., pp. 189–90), but it should reflect older usages.

[370] *Liber pont.*, 1: 396: "Gregorius . . . in patriarcho nutritus"; ibid, 2: 1 (on Leo III, pope in 795): "Quia parva aetate in vestario patriarchi enutritus"; ibid., 1: 440: "Stephanus [Stephen II] post patris transitum parvus derelictus in venerabili cubiculo Lateranensi pro doctrina apostolicae traditionis sub praedecessoribus beate memoriae pontificibus permansit"; ibid., p. 463 (on Paul I): "Ab ineunte aetate in Lateranensi patriarcho cum proprio seniore germano Stephano."

[371] Ibid., 1: 470.

[372] Ibid., p. 443: "Hic beatissimus papa omnes suos sacerdotes et clerum in Laterense patriarcho sedule aggregans ammonebat divinam totis nisibus sectari Scripturam et in lectione vacare spiritali ut efficaces invenirentur in omni responso et assertione adversariorum ecclesiae Dei."

[373] See Viscardi, *Le origini*, pp. 221ff. Except for a few comments in Duchesne's edition of the *Liber pontificalis*, p. clxi, the style and language of this document has never really been studied. We know one of the *primicerii notariorum* of the eighth century, Ambrose, whose epitaph boasts of his qualities as a teacher; see *Liber pont.*, 1: 457: "Suboles audiunt, intrinsecus gemunt de tali tantoque doctori privati."

[374] See, for example, the metrical inscription from Saint Clement, which dates from 741, or the inscription of the primicerius Ambrose. See also Fedor Schneider and Walther Holtzmann, *Die Epitaphien der Päpste* . . . , Texte zur Kulturgeschichte des Mittelalters, 6 (Rome, 1933).

(treasurer-paymaster) was in charge of the Lateran library[375] and perhaps was also charged with buying books and having them made.
Zachary enriched the library of Saint Peter with liturgical books.[376] In
741, a priest of Saint Peter offered the basilica of Saint Clement,[377] not
far from the Lateran, a series of books whose titles were listed in an
inscription: they were the books of the Old and New Testaments. A
manuscript bearing an ancient version of the Gospels was composed at
the monastery of Saint Mary Aracoeli under Gregory III.[378] All the
books we know to have been issued from Roman scriptoria during this
period are ecclesiastical: homilies by various Fathers[379] and Isidore of
Seville's *De ortu et obitu patrum.*[380] The profane books preserved at
Rome were reserved for exportation, as it were. The abbot of Corbie
brought some back from his trip in 741.[381] It was also significant that
Pope Paul I sent Greek grammatical and geometrical works to Pepin.[382]

Other schools, in addition to the episcopal school, must have existed
in Rome. But here, in the absence of texts, we are reduced to hypotheses. When Charlemagne came to Rome in 774, he was greeted by
the "children who were learning their letters."[383] Upon leaving the
city in 787, he brought back to France with him "masters of grammar
and computus."[384] These were most likely the pupils and masters of the

---

[375] *Liber pont.*, 1: 396: "Subdiaconus atque sacellarius factus bibliothecae illi est cura
commissa." This is the first mention of a librarian at the Lateran.

[376] Ibid., p. 432: "Hic in ecclesia praedicti principis apostolorum omnes codices domui
suae proprios qui in circulo anni leguntur ad matutinos armarium opere ordinavit."

[377] Henri Leclercq, "Chartes," *DACL*, III-1, 900: "Veteris novique testamentorum
denique libros Octateuchum Regum psalterium ac Profetarum Salomonem Esdram historiarum ilico plenos."

[378] See Paul Rabikauskas, *Der römische Kuriale in der päpstlicher Kanzlei*, Miscellanea
historice pontificiae, 20 (Rome, 1958), p. 42.

[379] Vat. lat. 3835 bears the subscription of Agimund, a priest of the basilica of Saint
Philip and Saint James.

[380] Vat. Palat. 277 dates from 740 (see *Laterculus imperatorum romanorum Malalianus*,
MGH, AA, XIII, 424). It is quite difficult to prove that Carolingian minuscule originated
in Rome. See Viscardi, *Le origini*, pp. 166ff., and Giorgio Cencetti, "Postilla nuova a un
problema paleografico: L'origine della minuscola carolina," *Nova historia* 8 (1955): 9–32.

[381] For this trip and Grimo of Corbie's acquisitions, see Olga Dobiache-Rojdestvenskaia, *Historie de l'atelier graphique de Corbie de 651 à 830, reflétée dans les manuscrits
de Léningrad* (Leningrad, 1934), p. 51, and Vanderhoven and Masai, *Regula Magistri*,
pp. 38, 39.

[382] Pope Paul, *Ep.* 24 (*MGH, Ep.*, III, 529): "Direximus . . . et libros, quantos reperire
potuimus: id est antiphonale et responsale, insimul artem gramaticam Aristolis, Dionisii
Ariopagitis [libros] geometricam, orthografiam, grammaticam, omnes Greco eloquio
scriptas." For the interpretation of this sentence, see below, sect. IV.D.

[383] *Liber pont.*, 1: 497: "[Papa] direxit universas scholas militiae una cum patronis
simulque pueris qui ad didicendas litteras pergebant."

[384] Adhemar of Chabannes, *Hist. libri tres*, II, 8 (*MGH, SS*, IV, 118): "Rex Karolus

elementary schools that had already been in existence for half a century. But while the texts mention the construction of churches and hospitals, and the organization of provisions, they never refer to the foundation of schools.[385] The tradition of family education had no doubt never disappeared among the Roman aristocracy. The *Liber pontificalis* reports that Hadrian, pope in 772, was raised and trained by his uncle, Duke Theodotus, after his father's death. It notes also that while still a layman he devoted himself to ecclesiastical studies and frequented the church of Saint Mark close by his uncle's house.[386] A priest from his church, then, could have given him the first elements of religious education. But where were Duke Theodotus and all the young aristocrats who were destined for public offices and who served in the public tribunals educated?[387] Some have answered that schools, even law schools, existed for laymen.[388] No text allows this supposition. Where, then, were the *cives honesti*, the Roman bourgeoisie known to us through the documents the *tabelliones* drew up for them, educated?[389] We do not know. It could be that some of them received elementary instruction from educated clerics and then went on to complete their education in their corporate milieu.

IV. CONTRASTS IN FRANKISH GAUL

Frankish Gaul cut a pale figure between England and Italy during the first half of the eighth century. The Merovingian dynasty disappeared in the midst of problems and invasions. Had it not been for the energy of the Austrasian mayors of the palace, especially Charles Martel,

---

iterum a Roma artis grammaticae et computatoriae magistros secum adduxit in Franciam, ut ubique studium litterarum expandere iussit."

385 *Liber diurnus*, LXVI (Sickel ed., p. 62): "Praeceptum de concedendo xenodochio." See the *Liber pont.*, 1: 440. For the organization of provisions and the foundation of hospitals in Rome, see René Vielliard, *Recherches sur les origines de la Rome chrétienne*, 2nd ed. (Rome, 1959), pp. 110ff.

386 *Liber pont.*, 1: 486: "Hic defuncto ejus genitore atque parvulus suae nobilissimae genetrici relictus, studiose a proprio. . . . Theodoto dudum consule et duce . . . nutribus atque educatus est. Nam a primaeva aetatis suae pueritiae, dum adhuc laicus existeret, spiritualibus studiis . . . sedule perseverans in ecclesia sancti Marci quae vicina domus suae esse videtur." A fresco from Santa Maria Antiqua contains a portrait of Theodotus and his family; see de Grüneisen, *Sainte-Marie-Antique*, 1: 119–96.

387 The Roman Council of 743, c. 12 (Mansi, XII, 382), forbade clerics from appearing before a civil judge.

388 Bertolini, *Roma*, p. 708.

389 For the tabellionate in Rome and Roman subscriptions, see de Boüard, "Les notaires de Rome au Moyen Age," *MEFR* 31 (1911): 298.

Gaul would have been divided up into a series of small principalities under local "tyrants."[390] Given these conditions, the cultural renewal we noted at the end of the seventh century was in danger of being cut short.

A. THE RUIN OF ROMAN GAUL

The regions that had been traditional refuges for culture after the fall of the Empire in the West—Aquitaine, Provence, and Burgundy—became victims of foreign invasions and civil wars.

Aquitaine had attempted to escape Frankish tutelage at the end of the seventh century.[391] But threatened by Arab invasion in the eighth century, its dukes appealed to the Franks, who used the opportunity to reconquer the province. Charles Martel and his son Pepin were to undertake successive campaigns between 731 and 768, sometimes annually, to seize Aquitaine. The political result was achieved, but one consequence of the reconquest was the disappearance of all cultural centers.[392] The only cultivated Aquitainians we know took refuge in Italy and contributed to the organization of Farfa.[393] Aquitaine was not to play any role in the intellectual and artistic life of Gaul for centuries hence.[394]

Provence was likewise a victim of the Arabs and Carolingians. Duke Mauront's attempt to erect an independent principality with Moslem help was quickly squashed by Charles Martel.[395] Provence, like Aquitaine, became a secondary province to Gaul: episcopal cities for many years were without bishops;[396] monasteries were in ruins. Lérins, which was restored in 671 by Agilus and at which Benedict Biscop was still able to find something to nourish his ascetic spirituality,[397] fell prey to

---

[390] For these events, see Lot, *Les destinées*, pp. 292–96, 394ff., and Pirenne, *Mahomet et Charlemagne*, pp. 174ff.

[391] We need a history of Aquitaine in the seventh and eighth centuries. We have but two works already cited (see above, chap. 6, n. 83) and Dom F. Chamard, "L'Aquitaine sous les derniers Mérovingiens," *RQH* 35 (1884): 36.

[392] Aquitainians remembered the "hostilitas Francorum." This expression is found in one of the eighth-century Arvernian formulae (*MGH, Leg. sect. V*, p. 28, l. 4).

[393] *Il Chronicon farfense*, ed. Balzani, 1: 33, noted that one of the first abbots of Farfa, Aunepertus (716–24), came from Toulouse, and that Fulcoald, Wandelbertus, and Alan were Aquitainians. See Hans Grasshoff, *Langobardisch-fraenkisches Klosterwesen in Italien* (Göttingen, 1907), p. 34.

[394] Even in the eleventh century, Adhemar of Chabannes would allude to the intellectual poverty of Aquitaine (*Historiarum libri tres, PL*, CXLI, 108–9). For the disruption of the workshops of Aquitainian sculptors at the beginning of the eighth century, see Raymond Lantier and Jean Hubert, *Les origines de l'art français* (Paris, 1947), p. 58.

[395] For this reconquest, see Buchner, *Die Provence*, p. 28.

[396] Duchesne, *Fastes épiscopaux*, 1: 235, 261.

[397] Bede, *Vita abb.*, 2 (p. 365). This event took place around 660. On Lérins during

the Saracen razzias. No important Provençal scriptorium is known, no literary work was produced. Provence was to remain outside the Carolingian renewal, its importance further diminished when the routes leading to Italy were displaced more to the north, toward Lyon and the Valais.

Even Lyon and the surrounding region were eclipsed during the first half of the sixth century. First in the grip of the tyrants Savaricus and Aymar of Auxerre, then threatened by the Saracens in 731, Lyon was retaken in 733 by Charles Martel, who installed his *leudes* in the town.[398] According to the chronicler Ado, the town was without a bishop for some time.[399] So was Vienne. One bishop of Vienne, Austrebertus, took refuge on his Norman properties, while another, Warnacharius, ended his days in the monastery of Agaune.[400] Only at the end of the eighth century would the Lyonnais regain its place in the religious history of Gaul.

In Burgundy, finally, after a period of renewal at the end of the seventh century, everything crumbled to pieces: Autun was devastated by Saracens in 731; the cathedral and its archives were burned;[401] Charles Martel retook the city and placed in it counts in his pay. Auxerre was also occupied by the Austrasians after the defeat of Savaricus and Aymar. Pepin the Short distributed the goods of the bishops to Bavarian chiefs and put his *fideles* in charge of Burgundian monasteries.[402]

Thus, Roman Gaul was brutally reincorporated into the *regnum Francorum* but at the expense of the region's place in cultural history.

B. THE DECLINE OF LAY AND CLERICAL CULTURE
IN BARBARIAN GAUL

The expeditions of the first Carolingians within and without the kingdom entailed a general upheaval of society. Clerics as well as laymen were involved in these wars. A new nobility enriched by the princes and closely bound to them replaced the ancient Romano-Frankish aris-

---

the eighth century, see Henri Moris, *L'abbaye de Lérins: Histoire et monuments* (Paris, 1909).

[398] Coville, p. 430.

[399] Ado, *Chronicon, PL*, CXXIII, 121.

[400] *Liber pont.*, 1: 421.

[401] "Et omnia instrumenta cartarum in eodem incendio exruta." For these events, see Maurice Chaume, "Les comtes d'Autun aux VIIIᵉ et IXᵉ siècles," *Mémoires de la Société éduenne* (1939), p. 333, and idem, *Les origines du duché de Bourgogne*, 2 vols. (Dijon, 1925–31), 1: 57–61.

[402] Rainogala and Alagus, *Gesta episc. Autisiod.*, 29 (*MGH, SS*, XIII, 395).

tocracy, with the consequence that the aristocracy abandoned certain Roman traditions, especially neglecting the education of children. We have already seen from a study of autograph signatures that until the middle of the seventh century laymen could still sign the documents they had prepared.[403] In Clotilda's charter of 673, there were fourteen autograph subscriptions. Beginning in the eighth century, however, the interested parties as well as the witnesses were content to place a cross at the bottom of documents. Thus, in the will of the Parisienne Erminentruda[404] and in documents in favor of the abbey of Wissembourg,[405] only the clerics subscribed with their own hand. The laymen who could write were very important individuals such as Count Eberhard (731) of Alsace;[406] Abbo, rector of Provence,[407] and Pepin of Herstal.[408] We could argue that the use of manual *signa* does not necessarily indicate ignorance on the part of those who traced them, but perhaps represents a new diplomatic technique—perhaps, but the new diplomatic technique resulted from a general ignorance of writing.

The disappearance of lay education brought about a major transformation of bureaucratic practices. Henceforth, only clerics would maintain registers and draw up documents. Clerics could be employed in the royal chancellery or in the count's tribunal before the eighth century, but they were still the exception. Rarely could they be found in such positions in the sixth century: Gregory of Tours related that a deacon left his church to serve in the administration of the public fisc, something Gregory thought was extraordinary.[409] The Church prohibited clerics from sitting on a tribunal.[410] The more frequent occurrence, on the contrary, was for former bureaucrats to become monks and clerics.[411]

---

403 See above, chap. 6, sect. III.B.

404 Pardessus, II, 258.

405 Albert T. Bruckner, ed., *Regesta Alsatiae aevi Merovingici et Karolini, 496–918* (Strasbourg, 1949), pp. 10–50.

406 Léon Levillain, Jeanne Vielliard, and Maurice Jusselin, "Charte du comte Eberhard pour l'abbaye de Murbach," *BECh* 99 (1938): 40.

407 *Monumenta novaliciensia vetustiora*, ed. Cipolla, 1: 12.

408 Pardessus, II, 298. During an illness, Pepin delegated Plectrude, his wife. We should also cite the subscription of a *venditor* in a charter of 723 from Saint Bertin (in *Les chartes de Saint-Bertin d'après le Grand cartulaire de Dom Charles-Joseph Dewitte . . .*, ed. Daniel Haigneré [Saint-Omer, 1886–99], XXIX). Is the reference, however, to a cleric?

409 Gregory of Tours, *De virtut. Juliani*, 17 (*MGH, SRM*, I-2, 571): "Relictam ecclesiam fisco se publico junxit."

410 *MGH, Leg. sect. III*, I, 182, 171: Auxerre, 573 (c. 34), Mâcon, 585 (c. 19).

411 Gregory of Tours, *Vitae patrum*, IV (*MGH, SRM*, I-2, 675, l. 4): "Proculus ex aerario presbyter." Jonas, *Vita Columbani*, II, 9 (ibid., IV-1, 123), recounted the story of a former notary of Theodoric II who became a monk at Luxeuil.

Clerics begin to appear in the offices in the seventh century.[412] In a letter a Provençal abbot wrote to Desiderius, then treasurer at court, the abbot asked for news of the *pueri* he had sent to help the king ("ad opera dominica"). The same Desiderius had a deacon in his service then.[413] Marculf prepared his formulary for a bishop.[414] In the eighth century, only clerics took up the pen. Clerics at Bourges, Sens, Tours, and Clermont found their models in the formularies that were being composed in the cities.[415] The diplomas from this period reveal that deacons and lectors were especially charged with the duties of the notariate because they were no doubt considered the most educated clerics.[416] It has been noted that the first Carolingians, unlike their Merovingian predecessors, did not have laymen in their service but, rather, used clerics to prepare their documents. This practice has been interpreted as a real "revolution" in royal administrative procedures.[417] There is no disputing the fact, however, that the change came about as a result of a general evolution which had begun at the end of the seventh century.

Clerics thus replaced laymen in the modest duties of the notary. Frankly, this is the only manifestation of their culture in the first half of the eighth century. Clergymen were also victims of the political turmoil and the serious material and moral crisis which afflicted the Frankish church.[418] The Carolingians profited from this crisis to place their creatures at the head of dioceses. Even the most important clerics resembled laymen in their ignorance and their way of life. In their dioceses, which they converted into veritable principalities, bishops spent their time hunting and fighting, quite unconcerned with their pastoral obligations.[419] Boniface's unflattering indictment of the Frankish church and of Milo of Triers and others like him ("Milo et ejusmodi

[412] *Form. And.*, 1 (*MGH, Leg. sect. V*, p. 4, l. 15): "Diaconus et amanuensis."

[413] Bertegyselus, *Ep.* II, 2 (*MGH, Ep.*, III, 204, ll. 6 and 12).

[414] See above, chap. 6, sect. III.D., for this formulary. An early eighth-century date is obviously preferable to a seventh-century date.

[415] See Buchner, *Die Rechtsquellen*, pp. 49ff.

[416] "Illo diacono atque professore" (formula from Bourges, *MGH, Leg. sect. V*, p. 176, l. 4). For Deacon-notaries, see charters from Wissembourg in 711, 731, 739, and a charter of Saint Bertin in 723; for lector-notaries, see the charters of Saint Bertin of 704, of Saint Germain-des-Prés of 697, of Saint Denis, etc.

[417] H. Sproemberg, "Marculf und die fränkische Reichskanzlei," *NA* 47 (1928): 127.

[418] Fliche-Martin, 5: 361ff.; Emile Lesne, *Histoire de la propriété ecclésiastique en France*, vol. 2, *Les étapes de la sécularisation des biens de l'Eglise du VIIIe au Xe siècle* (Lille, 1922).

[419] See Eugen Ewig's fine article on the Frankish episcopacy during this period, "Milo et eiusmodi similes," in *Sankt Bonifatius: Gedenkgabe zum 1200 Todestag* (Fulda, 1954), pp. 412–40.

similes") must be read in this connection.[420] No councils met between 696 and 742, and indeed, all religious life seems to have halted. Chroniclers did not hesitate to stigmatize the ignorance of these bishops: there was a Gauziolenus of Le Mans (743–77) who was an "illiterate and uncultured cleric,"[421] and a Ragenfridus of Rouen "as ignorant as his predecessors Grimo and Guido."[422] Unlettered bishops ordained the priest Aldebert, who preached heresy and revolt against the hierarchy throughout northern Gaul around 740.[423] Clerics followed the examples of their superiors. As in contemporary England, priests no longer knew Latin. There must have been many like the Bavarian cleric Boniface denounced, who baptized "in nomine patria et filia."[424] We can verify the ignorance of Latin in the liturgical works and in documents clerics prepared. The Latin language, which still had a certain hold in the seventh century, thanks to the survival of classical culture, was now liberated and in a giant step joined the spoken language. Whether one reads Austrasian or Neustrian documents, the degradation is the same.[425]

It has been argued that this evolution was felt less in the royal chancellery than in private notariates.[426] While, until the beginning of Charlemagne's reign, the Latin of private documents remained what it had been at the beginning of the eighth century, the Latin of the royal documents promulgated by Pepin was already much more correct.[427] How can this difference be explained? Were the clerics employed in the palace more educated than the others? Was the Carolingian palace a cultural asylum amidst general anarchy? Before answering these questions, we must turn to the monastic world and try to find out if it too had suffered from the crisis of Frankish culture. Perhaps there we shall find the first elements of an answer.

[420] MGH, Ep., III, 371. See ibid., p. 300, l. 14: "Episcopi ebriosi et incuriosi vel venatores et qui pugnant in exercitu armati." See also the preface of the Regula canonicorum, PL, LXXXIX, 1057.

[421] Actus pontificum Cenomannis, ed. Busson and Ledru, p. 245.

[422] Gesta abb. font., VIII (Lohier and Laporte ed., p. 60): "Erat namque ignarus litterarum sicuti predecessores sui Grimo et Vuido."

[423] For this individual, see Boniface's letters 57, 59, and 77 (MGH, Ep., III, 314, 316, 348) and the Roman Council of 745 (C. J. Hefele and Henri Leclercq, Histoire des Conciles d'après les documents originaux [Paris, 1908–10], 3, pt. 2: 873ff.).

[424] Boniface, Ep. 67 (MGH, Ep., III, 336, l. 20): "Sacerdos qui latinam linguam penitus ignorabat et dum baptizaret nesciens latini eloquii infringens linguam diceret: baptizo te in nomine patria et filia et spiritus sancti."

[425] See the examples given by Lot, "A quelle époque," pp. 139–44.

[426] Pei, Language of Eighth-Century Texts, pp. 364ff., 387.

[427] A bill of sale from 769 which has been published in Giry's Manuel de diplomatique, p. 439, can be compared with a judgment by Pepin in 759 (MGH, Dipl. karol., I-2, 17–18).

C. The Vitality of Monastic Culture in Gaul and Germany

Merovingian monasteries incontestably suffered during the first half of the eighth century. Their temporality had been diminished by the policy of secularization carried out by the Frankish princes;[428] laymen placed at the head of abbeys did not encourage religious life. Nevertheless, the revival of monastic culture we observed at the end of the seventh century continued (see Map 15). Monks were the only men of letters of the period, and in their scriptoria they recopied both ecclesiastical and profane works.

1. GAUL

All the active scriptoria belonged to monasteries north of the Loire, in particular, those within the borders of the former Neustria. Luxeuil had suffered from Arab incursions into Burgundy. While its production was not totally disrupted,[429] its activity was modest by comparison with that of its daughter house, Corbie. The scribes of Corbie, who had initially adopted Luxovian script,[430] soon invented a new kind of script by combining Anglo-Saxon and Roman elements.[431] It was certainly for the use of the scriptorium that the abbots had skins, papyrus, and gold pigment for illumination brought from their *cella* at Fos in 716.[432] Of course, not all the pre-Carolingian manuscripts Corbie possessed were made at the abbey itself.[433] Most were Italian and had been brought back by pilgrims,[434] but they served as models for the scribes. During Leutcharius' abbacy in the middle of the eighth century, the scriptorium was already in full operation.[435]

[428] See Lesne, *Les étapes*, and Jean Laporte, "Les monastères francs et l'avènement des Pippinides," *Revue Mabillon* 30 (1940): 1–30.

[429] The evangeliary of Autun (*CLA*, VI, 716), which was copied in 754 at Vosavio, seems to have come from Luxeuil; see *Les manuscrits à peintures en France du VIIe au XIIe siècle*, with Foreword and notes by Jean Porcher, Bibliothèque Nationale, Departement des manuscrits (Paris, 1954), p. 7. The same can be said for a Fulda manuscript (*CLA*, VIII, 1197) requested by a certain Ragyntrudis.

[430] As indicated in the Gregory of Tours manuscript that was begun at Luxeuil but finished at Corbie; see *CLA*, VI, xxii.

[431] In addition to the bibliographical references given by Lesne in *Les livres*, pp. 215ff., see A. Mundó's article, "Sur l'origine de l'écriture dite *ena* de Corbie," *Scriptorium* 11 (1957): 258–61.

[432] Léon Levillain, *Examen critique des chartes mérovingiennes et carolingiennes de l'abbaye de Corbie* (Paris, 1902), p. 236.

[433] See the list in Lesne, *Les livres*, p. 38.

[434] See above, n. 381. Some of these manuscripts may have come from Vivarium (Leningrad, Q. v. 1-6-10 and Q. v. 1-3). The fifth-century Livy (Paris, lat. 5730) came from Avellino, near Naples.

[435] Abbot Leutcharius, who attended the Council of Attigny in 765, was responsible

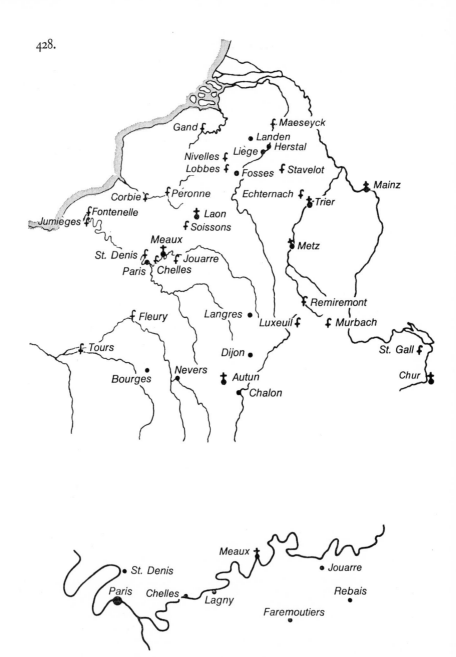

15. Centers of Monastic Culture in Northern Gaul in the Eighth Century

Laon, more to the east, boasted a scriptorium staffed by Anglo-Saxon trained scribes; from this center came works by Origen, Augustine, and Orosius, as well as Isidore of Seville's *De natura rerum*. The signature of a woman named Dulcia in the margin of this last manuscript suggests that it came from the abbey of Saint John, which Anstrude (died 707) had founded, rather than from the cathedral scriptorium.[436] In the region of Paris, the scriptoria of Chelles, Saint Denis, and Meaux were also active.[437]

The same was true of Fleury and Saint Martin, two monasteries located on the banks of the Loire. Fleury, founded in the middle of the seventh century, had rapidly established contact with Italy when, around 670–72, monks brought the relics of Saint Benedict from Monte Cassino to Fleury.[438] Sometime after the end of the seventh century, an Italian manuscript of Sallust was erased to make room for Jerome's commentary on Isaiah.[439] Most of the works recopied at Fleury were ecclesiastical except for an Oribasius manuscript of the seventh or eighth century and Isidore's *De natura rerum*.[440] The presence of this latter work is proof of contacts between Fleury and Spain, established no doubt when Spanish monks fled the Saracen invasion.

Saint Martin of Tours also benefited from the contributions of foreigners. The *archicantor* John, who taught Roman chant to the monks of Jarrow, wanted to be interred at Tours because of the warm welcome he found there on his way to England.[441] The famous *Pentateuch*, magnificently illustrated and perhaps the work of a Spanish painter, was

for the manufacture of a manuscript of Ambrose's works; see Lesne, *Les livres*, p. 218, and O. Dobiache-Rojdestvenskaia, "Un scribe corbéen au VIIIe siècle," *Paleographia latina* 5 (1927): 50. For the scriptorium at Corbie, see *CLA*, VI, xxiii, and Dobiache-Rojdestvenskaia, *Histoire de l'atelier graphique de Corbie*.

436 *CLA*, VI, 765. See Fontaine's edition of the *De natura rerum*, p. 30, for this manuscript.

437 Saint Denis is discussed later in this chapter. The *Gellone Sacramentary* may have been executed at Meaux or Cambrai; see J. Deshusses, "Le Sacramentaire de Gellone dans son contexte historique," *EL* 75 (1961): 193–209. For Chelles, see Bernhard Bischoff, "Die Kölner Nonnenhandschriften und das Skriptorium von Chelles," in *Karolingische und Ottonische Kunst* (Wiesbaden, 1957), pp. 345–411 (*Mittelalterliche Studien*, 1: 16–34).

438 Paul the Deacon, *HL*, VI, 2 (*MGH, SRL*, p. 165). See Fliche-Martin, 5: 518–19.

439 *CLA*, VI, 809; for the first Fleury manuscripts, see Pierre Courcelle, "Fragments patristiques de Fleury-sur-Loire," in *Mélanges dédiés à la mémoire de Félix Grat*, ed. E.-A. van Moé, J. Vielliard, and P. Marot, 2 vols. (Paris, 1946–49), 2: 145ff.

440 *CLA*, VI, xviii–xx.

441 Bede *HE*, IV, 16 (18) (p. 242). Abbot Agiricius' trip to Rome remains doubtful because the text which mentions it (Adeodatus, *Ep. ad universos galliae episcopos*, PL, LXXXVII, 1141) seems apocryphal.

at Tours at the end of the eighth century.[442] Irish influences are even more evident, since three manuscripts from the first half of the eighth century, one of which was Tiberius Donatus' commentary on the *Aeneid*, bear the mark of Irish hands.[443] Saint Martin's scriptorium was well organized during this period: about twenty scribes collaborated in the production of a Eugippius manuscript between 725 and 750.[444] As at Corbie, some of the scribes used a script which already presaged Carolingian minuscule.[445]

If we take into consideration the illuminated manuscripts that came from these different workshops, it can be argued that Merovingian painting, born at the end of the seventh century, enjoyed a brilliant career. A simple comparison, for example, of the frontispiece of Augustine's *Quaestiones in Heptateuchum* (attributed to Laon)[446] and a page from the *Gelasian Sacramentary* (from Saint Denis)[447] affirms that both manuscripts belong to the same "school." Influenced by the embroidery of Eastern textiles[448] and Coptic motifs, the painters decorated initials with interlace and with geometric and zoomorphic figures (birds, fish). Their choice of fresh colors—green, red, and yellow—gave the manuscripts "a delicate and charming gaiety."[449] The monks of northern Gaul had fashioned an art which contrasted with that of the Anglo-Saxons and the Italians and which would have continued to produce masterpieces had not Carolingian neoclassicism overwhelmed it.

The organization of a scriptorium did not always correspond to the literary activity of the monastic school.[450] Monks could be calligraphic

---

[442] See the bibliographical references in *CLA*, V, 693a–b, for this famous manuscript.

[443] See Lesne, *Les livres*, p. 52, and E. K. Rand, *A Survey of the Manuscripts of Tours* (Cambridge, Mass., 1929), pp. 91ff. The subscription of the evangeliary from Saint Gatien reminds one of hisperic Latin; see Rand, *A Survey*, p. 92.

[444] *CLA*, V, 682. See Edward Kennard Rand and Leslie Webber Jones, *Studies in the Script of Tours*, vol. 2, *The Earliest Book of Tours with Supplementary Descriptions of Other Manuscripts of Tours* (Cambridge, Mass., 1934), pp. 4–81. Abbot Wictbert (died 756), who was still copying manuscripts at the age of ninety, might have directed this scriptorium. For this abbot, who seems to have been allied to a Bavarian family, see H. Frank, *Die Klosterbischöfe d. Frankenreichs*, Beiträge zur Geschichte des alten Mönchtums und des Benediktinerordens, vol. 17 (Münster, 1932), pp. 56, 156ff.

[445] Rand and Jones, *The Earliest Book of Tours*, pp. 78–79.

[446] *CLA*, V, 630. The frontispiece is reproduced in *Les manuscrits à peintures en France du VIIe au XIIe siècle*, p. 6, plate A.

[447] Grabar and Nordenfalk, *Le haut Moyen Age*, p. 128.

[448] See especially the fabric from the tomb of Saint Merry (died 700), reproduced in Lantier and Hubert, *Les origines de l'art français*, p. 131.

[449] Grabar and Nordenfalk, *Le haut Moyen Age*, p. 133. Research continues on the origins of this little-known school of Merovingian painting.

[450] As A. Boutémy remarked in "Quelques directions à imprimer aux études de latin mé-

artists and painters without being lettered, as we saw in the case of Lindisfarne. In northern Gaul, however, such a contrast does not seem to have existed. One text, though from the ninth century, states that the nuns of Valenciennes, founders of the monastery of Alden-Eyck near Maeseyck (730), had received a good education and were also artists.[451] We know of several instances where manuscript copying went hand in hand with the production of literary works.

The monks of Saint Wandrille, while maintaining an active scriptorium and enriching their library with many kinds of books,[452] wrote several vitae at the requests of their abbots.[453] The same observation can be made of Laon.[454] At Lobbes, a Mosan monastery founded by Ursmer (died 713), Abbot Ermino (died 737) wrote a metrical poem in honor of the founder. Abbot Auso composed two vitae of high quality. During his period, a scriptorium was at work.[455] The same situation prevailed at Saint Denis, as we shall see. In some instances, we can see the relationship between the scriptorium and the school: scribes at Soissons and Corbie copied Caesarius' *Homilies* for monks who were preparing to evangelize the rural masses.[456] A Corbie manuscript required the joint efforts of a poet, a scribe, and a painter.[457]

---

diéval et de paléographie," in *Mélanges de philologie, de littérature et d'histoire anciennes offerts à J. Marouzeau* (Paris, 1948), p. 69.

[451] *Vita Harlindis et Reinulae, ASOB,* III, 656: "Legendo, modulatione cantus, psallendo (nec non quod nostris temporibus valde mirum est) etiam scribendo atque pingendo quod hujus aevi robustissimis viris oppido onerosum videtur." For this vita, see Léon van de Essen, *Etude critique et littéraire sur les vitae des saints mérovingiens de l'ancienne Belgique* (Louvain, 1907), pp. 109ff.

[452] The activity of this scriptorium is mentioned by Jonas of Fontenelle in the *Vita Vulframni (MGH, SRM,* V, 688) apropos of a young Frisian: "Quia erat in arte scriptoria eruditus, plurimos codices in praedicto transcripit monasterio." The *Gesta abb. font.,* IX, 2 (Lohier and Laporte ed., p. 66) reports that Abbot Wando (742–47) bought many books, and it even provides a list of them (see Lesne, *Les livres,* p. 582). Among them were three evangeliaries, Jordanes' *History of the Goths,* and the *History of Apollonius of Tyre.*

[453] See A. Legris, "Les vies interpolées des saints de Fontenelle," *AB* 17 (1898): 305. For the hagiographical work of the period, see František Graus, *Volk, Herrscher und Heiliger im Reich der Merowinger: Studien zur Hagiographie der Merowingerzeit* (Prague, 1965).

[454] The *Vita Sadalbergae* was written at the beginning of the eighth century; see Krusch, *MGH, SRM,* V, 40–66; VIII, 844.

[455] Auso, *Vita Wismari, MGH, SRM,* VI, 445: "Miracula etiam sui magistri, opere metrico, juxta elementorum summam optimus edidit." This poem in trochaic dimeters was published by Germain Morin, "La plus ancienne Vie de S. Ursmer: Poème de S. Ermin," *AB* 23 (1904): 315. Wilhelm Levison, "Ein neuer Hymnus auf Ursmar von Lobbes," *NA* 30 (1905): 141, did not think it authentic because its form was too literary. See *CLA,* I, 101, for the scriptorium.

[456] For Soissons, see above, n. 11. For Corbie, see *CLA,* V, 664.

[457] *CLA,* IV, 433. See above, n. 7. This illuminated manuscript carries an acrostic

It thus seems impossible to limit cultural life to the realms of painting and calligraphy in the Frankish monasteries of the first half of the eighth century. These monastic schools may not have had a Bede or a Boniface, but they did effectively lay the groundwork for the restoration of studies. While the secular clergy slumbered in ignorance, abbots tried to make their houses cultural bastions. They must have been encouraged by the monks who came from foreign countries, especially by the example of the Irishmen and Anglo-Saxons who settled in Germany.

2. GERMANY

Throughout the Merovingian period, the regions of Germany located across the Rhine were conquered by the Frankish kings without really ever being touched by Christian civilization. The kings did not attempt to integrate these areas, where they had never lived, into their own holdings but preferred instead to confide them to local chiefs.[458] While the local leaders were able to distinguish themselves from the masses—the tomb of Alamannic princes found at Wittislingen proves that they did[459]—the populace nevertheless continued to live as had their fifth-century ancestors. On this point, the evidence from cemeteries in the Moselle and Rhine regions is eloquent.[460] When Christianity finally reached these people, it was rapidly Germanized.[461]

Given these circumstances, the conquest of German lands—Thuringia, Alamannia, and Hesse—had to be repeated continually. The first Carolingians needed several campaigns to complete the conquest. In order to solidify Frankish domination, these regions had to be deeply Christianized. The princes were thus very much aware of the benefits that would accrue to them from the German missions of Irish and,

---

poem dedicated to Bishop Basinus (died 704). The manuscript of Gregory of Tours' *Historia Francorum* was written at Corbie, a royal foundation.

[458] Sprandel, *Der merovingische Adel*, pp. 110ff.

[459] Joachim Werner, *Das alemannische Fürstengrab aus Wittislingen* (Munich, 1950). A fibula bears this engraving: "Uffila vicat in d[e]o [fe]lix in[n]ocens funere capta fuit quo vi[ve]re dum potui fui fidelissima tuatisa in deo. Ardwig filius et Ferig filius et Viadis probissemam matrem et conjugem deposuerunt."

[460] Fritz Fremersdorf, *Das fränkische Reihengräberfeld von Köln-Müngersdorf* (Berlin, 1956); Walter Veeck, *Die Alamannen in Württemberg*, vol. 1 of *Germanische Denkmäler der Völkerwanderungzeit*, ed. H. Zeiss (Berlin and Leipzig, 1931).

[461] The Niederdollendorf stele is influenced more by Barbarian art than it is by Christianity. See *Mémorial d'un voyage*, p. 63. For Germany before the conversion, see S. Deel, *Die Germanen im Urteil des Bonifatius und in ihrer Wirkung auf seine Missionspraxis* (Heidelberg, 1939).

later, Anglo-Saxon monks at the end of the seventh century. This is not the place to study this missionary movement. Suffice it to recall that Pirmin (died 739) in the land of the Alamanns, Killian (died 689) in Thuringia, and Willibrord in Frisia (died 739) were the first to convert the German people before Boniface continued and completed their work from 716 until his death in 754.[462]

As in England a century before, the conversion was effected from monasteries. These establishments, generally located in forest regions (see Map 16), remind one of Anglo-Saxon or Columbanian foundations. They were primarily "seminaries" for missionaries, where children who had been locally recruited—generally ransomed slaves—were educated alongside young people from the missionaries' native land. Boniface twice speaks of Fulda's monastic schools.[463] At Fritzlar in Hesse, a priest and a deacon were to observe the Benedictine *Rule*, organize the liturgy, teach, and preach.[464] Sturm, a young Bavarian raised at Fulda, learned the Psalms and Scriptures—that is, the Latin of the Psalter and the principal rules of the sacred science—from the priest Wisbert.[465] Was this not the program of the first monasteries of the seventh century?

The comparison, however, ends there. Actually, the German monasteries became centers of studies even more rapidly than those of England. Willibrord, the apostle of Frisia, had had Wilfrid for a master at Ripon before going on to Egbert in Ireland. Hewald the Black, whose religious learning Bede praised, accompanied Willibrord to Frisia.[466] Boniface, as we know already, was a man of letters. When he solicited the help of his compatriots, he chose the most cultivated among them, those who were "as well trained in reading as in writing and the other arts."[467] He placed his disciple Lioba in charge of the abbey of Tauber-

[462] See Fliche-Martin, 5: 531ff.; Albert Hauck, *Kirchengeschichte Deutschlands* (Leipzig, 1887), 1: 346ff.; and Levison, *England*, pp. 49–83.

[463] Boniface, *Ep.* 93 (*MGH, Ep.*, III, 380, l. 22): "Quidam sunt monachi per cellulas nostras et infantes ad legentes litteras ordinati." He wrote, in regard to Lull, "Spero quod in illo habeant presbiteri magistrum et monachi regularem doctorem" (ibid., ll. 31–32).

[464] Idem, *Ep.* 40 (p. 289): "Regulam vestram vobis insinuent et spiritales horas et cursum aecclesiae custodiant et ceteros admoneant et magistri sint infantum et predicent verbum Dei fratribus."

[465] Eigil, *Vita Sturmi, MGH, SS,* II, 366.

[466] Bede, *HE,* V, 10 (p. 299): "Sacrarum litterarum erat scientia institutus."

[467] *Vita Bonifatii*, 6 (Levison ed., p. 34): "Ex Britanniae partibus servorum Dei plurima ad eum tam lectorum quam etiam scriptorum aliarumque artium eruditorum virorum congregationis convenerat multitudo."

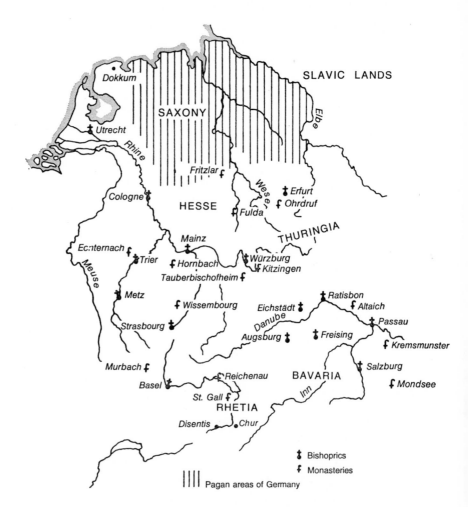

16. Cultural Centers in Eighth-Century Germany

bischofheim near Würzburg,[468] Chunihilt and Berthgyth in Thuringia,[469] and Tecla at Kitzingen.[470]

The abbots and abbesses of the new monasteries and convents soon
began to dream of building libraries and had books brought from England and Italy. Boniface asked Daniel of Winchester for the texts of
the six Prophets and appealed to Cuthbert at Jarrow and Egbert at
York for Bede's work, whose significance he had just discovered.[471] He
asked Duddo, a former pupil to whom he had dedicated a grammar,
for a commentary on Paul's Epistles and sought Gregory the Great's
letters from a Roman deacon.[472] When he went to Rome himself, he
brought back to Fulda the *Codex* of the Gospels that Victor of Capua
had revised in the sixth century.[473] Some of the works which were imported were obviously used by the teachers and missionaries. Boniface
asked Eadburg for a copy of the Epistle of Saint Peter written in golden
characters so that the pagans would give greater reverence to the words
of the apostle.[474] The books of Bede that interested him were those
useful to a preacher.[475] The homilies of Caesarius of Arles were brought
to Würzburg for the same purpose.[476] The missionaries, however, never
forgot that they were men of letters. Boniface completed his grammatical treatises with a work on grammar attributed to Augustine.[477] When
he trained his own disciples, he taught them not only Latin, exegesis,
and the art of preaching, but also poetry. He corrected the verses Abbess
Lioba sent him[478] and taught Lull and a certain Dombercht, "whom he
had trained, nourished, and loved," the rules of meter and grammar.[479]

[468] See above, sect. II.A.2, for this nun.
[469] Berthgyth, *Ep.* 147–48 (*MGH, Ep.*, III, 428–30); Otloh, *Vita Bonifatii*, I, 25 (Levison ed., p. 138, l. 4): "Sed Chunihilt et filia ejus Berhtgit valde eruditae in liberali scientia
in Thuringorum regione constituebantur magistrae."
[470] *Vita Bonifatii*, IV, 3 (Levison ed., p. 95).
[471] Boniface, *Ep.* 34 (p. 285); ibid., p. 348, l. 11.
[472] Ibid., pp. 285, 308. See above, n. 68, for Duddo.
[473] See Carl Scherer, "Die Codices Bonifatiani," in *Festgabe zum Bonifatius-Jubiläum,
1905*, ed Gregor Richter and Carl Scherer (Fulda, 1905), pp. 6–12. See above, chap. 5,
sect. IV.A, for this codex. It is difficult to know exactly when Isidore's *De natura rerum*
came to Fulda. Fontaine, in his edition of the work (p. 80), assumes that it came from
England to Fulda when the monastery was founded.
[474] Boniface, *Ep.* 35 (p. 286, l. 9).
[475] Ibid. 91 (p. 377, ll. 1–4): "Quod nobis predicantibus habile et manuale et utillimum
esse videtur, super lectionarium anniversarium et proverbia Salomonis."
[476] See Bernhard Bischoff, *Libri sancti Kiliani: Die Würzburger Schreibschule* (Wurz-
burg, 1952). Boniface consulted Caesarius' sermons (Levison, *England*, p. 140).
[477] Gebauer, *Prolegomena to the Ars grammatica Bonifatii*, p. 36.
[478] Lioba, *Ep.* 29 (p. 280). See above, n. 98.
[479] Lull, *Ep.* 98 and 103 (*MGH, Ep.*, III, 348, 389). According to the first letter, it seems
that Boniface taught meter to Lull during their stay in Rome. For Lull's culture, see

Boniface, like Columban, succumbed in his old age to his taste for poetry and sent several verses to Pope Zachary congratulating him on his accession.[480] He also composed enigmas on the virtues.[481] When he left for the mission that was to be his last, he brought a small library along with him.[482] According to one of his biographers, he fell beneath the blows of Frisian pagans, book in hand.[483]

We have lingered over Boniface's case because we know him best. We come to the same conclusion, however, if we look at the evidence concerning other missionaries. In distant Frisia, Gregory of Trier, a companion of Boniface, brought back many works from Rome for his monastery at Utrecht,[484] while his disciple Liudger, who studied with Alcuin for four years, came back from York with more manuscripts.[485]

A nun of Heidenheim, near Eichstädt, wrote the *Life* of Willibald and his brother Wynnebald.[486] The monasteries Pirmin founded in Alamannia were enriched with books: the famous *Codex Laudianus*, which Jarrow owned during Bede's time,[487] migrated to the monastery of Hornbach in the Palatinate, where Pirmin died.[488] The scriptorium at Murbach was active shortly after the monastery's foundation in 728.[489] Around 729, Pirmin brought several works with him to Reich-

---

Manitius, 1: 147–48, and Levison, *England*, pp. 144–45; for Domberecht, see Levison, p. 150.

[480] Boniface, *Ep.* 50 (*MGH, Ep.*, III, 302, ll. 1–6).

[481] Boniface, *Aenigmata, MGH, PAC*, I, 1–15. See above, n. 90, for these poems. There was a manuscript of the *Aenigmata* at Corbie from the middle of the eighth century; see *CLA*, V, 648.

[482] Willibald, *Vita Bonifatii*, ed. Levison, p. 50; "Thecas in quibus multa inerant librorum volumina." See Scherer, "Die Codices Bonifatiani," (see above, n. 473), and H. Schüling, "Die Handbibliothek des Bonifatius," *Archiv für Geschichte der Buchwesen* 4 (1961): 285–348.

[483] Otloh, *Vita Bonifatii*, II, 27 (Levison ed., p. 211).

[484] Liudger, *Vita Gregorii*, 8 (*MGH, SS*, XV-1, 73, 78). The *Enchiridion* of Augustine was among the books he left to his disciples.

[485] *Vita Liudgeri*, I, 12 (Diekamp ed., p. 17): "Habens secum copiam liborum." According to an hypothesis of Levison (*England*, p. 62), a Livy manuscript that belonged to the bishop of Dorstadt came from this collection; this suggestion, however, has not been universally accepted. The Evangeliary of Maeseyck probably did come from York, however; see above, n. 135.

[486] *MGH, SS*, XV-1, 86–117. Her name was Hugeburc according to B. Bischoff ("Wer ist die Nonne von Heidenheim?" *Studien und Mitteilungen zur Geschichte des Benediktinerordens und seiner Zweige* 49 [1931]: 387).

[487] See above, sect. II.B.1.

[488] *CLA*, II, 251.

[489] An extract from the *Moralia*, the late seventh-century "book of eclogues" by the Irishman Lathcen, might have been there already; see Lesne, *Les livres*, p. 711. Nevertheless, Lesne was mistaken to think that the manuscript of Jerome's letters, which was copied in 744, was from Murbach. It was copied at Tours; see *CLA*, VI, 762.

enau, some of which have come down to us.[490] The presence of Spanish works in this monastery is further proof of Abbot Pirmin's Visigothic origin.[491]

In the neighboring monastery of Saint Gall, a Columbanian creation established in the eighth century by Anglo-Saxons and Irishmen, there was an active scriptorium before the time of Winithar, the first known scribe.[492] The library might have been enriched with acquisitions from Italy, England, Ireland, and Spain.[493] Saint Gall, at the mouth of the upper valley of the Rhine, benefited from the influence of Rhaetia, which had maintained Roman traditions longer than elsewhere. This region, theoretically dominated by the Franks, was actually a principality under the direction of the bishop of Chur.[494] The will of Bishop Tello (died 765), an aristocrat from the illustrious family of the Victorids, speaks of *curiales*. Roman law was still applied here, and jurists in the mid-eighth century compiled Alaric's *Breviary* in a collection known as the *Lex Romana Curiensis*.[495] Chur long resisted Germanization because of its communications with northern Italy through the Splügen. Italian artists even came to work at Chur, while travelers brought back manuscripts from the other side of the mountains for the

[490] See Paul Lehmann, "Die mittelalterliche Bibliothek," in K. Beyerle, *Die Kultur der Abtei Reichenau* (Munich, 1925), p. 234, and T. Mayer, "Die Anfänge des Reichenau," *Zeitschrift für die Geschichte des Oberrheins* 21 (1953): 305–52. The first library at Wissembourg was definitely enriched by Primin and his disciples. See J. Semmler, "Studien zur Frühgeschichte der Abtei Weissembourg," *Blätter für pfälrische Kirchen und Geschichte* 24 (1957): 7–9.

[491] C. Jecker, "St. Pirmins Erden- und Ordensheimat," *Archiv für mittelrheinische Kirchengeschichte* 5 (1953): 9–41. F. Beyerle, however, opts for an insular origin; see "Bischof Perminius und die Gründüng der Abteien Murbach und Reichenau," *Zeitschrift für Schweizerischegeschichte* 27 (1947): 127–73. See also Arnold E. Angenendt, *Monachi peregrini: Studien zu Pirmin und den monastischen Vorstellungan des frühen Mittelalters* (Munich, 1972).

[492] H. Brauer, "Die Bücherei von St. Gallen und das althochdeutsche Schrifttum," *Hermaea* (1926); James M. Clark, *The Abbey of St. Gall as a Centre of Literature and Art* (Cambridge, 1926). Winithar is the first known scribe at St. Gall (Lesne, *Les livres*, pp. 301–2). The *Abrogans* glossary undoubtedly came from St. Gall; see Georg Baesecke, *Der deutsche Abrogans und die Herkunft des deutschen Schrifttums* (Halle, 1930).

[493] There is no proof that the papyrus fragment of Isidore's *Synonyma* (CLA, VII, 929) came from the British Isles. The fragments of the eleventh book of the *Origines* found at Saint Gall in 1940 and 1955, on the other hand, are of Irish origin. See Alban Dold and Johannes Duft, *Die älteste irische Handschriftenreliquie der Stiftsbibliothek St. Gallen mit Texten aus Isidors Etymologien*, Anhang von Heft 31 der Texte und Arbeiten, nebst einer Erweiterung (Beuron, 1955), and CLA, V, 995.

[494] Paul Edmond Martin, *Etudes critiques sur la Suisse à l'époque mérovingienne, 554–715* (Geneva, 1910), pp. 448ff.; Elizabeth Meyer-Marthaler, *Rätien im frühen Mittelalter* (Zurich, 1948); idem, *Römisches Recht in Rätien im frühen Mittelalter* (Zurich, 1968).

[495] See Buchner, *Die Rechtsquellen*, pp. 37–38. A charter from Chur is in the style of contemporary Italian documents; see ChLA, I, no. 4.

needs of the bishopric or of Disentis, the neighboring abbey.[496] Saint Gall later benefited from this relationship.

Bavaria, more to the east, also came under Italian influence. The duchy had looked more toward Italy than toward Gaul since the seventh century, as we have seen. Rome still lived in eighth-century Bavaria.[497] Charles Martel and Pepin once again brought the land under Frankish authority but maintained the national dynasty of the Agilolfians. The dukes, wanting to reorganize the Bavarian Church, which was still dependent on the metropolitan see at Aquilea, established contact with the popes. Theodon (died 717), Liutprand's brother-in-law, even asked Gregory II to attempt an ecclesiastical reorganization, a project which would only be achieved later by Boniface.[498] The dukes, meanwhile, founded monasteries at Mondsee, Nieder-Altaich, and Kremsmünster that were populated by Irish and Anglo-Saxon monks and rapidly became study centers.[499]

The Irish monk Fergil and his compatriot Dubda settled in Bavaria during this period. Fergil, who became bishop of Salzburg in 767, was very likely the same person as the Virgil Boniface denounced for having maintained "that there was another world and other men under the earth as well as a sun and a moon."[500] The scientific curiosity of the Irish, which Boniface certainly misinterpreted, thus found a welcome in Bavarian circles.[501]

[496] See Wilhelm Holmquist, *Kunstprobleme der Merovingerzeit* (Stockholm, 1939), pp. 210–13, and Bognetti, "S. Maria *foris portas* di Castelseprio," p. 528. For the foundation of Disentis, see Iso Müller, *Disentiser Klostergeschichte*, vol. 1 (Einseideln, 1952), and idem, "Zur rätisch-allemannischen Kirchengeschichte des 8. Jahrhunderts," *RSH* 2 (1952): 1–40.

[497] A Bavarian bill of sale from the region around Tegernsee proves that Roman juridical customs were still observed; see *Fonte iuris romani antejustiniani, pars tertia: Negotia*, ed. Vincenzo Arangio-Ruiz (Florence, 1943), no. 191, and Brunner, *Deutsche Rechtsgeschichte*, 1: 254. The names of the signatories were Roman: Mairanus, Floritus, Vigilius, Quartinus. The monuments of ancient Juvavum (Salzburg) were still standing in Saint Rupert's time (end of the seventh century). See Hauck, *Kirchengeschichte Deutschlands*, 1: 372–77. Rural traditions were more Roman than Germanic; see Eugen Ewig, "Das Fortleben römischer Institutionen in Gallien und Germanien," in *X Congresso internazionale di scienze storiche, Relazioni VI* (Florence, 1955), p. 583.

[498] Fliche-Martin, 5: 533, 539–40; Ernst Klebel, "Zur Geschichte des Christentums in Bayern vor Bonifatius," in *Sankt Bonifatius*, pp. 388–411.

[499] According to Konrad Beyerle, ed., *Lex Baiuvariorum* (Munich, 1926), p. lxv, the monks of Nieder-Altaich helped draw up the *Law of the Bavarians* around 740.

[500] Boniface, *Ep.* 80 (*MGH, Ep.*, III, 360, l. 21): "Quod alius mundus et alii homines sub terra sint seu sol et luna." For Virgil, see Delius, *Geschichte der irischen Kirche*, p. 112; H. Van der Linden, "Virgile de Salzbourg et les théories cosmographiques au VIIIe siècle," *BAB* (1914), pp. 163–87; and Paul Grosjean, "Virgile de Salzbourg en Irlande," *AB* 78 (1960): 92.

[501] Virgil, whom one Irish text calls "the geometer," is certainly the author of Aethicus

Bavarian clerics imitated the Irish literary style. A reading of the *Vita Corbiniani* of Bishop Arbeo of Freising (764–84) attests to the new success hisperic writings and the works of Virgil the Grammarian enjoyed.[502] Some historians have thought that Arbeo acquired his learning in northern Italy and that he had contacts with Pavia and Bobbio.[503] This could be, since there were strong ties between Bavaria and Lombard Italy; however, the presence of insular monks is sufficient to explain the reemergence of mannerism.

With Virgil of Salzburg and Arbeo of Freising a new period in cultural history begins. We are now in the midst of the Carolingian renewal.

Germany, thanks to monasticism, was in the vanguard of the intellectual renaissance during the first half of the eighth century. By a sort of compensation, the culture of Gaul, impoverished by the ruination of the southern provinces, found a new field of action in Germany. The renewal of monastic studies was soon to capture the entire Church, although indirectly. If cultivated monks had any influence during this period, it was primarily among princes, especially Carolingian princes.

D. The Frankish Court: A Cultural Center

Exercising power in the names of the Merovingian kings, the mayors of the palace maintained the traditions of the Merovingian court. In all likelihood, the only great change that accompanied the replacement of the ancient royal dynasty was a turnover in personnel, since the mayors of the palace had their own clientele. Aristocrats, as in earlier times, received their training from adolescence at court. Charles Martel welcomed young Gregory, descendent of an illustrious Austrasian fami-

---

Ister's cosmography. See Heinz Löwe, "Ein literarischer Widersacher des Bonifatius: Virgil von Salzburg und die Kosmographie des Aethicus Ister," *Abhandlungen der Akad. der Wissenschaften und der Literatur in Mainz* 11 (1951): 903–88. See Manitius, 1: 229–34, for Aethicus Ister's cosmography. J. Fontaine, in his edition of the *De natura rerum* (pp. 72–73), thinks that the Munich manuscript of this work (*CLA*, IX, 1294) was copied during Virgil's episcopate. The Pseudo-Isidorian *Liber de numeris* was undoubtedly composed in the entourage of the bishop of Salzburg; see Robert E. McNally, *Der irische "Liber de numeris": Eine Quellenanalyse des Pseudo-Isidorischen "Liber de numeris"* (Munich, 1957).

[502] See Krusch's preface, *MGH, SRM*, VI, 528ff., and Heinz Löwe, "Arbeo von Freising: Eine Studie zur Religiosität und Bildung im 8. Jahrhundert," *Rheinische Vierteljahrsblätter* 15–16 (1950–51): 87–120. Insular artists also came to Bavaria. The so-called chalice of Tassilo could have been made by someone in Virgil's circle; see Günther Haseloff, *Der Tassilokelch*, Münchener Beiträge zur Vor- und Frühgeschichte, vol. 1 (Munich, 1951).

[503] See Karl Kurt Klein, *Die Anfänge der deutschen Literatur: Vorkarlisches Schrifttum im deutschen Südostraum* (Munich, 1954), pp. 45ff.

ly, who was later to become Boniface's disciple and then abbot of Utrecht.[504] Chrodegang, another Austrasian, was also admitted to the court and named referendary by Charles before Pepin the Short made him bishop of Metz in 742. Paul the Deacon relates that Chrodegang spoke Latin with as much ease as he spoke his mother tongue, no doubt a very rare talent at court.[505] But we should not exaggerate. Perhaps Charles Martel was not that "brute, completely indifferent to intellectual life," some like to imagine.[506] He at least knew how to affix his signature to the bottom of documents he delivered.[507] There were cultivated men in his family entourage: his brother, the "illustrious count" Childebrand, eager to put the exploits of the Carolingian family into writing, had Pseudo-Fredegarius' history continued and did not neglect to recall that the Franks were descendents of the Trojans; his son, Nibelung, continued the chronicle after 751. Historiography thus was reappearing, thanks to the court.[508] In addition, certain important laymen had manuscripts executed in monastic scriptoria.[509]

We should add that during Charles' reign and, later, during that of his son, the palace became the new center of legal activity. The Salic law was then recopied, perhaps even glossed, and accompanied by the famous prologue a monk wrote glorifying the Franks.[510] *The Law of*

[504] Liudger, *Vita Gregorii*, 3 (*MGH, SS*, XV, 67). Gregory descended through his grandmother from Dagobert II; see Michael Tangl, "Studien zur Neuausgabe der Bonifatius-Briefe," *NA* 40 (1916): 769.

[505] Paul the Deacon, *Gesta ep. Mett.*, PL, XCV, 720: "Hic in palatio majoris Caroli ab ipso enutritus ejusdemque referendarius exstitit eloquio facundissimus patrio quamque etiam latino sermone imbutus." According to John of Gorze's tenth-century *Vita Chrodegangi* (*MGH, SS*, X, 552–72), Chrodegang would have been first raised at the abbey of Saint Trond. Roger, p. 427, notes that in his rule he cited a few verses from Eugenius of Toledo.

[506] The phrase is Etienne Delaruelle's ("Charlemagne et l'Eglise," *RHEF* 39 [1953]: 185).

[507] See the precept for Boniface (753), *MGH, Dipl. karol.*, I, no. 4, and Giry, *Manuel de diplomatique*, p. 715.

[508] Pseudo-Fredegarius, *Chron.*, 34 (*MGH, SRM*, II, 182): "Usque nunc inluster vir Childebrandus comes avunculus praedicto rege Pippino hanc historiam vel gesta Francorum diligentissime scribere procuravit. Abhinc ab inlustre viro Nibelungo, filium ipsius Childebrando itemque comite, succedat auctoritas." See *Wattenbach-Levison*, 2: 161ff., 180ff., for the historiography of this period.

[509] The daughter of a Frankish aristocrat ordered a work made for her at Luxeuil, according to the subscription of a Fulda manuscript bearing Isidore of Seville's *Synonyms* and the *Epistula Leonis* ("In honore dni nostri ihu xri ego Ragyndrudis ordinavi librum istum" [*CLA* VIII, 1197]). This woman corresponded with Lull; see Levison, *England*, p. 294.

[510] See Buchner, *Die Rechtsquellen*, p. 20. For the rhymed prose prologue, see *Wattenbach-Levison*, 1: 95–115. The allusion to the martyred victims of the Romans leads one to suspect that the prologue was the work of a monk of Saint Denis. See my "Le renouveau de la culture à la cour de Pépin," *Francia* 2 (1973).

the Alamanni was composed, while the laws of the Ripuarians were completed.[511] In providing justice, the princes were helped by *legis doctores*, an expression found in Frankish texts for the first time.[512]

This juridical activity must be seen in the context of the legal transformation occurring in Frankish Gaul. During this period, formularies preserving earlier documents were compiled throughout the kingdom of the Franks as if, during those troubled times, a need was felt to preserve models.[513] Eighth-century diplomas reveal that clerics and monks had not completely forgotten the rules of Roman law; even in such superficially Romanized areas as Flanders, the documents from Saint Bertin bespeak Roman influence. We can say the same for the documents that emanated from Wissembourg, Auxerre, and Autun.[514] It has been assumed that the redactors continued to refer to the *Romana auctoritas* in order to strengthen their documents without, however, really understanding the significance of what they were doing. Nevertheless, there were still several concepts that time had not obscured. The résumés of Alaric's *Breviary* from the early eighth century were not copied by clerics and monks interested merely in ancient texts: they had a practical application in mind.[515]

But at the same time there was a different development north of the Loire. Here, innovations contradicting Roman practices began to appear in documents dating from 708 and 723. Perhaps because of the economic upheaval of the period, the typical bill of sale gradually disappeared in the middle of the eighth century.[516] Wills, which had more or less preserved their Roman character from the time of the invasions, were markedly transformed in Burgundy and Dauphiné in the middle of the eighth century.[517]

---

[511] Buchner, *Die Rechtsquellen*, pp. 22–23, 31.

[512] Joseph Tardif, *Archives de l'Empire, Monuments historiques, Cartons des rois* (Paris, 1886), no. 54: "Sicut proceres nostri seu comis palatii vel reliqui legis doctores judicaverunt." This expression is found in Justinian's Code; see *ThLL*, V-1, 1773. It is also found in a diploma of 812 (*MGH, Dipl. karol.*, I, 422, l. 5).

[513] Buchner, *Die Rechtsquellen*, pp. 49ff.

[514] See J. F. Lemarignier, "Les actes de droit privé de l'abbaye Saint-Bertin au haut Moyen Age: Survivances et déclin du droit romain dans la pratique franque," *Revue internationale des droits de l'Antiquité* (1950): 37–53.

[515] Louis Stouff, "L'interprétation dans les formules et les chartes du VIe au XIe siècle," *AM* 1 (1889): 145. For the resumés, see Mommsen's preface to the *Theodosiani libri XVI*, 1: xxviii, 461, and Conrat, *Geschichte*, pp. 228–40. We must add the ninth-century *Breviary of Couches*; see A. Gouron, "Le Bréviaire d'Alaric de Couches-les-Mines," *Mémoires de la Société pour l'histoire du droit et des institutions des anciens pays bourguignons, comtois et romands* 29 (1957): 97.

[516] Lemarignier, "Les actes de droit privé," pp. 53–72.

[517] See G. Chevrier, "Déclin et renaissance du testament en droit bourguignon du VIIe

Neither clerics nor laymen could fuel the cultural enrichment of the Frankish court. The renewal came from the monastic world. Pepin of Herstal had encouraged Willibrord's missions, sent him to Rome, and in 700 established him at Echternach.[518] The disciples of the Anglo-Saxon monk remained faithful to the sons of Pepin and recorded the successes of the dynasty in their calendar.[519] Charles did for Boniface what his father had done for Willibrord.[520] Moreover, his confidence in the monastic life was such that he charged the monks of Saint Denis with the education of his son, Pepin.[521]

The significance of this decision cannot be overemphasized. First of all, in so acting, Charles Martel broke with the tradition of the Merovingian kings, who confided their children to governors, and followed instead the example of Anglo-Saxon princes, who, from the seventh century, had their children educated by monks. At the same time, the Carolingians forged strong bonds between their court and Saint Denis. This monastery already enjoyed the privilege of receiving the remains of kings and other major figures;[522] Charles Martel wanted to be interred there. Pepin sent the abbot of Saint Denis to Rome to obtain the pope's authorization to have himself elected king of the Franks. In 754, Pope Stephen II consecrated Pepin and his family at Saint Denis.[523] In gratitude for the monastery's many favors, Pepin undertook important building projects at Saint Denis, traces of which can still be seen.[524]

---

au XIIᵉ siècle," *Mémoires de la Société pour l'histoire du droit et des institutions des anciens pays bourguignons* 10 (1944–45), and idem, "L'évolution de l'acte à cause de mort en Dauphiné du VIIᵉ à la fin du XIᵉ siècle," *Recueil de mémoires et travaux publié par la Société d'histoire du droit . . . des anciens pays de droit écrit* 1 (1948): 9–27.

[518] Levison, *England*, pp. 56ff. We should also note the good relations between Pepin and the monks of Lobbes (*Vita Ermini, MGH, SRM*, VI, 445).

[519] Wilhelm Levison, "A propos du calendrier de S. Willibrord," *RB* 50 (1938): 37–41.

[520] Levison, *England*, pp. 74ff.

[521] According to Pepin (*MGH, Dipl. karol.*, I, 13), "ad monasterium beati domini Dionisii ubi enotriti fuimus." See Heinrich Hahn, *Jahrbücher des fränkischen Reichs, 741–752* (Berlin, 1863). One is astounded to see Manitius (1: 245) portray Pepin as an "illiterate." For an opposite view, see Paul Lehmann, "Das Problem der karolingischen Renaissance," *Settimane*, 1: 334. Carloman, Pepin's brother, who was to finish his days in Monte Cassino, must also have been raised at Saint Denis, while Jerome was raised at Saint Amand (*Versus libris saeculi octavi adiecti*, I [*MGH, PAC*, I, 89]).

[522] Léon Levillain, "Etudes sur l'abbaye de Saint-Denis à l'époque mérovingienne," *BECh* 82 (1921): 5–116; 86 (1925): 5–99; 87 (1926): 20–97, 245–346; 91 (1930): 5–65, 264–300. For the excavations and discovery of tombs at Saint Denis, see Edouard Salin, "Sépultures gallo-romaines et mérovingiennes dans la basilique de Saint-Denis," *Monuments et mémoires Piot* 49 (1957): 93–128.

[523] Lot, *Les destinées*, pp. 406, 410.

[524] Jules Formigé, *L'abbaye royale de Saint-Denis: Recherches nouvelles* (Paris, 1960), p. 59.

In addition, can we not assume that the Greek books sent by Pope Paul I to the king of the Franks[525] were intended, not for the "palace school," as is so often argued (even though the school never actually existed),[526] but rather for the library at Saint Denis? In fact, among these books were works attributed to Dionysius the Areopagite. The belief that the Areopagite was the same Dionysius as the apostle of the Gauls, whose relics were kept at Saint Denis, was undoubtedly already current.[527]

The library donation was justified, since Saint Denis was a center of studies. Of course, in the ninth century Hincmar recalled the misery of the monastery during Charles Martel's time and the abandonment of the library by monks little concerned with books.[528] But the situation might have improved during Pepin's reign. Pilgrims on their return from Rome brought with them the elements of the first collection of classics which were to be the glory of the abbey.[529] Furthermore, the scriptorium at Saint Denis began to produce its own texts during this period; perhaps the illuminated *Gelasian Sacramentary* already mentioned should be attributed to it.[530] The chronicle known as the *Liber historiae Francorum* was probably written about 727–36 by a monk from the monastery.[531] The author's citations reveal that he knew the work of Gregory of Tours and even of Isidore of Seville. His Latin was not yet of good quality, but there was some progress. Thirty years later the monks of the royal abbey were masters of their form.[532] Why not see the notaries who transformed the style of royal charters for the better as monks of Saint Denis?

---

[525] See above, n. 382.

[526] I cannot follow Erna Patzelt, *Die karolingische Renaissance* (Vienna, 1924), p. 80, on this subject. See Lesne, *Les écoles*, p. 43.

[527] Gabriel Théry, "L'entrée du Pseudo-Denys en Occident," in *Mélanges Mandonnet*, 2 vols. (Paris, 1930), 2: 23–25, discusses this gift without, however, linking it to the abbey of Saint Denis. Furthermore, he discounts Mabillon's argument (*ASOB*, II, xxxi, 536), according to which Pope Hadrian would have sent the Areopagite's works to Abbot Fulrad of Saint Denis. Contrary to what Théry maintained, however, the church of Saint Denis founded in Rome by Pope Paul I was not consecrated to Dionysius of Paris. See R. J. Loenertz, "Un prétendu sanctuaire romain de Saint-Denys de Paris," *AB* 66 (1948): 118–33.

[528] Hincmar of Reims, *Vita Remigii*, preface (*MGH*, *SRM*, III, 252, l. 25). See Lesne, *Les livres*, p. 29.

[529] See the list of pre-Carolingian manuscripts from Saint Denis in Lesne, *Les livres*, pp. 36–37.

[530] Antoine Chavasse, *Le sacramentaire gélasien* (Tournai, 1958), p. viii.

[531] *MGH*, *SRM*, II, 238ff. For the author, see Kurth, "Etudes critiques sur les *Gesta regnum Francorum*," in *Etudes franques*, 2: 31–65, and *Wattenbach-Levison*, 1: 114ff.

[532] See the *Clausula de unctione Pippini regis*, *MGH*, *SS*, XV-1, 1, which Levillain has studied (*BECh* 88 [1927]: 21ff.).

Monks from this monastery were not the only ones to influence Pepin. Chrodegang, founder of Gorze, became the king's counselor after Boniface's death and urged him to universalize Roman liturgical chant throughout Gaul.[533] Aldaric, who was named abbot of Saint Vaast (died 768), had a reputation for his knowledge of medicine.[534] Fergil the Irishman, later bishop of Salzburg, lived two years at court because, according to his *Vita*, King Pepin "liked his literary learning and his talents as a preacher."[535] Lastly, Ambrosius Autpertus, future abbot of Saint Vincent (Volturno), whose religious erudition was astonishing, may have spent his youthful years at court.[536]

If we admit that Pepin the Short's court was even a modest center of culture, we would expect that the prince would have favored ecclesiastical schools at the great reforming councils he called as mayor of Neustria at Boniface's request.[537] Now, at no time was there any question of obliging bishops to educate or to open schools. All the reformers' efforts bore more on the moral regeneration of the clergy than on their intellectual and dogmatic training: they chose first to reestablish the ecclesiastical hierarchy and to forbid clerics to practice magic, to hunt, to go to war, or to take a wife or a concubine before requiring that they become learned men. It sufficed that priests know the *Credo* and the *Pater* and that bishops supervise the manner in which they administered sacraments.[538] The first conciliar decisions concerning the organization of schools before those of Charlemagne were promulgated at Neuching in 772 through the impetus of Duke Tassilo of Bavaria.[539]

We must note, however, one individual initiative which would permit the clergy to rediscover its moral and intellectual dignity, the redaction of Chrodegang's rule.[540] The bishop of Metz was aware of the

---

[533] See above, n. 368.

[534] The *Miracula S. Vedasti*, MGH, SS, XV, 402, calls him a "probatissimus medicus." Even though this text was written about 875, it cannot be ignored.

[535] *Vita Virgilii*, MGH, SS, XI, 86: "Et quia litterarum scientia cum morum honestate in ipso exuberavit rex eum sicut tubam evangelicae predicationis libenter audiebat et secum fere duobus annis propter Dei amorem retinuit." Other Irishmen would later come to Saint Denis; see Lesne, *Les livres*, p. 51.

[536] Winandy, *Ambroise Autpert, moine et théologien*. For his beginnings at court, see the *Vita Ambrosii Autperti*, 2 (PL, LXXXIX, 1270). Winandy, p. 74, does not have much confidence in this text.

[537] Fliche-Martin, 5: 365ff.

[538] See the Council of Soissons, 744, c. 5 (Hefele and Leclercq, *Histoire des Conciles*, 3, pt. 2: 854).

[539] Ibid., pp. 971–72. The bishop was to have the priests read daily, to organize an episcopal school, and to recruit teachers.

[540] E. Mohrain, "Origine et histoire de la *Regula canonicorum* de St. Chrodegang,"

need for a rule of life, comparable to that of the monks, if the secular clergy were to rekindle a taste for religious activities. Chrodegang repeated efforts which had been attempted before him.[541] Like Augustine at Hippo and Caesarius at Arles, he sought to adapt a monastic rule for his clerics, choosing, obviously, the Benedictine rule for this purpose. The clerics of Metz were to live in common, to practice poverty, to follow the offices, and to devote time to reading, especially during Lent.[542] The books the bishop recommended for study were the Holy Scriptures and the works of the Fathers.[543] In addition, Chrodegang introduced Roman chant to Metz, had Romans come to Metz, and, conversely, sent missions to Rome.[544] The reputation of Metz was so great that Sigulf, an Anglo-Saxon friend of Alcuin, preferred to study in this Austrasian town rather than in Rome.[545] But whatever else might be said, Chrodegang did not provide for schools for young clerics. The articles in his rule concerning young clerics were not written until 816.[546]

Chrodegang's reform was not immediately adopted by the Frankish episcopacy. The intellectual tenor of the clergy during the reign of Pepin, however, contrasts happily with what we have observed during the reign of his predecessor. Frankish bishops at the synod of Gentilly (767) could hold their own with the Byzantines, who came to discuss the dogma of the Trinity and the cult of images.[547] When, during the following year, Pope Stephen III asked Pepin to send "bishops trained and versed in the divine writings and the institutes of the holy canons"[548] to a Roman council, he was in effect rendering homage to the reform undertaken by the Frankish king.

---

in *Miscelleanea Pio Paschini*, 2 vols. (Rome, 1948–49), 1: 173–85; Jean Baptiste Pelt, *Etudes sur la cathédrale de Metz*, vol. 1, *La liturgie* (Metz, 1937), pp. 7, 28.

[541] See Charles Dereine, "Chanoines," *DHGE*, 12: 358ff.

[542] *Regula canonicorum*, PL, LXXXIX, 1057 and 1073, preface and chap. XXXIV: "Scripturis enim sacris intenti decernimus ut omnes sint unanimes officiis in divinis, lectionibusque sacris assidu." Chapter XXXIV: "Lectioni vero clerici in his quadraginta diebus . . . a prima dicta usque ad tertiam plenam vacent."

[543] Ibid., chap. VIII.

[544] Paul the Deacon, *Gesta ep. Mett.*, PL, XCV, 709.

[545] *Vita Alcuini*, 8 (*MGH, SS*, XV-1, 189).

[546] *MGH, Leg. sect. III*, II, 312.

[547] Emile Amann, *L'époque carolingienne (757–888)*, vol. 6 of Fliche-Martin (Paris, 1947), pp. 24–25.

[548] *Liber pont.*, 1: 473: "Deprecans . . . ut aliquantos episcopos gnaros et in omnibus divinis scripturis atque sanctorum canonum institutionibus eruditos ac peritissimos dirigent ad faciendum in hanc Romanam urbem concilium."

Thanks to the action of Carolingian monks and princes, the first half of the eighth century was not the period "of barbarism and of sterility" that it has been typed.[549] We are already in the Carolingian renaissance.

[549] Dom G. Morin, "La plus ancienne Vie de S. Ursmer," *AB* 23 (1904): 317. F. Lot, in his *La fin du monde antique*, p. 439, wrote: "In the eighth century, night fell on Gaul."

CHAPTER TEN

Methods of Christian Education
in the Seventh and Eighth Centuries

We have just studied the organization of Christian culture in the various kingdoms of the Barbarian West during the seventh and eighth centuries with particular reference to masters and students, schools and programs. Our task is not yet finished. We cannot speak of education without knowing what methods teachers employed, what they thought of the child and the adolescent, and what educational techniques they used. Furthermore, we would not achieve the goal of this book if we were to remain within the confines of the monastic and episcopal schools: Christian education was addressed to all men, laymen as well as clergymen. We must try, then, to learn how the Church provided for the religious education of the Christian people.

1. PEDAGOGICAL METHODS

This heading is perhaps too ambitious. The masters of the seventh and eighth centuries were not theoreticians. The Christian education they organized was still too new for them to reflect on the training of youth in learned treatises. In the absence of educational manuals,[1] we must (with apologies to the reader) discuss scattered allusions and remarks which too often are only commonplaces. Even the vocabulary used to designate the different periods in the child's life is uncertain. Ancient authors adopted Hippocrates' theoretical but useful tripartite

[1] For the treatise *Institutionum disciplinae* attributed to Isidore, see chap. 6, n. 540.

division.[2] The child was called *infans* until he was seven years old; from seven to fourteen, he was a *puer*; beyond age fourteen he was called an *adolescens*. Gregory the Great twice repeated this definition, and later Isidore of Seville and Eugenius of Toledo also used it.[3] Isidore, however, noted that the Bible used the word *puer* to designate both the newborn and the adult who was faithful to God. The imprecision of biblical vocabulary perhaps explains the uncertainty of our authors. Virgil the Grammarian, for example, distinguished the *infans* from the *parvulus* in reference to small children.[4] Benedict's *Rule* and the *Rule* of the Master use the terms *infans*, *puer*, and *infantulus* for children younger than fifteen years.[5] Gregory of Tours mentioned an *adolescens* less than eight years old,[6] while an inscription used the term *infantia* for an adolescent.[7] Between seven and fourteen years, *infans, infantulus, juventus, ephebus, parvulus, perparvulus*, and *adolescens* were the terms generally used.[8] Alcuin, remembering a trip he made when he was thirty-six years old, wrote that he was an "adolescent" at the time.[9]

This said, let us first examine the situation of the child who had not yet reached the age of puberty. His education normally took place within the family. The Church reminded parents through the mouths of its preachers of their responsibility as educators.[10] Unfortunate was the lot of the father who neglected this task, for he ran the risk of barring his son from the celestial kingdom.[11] He had to raise his children with severity ("in disciplina et correctione"), as all the biblical

---

[2] Marrou, *Education*, p. 148.

[3] Gregory the Great, *Moral.*, XI, 46 (*PL*, LXXV, 981); *Hom. in Evang.*, I, 19 (*PL*, LXXVI, 1155): Isidore of Seville, *Origines*, XI, ii, 4; Eugenius of Toledo, *Satisfactio*, *MGH, AA*, XIV, 129.

[4] Virgil the Grammarian, *Epitomae*, II (Tardi ed., p. 41).

[5] Benedict, *Regula*, LXIII (Schmitz ed., p. 29): "Pueri parvi vel adolescentes"; ibid., LXX (p. 97): "Infantum vero usque quindecim annorum"; *Regula Magistri*, LIX (Vanderhoven and Masai ed., p. 263, l. 23): "Infantuli vero intra duodecim annos."

[6] Gregory of Tours, *Vitae patrum*, VIII, 2 (*MGH, SRM*, I-2, 692, l. 20). A sixth-century inscription describes a four-year-old child as an *adolescens*; see Le Blant, *NR*, no. 107.

[7] Le Blant, *NR*, no. 106.

[8] For *ephebus*, see *Vitas sanctorum*, I, 1 (Garvin ed., p. 139); *Vita Ursmari*, 1 (*MGH, SRM*, VI, 445). For *juventus*, see Joseph de Ghellinck, *"Juventus, gravitas, senectus,"* in *Studia medievalia in honorem R. P. Raymundi Josephi Martin, O. P.* (Bruges, 1949), pp. 38–59.

[9] Alcuin, *Ep.* 172 (*MGH, Ep.*, IV, 285).

[10] Caesarius of Arles, *Sermones* XIII, CXXVII (Morin ed., pp. 64, 502); Fulgentius of Ruspe, *Ep.* VII, 23, "De conjugali debito" (*PL*, LXV, 310); Gregory the Great, *Ep.* VI, 29 (*MGH, Ep.*, I, 407, l. 21).

[11] Gregory the Great, *Dial.*, IV, 19 (Moricca ed., p. 256); *Moral.*, I, 7–9, on Job, the model for fathers (*SC*, 32: 146–48).

texts recommended.[12] So that he would remember the punishment incurred by the high priest Helias for not having corrected his sons—who, as children, were sinners by nature—Gregory the Great and Isidore of Seville, following Augustine, repeated the story.[13] Hagiographers who wanted to show the special graces showered on the saint whose history they were writing took pleasure in reporting all the frivolities of his friends. Young Guthlac, for example, "did not imitate the impertinence of children, the extravagant gossip of women, the silly popular stories, the stupid sayings of peasants, the frivolous and lying chatter of parties, and the various cries of all sorts of birds, as was the custom to do at that age."[14] A good education necessitated the repression of all evil tendencies: the swaddling clothes which encircled the child's arms and feet were a symbol of discipline to Gregory the Great.[15] This severity, which was completely Roman, was reinforced by the Germanic tradition that gave the father or the uncle complete power over the child, who could be beaten, sold, and even killed by his father.[16]

Romano-Barbarian society was without pity for the child, whose fate, consequently, was often tragic among the lower classes. The birth of a child was a heavy burden on the family, so much so that civil and religious legislators continually had to decry abortion and infanticide.[17]

[12] These texts have been assembled in Isidore of Seville, *Liber de divinis scripturis*, PL, LXXXIII, 1203 (chap. 9, "De filio superbo"; chap. 12, "De correptione"; chap. 20, "Parvulos emandanda instantes"). See Donatien de Bruyne, "Etudes sur le *Liber de divinis scripturis*: Un abrégé du VIIᵉ siècle," *RB* 45 (1933): 124. The texts are also included in Augustine's *Speculum* (*CSEL*, 12: 3–285), which was well known during the period; see F. Weihrich, "Das *Speculum* des hl. Augustinus und seine handschriftliche Ueberlieferung," *Sitzungsberichte der Oesterreichischen Akademie der Wissenschaften zu Wien: Phil. hist. Klasse* 113 (1883): 33. See also chap. XXXI of the *Irish Canons*, copied in the middle of the eighth century in Cambrai (in *Die irische Kanonensammlung*, ed. Friedrich Wasserschleben [Leipzig, 1885], p. 105).

[13] Gregory the Great, *Moral*, IX, 21 (PL, LXXV, 876): "Damnantur parvuli ex sola culpa originali"; Isidore of Seville, *Sent.*, I, 13, 6 (PL, LXXXIII, 564): "Innoxios esse infantes opere non esse innoxios cogitatione."

[14] *Vita Gutlachi*, XII (Colgrave ed., p. 78). See the *Vita Siviardi*, *ASOB*, III-1, 486: "Et illud quod solet juvenilis aetas litteraturae disciplinam fugere ac laborem."

[15] Gregory the Great, *Moral.*, XXVIII, 17 (PL, LXXVI, 470): "Pannis quippe infantiae pedes ac brachia constringuntur ne huc atque illuc dis soluta libertate jactentur."

[16] See Henri Simonnet, *Le "mundium" dans le droit de famille germanique* (Paris, 1898).

[17] Laws against abortion are contained in *Leges Visigoth.*, VI, 3, 6 (*MGH, Leg. sect. I*, I); *Lex Baiuvariorum*, VIII, 18, 19, 20, 22, 23; *Lex Alaman.*, XC, XCII (ibid., V-1); Council of Lerida (524), c. 2; Caesarius of Arles, *Sermones* I, XIX, XLIV, LI, CC; Fortunatus, *Vita Germani*, I, 2 (*MGH, AA*, IV-2, 11); *Laws of Ine*, 9 (Haddan-Stubbs ed., 3: 214–19); Gregory of Tours, *Glor. martyr.*, 87 (*MGH, SRM*, I-2, 547). See laws against infanticide in Council of Lerida (524), c. 2, and Council of Toledo (589), c. 17; (Mansi, VIII, 612, and IX, 997). See P. Riché, "Problèmes de démographie historique du Haut Moyen Age, (Vᵉ–VIIIᵉ siècles)," *Annales de démographie historique* 3 (1966): 37–55.

Parents in seventh-century Gaul left their children to perish because of the added financial burden children imposed.[18] How many abandoned children,[19] children sold as slaves,[20] children exploited because they were born with some lucrative deformity,[21] and poor children[22] there were in the cities! The situation of children during this period—and, indeed, throughout the entire Middle Ages—reminds one of the situation still prevalent in many African and Asian countries.

The child could escape this fate, though, by entering a monastery, where he was fed, clothed, and (what seemed more important to him) provided with the means to attain his salvation and, indirectly, the salvation of his parents. There must have been many children in the monasteries, although obviously we can never know exactly what portion of the monastic population they comprised. Parents often offered their young sons and daughters to monasteries. Aristocrats, in particular, offered their children in fulfillment of a vow: if a descendent was born to them after many years of sterility,[23] if a son miraculously escaped death,[24] or if the outcome of a battle were favorable,[25] they thanked heaven by giving their child to God. Quite often, the influence of a great person—a Columban, for example—spurred them to part with a son or daughter.[26] Under these conditions we find children of all ages in monasteries. We even see young boys in convents in Ireland, Gaul, and Italy.[27] In the Spanish monasteries founded by Fructuosus, parents

[18] *Vita Bathildis*, MGH, SRM, II, 488: "Pessima et impia . . . consuetudo pro qua plures homines sobolem suam interire potius quam nutrire studebant." According to Roman law, the *capitatio* struck each child. This custom seems to have still been enforced in the seventh century; see Ferdinand Lot, *L'impôt foncier et le capitation personelle sous le Bas-Empire et l'époque franque* (Paris, 1928), p. 89.

[19] For the *alumni*, see the Council of Agde, c. 24; *Leges Visigoth.*, IV, 4 (*MGH, Leg. sect. I*, I); *Form. Tur.*, MGH, Leg. sect. V, p. 141; and Henri Leclercq, "Alumni," *DACL*, I-2, 1303–5.

[20] See the reflections of Jordanes, *Getica*, XXVI, 134 (*MGH, AA*, V-1, 93, ll. 9–11), and Gregory of Tours, *HF*, VI, 45 (p. 317).

[21] Gregory of Tours, *Mir. Mart.*, I, 40; II, 24 (*MGH, SRM*, I-2, 606, 617).

[22] Ibid., III, 16, 58 (pp. 636, 646).

[23] As in the case of Donatus of Besançon (see *Vita Columbani*, I, 14 [*MGH, SRM*, IV-1, 79]). The child was "given" to God but entered the monastery only after having been nursed by his mother ("matrique ad nutriendum reddit").

[24] Eddius, *Vita Wilfridi*, IX, XVIII (Colgrave ed., pp. 39–40).

[25] Bede, *HE*, III, 24 (Plummer ed., p. 179). King Oswy offered his one-year-old daughter after a victory.

[26] *Vita Columbani*, I, 14 (*MGH, SRM*, IV-1, 79). There were many children and adolescents with Burgundofara at Faremoutiers; see *Vita Columbani*, II, 12–13, 16–21 (pp. 131, 133, 135–41) for the beginnings of this abbey. See also James O'Carroll, "Sainte Fare et les origines," in *Sainte Fare et Faremoutiers* (Abbey of Sainte-Fare, 1956).

[27] For Ireland, see Aimée Lorcin, "La vie scolaire dans les monastères d'Irlande aux Ve–VIIe siècles," *RMAL* 1 (1945): 226. For Gaul, see *Vita Desiderii, mirac.*, IX, in *La*

who wished to become monks brought their children with them, although they were separated from them. The legislator did, however, allow children who were still of a tender age to see their parents when they wanted, so as not to create discontent among the monks.[28] When children could comprehend the rule, they were admitted into the monastery for good.[29] Abbots and monastic founders generally reacted against this tendency to transform the monastery into a "nursery": Caesarius of Arles and all who imitated his rule hoped that, if possible ("si potest fieri"), children would not be accepted before they were six or seven years old because only at that age could they learn to read and to obey.[30] Aurelian of Arles required the child to be eleven or twelve years old for admittance.[31]

When he became a monk at the ages just mentioned, the child had all the necessary opportunities to become a perfect Christian, since there was no other influence during his intellectual and moral training.[32] The abbot confided the child for his monastic training to an older monk, designated in the rules as the *formarius*, *senior*, or *decanus*.[33] As the last title indicates, the *decanus* was in charge of the education of ten monks. His role was more that of a boarding-school master than of a teacher: he had to teach his charges the rule, supervise them day and night, and keep them from joining other groups.[34] He was obviously

---

Vie de saint Didier, évêque de Cahors, 630–655, ed. René Poupardin (Paris, 1900), p. 51; *Vita Aldegondae*, 25 (*AS*, IV, 315). For Italy, see Gregory the Great, *Dial.*, III, 33 (p. 209): "Monasterium virginum in quo quidam puer parvulus erat." See also F. Kerlouegan, "Essai sur la mise en nourriture et l'éducation dans les pays celtiques d'après le témoignage des textes hagiographiques latins," *Etudes celtiques* 12 (1968–69): 101–46.

[28] Fructuosus, *Reg. mon. comm.*, 6 (*PL*, LXXXVII, 1115): "Illos tamen parvulos quos adhuc in crepundia videmus tenerculos propter misericordiam concessam habeant licentiam quando voluerint ad patrem aut matrem pergant, ne fortasse parentes pro ipsis in vitio murmurationis cadant; quia solet pro eis grandis in monasterio murmuratio evenire."

[29] Ibid.: "Sed inter utrosque foveantur quousque quantulumcumque regulam cognoscant et semper instruantur ut sive sint pueri sive puellae monasterio provocentur ubi habitare futuri erunt."

[30] Caesarius, *Statuta sanctarum virginum*, 6 (Morin ed., 2: 104).

[31] Aurelian, *Regula*, 17 (*PL*, LXVIII, 38): "Nisi ab annis decem et duodecim qui et nutriri non egeant et cavere nonverunt culpas."

[32] Bede, *Sup. parab. Salom.*, II, 22 (*PL*, XCI, 1002): "Quod adolescens quisque ceperit in senecta non mutaverit." Bede could speak from experience, since he had been a monk from his seventh year.

[33] The term *formarius*, or *formaria*, is found in *Regula Caesarii*, 37 (Morin ed., 2: 110), and Ferreolus, *Regula*, 17 (*PL*, LXVI, 965). *Decanus* is found in Fructuosus, *Reg. mon. comm.*, 12 (*PL*, LXXXVII, 1120); *Regula Magistri*, XI (Vanderhoven and Masai ed., p. 184); and Isidore of Seville, *Reg. mon.*, XIII, 1 (*PL*, LXXXIII, 883): "Decanus quasi rector et custos."

[34] Fructuosus, *Reg. mon. comm.*, 6 (*PL*, LXXXVII, 1116): "Qui et ipsi infantes suum

responsible to the abbot, who gave him whatever advice he needed.

Contrary to the educational traditions we have just discussed, moderation and discretion were recommended to the monastic educator in his relationships with children.[35] Screaming at children was superfluous because authority came from good example rather than from words.[36] Benedict in particular insisted on the virtue of *discretio*. Of course, the whip was needed for children below age fifteen, who could not comprehend moral chastisement, although even here Benedict recommended mildness in correction.[37] He devoted a chapter to the moderate attitude monks were to have toward those less than fifteen years old.[38] All the legislators who were influenced by the Benedictine rule retained the advice of the founder: the term *discretio* and the expression "ne quid nimis" frequently recur among them. Paul the Deacon, a famous Benedictine, wrote a commentary on the rule that was true to Benedict's attitude; he noted that beatings did more harm than good[39] and that the brutal master should be punished.[40] He also wanted pleasant living conditions for the child: comfortable garments, sufficient nourishment, and heat in the winter. He even provided for an hour of recreation a day and suggested that the abbot recompense the best behaved little monks by giving them sweets at dinner.[41] It could be objected that Paul's portrayal is a monk-humanist's description of an ideal monas-

---

habeant decanum qui plus de eis intelligit ut regulam super eos observet"; *Reg. mon.*, 6 (*PL*, LXXXVII, 1103): "Tam in cessione quam in operatione semper decania a decania segregata consistat. Juniores quique suos jugiter decanus ille commoneat."

[35] See Waldebert, *Reg. ad virgines*, 24 (*PL*, LXXXVIII, 1070): "De nutriendis infantibus. Debent enim nutriri cum omni pietatis affectu . . . in omnibus, virtutum custodia, discretio reperiatur." Gregory the Great wrote to the abbot of Lérins (*Ep.* XI, 9 [*MGH, Ep.*, II, 269, l. 6]): "Dulcedo cauta sit non remissa, correctio vero diligens sit non severa."

[36] *Reg. Pauli et Stephani*, 2 (Vilanova ed., p. 109): "Quales circa juvenes esse debeant seniores."

[37] Benedict, *Regula*, XXX (p. 50), concerns the punishment of children: "Omnis aetas vel intellectus proprias debet habere mensuras."

[38] Ibid., LXX (p. 97): "Infantum vero usque quindecim annorum aetate disciplinae diligentia ab omnibus et custodia sit sed et hoc cum omni mensura et ratione."

[39] Paul the Deacon, *Comm. Reg.*, XXXVII, in *Paulus Warnefridus: In sanctam Regulam commentarium editio archi-coenobii Casinensis monachi*, Bibliotheca Cassinensis, vol. 4 (Montecassino, 1880), p. 124: "Debet temperanter agere magister illorum erga illos et non illos flagellare nimis aut male tractare . . . quia post flagellum vel disciplinam statim ad vana revertuntur."

[40] Ibid., LXX (p. 169): "Quia si talis magister infantum fuerit qui quamvis nimis in ira accensus infantes aut percusserit . . . tolerandus est et correpiendus et ammonendus."

[41] See Butler, *Le monachisme bénédictin*, p. 336, and Mary Alfred Schroll, *Benedictine Monasticism as Reflected in the Warnefrid-Hildemar Commentaries on the Rule* (New York, 1941).

tery; however, we find the same desire to modify the child's obligations to fast and work in all the sixth- and seventh-century rules.[42]

Had the monks discovered the nature of the infant and all its richness? At the very least, they adhered more to the teachings of Christ than to Roman tradition.[43] Benedict rehabilitated the child in his rule and thought that the child's judgment should be respected, "since Samuel and David from their childhood judged the Elders."[44] He permitted young monks to give counsel "because the Lord often reveals what it is better to do to someone younger."[45] We should note in this regard that the child was often viewed as the interpreter of God's thought.[46] In the *Law of the Frisians*, a child drew the lot, while in various hagiographical texts, the intervention of a child is considered a sign from God.[47] The outstanding characteristic of childhood was innocence.

Two famous monks after Benedict—Columban and Bede—formulated the four characteristics of the child in the same terms: "He does not persevere in anger, he is not spiteful, he does not delight in the beauty of women, he says what he thinks."[48] Bede was one of the few

---

[42] Moderation in fasting is recommended for children in the *Regula Magistri*, LIX (Vanderhoven and Masai ed., p. 263, l. 32); Benedict, *Regula*, XXXVII (p. 57); and Isidore of Seville, *Reg. mon.*, XV, 3 (*PL*, LXXXIII, 881): "Tenerae aetatis fragilitas." See also the *Vita Samsoni*, 10 (Fawtier ed., p. 109). According to the appendix to *Theodore's Penitential*, IV (Haddan-Stubbs ed., 3: 211), children ate meat until they were fourteen years old. Moderate labor is prescribed in *Regula Magistri*, L (p. 251, 170). Gregory the Great forbade the presence of monks less than eighteen years old in the Palmarian islands and demanded that they be sent to Rome (*Ep.* I, 48 [*MGH, Ep.*, I, 75, l. 7]). Recreation seems to have been foreseen in Donatus of Besançon's *Reg. ad virgines*, 32 (*PL*, LXXXVII, 284): "Juvenculae quibus imponitur terminus ut non se appellent invicem."

[43] As had Leo the Great; see above, Introduction, n. 38. For the scriptural sources, see S. Legasse, *Jésus et l'enfant: Enfants petits et simples dans la tradition synoptique* (Paris, 1964).

[44] Benedict, *Regula*, LXIII (p. 88).

[45] Ibid., III (p. 14): "Saepe juniori dominus revelat quod melius est." Fructuosus, *Reg. mon. comm.*, 6 (*PL*, LXXXVII, 1116), referred to Christ's "sinite parvulos venire ad me." See P. Hofmeister, "Saepe juniori...," *Studien und Mitteilungen zur Geschichte des Benediktinerordens und seiner Zweige* 70 (1959): 159–68.

[46] P. Courcelle, "L'enfant et les 'sorts bibliques,' " *VChr* 7 (1953): 199.

[47] A child appeared to Saint Aldegundis (*Vita Aldegundis, MGH, SRM*, VI, 88). A three-year-old child turned Cuthbert away from brutal games by indicating his future mission to him (*Vita Cuthberti*, I, 3 [Colgrave ed., p. 64]).

[48] Columban, *Ep.* 2 (*MGH, Ep.*, III, 163, l. 29): "Infans humilis est, non laesus meminit, non mulierem videns concupiscit, non aliud ore aliud corde habet." Bede, *In Marc.*, *PL*, XCII, 230–31: "Puer non perseverat in iracundia, non laesus meminit, non videns pulchram mulierem delectatur, non aliud cogitat, aliud loquitur." Isidore of Seville had the same definition (*Quaestiones de veteri et novo Testamento*, XL [*PL*, LXXXIII, 207]): "Dic mihi, infans parvulus quantas virtutes habet? respondit IV: non laesus meminit,

eighth-century authors who argued in favor of the child. In a comment on Solomon's proverb "Stultitia colligata est in corde pueri," he explained that *pueri* did not mean young children but rather any young mind, since "we know many children endowed with wisdom."[49] Elsewhere, he stated that one of the characteristics of childhood is docility to the teaching of masters: "They do not contradict their teachers nor do they oppose him with arguments and speeches but faithfully absorb what is taught to them."[50]

The question of the child's innocence seems to have been a debated theme in insular monastic circles. An Irish text of the end of the seventh century focused on the *vera innocentia* by accumulating scriptural and patristic citations in support of different theses.[51] In England, some thought that it was useless to say masses for children who died before the age of seven—a neo-Pelagian position which elicited a strong reaction in *Theodore's Penitential*.[52]

These few clues sufficiently prove that monasticism evolved a new concept of the child which has too long been misunderstood. Monks throughout the Middle Ages would rise up against brutal masters and against ignorance of the nature of children. This new attitude merits a general study that would permit the revision of current opinions on medieval pedagogy.[53]

Monastic legislators were more severe toward adolescents, however, and shared with secular educators a basic distrust of this age group. In essence they thought that the young man had to be placed on guard against the sexual appetites that were awakening within him. Monks as well as clerics considered the body an enemy that had to be fought and tamed. Physical beauty was of no account; the senses endangered the soul. When Boniface consoled a blind friend, he wrote a "eulogy on

---

non perseverat in ira, non delectatur pulchra femina, non aliud cogitat vel aliud loquitur." For the authenticity of this work, see Berthold Altaner, "Der Stand der Isidorforschung," in *Miscellanea Isidoriana* (Rome, 1936), p. 10. There was thus a common source who—to believe Columban—would be Basil or Jerome (see *S. Columbani opera*, ed. Walker, p. 20).

[49] Bede, *Sup. parab. Salom.*, II, 23 (PL, XCI, 1004): "Multos novimus pueros sapientia praeditos."

[50] Bede, *In. Marc.*, PL, XCII, 231: "Parvulos in discendo non contradicit doctoribus neque rationes et verba componit adversum eos resistens, sed fideliter suscipit quod docetur."

[51] *Can. Hibern. liber*, LV (Wasserschleben ed., p. 216): (2) *De vera innocentia puerorum*; (3) *De pueris malis quamvis innocentis*; (4) *De vitiis quae adhaerent innocentiae puerorum*; (5) *De duobus generibus innocentiae.*

[52] *Theodore's Penitential*, V, 7 (Haddan-Stubbs ed., 3: 194): "Multi dicunt non licere pro infantibus missas facere ante VII annum sed tamen licet."

[53] There are some very brief remarks in Lesne, *Les écoles*, pp. 543–44.

blindness" in these terms: "What are the eyes of our body if not veritable windows of sin through which we look out on evil and those who commit it and, what is even worse, allow it to enter ourselves, the dirt we contemplate and covet."[54] The touch could lead to impurity: Nicetius of Lyon refused to take a child into his arms unless the child were wrapped in clothes.[55] The union of bodies, even if sanctified by the sacrament of marriage, was considered impure. The conjugal act was forbidden during Lent, on the eves of feasts, and on Sunday.[56] Gregory of Tours warned couples who did not observe this rule that they ran the risk of conceiving paralytics, epileptics, and lepers.[57] Thus, beginning with adolescence, the body had to be prepared by repressing "the flames of juvenile fervor through very severe discipline."[58] Hagiographers did not hesitate to show how their heroes achieved perfect chastity through will power.[59] Young girls were supposed to prefer virginity to a husband and to motherhood, the trials of which moralists loved to portray.[60]

Apprenticeship in chastity was vigorously pursued in the monasteries. Baths, which represented the cult of the body, were forbidden by legislators to all except the ill.[61] In the dormitory, the beds of the

[54] Boniface, *Ep.* 63 (*MGH, Ep.*, III, 330, ll. 10ff.).

[55] Gregory of Tours, *Vitae patrum*, VIII (*MGH, SRM*, I-2, 692): "Castitatem enim non modo hic custodiens verum etiam custodienti gratiam aliis jugiter praedicabat et a polluto tactu et verbis obscenis ut desisterent edocebat."

[56] On this question, see Peter Browe, *Beiträge zur Sexualethik des Mittelalters* (Breslau, 1932), and L. Godefroy, "Mariage," *DTC*, 9, pt. 2: 2117.

[57] Gregory of Tours, *Mir. Mart.*, II, 24 (*MGH, SRM*, I-2, 617, l. 23): "Sed quia dixi, parentibus ejus ob peccatum evenisse per violentiam noctis dominicae, cavete, o viri, quibus sunt conjuncta conjugia! Sat est aliis diebus voluptati operam dare; hunc autem diem in laudibus Dei inpolluti deducite. Quia cum evenerit exinde aut contracti, aut ephilentici, aut leprosi nascuntur."

[58] Gregory of Tours, *Vitae patrum*, VI (p. 680, l. 7): "Sciebat enim juvenilis fervoris flammas non aliter posse devincere nisi censurae canonicae et disciplinae severissimae subderetur."

[59] *Vita Maximi*, PL, LXXX, 31: "Postquam autem excessit ex ephebis luxuriae illecebras et blandimenta animi magisterio et censura edomabat, ut pollicitae virginitatis palmam incorruptae integritatis obtineret."

[60] There are many treatises *De virginitate* for the period. For the sixth century, see Avitus of Vienne (*MGH, AA*, IV-2, 275); Fortunatus, *Carm.* VIII, 3 (*MGH, AA*, IV-1, 181); and Leander of Seville, *De institutione virginum*, ed. Vega (Escorial, 1948). For the seventh century, Aldhelm, *De virginitate, I: Prosa* and *II: Carmen* (*MGH, AA*, XV, 226–323, 350–471), and Ildefonsus of Toledo, *De virginitate beatae Mariae: Historia de su tradición manuscrita, texto y comentario gramatical y estilístico*, ed. Vicente Blanco Garcia (Madrid, 1937). In his *De virginitate*, Fortunatus painted a frightening picture of what the married woman could expect; see *Carm.* VIII, 3, v. 355 (p. 190).

[61] Benedict, *Regula*, XXXVI; Waldebert, *Reg. ad virgines*, 15 (*PL*, LXXXVIII, 1065); Donatus of Besançon, *Reg. ad virgines*, 12 (*PL*, LXXXVII, 279); Fructuosus, *Reg. mon. comm.*, 6 (ibid., col. 1115); etc.

young were separated from one another by those of older monks,[62] and a lamp was kept burning at night.[63] Monastic legislators especially feared what an Irish text modestly called "children's games." Insular penitentials stipulated the punishments provided for young men guilty of homosexual relations.[64] Disturbing friendships between an older monk and a younger monk were also feared and severely repressed.[65] When an adolescent could prove that he no longer needed perpetual surveillance and a master, the abbot recommended him to an older monk, who, while allowing him more freedom of movement, was responsible for his education.[66]

But if the young monk could not observe the rule, especially in reference to chastity, could he leave the monastery and marry? The answers varied with the cases.[67] If the child had been offered to the monastery at an early age, when he was unable to accept his engagement personally, he could, according to some legislators, in good conscience either renew his commitment or leave the monastery. The monk's freedom of choice was always respected[68] although this liberal tendency seems

[62] Benedict, *Regula*, XXII; *Reg. Donati*, 65. Fructuosus, *Reg. mon. comm.*, 17, repeats a passage from Augustine's *Rule*, chap. 3.

[63] Waldebert, *Reg. ad virgines*, 14 (*PL*, LXXXVIII, 1065): "In schola qua dormitur per totam noctem lucerna ardeat."

[64] *Cummean's Penitential*, XI, *De ludis puerilibus*, ed. Ludwig Bieler, *The Irish Penitentials* (Dublin, 1963), pp. 126–29.

[65] Fructuosus, *Reg. mon. comm.*, 16 (*PL*, LXXXVII, 111): "Monachus parvulorum aut adolescentium consectator vel qui osculo, vel qualibet occasione turpe deprehendus fuerit inhiare . . . publice verberetur." Isidore, *Reg. mon.*, XVII, 3 (*PL*, LXXXIII, 886): "Si cum parvulis jocaverit, riserit vel eos osculatus fuerit . . . si cum altero in uno lecto jacuerit . . . excommunicatione purganda sunt." *Reg. mon. Tarnantensis* 13 (*PL*, LXVI, 980): "Qui cum junioribus verba otiosa narrare voluerit aut habere amicitias aetatis infirmae, increpationi, ut dignus est, subjacebit."

[66] Paul the Deacon, *Comm. Reg.*, LXIII, in *Paulus Warnefridus*, p. 159: "Adolescentes tamdiu debent esse sub custodia vel disciplina donec veniant ad illam aetatem in qua possunt credi sine magistris esse . . . ; si autem post quintum decimum annum visus fuerit ille juvenis bonus et sobrius ita ut non sit ille necesse magistros habere debet exire de illa disciplina et debet illum abba solummodo uni specialiter fratri bono et sanctae conversationis commendare, qui . . . illum custodiat et cum illo sedeat quando legit."
The *Consuetudines Cassiniensis*, chap. 7 (ed. Albers), provided for two supervisors for each adolescent.

[67] There are many works which treat oblation. Historians, however, do not agree on Benedictine oblation. See M. P. Deroux, *Les origines de l'oblature bénédictine: Etude historique* (Paris, 1927); D. Lentini, "Note sull'oblazione dei fanciulli nella regola di S. Benedetto," *Studia Anselmiana* 18–19 (1947): 195–225; Dom Stegmann, "Die Verbindlichkeit der Oblation nach *Regula Benedictina*," in Brechter, *Benedictus, der Vater des Abendlandes*, pp. 120–38. An important work has come out since these studies: see P. de la Garanderie, "Les oblations des mineurs dans l'Eglise depuis les origines à la fin du VIᵉ siècle" (thesis, Rennes, 1956).

[68] *Can. Hiber. liber*, LXVI, 16 (Wasserschleben ed., p. 221): "De juvenibus vota sua proferre debentibus, cum ad annos pubertatis venerint."

to have been abandoned in the eighth century. Gregory II, in response to Boniface, who had sought his opinion on the matter, wrote: "It is impious that children offered to God by their parents should abandon themselves to pleasure."[69] Spanish canonists and certain Merovingian councils had already adopted this position.[70] The question of freedom of choice for oblates, however, was never regularized and became the subject of controversies in the Carolingian period.[71]

Monastic legislators seem to have been less severe with regard to the oblation of girls.[72] This represented an exception to the general rule, since the manner of educating boys and girls was undifferentiated. In fact, the texts we have cited make no distinction: a masculine rule could be applied perfectly to the education of nuns. The ideal woman was the one who acquired masculine qualities and overcame the weakness that, to believe the etymology of *mulier*, characterized her sex.[73] Women thus "virilized" could be put in charge of double monasteries: a Hilda in England and a Gertrude in Gaul possessed talents worthy of abbots. Like their male counterparts, these women also acquired a literary culture. We have already referred to several examples of lettered women both within the world and removed from it.[74] The abbesses at Arles and Poitiers and the correspondents of Aldhelm and Boniface received a very masculine education.[75]

[69] *MGH, Ep.*, III, 276, l. 26: "Nefas est, ut oblatis a parentibus Deo filiis voluptatis frena laxentur."

[70] Fourth Council of Toledo (633), c. 49 (Mansi, X, 631): "Monachum aut paterna devotio, aut propria professio facit; . . . proinde his ad mundum reverti intercludimus aditum, et omnem ad saeculum interdicimus regressum." See Alonso, *La cura pastoral*, pp. 42–44. The Council of Orléans (549), c. 19, and Mâcon (583), c. 12 (*MGH, Leg. sect. III*, I, 107, 158) put the will of parents on the same plane as their children's wishes. See the Council of Paris (614), c. 13 (ibid., p. 190). *Theodore's Penitential*, XIV, 5 (Haddan-Stubbs ed., 3: 202) is clear on this point: "Infans pro infante potest dari ad monasterium Deo quamvis alium vovisset; tamen melius est votum implere."

[71] See especially Rabanus Maurus' famous treatise, *De oblatione puerorum*, PL, CVII, 419.

[72] Zachary, *Ep. ad Pippinum*, PL, LXXXIX, 938: "De his quae non coactae sed propria volontate virginitatis propositum susceperunt." He repeats a decretal of Leo I (*PL*, LIV, 1208).

[73] Caesarius, *Sermo* XLIII (Morin ed., p. 182): "Vir a virtute nomen acceperit et mulier a mollitie id est a fragilitate"; Isidore of Seville, *Origines*, XI, ii, 18: "Mulier vero a mollitie." See the allusions to weakness in *Form. Arvern.*, 2 (*MGH, Leg. sect. V*, p. 29) and Council of Orléans (533), c. 18 (*MGH, Leg. sect. III*, I, 63). The *Carmen in mulieres* attributed to Columban (*PL*, LXXX, 294), although certainly not one of his works, reflects the antifeminist currents in monastic circles.

[74] See above, chap. 6, sect. III.B, and chap. 9, sect. II.A.2.

[75] Paul Gide, *Etude sur la condition privée de la femme*, 2nd ed. (Paris, 1885), p. 213, seems to me to be mistaken when he speaks of "the inequality of the education offered to the two sexes."

Women played an active role in Barbarian society. They assumed political responsibility—the careers of Brunhilda, Fredegunda, and Theodelinda should be remembered in this light—and contributed to the conversion of princes and nations. But the chroniclers who portray women never allude to feminine charms. The only writer who felt and expressed them was the Italian Fortunatus, who perhaps could be considered the precursor of courtly literature,[76] although he left no school behind him. There was no place in this rude period for the literary expression of amorous sentiments.

We must ask, in conclusion, whether eighth-century men had definite ideas on the formation of men, particularly laymen. Unfortunately, we cannot answer this question in the absence of theoretical treatises. The saints' *Lives* we have are not at all useful, since the child and the young man begin to interest the hagiographer at the point when their character and way of life begin to contrast with that of the mass of their contemporaries. Married men and women appear here and there in the *Lives* but even they do not count, since they lead the lives of monks. All we know about the personalities of laymen is the warrior aspect. In the sixth and seventh centuries, the layman could express his ideals of life, that *dulcendo* dear to Fortunatus, through his literary culture.[77] In the eighth century, this was no longer possible. Religious sentiment, especially in an ascetical vein, is the only sentiment we encounter. We must await the Carolingian renaissance to rediscover a literary expression of the ideals of laymen.

II. EDUCATIONAL TECHNIQUES

A. ELEMENTARY EDUCATION

We must say at the outset that we have no theoretical treatise, no school manual, no student's notebook, and no iconographic representation of the school. The classroom itself cannot even claim a precise name, for the term *auditorium*, which had disappeared at the beginning of the sixth century,[78] had not been replaced, except by the word *schola*,

---

[76] Bezzola, 1: 55ff., refers to one of the rare texts which praise women, Antonina's epitaph (ed. Diaz y Diaz, *AW*, pp. 47–48). There are several pages on women during this period in Karl Weinhold, *Die deutschen Frauen in dem Mittelalter*, 2nd ed., 2 vols. (Vienna, 1882), and in M. L. Portmann, *Die Darstellung der Frau in der Geschichtschreibung des früheren Mittelalters*, Baseler Beiträge zur Geschichte 69 (Basel, 1958).

[77] Bezzola, 1: 53–54.

[78] The term is found in Ennodius, *Dictio* VIII (*MGH*, *AA*, VII, 78), and in Dracontius,

which had a variety of meanings at the time.[79] The school was probably included within the monastic or episcopal complex; the problem of the external school open to secular children had not yet been posed.[80] The schoolroom must still have been very small, like the buildings which surrounded it.[81] Perhaps there was a classroom for each "decade" in monasteries where there were many monks.[82]

We are a little better informed about the equipment of the schools. Like the young Roman, the student had to have tablets and a writing stylus. The wooden or bone tablets, which were covered with wax[83] and sometimes with leather on the outside,[84] were indispensable to the student[85] as well as to the man of letters because they permitted one to write a rough draft of a sermon, saint's *Life*, or other literary works.[86]

Romulea, I, 10 (*MGH, AA*, XIV, 133). It would reappear in the Carolingian period; see Lesne, *Les écoles*, p. 558. The word *gymnasium* was used to describe the study room in the *Notitia palatii*: "Hoc est locus ubi pueri discunt aliquid vel ludunt." But we do not know whether this text is pre-Carolingian. See S. Brugnoli, "Ancora sulla Notitia palatii," *Benedictina* 8 (1954): 71–76.

[79] Bede, in recopying classical terminology, used *schola* in the sense of "classroom"; see *In primam epistolam Petri, PL*, XCIII, 53: "Schola vocatur locus in quo adolescentes litteralibus studiis operam dare et audiendis magistris vacare solent unde schola vacatio interpretatur." See also the Cambridge glossary edited by J. H. Hessels, *An Eighth-Century Latin–Anglo-Saxon Glossary Preserved in the Library of Corpus Christi College, Cambridge (MS. no. 144)* (Cambridge, 1890), p. 74: "Ludus litterarum: scola legentium." But on p. 106 of this glossary, we read: "scola: doctrina." *Scola* generally meant simply a room (*Reg. mon. Tarnantensis*, 7 [*PL*, LXVI, 980]; *Reg. Caesarii*, 3) and even a dormitory (Waldebert, *Reg. ad virgines*, 12 [*PL*, LXXXVIII, 1053]; Council of Tours (567), c. 15 [*MGH, Leg. sect. III*, I, 126, l. 3]).

[80] Except in Ireland, where the school was sometimes located next to the monastery; see Lorcin, "La vie scolaire," p. 230.

[81] Seventh-century monastic churches were quite small (150–200 square meters). See J. Hubert, "Les églises et les bâtiments monastiques de l'abbaye de Manglieu au début du VIIIᵉ siècle," *BSAF* (1958), p. 95, n. 1.

[82] *Regula Magistri*, XLIV (Vanderhoven and Masai ed., p. 241): "Infantuli in decada sua in tabulis suis ab uno litterato litteras meditentur."

[83] We have two tablets from this period. One, in the National Museum in Dublin, bears verses from the Psalms; see R. A. S. Macalister, "Wooden Book with Leaves Indented and Waxed Found near Springmount Bog, Co. Antrim," *Journal of the Royal Society of Antiquaries of Ireland* 50 (1920): 160. The whalebone tablet found at Blyterburgh in Suffolk is in the British Museum. It is pierced by two holes, which suggests that it was originally folded. A schist tablet, found in an excavation, is also pierced and could have been used for writing; see Maurice Toussaint, *Répertoire archéologique du département de Seine-et-Marne* (Paris, 1953), p. 127. See above, chap. 6, sect. IV.B, for Visigothic slate tablets. See A. Blanchet, "Tablettes de cire à l'époque carolingienne," *AcIB* (1924), p. 163, for Carolingian tablets. The *Hisperica famina*, 20 (Jenkinson ed., p. 18) has a description of a tablet.

[84] Aldhelm, *Enigma* XXXII (*MGH, AA*, XV, 111): "Calciamenta mihi tradebant tergora dura."

[85] "Puerorum nutrices" Isidore of Seville called them (*Origines*, VI, ix, 1).

[86] Adamnan recorded Bishop Arculf's story on tablets; see *De locis sanctis*, preface (Meehan ed., p. 34). Willibald copied his rough draft of the *Vita Bonifatii* on tablets;

The man of letters guided his stylus over the tablet the way the peasant traced furrows with his plow.[87] The stylus (*graphium*) could be made of iron, bone, or silver.[88]

Both pupil and teacher could also use papyrus (*carta*) to practice writing and, especially, to prepare rough drafts. This material, which was used for documents and letters,[89] perhaps was still in use in the schools. Tree bark was substituted when papyrus was unavailable. Young Liudger, impatient to learn his letters, amused himself by "playing school" and gathering bark to make little books in which he traced characters.[90] Papyrus books—several fragments of which have come down to us,[91]—were still in circulation, although as books became increasingly rare and thus were borrowed many times to be recopied, parchment (*membrana*) replaced papyrus. Earlier, at the beginning of the sixth century, Caesarius of Arles had the text of his sermons recopied on parchment before circulating them.[92] Parchment had another advantage: it could be used several times. We have already mentioned the palimpsests scribes made, not to suppress an uninteresting text, but rather to recycle costly parchment.[93] Although we cannot determine

---

see *Vita Bonifatii*, ed. Levison, p. 105. The Basel papyrus studied by Perrat ("Des Pères du Jura à l'humaniste Grynaeus," *Bibl. HR* 12 [1950]: 149–62) bears the following phrase: "[Sermonem d]ei s[an]c[to]rum claudii ogentino ecc[les]ia cum cirea s[cripsi]." The preacher copied the text from the tablet onto papyrus. See Lesne, *Les écoles*, pp. 559–60 for the use of tablets.

[87] This metaphor, which Isidore of Seville used (*Origines*, VI, xiv, 7), enjoyed great success. See Curtius, p. 382.

[88] See above, chap. 8, n. 62, for the styli found in the ruins of the monastery of Whitby, and chap. 6, sect. III.B, for those from Merovingian tombs. Lull sent a silver stylus to an abbess in the middle of the eighth century; see *MGH, Ep.*, III, 338, l. 4.

[89] See H. Pirenne, "Le commerce du papyrus dans la Gaule mérovingienne," *AclB* (1928), pp. 178–91. The Basel papyrus discussed in n. 86 must be added to his examples. Writers often referred to papyrus as an intellectual symbol; see Gregory the Great, *Moral.*, XIII, 10 (*PL*, LXXV, 1024): "Per papyrum . . . saecularis scientia designatur."

[90] *Vita Liudgeri*, ed. Diekamp, pp. 12–13: "Qui statim ut ambulare et loqui poterat, coepit colligere pelliculas et corticis arborum quibus ad luminaria uti solemus et quidquid tale inveniri poterat, ludentibusque pueris aliis, ipse consuit sibi de illis collectionibus quasi libellos. Cumque invenisset sibi liquorem cum festucis imitabatur scribentes et afferebat nutrici suae quasi utiles libros custiendos."
Birch bark was used for pupils' notebooks in twelfth-century Novgorod (A. V. Artsikhovski, "La ville russe au Moyen Age," *MA* 65 [1959]: 459).

[91] Besides the works of Augustine and Isidore of Seville, see above, chap. 3, sect. I, and chap. 9, sect. IV.C.2, where we note Boethius' commentary on the *Topics* which was preserved at Saint Martin of Tours. See Lupus of Ferrières, *Ep.* 53 (in *Loup de Ferrières: Correspondance*, ed. Léon Levillain, 2 vols. [Paris, 1927–35], 1: 214–16).

[92] See above, chap. 4, sect. II.B.

[93] See above, chapt. 8, sect. III and n. 232, and Wattenbach, *Das Schriftwesen im Mittelalter*, p. 255. Gregory of Tours was afraid that the text of his *Histories* would be erased: "Ut nunquam libros hos abolere faciatis aut rescribi" (*HF*, X, 31 [p. 536]).

the price of parchment, we do know from several writers' complaints that parchment was costly;[94] we also know that it was worth enough to be considered a suitable gift.[95] Bird quills rather than the reed pens of the Ancients, were used to write on this material,[96] although the stylus was sometimes also used.[97]

Books were bound for protection by their owners in the Eastern fashion—a method which had not yet become universal[98]—and were kept in easily transportable chests (*arcae*), or less often, in armoires.[99] In monasteries, the librarian loaned out the books and took them back in at prescribed hours. When in use, books were to be placed on a stand: Eligius, according to his biographer, had a stand fixed on an axis—the ancestor of our revolving bookshelf—which allowed him to research easily among several works.[100]

Let us now turn to the classroom to try to picture children learning to read and write. The first step in reading was still the alphabet, which our texts designate as *elementa, notae litterarum*, or, more simply, *litterae*.[101] The child recopied the letters on his tablet, although Saint

[94] Braulio, *Ep.* 14 (Madoz ed., pp. 105–6): "Membrana nec nobis sufficient et ideo ad dirigendum vobis deficient, sed pretium direximus unde si jusseritis comparare possitis." See the complaint of the Toledan scribe above, chap. 8, n. 286. Scarcity of parchment forced some to write in minuscule; see Justus of Urgel's letter, *PL*, LXVII, 961. For the fabrication of parchment, see the Anglo-Saxon enigmas in *The Exeter Book, Part II*, trans. W. S. Mackie, Early English Text Society, Original Series, vol. 194 (London, 1934), p. 117.

[95] *Ep.* 142 (*MGH, Ep.*, III, 426, ll. 24–25): "Idque obsecro, ut, quando potueris me adiuvare in membranis scribendis, transmittas."

[96] Isidore of Seville, *Origines*, VI, xiv, 3. See also the enigmas of Tatwin (6) and Eusebius (35), ed. Adolf Ebert, *Sitzungberichte der sächsische Gesellschaft der Wissenschaften* 28 (1877): 33, 49. Earlier the *Anonymous of Valois* mentioned that Theodoric used a *penna* to sign his name; see above, chap. 2, n. 33.

[97] B. Bischoff, "Ueber Einritzungen in Handschriften des frühen Mittelalters," *Zentralblatt für Bibliothekswesen*, 54 (1937): 173–77 (*Mittelalterliche Studien*, 1: 88–92). For an example, see *CLA*, IV, no. 410a.

[98] See B. Van Regemorter, "Le codex relié depuis son origine jusqu'au Haut Moyen Age," *MA* 61 (1955): 1–26. Attala had Bobbio's books bound; see above, chap. 8, sect. III.

[99] *Vita Bonifatii*, 8 (Levison ed., p. 46, ll. 25 and 50): "Thecas, in quibus multa inerant librorum volumina." *Arcae* are mentioned in the *Regula Magistri*, XVII (Vanderhoven and Masai ed., p. 206): "Simul etiam arcam cum diversis codicibus membranis et chartis monastherii." See also Gregory of Tours, *HF*, IV, 46 (p. 181, l. 10).
Bede, *De orthographia*, has a definition of an *armarium*: "Locus ubi quarumcumque artium instrumenta ponuntur" (Keil, 7: 262). Lesne, *Les livres*, pp. 791–92, noted that representations of armoires for books are rare in pre-Carolingian manuscripts. The armoire portrayed on the frontispiece of this book comes from the *Codex Amiatinus*.

[100] *Vita Eligii*, I, 12 (*MGH, SRM*, IV, 679, l. 10): "Habebat . . . in cubiculo suo . . . sacros libros in gyro per axem plurimos quos post psalmodiam et orationem revolvens."

[101] Aldhelm, *Enigma* XXX (*MGH, AA*, XV, 110), uses *elementum* or *abecedarium*; Gregory of Tours, *Glor. confess.*, 39 (*MGH, SRM*, I-2, 772), speaks of "elementa litterarum, notae litterarum." See also *Vita Eugendi*, 4 (ibid., III, 155), and *Vitae patrum*, VII

Leobinus' hagiographer tells us that the young boy had neither tablets nor parchment and so carved his letters on his leather belt.[102]

After having learned his letters, the child went on to the syllables and the nouns. The antique technique was still in use in England. Bede relates that the bishop of Hexham cured a mute by making him attend a veritable reading lesson: "Say A, the mute said A, and B, he said B, and so he answered the bishop by giving him the name of each letter. The bishop then continued by asking him to read the syllables and words."[103] In the beginning of his *De arte metrica*, Bede studied the vowels, consonants, semivowels, and syllables.[104] The use of a syllabary, however, was often abandoned—it sufficed to learn the alphabet and go directly to reading. Samson the Gaul, after having learned the letters in one day, could use them in words within a week.[105] Sometimes the child had neither a syllabary nor an abecedary and thus learned to read from words, as in the case of Brachio, a slave Gregory of Tours mentioned. In order to learn how to read so he could pray like a monk, Brachio copied the characters he saw under the portraits of the Apostles and saints into a notebook and then explicated the names of the letters: "He read and wrote before he knew his alphabet."[106] The Lombard

---

(ibid., p. 692). The word *abgitorum*, which signified the alphabet as well as the ABC's of Christian doctrine, was used in Ireland; see Lorcin, "La vie scolaire," p. 231. Hugh Graham, *The Early Irish Monastic Schools: A Study of Ireland's Contribution to Early Medieval Culture* (Dublin, 1923), p. 18, cites the Würzburg gloss, "Abgitir crabaid initium fidei." See H. Thruston, "The Alphabet and the Consecration of Churches," *The Month* (1910), p. 621. We should also note the curious poem on the alphabet, *Versus cujusdam Scotti de alfabeto*, which appears to have been a seventh-century school exercise (ed. Baehrens, *Poet. lat. min.*, 5: 375). See Manitius, 1: 190–92, and Kenney, *Sources*, p. 275, no. 103.

[102] Fortunatus, *Vita Leobini*, MGH, *AA*, IV-2, 73: "Qui cum non haberet codicis aut tabelarum supplementum prout potuit apices in cingulo scripsit. . . . Postea pater litterarum lineas in tabulis decrevit." *Vita Brioci*, AB 2 (1883): 163 (a ninth-century *Life*): "In tabulis prout poterat, conabatur formare litterulas."

[103] Bede, *HE*, V, 2 (p. 284): "Addidit episcopus nomina litterarum: Dictio A, dixit ille A, Dictio B, . . . addidit et syllabas ac verba."

[104] *De arte metrica*, ed. Keil, 7: 228. Virgil the Grammarian studied the letters and syllables (*Epitomae*, II, III [Tardi ed., p. 40]).

[105] *Vita Samsoni*, ed. Fawtier, p. 40: "Sub uno eodem die vicinas eleas sub hebdomadis diebus harum litterarum distinctiones per conjonctiones verborum potuit scire." Fawtier thought that *eleas* was a contraction for *elementas* and that the number 20 was a reference to the ogamic alphabet, which included twenty letters.

[106] Gregory of Tours, *Vitae patrum*, XII (*MGH*, *SRM*, I-2, 713): "Nesciebat enim quid caneret quia litteras ignorabat; videns autem saepius in oratorium litteras super iconicas apostolorum . . . esse conscriptas, exemplavit eas in codice; cumque ad occursum domini sui clerici . . . convenirent, hic e junioribus . . . secretius interrogabat nomina litterarum et ob hac eas intelligere coepit. Antea autem inspirante Domino, et legit et scripsit quam litterarum seriem cognovit."

Vulfilaic, who taught himself how to read, also confessed ignorance of "the order of letters."[107] This method is no longer Roman, but it is not an entirely new method: even though the child learned to find letters in words, he nevertheless still began with the letters.[108]

In order to remember his letters, the student wrote them, following the models of characters traced by his master.[109] Sometimes, as in Roman schools, the child used a tablet—called a *productalis* in a glossary[110] —on which the letters he had to trace were engraved. The child probably first learned to write in cursive script, as in Roman times;[111] thus, part of his education took place in the scriptorium, where his master taught him the scripts that were then in use.[112]

As soon as the pupil knew his letters, he was immediately given his first book, the Psalter, a practice which came from the monastic tradition but which had become common in the schools as well as in private teaching: to know how to read was to know one's Psalter.[113] The master copied verses on the tablets, and the child had to learn them by heart, as young Moslems in our times learn to read and write by utilizing the

---

[107] *HF*, VIII, 15 (p. 381, ll. 3–5): "Jamque in majore aetate proficiens, litteras discere studui; ex quibus prius scribere potui quam ordinem scriptarum litterarum scirem."

[108] Scribes traced the alphabet to try out their pens. See Autun, ms. 20a (22), fol. 296r ("abc ecce magistrum") and Autun, ms. 27 (29), fol. 24. See also R. P. Robinson, "Manuscripts 27 and 107, Autun: A Study of Spanish Half-Uncial and Early Wisigothic Minuscule and Cursive Scripts," *Memoirs of the American Academy in Rome* 16 (1939): 62, pl. 43, 1; and Bernhard Bischoff, "Elementarunterricht und *Probationes Pennae* in der ersten Hälfte des Mittelalters," in *Classical and Mediaeval Studies in Honor of E. K. Rand*, ed. Leslie W. Jones, pp. 9–20 (*Mittelalterliche Studien*, 1: 74–87).

[109] *Vita Maclovii*, III, ed. François Plaine, *Bulletin de la Société archéologigue d'Ille-et-Vilaine* (1883), p. 138: "Et quando sanctus magister videbat quod s. Maclovius poterat litteras atque sermones intelligere, scripsit ei elementa in tabula cerea." This ninth-century *Life*, like many Breton saints' *Lives*, is later than our period; however, its testimony is certainly valid for the earlier period.

[110] Hessels, *An Eighth-Century Latin–Anglo-Saxon Glossary*, p. 98: "Productalem: strumentum infantium in scolis." Quintillian, *Inst. orat.*, I, 1, 27 (Bornecque ed., 1: 26), described this instrument without naming it.

[111] A comparison of the few fragments of cursive script from this period with fifth-century Roman cursive reveals that the *ductus* is the same in both scripts; see Jean Mallon, *Paléographie romaine* (Madrid, 1952), pp. 64–65.

[112] For the supposed relations between the school and the scriptorium, see above, chap. 9, sect. III.B. The major abbeys had a corps of specialized scribes. Abbot Cuthbert of Jarrow mentioned the *pueri* employed in the scriptorium (*Ep.* 116 [*MGH, Ep.*, III, 406, l. 11]). For child scribes, see Lesne, *Les livres*, p. 339, and idem, *Les écoles*, p. 576.

[113] Gregory of Tours, *Vitae patrum*, VIII, 2 (*MGH, SRM*, I-2, 692): "Studebat ut omnes pueros qui in domo ejus nascebantur . . . statim litteris doceret ac psalmis imbueret." The passage refers to Nicetius of Lyon, Gregory's uncle. I have collected the texts bearing on the study of the Psalter in Merovingian Gaul in "Le Psautier: Livre de lecture élémentaire," *Etudes mérovingiennes*, pp. 253–56. See Lorcin, "La vie scolaire," pp. 233–34, for Ireland.

surahs of the Koran. This technique was effective on three counts: the pupil learned to read and to write while at the same time becoming thoroughly familiar with the sacred text. The Psalter thus replaced the moral aphorisms such as the *Disticha Catonis* which in earlier times had been put in the hands of the young Roman.[114] All his life the pupil would remember the Psalter—it is not surprising to find citations from it on bits of tile, at the head of royal diplomas, and in the margins of manuscripts.[115]

Laymen thought it sufficient to learn a few Psalms in order to know how to read and write. Monks and clerics, however, had to learn the Psalms in order from Psalm 1 to Psalm 150[116]—a long and difficult study. Students who were not gifted took two to three years to accomplish this task, while others needed only six months to a year, generally considered a miraculously short period.[117] The *Rule* of the Master required that monks who were not *psaltarati* were to provide themselves with tablets covered with the Psalms when they traveled so that when they stopped, they could sharpen their memory either alone or with the help of a brother.[118]

Young monks helped each other study. "May each decade read and

---

[114] The *Disticha Catonis* were not entirely forgotten. Fortunatus cited them (see above, chap. 6, n. 133); the scribe of the Autun manuscript used them to try out his pen; and Julian of Toledo knew them (see M. Boas, "Cato und Julianus von Toledo," *RhM* 79 [1930]: 183–96). Eugenius' *monosticha* might have supplanted them, however; see the *Monosticha de decem plagis aegypti* and the poem *De inventoribus litterarum* (*MGH, AA,* XIV, 256–57). The *monosticha*, which contain Evagrius' sentences (see J. Leclercq, "L'ancienne version latine des sentences d'Evagre pour les moines," *Scriptorium* 5 [1951]: 195–213), could also be considered a work intended for elementary reading.

[115] The first verses of Psalms 105 and 106 were copied onto a diploma of 753 (*MGH, Dipl. karol.,* I, 6); this verse appears in Lyon, ms. 468 in cursive: "Jubelate dom omnes terras psalmum dicite nomine ejus." These are *probationes pennae.* See the tile from the church of Saint Samson-sur-Risle (Henri Leclercq, "Graffites," *DACL,* VI-2, 1538) and the brick from Barcelona (Mallon, *Paléographie romaine,* p. 64).

[116] *Vita Trudonis, MGH, SRM,* VI, 264: "Annali circulo revolute Trudo psalterium per ordinem pro dispositum est cantare praevaluit." *Reg. Pauli et Stephani,* 6 (Vilanova ed., p. 110): "Juniores et maxime qui adhuc psalmos discere meditantur per choros ex ordine et sine negligentia dicent."

[117] Gregory of Tours, *Vitae patrum,* XII (*MGH, SRM,* I-2, 713): "[Brachio] duos vel tres annos faciens, psalterium memoriae commendavit." Valerius of Bierzo, *Opuscula,* 49 (*PL,* LXXXVII, 450): "Tantam dispensatio divina dedit illi memoriae capacitatem ut intra medium annum peregrans eum canticis universum memoria retinet psalterium." *Vita Brioci, AB* 2 (1883): 163: "Psalmos quoque in spatio quinque mensium omnes . . . didicit."

[118] *Regula Magistri,* LVII (Vanderhoven and Masai ed., p. 261): "Si vero non fuerit [psaltaratus] tabulas a majore superposita psalmis secum portet . . . ut si cum litterato vadit cum ad refectione vel mansione applicaverit, ab eo tamen aliquantulum . . . meditetur."

listen together and may they teach the ignorant letters and Psalms one after the other," reads the *Regula Magistri*[119] in an example of mutual teaching, a practice which was to become common in the Middle Ages.[120] As in Roman times, however, the master taught only one pupil at a time. He dictated the Psalms the child was to write (which gave the master the title *dictator*) and then listened as the pupil read the text.[121]

Children also recited the Psalms aloud in order to remember them better. The ninth-century *Vita Maglorii* contains an episode in which a group of young monks asked permission to cross over to a nearby shore so they could recite aloud without disturbing their sleeping elders.[122] The memory was sharpened even during their naps: young Rusticula remembered the verses that her mistress continued to read to her while she slept on her mistress's knee, thus receiving hypnopedia without knowing it.[123] Some monks had remarkable memories: Abbot Achivus of Agaune could remember practically everything he read and

[119] Ibid., L (p. 247): "In una quoque decada ergo in his tribus horis, invicem et legant et audiant, vicebus litteras et psalmos ignorantibus ostendant." See Lorcin, "La vie scolaire," p. 231, n. 61, for Ireland.

[120] See Jacob Ackstaller, *Das Helfersystem in der mittelalterlichen Schulerziehung* (Innsbruck, 1934).

[121] The *Reg. Pauli et Stephani*, 15 (Vilanova ed., pp. 114–15), obliged the student to keep the same *dictator*: "De his qui psalmos discunt, ut dictatoribus delegati observent. Hi qui litteras vel psalmos discunt, illis observent ad excipiendum, quibus fuerint deputati: qui pro eis aut de negligentia arguendi sunt, aut in eorum eruditione et studio approbandi. Si autem discedens dictator pro se deputare neglexerit, ad patrem revertatur is qui excipit, ut ipse deputet pro absente qui ei dictare debeat, dum absens revertetur ad suum redeat dictatorem."

Valerius of Bierzo mentioned personal reading before the master (*Opuscula*, 49 [*PL*, LXXXVII, 450]): "Cum vero quodam die hora sexta diei ad operam sederem, et ille coram me legeret . . . mandavi illi electos psalmos recitare." See also Bede, *Sup. parab. Salom.*, II, 23 (*PL*, XCI, 1005): "Quando sederis ad legendum cum magistro . . . diligenter intellige quae scripta sunt"; and the *Vita Alcuini*, IV, 10 (*PL*, C, 96): "Legens igitur Joannis evangelium ante magistrum."

[122] *Vita Maglorii*, 24 (*AS*, Oct., X, 782): "Nunc parvuli monachi . . . sancti Maglorii pedes amplexati sunt dicentes 'beatissime pater, permitte nobis portum atque litus adire, ut garullitas nostrae vocis monachis quiescentibus somnum non possit eripere et ut securius alta voce legentes nostras lectiones valeamus commendari.'" The *Regula Magistri*, L (Vanderhoven and Masai ed., p. 247) stipulated that one monk would read in the study room while others listened to him: "Ne in uno redacta omnis congregatio suis sibi invicem vocibus obstrepent, id est lectionibus vacet unus de decem per loca et residui de suo numere audiant."

[123] Florentius, *Vita Rusticulae*, 6 (*MGH, SRM*, IV, 342): "Nam fertur aliquando dum infans psalmos pararet et ut adsolet infantia sompno occuparetur, recumbens in genua unius de sororibus psalmum et ipsa in aure dicebat. Quae mox ut expergefacta fuisset, tanquam si eum legisset, ita memoriter recensebat, implens illud scripturae dictum 'ego dormio et cor meum vigilat.'"

knew almost all the books of the Bible; Cassiodorus cited to his monks the example of a blind man who knew all the sacred texts.[124] In reading the literature of this period, we observe over and over again that scriptural citations came naturally to the pen of the writer. In the history of memorization, the men of the seventh and eighth centuries had no reason to envy the men of Antiquity.

In fact, their achievement was even greater, since oral reading was less and less practiced outside the classroom. We have already noted (Chapter 4) that personal and silent reading was imposed in the monasteries. Isidore, in the seventh century, showed that this kind of reading led to better comprehension of the text: when the reader's voice was hushed and the lips moved in silence, the *lectio* more easily penetrated the mind.[125] It was now customary to read alone, sometimes even while walking.[126] In a letter to Daniel of Winchester, Boniface asked for a manuscript written in very large characters because his sight had weakened and he could no longer make out small characters.[127] Thus the medieval cleric, a real reader, differentiated himself from the antique man of letters even on this point.

In addition to reading and writing, elementary teaching also included chant and computation, as we have already observed in reference to presbyteral schools.[128] The cantor had to content himself with teaching the notes and the manner of pitching the voice, without leading his students into the labyrinth of music theory. The *Vita Praejecti* notes that the masters sang the melodies several times, after which the children repeated them.[129] The calculation taught in the elementary schools was of the most basic and practical sort. The child could practice with tokens, as did young Samson,[130] and then learn digital computation, as

---

[124] *Vitae Abbatum Acaunensium*, 9 (*MGH, SRM*, III, 179, l. 12); Cassiodorus, *Inst.*, 1–5 (Mynors ed., pp. 22–23).

[125] Isidore of Seville, *Sent.*, III, 14, 9 (*PL*, LXXXIII, 689): "Acceptabilior est sensibus lectio tacita quam aperta. Amplius enim intellectus instruitur quando vox legentis quiescit et sub silentio lingua movetur, nam clare legendo et corpus lassatur et vocis acumen obtunditur."

[126] *Vita Columbani*, I (*MGH, SRM*, IV-1, 74, l. 16). Bede, *HE*, IV, 3 (p. 210) said that Chad of Lichfield read in the midst of a gale.

[127] Boniface, *Ep.* 63 (*MGH, Ep.*, III, 329, l. 32).

[128] See above, chap. 7, sect. II.A.

[129] *Vita Praejecti*, *MGH, SRM*, V, 228: "Jubetur puer sonum reddere quam vix puncto ore audierat decantari . . . mox igitur sancto se docente spiritu ita cantum memoriter reddidit, ut cuncti patenter agnoscerent quod illam melodiam magistralem in puero divinas pietas insudisset."

[130] *Vita Samsoni*, ed. Fawtier, p. 40: "Tesserasque agnovit totas." Fawtier thought that the reference was to squares bearing letters. But did not these squares really contain

had young Romans.[131] Bede described this method in his *De temporum ratione* and provided the rules by which the simple monk, using his fingers, could calculate rapidly the lunar and solar cycles.[132] The pupils might also have been invited to solve minor arithmetical problems like those that have been preserved for us under the names of Bede and Alcuin.[133] But these arithmetical puzzles were probably intended for more advanced children and really should be classified with the literary genre of the enigma rather than with the study of calculation.

Before leaving the subject of elementary education, let us describe the examinations that governed the student's progress. The child could recite his lesson in writing.[134] He could also recite orally before the abbot or bishop when the latter made his tour of the diocese.[135] In his commentary on Benedict's *Rule*, Paul the Deacon provided for examinations during the visits of particularly learned guests. The prior was to select the child to converse with the guest "on grammar, chant, computus, or any other discipline." The prior was also to attend the interview at a distance in order to see that the child responded correctly to his examiner. After the guest had left, the prior repeated the questions that the young monk could not answer.[136] Obviously, this was an ideal

---

figures? The definition from the Epinal glossary ("tessera: tasol quadrangulum") does not help us.

[131] See Charles W. Jones' preface to his edition of Bede's *De temporum ratione*, p. 174, and A. Cordoliani, "A propos du chapitre I du *De temporum ratione* de Bède," *MA* 54 (1948): 209–23. There are illustrated explanations of digital computus in the manuscripts; see Cordoliani's "Etudes du comput, I: Note sur le manuscrit latin 7418 de la Bibl. nat.," *BECh* 103 (1942): 61–62. The *Romana computatio*, in *Bedae pseudepigrapha*, ed. Jones, pp. 106ff., inspired Bede's treatise. See the references to ancient digital reckoning in the article "Digitus," *ThLL*, V-1, 11, 25, and the recent studies of A. Quacquarelli ("Ai margini dell'actio: La loquela digitorum," *Vetera Christianorum* 7 [1970]: 119–225) and E. Alföldi-Rosenbaum ("The Finger Calculus in Antiquity and the Middle Ages," *FS* 5 [1971]: 1–10).

[132] *De temporum ratione*, XIX (Jones ed., p. 218).

[133] Alcuin, *Disputatio puerorum*, PL, CI, 1143: "Aliae propositiones ad acuendos juvenes"; Manitius, 1: 289; Jones, *Bedae pseudepigrapha*, p. 52. There is nothing, however, on the study of fractions, which Aldhelm said he undertook with great difficulty (*Ep.*, *MGH, AA*, XV, 477). For the study of fractions in the early Middle Ages, see F. A. Jeldham, "Notation of Fractions in the Earlier Middle Ages," *Archeion* 8 (1927): 313–29, and Gottfried Friedlein's old work, *Die Zahlzeichen und das elementare Rechnen der Griechen und Römer und des christlichen Abendlandes vom 7. bis zur 13. Jahrhundert* (Erlangen, 1869).

[134] *Vita Maglorii*, *AS*, Oct., X, 702: "Cum quadam die a magistro lectionem reddere rogatus esset, inventa est in tabula ejus amplior quam ipse descripsisset litterarum insertio."

[135] The *Regula Magistri* mentions an examination before the abbot; see above, chap. 4, sect. I.C. The bishop of Trier had Gaugericus pass an exam; see chap. 7, sect. II.A.

[136] Paul the Deacon, *Comm. Reg.*, XXXVII, in *Paulus Warnefridus*, p. 124: "Post vero discessum hospitis debet illum prior admonere ubi negligenter interrogavit vel respondit . . . ut possit post modum petentibus reddere responsum."

toward which all masters were to strive. Paul the Deacon, as we have already said, portrayed what a true Benedictine monastery ought to be like.

It is difficult to assess the results of elementary education. To learn to read, write, chant, indeed to count, must have required a tremendous effort. We can be sure that many clerics and monks never went beyond this level.

B. "Secondary" and "Higher" Education

The distinction between elementary education and what can be called secondary education was not as clear as it had been in the time of the Roman school. Once the study of the Psalter was completed, the same master could invite the child to further his studies by first teaching him Latin. It was quite possible to know how to read, to know the Psalter by heart, and to know how to recite the office without really understanding Latin. When young Gregory, future abbot of Utrecht, was invited by Boniface to read a sacred text and then to explicate its contents in his own tongue, he confessed that he was unable.[137] The text remained a dead letter for those who received only elementary instruction. Anglo-Saxons and Franks, as well as Italians and Spaniards, had to learn the mechanisms and rules of a language that, at least from the sixth century, had become a foreign tongue to them.[138] Even in Ro-

---

[137] Liudger, *Vita Gregorii*, 2 (*MGH, SS*, XV-1, 67).

[138] Although they both derived from Latin, the popular tongues of Italy and Spain had already developed their own personalities by the eighth century. For the origin of Italian, see Charles H. Grandgent, *From Latin to Italian: An Historical Outline of the Phonology and Morphology of the Italian Language* (Cambridge, Mass., 1927); Carlo Battisti, *Avviamento allo studio del latino volgare* (Bari, 1955); and, most recently, Alfredo Schiaffini, "Problemi del passagio del latino all'italiano," in *Studi in onore di Angelo Monteverdi*, 2 vols. (Modena, 1959), 2: 691–715. Dag Norberg wrote that "the Italian language begins in the seventh century" ("Le développement du latin en Italie de Saint Grégoire le Grand à Paul Diacre," *Settimane*, 5: 495). Actually, though, it is difficult to date the beginnings of a language. Several words found in the Mozarabic *Orational* ("Separeba boves, alba trabuta araba stalbo versorio seneba et negro semen senunata" [*CLA*, IV, 515]) were long believed to have been a popular "Italian" quatrain from the beginning of the eighth century. But, as Curtius has shown (p. 383), this passage is really a copyist's aphorism in which he compared his pen to a plow and his manuscript to a field. The form of the aphorism, nonetheless, shows the evolution of Latin. See Alfredo Schiaffini, "I problemi dell'indovinello veronese," in *I mille anni della lingua italiana* (Milan, 1961), pp. 71–96, and Robert Louis Politzer, *A Study of the Language of Eighth-Century Lombardic Documents: A Statistical Analysis of the Codice paleografico lombardo* (New York, 1949).

For Spanish, see Ramón Menéndez Pidal, *Origines del Español*, 3rd ed. (Madrid, 1950), and M. C. Diaz y Diaz, "Movimientos fonéticos en el latin visigodo," *Emerita* 25 (1957): 369–86.

mance countries, the spoken dialect was very different from Latin.

To teach grammar, the master utilized the manuals already extant in the fifth and sixth centuries, beginning with the *Ars minor* of Donatus, but he attempted to facilitate their use by simplifying them. A work attributed to Bede that was used in monastic and episcopal schools, the *Cunabula grammaticae artis*, was a revision of Donatus. Its dialogue format and its simplicity clearly indicate that it was intended for beginners.[139] Anglo-Saxon masters, as we have seen,[140] composed treatises that were inspired by antique and modern classical grammatical manuals and that were true *Epitomes*, to repeat the title of Virgil the Grammarian's treatise.

We do not know whether the pupil learned these works by heart. We do know that he had to copy passages from them, thus compiling extracts of extracts, such as we see in the *Glosa de partibus orationis*, a compilation of various grammarians presented with no logical order in a Bobbio manuscript.[141] Another Italian manuscript, written in a cursive hand related to the script of diplomas, can be considered a fragment of a student's notebook.[142]

At the same time that the master taught the theory of the eight parts of speech, he taught his pupil Latin vocabulary. We do not know if he used bilingual manuals providing the essentials of ordinary vocabulary in the form of conversation such as Roman schoolboys used when they learned Greek.[143] Aelfric composed his *Colloquies* for young Anglo-Saxons of the tenth century; however, there is no trace of similar works for the seventh and eighth centuries.[144] The *Hisperica famina*, with its descriptions of scenes from daily life, especially school life, could be compared to the *Colloquies*. These strange writings, however, enjoyed success only in centers where the hisperic style was held in honor—centers which, happily for the future of culture, were located in Celtic countries and in Wessex.[145]

---

[139] *Cunabula grammaticae artis*, ed. Keil, 5: 325. The author addressed himself to the "parvulis et incipientibus."

[140] In chap. 9, sect. II.B.1.

[141] See A. Collignon, "Note sur une grammaire latine manuscrite du VIIIe siècle . . . ," *RPh*, n.s. 7 (1883): 13–22.

[142] *CLA*, II, 166. This manuscript is a double palimpsest. The grammatical fragments, which covered a historical text copied in the fifth century, were erased in the tenth century.

[143] Marrou, *Education*, pp. 356–57.

[144] William H. Stevenson, *Early Scholastic Colloquies* (Oxford, 1929); Marguerite-Marie Dubois, *Aelfric: Sermonnaire, docteur et grammairien* (Paris, 1943), pp. 200ff.

[145] Kenney, *Sources*, p. 256, n. 290.

It was, instead, in the glossaries that students learned vocabulary. Glossaries were of two types: one kind gave Latin words with their equivalents in the vulgar tongue, while the other explained rarely used Latin expressions with quite simple paraphrases.[146] The reading of glossaries allows us to judge the level of education in the centers where they were composed. In the Epinal glossary, which comes from Northumbria, we find the definition of terms such as *ariopagus* ("nomen curiae"), *bibliopola* ("qui codices vendit"), *filogoys* ("rationis vel verbi"), *platonis ideas* ("id est species"), and others.[147] The Cambridge glossary, which must have been used at Canterbury, explains *peripitegi* and *Epicurei* ("genus philosophrum"), *epifati*, and *laici*, among others.[148]

Men of letters who wanted to embellish their prose with rare and obscure words could readily find what they were looking for in glossaries: instead of *peccatum*, they wrote *peccamen*; instead of *canis*, *molossus*. Aldhelm and those who loved an affected style thus had a practical instrument at their disposal. Bede composed a work for the students at Jarrow which was jointly a glossary, a treatise on orthography, and a grammar. His *De orthographia* gives the explication of certain words in alphabetical order, as well as kinds of nouns, basic verb tenses, etymologies, and orthographic variants.[149] Here we are quite far from Cassiodorus' learned work on orthography.[150] Bede, in addition, cited several Greek words with their Latin translation. Clerics and monks used glossaries like Bede's to find the Greek terms that enriched their writings at a time when Greek was no longer taught in the schools.

Having acquired a basic vocabulary and the ability to construct short

[146] For early medieval glossaries, see Georg Goetz, ed., *Corpus glossariorum latinorum*, 7 vols. (Leipzig, 1888–1923), 4: 3ff., 101–298; W. M. Lindsay, *The Corpus, Epinal, Erfurt, and Leyden Glossaries* (Oxford, 1921); and idem, *The Corpus Glossary* (Cambridge, 1921). For Greek glossaries, see Hubert Le Bourdellès, "Naissance d'un serpent: Essai de datation de l'*Aratus Latinus* mérovingien," in *Hommages à Marcel Renard*, ed. J. Bibaux, 3 vols. (Brussels, 1969), 1: 506–14. Carlo Pascal published a fragment of a seventh-century Latin glossary (*Letteratura latina medievale: Nuovi saggi e note critiche* [Catania, 1909], app. 2, p. 191). A seventh-century Italian manuscript preserves a fragment of a glossary (*CLA*, VIII, no. 1106). Bern, 611, from a scriptorium in eastern France, contains a glossary, extracts from the *Origines*, fragments of a computus, metrics, etc.: see *CLA*, VII, 604a–b.

[147] Lindsay, *The Corpus, Epinal*, . . . ; Henry Sweet, *The Épinal Glossary: Latin and Old English of the Eighth Century* (London, 1883).

[148] Hessels, *A Eighth-Century Latin–Anglo-Saxon Glossary*; see *CLA*, II, 122.

[149] Bede, *De orthographia*, ed. Keil, 7: 262. This treatise was intended for children: "Ne puer legens erret" (ibid., 271, l. 19).

[150] See above, chap. 5, sect. IV.B.

Latin sentences, the student still could not read texts. To become a *lector*, he had to know accents and pauses—that is, he had to learn prosody.[151] This very long study was made easier for him by the poetical exercises he practiced in place of the study of rhetoric. Whoever could recite and then construct a poem was able to read and understand prose. Bede wrote his *De arte metrica* to help students with the different rules of prosody and meter[152] as taught by the most ancient grammarians, but like a master who was careful to facilitate the work of the less gifted, he remarked to those who still could not recognize short and long syllables that the first syllable of hexameters and pentameters was always long.[153] Aldhelm likewise provided a long list of words with their accentuation in his *De metris*.[154] By means of these empirical methods, the pupil could learn where to accent before he actually knew the rules contained in the manuals.

Practice could also teach him chant. Roger was correct when he said that the study of prosody was indispensable for the proper execution of the chants of the Church;[155] however, we could also argue that long periods spent in church habituated the young man's ear to Latin accentuation. It could be too that in the small elementary schools, the cantor might even have taught the first elements of prosody.[156]

In the antique school the second task of the grammarian was to explain the ancient authors. Such, however, was not the case in the episcopal and monastic schools, where, if the pupils were able to sample verses from pagan literature, they did so through the intermediary of grammarians and glossators. Explication was based, not on a text, but on a manual of grammar, and it was only in this way that the students could discover the classics.[157] Perhaps some examples in the manuals led them to search out the complete work in the library: Alcuin's biographer tells us that the young boy preferred to read Virgil rather than

---

[151] See Roger, pp. 350ff.

[152] Ibid., p. 363.

[153] Bede, *De arte metrica*, ed. Keil, 7: 234, ll. 10–14: "Sed qui necdum ad hoc pervenit, hunc interim hortamur syllabas omnium partium orationis ex principio versuum heroicorum diligentius scrutetur. Omnis enim versus hexameter . . . et pentameter . . . primam habet syllabam longam, quia vel a spondeo vel a dactylo incipit."

[154] Aldhelm, *De metris*, MGH, AA, XV, 161ff.

[155] See Roger, pp. 351–52. The study of prosody must have been pursued even more by the professional cantors in the major religious centers. Alcuin alluded to them at the school of York when he distinguished among "those who read, those who chant, and those who write" (*Ep.* 114 [MGH, Ep., IV, 169, l. 12]).

[156] See Lesne, *Les écoles*, p. 574. We mean, of course, prosody such as it existed in the Middle Ages.

[157] See Roger, pp. 351–52.

his Psalter.[158] But the importance of antique authors in the libraries of this period should not be exaggerated. If Aldhelm, Bede, Boniface, and even the Italian and Spanish masters could cite Virgil, Pliny, or Seneca, it was because they had used anthologies and florilegia, which, since they were school books, have not come down to us.[159] It is hazardous to try to reconstruct the library of a medieval author by using the *loci citati* in his writings as a starting point.[160]

It would be more certain, in the absence of library catalogues, to consult the list of manuscripts produced in the scriptoria or bought by bishops and abbots.[161] Of course, we do not have very many pre-Carolingian manuscripts, but those that have come down to us contain more pedagogical than classical works. Not all the codices in the ecclesiastical library were used by the master. When the abbot of Saint Wandrille bought the *History of the Goths* of Jordanes, the *History* of Apollonius of Tyre, and the *History* of Alexander, he did not intend these books for the students' library.[162] The medical treatises from Fleury and other centers were certainly reserved for the physician-monks in charge of the infirmary.[163] We can assume that the school library was becoming distinct from the general library, which only lettered clerics and monks used.

Texts counted for less than teachers in the seventh and eighth centuries. Teaching was without doubt oral, as Bede, master par excellence, tells us several times.[164] The treatises he wrote were the fruit of the courses he gave for the benefit of the best students.[165] The goal of grammatical and scientific studies was not—as in the antique school—to

---

158 *Vita Alcuini*, 5 (*MGH, SS*, XV-1, 187–88): "Virgilii amplius quam psalmorum amator conceditur puer Albinus."

159 We can count the *Codex Salmasianus*, which bears the *Latin Anthology* and other poems, as one of these manuals. So, too, Ansileubus' *Liber glossarum*. For the school manuals during Isidore's period, see J. Fontaine, *IS*, pp. 750ff.

160 Which is what Laistner did in his "Library of Venerable Bede," in Thompson, *Bede*, pp. 263–66.

161 See above, chap. 9, sects. II.A.4 and III.C. We know nothing about the commerce in books. Bischoff found in an eighth-century manuscript (*CLA*, IX, 1162) the note "Sigibertus bindit libellum," but he does not believe that organized commerce in books existed north of the Alps. See an allusion in Bischoff, "Biblioteche, scuole e letteratura nelle città dell'alto medio evo," *Settimane*, 6: 617.

162 See above, chap. 9, n. 452.

163 See above, chap. 9, sect. IV.C.1.

164 Bede, *De temporum ratione*, LV (Jones ed., p. 276): "Sed innumera hujusce disciplinae sicut et caeterarum artium melius vivae vocis alloquio quam stili signantis traduntur officio." See also ibid., XVI, 60 (p. 215).

165 Ibid., preface (p. 175): "De natura rerum et ratione temporum duos quondam stricto sermone libellos discentibus, ut rebar, necessarios composui."

furnish the student's mind with citations and references from his study of texts in order to make an erudite scholar of him, but rather to give him access to a higher level of teaching, the explication of the *divina pagina*.[166]

What do we know about exegetical teaching in the schools of this period? Truthfully, not very much. Here again, we must guard against judging instruction on the basis of lists of works contained in libraries. We know that the libraries contained the Fathers of the Church: Jerome, Ambrose, Augustine, Gregory, and Origen[167] were well represented. They were, as Boniface said, the masters of those who read the sacred word.[168] Obviously, biblical commentaries were not placed in the hands of students—indeed, some of the commentaries were hardly appropriate for students. Acca of Hexham asked Bede for a commentary on Saint Luke that would be more accessible to average readers than Ambrose's learned work.[169] The master of Jarrow composed patristic florilegia for his monks,[170] and even though the *De luminaribus ecclesiae* is not his, it does give us a good idea of what these works were like.[171] The master could also use the treatises of those Cassiodorus called the *introductores*—Eucherius, Junilius, or the *Clavis Scripturae*, which undoubtedly dates from the eighth century.[172] It is noteworthy that neither

---

[166] Willibald, *Vita Bonifatii*, 2 (Levison ed., p. 9), categorized grammar, rhetoric, metrics, and exegesis as *scripturarum eruditio*.

[167] See H. de Lubac, *L'exégèse médiévale* (Paris, 1961), 1: 223ff., for the significance of Origen during this period. Siegmund, *Die Ueberlieferung*, p. 110, discussed the manuscripts of Origenian translations.

[168] Boniface, *Ep.* 34 (*MGH, Ep.*, III, 285, l. 11): "Maxime in sanctorum Patrum spiritualibus tractatibus; quia spiritualis tractatus magister legentium sacrum eloquium esse dinoscitur."

[169] Bede, *In Luc.*, PL, XCII, 302. In this text Bede mentioned the four doctors Ambrose, Gregory, Augustine, and Jerome as a group for the first time.

[170] See M. T. A. Carroll, *The Venerable Bede: His Spiritual Teachings* (Washington, D.C., 1946), p. 49, and A. Wilmart, "La collection de Bède le Vénérable sur l'Apôtre," *RB* 38 (1926): 16–52.

[171] Paul the Deacon, *De gestis Langobardum*, PL, XCV, 552. So, too, does the *Collectanea*, PL, XCIV, 539–60 (*Clavis*, no. 1129). Isidore of Seville's *Quaestiones in vetus Testamentum* (PL, LXXXIII, 207–424) is a compilation of extracts from Origen, Ambrose, Jerome, Augustine, Fulgentius, and Gregory the Great. Isidore intended this work primarily for those "fastidiosis lectoribus qui nimium longitudinem sermonis abhorrent." For the patristic florilegia, see Joseph de Ghellinck, "Diffusion, utilisation et transmission des écrits patristiques," *Gregorianum* 14 (1933): 356–400, and idem, *Patristique et Moyen Age: Etudes d'histoire littéraire et doctrinale*, 3 vols. (Gembloux, 1946–49), 2: 181–377.

[172] Three sixth- and seventh-century manuscripts of Eucherius' works have come down to us; see *CSEL*, 31: vii. There is a seventh-century manuscript of Junilius' works at Munich, Clm. 14423, and one from the eighth century at St. Gall (ms 908). Aldhelm knew this author (*De metris, MGH, AA*, XV, 81, l. 17). On the *Clavis Scripturae*, a

the *De doctrina christiana* nor the first book of Cassiodorus' *Institutiones* were represented in the libraries or even cited by the exegetes of the period.[173] This lacuna alone is sufficient to induce doubt about the fruits of exegetical studies. Finally, among the manuals, we should note geographical works, such as Adamnan's and Bede's descriptions of the Holy Places[174] and Bede's list of biblical places at the end of his commentary on the Acts of the Apostles.[175]

Meditatio on Scripture could take several forms, although generally it must not have gone beyond the moral commentary. The author of the *Vita Gregorii*, a monk of Whitby at the beginning of the eighth century, saw in the *Moralia in Job* only a "medicine against the vices of men."[176] Still, some exegetes knew the tripartite and the quadripartite divisions of scriptural interpretation (*littera, allegoria, moralis, anagoge*).[177] Others turned to the traditional *quaestiones de sacra pagina*,[178] which led to a discussion of a biblical passage or of the correspondence between the two Testaments.[179] But these methods of

---

biblical glossary, see A. Wilmart, "Les allégories sur l'Ecriture attribuées à Raban Maur," *RB* 32 (1920): 51.

173 Pre-Carolingian manuscripts of the *De doctrina christiana* are scarcer than other manuscripts of Augustine's works. There is one from the fifth century (Leningrad, Q. v. I. 3), one from the sixth century (Milan, Ambr. G58), and one from the eighth century (Vatican, lat. 188).

174 See Manitius, 1: 85, 237, for these travels. The account of Willibald's voyage to the Holy Land (Hugeburc, *Vita Willibaldi*, 4 [*MGH, SS*, XV-1, 92–102]) and the *De locis sanctis* of Adamnan, recently reedited by D. Meehan (Dublin, 1958), can be added to this list. Adamnan added sketches but no general map to the descriptions which the traveler dictated to him. Maps were only rarely mentioned during this period. The *Vita Columbani*, I, 27 (*MGH, SRM*, IV-1, 104, l. 20) mentions a mappemonde. Pope Zachary had a map of the world designed for the Lateran which must have resembled the Byzantine mosaic at Madaba. For early medieval mappemondes, see Konrad Miller, *Mappae mundi: Die ältesten Weltkarten*, 6 vols. (Stuttgart, 1895–98), vol. 1, *Die weltkarte des Beatus* (776 n. Chr.). For the map that Isidore prepared, see R. Udhen, "Die Weltkarte des Isidorus von Sevilla," *Mnemosyne* 3 (1935–36): 1–28. See also the reproduction of an eighth-century mappemonde from an Albi manuscript in *Histoire universelle des explorations*, ed. Louis-Henri Parias, 4 vols. (Paris, 1955–56), 1: 256.

175 Bede, *Nomina regionum atque locorum de Actibus apostolorum* (ed. Laistner, in *Bedae venerabilis Expositio Actuum apostolorum et Retractatio*, pp. 147–58).

176 *Vita Gregorii*, ed. Gasquet, p. 36: "In languentium direxit mirabile morum, contra vitia humanorum medicamina animorum."

177 *Vita Bonifatii*, 2 (Levison ed., p. 9): "Historiae simplici expositione et spiritualis tripertita intelligentiae interpretatione imbutus." For the meaning of Scripture according to the Anglo-Saxons, see de Lubac, *L'exégèse médiévale*, 1: 147. Isidore knew only the tripartite division (ibid., p. 158).

178 For the *quaestiones*, see Bardy, "La littérature." For the dialogue technique, see Rudolf Hirzel, *Der Dialog: Ein literar-historischer Versuch*, 2 vols. (Leipzig, 1895).

179 See Braulio, *Ep.* 44 (p. 196), and Bede, *In libros Regum*, XXX (*PL*, CXI, 715). In his *Antikeimenon*, Julian of Toledo reviewed all the contradictions in the Bible and gave the Fathers' solutions. He was completely aware of the significance of what he was doing:

research, which later gave birth to true exegetical and theological science, were undoubtedly not applied in the schools. The teacher was satisfied to conduct a dialogue with his students, as he had when he taught grammar; his lessons resembled an interrogation rather than a *disputatio*. When Columban awakened the attention of his sleepy students by organizing discussions on different questions as games, one should not think that these discussions went beyond the elementary level.[180] We can judge what these dialogues represented by opening the *Quaestiones de veteri et novo Testamento* attributed to Isidore of Seville[181] or by reading the *Ioca monachorum*, which have survived in several fragments:[182] they were primarily puzzles and enigmas.

In conclusion, the teaching methods in the schools of the seventh and eighth centuries were still quite simple. The learning of the pupils depended upon the pedagogical talents of the master; he played the principal role, and without him nothing could be done.[183] It was he who transmitted the tradition of learning and dogma: "Be on guard against giving credence to your own discoveries rather than to the examples of your masters. The more one defends his own curiosity, the more he finds himself in error,"[184] said Aeneas, the supposed master of Virgil the Grammarian. Bede, the model master who held school every day,[185]

"Nonne stimulavit nos ad quaerendum?" (*PL*, XCVI, 668); "Haec sibi in verbis suis non discrepant, sed ad requirenda haec quasi discordantia studium nostrae mentis inflammatur" (ibid., col. 675).

180 Jonas, *Vita Columbani*, I, 3 (*MGH, SRM*, IV-1, 69): "Ut fieri adsolet cum ludendo magistri discipulos sciscitare conantur, ut de suo ingenio cognoscant vel flagrantem ubertate sensum vel neglegentiae somno torpentem, coepit ab eo ex difficilium quaestionum materia sensus querere."

181 Isidore of Seville, *Quaestiones de veteri et novo Testamento*, PL, LXXXIII, 201–7. For the authenticity of this work, see Altaner, "Der Stand der Isidorforschung," in *Miscellanea Isidoriana*, p. 10. We can also cite a dialogue attributed to Bede, *Quaestiones super Genesim* (*PL*, XCIII, 234–363).

182 *Ioca monachorum*, published by Wilhelm Meyer in *Romania* 1 (1872): 483, from a Sélestat manuscript: "Quis primus ex Deo precesset? Verbum. Quis semul natus et bis mortuos? Lazarus. . . . Quis prius rex factus est in Israel? Saul. . . . Quis dominum negavit? Petrus. Quanti milites deviserunt vistimenta Christi? IV." For the *Ioca monachorum* and pedagogical dialogues in general, see the introduction to Lloyd William Daly and Walther Suchier, *Altercatio Hadriani Augusti et Epicteti philosophi* (Urbana, Ill., 1939); Walther Suchier, *Das mittellateinische Gespräch Adrian und Epictitus, nebst verwandten Texten (Ioca monachorum)* (Tübingen, 1955), reprinted in *PL: Supplementum*, ed. A. Hamman, 4, pt. 2 (Paris, 1968): 917–23, 928–37; and *Clavis*, no. 1155f.

183 Braulio, *Vita Aemiliani*, 2 (*PL*, LXXX, 704): "Hoc credo nos facto instruens neminem sine magistrorum institutione recte ad beatam vitam tendere posse."

184 Virgil the Grammarian, *Epitomae*, V (Tardi ed., p. 69).

185 Cuthbert, *De obitu Baedae*, ed. Plummer, *Venerabilis Baedae . . .* , 1: clxii: "Nobis suis discipulis quotidie lectiones dabit."

praised the docility of his students and of young people in general. There were never controversies or objections to the words of the master. Neither revolts nor fights are ever mentioned in class: the students' tablets, which Pope Gregory II imagined would fly at the head of Emperor Leo the Iconoclast should he ever venture into a classroom,[186] rested peacefully on the knees of attentive children. This docility and submission to the teaching of the master, admirable in itself, was hardly conducive to the formation of a critical mind, an indispensable condition for the progress of learning.

The teacher had his preferred disciples to whom he transmitted his knowledge; indeed, in the absence of well-established school structures, he had to prepare a successor to himself. Around Bede, we can single out Deacon Wigbert, to whom Bede dedicated his *De arte metrica*,[187] and Deacon Cuthbert, who said himself that he passed his childhood "at the feet of the master."[188] Cuthbert later became abbot of Jarrow and concerned himself with diffusing Bede's work on the Continent.[189] Boniface's teaching was transmitted by his pupils Duddo and Lull, while that of Felix, the grammarian of Pavia, was transmitted by his nephew Flavian—who, in turn, passed it on to Paul the Deacon. We are beginning to witness the appearance of the genealogies of masters that writers in the Middle Ages liked to record.[190]

We should indicate yet another consequence of the strong ties that bound master and students, the tendency toward esotericism. The scholarly group was a closed one and jealousy guarded its secrets. Earlier, a curious passage in the *Regula Magistri* stated that when laymen were present at table with monks, the monks should choose an unusual reading so that the secrets of God and of monastic life would not be divulged.[191] In the eighth century, Bede provided for teaching in the

---

[186] Gregory II, *Ep. ad Leonem*, PL, LXXXIX, 516: "Obito scholas eorum qui elementis imbuuntur et dic, ego sum eversor et persecutor imaginum, et confestim tabella suas in caput tuum projicient."

[187] Keil, 7: 260, l. 3.

[188] Cuthbert, *Ep.* 116 (*MGH, Ep.*, III, 405): "Per experimentum ad pedes ejus nutritus, hoc quod narro, didici."

[188] Cuthbert, *Ep.* 116 (*MGH, Ep.*, III, 405): "Per experimentum ad pedes ejus nutripueris, juxta vires quod potui tuae dilectioni preparavi."

[190] See Gautbertus' famous *Grammaticorum* διαδοχή (Manitius, 2: 673–75), which presents a history of grammarians from the seventh through the tenth centuries but in a somewhat inexact fashion, as one can judge from the beginning of the *recapitulatio*: "Theodorus monacus et abbas Adrianus Aldhelmo instituerant grammaticam artem, Aldhelmus Bedam, Beda Rhabbanum [Rabanus Maurus], Rhabbanus, Alcuinum . . . ."

[191] *Regula Magistri*, XXIV (Vanderhoven and Masai ed., p. 219): "Propter detractionem futuram in saeculo cum secreta Dei saecularis agnoverit, si placuerit abbati aliam

language of fingers (*manualis loquela*), which, he said, could be used in the presence of persons who were indiscreet or dangerous.[192] To this secret language of gestures corresponded cryptography, which even the most learned monks used.[193] Virgil the Grammarian, attributing the art of cutting words (*scinderatio fonorum*) to his master Aeneas, had him say that "this language was created so as not to enable the young and fools to understand mysteries which are to be known only by the initiated."[194] Secret writing is a kind of game which all civilizations have practiced, especially when instruction is the privilege of a caste.[195] The period we are studying saw the appearance of a caste of learned men: the clerics of the seventh and eighth centuries jealously defended their privileges in the face of the great mass of those who did not have the opportunity to receive a literary, let alone a religious, education.,

III. RELIGIOUS EDUCATION OF LAYMEN

After the disappearance of antique educational traditions, laymen no longer had an opportunity for education except in ecclesiastical schools. We have already seen that the number of laymen who had been raised by monks and clerics was quite small. The only culture accessible to the great majority of laymen was religious culture—the culture which the Church desired to give all men no matter what their social standing or mental level in order to prepare them to live their faith in full awareness.

We would like to show in the following pages the way in which the layman—be he slave, *coloni*, or artisan—acquired his religious culture.

---

lectionem cujuscumque codicis legat ut secretum monasterii vel mensuras vitae sanctae constitutas in disciplinam ab inrisoribus non sciatur."

192 *De temporum ratione*, ed Jones, p. 181: "De computo vel loquela digitorum potest autem de ipso quem praenotavi computo quaedam manualis loquela tam ingenii exercendi quam ludi agendi gratia figurari." See E. M. Sanford, "De loquela digitorum," *Classical Journal* 23 (1928): 588–93. In this "language," a number is assigned to each letter (a=1; b=2; c=3; etc.). The number is translated by bending the finger as in digital computus. This practice is still observed in monasteries; see Gerard van Rijnberk, *Le langage par signes chez les moines* (Amsterdam, 1954).

193 Boniface, for example. See Levison, "St. Boniface and Cryptography," in *England*, pp. 290–94, and B. Bischoff, "Uebersicht über die nichtdiplomatischen Geheimschriften des Mittelalters," *MIOEG* 62 (1954): 1–27.

194 Virgil the Grammarian, *Epitomae*, XIII (Tardi ed., p. 111): "Ne mystica quaeque et quae solis gnaris pandi debent, passim ab infimis ac stultis facile repperiantur." One could cut words or syllables (for example, "ge, ve, ro, trum, quando, tum, a, fec, om, ni, libet, aevo," for "quandolibet vestrum, gero omni aevo affectum") or letters (for example, "RRR, SS, PP, MM, NT, EE, OO, A, V, I," for "spes Romanorum perit").

195 See Marcel Cohen, *Pour une sociologie du langage* (Paris, 1956), pp. 116–205, 211.

This inquiry has never been attempted because of the poverty of information at our disposal. Most have been content to say that Christianity was more practiced than known,[196] something that is true for all periods.

Should we, before undertaking this study, distinguish the countries that were already Christian at the time of the great invasions (Italy, Spain, and Gaul) from those where Christianity disappeared at the time of the invasions or where it had never been preached (northern Gaul, England, and Germany)? To use modern terminology, should we compare Christian lands to the still-pagan missionary lands? Certainly not. Paganism survived everywhere in the most diverse forms, in the towns as well as in the countryside. The sermons of Caesarius of Arles, the work of Martin of Braga at the beginning and middle of the sixth century, and the correspondence of Gregory the Great at the beginning of the seventh century show us that in Provence,[197] central Italy, Corsica, Sardinia,[198] and Galicia,[199] the rural populations had maintained their pagan customs. These customs did not disappear in the seventh and eighth centuries—quite the contrary: the Councils of Toledo in 589, 681, and 693 rose up against idolatry, the cults of stones and springs, and magical practices.[200] We see the same practices in Gaul and England.[201] The pagan practices listed by the Council of Leptinnes and by the *Indiculus* in the middle of the eighth century[202] were not unique to the newly converted countries. The ancient gods were not dead: their statues were honored, fountains were dedicated to them,[203]

---

[196] F. Lot, *La fin du monde antique*, p. 451.

[197] See Pelagius' letter to Sapaudus of Arles (*MGH, Ep.*, III, 443).

[198] Gregory the Great, *Ep.* VIII, 19 (Terracina); IV, 29, and IX, 204 (Sardinia); III, 59 (Sicily); VIII, 1 (Corsica) (*MGH, Ep.*, II, 21; I, 263; II, 191; I, 218; II, 1).

[199] Martin of Braga, *De correctione rusticorum*, ed. Barlow, pp. 188–89. See M. Meslin, "Persistances paiennes en Galice vers la fin du VIᵉ siècle," in Bibaux, *Hommages à Marcel Renard*, 2: 512–24.

[200] Council of Toledo (589), c. 14; (633), c. 29; (636), c. 4; (693), c. 2. See Stephen MacKenna, *Paganism and Pagan Survivals in Spain Up to the Fall of the Visigothic Kingdom* (Washington, D.C., 1938), pp. 84–107.

[201] See Vacandard, "L'Idolâtrie en Gaule," pp. 443ff.; Salin, 4: 19ff.; Gotfrid Storms, *Anglo-Saxon Magic* (The Hague, 1948); and Levison, "Venus a Man: From an Unpublished Sermon," in *England*, pp. 302–14.

[202] *Indiculus superstitionum et paganiarum, MGH, Leges*, I, 19ff. See Hefele and Leclercq, *Histoire des Conciles*, 3, pt. 2: 854–61, and especially Albin Saupe, *Der Indiculus superstitionum et paganiarum: Ein Verzeichniss heidnischer und abergläubischer Gebräuche und Meinungen aus der Zeit Karls des Grossen, aus zumeist gleichzeitigen Schriften erläutert*, Programm des städtischen Realgymnasium zu Leipzig (Leipzig, 1890–91).

[203] Vigilius of Auxerre's will (680) speaks of a fountain "quae vocatus Dianna." See Maximilien Quantin, ed., *Cartulaire général de l'Yonne*, 2 vols. (Auxerre, 1854–60), 1: 18.

banquets were offered to them,[204] and their temples were maintained.[205] Paganism reappeared in the towns during the celebrations commemorating the winter solstice and the Calends.[206] These holidays were even celebrated in Rome itself around the basilica of Saint Peter in the middle of the eighth century.[207] Of course, the same rituals were also practiced in Byzantium—almost officially, since the emperors took part in them.[208]

We can therefore study the methods of Christian instruction throughout the Barbarian West by considering one by one Christian initiation, then preaching, and finally, the liturgy.

A. Christian Initiation

In broaching this subject, we do not intend to deal with the different liturgical ceremonies by which the neophyte entered the Church.[209] Let us simply try to establish a precise notion of the doctrinal content of Christian initiation, a task all the more necessary because the fall of the Empire in the West modified the conditions of basic Christian training: the baptismal liturgy had been simplified, and the Church had opened its doors wider to unbelievers. The three years of the catechumenate were no longer required, as they had been during the first Christian centuries. Instead, pagans became Christians in a symbolic ceremony during Lent, after which they passed into the group of adepts, or *electi*. They then prepared for baptism and underwent various examina-

---

[204] Council of Clichy (626), c. 16 (*MGH, Leg. sect. III*, I, 199).

[205] See Gregory the Great, *Dial.*, II, 8, III, 7 (Moricca ed., pp. 95, 149), for temples to Apollo. The Pantheon in Rome remained a pagan temple until the seventh century, and Castor and Pollux were honored on an island in the Tiber at Ostia. For Gaul, see Elsmarie Knögel, *Schriftquellen zur Kunstgeschichte der Merowingerzeit*, Bonner Jahrbücher, vols. 140–41 (Darmstadt, 1936), pp. 59–61.

[206] The Council of Tours (567), c. 2 and c. 22, condemned the *Parentalia* and the *Kalendes* of January. See Martin of Braga, *De correctione rusticorum*, ed. Barlow, p. 189, for Galicia.

[207] Boniface, in a letter to Zachary, revealed that he was scandalized by these ceremonies: "Sicut adfirmant se vidisse annis singulis Romana urbe et juxta ecclesiam sancti Petri in die vel nocte quando kalendae januarii intrant paganorum consuetudine chorus ducere per plateas et adclamationes ritu gentilium et cantationes sacrilegas celebrare et mensas illa die vel nocte dapibus onerare" (*Ep.* 50 [*MGH, Ep.*, III, 301, l. 12]). The Council of Rome of 743 forbade these practices (*MGH, Leg. sect. III*, II, 16). See Schneider, *Rom und Romgedanke*, pp. 20ff., for pagan survivals in Rome.

[208] Fliche-Martin, 5: 473.

[209] See Duchesne, *Origines du culte chrétien*, pp. 309–60; B. Capelle, "L'introduction du catéchuménat à Rome," *RTAM* 5 (1933): 129–54; and P. de Puniet, "Catéchuménat," *DACL*, II-2, 2609–10. For the Middle Ages, see Peter Göbl, *Geschichte der Katechese im Abendlande vom Verfalle des Katechumenats bis zum Ende des Mittelalters* (Kempten, 1880), and J. D. C. Fischer, *Christian Initiation: Baptism in the Medieval West: A Study in the Disintegration of the Primitive Rite of Initiation* (London, 1965).

tions,[210] which now, rather than concentrating on exorcisms designed to tear the initiate from the powers of darkness, instead focused on the examinee's doctrinal knowledge. The Church seemed to attach less importance to initiation to the mysteries and to the discipline of the arcane and preferred to assure that future Christians and their leaders would have some knowledge of doctrine. During this period, the bishops' sermons dealt with Scripture in general[211] and on the two texts which the adept had to know, the *Symbol of the Apostles* and the *Pater*.[212] In his commentary on the *Symbol*, Ildefonsus of Toledo remarked that this short prayer could easily be memorized without the use of a text: believers "who were illiterate or too busy with worldly affairs and could thus not have direct contact with the Scriptures could remember this prayer and thereby have sufficient learning to attain salvation."[213] In Spain and southern Gaul, before the ceremony of baptism, the adepts proved that they knew the required prayers and were then allowed to receive the sacraments.

In Africa and in other Western lands, admission was even more simplified: it sufficed that the neophyte answer the questions of the priest or the bishop and prove that he knew the *Symbol* and the *Pater* for him to be baptized.[214] In his *De correctione rusticorum* Martin of Braga left a schema for baptism as it was practiced in his time; it was later repeated almost verbatim by Pirmin in his *Scarapsus*: " 'What is your name?' You answer yourself if you can or at least have your god-

---

[210] Dondeyne, "La discipline des scrutins dans l'Eglise latine avant Charlemagne," *RHE* 28 (1932): 1–33, 751, 787.

[211] See Caesarius of Arles' *Sermones*, ed. Morin, pp. 319ff. Bede noted that the four Gospels were sometimes explicated (*In Esdram*, II, 9 [*PL*, XCI, 867]). The *traditio psalmorum* was explicated in Naples; see Germain Morin, "Etude sur une série de discours d'un évêque (de Naples?) du VIe siècle," *RB* 8 (1894): 385–402.

[212] See Ildefonsus' commentary on the *Credo*, the *Liber de cognitione baptismi* (*PL*, XCVI, 111–72), and Fortunatus' commentary on the *Pater* and the *Credo* (*MGH, AA*, IV-1, 253–58).

[213] Ildefonsus, *Liber de cognitione baptismi, PL*, XCVI, 126–27: "Ad hoc autem sancti Patres, hoc non membranis sed memoriae commendare jusserunt. . . . In quo ideo ab apostolis breviatim collecta sunt ex omnibus Scripturis ut quia multi credentes vel litteras nescirent vel scientes occupati impedimento saeculi, Scripturas eis legere non liceret, hoc corde et memoria retinentes sufficientem sibi haberent scientiam salutarem." See the *Liber ordinum*, ed. Férotin, p. 164: "Symbolum . . . nemo scribit et legi possit . . . sit vobis codex vestra memoria."

[214] For Africa, see Ferrandus' letter to Fulgentius (*PL*, LXV, 378). For northern Italy, see B. Capelle, "Les *Tractatus de baptismo* attribués à saint Maxime de Turin," *RB*, 45 (1933): 108–18, and G. Morin, "Un *Ordo scrutinorum* de type inconnu jusqu'ici, d'après le Ms. Ambros. T 27 Sup.," *RB* 39 (1927): 56–80. For Spain, see Alonso, *La cura pastoral*, pp. 270ff. For southern Gaul, see Beck, *The Pastoral Care of Souls*, pp. 157ff.

father do it: 'My name is John.' The bishop will ask you, 'John, do you renounce the devil and his angels, his cult and his idols, his thefts and his frauds, his debaucheries, and drunkenness, and all his evil deeds?' You answer, 'I do renounce them.' After this, the bishop will again question you, 'Do you believe in the Almighty Father?' You answer, 'I believe.' 'And do you believe in Jesus Christ his only son?' You answer, "I believe.' And again, 'Do you believe in the Holy Spirit and the Holy Catholic Church?' You answer, 'I believe' "[215]

In England, the Council of Cloveshoe (747) recommended simply that priests and the faithful learn the *Credo* and the *Pater* in their native tongue.[216] Bede himself sent translations of two prayers to priests ignorant of Latin.[217] In Germany, it was apparently the same. A Wissembourg manuscript (incorrectly called a catechism) has a translation of and a Latin and German commentary on the *Credo* and the *Pater*.[218] This text was evidently intended for priests, who, after the reforming councils of the mid-eighth century, had to initiate neophytes to the two principal prayers.[219] Henceforth, preparation for baptism would be reduced to the minimum.

This simplification can be explained by the political and social transformations which followed the fall of the Roman Empire in the West and which led the Church to gather to its bosom a greater number of followers. The conversion of the pagans, which the princes supported in order to solidify their temporal domination, entailed an inevitable simplification—the pagans were, after all, a primitive people alien to all intellectual culture. In addition, in order to increase conversions, the Church admitted that baptisms might take place outside the baptistery of the cathedral church[220] and at times other than the Easter vigil.[221]

---

[215] Martin of Braga, *De correctione rusticorum*, ed. Barlow, p. 196; Pirmin, *Scarapsus*, ed. C. P. Caspari, in *Kirchenhistorische anecdota . . .* , vol. 1, *Lateinische Schriften* (Christiania, 1883).

[216] Council of Cloveshoe, 9 (Haddan-Stubbs ed., 3: 365).

[217] Bede, *Ep. ad Ecgbertum*, 5 (Plummer ed., p. 409): "Multis saepe sacerdotibus idiotis haec utraque et symbolum videlicet et Dominicam orationem in linguam Anglorum translatam obtuli."

[218] Paul Sprockhoff, *Althochdeutsche Katechetik: Literarhistorisch-stilistische Studien* (Rostock, 1912). Autun, ms. G3, contains an *ordo* for baptism intended for the use of priests; see André Wilmart, "Germain de Paris (lettres attribuées à saint)," *DACL*, VI-1, 1058.

[219] Boniface, *Sermo* 5 (*PL*, LXXXIX, 853), and the Council of 747, c. 16, 25, 26. Canon 27 contains an abjuration formula in the Germanic tongue; see Hefele and Leclercq, *Histoire des Conciles*, 3, pt. 2: 885–92. See also D. Kilfer, "Die Taufvorbereitung in der frühmittelalterlichen Benediktinermission," in *Benedictus, der Vater des Abendlandes*, ed. Suso Brechter (Munich, 1947), pp. 505–21.

[220] Gregory the Great mentioned rural baptisteries in his correspondence (VI, 22; VI,

The Church also demanded that henceforth children be baptized at an early age.[222] This led inevitably to a simplified baptismal rite. Religious and civil laws in England required, under pain of grave sanctions, that children be baptized within a month of birth.[223] Gregory the Great warned negligent parents that the salvation of their children would be in jeopardy if they were to die without baptism.[224] Nevertheless, many parents waited, sometimes for several years, before leading their children to the baptistery; in Gaul, for example, the aristocracy in particular wanted the child to respond to the bishop's questions himself and to be fully aware of the promises he was making.[225] The custom of baptizing young children, however, gradually became universal. The child was presented by his godparents, who had to recite the *Symbol* and the *Pater* for him[226] as well as to teach him those prayers later when he attained the age of reason.[227]

38; VIII, 1 [*MGH, Ep.*, I, 400, 415; II, 1]). See Charles Chazottes, *Sacerdoce et ministère pastoral d'après la correspondance de Saint Grégoire le Grand, 590–604* (Lyon, 1955). The future Chlothar II was baptized at Nanterre, according to Gregory of Tours, (*HF*, X, 28 [p. 522]): "Jussit baptisterium preparari in vico Nemptudoro".

221 Baptisms were performed at Christmas, at Pentecost, and on the eves of holy days, such as the feast of St. John.

222 Several texts mention the baptism of newborn children:
For Spain: Council of Gerona (517), c. 5; Council of Lerida (534), c. 13; Council of Toledo (681), c. 2; Council of Braga, II, c. 7; Ildefonsus, *Liber de cognitione baptismi*, XX (*PL*, XCVI, 120).
For Italy: Paul the Deacon, *HL*, V, 27 (*MGH, SRL*, p. 153): "Diaconos . . . qui infantulos baptizabant"; *Vita Caesarii*, II, 17. The *ordo Romanus*, XI, was composed during the second half of the sixth century especially for infant baptisms; see Andrieu, *Ordines Romani*, 1: 380ff.
For Gaul: Troianus of Saintes, *Ep.* 2 (*MGH, Ep.*, III, 437); Gregory of Tours, *HF*, VIII, 4 (p. 373); *Glor. confess.*, 47 (*MGH, SRM*, I-2, 777); *Vitae patrum*, II, 4 (ibid., p. 671); *Mir. Mart.*, II, 43 (ibid., p. 624); *Vita Amandi*, 15, 16 (*MGH, SRM*, V, 430).

223 *Laws of Ine*, 2 (Haddan-Stubbs ed., 3: 215). Ina's predecessor was baptized in Rome before his death; see Bede, *HE*, V, 7 (p. 292). See also *Theodore's Penitential*, I, 14, 28, 29 (Haddan-Stubbs ed., 3: 188–89). In the East, the Council of Quinisexta in 692 provided for sanctions if a child were not baptized during the first month after birth.

224 Gregory the Great, *Dial.*, IV, 33 (p. 277).

225 Chlothar II chose his own name; see Gregory of Tours, *HF*, X, 28 (p. 522). Fredegunda's ten-year-old son was baptized during an illness (ibid., V, 34 [p. 239, l. 15]). Eucherius of Orléans was several years old when he was baptized (*Vita Eucherii*, *MGH, SRM*, VII, 47). *Vita Geremari*, 8 (*AS*, Sept., VI, 699): "[Audoenus] suscipiens puerum, cathechizant eum preparatoque fonte baptismatis baptizavit."

226 Caesarius had earlier mentioned the role of godparents; see *Serm.* CCXXIX, 6 (Morin ed., p. 865, l. 12): "Ante omnia symbolum eis et orationem dominicam ostendite." See also Ildefonsus, *Liber de cognitione baptismi*, 94 (*PL*, XCVI, 145), and De Clercq, *La législation religieuse*, pp. 357–58.

227 Council of Cloveshoe, 11 (Haddan-Stubbs ed., 3: 366): "Symbolum quoque eis diligenter insinuant ut intelligant quid credere, quid sperare debeant, infantibusque illud vel eis qui eos in baptismate suscipere voluerint tradant, post haec legitimos professiones profiteri solerter instruant." See the letter of George of Ostia to Pope Hadrian (787) in

The child received no special religious education—nor would he throughout the entire Middle Ages.[228] His parents and godparents helped him to learn the minimum, and thus, he received the same education as adults. It now remains for us to examine this instruction.

B. TEACHING THROUGH PREACHING

One of the bishop's principal duties was to preach;[229] and kings, popes, and councils from the sixth to the eighth centuries called upon him to do so.[230] Gregory the Great particularly insisted on this point in his letters to his colleagues: "By your preaching, the unlettered learn what God wants."[231] The third part of the *Regula pastoralis* is a veritable treatise on preaching addressed to bishops.[232] But as the number of Christians grew, the bishop delegated preaching responsibilities to priests and asked them to seek inspiration from the sermons of the Fathers or even to improvise sermons themselves.[233] In his *Regula canonicorum*, Chrodegang deplored the fact that the Christian people did not hear the sacred word often enough and expressed the hope that his canons would preach twice a month. He added that it would be necessary to adapt preaching to each audience so that the faithful could understand the speaker.[234]

Mansi, XII, 937–50. For the teaching of the *Symbol*, see Friedrich L. Wiegand, *Die Stellung des apostolischen Symbols im kirchlichen Leben des Mittelalters* (Leipzig, 1899).

[228] Only rarely do the sources for our period mention children partaking in the sacraments. See the allusions to communion in the Council of Mâcon (585), the Council of Cloveshoe, 23 (Haddan-Stubbs ed., 3: 370), and the *Judicium Clementis*, 9 (Haddan-Stubbs ed., 2: 227). Roman children fasted on Holy Saturday (Gregory the Great, *Dial.*, III, 33 [p. 211, l. 9]).

[229] For fourth- and fifth-century preaching, see Gaudemet, *L'Eglise dans l'Empire romain*, pp. 593–97, and Probst, *Katechese und Predigt*. Anton Linsenmayer's book, *Geschichte der Predigt in Deutschland von Karl dem Grossen bis zum Ausgange des vierzehnten Jahrhunderts* (Munich, 1886) does not study the pre-Carolingian period; while F. R. Albert's work, *Die Geschichte der Predigt in Deutschland bis Luther* (Gütersloh, 1892), vol. 1, does so only very sketchily. There are a few references in M. Schian, "Predigt, Geschichte der christlichen," *Realencyklopädie für protestantische Theologie und Kirche*, ed. Albert Hauck, 15 (Leipzig, 1904): 639.

[230] *Form. Bitur.*, 5; Marculf, *Form.*, I, 5 (*MGH, Leg. sect. V*, pp. 45, 170). See Guntram's capitulary (*MGH, Capit.*, I, 11), the Council of Saint-Jean-de-Losne (673), and the letter of Pope Boniface IV to Florian of Arles (*MGH, Ep.*, III, 455): "Sermone vestro cottidie hi qui vobis caelesti gratia commissi sunt erudiantur."

[231] Gregory the Great, *Ep.* III, 13 (*MGH, Epist.*, I, 172): "Tua predicatione, qui litteras nesciunt, quid divinitus praecipiatur, agnoscant."

[232] See Dudden, *Gregory the Great*, 1: 229–38.

[233] See the Council of Vaison (529), c. 2; and, for Spain, Alonso, *La cura pastoral*, pp. 396ff. In Italy, Gregory forbade young clerics from preaching (*Moral.*, XII, 6 [*PL*, XXV, 953]; *Hom. in Ezech.*, II, 1[*PL*, LXXVI, 797]).

[234] See Chrodegang, *Regula canonicorum*, 44 and 83 (*PL*, LXXXIX, 1076, 1094).

METHODS OF CHRISTIAN EDUCATION

Obviously, that was the first rule that had to be observed. At the beginning of the sixth century, as we have already seen above, clerics and monks urged preachers to abandon the highly ornamented style which only a learned elite could understand. In the seventh century, Pseudo-Germanus hoped that the sermon would be neither so trivial as to shock the lettered nor so obscure as to repulse the less intelligent. During his period, however, it was only a question of oratorical style and not of language, since Latin was still understood.[235]

In northern Gaul and the newly converted lands, it was quite the contrary. We must ask, then, what language the preacher used—ask more than answer, since the texts provide only very sketchy information.[236]

In fact, no council during the Barbarian period ever mentioned the language of sermons. Not until 813, at the Council at Tours, were clerics asked to comment in the vulgar tongue (Romance or Teutonic) on the Gospels for the day.[237] Obviously this date does not represent the first time that vulgar tongues were used: fact, as always, preceded law. Two avenues were open to preachers: they could themselves speak in the popular language or they could use interpreters. What language did the Aquitainian Eligius use when he preached to his diocesans at Noyon? Although the texts tell us he preached in a simple language adapted to the people,[238] it is difficult to know whether he spoke in Latin or in the vulgar tongue. The remark, however, does allow us to assume that his vocabulary was close to the current language.[239] His successor, Mommelinus, according to his biographer, knew the *romana*

[235] Guntram addressed the *fideles* who had come together for the mass in Latin; see Gregory of Tours, *HF*, VII, 8 (p. 331).

[236] This is a question for all periods; see Christine Mohrmann, "Le problème du vocabulaire chrétien: Expériences d'évangelisation paléo-chrétiennes et modernes," in *Scientia missionum ancilla: Mélanges A. Mulders* (Nijmegen, 1953), pp. 254–62, reprinted in her *Etudes sur le latin des chrétiens* (Rome, 1958), pp. 113–22. M. Banniard is preparing a thesis entitled "Communication écrite et communication orale en Occident latin du IVᵉ au IXᵉ siècle" (University of Paris).

[237] Mansi, XIV, 85: "In rusticam Romanam linguam aut Theodiscam quo facilius cuncti possint intelligere quae dicuntur."

[238] *Vita Eligii, MGH, SRM*, IV, 757, l. 30: "Predixi vobis simpliciter, ut intellegere possitis." In a sermon that was reworked during the Carolingian period, Eligius was supposed to have said, "Ad vos simplici et rusticano utentes eloquio" (*Homilia XI: In Coena Domini, PL*, LXXXVII, 630).

[239] Lot, "A quelle époque," p. 105, n. 4, does not think so. Edouard de Moreau, *Histoire de l'Eglise en Belgique*, 5 vols. (Brussels, 1945–52), 1: 109, posed this question in relation to Saint Amandus but did not resolve it. Amandus had among his collaborators clerics and monks from the country, who could have spoken the popular tongue.

lingua and *theutonica*.[240] The transformation of Latin into a pre-Romance language occurred much more rapidly in the northern portions of Gaul than in the south. It is unthinkable that missionary bishops did not use a tongue which all could understand.

Of course, they could have used interpreters. When the Irishman Aidan came to convert the Northumbrians, King Oswald, who had spent his youth among the "Scots," supplied him with an intermediary to communicate with his magnates.[241] In order to evangelize the Frisians, Wulfram of Sens needed an interpreter.[242] In monasteries that prepared missionaries and taught them how to preach,[243] the study of foreign languages could have been made easier when former young pagans, newly converted, were brought up alongside the monks. Eligius, Amandus, and Wulfran, in fact, ransomed Frisian and Saxon slaves, whom they educated and made close collaborators.[244]

No sermon in a non-Latin language has come down to us from this period. They must have been improvised orally from Latin texts, of which we do have some copies: fragments of Eligius' sermons,[245] Pirmin's *Scarapsus*,[246] and the curious Anglo-Saxon sermon published by Wilhelm Levison.[247] Until the twelfth century Latin sermons would continue to serve as schemas for the sacred orator when he improvised before the faithful.[248]

What were the most familiar themes used by the preachers? Here, again, we must distinguish between periods. In the sixth century in Italy, southern Gaul, and Africa, preachers most often commented on

[240] *Vita Mommelini, AS, Belgii*, IV, 403–4: "Cujus Eligii in loco fama bonorum operum quia praevaletit non tantum in theutonica sed etiam in romana linguae." Saint Gall was reputed for his knowledge of the vulgar tongue, but the source of this information is rather late (*Vita S. Galli, MGH, SRM*, IV, 260).

[241] Bede, *HE*, III, 3 (p. 132): "Evangelizante antistite qui Anglorum linguam perfecte non noverat, ipse rex suis ducibus ac ministris interpres verbi existeret caelestis."

[242] Jonas of Fontenelle, *Vita Vulframni, MGH, SRM*, V, 665, ll. 27–28: "Respondebat autem dux [a Frisian] patrio sermone."

[243] At Saint Wandrille, for example ("De eodem loco cooperatores verbi strenuos et ad praedicandum idoneos" [ibid., p. 664]), and in Egbert's Irish monastery ("Electis sociis strenuissimis et ad praedicandum verbum idoneis" [Bede, *HE*, V, 9]).

[244] *Vita Eligii*, I, 10 (*MGH, SRM*, IV, 677); *Vita Amandi*, I, 9 (ibid., V, 480); *Vita Vulframni*, ibid., p. 666.

[245] *Vita Eligii*, II, 16 (ibid., IV, 705–8).

[246] Pirmin, *Scarapsus*, ed. Caspari, in *Kirchenhist. anecdota*, vol. 1; Ursmar Engelmann, *Der heilige Pirmin und seine Missionsbüchlein* (Constance, 1959).

[247] Levison, "Venus a Man: From an Unpublished Sermon," in *England*, pp. 302–14.

[248] See Albert Lecoy de la Marche, *La chaire française au Moyen Age*, 2nd ed. (Paris, 1886), pp. 47ff.

Holy Scripture.[249] Gregory the Great, who introduced the Romans to the riches of the book of Ezechiel and the Gospels, thought that the Scriptures had the unique ability to speak to the lettered as well as to the *rudes*. Like a revolving wheel, Scriptures were offered to all kinds of believers.[250] One might find a *historia* where another would find moral instruction and where the most polished would find allegorical and mystical meaning.[251] Isidore of Seville also insisted on the vast field which Scriptures offered to the *viri perfecti* as well as to the *simplices*.[252] The faithful, then, were invited to read the Bible or, if they were illiterate, to have the sacred text read to them by someone else.[253] Gregory the Great gave the example of an illiterate paralytic who bought manuscripts of the Scriptures and asked those who had gathered around him to read passages to him so that eventually he knew the entire Bible.[254]

This was an exceptional, indeed miraculous, case because in general the biblical culture of laymen was quite limited. If they were lettered, they could remember the Psalms they had learned in their childhood, but if they were not, their knowledge would come only from preaching. After the sixth century, preachers' themes were rarely taken from the Bible. If Bede translated the Gospel of Saint John into the vulgar tongue, it was not, as we have seen, for laymen but for clerics who did not know Latin. If laymen consulted the Bible or had it consulted for them, it was solely in order to try to unmask the future. The Church

[249] In addition to the sermons of Caesarius of Arles, see those of Sedatus of Nîmes (*Clavis*, no. 1005), John of Naples (ibid., no. 915), and Fulgentius (ibid., no. 828).

[250] Gregory the Great, *Hom. in Ezech.*, VI, 7 (*PL*, LXXVI, 831): "Rota ergo quasi per terram trahitur quia parvulis humili sermone concordat et tamen magnis spiritalia infundens quasi circulum in altum levat." See also *Moral.*, XX, 1 (ibid., 135).

[251] *Hom. in Ezech.*, I, 7, 10 (ibid., 844): "In una enim eademque scripturae sententia alias sola historia pascitur, alius typicam alias vero intelligentiam per typum contemplativam quaerit." See de Lubac, *L'exégèse médiévale*, 2: 426ff., for the literal interpretation (*historia*) of Scripture. We should note that Gregory had in mind only the Bible and not exegetical commentaries. He rebuked Marinian of Ravenna for having publicly read his *Moralia* (*Ep.* XII, 6 [*MGH, Ep.*, II, 352]): "Quia non est illud opus populare et rudibus auditoribus impedimentum magis quam provectum generat."

[252] Isidore of Seville, *Sent.*, I, 18, 3 (*PL*, LXXXIII, 576): "In scripturis sanctis quasi in montibus excelsis et viri perfecti . . . et simplices quasi parva animalia inveniunt modicos intellectus ad quos humiles ipsi refugiant." Ibid., 4: "Scriptura sacra infirmis et sensu parvulis secundum historiam humilis videtur in verbis." Ibid., III, 43: "Rudibus populis seu carnalibus plana et communia non summa atque ardua praedicanda sunt."

[253] See Caesarius of Arles' advice in chap. 3, sect. II, above.

[254] Gregory the Great, *Dial.*, IV, 15 (p. 250): "Nequaquam litteras noverat sed scripturae sacrae sibimet codices emerat et religiosos quosque in hospitalitatem suscipiens, hos coram se studiose legere faciebant . . . ut plene sacram scripturam disceret."

fought in vain against the practice of "biblical lots," which reduced the sacred Book to the level of a book of magic.[255]

In order to reach his public better, the preacher preferred to use examples drawn from the *passiones* and the *vitae sanctorum*. The hagiographical literature that enjoyed so much success during this period was not intended only for clerics and monks: hagiographers quite often alluded to lay readers who read or listened to their stories.[256] Reading a vita was good fare for the moral formation of the faithful.[257] When Gregory the Great composed his *Dialogues*, he especially had in mind the masses and those who were more sensitive to exempla than to doctrinal statements.[258] In order to place himself at the level of his listeners, he deliberately used, like many hagiographers, that simple and popular tone for which certain historians have chastised him.

Exempla became so necessary for instruction that extracts from hagiographical texts were incorporated into the liturgy. In fifth-century Rome, the *vitae sanctorum* were not used in the Office because of the doubtful sources of some of the texts. But in Spain—and, shortly afterwards, everywhere else—the *Acts of the Martyrs* and the vitae took their place in the Office.[259] Bishops had passionals compiled,[260] while hagi-

---

[255] For the *sortes sanctorum* and the *sortes biblicae*, see Henri Leclercq, "Sortes sanctorum," *DACL*, XV-2, 1590–92, and P. Courcelle, "L'enfant et les 'sorts bibliques,'" *VChr* 7 (1953): 204, 220.

[256] Gregory of Tours, *Glor. martyr.*, 63 (*MGH, SRM*, I-2, 531): "Mos namque erat hominum rusticorum, ut sanctos Dei, quorum agones religunt, attentius venerentur"; *Vita Sulpicii, PL*, LXXX, 574: "Tamen vel sermonem tenuem devotae plebis auribus tentamus inferre."

[257] *Vita Eutropii*, in *Gallia christiana novissima*, ed. Albanés, 6: 10: "Illa magis narranda sunt quae exemplis suis excitant, instruant, et aedificent audientes." See also the preface to the *Vita Viviani, MGH, SRM*, III, 94.

[258] Gregory the Great, *Hom. in Ezech.*, II, 7 (*PL*, LXXVI, 1014): "Plus enim plerumque exempla quam ratiocinationis verba compungunt." See also the *Hom. in Evang.*, II, 37 (ibid., 1290), and *Dial.*, preface (p. 15): "Sunt nonnulli quod ad amorem patriae coelestis plus exempla quam praedicamenta succendunt." Maximus of Turin expressed the same ideas in *Sermo* LXXXVII (*PL*, LVII, 706): "Quod utile est mihi, melius disco exemplo sanctorum quam assertione verborum." See also Sisebut in his *Vita Desiderii episc. Viennensis, MGH, SRM*, III, 631: "Exemplo magis quam verbis edocuit, sciens dominum adfuturum non tam eloquia quaesiturum quam opera"; and *Vita Aredii*, 2 (*MGH, SRM*, III, 582, l. 16): "Plus namque aedificat exemplum boni operis cum simplicitate vigoris, quam multa praedicatio cum tumore vanae gloriae." For the fate of exempla, see J.-Th. Welter, *L'exemplum dans la littérature religieuse et didactique du Moyen Age* (Paris, 1927).

[259] See Baudouin de Gaiffier, "La lecture des Actes des Martyrs dans la prière liturgique en Occident," *AB* 72 (1954): 134–66.

[260] See the list in *Clavis*, nos. 2076ff.

ographers expressed the hope that their works would be read and commented on before the Christian people.[261]

Finally, preachers could also give moral guidance to the people without using exempla. Cassiodorus had earlier commanded the monks of Vivarium to teach their peasants "good morals": not to steal, not to be idolatrous, to call upon God to fructify the fields.[262] Two centuries later (also in southern Italy) Abbot Ambrosius Autpertus made similar recommendations to the laymen of Beneventum: they were not to covet or seize the property of another by theft, fraud, lies, or perjury; they should be happy with their own wives, observe the Lenten fast, and make retribution for their faults by almsgiving.[263] The preachers of northern Gaul and of Germany used this language even more skillfully. The sermons of Eligius and Boniface and Pirmin's *Scarapsus* exhibit more than one common trait:[264] the preacher recalled the promise made at baptism; exhorted the faithful to abandon pagan practices; and painted a portrait of the true Christian as one who goes to church regularly, lives chastely, teaches his sons the *Credo* and *Pater*, and makes them fear God and avoid the principal vices.[265] The major themes of Christian life, based on the observance of moral obligations rather than on the adherence to a divine mystery, were thus delineated; antique moralism lived on in Christian sermons.[266]

261 Alcuin, *Vita Willibrordi*, preface (*AS*, Nov., III, 435): "Unam quoque priori libello superaddidi omeliam quae utinam digna esset tuo venerando populo praedicari." For popular culture, see J. Le Goff, "Culture clericale et traditions folkloriques dans la civilisation mérovingienne," *Annales* 22 (1967): 780–91.

262 Cassiodorus, *Inst.*, I, 32, 2 (p. 79): "Ipsos autem rusticos qui ad vestrum monasterium pertinent, bonis moribus erudite . . . furta nesciant, lucos colere prorsus ignorent . . . sciant etiam Deum ubertatem agris eorum dignanter infundere si eum fideliter consueverint invocare."

263 Ambrosius Autpertus, *De cupiditate*, PL, LXXXIX, 1290.

264 *Vita Eligii*, MGH, SRM, IV, 753, l. 10: "Qui et ipse caste vivit et filios vel vicinos suos docet ut caste et cum timore dei vivant . . . qui postremo symbolum vel orationem dominicam memoriter tenit et filios ac filias eodem docet."

265 Pirmin's *Scarapsus* (ed. Caspari, in *Kirchenhist. anecdota*, vol. 1) gave a list of eight vices to avoid. The Wissembourg "Catechism" cites twenty such vices (see above, sect. III.A, for this text). For Boniface's sermons, see Franz Flaskamp, *Die Missionsmethode des hl. Bonifatius*, 2nd ed. (Hildesheim, 1929); Wilhelm Konen, *Die Heidenpredigt in der Germanenbekehrung* (Düsseldorf, 1909); and J. Lortz, "Untersuchungen zur Missionsmethode und zur Frömmigkeit des hl. Bonifatius nach seinen Briefen," in *Willibrordus: Echternacher Festschrift*, ed. N. Goetzinger (Luxembourg, 1940), pp. 247–83. For the missionaries' methods, see W. H. Fritze, "Universalis gentium confessio: Formeln Träger und Wege universalmissionarischen Denkens im 7. Jahrhundert," *FS* 3 (1969): 78–130, and H. Löwe, "Pirmin, Willibrord, und Bonifatius: Ihre Bedeutung für die Missionsgeschichte ihrer Zeit," *Settimane*, 14: 249ff.

266 A *Liber de moribus* attributed to Martin of Braga (*PL*, LXXII, 29) consists of ex-

If the preacher used the Bible, he chose his references chiefly from the sapiential books. Boniface asked one of his compatriots for Bede's *Commentary on the Book of Proverbs*, a work which seemed to him particularly useful and manageable for his preachers.[267] If, on the other hand, the preacher was influenced by classical sermons—those of Caesarius of Arles, for example—he chose the pages that contained the most moralizing and those that denounced the absurdity of pagan practices.[268] The *sermones de Scriptura* were in general seldom used. The spiritual poverty of the sermons of this period quite possibly might have led the Church to encourage the manufacture of homilaries that gathered together the Fathers' texts for use by preachers. These florilegia, in fact, began to appear in Italy during the mid-eighth century and multiplied during the Carolingian period.[269]

C. Religious Instruction through Image and Song

In order to familiarize the faithful with biblical themes, the Church could use what has been called "mute preaching"—that is, the image.[270] From the fourth century on, Western clerics knew how to use the representations that decorated church walls,[271] but only in the pontificate of Gregory the Great would the pedagogical role of religious painting be affirmed. In a letter to the bishops of Marseille, who worried that the faithful would adore images, the pope recommended that the images not be suppressed "so that the illiterate will at least read by looking at the walls. . . . It is one thing to adore images and another to learn through the story represented by the image what one must adore."[272] Gregory's missionaries to England used sacred images to

---

tracts from Seneca, Lactantius, Ausonius, and others. See Schanz, IV-2, 626, and Barlow, *Martini episc. Bracarensis*, p. 285.

[267] Boniface, *Ep.* 91 (*MGH, Ep.*, III, 377, l. 3): "Quod nobis predicantibus habile et manuale et utillimum esse videtur."

[268] See Levison, *England*, pp. 140, 306ff., for the use Anglo-Saxon preachers made of Caesarius.

[269] The homilaries were composed at Farfa and Rome; see J. Leclercq, "Tables pour l'inventaire des homéliaires manuscrits," *Scriptorium* 2 (1948): 195–214.

[270] There has been no general study on this subject. See the few texts cited by L. Gougaud, "Muta predicatio," *RB* 42 (1930): 168, and Knögel, *Schriftquellen zur Kunstgeschichte der Merowingerzeit*, pp. 50–51.

[271] See Henri Leclercq, "Images," *DACL*, VII-1, 180–302.

[272] Gregory the Great, *Ep.* IX, 208 (*MGH, Ep.*, II, 195): "Idcirco enim in ecclesiis adhibetur ut hi qui litteras nesciunt saltem in parietibus videndo legant quae legere in codicibus non valent." Ibid. XI, 10 (p. 270): "Aliud est enim picturam adorare, aliud picturae historia quid sit adorandum addiscere . . . quia in ipsa ignorantes vident, quod se qui debeant, in ipsa legunt qui litteras nesciunt."

support their preaching: Augustine carried a painting of Christ before him when he approached the king of Kent for the first time.[273] The Evangeliary of Cambridge, illustrated with scenes from the life of Christ, could also have been used for the Christian training of pagans.[274] At Jarrow at the end of the seventh century, Abbot Benedict Biscop decorated his monastery with paintings brought from Rome. Bede says that Benedict wanted to make clear the parallels between the two Testaments: on one side, Isaac was represented carrying the wood intended for his sacrifice, and on the other, Christ carrying his cross; to one side was the bronze serpent of Moses, and on the other, the cross of the Son of Man.[275] Bede tells us that they were thus located not only for decoration but so that everyone who entered the church, even the illiterate, could see them and profit from them.[276]

In the eighth century, the iconoclastic quarrel gave the Roman Church in the West the opportunity to reaffirm its position on the pedagogical role of images. Pope Gregory II wrote to Emperor Leo the Isaurian that "men and women hold newly baptized infants in their arms while accompanied by young children and teach them by raising their minds and hearts to God while pointing out images to them with their fingers."[277] In short, the Church took advantage of the particular taste which the Barbarians, like all primitive peoples, had for the representational image.[278]

The Church also utilized the Barbarians' aptitude for song and dance. While we have no texts of secular songs from this period,[279] we

---

[273] Bede, HE, I, 25 (p. 46): "Veniebant . . . ferentes . . . imaginem domini salvatoris in tabula depictam."

[274] See Francis Wormald, The Miniatures of the Gospels of Saint Augustine (Cambridge, 1954). One wonders whether the development of pre-Carolingian miniatures was linked to general religious instruction.

[275] Bede, Vita abb., 9 (Plummer ed., p. 373).

[276] Ibid.: "Quatenus intrantes ecclesiam omnes etiam litterarum ignari contemplarentur aspectum." See also Homel., I, 13 (CCL, 122: 93, l. 181): "Quae non ad ornamentum solummodo ecclesiae, verum et ad instructionem intuentium proponerentur."

[277] Gregory II, Ep. ad Leonem, PL, LXXXIX, 521: "Viri ac mulieres pueros parvulos nuper baptizatos in ulnis tenentes, itemque florentes aetate juvenes . . . indicatis digito historiis eos aedificant."

[278] Gregory the Great. Ep. XI, 10 (MGH, Ep., II, 270): "Unde precipue gentibus pro lectione pictura est." See the episode reported by Paul the Deacon (HL, IV, 16 [MGH, SRL, p. 121]) in which a duke from Spoleto was converted after viewing the frescoes in Santa Sabina in Spoleto.

[279] Except perhaps for four verses from "Saint Faro's cantilena" preserved in Latin in a ninth-century text; see Vita Faronis, 78 (MGH, SRM, V, 193). René Louis, in De l'histoire à la legende: Girart, comte de Vienne . . . , 2 vols. (Auxerre, 1947), 1: 298–300, thinks that this text is a translation from the original "roman," but debate still continues on this point.

do know that they enjoyed great success. Wandering singers and dancers provided recreation for people in the country and in towns.[280] At weddings, funerals, and seasonal feasts, and even upon the return of a victorious king, the people exhibited their feelings by singing to the lyre or cithara and by clapping their hands and dancing.[281] The Church had to intervene to stop these practices, which seemed so unworthy of Christians. Songs and dances in the antique tradition were, in fact, quite often erotic:[282] conciliar texts speak of the "saltationes" and "turpes cantici," of "amatoria turpia," "ebrietas," and "scurrilitas."[283] In addition, clerics joined in these celebrations as musicians and dancers,[284] while the people abandoned themselves to these kinds of festivities not only on the occasion of antique pagan feasts but also during the vigils which preceded religious feasts.[285]

[280] Edict of Childebert I, *MGH, Capit.*, I, 2, l. 38: "Bausatrices per villas ambulare." *Vita Radegundis*, I, 36 (*MGH, SRM*, II, 375): "Inter corandas et citharas dum circa monasterium a saecularibus multo fremitu cantaretur." One of the nuns recognized an air which she used to sing, "unum de meis canticis." Godefroid Kurth, *Histoire póetique des Merovingiens* (Paris, 1893), p. 491, thought without sufficient reason that the reference was to religious songs.

[281] Wedding songs are mentioned by the Council of Vannes (465), c. 11; the Council of Agde (506), c. 39; the Council of Auxerre (518), c. 40; the Council of Merida (546); Isidore of Seville, *Origines*, I xxxix; and the Council of Toledo (569), c. 22; and songs for seasonal celebrations are noted by Isidore of Seville in *De eccl. off.*, I, 41, 2 (*PL*, LXXX, 775), and in *Origines*, X, 109. For these celebrations, see above, sect. III. For celebrations upon the return of a king, see *Vitas sanctorum*, ed., Garvin, p. 246, l. 29 ("Cum omne plebe plaudentes manibus ymnizantesque venerunt"), and Julian of Toledo, *Historia de Wambae regis Gothorum Toletani expeditione, MGH, SRM*, V, 500. The cithara is mentioned by Braulio in the *Vita Aemiliani, PL*, LXXX, 703, and the lyre by Valerius of Bierzo in *Ordo querimoniae, PL*, LXXXVII, 443.

[282] See the sermon published by J. Leclercq, "Sermon ancien sur les danses déshonnêtes," *RB* 59 (1949): 196–201, which is dated to the fifth or sixth century and perhaps is Spanish.

[283] *Turpes cantici*: Council of Toledo (589), c. 23, in Mansi, IX, 999. *Amatoria turpia*: Isidore of Seville, *Reg. mon.*, V, 5 (*PL*, LXXXIII, 874); Augustine, *De opere monach.*, XVII, 20 (ed. A. Zycha, *CSEL*, vol. 41) and repeated in the *Institutionum disciplinae*, ed. A. E. Anspach, *RhM* 67 (1912): 566. *Amatoriae cantiones: Reg. mon. Tarnantensis*, 8 (*PL*, XVI, 980). "Cum choreis femineis turpia . . . decantare videantur" (Council of Chalon [639], *MGH, Leg. sect. III*, I, 212); "cum ebrietate scurrilitate vel canticis" (Edict of Childebert I, *MGH, Capit.*, I, 2, l. 38); "ad excitandam libidinem nugatoribus cantionibus proclamare" (Licinianus of Carthagena's letter to the bishop of Ibiza, ed. Madoz, p. 128); "si quis in quacumque festivitate ad ecclesiam veniens pallat [psallit] foris aut saltat aut cantat orationes amatorias" (*Judicium Clementis*, 20 [Haddan-Stubbs ed., 2: 227]).

[284] See above, chap. 9, sect. II.B.2. Valerius of Bierzo gives us a detailed description of the scandalous dance a priest performed in front of him (*Ordo querimoniae*, 34 [*PL*, LXXXVII, 443]).

[285] See the Councils of Toledo (589) and of Braga (572), in Mansi, IX, 999, XII, 371; the Council of Auxerre (573), *MGH, Leg. sect. III*, I, 180, for a choir composed of laymen and for songs sung by young women in churches; and the Council of Chalon (639),

The repeated conciliar interdictions clearly prove that it was impossible to eliminate these rites. The Church thus used deeply rooted customs when it invited the faithful to participate actively in the liturgy. This transposition conformed to the general policy of the bishops and popes of the period: rather than forcing the laity to break with antique traditions, they thought it better to use those traditions to organize the cult of God. In Rome in the fifth century, the Christian calendar was aligned with the calendar of important pagan feasts.[286] In his directives to Augustine of Canterbury, Gregory the Great urged him not to extirpate pagan customs immediately, but rather to Christianize them.[287]

We can best see this effort at adaptation in Visigothic Spain, where, in order to replace the epithalamia and threnodies still in use, clerics composed poems and benedictions that the *Liber ordinum*, a veritable *cathemerinon*, has preserved for us.[288] All of life's great events were accompanied by sacred songs: the priest blessed the fields, the vines, the marriage bed, and the shaving of the first beard.[289]

The liturgy of the Visigothic Church, which was perhaps influenced by the Byzantine liturgy, gave great emphasis to song. Lettered bishops turned musician and wrote religious offices which unfortunately have not survived.[290] Can we assume that these chants were accompanied by sacred dances? A bas-relief from a church in Galicia that portrays dancers expressing their faith by harmonious gestures, in the manner of David before the sacred Ark, might support this hypothesis, although it is the only known Western example.[291] Can we be sure, however,

---

ibid., p. 212. Eligius was interrupted in the midst of a sermon by some men who began to dance ("modis diversis debaccare"; *Vita Eligii*, II, 22 [*MGH, SRM*, IV, 712, l. 19]).

[286] Duchesne, *Origines du culte chrétien*, pp. 295–305; André Festugière, *L'enfant d'Agrigente* (Paris, 1941); R. N. Bonet-Llach, *Die sanctificatione festorum in Ecclesia catholica, a primordis ad s. VI inclusive* (Ripoll and Gerona, 1945).

[287] Gregory the Great, *Ep.* XI, 56 (*MGH, Ep.*, II, 331), cited by Bede, *HE*, I, 30 (p. 65). Some Christian holy days in England were named after pagan ceremonies (Easter, Yule).

[288] J. Scudieri Ruggieri, "Alle fonti della cultura ispano-visigotica," *SM* 16 (1943–50): 34ff.

[289] *Liber ordinum*, ed. Férotin, p. 433, "Ordo ad thalamum benedicendum"; p. 434, "Ordo arrarum"; p. 436, "Ordo ad benedicendum eos qui noviter nubunt"; p. 166, "Benedictio seminis." The *Gelasian Sacramentary*, 89 (in *Le sacramentaire gélasien*, ed. Antoine Chavasse [Tournai, 1958], pp. 461–69), has a "benedictio pomorum arbores."

[290] See above, chap. 8, sect. IV.B. For the Holy Friday ceremonies in Spain, see Duchesne, *Origines du culte chrétien*, pp. 463–65.

[291] The bas-relief discovered in the church of St. Eulalia in Boveda (Lugo) has been reproduced in Garcia Villada, *Historia eclesiástica*, 2, pt. 2: 252. For sacred dance, see Emile Bertaud, "Danse religieuse," *DSp*, 3: 25–26, and L. Gougaud, "La danse dans les églises," *RHE* 15 (1914): 1–22, 229–45.

that during the course of Rogations or during pilgrimages to the tombs of saints, the faithful did not express their religious feelings by appropriate physical movements? We should also note in this regard that the non-Roman liturgy, especially the Gallican liturgy, made the mass a veritable drama by increasing the number of incensements, processions, benedictions, and chants.[292]

The faithful participated in the liturgy everywhere and sung the hymns that were multiplying throughout the period.[293] The hymns were very successful, but it was necessary to control their origin and admit only those hymns whose authors were known and whose form was correct.[294] English monks encouraged the development of sacred poetry in the national tongue so that laymen and clerics would abandon profane songs. Caedmon in the seventh century and Aldhelm and Bede in the following century were, as we have seen, creators of this new popular religious poetry.

It is difficult to determine whether the religious culture that the laity received through preaching and through participation in the liturgy enabled them to have a personal religious life. Their religious education, we should note, was more collective than individual. The Church could not train the many faithful as it really wanted because it lacked priests or because the priests were incapable of training the laity.[295] Consequently, the Church, with the help of princes,[296] sur-

---

[292] See Jungmann, *Missarum sollemnia*, I: 109, and Henri Leclercq, "Gallicane (liturgie)," *DACL*, VI-1, 473–593. For the participation of the people, see Georg Nickl, *Der Anteil des Volkes an der Messliturgie im Frankenreich von Chlodwig bis auf Karl den Grossen* (Innsbruck, 1930).

[293] Caesarius of Arles had the faithful sing (*Vita Caesarii*, I, 19 [Morin ed., p. 303]). In Paris, Germanus had both the people and the children sing; see Fortunatus, *Carm.* II, 9, v. 69 (*MGH, AA*, IV-1, 39): "Plebs psallit et infans." Bishop Exocius of Limoges composed songs for the faithful (ibid., IV, 6, v. 13 [p. 83]: "Recreans modulamine cives"). Bishop Chalactericus of Chartres (ibid., p. 84, l. 15) and Nicetius of Lyon (*CIL*, XIII, 2400) did the same.

[294] The Council of Tours (567), c. 24, *MGH, Leg. sect. III*, I, 133, required "[hymnos] qui digni sunt forma cantari." The Council of Braga (561), c. 12, was more rigorous: "Nihil poetice compositum in ecclesia psallatur." This interdiction was followed by a reference to the Council of Laodicea. Braga and Tours were in contact during this period, but we do not know whether they influenced each other. At the Fourth Council of Toledo (633), c. 13, the rigorists even wanted to forbid the hymns of Hilary and Ambrose. For the diffusion of hymns, see Corbin, *L'Eglise à la conquête de sa musique*, pp. 126ff.

[295] See Bede's complaints in his *Ep. ad. Ecgbertum*, 5–17 (Plummer ed., pp. 408–23), and in *In Samuel*, *PL*, XCI, 590; and Boniface, *Ep. 91* (*MGH, Ep.*, III, 377, l. 11): "Propter raritatem sacerdotum."

[296] Isidore had previously insisted on collaboration between the princes and the Church in his *Sent.*, III, 51 (*PL*, LXXXIII, 723). See also Boniface, *Ep. 63* (*MGH, Ep.*, III, 329, l. 14): "Sine patrocinio principis Francorum nec populum aecclesiae regere nec presbiteros vel clericos, monachos vel ancillas Dei defendere possum."

rounded Christians from their baptism with well-defined obligations (Sunday as a day of rest, attendance at mass, communion three times a year)[297] and required them to respect natural laws rather than to adhere to mysteries which were foreign to them. Laymen, who could no longer know the Bible and doctrine personally, attended mass without being able to participate actively in it. When the Roman liturgy gained sway over the West, the altar was pushed to the back of the apse, and the ceremony became an affair for clerics.[298] The gulf between the layman and the cleric grew wider and wider.

While laymen at the end of the Roman Empire could take part in the election of the bishop, play an active role in the councils, administer the goods of the Church, and even "preach" with the permission of the priest,[299] laymen of the eighth century were considered irresponsible minors who were to venerate priests and obey their orders.[300] More than this, the lay state was regarded as a concession to human weakness. Bede, speaking of those who had not yet left the world ("in populari adhuc vita continentur"), betrayed his regret that society was not composed entirely of monks and clerics.[301] Monks and clerics increasingly formed an order apart, distinguished by their dress, their way of life, their legal privileges, and—especially after the Carolingian reform—by their culture.[302] We are already in the Middle Ages.

[297] See Jean Chélini, "La pratique dominicale dans l'Eglise franque sous le règne de Pépin," *Revue d'histoire de l'Eglise de France* 42 (1956): 161–74, and P. Riché, "Vie spirituelle aux 6e–8e siècles," and "Vie spirituelle des laïcs du 9e au 12e siècle," both in *Histoire spirituelle de la France* (Paris, 1964), pp. 45–63, 111–24.

[298] For this development, see Jungmann, *Missarum sollemnia*, 1: 116. The Carolingian Church tried to involve the people more actively in the mass (ibid., pp. 289–90).

[299] *Statuta ecclesiae antiqua*, 38, in *S. Caesarii opera omnia*, ed. Morin, 2: 93: "Laicus praesentibus clericis, nisi ipsis probantibus, docere non audeat."

[300] A layman who encountered a priest was supposed to dismount from his horse to greet the clergyman; see Council of Mâcon (585), c. 15 (*MGH, Leg. sect. III*, I, 170).

[301] Bede, *Ep. ad Ecgbertum*, 5 and 15 (Plummer ed., pp. 409, 418): "Qui in populari adhuc vita continentur de laicis, id est in populari adhuc vita constitutis." In his *Ecclesiastical History*, V, 23 (p. 351), Bede was overjoyed that laymen and their children preferred entering the cloister to practicing military skills.

[302] In the middle of the eighth century, society was thought to consist of two orders, the *oratores* and the *bellatores*. See M. David, "Les Laboratores," in *Etudes d'histoire du droit privé offertes à Pierre Petot* (Paris, 1958), p. 110.

Conclusion

On the eve of the disappearance of the Roman Empire in the West, the antique educational system was still very much alive, its prestige intact. By the time of Charlemagne's reign, however, it had ceased to exist. In its place was a new educational system that was destined to influence Western cultural history until the twelfth century: written civilization had been destroyed; education for laymen was the exception rather than the rule; only an elite of clerics, monks, and princes had access to intellectual culture.

The change came about very slowly during the two and a half centuries which separate Antiquity from the Middle Ages. The antique educational system survived the Barbarian invasions only, regrettably, to be abandoned by men in the West. The antique school survived and continued to flourish in the fifth century. As long as the Germans remained Arians, they did nothing to save antique culture—but neither did they destroy it. Only Theodoric—who, as master of Italy, considered himself heir to the emperors—bestirred himself to protect educational institutions.

In Gaul until the beginning of the sixth century, in Italy until the beginning of the seventh century, and in Africa until the Arab invasions, the schools of the grammarians and rhetors remained open and carried on the traditional program of study. Where a school was unable to survive the disruptions, classical culture found refuge among the great aristocratic families: the "senators" of southern Gaul until the middle of the seventh century and the Hispano-Gothic nobility until the beginning of the eighth century still displayed a taste for good style and the habits of antique men of letters. In the lands under Germanic influence, the most civilized laymen mastered writing and gave their children a minimum of religious and profane culture.

At the same time, the influence of antique education marked clerical and monastic culture: Gregory the Great and Cassiodorus at the end of the sixth century and Isidore of Seville and his followers in the seventh century seem to me to be heirs of the classical authors. If they contributed to the formation of medieval culture, they did so by transmitting the legacy of the past rather than by inventing a new system of thought. They were more in line with Augustine than with the real "founders of the Middle Ages,"[1] the Anglo-Saxon and Irish monks. True to the example of Gregory, Cassiodorus, and Isidore, some clerics and monks remained faithful to classical forms in their poems and discourses, but fettered by their early education, they were unable to create a genuinely Christian culture based on the Bible.

The need for a truly Christian culture was felt even before the ruin of the antique school, to which the Christian school stood not as an heir but as a rival. By the beginning of the sixth century, monastic reformers and others influenced by the monks created centers of study for parish and episcopal clergy that dispensed an ascetical culture and introduced the clergy to biblical studies. These schools, however, never produced the desired results; too concerned with pastoral needs, they could not become centers of sacred study. Similarly, the Christian "university" Cassiodorus planned for Rome never saw the light of day. Even his foundation at Vivarium, intended for a few monks, was without a future. The instruction organized in the great Spanish monasteries was reserved for an elite group of clerics and monks, and the work of the most famous Spaniard, Isidore of Seville, was in most respects turned toward the past.[2]

The honor for having first successfully applied the principles of Christian culture belongs to the Barbarian Celts and Anglo-Saxons. When Isidore died in 636, the king of East Anglia was founding his religious school, Irishmen were settling at Lindisfarne, and the disciples of Columban were establishing centers for asceticism in Gaul and Italy —all of which taught only sacred literature. It was in the "desert" that the West rethought its culture.

---

[1] To borrow from the title of E. K. Rand's *Founders of the Middle Ages*.

[2] For the transitional culture of Isidore, see J. Fontaine, *IS*, pp. 807ff. I find it difficult to place Isidore in the medieval tradition, as do Henri Marrou and Jean Chatillon, "Patristique et Moyen Age," *RMAL* 4 (1948): 12.

The period of contemplation ended about 680, when, as a consequence of intellectual exchanges between the Mediterranean and Nordic worlds, monasteries were no longer content with ascetic culture and began to open their doors to literary studies, thereby reforging links with the antique educational program. Monastic learning—centered on grammar, computus, and chant—had as its essential goal the study of the Bible and the celebration of the liturgy, in which "the love of learning and the desire for God are reconciled."[3]

When Charlemagne became king of the Franks, the great monasteries which were to effect the Carolingian renaissance were already active: monks were copying manuscripts at Corbie, Saint Martin of Tours, Saint Gall, Fulda, and Bobbio, sometimes employing a new script. Charlemagne's future collaborators had already begun their literary careers: Paul the Deacon was in the service of Lombard princes; in 767 at Pavia, Alcuin, master at the school of York, met Peter of Pisa, a luminary in the renewal of grammatical studies in northern Italy. Finally, Hellenism had made its reappearance in Rome.

Given these conditions, the first Carolingian renaissance—that of Charlemagne—does not seem to me as original as is usually claimed.[4] What impressed his contemporaries and what still engages the interest of modern historians is Charlemagne's educational legislation. Yet bishops and princes in England, Bavaria, and Gaul had already taken measures obliging clerics and monks to educate themselves. Charlemagne continued this work by restoring parish and episcopal schools as they had been organized in the seventh century. The proposed program of studies was as yet modest: "In each bishopric and in each monastery may the Psalms, the *notae* [stenography], chant, computus, and grammar be taught; and may the books be carefully corrected."[5] What is new is the word *each*—studies were not to be the privilege of a few centers, as we saw in earlier times. The goal of studies, however, remained unchanged: clerics and monks were to be educated so that they could understand the Bible and celebrate the cult of God. Certain

---

[3] Leclercq, *L'amour des lettres*, p. 235.

[4] I do not want to get into the semantic quarrel concerning the Carolingian Renaissance. For a different view of this question, see Lehmann, "Das Problem der karolingischen Renaissance," pp. 310–58, and A. Monteverdi, "Il problema del Rinascimento carolino," *Settimane*, 1: 359–72.

[5] *Admonitio generalis, MGH, Capit.*, I, 60: "Psalmos, notas, cantus, compotum, grammaticam, per singula monasteria vel episcopia et libros catholicos bene emendate." For Charlemagne's educational legislation, see Lesne, *Les écoles*, p. 15.

phrases in Charlemagne's capitularies seem even to come directly from Bede or Aldhelm.[6]

Charlemagne wanted to be more than simply a legislator. He gathered together scholars from all countries in an effort to make his court an important cultural center. Here he seems to me to be closer to Kings Theodoric and Sisebut than to the Roman emperors he sought to imitate. Like the Barbarian princes, Charlemagne loved to discuss astronomy and scientific questions.[7] Indeed, the literary games that were organized at the court remind us of the verbal exercises of Ennodius and Fortunatus. The riddles of Alcuin plagiarize those of Virgil the Grammarian and of the Anglo-Saxons.[8] The mannerism and the preciosity so often mentioned in this book are elements of the Carolingian renaissance. Even the favorite literary genres—hagiography, letters, and poetry[9]—are literary forms we have already encountered throughout the Barbarian West. In restoring classical Christian poetry, the Carolingians imitated Avitus of Vienne, Arator, Aldhelm, and Eugenius of Toledo.[10] Monks at Saint Gall recopied Austrasian and Visigothic letters which they thought were worthy rhetorical models.[11]

In their literary enthusiasm, the Carolingians believed that they had rediscovered the works of antique authors. In fact, they were primarily reading the works of the heirs of these authors: Cassiodorus, Isidore of Seville, and the Visigothic men of letters.[12] Like them, the Carolingians were interested neither in philosophy nor in true scholarship: in their theological treatises they appealed more to the authority of the Fathers

[6] See the capitulary *Ep. de litteris colendis*, MGH, *Capit.*, I, 79: "Cum enim in sacris paginis schemata, tropi, et cetera his similis inserta inveniantur, nulli dubium est quod ea unusquisque legens tanto citius spiritaliter intellegit, quanto prius in litterarum magisterio plenius instructus fuerit." This passage can be compared with Aldhelm's text cited above, chap. 9, n. 198.

[7] For the questions Charlemagne asked Alcuin, see Bezzola, 1: 120, n. 3.

[8] Ozanam, *La civilisation chrétienne*, p. 550, has already made this comparison.

[9] Joseph de Ghellinck, *Littérature latine au Moyen Age* (Paris, 1939), 1: 132ff.

[10] Theodulf of Orléans pilfered from his compatriot, Eugenius of Toledo; see Manitius, 1: 540. A Carolingian manuscript, Paris, Bibliothèque Nationale, lat. 8093, contains an anthology of Spanish poets. For the Carolingian manuscripts of Avitus, see Peiper, *MGH, AA*, VI-2, xiv ff.

[11] Sangallensis 190 has preserved these collections for us.

[12] For Cassiodorus' influence, see Leslie W. Jones, "The Influence of Cassiodorus on Medieval Culture," *Speculum* 20 (1945): 433–42, and ibid. 22 (1947): 252–56; and Bronislas Gladysz, *Cassiodore et l'organisation de l'école médiévale*, Collectanea Theologica, XVII-1 (Lvov, 1936). For Isidore's influence, see A. Anspach, "Das Fortleben Isidors im VII bis IX Jahrhundert," in *Miscellanea Isidoriana*, pp. 323–56; B. Bischoff, "Die europaische Verbreitung der Werke Isidors von Sevilla," in Diaz y Diaz, *Isidoriana*, pp. 317–44 (*Mittelalterliche Studien*, 1: 171–94); and M. Reydellet, "La diffusion des Origines d'Isidore de Séville au haut Moyen Age," *MEFR* 78 (1966): 383–437.

than to their own thought.[13] In short, Carolingian culture under Charlemagne remained, as in the past, literary and rhetorical.

The first Carolingian renaissance, it seems to me, was the product of the different renaissances we have studied. Charlemagne's contemporaries benefited from the many experiments of the Barbarian period. Their own work is a brilliant culmination rather than a point of departure. Only when schools multiplied and when antique works were recopied from accurate manuscripts would the real Carolingian renaissance—the renaissance of the ninth century—begin.

---

[13] Alcuin's *De dialectica*, PL, CI, 951, is essentially a cento of texts from Cassiodorus and Isidore. His *De Trinitate*, usually considered one of the first theological works of the Middle Ages, repeats definitions from Augustine (see Manitius, 1: 287–88).

Bibliography

I. SOURCES

Only those sources which have been recently edited or which are not found in the major source collections (*MGH*, *CSEL*, *PL*, or *PG*) are listed here.

Actus pontificum Cenomannis in urbe degentium. Ed. G. Busson and A. Ledru. Archives historique du Maine, vol. 2. Le Mans, 1901.

Adamnan. *De locis sanctis.* Ed. D. Meehan. Scriptores latini Hiberniae, vol. 3 Dublin, 1958.

————. *Vita Columbae.* Ed. Joseph Thomas Fowler. Oxford, 1894.

Anonyme de Cordoue: Chronique rimée des derniers rois de Tolède. Ed. Julius Tailhan. Paris, 1885.

Anthologia latina. Ed. Franz Buecheler and Alexander Riese. Vol. 1, Leipzig, 1894.

Bede, *De arte metrica.* In Keil, 7: 227–60.

————. *Liber de schematibus et tropis.* In *Rhetorici latini minores,* ed. Karl Halm, pp. 607–18. Leipzig, 1863.

————. *Opera homiletica.* Ed. D. Hurst. In *CCL,* 122: 1–378. Turnhout, 1955.

————. *Opera rhythmica.* Ed. J. Fraipont. In ibid., pp. 407–70.

————. *De orthographia.* In Keil, 7: 261–94.

————. *Retractatio in Actus apostolorum.* In *Bedae venerabilis Expositio Actuum apostolorum et Retractatio,* ed. M. L. W. Laistner, pp. 93–146. Cambridge, Mass., 1939.

————. *De temporibus liber.* In *Bedae Opera de temporibus,* ed. Charles W. Jones, pp. 295–303. Cambridge, Mass., 1943.

————. *De temporum ratione.* In ibid., pp. 174–291.

————. *Venerabilis Baedae Historiam ecclesiasticam gentis Anglorum, Historiam abbatum, Epistolam ad Ecgbertum una cum Historia abbatum auctore anonymo.* Ed. Charles Plummer. 2 vols. Oxford, 1896. This work includes the following:

    Epistola Baedae ad Ecgbertum episcopum. In ibid., 1: 405–23.

    Historia ecclesiastica gentis anglorum (= *HE*). In ibid., 1: 5–360.

    Vita beatorum abbatum Benedicti, Ceolfridi, Eosterwini, Sigfridi atque Hwaetberhti (= *Vita abb.*). In ibid., 1: 364–87.

————. *Vita Cuthberti.* Ed. Bertram Colgrave. Cambridge, 1940.

Benedict of Nursia. *S. Benedicti Regula monachorum.* Ed. Philibert Schmitz. Maredsous, 1955.

Boethius. *De institutione arithmetica.* Ed. Gottfried Friedlein. Leipzig, 1867.

————. *Opuscula sacra.* Ed. Rudolf Peiper. Leipzig, 1871.

Braulio of Saragossa. *Epistolae.* In *El epistolario de San Braulio de Zaragoza,* ed. José Madoz. Biblioteca de antiguos escritores cristianos españoles, vol. 1. Madrid, 1941.

Caesarius of Arles. *Sancti Caesarii opera omnia.* Ed. Germain Morin. 2 vols. Maredsous, 1937–42.

————. *De mysterio S. Trinitatis.* In ibid., 2: 165–80.

————. *Regula monachorum.* In ibid., pp. 149–55.

————. *Sermones.* Vol. 1 of ibid.

————. *Sermones au peuple, I.* Ed. Marie-José Delage. In *SC,* vol. 175. Paris, 1971.

————. *Statuta sanctarum virginum.* In *S. Caesarii opera omnia,* ed. Morin, 2: 101–29.

Canones Hibernenses liber. In *Die irische Kanonensammlung,* ed. Friedrich Wasserschleben. 2nd ed. Leipzig, 1885.

Cassiodorus. *Expositio psalmorum.* Ed. M. Adriaen. In *CCL,* vols. 97–98. Turnhout, 1958.

————. *Cassiodori Senatoris Institutiones Edited from the MSS.* Ed. Roger Aubrey Baskerville Mynors. Oxford, 1937.

————. *De orthographia.* In Keil, 7: 143–260.

Chartae latinae antiquiores: Facsimile Editions of the Latin Charters Prior to the Ninth Century. Ed. Albert T. Bruckner and Robert Marichal. Olten and Lausanne, 1954–.

Codice diplomatico longobardo. Ed. Luigi Schiaparelli. Fonti per la storia d'Italia, vols. 62–63. Rome, 1929–33.

Codices latini antiquiores: A Paleographical Guide to Latin Manuscripts Prior to the Ninth Century. Ed. Elias Avery Lowe. 11 vols. with a *Supplement.* Oxford, 1934–71.

Codices lugdunenses antiquissimi: Le scriptorium de Lyon, la plus ancienne école calligraphique de France. Ed. Elias Avery Lowe, Lyon, 1924.

Columban. *Sancti Columbani opera.* Ed. G. S. M. Walker. Scriptores latini Hiberniae, vol. 2. Dublin, 1957.

Concilios visigóthicos e hispano-romanos. Ed. José Vives, Tomás Marin, and Gonzalo Martínez Díez. España cristiana, Textos, I. Barcelona, 1963.

Corpus iuris civilis. Ed. Theodor Mommsen, Paul Krüger, Rudolf Schöll, and Wilhelm Kroll. 3 vols. Berlin, 1908–12.

Defensor of Ligugé. *Scintillarum liber.* Ed. A. M. Rochais. In *CCL,* 117: 1–308.

Eddius. *Vita Wilfridi.* In *The Life of Bishop Wilfrid by Eddius Stephanus,* ed. Bertram Colgrave. Cambridge, 1927.

Eusebius (Hwaetberhtus). *Aenigmata.* Ed. Adolf Ebert. *Sitzungberichte der sächsische Gesellschaft der Wissenschaften* 28 (1877): 20–56.

Eutropius of Valencia. *Epistulae.* In Diaz y Diaz, *AW,* pp. 20–25.

Ferrandus. *Vita Fulgentii.* In *Vie de saint Fulgence de Ruspe,* ed. and trans. Gabriel G. Lapeyre. Paris, 1929.

Fulgentius the Mythographer. *Opera.* Ed. Rudolf Helm. Leipzig, 1898.

Gesta sanctorum patrum fontanellensis coenobii (Gesta abbatum fontanellensium). Ed. F. Lohier and J. Laporte. Paris and Rouen, 1936.

Gregory the Great. *Gregorii Magni Dialogorum libri iv* (= *Dial.*). Ed. Umberto Moricca. Fonti per la storia d'Italia, vol. 57. Rome, 1924.

―――. *Moralia in Job.* Books I and II. Ed., with French trans., by A. de Gaudemaris and Robert Gillet, as *Morales sur Job, I–II*. In *SC*, vol. 32. Paris, 1950.

Hisperica famina. Ed. Francis John Henry Jenkinson. Cambridge, 1908.

Institutionum disciplinae. Ed. A. E. Anspach. *RhM* 67 (1912): 556–68. Also ed. P. Pascal, in *Traditio* 13 (1957): 425–31.

Isidore of Seville. *De natura rerum*. In *Isidore de Seville: Traité de la nature*, ed. Jacques Fontaine. Bordeaux, 1960.

―――. *Origines*. In *Isidori Hispalensis episcopi Etymologiarum sive Originum libri xx*. Ed. W. M. Lindsay. 2 vols. Oxford, 1911.

―――. *Versus in bibliotheca*. In *Isidor-Studien*, ed. Charles H. Beeson, pp. 133–66. Munich, 1913.

Junilius. *Instituta regularia divinae legis*. In *Theodor von Mopsuestia und Junilius Africanus als Exegeten . . .* , ed. H. Kihn, pp. 465–528. Freiburg-im-Breisgau, 1880.

Leander of Seville. *De institutione virginum et de contemptu mundi*. Ed. Ángel Custodio Vega. Scriptores ecclesiastici hispano-latini veteris et medii aevi, fascs. 16–17. Escorial, 1948.

Liber ordinum. In *Le "Liber ordinum" en usage dans l'Eglise wisigothique et mozarabe d'Espagne du cinquième au onzième siècle*, ed. Marius Férotin. Monumenta ecclesiae liturgica, vol. 5. Paris, 1904.

Liber pontificalis. Ed. Louis Duchesne and Cyrille Vogel. 3 vols. Paris, 1955–57.

Licinianus of Carthage. *Epistulae*. In *Liciniano de Cartagena y sus cartas*, ed. José Madoz. Estudios Onienses, I, 4. Madrid, 1948.

Martin of Braga. *Martini episcopi Bracarensis Opera omni*. Ed. Claude W. Barlow. Papers and Monographs of the American Academy in Rome, vol. 12. New Haven, 1950.

Oracional visigótico. In *Monumenta hispaniae sacra*, ed. José Vives, vol. 1. Barcelona, 1946.

Procopius of Caesarea. *Procopii Caesariensis Opera omnia*. Ed. Jacob Haury. 3 vols. in 4. Leipzig, 1905–13. This work includes the following:
Anecdota. In ibid., vol. 3, pt. 1.
Bellum gothicum. In ibid., vol. 2.
Bellum vandalicum. In ibid., 1: 307–551.

Regula Benedicti. Ed. Adalbert de Vogüé, as *La Règle de saint Benoît*. In *SC*, vols. 181–86. Paris, 1972.

Regula Magistri. Ed. Adalbert de Vogüé, as *La Règle du Maître*. In *SC*, vols. 105–7. Paris, 1964–65.

Regula Magistri: Edition diplomatique des manuscrits latins 12.205 et 12.634 de Paris. Ed. Hubert Vanderhoven and François Masai, with the collaboration of Philip B. Corbett. Publications de *Scriptorium*, vol. 3. Brussels, 1953.

Regula Pauli et Stephani. Ed. J. Evangelista M. Vilanova. Scripta et documenta, vol. 11. Abadía de Montserrat, 1959.

Sidonius Apollinaris. *Sidoine Apollinaire: Lettres*. Ed. and trans. into French by André Loyen. 2 vols. Paris, 1970.

Sisebut. *Carmen de eclipsibus solis et lunae*. In Isidore of Seville, *De natura rerum*, ed. Jacques Fontaine. Bordeaux, 1960.

Tatwin of Canterbury. *Opera omnia*. Ed. Maria De Marco. In *CCL*, vol. 131. Turnhout, 1968.

Theodosiani libri XVI cum Constitutionibus Sirmondianis et Leges novellae. Ed. Theodor Mommsen and Paul M. Meyer. 2 vols. Berlin, 1905.

Virgil the Grammarian. *Epitomae.* In *Les "Epitomae" de Virgile de Toulouse: Essai de traduction critique avec une bibliographie, une introduction, des notes,* trans. Dominique Tardi. Paris, 1928.

————. *Epitomae et epistolae.* In *Virgilii Maronis grammatici Opera,* ed. Johan Huemer. Leipzig, 1886.

Vita Caesarii. In *Sancti Caesarii opera omnia,* ed. Germain Morin, 2: 296–345. Maredsous, 1942.

Vita Ceolfridi. In *Venerabilis Baedae,* ed. Charles Plummer, 1: 388–404. Oxford, 1896.

Vita Fructuosi. In *The Vita Sancti Fructuosi: Text with a Translation, Introduction, and Commentary,* ed. Frances Clare Nock. Washington, D.C., 1946.

Vita Gregorii. In *A Life of Pope St. Gregory the Great, Written by a Monk of the Monastery of Whitby (Probably about A.D. 713),* ed. Francis Aidan Gasquet. Westminster, 1904.

Vita Guthlachi. In *Felix's Life of Saint Guthlac,* ed. and trans. Bertram Colgrave. Cambridge, 1956.

Vita Liudgeri. Ed. Wilhelm Diekamp. In *Die Geschichtsquellen des Bisthums Münster,* 4 (Münster, 1881): 54–83.

Vita Samsoni. In *La vie de saint Samson: Essai de critique hagiographique,* ed. Robert Fawtier. Paris, 1912.

Vita sancti Ansberti archiepiscopi Rotomagensis ab interpolationibus pura, AB 1 (1882): 179–91.

Vitae sancti Bonifatii archiepiscopi Moguntini. Ed. Wilhelm Levison. Hannover and Leipzig, 1905.

Vitas sanctorum patrum emeretensium. In *The "Vitas sanctorum patrum emeretensium": Text and Translation with an Introduction and Commentary,* ed. Joseph N. Garvin. The Catholic University of America Studies in Medieval and Renaissance Latin Language and Literature, vol. 19. Washington, D.C., 1946.

II. MODERN AUTHORS

In the following list of books that I have found useful, those bearing on intellectual culture in general have been marked with an asterisk; a double asterisk denotes those works that treat instruction and education in particular.

Åberg, Nils. *The Occident and the Orient in the Art of the Seventh Century.* Vol. 1, *The British Isles,* Stockholm, 1949. Vol. 2, *Lombard Italy,* Stockholm, 1945. Vol. 3, *The Merovingian Empire,* Stockholm, 1947.

**Adamson, J. W. *The "Illiterate Anglo-Saxon" and Other Essays on Education.* Cambridge, 1946.

**Albert, F. R. *Die Geschichte der Predigt in Deutschland bis Luther.* Vol. 1, *Die Zeit von Karl der Grossen, 600–814,* Gütersloh, 1892.

Alonso, Justo Fernandez. *La cura pastoral en la España romano-visigoda.* Instituto español de estudios eclesiásticos, vol. 2. Rome, 1955.

Andrieu, M., ed. *Les Ordines Romani du Haut Moyen Age.* 4 vols. Louvain, 1930–56.

**Appuhn, Albert. *Das Trivium und Quadrivium in Theorie und Praxis.* Vol. 1,

Das Trivium: Ein Beitrag zur Geschichte des höheren Schulwesens im Mittel-alter. Erlangen, 1900.

Astuti, Guido. *Lezioni di storia del diritto italiano: Le Fonti (Età romano-barbarica).* Padua, 1953.

Atti del I Congresso internazionale di studi longobardi. Spoleto, 1951.

Atti del II Congresso internazionale di studi longobardi. Spoleto, 1953.

Atti del III Congresso internazionale di studi sull'alto medioevo (14-18 ottobre 1956). Spoleto, 1959.

Avalle, D'Arco Silvio. *Protostoria delle lingue romanze.* . . . Turin, 1965.

*Balogh, J. *"Voces paginarum: Beiträge zur Geschichte des lauten Lesens und Schreibens."* Philologus 82 (1927): 83–202.

*Bardy, Gustave. "La littérature des *quaestiones et responsiones* sur l'Ecriture sainte." *Revue biblique* 41 (1932): 210–36, 341–69.

**———. "Les origines des écoles monastiques en Occident." *SE* 5 (1953): 86–104.

*Barlow, Claude W. "The Literary Heritage of Spain, 360–600 A.D." *Folia: Studies in the Christian Perpetuation of the Classics* 1 (1946): 101–11.

———. *Martini episcopi Bracarensis opera omnia.* Papers and Monographs of the American Academy in Rome, vol. 12. New Haven, 1950.

**Bassi Costa, Maria M. *Le origini dello studio di Pavia: Formazione della scuola di Pavia nell'alto medio evo.* Annali della biblioteca governativa e libreria civica di Cremona, vol. 4, fasc. 1. Cremona, 1951.

Battifol, Pierre. *Saint Grégoire le Grand.* 2nd ed. Paris, 1928. (English trans. by John L. Stoddard. London, 1929).

Beck, H. G. J. *The Pastoral Care of Souls in South-East France during the Sixth Century.* Rome, 1950.

*Beeson, Charles H. "The *Ars grammatica* of Julian of Toledo." In *Miscellanea Francesco Ehrle,* pp. 50–70. Vol. 37 of *ST.* Rome, 1924.

**———. "The *Institutionum disciplinae* and Pliny the Younger." *CPh* 8 (1913): 93–98.

———. *Isidor-Studien.* Quellen und Untersuchungen zur lateinischen Philologie des Mittelalters, vol. 4, pt. 2. Munich, 1913.

Bertolini, Ottorino. *Roma di fronte a Bisanzio e ai longobardi.* Vol. 9 of *Storia di Roma.* Bologna, 1941.

Besse, Jean Martial Léon. *Les moines de l'ancienne France: Période gallo-romaine et mérovingienne.* Archives de la France monastique, vol. 2. Paris, 1906.

Besta, Enrico. *Storia del diritto italiano: Diritto pubblico.* 2 vols. Milan, 1949–50.

*Bezzola, Reto R. *Les origines et la formation de la littérature courtoise en Occi-dent, 508–1200.* Vol. 1, *La tradition impériale de la fin de l'Antiquité au XIe siècle.* Vol. 2, pts. 1 and 2, *La société féodale et la transformation de la lit-térature de cour.* Bibliothèque de l'Ecole des Hautes Etudes, fascs. 286 and 313. Paris, 1944, 1960.

*Bischoff, Bernhard. "Das griechische Element in der abendländischen Bildung des Mittelalters." *BZ* 44 (1951): 29–55. Reprinted in B. Bischoff, *Mittelalterliche Studien: Ausgewählte Aufsätze zur Schriftkunde und Literaturgeschichte,* 2: 246–75. 2 vols. Stuttgart, 1966–67.

Blair, Peter Hunter. *An Introduction to Anglo-Saxon England.* Cambridge, 1956.

Bognetti, Gian Piero; Chierici, Gino; and Capitani d'Argazo, Alberto de. *Santa Maria di Castelseprio.* Milan, 1948.

Bognetti, Gian Piero. *L'età longobarda.* 4 vols. Milan, 1966–68.

————. "S. Maria *foris portas* di Castelseprio e la storia religiosa dei Longobardi." In Gian Piero Bognetti, Gino Chierici, and Alberto de Capitani d'Argazo, *Santa Maria di Castelseprio*, pp. 11–511. Milan, 1948.

Bolton, W. F. *A History of Anglo-Latin Literature, 597–1066*. Vol. 1, *597–740*, Princeton, 1967.

*Bonnet, Max. *Le latin de Grégoire de Tours*. Paris, 1890.

Boüard, Alain de. *Manuel de diplomatique française et pontificale*. Vol. 1, *Diplomatique générale*, Paris, 1929. Vol. 2, *L'acte privé*, Paris, 1948.

Brechter, Suso. "Sankt Benedikt und die Antike." In *Benedictus, der Vater des Abendlandes, 547–1947: Weihegabe der Erzabtei Sankt Ottilien zum 1400 Todesjahr*, ed. S. Brechter. Munich, 1947.

Bresslau, Harry. *Handbuch der Urkundenlehre für Deutschland und Italien*. 2 vols. Leipzig and Berlin, 1889–1931.

Browe, Peter. *Beiträge zur Sexualethik des Mittelalters*. Breslau studien zur historischen Theologie, vol. 23. Breslau, 1932.

Brunner, Heinrich. *Deutsche Rechtsgeschichte*. 2 vols. 2nd ed. Leipzig, 1906–28.

*Bruyne, Edgar de. *Etudes d'esthétique médiévale*. Vol. 1, *De Boèce à Jean Scot Erigène*. Recueil de travaux de la Faculté de Philosophie et Lettres de l'Université de Gand, vol. 97. Bruges, 1946.

Buchner, Rudolf. *Die Provence in merowingischer Zeit: Verfassung, Wirtschaft, Kultur*. Arbeiten zur deutschen Rechts- und Verfassungsgeschichte, vol. 9. Stuttgart, 1933.

————. *Die Rechtsquellen*. Supplement to *Wattenbach-Levison: Deutschlands Geschichtsquellen im Mittelalter: Vorzeit und Karolinger*. Ed. Wilhelm Levison and Heinz Löwe. Weimar, 1953.

————. Review of *Education et culture*. *Historische Zeitschrift* 201 (1965): 392–95.

Butler, Edward Cuthbert. *Le monachisme bénédictin*. French trans. by C. Grolleau. Paris, 1924. (In English as *Benedictine Monachism: Studies in Benedictine Life and Rule*. 2nd ed. London and New York, 1924).

Cantor, Moritz. *Die römischen Agrimensoren und ihre Stellung in der Feldmesskunst: Eine historisch-mathematische Untersuchung*. Leipzig, 1875.

————. *Vorlesungen über Geschichte der Mathematik*. Vol. 1. 3rd ed. Leipzig, 1907.

*Cappuyns, Maieul. "Capella (Martianus)." *DHGE*, 11: 835–43.

*————. "Cassiodore." *DHGE*, 11: 1349–1408.

Chadwick, Owen W. *John Cassian: A Study in Primitive Monasticism*. Cambridge, 1950.

Classen, Peter. "Kaiserreskript und Königsurkunde: Diplomatische Studien zum römisch-germanischen Kontinuitätsproblem." *Archiv für Diplomatik* 1 (1955): 1–87; 2 (1956): 1–115.

**Clerval, A. *Les écoles de Chartres au Moyen Age du Ve au XVIe siècle*. Chartres, 1895.

Conrat, Max. *Geschichte der Quellen und der Literatur des römischen Rechts im früheren Mittelalter*. Leipzig, 1891.

*Corbin, Solange. "La notation musicale neumatique dans les quatres provinces lyonnaises." Thesis, University of Paris, 1957.

————. *L'Eglise à la conquête de sa musique*. Paris, 1960.

Cottineau, L. H. *Repertoire topo-bibliographique des abbayes et prieurés*. 2 vols. Mâcon, 1935–39.

Courcelle, Pierre. *Histoire littéraire des grandes invasions germaniques.* 3rd ed. Paris, 1964.

—————. *La Consolation de la Philosophie dans la tradition littéraire: Antécédents et postérité de Boèce.* Paris, 1967.

—————. *Les lettres grecques en Occident de Macrobe à Cassiodore.* 2nd ed. Paris, 1948. (In English as *Late Latin Writers and Their Greek Sources.* Trans. Harry E. Wedeck. Cambridge, Mass., 1969.)

—————. Reviews of *Education et culture. BECh* 120 (1962): 213–17; *REA* 65 (1963): 127–32.

Courtois, Christian. *Les Vandales et l'Afrique.* Paris, 1955.

Courtois, C.; Leschi, L.; Perrat, C.; and Saumagne, C. *Tablettes Albertini: Actes privés de l'époque vandale, fin du Ve siècle.* Paris, 1952.

Coville, Alfred. *Recherches sur l'histoire de Lyon du Ve au IXe siècle (450–800).* Paris, 1928.

*Curtius, Ernst Robert. *La littérature européenne et le Moyen Age latin.* Trans. J. Bréjoux. Paris, 1956. (In English as *European Literature and the Latin Middle Ages.* Trans. Willard R. Trask. New York, 1953.)

De Clercq, Carlo. *La législation religieuse franque de Clovis à Charlemagne: Etude sur les actes des conciles et des capitulaires, les statuts diocésains et les règles monastiques, 507–814.* Université de Louvain, Recueil des travaux, 2nd series, fasc. 38. Louvain and Paris, 1938.

Delius, Walter. *Geschichte der irischen Kirche von ihren Anfängen bis zum 12. Jahrhundert.* Munich, 1954.

*Denk, Victor Martin Otto. *Geschichte des gallo-fränkischen Unterrichts- und Bildungswesens von den ältesten Zeiten bis auf Karl den Grossen mit Berücksichtigung der literarischen Verhältnisse.* Mainz, 1892.

Diaz y Diaz, Manuel C. *Anecdota Wisigothica, I: Estudios y ediciones de textos literarios menores de época visigoda.* Acta Salmanticensia, filosofia y letras, vol. 12, pt. 2. Salamanca, 1958.

—————. *Index scriptorum latinorum medii aevi hispanorum.* Madrid, 1959.

Diehl, Charles. *Etudes sur l'administration byzantine dans l'exarchat de Ravenne.* Paris, 1888.

*Dobiache-Rojdestvenskaia, Olga. *Histoire de l'atelier graphique de Corbie de 651 à 830, reflétée par les manuscrits de Léningrad.* Leningrad, 1934.

*Dornseiff, Franz. *Das Alphabet in Mystik und Magie.* 2nd ed. Berlin, 1925.

Duchesne, Louis M. *Fastes épiscopaux de l'ancienne Gaule.* 3 vols. 2nd rev. ed. Paris, 1907–15.

—————. *L'Eglise au VIe siècle.* Paris, 1925.

—————. *Origines du culte chrétien: Étude sur la liturgie latine avant Charlemagne.* 5th ed. Paris, 1925. (In English as *Christian Worship, Its Origins and Evolution: A Study of the Latin Liturgy to the Time of Charlemagne.* Trans. M. L. McClure. 5th ed. London, 1949.)

Dudden, F. Homes. *Gregory the Great: His Place in History and in Thought.* 2 vols. London, 1905.

*Duhem, Pierre. *Le systeme du monde: Histoire des doctrines cosmologiques de Platon à Copernic.* Vol. 3, *L'astronomie latine au Moyen Age,* Paris, 1915.

Ensslin, Wilhelm. *Theodorich der Grosse.* Munich, 1947.

Estudios sobre la España Visigoda: I semana internacional de estudios visigoticós, 9 al 13 de octubre 1967. In *Anales Toledanos* 3 (1971).

Etudes mérovingiennes: Actes des journées de Poitiers, 1–3, mai 1952. Paris, 1953.

Ewig, Eugen. "Résidences et capitales pendant le Haut Moyen Age." *RH* 230 (1963): 25–72. (Partial English trans. by Sylvia L. Thrupp, "Residence and Capital in the Early Middle Ages [Ostrogoths and Visigoths]." In *Early Medieval Society*, ed. Sylvia L. Thrupp, pp. 163–73. New York, 1967.)

————. *Trier im Merovingerreich: Civitas, Stadt, Bistum.* Trier, 1954.

Fiebiger, Otto, and Schmidt, Ludwig. *Inschriftensammlung zur Geschichte der Ostgermanen.* Kaiserliche Akademie der Wissenschaften in Wien. Philosophisch-historische Klasse. Denkschriften, vol. 60, pt. 3. Vienna, 1917.

Fliche, Augustin, and Martin, Victor, eds. *Histoire de l'Eglise depuis les origines jusqu'à nos jours.* Vol. 4, *De la mort de Théodose à l'élection de Grégoire le Grand (395–590)*, by Pierre de Labriolle, Gustave Bardy, and Jean Rémy Palanque, Paris, 1948. Vol. 5, *Grégoire le Grand, les Etats barbares et la conquête arabe (590–757)*, by Louis Bréhier and René Aigrain, Paris, 1938.

*Fontaine, Jacques. *Isidore de Séville et la culture classique dans l'Espagne wisigothique.* Paris, 1959.

*————. "Isidore de Séville et l'astrologie." *REL* 31 (1953): 271–300.

*Fournier, Paul, and Le Bras, Gabriel. *Histoire des collections canoniques en Occident depuis les Fausses Décrétales jusqu'au Décret de Gratien.* Vol. 1, *De la réforme carolingienne à la réforme grégorienne*, Paris, 1931.

Galy, Charles. *La famille à l'époque mérovingienne: Etude faite principalement d'après les récits de Grégoire de Tours.* Paris, 1901.

Garcia Villada, Zacarias. *Historia eclesiástica de España.* Vol. 2, pts. 1 and 2, *Epoca visigotica*, Madrid, 1933.

Gaudemet, Jean. *Histoire du droit et des Institutions de l'Eglise en Occident.* Vol. 3, *L'Eglise dans l'Empire romain, IVe–Ve siècles*, Paris, 1958.

————. Review of *Education et culture.* *RHDE* (1962), pp. 629–32.

*————. "Survivances romaines dans le droit de la monarchie franque du Ve au Xe siècle" *RHD* 23 (1955): 149–206.

*Ghellinck, Joseph de. *Littérature latine au Moyen Age.* Vol. 1, *Depuis les origines jusqu'à la fin de la renaissance carolingienne*, Paris, 1939.

*Giesebrecht, Wilhelm von. *De litterarum studiis apud Italos primis Medii Aevi saeculis.* Berlin, 1845. (Italian trans. by C. Pascal. Florence, 1895.)

*Gilson, Etienne. *La philosophie au Moyen Age: Des origines patristiques à la fin du XIVe siècle.* 2nd ed. Paris, 1944.

Giry, Arthur. *Manuel de diplomatique.* Paris, 1894.

*Gorce, Denys. *La "lectio divina" des origines du cénobitisme à St. Benoît et Cassiodore.* Vol. 1 (only volume to appear), *Saint Jérôme et la lecture sacrée dans le milieu ascétique romain*, Paris and Wépion-sur-Meuse, 1925.

Gose, Erich. *Katalog der frühchristlichen Inschriften in Trier.* Trierer Grabungen und Forschungen, vol. 3. Berlin, 1958.

Gougaud, Louis. *Les chrétientés celtiques.* 2nd ed. Paris, 1911. (The English edition, *A History of the Churches of the Celts: Their Origin, Their Development, Influence, and Mutual Relations*, trans. Maud Joynt [London, 1932], has supplementary material.)

*Grabar, André, and Nordenfalk, Carl. *Le haut Moyen Age du quatrième au onzième siècle: Mosaiques et peintures murales*, by André Grabar; *L'enluminaire*, by Carl Nordenfalk. Les grandes siècles de la peinture. Geneva, 1957. (In English as *Early Medieval Painting from the Fourth to the Eleventh Century.* Trans. Stuart Gilbert. Geneva, 1957.)

*Grattan, J. H. G., and Singer, Charles. *Anglo-Saxon Magic and Medicine: Illus-

trated Specially from the Semi-Pagan Text "Lacnunga." Publications of the Wellcome Historical Museum, n.s., no. 3. London, 1952.

*Grosjean, Paul. "Sur quelques exégètes irlandais du VIIe siècle." *SE* 7 (1955): 67–97.

Grosse, Roberto, ed. *Las fuentes de la época visigoda y bizantinas: Edición y comentario.* Fontes Hispaniae Antiquae, fasc. 9. Barcelona, 1947.

Guilhiermoz, Paul. *Essai sur l'origine de la noblesse en France au Moyen Age.* Paris, 1902.

**Haarhoff, Theodore. *Schools of Gaul: A Study of Pagan and Christian Education in the Last Century of the Western Empire.* Oxford, 1920.

Haddan, Arthur West, and Stubbs, William, eds. *Councils and Ecclesiastical Documents Relating to Great Britain and Ireland.* 4 vols. Oxford, 1869–78.

*Hagendahl, Harald. *La correspondance de Ruricius.* Acta Universitatis Gotoburgensis, vol. 3. Göteborg, 1952.

Hahn, Heinrich, *Bonifaz und Lul: Ihre angelsächsischen Korrespondenten.* Leipzig, 1883.

*Halm, Karl, ed. *Rhetorici latini minores.* Leipzig, 1863.

Hartmann, Ludo Moritz. *Geschichte Italiens im Mittelalter.* 2 vols. Leipzig, 1879–1900.

Hauck, Albert. *Kirchengeschichte Deutschlands.* Vol. 1. Leipzig, 1887.

*Heerklotz, Alexander Theodore. *Die Variae des Cassiodorus Senator als kulturgeschichtliche Quelle.* Heidelberg, 1926.

Hefele, Charles Joseph [and Leclercq, Henri.] *Histoire des Conciles d'après les documents originaux: Nouvelle traduction française faite sur la 2. éd. allemande. . . .* Vols. 2–3. Paris, 1908–10.

*Henry, Françoise. *Art irlandais.* Dublin, 1954.

Herwegen, Ildefons. *Saint Benoît.* French trans. A. Alibertis and N. de Varey. Paris, 1935. (In English as *St. Benedict: A Character Study.* Trans. Peter Nugent. London, 1924.)

―――. *Sinn und Geist der Benediktinerregel.* Einsiedeln, 1944.

*Heusler, Andreas. *Die altgermanische Dichtung.* Wildpark and Potsdam, 1926.

*Hörle, Georg Heinrich. *Frühmittelalterliche Mönchs- und Klerikerbildung in Italien: Geistliche Bildungsideale und Bildungseinrichtungen vom 6. bis zum 9. Jahrhundert.* Freiburger theologische Studien, vol. 13. Freiburg-im-Breisgau, 1914.

Hubert, Jean. *L'architecture religieuse du haut Moyen Age en France: Plans, notices, et bibliographie.* Paris, 1952.

*―――. *L'art pré-roman.* Paris. 1938.

Hubert, Jean; Porcher, Jean; and Volbach, Wolfgang Fritz. *L'Europe des Invasions.* Paris, 1968. (In English as *Europe of the Invasions.* Trans. Stuart Gilbert and James Emmons. New York, 1969).

Illmer, Detlef. *Formen der Erziehung und Wissensvermittlung im frühen Mittelalter: Quellenstudien zur Frage der Kontinuität des abendländischen Erziehungswesens.* Münchener Beiträge zur Mediävistik und Renaissance-Forschung, vol. 7. Munich, 1971.

Isidoriana: Colleción de estudios sobre Isidoro de Sevilla, publicados con ocasión del XIV centenario de su nacimiento. Ed. M. C. Diaz y Diaz. Leon, 1961.

*Jackson, Kenneth H. *Language and History in Early Britain: A Chronological Survey of the Brittonic Languages, First to the Twelfth Century.* Edinburgh and London, 1953.

*Jahn, Otto. "Ueber die Subscriptionen in den Handschriften römischer Classi-ker." *Berichte über die Verhandlungen der königlich-sächsischen Gesellschaft der Wissenschaften zu Leipzig, Philologisch historische Classe* 3 (1851): 327–72.

*Jones, Charles W. *Bedae pseudepigrapha: Scientific Writings Falsely Attributed to Bede.* Ithaca, 1939.

Jungmann, Josef Andreas. *Missarum sollemnia: Explication génétique de la Messe romaine.* Translated from the German. 3 vols. Paris, 1951–54.

Katz, Solomon. *The Jews in the Visigothic and Frankish Kingdoms of Spain and Gaul.* Cambridge, Mass., 1937.

**Kaufmann, Georg. *Rhetorenschulen und Klosterschulen oder heidnische und christliche Cultur in Gallien während des 5. und 6. Jahrhunderts.* Historisches Taschenbuch, vol. 4. Leipzig, 1869.

*Keil, Heinrich, ed. *Grammatici latini.* 7 vols. Leipzig, 1855–80.

Kenney, James F. *The Sources for the Early History of Ireland: Ecclesiastical (An Introduction and Guide).* New York, 1929. Reprinted, New York, 1966.

*Koebner, Richard. *Venantius Fortunatus: Seine Persönlichkeit und seine Stellung in der geistigen Kultur des Merowingerreiches.* Beiträge zur Kulturgeschichte des Mittelalters und der Renaissance, vol. 22. Leipzig and Berlin, 1915.

**Konen, Wilhelm. *Die Heidenpredigt in der Germanenbekehrung.* Düsseldorf, 1909.

Kurth, Godefroid. *Etudes franques.* 2 vols. Paris and Brussels, 1919.

*Labriolle, Pierre de. *Histoire de la littérature latine chrétienne.* 2 vols. 3rd ed., rev. and supplemented by Gustave Bardy. Paris, 1947.

*Laistner, M. L. W. "Antiochene Exegesis in Western Europe during the Middle Ages." *Harvard Theological Review* 40 (1947): 19–31.

*————. "Bede as a Classical and Patristic Scholar." *Transactions of the Royal Historical Society* 16 (1933): 69–94.

*————. *Thought and Letters in Western Europe, A.D. 500 to 900.* 2nd rev. ed. London and Ithaca, 1957.

Lapeyre, Gabriel G. *Saint Fulgence de Ruspe: Un évêque catholique africain sous la domination vandale.* Paris, 1929.

Larès, Micheline. *Bible et civilisation anglaise: Naissance d'une tradition (Ancien Testament)* Publications de la Sorbonne, Littératures, 6: Etudes Anglaises, 54. Paris, 1974.

Lauer, Philippe, and Samaran, Charles. *Les diplómes originaux des rois mérovin-giens.* Paris, 1908.

Le Blant, Edmond, ed. *Inscriptions chrétiennes de la Gaule antérieures au VIIIe siècle.* 2 vols. Paris, 1856–65.

————, ed. *Nouveau recueil des inscriptions chrétiennes de la Gaule antérieures au VIIIe siècle.* Paris, 1892.

*Leclercq, Jean. *L'amour des lettres et le désir de Dieu: Initiation aux auteurs monastiques du Moyen Age.* Paris, 1957. (In English as *The Love of Learning and the Desire for God: A Study of Monastic Culture.* Trans. Catharine Misrahi. 2nd rev. ed. New York, 1974.)

*Lehmann, Paul. *Parodistische Texte.* Munich, 1923.

*————. "Das Problem der karolingischen Renaissance." *Settimane,* 1 (1954): 309–58.

**Lesne, Emile. *Les écoles de la fin du VIIIe siècle à la fin du XIIe siècle.* Vol. 5 of *Histoire de la propriété ecclésiastique en France.* Lille, 1940.

*————. *Les livres, scriptoria et bibliothèques du commencement du VIIIe siècle* *à la fin du XIIe siècle.* Vol. 4 of *Histoire de la propriété ecclésiastique en France.* Lille, 1938.

Levison, Wilhelm. *England and the Continent in the Eighth Century.* Oxford, 1946.

Lloyd, John Edward. *A History of Wales from the Earliest Times to the Edwardian Conquest.* 2 vols. London, 1939.

**Lorcin, Aimée. "La vie scolaire dans les monastères d'Irlande aux Ve–VIIe siècles." *RMAL* 1 (1945): 221–36.

Lortz, J. "Untersuchungen zur Missionsmethode und zur Frömmigkeit des hl. Bonifatius nach seinen Briefen." In *Willibrordus: Echternacher Festschrift,* ed. N. Goetzinger, pp. 247–83. Luxembourg, 1940.

Los monjes y los estudios. IV Semana de estudios monasticos, Poblet, 1961. Abadia de Poblet, 1963.

Lot, Ferdinand. *La fin du monde antique et le début du Moyen Age.* 2nd ed. Paris, 1951. (In English as *The End of the Ancient World and the Beginnings of the Middle Ages.* Trans. Philip and Mariette Leon. London and New York, 1931. Harper Torchbook ed., with an Introduction by Glanville Downey, New York, 1961.)

———. *Les destinées de l'Empire en Occident de 395 à 888.* Vol. 1, pt. 1, of *Histoire du Moyen Age,* ed. Gustave Glotz, 2nd ed., Paris, 1940.

———. *Les invasions germaniques: La pénétration mutuelle du monde barbare et du monde romain.* Paris, 1945.

*———. "A quelle époque a-t-on cessé de parler latin?" *ALMA* 6 (1931): 97–159.

*Loyen, André. *Sidoine Apollinaire et l'esprit précieux en Gaule aux derniers jours de l'Empire.* Paris, 1943.

*Lubac, Henri de. *L'exégèse médiévale: Les quatre sens de l'Ecriture.* Vol. 1, pts. 1 and 2; vol. 2, pt. 1. Paris, 1959–61.

Lynch, C. H. *Saint Braulio, Bishop of Saragossa (631–651): His Life and Writings.* Washington, D.C., 1938. Revised and augmented Spanish edition by Pascual Galindo, *San Braulio obispo de Zaragoza (631–651): Su vida y sus obras.* Madrid, 1950.

*Maassen, Friedrich. *Geschichte der Quellen und der Literatur des canonischen Rechts im Abendlande bis zum Ausgange des Mittelalters.* Vol. 1, *Die Rechtssammlungen bis zur Mitte des 9. Jahrhunderts,* Graz, 1870.

McGuire, Martin. *Introduction to Mediaeval Latin Studies: A Syllabus and Bibliographical Guide.* Washington, D.C., 1964.

MacKenna, Stephen. *Paganism and Pagan Survivals in Spain up to the Fall of the Visigothic Kingdom.* The Catholic University of America, Studies in Medieval History, n.s., vol. 1. Washington, D.C., 1938.

Maillé, Geneviève Aliette (de Rohan-Chabot), marquise de. *Les cryptes de Jouarre.* Paris, 1971.

———. *Recherches sur les origines chrétiennes de Bordeaux.* Paris, 1960.

Mâle, Emile. *La fin du paganisme en Gaule et les plus anciennes basiliques chrétiennes.* Paris, 1950.

*Mallon, Jean. *Paléographie romaine.* Scripturae, monumenta, et studia, vol. 3. Madrid, 1952.

Malnory, Arthur. *Saint Césaire, évêque d'Arles, 503–543.* Paris, 1894.

**Manacorda, Giuseppe. *Storia delle scuola in Italia.* Vol. 1, *Il medio evo.* Vol. 1, pt. 1, *Storia del diritto scolastico.* Vol. 1, pt. 2, *Storia interna della scuola medi-*

oevale italiana e dizionario geografico delle scuole italiane nel medio evo. Milan, 1913.

*Manitius, Max. *Geschichte der lateinischen Literatur des Mittelalters.* 3 vols. Munich, 1911–31.

*Mariétan, Joseph. *Problème de la classification des sciences d'Aristote à saint Thomas.* Paris and Saint Maurice, 1901.

Marini, Gaetano. *I papiri diplomatici.* Rome, 1805.

*Marrou, Henri. "Autour de la bibliothèque du pape Agapit." *MEFR* 48 (1931): 124–69.

**———. *Histoire de l'éducation dans l'Antiquité.* Paris, 1948. 6th ed., Paris, 1965. (In English as *A History of Education in Antiquity.* Trans. of 3rd French ed. by George Lamb. New York, 1956.)

*———. *Saint Augustin et la fin de la culture antique.* Paris, 1937. 2nd ed. with *Retractatio,* Paris, 1949.

*Masai, François. *Essai sur les origines de la miniature dite irlandaise.* Brussels, 1947.

———. Review of *Education et culture.* *RBPh* 42 (1964): 160–62.

Mélanges colombaniens: Actes du Congrès international de Luxeuil, 20–23 juillet 1950. Paris, 1951.

Mémorial d'un voyage d'études de la Société nationale des antiquaires de France en Rhénanie, juillet 1951. Paris, 1953.

Menéndez Pidal, Ramón. *Historia de España.* Vol. 2, *Espana romana.* Vol. 3, *España visigoda.* Madrid, 1935–40.

**Mengozzi, Guido. *Ricerche sull'attività della scuola di Pavia nell'alto medio evo.* Pavia, 1924.

Mentz, A. "Die tironischen Noten: Eine Geschichte der römischen Kurzschrift." *AFU* 16 (1939): 287–384; 17 (1941–42): 155–302.

Meyer-Marthaler, E. *Rätien im frühen Mittelalter.* Zurich, 1948.

Miscellánea Isidoriana: Homenaje a S. Isidoro de Sevilla en el XIII centenario de su muerte, 636, 4 de Abril, 1936. Rome, 1936.

Molinier, Auguste. *Les sources de l'histoire de France des origines aux guerres d'Italie (1494).* Vol. 1. *Epoque primitive: Mérovingiens et carolingiens,* Paris, 1901.

Moricca, Umberto. *Storia della letteratura latina cristiana.* Vols. 2–3. Turin, 1928–32.

Musset, Lucien. *Les invasions: Les vagues germaniques.* Nouvelle Clio: Histoire et ses problems, ed. Robert Boutrache and Paul Lemerle, no. 12. Paris, 1965.

*Norberg, Dag. *Introduction à l'étude de la versification latine médiévale.* Studia latina Stockholmiensia, vol. 5. Stockholm, 1958.

*———. *La poésie latine rythmique du haut Moyen Age.* Studia latina Stockholmiensia, vol. 2. Stockholm, 1953.

———. *Syntaktische Forschungen auf dem Gebiete des Spätlateins und des frühen Mittellateins.* Uppsala, 1943.

*Norden, Eduard. *Die antike Kunstprosa vom VI. Jahrhundert v. Chr. bis in die Zeit der Renaissance.* Vol. 2. 3rd ed. Leipzig, 1918.

Ogilvy, J. D. A. *Books Known to Anglo-Latin Writers from Aldhelm to Alcuin (670–804).* Cambridge, Mass., 1936.

**Ozanam, Antoine Frédéric. "Des écoles et de l'instruction publique en Italie aux temps barbares." In *La civilisation au cinquième siècle,* 2: 401–94. Paris, 1873.

————. *Etudes germaniques.* Vol. 2, *La civilisation chrétienne chez les Francs,* 6th ed., Paris, 1893.

**Paré, Gerard; Brunet, Adrien; and Tremblay, Pierre. *La Renaissance du XIIe siècle: Les écoles et l'enseignement.* Paris and Ottawa, 1933.

Patzelt, Erna. *Die karolingische Renaissance.* Vienna, 1924. 2nd ed., Graz, 1967.

*Pei, Mario. *The Language of the Eighth-Century Texts in Northern France: A Study of the Original Documents in the Collection of Tardif and Other Sources.* New York, 1932.

Peitz, Wilhelm M. *Dionysius Exiguus-Studien.* Berlin, 1960.

Perez de Urbel, Justo. *Los monjes españoles en la edad media.* 2 vols. Madrid, 1933–34.

Piganiol, André. *L'Empire chrétien, 325–395.* Vol. 4 of *Histoire romaine,* ed. G. Glotz. Paris, 1947.

**Pirenne, Henri. "De l'état de l'instruction des laiques a l'époque mérovingienne." *RB* 46 (1934): 165–77.

————. *Mahomet et Charlemagne.* Paris and Brussels, 1937. (In English as *Mohammed and Charlemagne.* Trans. Bernard Miall. New York and London, 1939.)

Prinz, Friedrich. *Frühes Mönchtum im Frankenreich: Kultur und Gesellschaft in Gallien, den Rheinlanden und Bayern am Beispiel der monastischen Entwicklung, 4. bis 8. Jahrhundert.* Munich, 1965.

**Probst, Ferdinand. *Katechese und Predigt von Anfang der IV bis zum Ende der VI Jahrhundert.* Breslau, 1884.

*Raby, F. J. E. *A History of Christian Latin Poetry from the Beginnings to the Close of the Middle Ages.* 2nd ed. Oxford, 1953.

*————. *A History of Secular Latin Poetry in the Middle Ages.* 2 vols. 2nd ed. Oxford, 1957.

**Rand, Edward Kennard. *Founders of the Middle Ages.* Cambridge, Mass., 1928.

Riché, Pierre. *De l'éducation antique à l'éducation chevaleresque.* Paris, 1968.

————. "Enseignement du droit en Gaule du VIe au XIe siècle." In *Ius Romanum medii aevi,* I, 5 b *bb.* Société d'histoire des droits de l'Antiquité. Milan, 1965.

**————. "L'instruction des laics en Gaule mérovingienne au VIIe siècle." In *Settimane,* 5 (1958): 873–88.

**————. "La survivance des écoles publiques en Gaule au Ve siècle." *MA* 63 (1957): 421–36.

Roeder, Fritz. *Die Familie bei den Angelsachsen: Ein kultur- und litterarhistorische Studie auf Grund gleichzeitigen Quellen.* Part 1, *Mann und Frau.* Studien zur englischen Philologie, vol. 4. Halle, 1899.

**Roger, Maurice. *L'enseignement des lettres classiques d'Ausone à Alcuin: Introduction à l'histoire des écoles carolingiennes.* Paris, 1905.

Rossi, Giovanni Battista de. *Inscriptiones christianae urbis Romae septimo saeculo antiquiores.* 2 vols. Rome, 1857/61–88.

*Ruffini, Mario. *Le origini letterarie in Spagna.* Vol. 1, *L'epoca visigotica,* Turin, 1951.

Salin, Edouard. *La civilisation mérovingienne d'après les sépultures, les textes et le laboratoire.* 4 vols. Paris, 1950–59.

**Salvioli, Giuseppe. *L'istruzione pubblica in Italia nei secoli VIII, IX, e X.* Florence, 1898.

**Sandys, John Edwin. *A History of Classical Scholarship.* 3rd ed. Vol. 1, *From the VIth Century B.C. to the End of the Middle Ages,* Cambridge, 1921.

*Sarton, George. *Introduction to the History of Science.* Vol. 1, *From Homer to Omar Khayyam,* Baltimore, 1927.

Saupe, Albin. *Der Indiculus superstitionum et paganiarum: Ein Verzeichniss heidnischer und aberglaübischer Gebräuche und Meinungen aus der Zeit Karls des Grossen, aus zumeist gleichzeitigen Schriften erläutert.* Programm des städtischen Realgymnasium zu Leipzig. Leipzig, 1890–91.

*Schanz, Martin. *Geschichte der römischen Literatur bis zum Gesetzgebungswerk des Kaisers Justinian.* Vol. IV, *Die römische Literatur von Constantin bis zum Gesetzgebungswerk Justinians,* pt. 1, *Die Literatur des vierten Jahrhunderts,* 2nd ed., Munich, 1914; pt. 2, with Carl Hosius and Gustav Krüger, *Die Literatur des fünften und sechsten Jahrhunderts,* Munich, 1920.

Schmidt, Ludwig. *Geschichte der Wandalen.* 2nd ed. Munich, 1942.

———. *Die Ostgermanen.* Munich, 1934.

Schneider, Fedor. *Rom und Romgedanke im Mittelalter: Die geistigen Grundlagen der Renaissance.* Munich, 1926.

Schubert, Hans von. *Geschichte der christlichen Kirche im Frühmittelalter.* Tübingen, 1921.

Séjourné, Paul. *Le dernier Père de l'Eglise, saint Isidore de Séville: Son rôle dans l'histoire du droit canonique.* Paris, 1929.

Settimane di studio del Centro italiano di studi sull'alto medioevo.

———. Vol. 1, *I problemi della civiltà carolingia,* Spoleto, 1954.

———. Vol. 2, *I problemi comuni dell'Europa post-carolingia,* Spoleto, 1955.

———. Vol. 3, *I Goti in Occidente: Problemi,* Spoleto, 1956.

———. Vol. 4, *Il monachesimo nell'alto medioevo e la formazione della civiltà occidentale,* Spoleto, 1957.

———. Vol. 5, *Caratteri del secolo VII in Occidente,* Spoleto, 1958.

———. Vol. 6, *La città nell'alto medioevo,* Spoleto, 1959.

———. Vol. 7, *Le chiese nei regni dell'Europa occidentalo e i loro rapporti con Roma sino all'800,* Spoleto, 1960.

———. Vol. 9, *Il passagio dall'Antichitá al medioevo in Occidente,* Spoleto, 1962.

———. Vol. 14, *La conversione al cristianesimo nell'Europa dell'alto medioevo,* Spoleto, 1967.

———. Vol. 19, *La scuola nell'Occidente latino dell'alto medioevo,* Spoleto, 1972.

———. Vol. 20, *I problemi dell'Occidente nel secolo VIII,* Spoleto, forthcoming.

*Siegmund, Albert. *Die Ueberlieferung der griechischen christlichen Literatur in der lateinischen Kirche bis zum zwölften Jahrhundert.* Munich, 1949.

Silvestre, Hubert. Review of *Education et culture. RHE* 58 (1963): 576–82.

Simonnet, Henri. *Le "mundium" dans le droit de famille germanique.* Paris, 1898.

*Smalley, Beryl. *The Study of the Bible in the Middle Ages.* Oxford, 1952.

**Specht, Frantz Anton. *Geschichte des Unterrichtwesens in Deutschland von der ältesten Zeiten bis zur Mitte des dreizehnten Jahrhunderts.* Stuttgart, 1885.

Spörl, Johannes. "Gregor der Grosse und die Antike." In *Christliche Verwicklichung: Festschrift Romano Guardini,* ed. Karlheinz Schmidthues, pp. 198–221. Rothenfels, 1935.

Sprandel, Rolf. *Der merovingische Adel und die Gebiete östlich des Rheins.* Forschungen zur oberrheinischen Landesgeschichte, vol. 5. Freiburg-im-Breisgau, 1957.

Stein, Ernst. *Histoire du Bas-Empire.* French translation under the direction of Jean-Remy Palanque. Vol. 1, *De l'Etat romain à l'Etat byzantin.* Vol. 2, *De la disparition de l'Empire d'Occident à la mort de Justinien.* Paris, 1949–59.

*Steinacker, Harold. "Die römische Kirche und die griechischen Sprachkenntnisse des Frühmittelalters." In *Festschrift Theodor Gomperz,* pp. 324–41. Vienna, 1902. Completed in *MIOEG,* 62 (1954): 28–66.

Stenton, F. M. *Anglo-Saxon England.* 2nd ed. Oxford, 1947.

Stevens, Courtenay Edward. *Sidonius Apollinaris and His Age.* Oxford, 1933.

Storms, Gotfrid. *Anglo-Saxon Magic.* The Hague, 1948.

Straeten, J. van der. Review of *Education et culture. AB* 81 (1963): 295–99.

Stroheker, Karl Friedrich. *Germanentum und Spätantike.* Zurich and Stuttgart, 1965.

———. *Der senatorische Adel im spätantiken Gallien.* Tübingen, 1948.

Sundwall, Johannes. *Abhandlungen zur Geschichte des ausgehenden Römertums.* Helsinki, 1919.

*Tardi, Dominique. *Les Epitomae de Virgile de Toulouse: Essai de traduction critique avec une bibliographie, une introduction, des notes.* Paris, 1928.

———. *Fortunat: Etude sur un dernier représentant de la poésie latine dans la Gaule mérovingienne.* Paris, 1927.

Thompson, A. Hamilton, ed. *Bede, His Life, Times, and Writings: Essays in Commemoration of the Twelfth Centenary of His Death.* Oxford, 1935. New York, 1966.

Tjäder, Jan Olof, ed. *Die nichtliterarischen lateinischen Papyri Italiens aus der Zeit 445–700.* Acta instituti Romani regni sueciae, series in quarto, vol. 19, pts. 1–3. Lund, 1954–55.

Traube, Ludwig. *Vorlesungen und Abhandlungen.* Ed. Franz Boll. Vol. 2. Munich, 1911.

Vacandard, Elphège. "L'idolâtrie en Gaule au VIᵉ et au VIIᵉ siècle." *RQH* 65 (1899): 424–54.

**———. "La *scola* du palais mérovingien." *RQH* 61 (1897): 490–502.

———. "Encore un mot sur la *scola* du palais mérovingien." *RQH* 62 (1898): 546–51.

———. "Un dernier mot sur l'école du palais mérovingien." *RQH* 76 (1904): 549–53.

———. *Vie de saint Ouen, évêque de Rouen.* Paris, 1902.

Vercauteren, Fernand. *Les "Civitates" de la Belgique seconde.* Brussels, 1934.

*Vielliard, Jeanne. *Le latin des diplômes royaux et des chartes privées de l'époque mérovingienne.* Paris, 1927.

*Viscardi, Antonio. *Le origini.* Vol. 1 of *Storia letteraria d'Italia.* 3rd ed. Milan, 1939.

Vives, José. *Inscripciones cristianas de la España romana y visigoda.* Barcelona, 1942.

Vogel, Cyrille. *La discipline pénitentielle en Gaule, des origines à la fin du VIIᵉ siècle.* Paris, 1952.

———. *Le pécheur et la pénitence dans l'Eglise ancienne.* Paris, 1966.

———. *Le pécheur et la pénitence au Moyen Age.* Paris, 1969.

**Voigt, E. "Das erste Lesebuch des Triviums in der Kloster- und Stiftsschulen des Mittelalters." *Mitteilungen der Gesellschaft für deutsche Erziehungs- und Schulgeschichte* 1 (1891).

*Vyver, André van de. "Cassiodore et son oeuvre." *Speculum* 6 (1931): 244–92.
*————. "Les étapes du développement philosophique du Haut Moyen-Age."
    RBPh 8 (1929): 425–52.
*————. "L'évolution scientifique du Haut Moyen Age." *Archeion* 19 (1937):
    12–20.
Wasserschleben, Friedrich Wilhelm Hermann. *Die Büssordnungen der abend-*
    ländischen Kirche. Halle, 1851.
*Wattenbach, Wilhelm. *Das Schriftwesen im Mittelalter.* 3rd ed. Leipzig, 1896.
Wattenbach-Levison: Deutschlands Geschichtsquellen im Mittelalter: Vorzeit und
    Karolinger. Ed. Wilhelm Levison und Heinz Löwe. Pts. 1–2. Weimar, 1952–53.
Wiegand, Friedrich L. *Die Stellung des apostolischen Symbols in kirchlichen*
    Leben des Mittelalters. Studien zur Geschichte der Theologie und der Kirche,
    vol. 4, pt. 2. Leipzig, 1899.
**Wilde, W. H. "Decadence of Learning in Gaul in the Seventh and Eighth
    Centuries as Viewed Especially in the Lives of the Saints." *American Journal*
    of Theology 7 (1903): 443–51.
*Zimmermann, E. H. *Vorkarolingische Miniaturen.* Plates, 4 vols.; text, 1 vol.
    Berlin, 1916–18.

Index

Index

PERSONS

PLACES AND SUBJECTS

Education and Culture in the Barbarian West, Sixth through Eighth Centuries was cast on the Linotype in eleven-point Granjon with two-points spacing between the lines. Garamond was selected for display.

The Granjon type design came into being in 1924 through the hands of George W. Jones, one of England's great printers. Granjon continues to meet the most exacting requirements for fine books, a tribute to the honest design and legibility distinguishing this type.

This book was designed by Larry Hirst, manually composed and printed letterpress at Heritage Printers, Inc., Charlotte, North Carolina. It was bound by Carolina Ruling and Binding Co., Inc., also of Charlotte. The paper, bearing the watermark of the South Carolina Press Colophon was developed by the S.D. Warren Company for an effective life of at least 300 years.

UNIVERSITY OF SOUTH CAROLINA PRESS / COLUMBIA